AGENCY AND PARTNERSHIP

Cases and Materials

Michael L. Closen
Professor of Law
The John Marshall Law School

and

Gary S. Rosin
Professor of Law
South Texas College of Law

CAROLINA
ACADEMIC
PRESS
700 KENT ST.
DURHAM, NC
27701

International Standard Book Number: 0-89089-515-5
Library of Congress Card Catalog Number: 92-71956

Carolina Academic Press
700 Kent Street
Durham, North Carolina 27701
(919) 489-7486 FAX (919) 493-5668

Summary of Contents

Table of Contents

Table of Cases

Principal cases are in bold.

Preface

We are pleased to present this edition of our casebook on the law of agency and partnership. We sincerely appreciate the confidence displayed in us by Carolina Academic Press, and we must especially note our genuine indebtedness to the publishers of the first edition of the book for their continued cooperation and support. The first edition was authored by Professor Closen and published in 1984 by Butterworth Publishing.

As the title indicates, this book treats the closely related subjects of agency and partnership law. The significance of these subjects is readily apparent. Almost all commercial and many noncommercial activities are carried out by agents or servants—employees acting for their employers. Far more than one hundred million Americans serve as employees each year. More than a million businesses are operated as partnerships, and partnership law constitutes a special branch of the law of agency. Hence, these subjects are unquestionably worthy of study, and it is appropriate to consider them in a single law school course. This book reflects the belief of the authors that the course in agency-partnership provides essential foundation materials of a sound legal education in commercial/business law.

We share the concern that our students be prepared for the practice of law, and even for more advanced courses in law school, with materials that emphasize the modern law of agency and partnership. We have found that the fundamentals of this course can be comprehensively addressed in a contemporary fashion, principally from recent cases.

Virtually all principal cases in this volume were decided in the decades of the 1970s, 1980s, and 1990s and most since 1980. The recent decisions are more relevant and thus more interesting and instructive about the factual and legal contexts that today's students will later encounter. Additionally, the recency of these materials should help students to appreciate the continuing vitality of the subjects addressed in this book. *See* Closen, *Teaching with Recent Decisions: A Survey of Past and Present Practices*, 11 FLA. ST. U.L. REV. 289 (1983). Liberal reference has been made to the Restatement (Second) of Agency. Although we also refer to the Restatement (Second) of Torts, citations to the "Restatement" without differentiation refer to the Restatement (Second) of Agency. In the partnership portion of the materials, liberal reference has been made to the Uniform Partnership Act, the Uniform Limited Partnership Act, the Revised Uniform Limited Partnership Act, and the Revised Uniform Partnership Act. (All of these partnership statutes appear in the statutory supplement to this casebook.)

One of our major tasks has been to keep the materials down to manageable size for a single-volume casebook without sacrificing thoroughness of coverage. Consequently, we have had to be very selective. The materials chosen have been generously and liberally edited, usually without any indication. Almost all citations to authority and footnotes have been omitted, and the original footnote numbers from the cases appear on the footnotes that have been retained. Any reader wishing to conduct further research or to cite the material included here must, therefore, consult the original sources. We have abandoned almost entirely the use of ellipses. But, we should hasten to add that the accuracy and soundness of our final product has not been diminished.

Several acknowledgments are due for the assistance provided to us over the years that it has taken to complete this project. Professor Closen has had the full support and encouragement of Dean Howard Markey, Associate Dean R. Gilbert Johnston, and his colleagues on the faculty at The John Marshall Law School. Particular mention is deserved by his colleagues who teach agency and partnership law, for they offered considerable guidance and encouragement. They are Professors John Ingram and Randall Peterson. Over the years, several able student research assistants have made important contributions, including Cory Aronovitz, Grant Dixon, John Furnari, Michael Osty, and Anthony Perniciaro. The typing of these materials was accomplished by a group of very capable secretaries, Gwen Konigsfeld, Joanne Sorce, Yolanda Aparicio, and Nancy Ruberry.

Professor Rosin wishes to express his appreciation for the support and encouragement of Dean William L. Wilks and his colleagues on the faculty at South Texas College of Law. In preparing these materials he was assisted by Ms. Terry L. Velligan, his student research assistant. Special thanks to Ms. Diane Lee, faculty secretary, for her many long hours at the word processor.

Our grateful acknowledgment is hereby extended to the American Law Institute for permission to reprint selected portions of the Restatement (Second) of Agency and the Restatement (Second) of Torts, and to the National Conference of Commissioners on Uniform State Laws for permission to reprint the uniform partnership statutes.

The preparation of this casebook has been challenging, interesting, and rewarding for us, and we hope that readers who study this book will find it profitable as well.

April 1992

Michael L. Closen
Gary S. Rosin

AGENCY
AND
PARTNERSHIP

Chapter 1

Contractual Dealings by Agents

A. The Agency Relationship

Since the time human affairs became so complex that a person was no longer able to undertake them alone, people have required the assistance of others. Sometimes people have shared responsibilities equally with others who had similar goals; sometimes they have enlisted the assistance of others who became subservient to their authority. Section 1(1) of the Restatement of Agency 2d (Restatement) defines "agency" as follows:

> Agency is the fiduciary relation which results from the manifestation of consent by one person [the principal] to another that the other [the agent] shall act on his behalf and subject to his control, and consent by the other so to act.

The study of agency law is the study of the mutual rights and obligations arising out of interactions between principals, agents, and third persons. An agency creates a *triangular* set of relations: those between the principal and third persons; those between the agent and the third persons; and those between the principal and the agent.

Often, the agent acts as an intermediary in contractual dealings between the principal and a third person. Indeed, one of the central purposes of agency is to relieve the principal of the need to deal directly with third persons. Contractual dealings raise issues of the liability of each of the principal, the agent, and the third person.

However, the agency relationship is not limited to persons appointed to undertake contractual dealings, but includes persons employed by a principal to perform *any* service on his or her behalf. Where a principal controls or has the right to control the agent's *physical conduct* in the performance of services for the principal, the principal is called a *master* and the agent is called a *servant*. Restatement §§ 2(1)-(2). Where the principal does *not* have such right of control, the agent is called an *independent contractor*. Restatement § 2(3). Although the services of either a servant or an independent contractor *may* involve contractual dealings, the chief issue with respect to servants and independent contractors is liability *in tort* for the conduct of such persons. Liability in tort for the conduct of servants or independent contractors will be discussed in chapters 7 through 9.

B. Liability of Principal

Kasselder v. Kapperman

316 N.W.2d 628 (S.D. 1982)

DUNN, Justice.

This is an appeal from an order and judgment entered in favor of appellees Alice and Gene Kasselder, doing business as A & G Diesel Truck Repair (Truck Repair), for repairs performed on a Galion road grader owned by appellee Jerome Kapperman (Kapperman).

Kapperman owns a Galion road grader which had a defective engine. Appellant James Schladweiler (Schladweiler) offered to purchase the grader for the sum of $8,500, if the grader was in running condition. Kapperman said he would pay up to $3,000 to have the engine repaired and Schladweiler said he could have it repaired for less than that sum at Truck Repair in Mitchell, South Dakota. Kapperman shipped the grader from Minnesota to Schladweiler's residence in Mitchell.

At the request of Schladweiler, Truck Repair's mechanics took the engine apart and discovered that it was not repairable. They suggested to Schladweiler that a new engine be purchased for $7,000. Schladweiler informed Kapperman of this information and Kapperman said he was not interested in spending that much money. Kapperman tried to locate a used engine that could be rebuilt, but was unsuccessful. The mechanics located a used engine in Omaha, Nebraska, and told Schladweiler the cost of repairs would be $1,000 to purchase the engine, $1,300 for labor, and the cost of oil and gaskets. Schladweiler informed Kapperman of this estimate and Kapperman approved the purchase of the engine but specified that he would not pay more than $3,000 in repair costs.

A short time later, the mechanics contacted their supplier in Sioux Falls, South Dakota and were informed that the supplier had repaired a similar engine for $5,000, which did not include repairing the cylinder head. The Omaha engine had a cracked cylinder head. Truck Repair relayed this estimate to Schladweiler. Schladweiler authorized the repairs, but did not inform Kapperman of this increased bid. The repairs to the engine took several months and Schladweiler periodically followed the progress of the repairs. At no time did Truck Repair discuss the cost of repairs with Kapperman. When the repairs were finally completed, the total cost was $6,441.06. Neither Kapperman nor Schladweiler would pay the bill.

The trial court found for Truck Repair and entered an order and judgment against Schladweiler in the amount of $3,441.06 plus interest and against Kapperman in the amount of $3,000 plus interest.

Schladweiler's only contention is that the evidence presented at trial was insufficient to support the trial court's finding that he was liable for $3,441.06, plus interest, of the Truck Repair bill. He alleges that his agency relationship with Kapperman should have precluded his liability.

An agency relationship is defined by SDCL 59-1-1 as "the representation of one called the principal by another called the agent in dealing with third persons." An agency relationship is either actual or ostensible. It is actual when the principal appoints the agent. It is ostensible when the principal by conduct or want of ordinary care causes a third person to believe another, who is not actually appointed, to be his agent.

To determine whether an agency relationship has in fact been created, we examine the relations of the parties as they exist under their agreement or acts. Agency

> is a legal concept which depends upon the existence of required factual elements: The manifestation by the principal that the agent shall act for him, the agent's acceptance of the undertaking, and the understanding of the parties that the principal is to be in control of the undertaking.

Watkins Co. v. Dutt, 84 S.D. 453, 457, 173 N.W.2d 41, 43 (1969).

The evidence indicates that this was not an ostensible agency. Kapperman made no representations or actions to cause Truck Repair to believe that Schladweiler was his agent. In fact, Kapperman did not deal with Truck Repair until after he received the final bill from them. The only proof introduced at trial supporting an agency relationship in excess of $3,000 was the words and actions of Schladweiler. Ostensible agency for which a principal may be held liable must be traceable to the principal and cannot be established solely by the acts, declarations or conduct of an agent.

The evidence indicates that an actual agency relationship did exist between Kapperman and Schladweiler but only to the extent of $3,000. Kapperman allowed Schladweiler to act for him regarding repair of the grader but specified that he would not pay more than $3,000 for repair costs. Schladweiler agreed to represent Kapperman in the transaction with Truck Repair. However, Schladweiler exceeded the scope of his agency authority when he authorized repairs exceeding the scope of his agency authority when he authorized repairs exceeding $3,000 and failed to consult with Kapperman regarding the increased expenditures. Under SDCL 59-6-2,

> [w]hen an agent exceeds his authority, his principal is bound by his authorized acts so far only as they can be plainly separated from those which are unauthorized.

We hold that the trial court was correct in its determination that Schladweiler was liable for $3,441.06, plus interest, of the Truck Repair bill, because this sum represented the portion of the bill resulting from his unauthorized acts as agent.

We affirm the judgment and order of the trial court.

Notes

1. "Authority" is the agent's power to bind the principal "by acts done in accordance with the principal's manifestations of consent" to the agent. Restatement § 7. A principal is bound by the authorized acts of his or her agent in entering into contracts on the principal's behalf. Restatement §§ 140, 144, & 159. Under certain circumstances agents may have *power* to bind the principal by *unauthorized* acts, such as where the agent has *apparent authority* or *inherent agency power*, or where the principal is *estopped* from denying the agent's authority. Restatement §§ 8, 8A, & 8B. Chapter 2 discusses at greater length the creation and interpretation of authority, as well as an agent's power to bind the principal by unauthorized acts.

2. Where an agent enters into an unauthorized contract without having the power to bind the principal, the principal is not bound by the contract as actually made by the agent, or as it would have been made if the agent had acted within his or her authority. Restatement § 143(1). As indicated in *Kasselder v. Kapperman,*

> Where the only difference between the contract as authorized and the contract as made is a difference as to amount, or the inclusion or exclusion of a separable part, the principal is liable upon the contract as it was authorized to be made, provided that the other party seasonably manifests his willingness to accept the contract as authorized.

Restatement § 143(2).

3. At common law, a principal is *not* bound by the authorized contracts of his or her agent where the contract is under seal or is a *negotiable instrument*. Restatement §§ 151 & 152. Section 3-401 and Official Comment 1 of the *1990 Official Text* of the Uniform Commercial Code change this rule and hold the principal liable on negotiable instruments signed by an authorized agent, regardless of whether the principal's name appears on the instrument.

4. A principal must have the capacity to give a legal consent, as well as capacity to do the act that he or she is authorizing the agent to do. An infant, for instance, can employ an agent with authority to make fully enforceable contracts for necessities, but the contracts of the agent for other types of subject matter would be voidable at the election of the infant. *See* Restatement § 20.

To be an agent, a person needs only the physical or mental capability to do the thing he or she has been appointed to do. Hence, almost anyone can serve as an agent. Even an infant or an insane person might well have the capacity to bind a principal to a contract (or to cause tort liability for a master where they act as servants). *See* Restatement § 21.

Dyer v. Johnson

757 P.2d 178 (Colo. App. 1988)

real property purchase. Not up to code after fire.

STERNBERG, Judge.

Following a trial to the court, a judgment was entered awarding damages to the purchasers of real property against the sellers and their agent and broker. The sellers and the purchasers appeal.

The plaintiffs, Robert J. Dyer III and Eva O. Dyer (purchasers), were interested in buying rental property, and to that end, contacted Peter Kantor (agent), an employee of Peter Kantor International, Inc. (broker). Kantor showed the purchasers a property that Ned B. Johnson and Helene Johnson (sellers) had listed with Kantor for sale. The property had been damaged by fire, and the agent, according to the purchasers, told them it had been reconstructed and brought "totally up to code." The purchasers asserted that the agent told them there was a written appraisal on the property for $220,000. Following negotiations, the purchasers bought the property for $160,000 on January 18, 1980.

Thereafter, the purchasers discovered that the property did not comply with the building code, and that there was no written appraisal of $220,000. The purchasers returned the property to the sellers, who thereafter sold it to a third party. The purchasers filed this suit to recover their out-of-pocket expenses. The sellers counterclaimed against the purchasers and cross-claimed against the agent and broker.

The case was initially tried to a jury which returned a verdict in favor of the purchasers; however, the court granted the sellers' motion for a new trial based on an error in an instruction and the court's conclusion that the verdicts were inconsistent.

The purchasers filed a motion for summary judgment against the agent, broker, and sellers, which was granted, leaving for determination the issue of damages, the sellers' counterclaim, and the sellers' cross-claim. After a trial to the court, judgment was entered in favor of the purchasers and against the sellers, agent, and broker, jointly and severally, for $34,000. The court entered judgment in favor of the sellers on their cross-claim against the agent and broker, finding them to be jointly and severally liable for $17,000. All other claims were dismissed.

On appeal, the sellers contend that the trial court erred in finding them liable for the misrepresentations of the agent.

Generally, a principal may not be bound by the false representations of his agent made without his knowledge, consent, or authority. However, an exception to this rule exists if an agent has apparent authority to make a representation, the question whether such authority existed being one of fact. A principal may be held liable for the tortious conduct of an agent if the conduct was within the scope of employment. An agent is acting within the scope of employment if he is doing what is necessarily incidental to the work that has been assigned to him or which is customarily within the business in which the employee is engaged.

In *Byrn v. Walker*, 275 S.C. 83, 267 S.E.2d 601 (S.C. 1980), the court reached a similar result, reasoning that:

> If the representations are made by the agent as a part of the negotiation for the purpose of bringing about the sale, and by means of this it is brought about, the conveyance made, and the proceeds of the sale received, this brings the case within the general rule that a principal is responsible for such acts of his agent as are done within the scope of his authority, whether authorized or not, except by the general authority to do the principal act.

The agent's misrepresentations at issue here, and the context in which they were made, were such that the trial court properly held sellers liable for them.

[We] agree with the sellers that the trial court erred in not requiring the agent and broker to indemnify them fully for the damages awarded to the purchasers. The damage award against the sellers was for $34,000. The basis of the sellers' liability was the acts of the agent and broker leading to application of the doctrine of respondeat superior; thus, we conclude the trial court erred in not entering judgment against the agent and broker for the full amount of the judgment against the sellers.

The judgment in favor of the purchasers is affirmed. The judgment on the cross-claim is reversed and the cause is remanded with directions to award the sellers a judgment against the broker and agent for the full amount of the judgment entered against sellers in favor of the purchasers.

Note

In chapter 7 we will study *respondeat superior*, the liability of a master for torts committed by a servant in the scope of his or her employment. As we will see, *respondeat superior* is largely based on the master's right to control the servant's physical conduct in the performance of the work assigned to the servant. Is the principal's liability in *Dyer v. Johnson* based on *respondeat superior*? That is, is the principal liable because of the right to control the agent's physical conduct? What is the relevance of the agent's *authority or apparent authority* to make the misrepresentation?

C. Liability of Third Person to Principal

Third persons dealing with an agent may not know they are dealing with an agent. Where the third person has no notice that the agent is acting for a principal, the principal is said to be "*undisclosed.*" Restatement § 4(3). Even where third persons know they are dealing with an agent, they may not have notice of the identity of the principal. In that situation the principal is said to be "*partially disclosed.*" Restatement § 4(2). Where the third person has notice *both* that the agent is acting for a principal *and* of the principal's identity, the principal is said to "*disclosed.*" Restatement § 4(1). To complicate matters further, even where the principal is disclosed in the sense that the third person has notice of the agency and of the principal's identity, the *written agreement* may not fully disclose the principal.

To what extent does the degree of disclosure of the principal affect the principal's ability to enforce a contract entered into by the agent on the principal's behalf?

Comind, Companhia de Seguros v. Sikorsky Aircraft Division of United Technologies Corp.

116 F.R.D. 397 (D. Conn. 1987)

CLARIE, Senior District Judge.

The defendants, [Sikorsky Aircraft Division of] United Technologies Corporation (UTC) and United Technologies International, Inc. (UTI), move for summary judgment pursuant to Rule 56 of the Federal Rules of Civil Procedure.

The present controversy stems from the crash of a helicopter owned and operated by Votec Servicos Aeros Regional, S.A. (VOTEC), a Brazilian Corporation with its principal place of business in Brazil. The helicopter was insured by Comind, Companhia de Seguros (Comind), also a Brazilian corporation with its principal place of business in Brazil. The defendants, UTI and UTC, are both Delaware corporations, with principal places of business in Connecticut.

In September of 1975, VOTEC entered into a sales agreement with UTI to purchase several helicopters made by UTC. On or about September 14, 1979, VOTEC accepted delivery of the helicopter at issue here. VOTEC paid roughly $1,600,000.00 for this helicopter. Subsequently, on March 20, 1980, the helicopter crashed off the coast of Brazil. Approximately 14 deaths resulted and the helicopter was completely destroyed. Comind, VOTEC's insurer, paid VOTEC for the loss of the helicopter. Comind is now suing UTI as the seller, and UTC as the manufacturer of the helicopter, seeking to recover the amount it paid to VOTEC plus costs and interest. Comind claims complete subrogation rights, and seeks to impose liability on UTI and UTC under a variety of theories.

The evidence available to the Court at this time suggests that the crash was caused by the failure of a small part within the rotary mechanism that held the helicopter's blades in place. This part is known as the "bearing inner race." The plaintiff has made numerous claims arising from its allegation that the helicopter was defective. First, it argues that the defective condition constitutes a breach of warranty; second, it alleges negligence on the part of the defendants; and third, it seeks to impose liability under strict products liability theory. The defendants seek summary judgment on each of Comind's claims, arguing that the sales contract's warranty and tort disclaimer provisions bar such claims. The plaintiff, however, contends that these disclaimer provisions are unenforceable; and, additionally, that even if UTI may enforce the disclaimer provisions, UTC may not since it was not a party to the agreement. UTC argues that UTI acted as its agent in the matter and that it is therefore entitled to enforce the disclaimers on its own behalf.

The defendants contend that UTI acted as UTC's agent in entering into the sales contract with VOTEC, and that therefore UTC may take advantage of the contract's disclaimer provisions. The Court agrees and finds that summary judgment is appropriate on [the issue of whether UTI acted as UTC's agent].

In Connecticut the general rule is that "the contract of an agent is in law the contract of the principal." *Robert Lawrence Associates, Inc. v. Del Vecchio,* 178 Conn. 1, 13, 420 A.2d 1142 (1979) (citing 2 Restatement, Second, Agency § 302). There are several exceptions to this rule, the first of which is that a principal is not bound to the contract, absent ratification, if the agent exceeded its authority in making the contract. Also, a principal is not a party if specifically excluded as a party in the contract. 1 Restatement, Second, Agency § 147. Finally, the principal is not entitled to benefit from the contract if the principal was an undisclosed principal hiding behind its agent for fraudulent or dishonest purposes.

With regard to the issue of whether UTI acted within its authority, the Court finds that UTC granted UTI the authority to engage in the transaction at issue, and that UTI acted within its authority in entering into the agreement.

The Restatement defines authority as the power of the agent to affect the legal relations of the principal by acts done in accordance with the principal's manifestations of consent to him. *Id.* § 7. In other words, the agent's powers flow from and are defined by the particular consent given. Where the consent is not written or otherwise stated with particularity, its nature is to be inferred from the principal's "manifestations of consent," meaning "conduct from which, in light of the circumstances, it is reasonable to infer consent." 1 Restatement, Second, Agency § 7, comment b. Therefore, the Court looks to the conduct of the principal, UTC, to define the scope of UTI's authority in handling UTC's affairs.

The issue of the scope of the agent's authority is closely related to the issue of consent to the agency. Factually, whether or not UTI acted within its authority in entering into the sales contract is beyond dispute. It is unrefuted that, at UTC's behest, UTI was engaged exclusively in the business of selling UTC's products, of which the accident aircraft was one. UTI sold such products to UTC's international customers, of which VOTEC was one. Although the nature and extent of an agent's authority is typically a question of fact, a review of the record establishes that the Court's conclusion is supported and unrefuted. The Court therefore finds that UTI acted within its authority in conducting the transaction on behalf of UTC.

With regard to the issue of fraudulent non-disclosure, the Court finds that UTC was a disclosed principal, and as such cannot be accused of hiding its identity for dishonest purposes. As the Restatement explains,

> [i]f, at the time of the transaction conducted by an agent, the other party thereto has notice that the agent is acting for a principal and of the principal's identity, the principal is a disclosed principal.

1 Restatement, Second, Agency § 4. Notice does not have to be in writing, nor does it have to be "actual" notice. As explained in comment d,

> [i]f the manifestations of the principal or agent are such as reasonably to indicate to the other party the identity or existence of the principal, the latter is disclosed or partially disclosed, and this is true although the other party believes that he is dealing with the agent alone. If the manifestation as to agency is ambiguous, the belief of the other party, if reasonable, is conclusive.

Id., comment d. The contract itself does not disclose that UTC was the principal in the transaction. Nor is the Court aware of any other documents that were shown to VOTEC that state that UTI was acting as the agent of UTC. However, notice may be had by means other than written notice. The unrefuted evidence reveals that VOTEC knew of UTC's existence and the scope of UTC's control. VOTEC had made other purchases from UTC through UTI in the past, and knew of the interrelationship between the parent and subsidiary. The Court finds that VOTEC had actual knowledge both of the existence of UTC, and that UTI acted on UTC's behalf.

With regard to the final element, the law presumes that the principal is a party unless explicitly excluded by agreement. 1 Restatement, Second, Agency § 147 (a disclosed principal is a party to the contract "unless otherwise agreed"). The preamble of the contract in question defines the seller of the aircraft as UTI, and the buyer as VOTEC. It makes no mention of UTC as either the principal or as the seller. Comind argues that this suggests that UTC was excluded. However, evidence that the principal was never actually mentioned in the contract, while perhaps indicative of an intent to limit the parties to those actually named, "is not sufficient to rebut the inference that a disclosed principal is a party to a contract made by his agent." 1 Restatement, Second, Agency § 149, comment a.

Comind also argues that the contract is an "integrated" contract, and that it therefore would be improper to expand the definition of the parties to include UTC. On the contrary, the mere fact that a contract is integrated is insufficient to exclude the principal as a party even where the parties are defined. 1 Restatement, Second, Agency § 154, comment b. While it is true that special rules apply to integrated contracts regarding the use of non-textual evidence to show whether or not the parties intended other than what they actually stated, these rules are inapplicable to the issue presented here. The Court does not presently address the question of the admissibility of extrinsic evidence in conflict with the text of an agreement. It deals with the presumption that a principal is in law a party to its agent's contract. The facts demonstrate that the contract contains no language expressly limiting the parties to the named buyer and seller. And as explained in the Restatement, under the rule stated in section 149, the fact that the agent appears to be a party and that the principal's name does not appear in the integrated instrument is not sufficient to exclude the principal as a party. The instrument may be so worded, however, as to exclude him. 1 Restatement, Second, Agency § 154, comment b. Furthermore, the fact that the contract is final with regard to some matters is not to be taken as an expression of finality with regard to matters not specifically addressed in the contract. Because the contract does not explicitly exclude UTC as a party, and because it does not mention any express limitations on who may be a party to it, the mere fact that the parties are defined and that the contract is integrated is insufficient as a matter of law to exclude UTC as a party.

Comind next suggests that the express provisions of the contract, in particular the anti-assignment clause, establish that UTC is excluded on the face of the document. The Court is obliged to scrutinize the contract to determine if indeed Comind has raised a genuine issue of interpretation.

An integrated contract is a "writing or writings constituting a final expression of one or more terms of an agreement." 2 Restatement, Second, Contracts § 209. Furthermore,

> [a] completely integrated agreement is an integrated agreement adopted by the parties as a complete and exclusive statement of the terms of the agreement.

2 Restatement, Second, Contracts § 210.

[T]he Court finds that the UTI-VOTEC contract is a completely integrated agreement.

In interpreting the express provisions of the contract, the Court recognizes that such interpretation is directed to discovering "the meaning of the terms of the writing in light of the circumstances [presented]." 2 Restatement, Second, Contracts § 212. The Court is also mindful that any interpretation that depends upon a choice between reasonable inferences drawn from the evidence presented is a question of fact. However, the Court finds that the evidence establishes that the contract does not exclude UTC as a principal, including the anti-assignment clause, and that any claim to the contrary is entirely unsupported. Furthermore, the Court declines to add such an exclusion to the contract.

Because the contract does not expressly exclude UTC as a principal, and because the law presumes a principal is a party even if not mentioned in the contract itself (regardless of whether the contract is integrated or not); and further because there is no evidence in the record sufficient to rebut this presumption, the Court concludes that UTC is a proper party to the contract.

With regard to whether UTC is entitled to enforce the disclaimer provisions as a defense, Comind argues that UTC has no such right as a matter of law. Comind argues that even if UTC is a principal to the contract it nevertheless may not assert the contract's disclaimer provisions as a defense to Comind's claims.

A principal, as a proper party to a contract, may sue and be sued on that contract. 1 & 2 Restatement, Second, Agency §§ 140, 292. Where the principal is the party bringing the suit, the law treats the action exactly as though the agent had brought the suit, including the preservation on the defendant's behalf of all defenses that the defendant could have brought to bear against the agent. Nevertheless, Comind argues that when the principal is the one being sued, it is not entitled to claim any such defenses, including those arising from the contract itself. The Court finds that if Comind were to prevail on this argument, such would create a gross inconsistency within the law of agency. The Court therefore holds that under Connecticut law, where the principal is a proper party to a contract, the principal is entitled to assert the valid provisions of the contract in its defense just as surely as it would be able to assert such provisions if it were the plaintiff.

However, it is axiomatic that a party may not enforce an invalid provision. The Court therefore addresses the issue of whether UTC's disclaimer provisions are enforceable in and of themselves.

The plaintiff, Comind, has brought suit against the defendants claiming negligence, breach of warranty, and strict products liability. The defendants raise the provisions of the sales contract, which purport to disclaim or limit all such liability, as an absolute defense. The defendants request summary judgment claiming that these disclaimers and limitations are valid and enforceable as a matter of law, and that no genuine issue of material fact exists regarding their enforceability. Comind claims that each of the disclaimer and limitation provisions are fatally flawed and, accordingly, claims the existence of genuine issues of fact which, if resolved in Comind's favor, would defeat the purported effect of these provisions. The Court finds that there is merit to the plaintiff's claims and therefore denies summary judgment on these issues.

For the foregoing reasons, the defendants' motion for summary judgment is granted on the issues of agency; the motion is denied in all other respects.

SO ORDERED.

Note

Under Restatement section 292

> [t]he other party to a contract made by an agent for a disclosed or partially disclosed principal, acting within his authority, apparent authority or other agency power, is liable to the principal as if he had contracted directly with the principal, unless the principal is excluded as a party by the form or terms of the contract.

In *Comind, Companhia de Seguros v. Sikorsky Aircraft Division of United Technologies Corp.*, the agent and the third person entered into a written contract that *not only* failed to name the principal as a party, *not only* failed to expressly grant the principal any rights, *but also* contained a clause that the contract could not be assigned. On what basis did the court conclude that the contract did *not* exclude UTC as a party? Is UTC in privity of contract with VOTEC? Does giving UTC rights under the contract violate the parol evidence rule?

Kelly Asphalt Block Co. v. Barber Asphalt Paving Co.

211 N.Y. 68, 105 N.E. 88 (1914)

CARDOZO, J.

The plaintiff sues to recover damages for breach of an implied warranty. The contract was made between the defendant and one Booth. The plaintiff says that Booth was in truth its agent, and it sues as undisclosed principal. The question is whether it has the right to do so.

The general rule is not disputed. A contract not under seal, made in the name of an agent as ostensible principal, may be sued on by the real principal at the latter's election. The defendant says that we should establish an exception to that rule, where the identity of the principal has been concealed because of the belief that, if it were disclosed, the contract would not be made. We are asked to say that the reality of the defendant's consent is thereby destroyed, and the contract vitiated for mistake.

The plaintiff and the defendant were competitors in business. The plaintiff's president suspected that the defendant might refuse to name him a price. The suspicion was not based upon any previous refusal, for there had been none; it had no other origin than their relation as competitors. Because of this doubt the plaintiff availed itself of the services of Booth, who, though interested to the defendant's knowledge of the plaintiff's business, was also engaged in a like business for another corporation. Booth asked the defendant for a price and received a quotation, and the asphalt blocks required for the plaintiff's pavement were ordered in his name. The order was accepted by the defendant, the blocks were delivered, and payment was made by Booth with money furnished by the plaintiff. The paving blocks were unmerchantable, and the defendant, retaining the price, contests its liability for damages on the ground that if it had known that the plaintiff was the principal it would have refused to make the sale.

We are satisfied that upon the facts before us the defense cannot prevail. A contract involves a meeting of the minds of the contracting parties. If 'one of the supposed parties is wanting,' there is an absence of 'one of the formal constituents of a legal transaction.' *Rodliff v. Dallinger,* 141 Mass. 1, 6, 4 N.E. 805, 807 (55 Am. Rep. 439). In such a situation there is no contract. A number of cases are reported where A has ordered merchandise of B, and C has surreptitiously filled the order. The question has been much discussed whether C, having thrust himself without consent into the position of a creditor, is entitled to recover the value of his wares. That question is not before us, and we express no opinion concerning it. We state it merely to accentuate the distinction between the cases which involve it and the case at hand. Neither of the supposed parties was wanting in this case. The apparent meeting of the minds between determinate contracting parties was not unreal or illusory. The defendant was contracting with the precise person with whom it intended to contract. It was contracting with Booth. It gained whatever benefit it may have contemplated from his character and substance. An agent who contracts in his own name for an undisclosed principal does not cease to be a party because of his agency. Indeed, such an agent, having made himself personally liable, may enforce the contract though the principal has renounced it. As between himself and the other party, he is liable as principal to the same extent as if he had not been acting for another. It is impossible in such circumstances to hold that the contract collapses for want of parties to sustain it. The contractual tie cannot exist where there are not persons to be bound; but here persons were bound, and those the very persons intended. If Booth had given the order in his own right and for his own benefit, but with the expectation of later assigning it to the plaintiff, that undisclosed expectation would not have nullified the contract. His undisclosed intention to act for a principal who was unknown to the defendant was equally ineffective to destroy the contract in its inception.

If therefore the contract did not fail for want of parties to sustain it, the unsuspected existence of an undisclosed principal can supply no ground for the avoidance of a contract unless fraud is proved. We must distinguish between mistake, such as we have been discussing, which renders the contract void ab initio, because the contractual tie has never been completely formed, and fraud which renders it voidable at the election of the defrauded party. *Rodliff v. Dallinger,* 141 Mass. 1, 6, 4 N.E. 805, 807 (55 Am. Rep. 439). In the language of Holmes, J., in the case cited:

> Fraud only becomes important, as such, when a sale or contract is complete in its formal elements, and therefore valid unless repudiated, but the right is claimed to rescind it.

If one who is in reality an agent denies his agency when questioned, and falsely asserts that his principal has no interest in the transaction, the contract, it may be said, becomes voidable, not because there is a want of parties, but because it has been fraudulently procured. When such a case arises, we shall have to consider whether a misrepresentation of that kind is always so material as to justify rescission after the contract has been executed. But no such situation is disclosed in the case at hand. Booth made no misrepresentation to the defendant. He was not asked anything, nor did he say anything, about the plaintiff's interest in the transaction. Indeed, neither he nor the plaintiff's officers knew whether the defendant would refuse to deal with the plaintiff directly. They suspected hostility, but none had been expressed. The validity of the contract turns thus, according to the defendant, not on any overt act of either the plaintiff or its agent, but on the presence or absence of a mental state. We are asked to hold that a contract complete in form becomes a nullity in fact because of a secret belief in the mind of the undisclosed principal that the disclosure of his name would be prejudicial to the completion of the bargain. We cannot go so far.

It is unnecessary, therefore, to consider whether, even if fraud were shown, the defendant, after the contract was executed, could be permitted to rescind without restoring the difference between the price received for the defective blocks and their reasonable value. It is also unnecessary to analyze the evidence for the purpose of showing that the defendant, after notice of the plaintiff's interest in the transaction, continued to make delivery, and thereby waived the objection that the contract was invalid.

The judgment should be affirmed, with costs.

Notes

1. Restatement section 320 provides that

> [a] person who makes a contract with an agent of an undisclosed principal, intended by the agent to be on account of the undisclosed principal and within the power of such agent to bind his principal, is liable to the principal as if the principal himself had made the contract with him, unless he is excluded by the form or terms of the contract, unless his existence is fraudulently concealed or unless there is set-off or a similar defense against the agent.

Under Restatement section 304,

> [a] person with whom an agent contracts on account of an undisclosed principal can rescind the contract if he was induced to enter into it by a representation that the agent was not acting for a principal and if, as the agent or principal has notice, he would not have dealt with the principal.

In *Kelly Asphalt Block Co. v. Barber Asphalt Paving Co.*, the Court reasons that neither the principal nor the agent *knew* that the third person would not deal with the principal. Did either the principal or the agent have *notice* of the third person's reluctance (under Restatement section 9(1), a person has *notice* of a fact if the person knows it, has reason to know it, should know it, has been given a notification of it)?

2. Would the court in *Kelly Asphalt Block Co. v. Barber Asphalt Paving Co.* have reached the same result if the third person were *suing to rescind* the contract, instead

of trying to avoid responsibility for breach of warranty while retaining the sales proceeds?

3. Big Amusement, Inc., the operator of a world-famous amusement park in Southern California, plans to open a major amusement park just outside a city in northern Florida. Big Amusement, Inc., hires Agent to purchase the necessary property, but directs Agent not to reveal Big Amusement's identity. Agent approaches Owner, who owns some suitably located agricultural land, and offers to buy the property at the market price for agricultural land. Owner believes Agent is acting on his or her own behalf, but does not ask Agent if that is the case. After the sale, Owner discovers that Big Amusement, Inc. is the true purchaser. Owner sues for rescission, claiming that Owner would have insisted on a higher price if Owner had known this. What result? Would your answer change if Owner would have objected to the sale because he did not want to live next door to a major amusement park? Has there even been a misrepresentation? *See* Restatement § 304 comments a and c.

4. As discussed in *Comind, Companhia de Seguros v. Sikorsky Aircraft Division of United Technologies Corp.*, if the contract entered into by the agent provides that the contract cannot be assigned, the principal is *not* excluded *per se.*

> A clause in the contract against assignment does not of itself prevent the principal from bringing suit upon the contract. The existence of such a clause, however, may be considered as evidence that the parties intended to exclude the principal or that failure to reveal the existence of a principal is fraudulent within the rule stated in Section 304 *if there is other evidence to that effect.*

Restatement § 303 comment c (emphasis added). *See Cooper v. Epstein,* 308 A.2d 781 (D.C. Ct. App. 1973) (question of whether non-assignability clause excluded principal is a question of fact and summary judgment should not have been entered).

5. *Birmingham Matinee Club v. McCarty*, 152 Ala. 571, 44 So. 642 (1907), involved a suit by a principal for breach of a contract made by an agent in his own name for the sale of the principal's lands that called for the agent to convey unencumbered title *via* a warranty deed. The court invoked the rule preventing enforcement of the contract by an undisclosed principal where the contract involves elements of personal trust and confidence as a consideration moving from the undisclosed principal's agent to the other party to the contract:

> The reason for this exception is manifest. If the party contracting without knowledge of the agency were bound to take the service or conveyance or property from the undisclosed principal, the well-recognized rule that one may determine for himself with whom he will deal or contract would be directly infracted; and the elements of the contract reasonably attributable to personal confidence and trust, including the financial responsibility of the agent with whom one deals as principal, would be stricken of force to which, under all principles of substantial justice and right, the relying party is entitled to the benefit.

Note that the undisclosed principal will *only* be denied the right to enforce the contract where the portion of the contract calling for personal trust and confidence remains *executory*; once that portion of the contract has been performed, the principal will be at liberty to enforce the contract. *See Strand v. Courier,* 434 N.W.2d 60 (S.D. 1988).

6. In *Hammon v. Paine*, 56 F.2d 19 (1st Cir. 1932), Hammon desired to engage in stock transactions but not in her own name. She turned over 5,000 shares of her stock to Cunniff to act on her behalf in trading. Cunniff employed the defendants, Paine, Webber & Co., as his brokers. Cunniff did not disclose the existence of Hammon. For a number of years, Cunniff had dealt with the defendants and had established accounts of his own numbered one to five. Hammon did not know this. Cunniff established account number six in order to deal with Hammon's stock. When Hammon requested return of her stock and the cash proceeds from the stock transactions, she was unable to receive a full return because Cunniff had a deficit in account five. Therefore, the defendants transferred part of the stock and cash from account six to cover the deficit in account five. Hammon sued to recover from the defendants and lost in the trial court. Hammon contended that she was the undisclosed principal of Cunniff and was therefore entitled to recover her stock and cash. The appellate court rejected her argument:

> One dealing with the agent of an undisclosed principal can do no other than treat the agent as the principal, and he cannot be deprived of any rights which have attached during such dealings when later the real party in interest claims the benefit of the transactions.

Restatement section 306 provides:

> (1) If the agent has been authorized to conceal the existence of the principal, the liability to an undisclosed principal of a person dealing with the agent within his power to bind the principal is diminished by any claim which such person may have against the agent at the time of making the contract and until the existence of the principal becomes known to him, if he could set off such claim in an action against the agent.
>
> (2) If the agent is authorized only to contract in the principal's name, the other party does not have set-off for a claim due him from the agent unless the agent has been entrusted with the possession of chattels which he disposes of as directed or unless the principal has otherwise misled the third person into extending credit to the agent.

D. Liability of Agent to Third Persons

Clark v. Maddux

118 Ill. App. 3d 546, 454 N.E.2d 1179 (1983)

Pl. sued Atty for expert fees. Atty claimed client liable.

SEIDENFELD, Presiding Justice:

The plaintiff, a medical doctor, sued defendant, a lawyer, to recover a fee for review of medical information in connection with a medical malpractice case. The defendant appeals from the judgment of $4,350 and costs entered for the plaintiff, contending that he acted for a disclosed principal, his client, and therefore was not personally liable.

At trial plaintiff testified that he had a discussion with Shelley Gardner, who identified herself as an attorney from defendant's office. Gardner said the firm represented a case that she wished to discuss; he agreed to review the records involved in the case. He testified that there was "no real indication who was going to pay" his fee, but that it was his "assumption" that defendant's office would pay "since she agreed to the fee." He stated that at the time of conversation, there was no discussion of whether a suit had been filed; only that the firm represented the patient. He did testify, however, that "the malpractice case was directed against a doctor," naming him; that there was a "pending suit"; and that Gardner "indicated that they were suing a physician."

Gardner testified that she told Clark that Jenkins was a poor woman who was frequently unable to work. She testified that the firm's practice is to explain to the client that although costs may be advanced, the client is ultimately responsible. She testified that, in her conversation with plaintiff, she told him that she represented Arnetta Jenkins, who had a claim against the named doctor. She identified herself as an attorney working on behalf of Jenkins and informed Clark that a lawsuit had been filed. She never agreed to become personally liable for the plaintiff's services or to make the defendant personally liable. She had a conversation with Jenkins within two weeks after meeting with Clark; she gave Jenkins a status report, told her she had retained a physician, and, she was "sure" she told her what his charges were.

In his discovery deposition, some of which was read into evidence, defendant admitted that his firm had not asked Arnetta Jenkins to reimburse the firm for costs, as she would not be able to afford it.

Also in evidence was a letter sent by defendant in response to plaintiff's bill, over Gardner's signature. In substance the letter confirmed that an hourly charge of $300 had been agreed upon but protested the extensive literature research and medical report as allegedly not needed or authorized. The letter also stated that in the experience of the attorneys they had never been previously billed for secretarial copying services, and that the bill was "far in excess of the normal for initial interviews." An adjustment was requested.

The long settled rule in Illinois is that

> [w]here an agent in making a contract discloses his agency and the name of his principal[,] the agent is not liable on the contract unless he agrees to become personally liable.

The rule has been applied in various cases involving attorneys. In *Petrando v. Barry* (1955), 4 Ill. App. 2d 319, 124 N.E.2d 85, a printer sued an attorney for the cost of printing briefs, abstract, petition for rehearing, and petition for leave to appeal. The name of the attorney's client appeared on the cover pages of the printed materials and the plaintiff's business largely was of printing such materials. In holding for the attorney the court noted that the attorney-client relationship in some of its aspects is a relationship of agency, and that the printer was necessarily aware of the attorney's representative capacity. The fact that the plaintiff had billed the attorney or that the attorney rather than the client placed the printing order was held not critical, absent proof that the credit was given expressly or exclusively to the attorney with further proof that he intended to assume personal liability. In *International Service Corp. v. Ooms* (1969), 105 Ill. App. 2d 391, 245 N.E.2d 571, the plaintiff sued the defendant attorney for investigative work in a civil action, performed at the attorney's request. The court, noting the applicability of agent-principal rules to the attorney-client relationship, held that the defendant was not personally liable because he employed plaintiff while acting as an attorney for a client and the plaintiff was aware of this relationship. It made no difference that the plaintiff dealt directly with the defendant and not with the client. In *McCorkle v. Weinstein* (1977), 50 Ill. App. 3d 661, 662-64, 365 N.E.2d 953, the plaintiff, a court reporter, sued an attorney for the value of the court reporting services rendered in connection with a proceeding before the Pollution Control Board. The court affirmed a holding for the defendant even though the defendant was billed for the services and the defendant had initially requested the services. The court expressly rejected an argument also made by the plaintiff in this case that the promise of the attorney to pay be implied from the conduct of the parties, custom, and a consideration of the nature of the attorney's role in litigation and society generally. In *Association Claims Service v. Rinella & Rinella* (1979), 79 Ill. App. 3d 1023, 398 N.E.2d 1211, a law firm employed the plaintiff to serve subpoenas in a case. The plaintiff sued to recover for its services but the court held that the law firm was not liable because it employed plaintiff while acting as an agent for a client, a disclosed principal.

There is no doubt that Gardner told plaintiff that defendant was representing Arnetta Jenkins. Her name also was on the medical records given to plaintiff. Plaintiff admitted that Gardner told him that defendant's firm was representing Jenkins and, in fact, plaintiff conceded on cross-examination that he was told that a suit had been filed. Gardner testified that she told plaintiff that defendant represented Jenkins and that a suit had been filed. There was no showing, and no finding, that defendant had taken himself out of the disclosed principal rule by agreeing to be personally liable. Plaintiff testified only that he "assumed" that defendant would be liable. Gardner testified that she told plaintiff that Jenkins would ultimately pay. The letter from Gardner to Clark contests the reasonableness and propriety of the fee but it is not inconsistent with the position that, in accordance with the employment agreement, Jenkins was remaining liable although defendant was advancing costs. Defendant was thus not personally liable for the plaintiff's charges.

The judgment of the Circuit Court of DuPage County is reversed.

Copp v. Breskin

56 Wash. App. 229, 782 P.2d 1104 (1989)

WEBSTER, Judge.

Breskin & Robbins, a law firm, appeals a summary judgment in favor of Harley Copp, an expert witness hired by the firm on behalf of a client. Copp successfully claimed $14,789 for expert services.

Breskin & Robbins advised Copp before hiring him that fees "were being paid, and were to be paid" by the client. Copp says he would never accept employment if an attorney's obligation were dependent on reimbursement from a client. He made this policy known.

Breskin & Robbins concedes by way of deposition that, absent an agreement to the contrary, a provider of litigation services can expect an attorney in King County to pay the provider's bill whether or not the client reimburses the attorney. Copp, a California resident, is aware of a similar custom.

Copp sent Breskin & Robbins an initial bill which the firm paid with a "trust check" for $1,424. An accompanying letter assured Copp that any future charges would be paid within 30 days of his testimony. Breskin & Robbins claims it gave the assurance on behalf of the client and did not intend a guaranty. The client paid some of Copp's bills directly while he was in town for the trial. After trial, Copp sent Breskin & Robbins a final bill. He said he expected payment within 30 days, as previously agreed.

Breskin & Robbins replied that the client was willing to pay only 30 per cent of the bill. The firm offered to commence litigation on Copp's behalf, and eventually sued the client on its own behalf. It claimed $37,000 in litigation expenses allegedly incurred at the client's request, including amounts owing to Copp.

Subsequently, Copp filed this action against Breskin & Robbins. Breskin & Robbins admitted the amount owed, but averred as an affirmative defense that it hired Copp as agent of a disclosed principal, the client.

Breskin & Robbins relies on dictum to the effect that an attorney, as agent of a client, is not responsible for litigation costs, such as expert witness fees, unless the attorney personally agrees with the litigation service provider to pay them. *See Christensen, O'Connor, Garrison & Havelka v. Department of Rev.*, 97 Wash. 2d 764, 769-70, 649 P.2d 839 (1982). The *Christensen* dictum might be persuasive if it were not for a subsequent case which dealt with the same issue (whether reimbursements for costs advanced on behalf of a client are subject to business and occupation tax) but which disclaimed any ruling on the issue presented in this case. *See Walthew, Warner, Keefe, Arron, Costello & Thompson v. Department of Revenue*, 103 Wash. 2d 183, 190, 691 P.2d 559 (1984). *Walthew* held, as did *Christensen*, that reimbursements for litigation costs are exempt from B & O tax because the attorney receiving the reimbursement is not ultimately responsible for those costs. However, *Walthew* retracted the agency reasoning in *Christensen*, together with the suggestion that reimbursements might be taxable if an attorney agrees to pay them personally, holding instead that reimbursements for costs are per se exempt from B & O tax.

Walthew relied on the Code of Professional Responsibility, now the Rules of Professional Conduct, which forbid attorneys from advancing or otherwise paying the costs of litigation unless the client remains ultimately liable for them. *Walthew*, at 188, 691 P.2d 559 (discussing DR 5-103, now RPC 1.8(e)). Washington State Bar Association, Ethics Opinion 140 (1969), states:

> [W]hen the attorney has directly and personally ordered or arranged for services in circumstances under which the attorney did not make it clear (if such were [the] intent) to the person rendering the services that such person must look to the client alone for payment, the attorney has been derelict in preserving a good public image of the legal profession. *The primary responsibility of making it clear that the attorney acts in an agency capacity with no personal liability rests upon the attorney.* If [the attorney] has been derelict herein, others may reasonably be misled into believing that the attorney is agreeing to pay or to guarantee the payment of the obligation so created. In this circumstance it would be the ethical obligation of the attorney to pay such indebtedness and then look to [the] client for reimbursement and assume the risk of nonpayment.

(Emphasis added). The Rules of Professional Conduct prohibit attorneys from using the ignorance of litigation service providers to their financial advantage. Attorneys may not engage in conduct involving dishonesty, fraud, deceit, or misrepresentation. RPC 8.4(c). They must prevent or correct misunderstandings when the client's legitimate interests are not jeopardized. RPC 4.1, 4.3. They must avoid means that burden third persons without justification. RPC 4.4. The rules do not "undertake to define standards for civil liability of lawyers," RPC, Preliminary Statement, but that is often a necessary or logical consequence of upholding them.

Other jurisdictions are split as to whether an attorney is responsible to an expert or other service provider in the absence of a disclaimer. *See Annot., Attorney's Personal Liability for Expenses Incurred in Relation to Services for Client,* 66 A.L.R. 4th 256 (1988). Since 1955, three jurisdictions deciding the issue as a matter of first impression have reasoned that the attorney is an agent of a disclosed principal and, as such, is not liable unless the attorney expressly or impliedly agrees to be bound. *See Free v. Wilmar J. Helric Co.,* 70 Or. App. 40, 688 P.2d 117 (1984); *Hasbrouck v. Krsul,* 168 Mont. 270, 541 P.2d 1197 (1975); *see also Soro v. Bank of Miami,* 537 So. 2d 1135 (Fla. App. 1989) (agreement to be bound). During the same period, nine jurisdictions considering the issue anew or for the first time have held that formal agency reasoning does not accurately reflect the attorney's role as a strategist in litigation or the common understanding of litigation service providers. *See Gualtieri v. Burleson,* 84 N.C. App. 650, 353 S.E.2d 652 (1987); *Ingram v. Lupo,* 726 S.W.2d 791 (Mo. App. 1987) (rejecting earlier cases); *Gaines Reporting Serv. v. Mack,* 4 Ohio App. 3d 234, 447 N.E.2d 1317 (1982); *Theuerkauf v. Sutton,* 102 Wis. 2d 176, 306 N.W.2d 651 (1981); *Molezzo Reporters v. Patt,* 94 Nev. 540, 579 P.2d 1243 (1978); *C.C. Plumb Mixes, Inc. v. Stone,* 108 R.I. 75, 272 A.2d 152 (1971); *Roberts, Walsh & Co. v. Trugman,* 109 N.J. Super. 594, 264 A.2d 237 (1970); *Burt v. Gahan,* 351 Mass. 340, 220 N.E.2d 817, 15 A.L.R.3d 527 (1966); *see also In re Peters,* 332 N.W.2d 10, 17 (Minn. 1983) (disciplinary proceeding). The clear trend is to hold the attorney liable. One court, bound by prior cases siding with the attorney, nevertheless expressed the view that the attorney should be liable in the absence of a disclaimer, because the service provider deals with the attorney, not the client, and generally accepts employment based on the attorney's credit, not the client's. *See Rayvid v. Burgh,* 37 Misc. 2d 963, 234 N.Y.S.2d 868 (1962).

Justification for the disclosed agency rule is the probable intention of the parties, objectively manifested. Restatement (Second) of Agency § 320, Comments a-c; § 321, Comment a; § 328, Comment a (1958). When the circumstances indicate a probable intention that is contrary to the general rule, the reason for the rule is gone, and the rule should be modified to reflect this fact. Otherwise, the purpose of the rule—giving effect to the intentions of the parties—is lost. When a litigation service provider contracts with an attorney based on the attorney's credit, and the attorney is aware, or should be aware of this, it should not matter that the client's identity is known. The service provider reasonably expects that the attorney will be responsible, as surety or guarantor of the client's performance, RPC 1.8(e), and any contrary expectation of the attorney is unreasonable, if not fraudulent.

An agent may guarantee performance by the principal, and the existence of a guarantee "may be shown by proof of a custom to that effect." Restatement (Second) of Agency § 328, Comment b. Custom is determinative of the parties' intent where both parties are aware of it, and neither knows or should know that the other party has an intention contrary to it.

Here, Copp's testimony establishes that he relied upon a custom whereby experts look to attorneys for payment of their fees. Breskin & Robbins was aware of an identical custom locally. The statement that litigation costs were being paid and were to be paid by the client does not address the situation when the client is unwilling or unable to pay. Therefore, under the circumstances of this case, it was insufficient as a matter of law to apprise Copp of a change from customary practice. Copp accepted employment before meeting the client, and he sent bills to Breskin & Robbins, which the firm paid. This put the firm on notice that he was relying on its credit, not the client's, making an express disclaimer of responsibility essential to avoid liability. Breskin & Robbins assured Copp that any future charges would be paid within 30 days of his testimony. This assurance, on the firm's letterhead and signed "BRESKIN & ROBBINS /s/ Howard Breskin," did not disclose the agency character in which it was allegedly made. It is completely consistent with the customary practice of a firm pledging its credit to obtain expert services.

Breskin & Robbins advanced several thousand dollars by itself and through an associated attorney. This conflicts with the firm's assertion that the client alone was paying, and alone was expected to pay, the expenses of litigation. The advancements reveal the firm's personal interest in the litigation—established by a contingency fee agreement—evidencing an intent by the firm to become a party to the contract with Copp.

Breskin & Robbins offered to commence litigation against the client on Copp's behalf without any indication that there would be a charge for this service. The firm's offer reveals an understanding on its part that it was indebted to Copp. The lawsuit commenced by Breskin & Robbins on its own behalf against the client admits amounts owing to Copp as its damages. The firm would not have acted in this way if it believed it had adequately apprised Copp of an intention not to be liable for his services.

We hold that in these circumstances an attorney owes an expert or other litigation service provider an express disclaimer of responsibility if the attorney intends not to be bound by a contract for litigation services. This reflects the modern trend, which is to hold the attorney liable in the absence of an express disclaimer or other clear indication not to be bound. Putting the burden on the attorney promotes public trust and confidence in the legal profession, the supervision of which is the exclusive province and responsibility of the courts. Public trust in the profession and the courts would be "greatly endangered and jeopardized" by a technical defense of disclosed agency. Ethics Opinion 140.

The judgment is affirmed.

Note

Copp v. Breskin states that it is "rejecting" the agency rule that, unless otherwise agreed, an agent acting on behalf of a disclosed principal is not a party to the contract (and thus not liable on it). Is the reasoning in *Copp v. Breskin* inconsistent with *Clark v. Maddux*? *See* Restatement § 320.

Robert T. Reynolds Associates, Inc. v. Asbeck

23 Conn. App. 247, 580 A.2d 533 (1990)

DALY, Judge.

The plaintiff instituted this contract action against the defendant for the recovery of sums due for advertising services. The defendant pleaded, by way of special defense, that the plaintiff was either estopped from holding him personally liable on the agreement or had waived the right to do so. The trial court rendered judgment for the plaintiff and awarded $31,453.93 in damages, together with statutory interest. On appeal, the defendant claims that the trial court (1) should not have found him personally liable.

The trial court found the following facts that are relevant to the first claim. In January, 1984, the plaintiff started doing business with Acousticon Electronics (AE), a company that employed between forty-five and fifty people and that was involved in the manufacturing of hearing aids. Although AE was a trade name, there was no certificate of that name filed in Waterbury, its principal place of business. From January through June, 1984, the plaintiff provided advertising services for AE. During this time period, Robert T. Reynolds, the plaintiff's president, worked directly with Niles Floyd, vice president of AE, and communicated with Robert Teal, AE's president, on billing matters. Some time in January, 1984, Reynolds was told by either Teal or Floyd that AE was not a corporation. This was stated in connection with a logo that was being made for AE. When the plaintiff first started doing business with AE, the plaintiff did not request, or perform, a credit check, or require personal guarantees. Payment for those services was made.

In July, 1984, the defendant first heard about AE when he met with Teal regarding possible employment. Following this meeting, the defendant went to Birmingham, Alabama, where he met with Charles Speir, whom the defendant understood to be in the process of buying J.S. Sales Corporation. The defendant entered into a verbal three year employment contract with Speir and was paid by J.S. Sales Corporation.

The defendant began his employment as president of AE in August, 1984. He was put in charge of trying to resolve AE's financial difficulties. Shortly after analyzing the needs of AE, the defendant contacted Reynolds to obtain advertising services, advising Reynolds that he was the president of AE. The defendant authorized, reviewed and approved the advertising services at issue. The plaintiff provided these services and billed the defendant. During the period that the plaintiff provided services at the defendant's request, the defendant did not inform the plaintiff that he was the agent for any other entity. The defendant made partial payment but when pressed for the rest of the money, he merely made reference to "money" people, but never disclosed their identity or involvement.

The trial court found that there was a meeting of the minds to form a contract, and that the defendant's special defenses were without merit. In addition, the court found that, even if the defendant had shown that an agency relationship existed with J.S. Sales Corporation, a corporation that sold its assets at public auction under the name J.S. Sales Corporation International d/b/a Acousticon Electronics, the defendant's failure to disclose a principal to the plaintiff caused him to remain personally liable.

In this first claim, the defendant asserts three theories as to why he should not be personally liable.

He first argues that the court should not have found that there was mutual assent to form a contract since he never intended to contract on his behalf. We disagree.

The defendant essentially argues that the plaintiff, as part of its duty to be reasonably certain of the identity of the party with whom it was contracting, should have been more diligent in ascertaining whether the defendant intended to bind himself or a corporation. The defendant argues that because of evidence that shows that the plaintiff was not diligent in doing this, the plaintiff failed to prove this essential element of a contract and thus no contract existed to bind him. This argument fails for two reasons.

First, to impose such a duty on the plaintiff under the guise of mutual assent would impermissibly shift the burden of proving notice of agency away from the party asserting its existence. The law is clear that the burden of proving agency is on the party asserting its existence. See *Botticello v. Stefanovicz*, 177 Conn. 22, 26, 411 A.2d 16 (1979).

Further, the defendant's claim that the plaintiff had a duty to discover in what capacity the defendant was acting in order to meet its burden of proving mutual assent is contrary to this court's statements in *New England Whalers Hockey Club* [*v. Nair*, 1 Conn. App. 680, 474 A.2d 810 (1984)]:

> To avoid personal liability, it is the duty of an agent to disclose both the fact that he is acting in a representative capacity and the identity of his principal, since the party with whom he deals is not required to discover or to make inquiries to discover these facts. Therefore, 'where the agent contracts as ostensible principal, regardless of his intention and notwithstanding his lack of personal interest in the consideration he will be personally liable on the contract as if he were the principal.' 3 C.J.S., Agency § 369.

Accordingly, the defendant's first theory of avoiding personal liability is without merit.

The defendant next argues that, because the plaintiff had notice that the defendant was acting in the capacity of an agent, he should not be personally liable. Here, the defendant argues that his consistent use of the words "its president" when dealing with the plaintiff and the fact that the name "Acousticon Electronics" appeared on all invoices and correspondence constituted notice that he was not making a personal promise and, therefore, should not be personally liable. The defendant relies on *Jacobs v. Williams*, 85 Conn. 215, 82 A. 202 (1912), for his assertion that the plaintiff had proper notice that he made a corporate obligation and not a personal obligation. That case is distinguishable from the present case. In *Jacobs*, the name of the alleged principal, the Glastonbury Power Company, appeared directly above the signatures of the two officers who also signed in their representative capacity. Further, the court in that case relied on the following rule:

> [W]here the corporation appears as the primary signer, the almost universally accepted and reasonable rule of construction is that where the signature is that of the corporation, and the name or names of one or more of its officers in their official capacity are appended as subscribing agents the corporation will be regarded as the signer and obligor, and the individuals will not be obligated, unless other language or the general tenor of the writing indicates a contrary intent.

In this case, the court found that AE was not a corporation. This finding is supported by the evidence. Thus, although the name of the business, "AE," may have been present in the correspondence between the parties, there was no evidence submitted to show that this business was a corporation. The only evidence indicating the possibility that this was a corporate obligation was that the correspondence was signed by the defendant as president. The proper name of the alleged corporation, however, was J.S. Sales Corporation International d/b/a Acousticon Electronics. The name of that corporation never appeared in any correspondence concerning this contract. Because this was not a corporate obligation, the mere fact that the defendant signed in a representative capacity will not permit him to avoid personal liability.

Last, the defendant argues that the plaintiff had notice of both the fact of his agency and the identity of his principal because the plaintiff knew that it was dealing with a certain principal and had previous dealings of the same nature through the agent's predecessor.

While it is true that

> [a]n agent, by making a contract only on behalf of a competent disclosed principal whom he has the power to bind, does not thereby become liable for its nonperformance;

whether there was a nondisclosure of a competent principal so that the plaintiff might hold the defendant personally liable on the contract is a question of fact for the trial court.

The evidence showed that neither the defendant nor his alleged predecessors, Teal or Floyd, informed the plaintiff that a corporation existed.

The trial court's decision was not clearly erroneous.

Notes

1. Under Restatement section 4, a principal is at least partially disclosed where the third person has *notice* the agent is acting for a principal, and (fully) disclosed where the third person also has *notice* of the identity of the principal. As discussed earlier, persons have "notice" of a fact when they know it, have *reason to know* it, or *should know* it. In *J. T. Doiron, Inc. v. Lundin,* 385 So. 2d 450 (La. Ct. App. 1980), an officer of a corporation employed an appraiser to appraise real property owned by the corporation. The corporation met with the officer in the corporate offices and was introduced to its president. The property (or at least a portion of it) was carried in the name of the corporation on the tax rolls. The appraiser billed the corporation, but when the corporation failed to pay, the appraiser sued the officer. The court held that the officer had (fully) disclosed the principal, stating that even where there is no "straightforward disclosure,"

> an agent may still be able to escape individual liability by proving that sufficient indicia of the agency relationship were known by the third party to put him on notice of the principal/agent relationship. Express notice of the agent's status and the principal's identity is unnecessary if [the] facts and circumstances surrounding the transaction, combined with the general knowledge that persons in that type of business are usually acting as agents, demonstrate affirmatively that the third person should be charged with notice of the relationship.

In *Robert T. Reynolds Associates, Inc. v. Asbeck*, why wasn't Mr. Reynolds's disclosure that he was acting as president of "Acousticon Electronics" sufficient disclosure of his principal as to relieve him of liability on the contract?

2. *Unless otherwise agreed*, an agent acting for a *partially* disclosed principal is a party to a contract entered into on behalf of the principal. Restatement § 321. According to Comment a to section 321

> The inference of an understanding that the agent is a party to the contract exists unless the agent gives such complete information concerning his principal's iden-

> tity that he can be readily distinguished. If the party has no reasonable means of ascertaining the principal, the inference is almost irresistible and prevails in the absence of an agreement to the contrary.

Why should the inference that the agent is a party to the contract be "almost irresistible" when the third person knows the agent is acting for a principal?

Benner v. Farm Bureau Mutual Insurance Co.

96 Idaho 311, 528 P.2d 193 (1974)

BAKES, Justice.

This action arises out of an alleged oral contract of insurance. George M. Benner and Sherrin Benner, husband and wife, plaintiffs, respondents and cross-appellants in this action, had purchased a homeowners insurance policy in June of 1970 from insurance agent Warren Bauman, defendant, respondent and cross-respondent, who sold insurance exclusively for and was the exclusive agent in the area for Farm Bureau Mutual Insurance Company of Idaho, Inc., defendant, appellant and cross-respondent. The policy provided for $15,000 coverage on the Benners' home in Samuels, Idaho, $6,000 coverage on the contents of the home and $1,000 coverage (with $100 deductible) upon possessions outside the home. The policy was to be in force for a year; it was renewed upon the same terms a year later in 1971.

During the summer of 1971 the Benners sought to sell their home in Samuels. The buyers they found were initially unable to secure financing and the Benners agreed to rent the house to them on a temporary basis until all the necessary loans were approved. During the period in which the future buyers would be renting their home in Idaho, the Benners wished to continue the insurance upon the house, but they wished to insure their own personal belongings, which they would take with them to California rather than the renters' possessions in the Samuels house.

To achieve this result, Sherrin Benner testified that in a telephone call with Bauman she asked him if the coverage under the policy could be split between the house in Samuels and the possessions that they were taking to California. She testified that Bauman responded, "Fine, Mrs. Benner, I will take care of everything." Bauman, on the other hand, testified that he remembered Sherrin Benner telling him that she and her family were moving to California and that they wished to retain coverage on the home while they were renting it. He testified that neither insurance of personal property to be taken to California nor splitting the coverage was discussed and that he did not agree to insure personalty outside the state of Idaho.

The Benners moved to California in September of 1971. A month later, on October 27, the house they were renting burned and all of its contents, which the Benners valued at over $10,000, were destroyed. The Benners submitted a $6,000 claim for the loss to Farm Bureau. Farm Bureau refused to pay $6,000, offering the Benners $900 ($1,000 minus the $100 deductible), the coverage the Benners had in their written policy for losses outside the home.

The court found that in the telephone call with Bauman that Sherrin Benner had entered into an oral contract with Farm Bureau to insure their personalty in California for $6,000. The court further found that over $6,000 damage to the possessions had occurred. Accordingly, the court held Farm Bureau liable to the Benners for $6,000 under the contract, and judgment was entered against Farm Bureau for $6,000.

However, the court found Bauman neither liable to the Benners under the contract of insurance nor liable to reimburse Farm Bureau for its payments under the contract.

Farm Bureau assigns several errors relating to the trial court's finding that a binding new or modified contract of insurance was entered into that was to cover personal property to be taken to California. In another case involving an insurance agent acting outside of the scope of his authority in direct opposition to his company's instructions, this Court approved the following instruction given by the trial court:

> An insurance company is bound by all acts, contracts or representations of its agent which are within the scope of his apparent authority, notwithstanding the fact that they may be in violation of private instructions or limitations upon his authority, unless the person with whom the agent is dealing has either actual or constructive knowledge of the agent's limitation of authority.

The trial court was presented with substantial though conflicting evidence supporting a finding that a representation of insurance coverage upon the personalty in California was made by an agent apparently authorized to offer such coverage to one unaware of the limitations upon the agent's authority. Thus, the trial court's finding that a contract of insurance was entered into was supported by substantial, competent evidence.

Farm Bureau also assigns error dealing with the trial court's rulings upon the liability of the agent Bauman. Bauman testified that he was not licensed to sell insurance covering property in California. Bauman's agreement with Farm Bureau denied him authority to alter existing insurance contracts and required him to report all new insurance contracts he issued. Given these restrictions upon the agent's authority, Farm Bureau claims that Bauman is liable to it for any liability incurred to the Benners because Bauman (1) exceeded his authority by contracting to insure property in California; (2) altered the contract without Farm Bureau's permission; and (3) failed to report the new contract.

We agree with Farm Bureau that their agent is liable to it for any losses resulting from his entering into contracts obligating Farm Bureau in contravention of an agency agreement with Farm Bureau. In *Crawford v. DiMicco,* 216 So. 2d 769 (Fla. App. 1968), the District Court of Appeals of Florida, in a case in which an insurance agent had insured a boat without first subjecting the boat to an inspection as required by the agent's agreement with the insurance company, said that

> [an agent] may not proceed without or beyond his authority, particularly where he has been forbidden to act and [if by] so proceeding, his actions caused loss to his principal, the agent is fully accountable to the principal therefor.
>
> [U]nless and until the principal with full knowledge of all the applicable facts waived the breach of its instructions, ratified or adopted the agent's act as its own the agent became and remained liable to the principal for the damages incurred in acting without authority to the disadvantage of its principal.

Because Bauman acted without the scope of his authority and Farm Bureau did not waive or ratify this breach of the agency agreement, Bauman is liable to Farm Bureau for the loss his entering into the contract caused the company.

Finally, we disagree with the Benners' contention that the agent Warren Bauman is liable to them for entering into this contract without the scope of his authority. As a general rule one purporting to be an agent is liable to a third party when the purported agent has attempted to bind a principal by an agreement which the agent is not authorized to enter into because the purported agent has breached an implied warranty of authority. Restatement of Agency 2d, § 329. In this case the agent Bauman was found to have contracted in a manner he was not authorized to do by his principal Farm Bureau, but nevertheless Farm Bureau was obligated upon the contract because Bauman was acting within the scope of his apparent authority. Bauman did not breach a warranty of authority to the Benners because the Benners were able to hold Farm Bureau to the contract which he entered into with them. The rule holding an agent liable to a third party for entering into a contract which the agent was not authorized to enter into was not intended to apply to the situation where the principal was nevertheless bound as if the agent were authorized to reach such an agreement with the third party.

Farm Bureau had clothed Bauman with sufficient authority that the company could not assert against third parties that Bauman was not authorized to enter into the contract in question. The Benners' recovery against Farm Bureau was based upon their justifiable reliance on this apparent agency. Because, from the Benners' point of view, Bauman bound his principal as he impliedly warranted he would, the Benners have no more claim against him than they would have against any other agent contracting on a principal's behalf. The Benners are not entitled to judgment against Bauman.

Judgment reversed in part and affirmed in part.

Notes

1. In *Benner v. Farm Bureau Mutual Insurance Co.*, the court follows Restatement section 329 in holding that an agent does *not* violate his or her implied warranty of *authority* where the agent had power to bind the principal by an *unauthorized act.* The Restatement reasons that

> if the principal becomes a party [to the transaction], the rights of the other party are not affected by the fact that the agent committed a wrong to his principal.

Restatement § 329 comment f. In *Benner v. Farm Bureau Mutual Insurance Co.*, did the fact that Bauman was acting outside the scope of his authority from Farm Bureau Mutual Insurance Co. harm the Benners in any way?

2. Suppose that an agent in good faith enters into a contract on behalf of his principal without knowing that the principal has died. As discussed in chapter 5, the occurrence of certain events, such as the *death* of the principal, *automatically and without notice* terminate by operation of law the agent's power to bind the principal, so the agent has *not* bound the principal. Has the agent violated the implied *warranty* of authority? *See* Restatement § 329 comments b and d.

3. May an agent *disclaim* the Restatement section 329 implied warranty of authority?

E. Election of Remedies

Bryans Road Building & Supply Co. v. Grinder

46 Md. App. 10, 415 A.2d 615 (1980)

WILNER, Judge.

The "nice sharp quillets of the law"[1] are both weapon and shield, thrust and parry. Or, as appellant would say in this case, "my technicality prevails over your technicality." In the end, it is the Court's technicality, unrecognized as yet by either party, that will prevail.

This proceeding commenced on May 1, 1978, when appellant, a building supply company, sued Elvin Grinder, individually and trading as Grinder Construction, for some $5,900. The suit was for goods sold and delivered on a long-standing open account. Attached to the Declaration was a motion for summary judgment, accompanied by an affidavit and copies of monthly statements sent to Elvin Grinder showing the periodic status of the account and the final balance due.

On June 20, 1978, Mr. Grinder, individually, filed a general issue plea to the Declaration and an answer to the motion for summary judgment. In this answer, Grinder asserted that, since May 1, 1973 (a date earlier than any of the purchases sued upon), he had made all purchases from appellant on behalf of a corporation known as G. Elvin Grinder Corporation, Inc., of which he was president, that he never guaranteed the corporate obligation personally, and that he was not, therefore, liable for its indebtedness in his individual capacity. With this assertion, he sought to defeat summary judgment on the basis of having raised a genuine dispute of material fact. The court agreed, and denied appellant's motion.

Appellant responded with an Amended Declaration in which it (1) expanded its action against Grinder individually with a claim that the corporation was his "alter ego," that Grinder undercapitalized the corporation during its corporate life, and that he caused it to incur debts when there was no reasonable possibility that it had sufficient assets to cover those debts, and (2) brought the corporation in as an additional defendant. Appellant moved for summary judgment against the defendant corporation, relying primarily upon Grinder's admissions contained in his answer (and affidavit) filed in response to appellant's earlier motion against him. As the corporation was penniless and defunct, no one opposed this new motion; and, on May 25, 1979, it was routinely granted. On that day, judgment in the amount of $5,912.68 was entered against G. Elvin Grinder Construction, Inc. Trial of the case against Grinder individually had previously been set for June 4, 1978, and no attempt was made to disturb that proceeding.

Grinder's defense to the claim was that, by taking judgment against the corporation, appellant had, at least implicitly, recognized the existence of the corporation and the status of the account in question as a corporate one. Otherwise, he argued, appellant had no right to a judgment against the corporation. Thus, by seeking and taking the judgment, appellant was estopped from claiming that the account was an individual one and pursuing judgment against Grinder individually.

---

1. See Shakespeare's Henry VI, Part I, Act II, Scene IV, response of the Earl of Warwick.

The court saw the case as involving [the following issue]: if Grinder, individually, was acting as agent for the corporation and the corporation at the time was an undisclosed principal, did the taking of judgment against the principal constitute an election sufficient to preclude judgment also against the agent? [T]he court concluded that the matter was controlled by the doctrine of "election" enunciated most recently in *Traylor v. Grafton*, 273 Md. 649, 332 A.2d 651 (1975), and entered judgment in favor of Grinder.

(1) Appellee's Technicality.

In *Codd Company v. Parker*, 97 Md. 319, 325, 55 A.623, 624 (1903), the Court made clear that

> where an agent contracts in his own name, without disclosing his interest, though in fact for the exclusive benefit of another person, who is afterwards discovered, the creditor may sue either, but after he has elected whom to sue, and has sued either the agent or principal to final judgment, he cannot after that sue the other, whether the first suit has been successful or not.

See also Wheaton Lumber Co. v. Metz, 229 Md. 78, 181 A.2d 666 (1962). The "bottom line" of it, as stated in *Traylor* is this:

> If the third party contract[s] with an agent for an undisclosed principal, he may hold the agent or, upon discovery, the principal, but the third party cannot recover from both. If the third party elects to hold the agent, the principal is discharged; and, conversely, if he elects to hold the principal, the liability of the agent is at an end.

The third party is entitled to join both principal and agent as co-defendants in a single action, and he may thus proceed against both. The election does not occur "until he takes a final judgment against the one he thus elects to hold to the exclusion of the other." It is thus the final judgment that constitutes the election and bars recovery against the alternative defendant.

This doctrine—appellee's "technicality"—can come into play in a number of factual settings. In *Codd Company v. Parker*, the plaintiff had recovered judgment against the principal before suit was ever filed against the agent. The defense of discharge based on election thus existed at the time the second suit was filed. By way of contrast, in *Wheaton Lumber Co.*, principal and agent were joined as co-defendants in the same action, but judgment against one was entered upon pre-trial motion.[4] In

4. The actual holding in *Wheaton* was that the election doctrine of *Codd* was not applicable. The plaintiff (Wheaton) had initially sued two defendants on an open account. In count one, it alleged that Rothman had been the purchaser; in count two, it alleged that Metz and Mood, trading as Best Window Co., had purchased the goods through Rothman, their agent. Wheaton recovered a default judgment against Rothman. Subsequently, as the result of discovery, Wheaton learned that the real purchaser may have been a corporation known as Best Construction Company, to which Best Window Co. had transferred its business; and it then filed an amended declaration adding the corporation. On the day of trial, the court granted defendants' motions for summary judgment on the premise that, by taking judgment against Rothman, the agent, plaintiff had made an election and was not entitled to proceed against the alleged principals.

The Court of Appeals reversed on the grounds that (1) with respect to Best Window Co., the account was in its name, and it was therefore not an undisclosed principal to which the election doctrine applied; and (2) as to Best Construction Company, Wheaton was not aware that situation, as in the one subjudice, the defense of election (and thus of discharge) arose during the proceeding and did not exist *ab initio*. This distinction is critical when considering,

(2) Appellant's Technicality.

It will be recalled that Grinder's only plea to the Declaration and Amended Declaration was the general issue—"not indebted as alleged." Maryland Rule 342 b.3 provides that "[u]nder a general issue plea any matter of defense shall be admissible in evidence, *except such matters as must be specially pleaded pursuant to section c of this Rule*." (Emphasis supplied.) Section c.1 of Rule 342 states, in relevant part:

> The following matters of defense *must* be specially pleaded in an action ex contractu: Pleas Puis Darrein Continuance. Any defense on the merits arising after suit brought.

(Emphasis on "must" supplied.)

This part of Rule 342 c serves merely to codify and perpetuate the common law plea puis darrein continuance (since the last continuance), which has been accepted as part of our system of common law pleading at least since *Agnew v. Bank of Gettysburg*, 2 Har. & G. 479 (1828).

This "doctrine," the court said at p. 492, is "founded in justice, and calculated to prevent surprise." It served not only to prevent the defendant from offering evidence of the new circumstance raised in defense (expiration of the plaintiff bank's charter after suit was filed), but also from availing himself of the fact to nonsuit the plaintiff. "Whether the bank was dissolved or not pending the suit, was not in issue, and the fact of the dissolution of the charter having taken place after the commencement of the action, was not pertinent to the issue, and was not in evidence before the jury."

It is evident, therefore, that, if the election doctrine was applicable in the first instance, as the court below believed, so was Maryland Rule 342, which would, in that event, have served to preclude appellee from relying on the doctrine. But, as we earlier noted, there is yet to be considered,

(3) The Court's Technicality.

In quoting from *Codd* and *Traylor* we have carefully underscored the language which makes clear that the election between agent and undisclosed principal does not occur until the plaintiff takes final judgment against one or the other. There has never, in the Maryland cases, been any question about that. Until a final judgment, the plaintiff may proceed merrily against both agent and principal.

In such a case, of course, multiple claims—independent claims against two or more parties—are involved. This brings into play Maryland Rule 605a (Multiple Claims—Judgment Upon), which provides:

> Where more than one claim for relief is presented in an action, whether as an original claim, counterclaim, cross-claim, or third-party claim, the court may

---

of its existence at the time it took judgment against Rothman, and the election doctrine applies only when the plaintiff knows of the previously undisclosed principal when he takes a final judgment.

See however, Garfinkel v. Schwartzman, 253 Md. 710, 254 A.2d 667 (1969), where principal and agent were also joined in a single action. At the conclusion of the case, final judgment was entered against the principal, but, on directed verdict, in favor of the agent. On appeal by the plaintiff, the Court held that the plaintiff could not recover from both, and that, by taking the judgment against the principal, the agent's liability was extinguished.

direct the entry of a final judgment upon one or more but less than all of the claims only upon an express determination that there is no just reason for delay and upon an express direction for the entry of judgment. In the absence of such determination and direction, any order or other form of decision, however designated, which adjudicates less than all the claims shall not terminate the action as to any of the claims, and the order or other form of decision is subject to revision at any time before the entry of judgment adjudicating all the claims.

The record before us reveals that no "express determination" of the type referred to in Rule 605a was made with respect to the summary judgment taken against the corporation; nor does it appear that there was "an express direction for the entry of [such] judgment." It was therefore not a final judgment when entered, but was subject to revision until the case against Grinder individually was resolved by final judgment.

In the circumstances of this case, therefore, appellant's election as between the agent and the principal remained open and viable at the conclusion of its case against the agent, and was not foreclosed by the mere entry of a revisable, non-final summary judgment against the principal. The election doctrine, which formed the basis of the court's ultimate ruling, was simply not applicable.

It is inferable that, where both principal and agent have been joined in a single action, the proper time for election is at the end of the case—before any final judgments are entered. The existence of a judgment previously entered on motion presents somewhat of a "wrinkle" in this approach, of course, but not a significant or fatal one, so long as that judgment is not final. It would have been possible, and, we think, proper, for appellant to have made its election—to rest on the corporate judgment and forego the individual one or, conversely, to request the court to strike the corporate judgment and proceed against Grinder individually—at the conclusion of trial.

Because this was not done, the record before us is, from a technical and formal point of view, unclear. Although we have serious doubt that appellant intended to opt (or, if given the opportunity, would actually opt) to hold a defunct and worthless corporation in lieu of the individual whose credit supported the account, it has taken no affirmative steps to forego the judgment against the corporation. With neither party, nor the court, fully appreciating the problem until both judgments had been entered, it would be a triumph of legal fiction over justice for us to assume, as ultimately did the trial court, that appellant made a knowing election in favor of the penurious defendant.

In light of this record, this seems an appropriate case in which to invoke Maryland Rule 1071a and to remand the matter, without affirmance or reversal, in order to permit appellant to make its election. If, at a proceeding held for that purpose, it opts to hold Grinder individually, the court should reinstate the original judgment entered against that individual and strike the judgment against the corporation. If, perchance, appellant should elect to hold the corporation, the existing judgments should stand.

Notes

1. An agent acting for an undisclosed or partially disclosed principal generally is *not* relieved from liability on the contract short of a final judgment against the principal. This is true even though the third person may have indicated that he or she was going to hold the principal liable. The agent is only relieved from liability by conduct short of taking a final judgment against the principal

> *to the extent that he is prejudiced* thereby if he changes his position in *justifiable reliance* upon a manifestation of the [third person] that he will look *solely* to the principal for performance.

Restatement § 336 (emphasis added).

In *Newark Parafinne Paper Co. v. Dugan*, 162 N.J. Super. 575, 394 A.2d 114 (1978), an agent had entered into a lease in the agent's own name, but on behalf of an undisclosed principal. After the principal had defaulted in the payment of rent, the landlord asserted a landlord's lien against $2,400 worth of the principal's property (as opposed to $66,000 due under the lease). The court held the agent was still liable reasoning that (i) the landlord's conduct was *not* a *definite* manifestation of an election to hold *only* the principal liable sufficient to permit the agent to rely on it, and (ii) in any event, there was no showing that the agent had in fact changed position in reliance on the manifestation.

2. The election of remedies can also apply to release an *undisclosed principal* from liability to the third person, but only so long as the third person *knows* of the identity of the principal. Restatement §§ 209 & 210.

Orrock v. Crouse Realtors, Inc.

823 S.W.2d 40 (Mo. App. 1991)

CRANE, Judge.

Plaintiffs Alexander J. Orrock, Jr. and L. Charlene Orrock appeal from the order of the Circuit Court of Lincoln County sustaining the motion of defendant Crouse Realtors, Inc. for summary judgment in their action for breach of a residential sales contract and negligent and intentional misrepresentations in connection therewith. Defendant's motion alleged that the action, which sought to impose liability on defendant as a result of the acts of its agent, Michael Flynn, was barred because plaintiffs had previously obtained judgment against the agent for those acts.

Prior to the filing of this petition, plaintiff filed a petition in St. Louis County against defendant Crouse, another real estate agency, and Crouse's agent Michael Flynn. This petition alleged that defendant Crouse, acting through its agent Michael Flynn, breached a residential sales contract between the parties and made intentional and negligent misrepresentations with respect to the quality of the residence being purchased. On January 9, 1989, the plaintiffs took a default judgment against Flynn on the breach of contract count and the intentional misrepresentation count and dismissed all claims against Crouse and the other real estate company.

On November 21, 1990 plaintiffs filed this action in Lincoln County naming Crouse as the sole defendant. The Lincoln County petition again alleged that Crouse, acting through its agent Flynn, breached a residential sales contract between the parties and made intentional and negligent misrepresentations. Defendant Crouse moved for summary judgment on the grounds that the previous judgment against the agent constituted an election of remedies and thus barred the claim against Crouse as principal. Crouse did not allege in his motion that the judgment was satisfied and nothing else in the record indicates that the judgment was satisfied. Therefore, for the purposes of this motion, we assume the prior judgment is unsatisfied.

The prior judgment was based upon one count of intentional misrepresentation and one count of breach of contract. We first consider whether the entry of judgment against the agent on the intentional misrepresentation count constitutes an election of remedies which bars a subsequent action for intentional misrepresentation against the principal for misrepresentations made by that agent. The applicable rule is that if there is election to pursue one of two inconsistent theories, mere entry of judgment bars suit on the second theory. However, if there is an election between two consistent theories, only satisfaction of a judgment bars proceedings under the second theory.

This case does not involve an election of inconsistent remedies. The test of inconsistency is that one theory of recovery must allege what the other denies, or that the theory of one must be repugnant to the other. The plaintiffs obtained judgment against the agent and now bring suit against the principal under the same theories of law. Under these principles it is clear that "[A] person injured by the act of an agent for which the principal is liable can bring separate actions against either one." Seavey, *Agency* § 95, p. 170 (1964 Hornbook Edition).

Since the remedies against the principal and agent were consistent, only satisfaction of the claim against the agent would bar an action on the same claim against the principal.

> If the principal is liable solely because of the agent's conduct the satisfaction of judgment against one of them bars an action against the other.

Seavey, *supra*. Since the judgment against the agent on the intentional misrepresentation count was not satisfied, an action against the principal on this theory is not barred.

We next consider the breach of contract count. Defendant Crouse argues that the action against it was barred by the entry of judgment against its agent, citing *Stambaugh v. Wedlan,* 371 S.W.2d 361, 362-63 (Mo. App. 1963), for the rule that

> a person who has dealt with an agent of an undisclosed principal may elect to hold either the agent or principal [liable], he cannot hold both.

While this is a correct rule of law, it applies only where the principal is undisclosed. An undisclosed principal is discharged from liability upon a contract if the third party, knowing the identity of the principal, obtains a judgment for breach of contract against the agent who made the contract. Restatement (Second) of Agency § 210 (1957). This is because the liability of the agent and the undisclosed principal is an alternative and not a joint liability. It is clear from the pleadings that the St. Louis County action against Flynn was not premised on Crouse being an undisclosed principal.

Where the principal is disclosed, other rules govern the effect of the previous judgment. *See* Restatement (Second) of Agency § 184 comments a, b (1957). The application of these rules depends on the basis for the agent's contractual liability in the prior action. It is significant whether the agent was a party to the contract, and, if so, whether the agent was a joint contractor with the principal or if the third unsatisfied party had a separate contract with each. In either case, an unsatisfied judgment does not bar the third party from proceedings against the principal.

> Recovery of judgment against the agent of a disclosed or partially disclosed principal for failure of performance of a contract to which the agent is a party does not thereby discharge the principal.

Restatement (Second) of Agency § 184.

> If the agent is separately liable, the other party has two separate causes of action although based upon the same claim and only satisfaction of the judgment against the agent terminates the liability of the principal.

Restatement, *supra,* § 184, comment c. Because the principal was disclosed, the trial court erred in granting summary judgment.

The judgment of the trial court is reversed and the case is remanded.

Chapter 2

Power of Agents to Bind Principals

A. Authority

1. Express Authority

Authority (often referred to as *actual* authority) is "the power of the agent to affect the legal relations of the principal by acts done in accordance with the principal's manifestations of consent to him." Restatement § 7.

a. Creation

Generally, authority can be created by *any* "written or spoken words or other conduct of the principal." Restatement § 26. That is, no formalities are usually required to vest authority in an agent. In some circumstances, however, formalities of appointment are required.

Estate of Giannopoulos

89 Misc. 2d 961, 392 N.Y.S.2d 828 (Surrogate's Court 1977)

LOUIS D. LAURINO, Surrogate.

A firm of New York attorneys seeks to have the court entertain an application regarding the widow's alleged right of election to take against the decedent's Will. The widow, 'ARETI GIANNOPOULOS,' 'ARETI JANOPULLI' or 'ARETI GIANNOPULOS,' is a resident of Albania. The firm's authority to represent her is based upon a power of attorney allegedly executed by her in Albania. This 'power of attorney' was filed for recording by the firm with a clerk of the court.

EPTL 13—2.3 provides that every power of attorney relating to an interest in an estate shall be in writing and acknowledged or proved in the manner prescribed by the laws of this state for the recording of a conveyance of real property and shall be recorded in the Surrogate's Court having jurisdiction. The statute also provides that the Surrogate may inquire into the validity of the power of attorney and prescribe rules consistent with the section.

In examining the power of attorney and the documents accompanying it in connection with the present application, the court finds that they do not comply with the various sections of the Real Property Law, the CPLR and the Uniform Rules [for All Surrogate's Courts in the Second Department] involved and that the instrument and accompanying papers should not have been accepted for filing.

Section 1830:33(b) of the Uniform Rules regarding the filing and recording of powers of attorney provides:

> The person offering the instrument for filing or recording shall furnish an affidavit of the attorney-in-fact, stating the circumstances under which the power of attorney was procured; the post office address of the grantor, the amount of his interest and relationship, if any, to decedent; the financial arrangement and exact terms of compensation of the attorney-in-fact or of any other person concerned with the matter; disbursements to be charged to the grantor; a copy of any agreement concerning compensation; name of any attorney representing the attorney-in-fact.

A member of the law firm to which the power allegedly runs has supplied an affirmation in connection with this rule. The only address given for the alleged grantor, 'Mrs. Giannopulos,' is 'Fier, Albania,' which is also the only address given for the grantor in the power itself. It might be argued that there are no house numbers in Fier, Albania, except that the application which the court is asked to entertain regarding the right of election contains the house numbers of a number of other persons residing in Fier.

The affirmation states the circumstances under which the power of attorney was received:

> We received this power of attorney in the normal course of business relationships with forwarders from Albania known as Shoqeria Komisionaria, who first apprised us of this estate and asked us to protect the interests of our client by letter dated October 20, 1975.

No attempt is given to explain who or what 'Shoqeria Komisionaria' is or what their interest is in the matter, financial or otherwise.

The affirmation goes on to state that the attorneys will receive no fees as attorney-in-fact and that as attorneys-at-law they will receive 20% of the net to their client, together with out-of-pocket expenses. There is nothing in the alleged power of attorney that reflects that such an arrangement has been agreed to by their alleged client, nor is a copy of any such agreement attached to the affirmation.

The translation accompanying the power of attorney is also defective. CPLR 2101 provides that when a paper served or filed is in a foreign language, it shall be accompanied by an English translation and an affidavit [under oath or an affirmation under pain of perjury] by the translator setting forth his qualifications and that the translation is accurate.

The translation of the main body of the power of attorney from Albanian to English was allegedly made by a lawyer residing in Albania, a country with which the United States does not maintain diplomatic relations. More importantly, the statement of the translator as to his qualifications and the accuracy of the translation is not given under oath or an affirmation under pain of perjury. There is a mere acknowledgement of his signature before a notary.

Section 312(2) of the Real Property Law sets forth the [required] contents of a certificate of authentication accompanying a certificate of acknowledgement made before a notary in a foreign country. The certificate of authentication accompanying the certificate of acknowledgement of the notary public before whom the widow allegedly appeared does not comply with this section. This failure to comply with the Real Property Law would in and of itself be sufficient reason to refuse to record the power of attorney. The signature of 'Mrs. Giannopoulos' and the acknowledgement before the 'notary' also raise grave questions as to whether the grantor knew what she was doing at the time of signing. The acknowledgement refers to the identity of the signer and states she is of full legal capacity and that she 'executed the foregoing instrument and signed same in my presence as her free act and deed.'

The Albanian text under which the signature of the alleged grantor appears is written in the Latin Alphabet. Yet the signature is written in the Greek Alphabet. As far as indicating any understanding of what was being signed, it is then the equivalent of the illiterate's 'X.' In spite of this, there is no statement by the notary that the document was read to her or explained to her.

Based on all of the above, the court finds that this power of attorney was improperly accepted by the clerk for filing and recording.

As to the application made by the firm of attorneys to determine the validity of the widow's right of election and for other relief, without the power of attorney there is nothing to show under what authority these attorneys are acting.

Accordingly, the application is not entertained, as the firm is without legal authority to appear in this matter.

Notes

1. What is the source of the requirement that the power of attorney in *Estate of Giannopoulos* be given in a certain manner?

2. Suppose that a principal wishes to authorize an agent to take an action that itself requires formalities of action, such as a contract required to be in writing under the Statute of Frauds. Do those formalities of action apply to the principal's authorization of the agent? That is, must the form of authorization be of *equal dignity* to the underlying act?

At *common law,* equal dignity is *only* required for *contracts under seal.* Thus, a *written* contract signed by agent orally authorized to do so satisfies the Statute of Frauds. *E.g., Little v. Clark,* 592 S.W.2d 61 (Tex. Civ. App. 1979) (*contract* for sale of land).

However, in most states equal dignities in the authorization of an agent are required, at least for certain actions. Equal dignities are frequently required by statute as to such matters as *deeds*, contracts for the sale of land, or other contracts within the Statute of Frauds. The actions that require equal dignities vary from state to state.

Also, where equal dignities are required, action on behalf of *corporate* principals raise special problems. A corporation is only a legal entity; it has no body. Of necessity, corporate action requires that *someone* act on behalf of the corporation. How, then, can the corporation meet the equal dignities requirement? This problem is handled by deeming that the acts of certain persons are *in themselves* the acts of the corporation. For example, under corporate law, the management of corporate business is entrusted to its *board of directors*. The board of directors is not, as such, an *agent* of the corporation, Restatement § 14C. Rather, it is that *part* of the corporation that acts on its behalf. Second, under many state statutes, the authorized acts of certain *officers* are deemed to be the acts of the corporation, so that the authority of such officers to act need not be evidenced separately. For example, while Texas law requires that an agent's authority to sign a *deed* must be evidenced in recordable form (in writing, acknowledged, etc.), a corporate officer's deed is recordable if the officer acknowledges the deed as the act of the corporation. Such deeds are *prima facie* evidence of approval of the deed by the board of directors. TEX. REV. CIV. STAT. ANN. art. 1396-5.09 (Vernon's 1980).

b. Interpretation

Even where the grant is spelled out in a written document, there may be problems due to the uncertainty and limitations of language. Interpretation of written instruments is often a difficult matter. In hindsight, it may be discovered that the principal and agent did not have a mutual understanding of the extent of the authority. The instrument may be incomplete due to clerical error or faulty judgment of the principal in anticipating the circumstances that the agent might encounter. The principal may have supplemented the written grant of authority with amendments or limitations presented orally.

King v. Bankerd

303 Md. 98, 492 A.2d 608 (1985)

COLE, Judge.

The single issue presented in this case is whether a power of attorney authorizing the agent to "convey, grant, bargain and/or sell" the principal's property authorizes the agent to make a gratuitous transfer of that property.

The facts are uncomplicated. Howard R. Bankerd and his wife, Virginia, owned, as tenants by the entirety, a home in Montgomery County, Maryland. They resided there until 1966 when Mrs. Bankerd moved out as a result of marital problems. Bankerd continued to live at the property until July 1968, when he "left for the west." Mrs. Bankerd thereupon resumed residency of the property. For the ensuing twelve years, Bankerd lived at various locations in Nevada, Colorado, and Washington, and he made no payments on the mortgage, for taxes, or for the maintenance and upkeep of the home.

Before Bankerd's departure, he executed a power of attorney to Arthur V. King, an attorney with whom he was acquainted. From 1971 to 1974, Bankerd did not communicate or correspond with King in any manner. In 1975, however, King sent Bankerd a letter enclosing an updated power of attorney because the Washington Suburban Sanitary Commission was about to put a sewer adjacent to the subject property, and King believed the new power would be beneficial. This power of attorney, which is the center of the instant litigation, was executed by Bankerd and returned to King. Dated October 30, 1975, this power of attorney provides:

> KNOW ALL MEN BY THESE PRESENTS, that I, Howard R. Bankerd, hereby make, constitute and appoint ARTHUR V. KING, my attorney for me, and in my name to convey, grant, bargain and/or sell the property designated in the Montgomery County land record as Lot 9 of an unrecorded subdivision as recorded in Liber 3027 at folio 293, situated at 14026 Travilah Road, Rockville, Maryland on such terms as to him may seem best, and in my name, to make, execute, acknowledge and deliver, good and sufficient deeds and conveyances for the same with or without covenants and warranties and generally to do and perform all things necessary pertaining to the future transfer of said property, and generally to do everything whatsoever necessary pertaining to the said property.

After granting this power of attorney, Bankerd had no further communication with King until 1978.

Mrs. Bankerd, who as noted above had been residing at and maintaining the subject property since 1968, requested King in September 1977 to exercise the power of attorney and to transfer Bankerd's interest in the property to her. King was aware that Mrs. Bankerd was nearing retirement and that she was "saddled" with a property she could neither sell nor mortgage. Consequently, King attempted to locate Bankerd. King wrote to Bankerd on at least two occasions at a Carson City, Nevada hotel where Bankerd had been living. Only one letter was returned. King sent a third letter to Bankerd to another Carson City address, but that letter was also returned. King also made several other efforts, albeit unsuccessful, to obtain Bankerd's address.

Mrs. Bankerd informed King that her husband had once attempted to give the property away to a neighbor on the condition that the neighbor assume the mortgage payments. Consequently, King asserted that he believed Bankerd "didn't give a damn" about the property, that Bankerd had abandoned his interest in the property, and that given Bankerd's age (approximately sixty-nine years), King believed that Bankerd might even be deceased. King therefore conveyed Bankerd's interest in the property to Mrs. Bankerd by deed dated June 21, 1978. Mrs. Bankerd paid no consideration for the transfer and King received no compensation for the conveyance on behalf of Bankerd. Mrs. Bankerd thereafter sold the property to a third party for $62,500.

In 1981 Bankerd filed suit against King alleging breach of trust and breach of fiduciary duty in King's conveyance of Bankerd's interest in the subject property in violation of the power of attorney. After the completion of the discovery proceedings each party moved for summary judgment. [T]he trial court granted summary judgment to Bankerd against King and awarded $13,555.05 in damages on the basis that King had negligently violated the fiduciary relationship that existed between those two parties. The Court of Special Appeals affirmed, holding that the broad language of the power of attorney did not authorize the conveyance without consideration in favor of Bankerd.

King basically contends that the language contained in a document granting a broad power of attorney be viewed in light of the surrounding circumstances to determine whether the attorney in fact had authority to transfer the property without consideration. Based on this contention, King concludes that the second power of attorney did not as a matter of law preclude him from gratuitously transferring Bankerd's property.

Similar to other jurisdictions, Maryland appellate courts have had relatively few occasions to analyze powers of attorney. Because we last addressed the substantive law relating to powers of attorney over a half century ago, we shall review the relevant rules relating to powers of attorney.

Broadly defined, a power of attorney is a written document by which one party, as principal, appoints another as agent (attorney in fact) and confers upon the latter the authority to perform certain specified acts or kinds of acts on behalf of the principal. This instrument creates a principal-agent relationship. *See* Restatement (Second) of Agency §§ 1, 34 (1958) (Restatement).

Various rules govern the interpretation of powers of attorney. [O]ne "well settled" rule is that powers of attorney are "strictly construed as a general rule and [are] held to grant only those powers which are clearly delineated[.]" [*Klein v. Weiss*, 284 Md.

36, 61, 395 A.2d 126, 140 (1978).] Although our predecessors recognized this rule over a century ago in *Posner v. Bayless*, 59 Md. 56 (1882), they were careful to note that the rule of strict construction "cannot override the general and cardinal rule" that the court determine the intention of the parties. To ascertain this intent, the *Posner* Court emphasized that the language used in the instrument and the object to be accomplished be viewed in light of the surrounding circumstances. Other courts of last resort have likewise embraced the rule of strict construction of powers of attorney. *See generally* Comment, Construction of Written Powers of Attorney, 18 Ohio St. L.J. 129, 130 (1957) (American courts follow the strict construction principle).

Another accepted rule of construction is to discount or disregard, as meaningless verbiage, all-embracing expressions found in powers of attorney. Restatement, § 34 comment h. Because powers of attorney are ordinarily very carefully drafted and scrutinized, courts give the terms used a technical rather than a popular meaning. Restatement, § 34 comment h. In addition, ambiguities in an instrument are resolved against the party who made it or caused it to be made, because that party had the better opportunity to understand and explain his meaning. *Id.* Finally, general words used in an instrument are restricted by the context in which they are used, and are construed accordingly.

In accordance with these principles, nearly every jurisdiction that has considered the issue has concluded that a general power of attorney authorizing an agent to sell and convey property, although it authorizes him to sell for such price and on such terms as to him shall seem proper, does not authorize the agent to make a gift of the property, or to convey or transfer it without a present consideration inuring to the principal. *See, e.g.*, Annot., 73 A.L.R. 884 (1931).

[W]e conclude that an agent holding a broad power of attorney lacks the power to make a gift of the principal's property, unless that power (1) is expressly conferred, (2) arises as a necessary implication from the conferred powers, or (3) is clearly intended by the parties, as evidenced by the surrounding facts and circumstances.

[T]he power to make a gift of the principal's property is a power that is potentially hazardous to the principal's interests. Consequently, this power will not be lightly inferred from broad, all-encompassing grants of power to the agent. [I]t is difficult to imagine how a gift of the principal's real property would be to the benefit of the principal when the power of attorney does not authorize such a gift or the principal does not intend to authorize such a gift.

The general power of attorney executed by Bankerd authorized King to "convey, grant, bargain and/or sell" the subject property "on such terms as to him may seem best." A strict construction of this broad language, however, makes clear that the instrument did not expressly authorize a gratuitous transfer of property. [W]e decline to interpret this broad, all-encompassing language as authority for the agent to make a gift of the principal's property.

The facts and surrounding circumstances presented in this case do not give rise to any fact or inference that King was authorized to make a gift of Bankerd's real property. In arguing that his conduct was reasonable under the circumstances, King points to his "beliefs" that Bankerd had abandoned the property, that Bankerd did not care about the property, and that Bankerd might be deceased. These arguments completely miss the mark. King's conduct could only be "reasonable" if Bankerd intended for King to give the property away. Although the facts and surrounding circumstances to which King points suggest reasons why he made the gift, they do not support an inference that Bankerd intended to authorize the gift.

In sum, there is no genuine dispute as to any material fact. [T]he facts are not susceptible of more than one permissible inference. [T]he trial court did not err in granting Bankerd's motion for summary judgment.

Notes

1. *King v. Bankerd* involved a suit by the principal against the agent for breach of duty in making a gift. Would the result change in a suit against the *donee*?

2. *De Bueno v. Castro*, 543 So. 2d 393 (Fla. App. 1989), *upheld* a transfer without consideration of real property owned by the principal, a foreign national, under a power of attorney granting the agent the authority, among other things

> to represent me, claim for me and protect all my rights, interests and actions in everything concerning the business and interests that I have at present and that I might have in the future[, and,] in general, power of attorney to do, in respect and concerning my properties and rights, all and everything that I could do in my own benefit and without limitations.

The agent conveyed the property to a corporation owned by the principal's children from a former marriage. After the principal's death, his widow challenged the transfer. The trial court found that the principal not only had consented to the transfer, but had informally requested the agent to make the transfer as an estate-planning device.

Is the result in *DeBueno v. Castro* consistent with the principles stated in *King v. Bankerd*?

3. A principal and agent should not rely on a court applying a broadly worded general power of attorney to unusual acts, such as a gift. For example, in *Von Wedel v. McGrath*, 180 F.2d 716 (3d Cir. 1950), the principal, a German national leaving the United States on the eve of World War II, made a general power of attorney authorizing his agent, among other things, "to do any and all acts which I could do if personally present." The power of attorney then set forth a "non exclusive" list of specific powers that the court characterized as "ordinary business powers." After the outbreak of World War II, a statute was enacted under which the U.S. property of German nationals was forfeited to the government. Before that law was enacted, the agent attempted to transfer all of the principal's property to the principal's wife, a U.S. national. Despite the broad language of the power of attorney, and despite testimony that such a gift was among the purposes of the power of attorney, the court limited the power of attorney to the kinds of "ordinary business powers" as were specifically outlined in the power of attorney. Because gifts of the principal's property are not in the ordinary course of business, they were not within the scope of authority granted by the power of attorney.

4. Suppose that after a principal has authorized an agent to act on the principal's behalf in certain matters, the agent encounters unforeseen circumstances not covered by the principal's instructions. Suppose further that it is impracticable for the agent to communicate with the principal. Under Restatement section 47, the agent would be authorized to take such acts as the agent "reasonably believes necessary to prevent substantial loss to the principal with respect to the interests committed to [the agent's]

care." Could Restatement section 47 have been applied to uphold the gifts in the *Von Wedel* case?

2. Implied Authority

Mill Street Church of Christ v. Hogan

785 S.W.2d 263 (Ky. App. 1990)

HOWARD, Judge.

Mill Street Church of Christ and State Automobile Mutual Insurance Company petition for review of a decision of the New Workers' Compensation Board [hereinafter "New Board"] which had reversed an earlier decision by the Old Workers' Compensation Board [hereinafter "Old Board"]. The Old Board had ruled that Samuel J. Hogan was not an employee of the Mill Street Church of Christ and was not entitled to any workers' compensation benefits. The New Board reversed and ruled that Samuel Hogan was an employee of the church.

Samuel Hogan filed a claim for workers' compensation benefits for an injury he received while painting the interior of the Mill Street Church of Christ on December 15, 1986. In 1986, the Elders of the Mill Street Church of Christ decided to hire church member Bill Hogan to paint the church building. The Elders decided that another church member, Gary Petty, would be hired to assist if any assistance was needed. In the past, the church had hired Bill Hogan for similar jobs, and he had been allowed to hire his brother, Sam Hogan, the respondent, as a helper. Sam Hogan had earlier been a member of the church but was no longer a member. The church, at the time the painting project was undertaken, had switched to an Elder form of church government. At the time Bill Hogan was employed for other projects, the church operated under a congregational form of church government.

Dr. David Waggoner, an Elder of the church, soon contacted Bill Hogan, and he accepted the job and began work. Apparently Waggoner made no mention to Bill Hogan of hiring a helper at that time. Bill Hogan painted the church by himself until he reached the baptistery portion of the church. This was a very high, difficult portion of the church to paint, and he decided that he needed help. After Bill Hogan had reached this point in his work, he discussed the matter of a helper with Dr. Waggoner at his office. According to both Dr. Waggoner and Hogan, they discussed the possibility of hiring Gary Petty to help Hogan. None of the evidence indicates that Hogan was told that he had to hire Petty. In fact, Dr. Waggoner apparently told Hogan that Petty was difficult to reach. That was basically all the discussion that these two individuals had concerning hiring a helper. None of the other Elders discussed the matter with Bill Hogan.

On December 14, 1986, Bill Hogan approached his brother, Sam, about helping him complete the job. Bill Hogan told Sam the details of the job, including the pay, and Sam accepted the job. On December 15, 1986, Sam began working. A half hour after he began, he climbed the ladder to paint a ceiling corner, and a leg of the ladder broke. Sam fell to the floor and broke his left arm. Sam was taken to the Grayson County Hospital Emergency Room where he was treated. He later was under the care of Dr. James Klinert, a surgeon in Louisville. The church Elders did not know that

Bill Hogan had approached Sam Hogan to work as a helper until after the accident occurred.

After the accident, Bill Hogan reported the accident and resulting injury to Charles Payne, a church Elder and treasurer. Payne stated in a deposition that he told Bill Hogan that the church had insurance. At this time, Bill Hogan told Payne the total number of hours worked which included a half hour that Sam Hogan had worked prior to the accident. Payne issued Bill Hogan a check for all of these hours. Further, Bill Hogan did not have to use his own tools and materials in the project. The church supplied the tools, materials, and supplies necessary to complete the project. Bill purchased needed items from Dunn's Hardware Store and charged them to the church's account.

It is undisputed in this case that Mill Street Church of Christ is an insured employer under the Workers' Compensation Act. Sam Hogan filed a claim under the Workers' Compensation Act. The Old Board decided the case in favor of the Petitioners on June 20, 1988. The New Board reversed and entered its final order in favor of Sam Hogan on January 20, 1989. It remanded Samuel Hogan's claim to an administrative law judge for determination of compensation benefits to which Samuel Hogan may be entitled. The Petitioners now ask this Court to review and reverse the decision of the New Board.

Petitioners argue that the New Board also erred by applying the doctrine of implied authority as a basis for creation of an employment relationship between Sam Hogan and Mill Street Church of Christ.

[E]mployees covered [under the Kentucky Workers' Compensation Act] include:

> every person, including a minor, whether lawfully or unlawfully employed, in the service of an employer under any contract of hire or apprenticeship, express or implied, and all helpers and assistants of employees whether paid by the employer or employee, if employed with the knowledge, actual or constructive of the employer.

Petitioners argue that the New Board erred by finding that a person hired under implied authority of an agent could be an employee for the purposes of this statute.

The statute specifically mentions that the contract of employment can be either express or implied. Additionally, the statute specifically applies to all helpers and assistants of employees whether paid by the employer or employee. Petitioners argue that the employee must be employed with the actual or constructive knowledge of the employer. They contend that the facts of this case cannot meet this test. We find that the Mill Street Church of Christ had knowledge that Bill Hogan would have to hire a helper as in the past. Since he had hired his brother in the past, and had not been instructed differently this time, the church should be imputed with the knowledge if it is found that its agent had the authority to hire a helper.

As part of their argument, petitioners argue the New Board also erred in finding that Bill Hogan possessed implied authority as an agent to hire Sam Hogan. Petitioners contend there was neither implied nor apparent authority in the case at bar.

It is important to distinguish implied and apparent authority before proceeding further. Implied authority is actual authority circumstantially proven which the principal actually intended the agent to possess and includes such powers as are practically necessary to carry out the duties actually delegated. Apparent authority on the other hand is not actual authority but is the authority the agent is held out by the principal as possessing. It is a matter of appearances on which third parties come to rely.

Petitioners attack the New Board's findings concerning implied authority. In examining whether implied authority exists, it is important to focus upon the agent's understanding of his authority. It must be determined whether the agent reasonably believes because of present or past conduct of the principal that the principal wishes him to act in a certain way or to have certain authority. The nature of the task or job may be another factor to consider. Implied authority may be necessary in order to implement the express authority. The existence of prior similar practices is one of the most important factors. Specific conduct by the principal in the past permitting the agent to exercise similar powers is crucial.

The person alleging agency and resulting authority has the burden of proving that it exists. Agency cannot be proven by a mere statement, but it can be established by circumstantial evidence including the acts and conduct of the parties such as the continuous course of conduct of the parties covering a number of successive transactions. Specifically one must look at what had gone on before to determine if the agent had certain authority. If considering past similar acts done in a similar manner, [and if] it is found that the present action was taken [within] the apparent scope of the agent's authority, the act is binding upon the principal.

In considering the above factors in the case at bar, Bill Hogan had implied authority to hire Sam Hogan as his helper. First, in the past the church had allowed Bill Hogan to hire his brother or other persons whenever he needed assistance on a project. Even though the Board of Elders discussed a different arrangement this time, no mention of this discussion was ever made to Bill or Sam Hogan. In fact, the discussion between Bill Hogan and Church Elder Dr. Waggoner indicated that Gary Petty would be difficult to reach and Bill Hogan could hire whomever he pleased. Further, Bill Hogan needed to hire an assistant to complete the job for which he had been hired. The interior of the church simply could not be painted by one person. Maintaining a safe and attractive place of worship clearly is part of the church's function, and one for which it would designate an agent to ensure that the building is properly painted and maintained.

[Affirmed.]

B. Power of Agents to Bind Principal by Unauthorized Acts

An agent's power to bind the principal is the agent's *ability* to do so. *Authority* is the power to bind that results from the principal's "manifestations" to the agent of the principal's *consent* to be bound. *Compare* Restatement § 6 *with* Restatement § 7. Thus, an agent authorized to bind the principal has the power to do so.

But is the converse true? Does an agent have the *power* to bind the principal even though the agent was not *authorized* to do so? The use of agents to conduct business inevitably involves the risk that the agents will sometimes exceed their authority to bind the principal. Under what circumstances should the principal—or the third person dealing with the agent—bear the risk of unauthorized actions?

1. Apparent Authority and Estoppel

Hamilton Hauling, Inc. v. GAF Corp.

719 S.W.2d 841 (Mo. App. 1986)

DIXON, Judge.

Plaintiff Hamilton Hauling, Inc., appeals from a jury verdict for defendant GAF Corporation in a contract action. The only claims of error relate to instructions. Fundamental to the instruction issue is whether John Bajt, an agent of GAF, had the authority to execute a contract on behalf of GAF. The contract in question required GAF, a manufacturer, to purchase a minimum of over $800,000 of raw materials annually from Hamilton Hauling for a period of ten years.

Bajt was a purchasing agent or buyer at GAF's Kansas City plant from 1973 until 1980. Duties of a purchasing agent generally included the acquisition and purchase of all raw materials and related supplies necessary to sustain plant production on a day-to-day basis.

In that capacity, Bajt conducted all negotiations and sales transactions with various vendors for the purchase of raw materials, particularly wood chips, for the Kansas City plant. In the last year of his employment, Bajt purchased approximately $6,000,000 worth of raw materials to be used in production at the plant. None of these purchases were by any document other than a purchase order pursuant to Bajt's actual authority.

The evidence showed that under GAF's internal policy, buyers at Bajt's level had authority to make purchase orders not exceeding $25,000 in amount or one year in duration. Any order or contract exceeding those limits had to be approved in advance by GAF's corporate headquarters. All purchase orders were eventually sent to corporate headquarters for review. Bajt acknowledged the $25,000 limit on the purchase of items for maintenance, repair and operations but denied that it applied to the acquisition of raw materials. No evidence was presented to show that buyers like Bajt customarily entered into long term contracts or contracts involving amounts over $25,000. In all his years with GAF, Bajt never entered into any long term contract except the one at issue in this case.

Hamilton Hauling, solely owned by Warren Hamilton, had supplied a variety of goods and services to GAF and its corporate predecessors at the plant since 1954. During his course of business with GAF, Hamilton had dealt with three different purchasing agents. Hamilton had never had a long term contract with GAF but dealt with it consistently on a purchase order basis. A purchase order could be cancelled by GAF at any time. Hamilton was aware that GAF had at one time entered into a contract with another wood chip vendor prior to the time the agreement here was executed. Bajt was also aware of that contract and knew that it had been signed at corporate headquarters.

A continuous, uninterrupted supply of wood chips was essential to meet the production demands of the plant. The harsh winter of 1978/1979 adversely affected GAF's ability to obtain an adequate supply of wood chips. Bajt negotiated with Hamilton for several months encouraging him to go into the wood chip business so that Bajt might obtain a dependable supplier of wood chips. Hamilton was wary about supplying wood chips to GAF on a purchase order basis because he previously had been cancelled twice by GAF on orders involving delivery of raw materials. Preparation by Hamilton to supply GAF with the needed wood chips would be costly, and Bajt was aware of that. On February 1, 1979, Bajt and Hamilton entered into a contract to purchase which required GAF to purchase approximately 26,000 tons of wood chips annually from Hamilton at a minimum cost of more than $800,000 per year for 10 years. The agreement was drawn up by Hamilton's attorney and signed by Bajt in Hamilton's office. Bajt left the original agreement with Hamilton. The agreement was subject to renegotiation of price increases at six-month intervals.

Bajt admitted that he never sent a copy of the contract to GAF's corporate headquarters. No one at GAF seemed to know about the agreement other than Bajt's secretary. Hamilton acknowledged that he never told his two associates in the wood chip business that he had a contract with GAF; in fact, he indicated to them that he only had a purchase order.

After the execution of the agreement, Bajt continued to issue standard purchase orders for all wood sold to GAF by Hamilton, and the purchase orders were routinely sent to GAF's corporate headquarters. The wood supplied by Hamilton pursuant to the purchase orders issued after the signing of the agreement was inconsistent with the tonnage requirements specified in the agreement. Bajt was terminated by GAF in September 1980 and in December 1980, GAF notified Hamilton Hauling that no further deliveries of wood chips would be accepted. Hamilton produced the contract. GAF disclaimed any knowledge of the contract and denied the authority of Bajt to have made such a contract on its behalf.

At trial Hamilton testified that Bajt had told him that he had authority to execute the contract and Hamilton believed him. There was substantial evidence, however, that Hamilton was aware of limitations on Bajt's authority to contract. Both of Hamilton's associates in the wood chip business testified that they had informed Hamilton of conversations with Bajt in which Bajt had indicated his limited authority to contract. These conversations took place prior to the execution of the agreement between Hamilton and Bajt.

Hamilton acknowledged that he had entered into contracts with two other corporations and in each instance the contract had been prepared and executed at the corporate headquarters of the respective company rather than by the local plant manager. It was Hamilton Hauling's theory throughout the trial that Bajt bound GAF because he acted with apparent authority.

On appeal, Hamilton Hauling complains that the instruction given by the trial court defining apparent authority was erroneous. [I]nstruction [9] reads as follows:

> Acts are within an employee's apparent authority even though not specifically authorized if:
>
> 1. The defendant GAF Corporation knowingly permitted its employees to so act, and
>
> 2. Hamilton Hauling, Inc. knew that GAF Corporation knowingly permitted its employees to so act, and
>
> 3. Hamilton Hauling, Inc. acting reasonably and in good faith, actually believed that GAF employees had the authority to so act, and
>
> 4. Hamilton Hauling, Inc. relied on the authority of GAF Corporation's employees, and

5. Hamilton Hauling, Inc. will be damaged if said acts of GAF Corporation's employees are not binding on GAF Corporation.

Hamilton Hauling urges the instruction is erroneous because of the requirement that the jury find that Hamilton Hauling knew that GAF had knowingly permitted Bajt to contract. Hamilton Hauling says that this requirement is contrary to law and that Instruction A [offered by Hamilton] had no such requirement [and] should have been given. The tenor of the Hamilton Hauling argument is that Bajt's apparent authority arose from his position as a buyer and his actions in that position.

GAF contends that given the specific limitations on Bajt's authority there must be proof that GAF had acquiesced in Bajt's overstepping of his authority. GAF also contends the acquiescence must be known to Hamilton Hauling.

The nub of the issue as to the instructional error turns on the positions of the parties as to the definition of apparent authority to be applied in the case.

Some review of the principles governing apparent agency will aid in the consideration of the issue. In the area of agency, Missouri courts have relied extensively on the RESTATEMENT (SECOND) OF AGENCY (1957).

It is generally held that when a principal "holds out" another as possessing certain authority, thereby inducing others reasonably to believe that authority exists, the agent has apparent authority to act even though as between himself and the principal, such authority has not been granted. Apparent authority differs from actual authority in that the principal communicates directly with a third person to create apparent authority; to create actual authority, the principal communicates directly with the agent. RESTATEMENT (SECOND) OF AGENCY § 8 comments a and e.

When a principal has by his voluntary act placed an agent in such a situation that a person of ordinary prudence, conversant with business usages and the nature of the particular business, is justified in presuming that such agent has authority to perform a particular act on behalf of his principal, the principal is estopped, as against such innocent third person, from denying the agent's authority to perform the act.

The "holding out" of the agent's authority by the principal party may be by action or inaction. The principal may directly communicate the authority to a third party or knowingly permit the agent to exercise such authority. *See Continental-St. Louis Corp. v. Ray Scharf Vending Co.*, 400 S.W.2d 467, 470 (Mo. App. 1966). The *Continental-St. Louis Corp.* court quotes 3 Am. Jur. 2d Agency § 74 (now § 79) as saying:

> [T]he rule is that if a principal acts or conducts his business, either intentionally or through negligence, or fails to disapprove of the agent's act or course of action so as to lead the public to believe that his agent possesses authority to act or contract in the name of the principal, such principal is bound by the acts of the agent within the scope of his apparent authority as to any person who, upon the faith of such holding out, believes, and has reasonable ground to believe, that the agent has such authority, and in good faith deals with him.

It must be emphasized that the third party must reasonably rely on the authority held out by the principal. The third party must know of facts demonstrating the principal's consent to the agent's actions.

Apparent authority exists only to the extent that it is reasonable for the third person dealing with the agent to believe that the agent is authorized.

RESTATEMENT (SECOND) OF AGENCY § 8 comment c. Further, the third party must actually believe the agent to be authorized. *Id.* Apparent authority is that which a reasonably prudent man, using diligence and discretion, in view of the principal's conduct would suppose the agent to possess.

> [T]he party who claims reliance [on an agent's apparent authority] must not have closed his eyes to warning or inconsistent circumstances. Authority is not 'apparent' simply because the party claiming has acted upon his conclusions [nor] simply because it looked so to him. It is not a situation where one may read while he runs. It is only where a person of ordinary prudence, conversant with business usages and the nature of the particular business, acting in good faith, and giving heed not only to opposing inferences but also to all restrictions brought to his notice, would reasonably rely, that a case is presented within the operation of the rule.

Mechem on Agency (2nd Ed.), Vol. 1, Sec. 726, p. 513.

Where the agent has some present actual authority, apparent authority may arise in any of three ways. The basic requirement for the creation of apparent authority is that it is the principal who is responsible for the information received by the third party. RESTATEMENT (SECOND) OF AGENCY § 27 comment a. The principal must have intentionally caused the third party to believe that the agent is authorized to act for the principal or he should have realized his conduct would create such a belief on the part of the third party. *Id.* The information received by the third person may come directly from the principal by letter or word of mouth, from authorized statements of the agent, from documents or other indicia of authority given by the principal to the agent, or from third persons who have heard of the agent's authority through authorized or permitted channels of communication. Likewise, as in the case of authority, apparent authority can be created by appointing a person to a position, such as that of manager or treasurer, which carries with it generally recognized duties; to those who know of the appointment there is apparent authority to do the things ordinarily entrusted to one occupying such a position, regardless of unknown limitations which are imposed upon the particular agent. So, too, a person who permits another to do an act in such a way as to establish in a community a reputation of having authority to act, either by directing the agent so to represent, or by directing him to act and doing nothing to prevent the spread of such information by the agent or by others, creates apparent authority with respect to those who learn of the reputation. Third persons who are aware of what a continuously employed agent has done are normally entitled to believe that he will continue to have such authority for at least a limited period in the future, and this apparent authority continues until the third person has been notified or learns facts which should lead him to believe that the agent is no longer authorized. *Id.*

Establishment of apparent authority by direct, express statements is obvious. The other methods of creating apparent authority—by "position" and by "prior acts" have both been recognized by Missouri courts.

Wynn v. McMahon Ford Co., 414 S.W.2d 330 (Mo. App. 1967), exemplifies the apparent authority that may be generated by an agent's position. In *Wynn,* defendant's agent, designated as used car sales manager, was placed by defendant in a managerial position. The court found that persons dealing with the agent could reasonably believe that he had authority to conclude sales transactions. According to the RESTATEMENT (SECOND) OF AGENCY § 49 comment c,

> [i]f a principal puts an agent into, or knowingly permits him to occupy, a position in which according to the ordinary habits of persons in the locality, trade or profession, it is usual for such an agent to have a particular kind of authority, anyone dealing with him is justified in inferring that he has such authority, in the absence of reason to know otherwise.

Another way apparent authority may be created is by acquiescence of the principal in prior acts of an agent.

> [W]herever a person has knowingly and without dissent permitted [an]other to act as his agent in such capacity, or where his habits and course of dealing have been such as to reasonably warrant the presumption that such other was his agent, authorized to act in that capacity, whether it be a single transaction or a series of transactions, his authority to act for him in that capacity will be conclusively presumed so far as it may be necessary to protect the rights of third persons who have relied thereon in good faith and in the exercise of reasonable prudence; and he will not be permitted to deny that such other was his agent, authorized to do the act he assumed to do, provided that such act is within the real or apparent scope of the presumed authority.

Bennett v. Potashnick, 214 Mo. App. 507, 514, 257 S.W. 836, 838 (1924). Apparent authority may result from a prior relation of agent and principal. The principal by allowing an agent to carry out prior similar transactions may create an appearance of authority of the agent to carry out such acts. As it is expressed by the RESTATEMENT,

> a person who permits another to do an act in such a way as to establish in a community a reputation for having authority to act, creates apparent authority with respect to those who learn of the reputation.

RESTATEMENT (SECOND) OF AGENCY § 27 comment a.

Hamilton Hauling argues that since Bajt was a purchasing agent, the authority to contract upon behalf of GAF is inferable from the position he held. Hamilton Hauling's theory of apparent authority was not supported by the evidence.

Apparent authority could only have resulted from some act or failure to act on the part of GAF. Hamilton testified that Bajt told him he had the authority to contract and Hamilton believed Bajt. Bajt's unauthorized representations are totally immaterial on the issue of apparent authority.

Hamilton Hauling claims Bajt's authority came from his position; however, there was no evidence of any sort in this case as to the usual authority of purchasing agents generally. There was nothing to support an inference that a vendor dealing with a purchasing agent expects that agent to have the power to make a contract like the long term agreement in evidence. There was evidence that Bajt had twice exceeded the company-imposed limits on his authority in making purchase orders. No purchase order represented a long-term contract and all purchase orders contained explicit limitations on the purchase including the right to cancel. There was no evidence that Bajt had ever entered into a long term contract on behalf of GAF; in fact, Bajt admitted that in all his years at GAF, he had not made any other such contract. Bajt was not clothed with apparent authority by virtue of his position.

Moreover, there was no evidence to support Hamilton's claim that he reasonably relied on Bajt's authority. Hamilton admitted that the contracts he had entered into with other corporations were signed at corporate headquarters, not locally. Apparent authority is not a "situation" where one can "read while he runs."

The judgment favoring GAF is affirmed.

Notes

1. Apparent authority is the basic doctrine used by the Restatement to allocate the risk of an unauthorized transaction entered into by an agent. Under Restatement sections 8 and 27 an agent's power to bind the principal by an unauthorized action is based on the *principal's manifestations*—written or spoken words or other conduct—to third persons. However, a *third person* dealing with an agent has a correlative *duty* to act reasonably in interpreting the principal's conduct; the third person must reasonably believe, based on the principal's conduct and in light of all accompanying circumstances, that the principal consents to being bound by the particular act in question. Restatement §§ 27, 34, 49.

One corollary of these principles is that apparent authority *cannot* be based solely on the *agent's* conduct. That is, a third person cannot reasonably believe the principal consents where the principal has not taken any action on which such a belief could be based. *E.g., Southwest Land Title v. Gemini Financial,* 752 S.W.2d 5 (Tex. App. 1988); *Barnes v. Treece,* 15 Wash. App. 437, 549 P.2d 1152 (1976).

Is the principle that third persons owe a *duty* to act reasonably in determining the scope of an agent's authority inconsistent with the principle from chapter 1 that third persons are the *beneficiaries* of an implied warranty of authority?

2. In *Hamilton Hauling, Inc. v. GAF Corp.,* when GAF appointed Bajt as its purchasing agent, what, if anything, was it "manifesting" to third persons about Bajt's authority to bind GAF?

3. Traditionally, corporate officers—including a president—were viewed as having *neither* implied authority *nor* power to bind by an unauthorized act solely by virtue of holding corporate office. *See* H. Henn & J. Alexander, Laws of Corporations 595-604 (3d ed. 1983). The *modern trend* is to give the president both implied and apparent authority to conduct ordinary business transactions. *Id.*

Under either the traditional or the modern view, a corporate officer, just as any other agent, may have *apparent authority* based on how the corporation in fact conducts its business, such as by customarily permitting its president to enter into ordinary business transactions.

Fennell v. TLB Kent Company

865 F.2d 498 (2d Cir. 1989)

MAHONEY, Circuit Judge:

This is an appeal from a final judgment of the United States District Court for the Southern District of New York, which dismissed plaintiff's action and approved a $10,000 settlement agreement. The attorneys for the parties negotiated a settlement and reported it to the court by telephone. [T]he district court dismissed the action and approved the settlement, finding that plaintiff's attorney had apparent authority to settle the case and plaintiff was accordingly bound by the settlement agreement.

Plaintiff-appellant Louis Fennell commenced this action against his employer, alleging wrongful discharge because of his race and age. Fennell was represented by C. Vernon Mason and several of his associates, including Fred K. Brewington.

On January 16, 1987, Brewington and Eugene Frink, defendants' attorney, agreed to settle the case for $10,000 during a telephone conversation. The settlement was reported to the court by both attorneys in a telephone conference call on January 20, 1987. The district court issued an order of dismissal on the same day.

Fennell [contends] that he had told Brewington on January 16, 1987 that he would not approve a $10,000 settlement, but he was willing to settle the case out of court "with the intentions of getting it out of the way and behind me." He also claimed that he had told Mason on January 20, 1987 that $10,000 was not a satisfactory settlement, and that he had tried several times in early February, 1987 to contact Mason's office by telephone about the case, but elicited no response. Fennell further stated that he had gone to Mason's office on February 20, 1987, at which time Mason informed him that the case had been settled for $10,000, whereupon Fennell reiterated his dissatisfaction with that settlement.

On February 27, 1987, Fennell wrote Mason expressing his dissatisfaction with the settlement agreement and indicating that he had "no further use of [Mason's] services." A copy of this letter was sent to the district court and received there on March 3, 1987. On March 20, 1987, Brewington wrote to the district court requesting that the "matter be restored to the calendar as the settlement which was authorized and accepted by our client is no longer acceptable to him," and that Mason and his associates be released by the court as counsel to Fennell.

[T]he district court held a hearing on June 16, 1987 to determine whether Fennell's case should be restored to the calendar. At the conclusion of the hearing, the district court dismissed the action and approved the settlement. This ruling was based upon a finding that Fennell's attorney had been clothed with "apparent authority" when he settled the case.

[T]wo circuits have ruled that where an action is based upon federal law, the authority of an attorney to settle that action is a federal question. In the absence of weighty countervailing considerations, we are inclined to follow our sister circuits in deeming federal law applicable to the question before us. In any event, to the extent that deference might be accorded to New York precedents concerning what is at root a fairly general question of agency law, the outcome would in our view be the same.

We begin with the undisputed proposition that the decision to settle is the client's to make, not the attorney's. On the other hand, if an attorney has apparent authority to settle a case, and the opposing counsel has no reason to doubt that authority, the settlement will be upheld.

The district court made the following findings concerning the issue of apparent authority: 1) that Mason and his associates represented Fennell "in dealing with the other side," 2) that they were authorized to appear at conferences for him, 3) that Fennell knew that settlement was being discussed, 4) that Fennell did not tell his counsel not to continue discussing settlement, 5) that Fennell would have accepted a higher settlement figure ($50,000-75,000), and 6) that Fennell did not tell defendants' counsel that the authority of plaintiff's counsel was limited in any way. The district court concluded that Fennell's counsel "had every appearance of being authorized to make a binding agreement with [defendants' counsel]."

Apparent authority is

> the power to affect the legal relations of another person by transactions with third persons, professedly as agent for the other, arising from and in accordance with *the other's manifestations* to such third persons.

Restatement (Second) of Agency § 8 (1958) (emphasis added). Further, in order to create apparent authority, the *principal must manifest to the third party* that he "consents to have the act done on his behalf by the person purporting to act for him." *Id.* § 27. Second Circuit case law supports the view that apparent authority is created only by the representations of the principal to the third party, and explicitly rejects the notion that an agent can create apparent authority by his own actions or representations.

In this case, taking the facts as the district court found them, Fennell made no manifestations to defendants' counsel that Mason and his associates were authorized to settle the case. Fennell's attorneys accordingly had no apparent authority to settle the case for $10,000 without Fennell's consent. The district court's findings that Mason and his associates represented Fennell, and that they were authorized to appear at conferences for him, do not prove otherwise. A client does not create apparent authority for his attorney to settle a case merely by retaining the attorney.

Further, the court's findings that Fennell knew settlement was being discussed, did not ask his attorneys not to discuss settlement, would have accepted a higher settlement figure, and did not tell defendant's counsel that the authority of plaintiff's counsel was limited in any way, do not lead to a different outcome. These findings involve only discussions between Fennell and his attorneys or things that Fennell did not say to opposing counsel. None of these findings relates to positive actions or manifestations by Fennell to defendants' counsel that would reasonably lead that counsel to believe that Fennell's attorneys were clothed with apparent authority to agree to a definitive settlement of the litigation.

Finally, we note that the application of state law would not yield a contrary result. Defendants contend that *Hallock v. State,* 64 N.Y.2d 224, 474 N.E.2d 1178, 485 N.Y.S.2d 510 (1984), would call for a decision in their favor if New York law were considered applicable. We disagree.

Hallock held that a stipulation of settlement made by counsel in open court may bind his clients even where it exceeds his actual authority, provided that there is apparent authority. In that case, however, an applicable court rule required that attorneys attending pretrial conferences have authority to enter into binding court settlements on behalf of their clients, a co-plaintiff attended the conference from which Hallock was absent because of illness, and more than two months passed before plaintiffs made any objection to the settlement. We do not think the rule stated in *Hallock* would apply here.

We realize that the rule we announce here has the potential to burden, at least occasionally, district courts which must deal with constantly burgeoning calendars. A contrary rule, however, would have even more deleterious consequences. Clients should not be faced with a Hobson's choice of denying their counsel all authority to explore settlement or being bound by any settlement to which their counsel might agree, having resort only to an action against their counsel for malpractice. In any event, even if we were to consider such a rule advisable, the applicable precedents and settled principles of agency law would preclude its adoption.

Reversed and remanded for further proceedings not inconsistent herewith.

Notes

1. Why did the attorney in *Hallock* have apparent authority to settle, while the attorney in *Fennell v. TLB Kent Co.* did not?

2. Note that some cases hold that where a party's attorney announces a settlement, in open court, the settlement will be presumed valid unless the party can prove the attorney had no authority to settle. *See, e.g., Kazale v. Flowers,* 541 N.E.2d 219 (Ill. App. 1989).

3. *Menard & Co. Masonry v. Marshall Building,* 539 A.2d 523 (R.I. 1988) involved a dispute growing out of the construction of a building. The general contractor on the project, Con-Sul, Inc. (Consul), contracted with Marshall Building Systems, Inc. (Marshall), to perform most of the work. Marshall entered into a contract "sub-contracting" certain masonry work to Menard & Co. Masonry Building Contractors (Menard).

During construction, Con-Sul, the general contractor, called a meeting to discuss the completion of a wall needed to support equipment that was to be delivered in a few days. The meeting was attended by (i) Con-Sul's project manager (Pickett), (ii) Marshall's project manager (Stone) and Copithorne (who had represented Marshall in the negotiations with Menard and who had executed the contract with Menard), and (iii) by Menard's project manager (Cillino). Con-Sul insisted that Menard work overtime if necessary to finish the wall. Menard's representative, Cillino, pointed out that the Menard-Marshall subcontract did not cover overtime expenses. At this point Copithorne assured Cillino that Menard would be paid for the overtime.

When Menard submitted invoices for the overtime work, Marshall refused to pay for them because the overtime had not been authorized by a written "change order," as required by the subcontract.

After the jury returned a verdict that Marshall was liable to Menard for the overtime, the trial court entered a directed verdict in favor of Marshall on the basis that there was no evidence from which the jury could conclude that Copithorne was authorized to agree to overtime. On appeal, the Rhode Island Supreme Court held that there was sufficient evidence of apparent authority to support the jury verdict:

> That Copithorne had authority to negotiate and execute the subcontract is undisputed by Marshall. Nor has Marshall shown that it communicated a subsequent limitation on Copithorne's authority to Marshall. He attended the meeting at which Menard was directed to perform overtime as Marshall's authorized representative. Thus, we conclude that Menard offered evidence upon which reasonable persons could differ, sufficient to defeat a motion for a directed verdict.

What is the basis of the holding in *Menard & Co. Masonry*? Does the fact that Copithorne had authority to enter into the original contract with Menard give him apparent authority to agree to a change? What other facts would you want to know in determining whether Copithorne had apparent authority? *See* Restatement § 51 comment c & Illustration 4.

Metalworking Machinery Co., Inc. v. Fabco, Inc.

17 Ohio App. 3d 91, 477 N.E.2d 634 (1984)

COLE, Judge.

This is an appeal taken from a decision of the Court of Common Pleas of Hancock County, wherein summary judgment was granted in favor of plaintiff, Metalworking Machinery Company (Metalworking), in the amount of $15,000, plus defendant, Yoder Machinery Company (Yoder).

The basic relevant facts in this case were stipulated to by the parties and are as follows.

On August 10, 1979, Metalworking purchased from East Coast Steel Company of Columbia, South Carolina (East Coast), a two wheel "Wheelabrator" metalworking machine[, for a] purchase price [of] $15,000. No certificate of title or bill of sale was involved.

On April 4, 1980, Yoder purchased the same metalworking machine from East Coast, said machine never having been picked up by Metalworking. Subsequently, in the usual course of its business, Yoder sold the same "Wheelabrator" to defendant/third party plaintiff, Fabco, Incorporated (Fabco), for a price of $31,500. Fabco also expended a substantial amount of money in rehabilitating and putting into service the machine.

It was also stipulated that East Coast was a manufacturing company and that the "Wheelabrator" machine was not sold by East Coast in the ordinary course of its business.

Upon motions for summary judgment made by all of the parties, the trial court ordered that summary judgment be granted to the plaintiff, Metalworking, against Fabco, and further that summary judgment be granted to Fabco against Yoder. Both summary judgments granted were in the amount of $15,000.

The specific finding of the trial court to which Yoder now addresses its appeal is that there was no estoppel created by the fact situation upon which Yoder can rely as a defense.

It is appellant's argument that the plaintiff Metalworking should be estopped from asserting the fact of its own ownership of the machine because it, by leaving the machine in the possession of East Coast for some nine months, created an appearance of authority in East Coast to sell that machinery.

Metalworking became the owner of the "Wheelabrator" on August 10, 1979. R.C. 1302.44(A) provides:

> A purchaser of goods acquires all title which his transferor had or had power to transfer.

Assuming as we must that the transferor East Coast had title, this passed to Metalworking and no title remained in East Coast. It is clear that Yoder in fact acquired no title, since on April 4, 1980, East Coast had no interest to transfer.

What East Coast did have was possession, the machine having been left with it. Was the act of Metalworking in leaving possession with East Coast a sufficient basis upon which to create an estoppel of Metalworking to assert its actual ownership?

In 42 Ohio Jurisprudence 3d, at 85, Section 54, it is stated:

> It is only when the owner, by his own affirmative act, has conferred the apparent title and absolute ownership upon another, upon the faith of which the chose in action has been purchased for value, that he is precluded from asserting his real title.

Here we are concerned with personalty but the principle applies. There needs to be some affirmative act on which to base estoppel. There is no affirmative act by Metalworking. It simply left the machine in situs. It did nothing actively to clothe East Coast with any authority to sell. Appellant argues that Metalworking was negligent in letting the machine sit in Coast's possession for nine months. However, there is nothing in the factual situation as stipulated to show the appellant was aware of this length of possession or relied on it. Had the sale taken place on succeeding days the situation would be the same so far as the length of possession without title by East Coast is concerned. There is no causal relationship between the length of time and the ultimate purchase. The causal relation asserted concerns only the fact of possession by East Coast, not the duration of that possession.

Thus, the issue narrows to the question whether or not simply possession by East Coast with permission by Metalworking without more and without respect to the duration of possession is a sufficient basis for estopping Metalworking from asserting its title.

In 28 American Jurisprudence 2d (1966) 686, Estoppel and Waiver, Section 63, it is said:

> Although mere possession and control of personal property are not ordinarily sufficient to estop the real owner from asserting his title against a person who has dealt with the one in possession on the faith of his apparent ownership, slight additional circumstances may turn the scale against the owner and estop him from asserting title against one who has purchased the property in good faith.

Here, however, there is nothing but possession involved. There are no indicia of ownership nor title documents entrusted to the possessor. The Ohio Uniform Commercial Code is quite clear that to create apparent authority to sell there must be more than simple possession. There must be a merchant of a specific type. R.C. 1302.44(B) states:

> Any entrusting of possession of goods to a merchant who deals in goods of that kind gives him power to transfer all rights of the entruster to a buyer in ordinary course of business.

Here the facts explicitly negate the application of this section as it is stipulated that East Coast was a manufacturing company and like machinery was not sold by it in the ordinary and usual course of its business.

There is evidence of no other act by Metalworking which could constitute this "slight additional circumstance."

[T]here is no evidence sufficient to warrant a finding of estoppel.

Judgment affirmed.

Notes

1. The Restatement distinguishes between apparent authority and estoppel. Under Restatement section 8B(1):

> A person who is not otherwise liable as a party to a transaction purported to be done on his account, is nevertheless subject to liability to persons who have changed their positions because of their belief that the transaction was entered into by or for him, if
>
> (a) he intentionally or carelessly caused such belief, or
>
> (b) knowing of such belief and that others might change their positions because of it, he did not take reasonable steps to notify them of the facts.

Estoppel differs from apparent authority in a couple of particulars. First, estoppel can be based on omissions, not just affirmative conduct. That includes situations in which the principal is aware that third parties might believe someone to have authority, and the principal fails to act reasonably to protect third parties. Second, while merely entering into a contract based on a reasonable belief of authority is sufficient to invoke apparent authority, it is *not* a change in position sufficient to invoke *estoppel.* Thus, in estoppel, while the conduct necessary to charge a principal is lower then in apparent authority, the third party must show something additional: a detrimental change in position.

The lines between apparent authority and estoppel are not all that clear. In fact, many opinions treat apparent authority and estoppel as a single doctrine (sometimes called "*ostensible* authority").

2. Why does possession of property not create apparent authority or estoppel as to the possessor's power to sell the property?

3. Thief steals a stereo from Owner, then sells it to Merchant, who sells used stereos. Assuming Buyer buys in the ordinary course of business, does Merchant have power to transfer to Buyer Owner's title to the stereo? Why or why not?

4. Suppose instead that Merchant not only sells stereos, but also repairs them. If Owner leaves a stereo with Merchant to be repaired, does Merchant have the power to transfer Owner's title by a sale in the ordinary course of business? What is the source of that power—apparent authority or estoppel?

Goldstein v. Hanna

97 Nev. 559, 635 P.2d 290 (1981)

GUNDERSON, Chief Justice:

Appellants, Ronald and Mary Goldstein, sued respondent, Fuad Hanna, to compel specific performance of an option to purchase Hanna's condominium. The district court entered judgment in favor of Hanna.

On or about December 10, 1977, the parties entered into a lease relating to Hanna's condominium in Clark County, Nevada. The lease granted the Goldsteins an option to purchase the condominium, and declared

> the option may be exercised at any time after December 1, 1977 and shall expire at midnight December 9, 1978 unless exercised prior thereto.

Callahan Realty conducted all negotiations on behalf of respondent Hanna, and was designated in the agreement as his authorized agent. The Goldsteins dealt exclusively with Callahan Realty, both as tenants and prospective purchasers. They had no direct dealings with Hanna until after August 1978.

In the summer of 1978, the Goldsteins exercise[d] their option to purchase. They contemplated a purchase from Hanna, with a simultaneous sale from themselves to another purchaser. To effectuate this double sale, Callahan Realty established two escrows, both with closing dates of August 29, 1978. Shortly before the escrows were to close, however, the ultimate purchaser declined to perform.

Three days before their escrow with Hanna was due to close, the Goldsteins contacted Mr. Callahan. They advised Callahan [that] they would purchase the condominium themselves, rather than find another purchaser.[1] Callahan informed the Goldsteins that they need not consummate the purchase by August 29, because their option would continue to be valid under the terms of the lease until December 9, 1978. To insure that respondent Hanna shared this understanding of the option terms, Mr. Goldstein requested Callahan call Hanna, in his presence, and confirm the agent's representations.

Callahan called Hanna and advised him that the ultimate purchaser would not close escrow as planned. Callahan also told Hanna that the Goldsteins' option to purchase would still be in effect until expiration of the lease term. Although Hanna testified at trial that he never authorized Callahan Realty to extend the escrow, the record indicates he never asserted that the option would not remain viable following termination of the pending escrow. On this issue, it appears he remained silent, and thus permitted the Goldsteins to rely on Callahan's representations.

On August 31, Hanna notified the escrow holder to consider the escrow cancelled. On September 15, however, Hanna called the Goldsteins on at least two occasions and attempted to purchase their option rights in the property.[2] After the Goldsteins rejected Hanna's offer, they learned that Hanna purportedly had cancelled the escrow. Hanna then refused to participate in a second escrow initiated by the Goldsteins.

In our view, this case does not turn on whether Callahan correctly advised the Goldsteins concerning their contract with respondent Hanna. Nor need we decide whether Callahan had actual authority to alter the contract's terms. The doctrine of equitable estoppel clearly precludes Hanna from claiming that the Goldsteins' rights under the lease-option agreement expired on August 29, 1978.

According to § 8B(1) of the Restatement (Second) of Agency (1958), an equitable estoppel arises under the following circumstances:

> A person who is not otherwise liable as a party to a transaction purported to be done on his account, is nevertheless subject to liability to persons who have changed their positions because of their belief that the transaction was entered into by or for him, if
>
> (a) he intentionally or carelessly caused such belief, or

1. The uncontroverted testimony of Ronald Goldstein reflects that he was prepared to fund the escrow himself when the ultimate purchaser declined to perform.

2. Appellants' uncontradicted testimony is as follows: "Mr. Hanna offered to buy our interest out. Maybe I am not using the right phrase. He offered us money to leave the property. He said that he wanted the place for himself."

(b) knowing of such belief and that others might change their positions because of it, he did not take reasonable steps to notify them of the facts.

Where there is a duty to speak, silence can raise an estoppel quite as effectively as can words. A duty to speak arises when another is or may come under a misapprehension regarding the authority of the principal's agent. Under such circumstances, the principal is obligated to exercise due care, and to conduct himself as a reasonably prudent business person with normal regard for the interests of others. Restatement (Second) of Agency § 8B comment d. Thus,

> a person remaining silent when he ought, in the exercise of good faith, to have spoken, will not be allowed to speak when he ought, in the exercise of good faith, remain silent.

Gardner v. Pierce, 22 Nev. 146, 36 P. 782 (1894). Similarly, silence or failure to repudiate an agent's representations can give rise to an inference of affirmation. According to § 94, comment a, of the Restatement (Second) Agency (1958):

> Silence under such circumstances that, according to the ordinary experience and habits of men, one would naturally be expected to speak if he did not consent, is evidence from which assent can be inferred. Such inference may be made although the purported principal had no knowledge that the other party would rely upon the supposed authority of the agent; his knowledge of such fact, however, coupled with his silence, would ordinarily justify an inference of assent by him.

In the instant case, during his telephone conversation with Callahan, Hanna made no effort to assure that the Goldsteins were not misled or lulled by his agent's representations.[3] Hanna knew the Goldsteins might not hasten to complete the August escrow while assuming they still had several months to exercise the option. Consequently, Hanna's silence and acquiescence in his agent's representations manifestly caused the Goldsteins to do what they otherwise would not have done, *i.e.*, to permit, at least arguably, a lapse of their valuable option rights.[4]

> Persons ordinarily express dissent to acts done on their behalf which they have not authorized or of which they do not approve.

---

3. The uncontroverted testimony of Mr. Goldstein indicates:

> "A. I was concerned having, on Callahan's advice, used the last month's rent, in restoring this so as not to be in default of the agreement, and he called Mr. Hanna at that time, at my insistence, in my presence he phoned him, and advised him of the problem, that there would be a delay in the closing of the escrow and that and he informed Mr. Hanna on the phone that evidently he asked if this invalidated it, and he told him it did not, it was good until the end of November."
>
> "Q. What did Mr. Callahan indicate to you after the telephone conversation?"
>
> "A. No problem. This is the basic phrase he used, no problem, we will go ahead and obtain a new buyer."

4. The record indicates that but for Hanna's silence the Goldsteins would have completed the escrow as scheduled. When Hanna informed the Goldsteins in mid-September 1978 that he did not intend to go through with an escrow with them, the Goldsteins promptly deposited with Western Title Company the necessary $82,000.00 to fulfill their part of the option agreement.

Restatement (Second) of Agency § 43 comment a. (1958). The doctrine of equitable estoppel is properly invoked whenever

> unconscionable injury would result from denying enforcement of the contract after one party has been induced by the other seriously to change his position in reliance on the contract.

Alpark Distributing Inc. v. Poole, 95 Nev. 605, 600 P.2d 229 (1979). In the case at bar, the detriment suffered by the Goldsteins involves the loss of the benefit of their bargain: the right to purchase the property for a specified sum.

Thus, we need not decide whether or not Callahan Realty would have had actual authority, acting alone, to extend the Goldsteins' right to exercise the option or to interpret the contract's meaning. In effect, Hanna imbued his agent, Callahan, with apparent authority to make the representations upon which the Goldsteins relied.

> Apparent authority (when in excess of actual authority) proceeds on the theory of equitable estoppel; it is in effect an estoppel against the owner to deny agency when by his conduct he has clothed the agent with apparent authority to act.

Ellis v. Nelson, 68 Nev. 410, 233 P.2d 1072 (1951).

We therefore conclude that the doctrine of equitable estoppel precludes Hanna from claiming a forfeiture of the Goldsteins' option rights. The cause is reversed and remanded for further proceedings consistent with this opinion.

MANOUKIAN, Justice, dissenting:

As we stated in *Tsouras v. Southwest Plumbing & Heating,* 94 Nev. 748, 751, 587 P.2d 1321, 1323 (1978):

> It is indispensable to keep in mind here that, as against the principal, there can be reliance only upon what the principal himself has said or done, or at least said or done through some authorized agent. The acts of the agent in question can not be relied upon as alone enough to support an estoppel. If his acts are relied upon there must also be evidence of the principal's knowledge and acquiescence in them.

Contrary to the majority view, appellants have failed to present any evidence of actions on the part of respondent which could be construed as clothing Callahan with the apparent authority to either extend the escrow or renew the option. Indeed, on cross-examination, Callahan testified that he had no authorization to extend the escrow, and that in the event appellants failed to timely comply, Hanna had instructed him to cancel the escrow.[4] Any representations that Callahan made regarding any extension of the escrow or regarding the option

> were merely hearsay, and, however much the (Goldsteins) may have been lured into relying upon them, they did not affect the rights of the (seller).

Tsouras v. Southwest Plumbing & Heating.

---

4. Callahan also testified that customarily brokers are without the authority to extend an escrow.

I would reject as unmeritorious the claim of equitable estoppel. Hanna failed to take any action, express or implied, that could be construed as clothing Callahan with the necessary authority. It necessarily follows that appellants' reliance was inappropriate, as application of the doctrine of estoppel would require that Hanna know about and acquiesce to any assertion on which the Goldsteins purportedly relied.

I would affirm the judgments of the trial court.

Note

May an imposter cause liability for another on an agency theory? In *Hoddeson v. Koos Bros.*, 47 N.J. Super. 224, 135 A.2d 702 (1957), Mrs. Hoddeson, a customer of a large furniture store, alleged that when she entered the store, she was assisted by a distinguished looking gentleman in a light blue suit, that he took her order for certain furniture, that he accepted her payment in full in cash, and that the furniture was never delivered. The store claimed Mrs. Hoddeson was swindled by an imposter. The trial court dismissed the purchaser's complaint. On appeal, the complaint was reinstated:

> [T]here was evidence that the person whose identity is undisclosed approached Mrs. Hoddeson and her aunt in the store, publicly exhibiting the mannerisms of a salesman; inquired if he could be of service; upon being informed of the type of the articles in which Mrs. Hoddeson was interested, he was not only sufficiently acquainted with their description, but also where in the department they were respectively on display, guiding them without hesitation to the location of the mirror and then to that of the indicated bedroom furniture; he represented that those articles were not then available in stock, which significantly the store records disclosed to be true; his prophetic representation concerning their prospective arrival in stock proved to be prescient, unless he gleaned that information from the price tag; he accurately calculated their true sales prices and openly received the cash. Those activities precisely characteristic of the common experiences and practices in the trade were conspicuously pursued in market overt during a period of 30 to 40 minutes.
>
> The point here debated is whether or not the evidence circumstantiates the presence of apparent authority.
>
> Let us hypothesize for the purposes of our present comments that the acting salesman was not in fact an employee of the defendant, yet he behaved and deported himself during the stated period in the business establishment of the defendant in the manner described by the evidence adduced on behalf of the plaintiffs, would the defendant be immune as a matter of law from liability for the plaintiffs' loss? The tincture of estoppel that gives color to instances of apparent authority might in the law operate likewise to preclude a defendant's denial of liability. It matters little whether for immediate purposes we entitle or characterize the principle of law in such cases as 'agency by estoppel' or 'a tortious dereliction of duty owed to an invited customer.' That which we have in mind are the unique occurrences where solely through the lack of the proprietor's reasonable surveillance and supervision an impostor falsely impersonates in the place of business an agent or servant of his. Certainly the proprietor's duty of care and precaution for the safety and security of the customer encompasses

more than the diligent observance and removal of banana peels from the aisles. Broadly stated, the duty of the proprietor also encircles the exercise of reasonable care and vigilance to protect the customer from loss occasioned by the deceptions of an apparent salesman. The rule that those who bargain without inquiry with an apparent agent do so at the risk and peril of an absence of the agent's authority has a patently impracticable application to the customers who patronize our modern department stores.

Our concept of the modern law is that where a proprietor of a place of business by his dereliction of duty enables one who is not his agent conspicuously to act as such and ostensibly to transact the proprietor's business with a patron in the establishment, the appearances being of such a character as to lead a person of ordinary prudence and circumspection to believe that the impostor was in truth the proprietor's agent, in such circumstances the law will not permit the proprietor defensively to avail himself of the impostor's lack of authority and thus escape liability for the consequential loss thereby sustained by the customer.

2. Inherent Agency Power

Cange v. Stotler & Co., Inc.

826 F.2d 581 (7th Cir. 1987)

CUMMINGS, Circuit Judge.

Plaintiff has sued defendant Stotler and Company, a futures commission merchant ("FCM"), to recover for "fraudulent and unauthorized trades for gold and silver futures contracts" charged to plaintiff's account with defendant. The complaint alleges misconduct of Dwight Wilson and Wilpadco, Inc., purportedly agents of defendant. Wilpadco was said to be wholly controlled by Wilson.

According to the complaint and plaintiff's affidavit filed in opposition to the motion to dismiss, plaintiff opened an account with defendant Stotler and Company through its agent Wilson and his company Wilpadco in early 1981 when a Stotler and Company Customer's Agreement was signed by one of defendant's partners and plaintiff. During four weeks in September 1982, nine unauthorized trades for the sale and purchase of gold and silver futures were charged to plaintiff's account with defendant, causing him losses of $59,150. These transactions were conducted by Wilson and Wilpadco, with commissions going to defendant. Plaintiff contends that he never traded in gold and silver futures. Wilson on his own initiative allegedly called plaintiff and told him of the first few trades and said they would be reversed since they were defendant Stotler and Company's mistakes. Plaintiff then discovered more unauthorized trades on his statement from defendant and in September and October 1982 notified Wilson who again told him that the trades were defendant's mistakes and would be reversed. The losses from the unauthorized trades remained on later statements but Wilson reassured him that defendant would refund the losses from those trades and later that the trades had in fact been reversed out but that plaintiff was misreading the statements.

When plaintiff's accountant discovered in August 1983 that the unauthorized trades still had not been reversed out, plaintiff wrote a letter to defendant requesting reimbursement and had that letter hand-delivered to Wilson. Allegedly, Wilson admitted that the trades were unauthorized and in late August 1983 he and Wilpadco apparently arranged for $15,483.21 to be transferred to plaintiff's account with defendant. Wilson also orally agreed to pay $5,000 a month into plaintiff's account with defendant to reimburse the remaining amount owed to plaintiff. When Wilson failed to make the September and October payments, plaintiff in November 1983 had Wilson sign an agreement to reimburse the rest of the charges plus interest in monthly payments of $1,000, with the first due on December 1, 1983. Wilson and Wilpadco are said to have acted with "express, implied or apparent authority" of defendant, and none of the three has made any subsequent payments to plaintiff.

The complaint charges violations of the [federal] Commodity Exchange Act, common law fraud, breach of fiduciary duty, violations of the Illinois Consumer Fraud and Deceptive Business Practices Act, and breach of the repayment agreement.

Prior to answering the complaint, defendant filed a motion to dismiss, relying on a one-year limitation clause in paragraph 14 of the Customer's Agreement with plaintiff.

The district court here erred in holding that defendant could not be estopped from asserting the limitation period due to defendant's lack of knowledge of or participation in its independent agent's conduct. Defendant admits that for purposes of this motion to dismiss or summary judgment motion Wilson must be assumed to be the agent of Stotler and Company, as the complaint alleges, and in fact there is much evidence to support the existence of an agency relationship: Wilson handled plaintiff's account with Stotler and Company; the Customer Agreement he gave plaintiff had Stotler and Company's name on it; the trades he executed on plaintiff's account were reflected on Stotler and Company confirmation slips and account statements; and Stotler and Company received commissions for executing the trades.

Plaintiff's first six counts are solely based on his losses from the alleged unauthorized trades made in violation of federal and state statutes and common law. The Commodity Exchange Act prohibits the cheating or defrauding of investors, and the knowing and deliberate execution of unauthorized trades, even if not done out of an evil motive or intent to injure the customer, violates that prohibition. The unauthorized trades were made through plaintiff's account with defendant by defendant's agent in charge of that account and presumably were acts within the scope of Wilson's agency with Stotler and Company. The fact that the agent's actions were illegal and fraudulent does not relieve the FCM, as the agent's principal, of civil liability under the vicarious liability principles [of the Commodity Exchange Act]. Nor does it matter that the FCM had no prior knowledge of the illegal acts and did not take commissions from the defrauded customer or otherwise benefit financially from the illegal acts.

The unauthorized trades by Wilson could be found to be within the scope of his agency with Stotler and Company and so too could his conduct that is alleged to have caused plaintiff not to file suit within the one-year limitations period. Wilson's acknowledgments that the trades were unauthorized and that plaintiff's correct account balance was different from that sworn on the account statements prepared by Stotler and Company could be found to be within the scope of his agency with Stotler and Company. For example, in a reparations case brought by a customer challenging unauthorized trades that an FCM's agent made, the Commodity Futures Trading Commission decided that the agent's admissions to the customer concerning the unauthorized nature of the trades, the consequent inaccuracies in the account statements issued by the FCM, and the amount owed, as reflected in a promissory note signed by the agent, were admissible against the FCM. The Commission reasoned that

> since the reporting of equity balances is a matter generally within the scope of an account executive's agency, his statements relating to the amount in complainant's accounts are admissible against [the FCM]

to prove the FCM's liability for the losses. *Stoller v. Siegel Trading Co.*, Comm. Fut. L. Rep. (CCH) ¶ 22,224, at 29,204 (CFTC June 6, 1984).

Wilson's promises to plaintiff that the losses from the unauthorized trades would be refunded could also be found to be acts within the scope of his agency with defendant and, as such, would be admissible to estop defendant's assertion of a limitations defense. A customer has an "absolute right not to incur liability for any trade not authorized by him." The failure of the FCM's agent to inform the customer of this absolute right to a refund can defeat the FCM's otherwise valid defense, based on a customer's untimely request for a refund, that the customer ratified the trade. Because the FCM or its agent must ensure that the customer understands the right to a refund, it is expectable that when unauthorized trades occur, the FCM's agent handling the account will tell the customer that the losses from any unauthorized trades will be refunded and statements and promises to that effect could certainly be within the scope of the agency.

Here the trier of fact could find that Wilson's statements of the "correct" account balance and his promises of a refund for the unauthorized trades were acts within the scope of the inherent agency power of a person like Wilson handling a customer's account for an FCM. *See* Restatement (Second) of Agency §§ 8A, 161 (1958). Stotler and Company allowed Wilson to act as its agent in handling plaintiff's account, and absent proof that Stotler and Company informed plaintiff that Wilson would not have the customary power of a person in a similar agency relationship, the defendant is bound by the acts of its agent no matter its secret limitations to the contrary. This Court has before observed that

> [t]he powers of an agent are, prima facia, coextensive with the business intrusted to his care, and will not be narrowed by limitations not communicated to the person with whom he deals.

Lumbermen's Mut. Ins. Co. v. Slide Rule & Scale Eng'g Co., 177 F.2d 305, 309 (7th Cir. 1949). Judge Learned Hand articulated this concept of inherent agency power when he upheld a jury verdict for plaintiff based on a contract the jury found to be an unconditional engagement for a singing tour despite the principal's instructions to its agent to engage the singer only for such recitals as he could later persuade record dealers to book her for, instructions which were not told to plaintiff. *Kidd v. Thomas A. Edison, Inc.*, 239 F. 405 (S.D.N.Y. 1917), affirmed, 242 F. 923 (2d Cir. 1917). He reasoned that the scope of an agency must be measured

> not alone by the words in which it is created, but by the whole setting in which those words are used, including the customary powers of such agents

and thus the contract was enforceable because

> the customary implication would seem to have been that [the agent's] authority was without limitation of the kind here imposed.

The principal benefits from the existence of inherent authority because

> [t]he very purpose of delegated authority is to avoid constant recourse by third persons to the principal, which would be a corollary of denying the agent any latitude beyond his exact instructions.

The trier of fact could find that it is within the customary authority of an FCM's agent handling a customer's account to make statements of the account's correct balance and to promise refunds for losses from unauthorized trades. Thus the plaintiff's reliance on those statements and promises, notwithstanding contrary figures listed on the account statement issued by Stotler and Company, could be found to be reasonable. As such, the plaintiff's failure to bring suit within the one-year limitations period could be found to be attributable to Wilson's statements, and Stotler and Company would be estopped from asserting the bar of the limitations period. Here there were triable issues of fact regarding whether Wilson's acts dissuading plaintiff from timely bringing suit were within the scope of Wilson's agency with defendant and therefore summary judgment should have been denied on the first six counts.

Defendant argues that Wilson lacked the "apparent authority" for his actions to estop Stotler and Company from asserting the bar of the limitations period. First, defendant argues that plaintiff has failed to show "a single action on Stotler's part to create apparent authority" of Wilson but plaintiff need not prove any actions on Stotler and Company's part besides its allowing Wilson to act as its agent for handling plaintiff's account because the trier of fact could find Wilson's statements within his inherent authority. Representations of the principal to the third party are central for defining apparent authority, but in contrast, inherent authority originates from the customary authority of a person in the particular type of agency relationship and no representations beyond the fact of the existence of the agency need be shown. *See* Restatement (Second) of Agency § 161 comment b (1958). *Compare id.* at § 8 *with id.* at § 8A. *See generally id.* at §§ 194-195 (inherent agency power can subject undisclosed principal to liability for acts of his or her agent).[7] Plaintiff has provided evidence of the existence of the agency and it is a triable issue of fact whether the acts fall within such an agent's customary authority; therefore, this first argument is meritless.

Notes

1. As noted in *Cange v. Stotler & Co., Inc.*, under Restatement section 161, inherent agency power is based on the customary authority of a general agent. A "general" agent is an agent authorized to conduct a *series* of transactions involving a *continuity of service*. Restatement § 3(1). A "special" agent is an agent authorized to conduct only a single transaction *or* authorized to conduct a series of transactions *not* involving a continuity of service. Restatement § 3(2).

2. Restatement section 8A indicates that inherent agency power is *distinct from* actual authority, apparent authority, and estoppel to deny authority, and derives solely from the general agency relationship itself. Yet is not inherent agency power analogous to the kind of *apparent authority,* discussed in *Hamilton Hauling, Inc. v. GAF Corp.*,

---

7. Inherent authority not only can differ from apparent authority but also from actual authority. Unlike actual authority, inherent authority cannot be limited by secret instructions to an agent restricting his or her customary authority. Kidd v. Thomas A. Edison, Inc., 239 F. at 406; see Restatement (Second) of Agency §§ 8A, 161 comment b (1958).

that arises by appointing the agent to a position customarily carrying with it certain authority?

3. Judge Learned Hand's opinion in *Kidd v. Thomas A. Edison, Inc.* (discussed by the court in *Cange v. Stotler & Co., Inc.*), is widely cited as the origin of the doctrine of inherent agency power. In order to sell the Edison phonograph, Edison conceived the idea of engaging some of the most popular singers to give recitals. The artist would sing, and the same song would be immediately reproduced by the phonograph, giving the audience an opportunity to compare the voice of the phonograph with the voice of the singer.

As a part of his duties as general supervisor of Edison's musical division, Fuller was given general responsibility for arranging the "tone-test" recitals, including authority to contract with the artists. Kidd claimed that Fuller had contracted for Edison to pay her $300 per week from October 15 to April 1, regardless of whether Edison Company booked any recitals. Edison argued Fuller was only authorized to agree to pay singers for those weeks during which she was booked for a recital.

Judge Hand characterized the question as one of apparent authority, but in the course of his opinion gave his views as to when a principal should be bound by an agent's unauthorized acts:

> If estoppel is the basis of all apparent authority, it existed here. Yet the argument involves a misunderstanding of the true significance of the doctrine. It is a fiction to say that the principal is estopped where he has not communicated with the third person and has thus misled him. There are, indeed, the cases of customary authority, which perhaps come within the range of a true estoppel; but in other cases the principal may properly say that the authority he delegated must be judged by his directions, taken together, and that it is unfair to charge him with misleading the public because his agent, in executing that authority, neither observed nor communicated an important part of his directions. Certainly it begs the question to assume that the principal has authorized his agent to communicate a part of his authority and not to disclose the rest.
>
> The considerations which have made the rule survive are apparent. If a man selects another to act for him with some discretion, he has by that fact vouched to some extent for his reliability. While it may not be fair to impose upon him the results of a total departure from the general subject of his confidence, the detailed execution of his mandate stands on a different footing. The very purpose of delegated authority is to avoid constant recourse by third persons to the principal, which would be a corollary of denying the agent any latitude beyond his exact instructions. Once a third person has assured himself widely of the character of the agent's mandate, the purpose of the relation demands the possibility of the principal's being bound through the agent's minor deviations.
>
> In the case at bar, there was no question of fact for the jury touching the scope of Fuller's authority. His general business covered the whole of the tone-test recitals; on him was charged the duty of doing everything necessary in the premises, without recourse to anyone else. It would certainly have been quite contrary to the expectations of the defendant if any of the prospective performers at the recitals had insisted on verifying directly with Maxwell the terms of his contract. It was precisely to delegate such negotiations to a competent substitute that they chose Fuller at all.

Zanac, Inc. v. Frazier Neon Signs, Inc.

134 Ga. App. 501, 215 S.E.2d 265 (1975)

MARSHALL, Judge.

The main issue in this appeal is whether Zanac's agent had authority to bind it to a contract for repairs of a sign at Zanac's restaurant.

Frazier brought his action on account, and on quantum meruit against Zanac, Inc., and its employee, Robert Spears, and Zanac's restaurant, Seven Steers, at which Spears worked. Spears was not served and did not appear as a witness.

Following a trial without a jury, the trial court entered the following findings of fact and conclusion of law:

> The Plaintiff furnished merchandise and services to Defendant Zanac, Inc. as set forth on Plaintiff's invoice no. 2760, dated October 20, 1970, the same being repair of neon sign at Seven Steers Restaurant. Said services and merchandise were furnished by Plaintiff pursuant to the request of Robert Spears, as employee of Defendant corporation, and Assistant Manager of the restaurant. Said Spears had the authority, according to the testimony of Defendant's President, Louis Zakas, to take deliveries of merchandise, hire and fire waitresses, busboys and other employees and to do other things that had to be done. Additionally, Spears was expressly authorized by Zakas to take a bid from Plaintiff for the job.
>
> The Court finds that Defendant's employee, Robert Spears, had the authority to contract for the merchandise and services performed by Plaintiff and that the acts of said Spears were within the scope of his authority.

These facts are not disputed by the parties and are supported by the record. Zanac contends that the evidence did not support the trial court's conclusion of law that Spears had agency authority to make the contract for repairs.

There is no question that Spears was the agent of Zanac; the question is whether there is sufficient evidence to show that this agent had authority to bind his principal, Zanac, to the contract with Frazier. Zanac's president stated he gave authority to Spears "to price out the job" but denied ever giving any of his employees, including Spears, authority "to spend my money." Frazier's president testified:

> Mr. Spears asked me to come and give him a price on repairing the sign. And I sent my truck crew of men out there and came up with a number of bad transformers and broken and burned out neons. And I told Mr. Spears that I couldn't give him a price, a total price to repair the sign, but I would repair it for so much for each unit of glass, and so much for each transformer I had to install in the sign. And he said, well, he'll have to clear that with Mr. Zakas [the president of Zanac]. And he let me, he would let me know. So, three days later, he called me back and said, 'Mr. Zakas said it was all right. Go ahead and repair the sign.'

We are not dealing with apparent authority in this case, since Zanac at no time manifested to Frazier that Spears was authorized to contract for the services rendered. *See* Restatement 2d, Agency, § 8 (1958). Nor may Spears' authority to contract be inferred from his authority to solicit bids for the job. *See* Restatement 2d, Agency,

§ 50 (1958). And it is questionable whether Spears' authority as an "assistant manager" included authority to "make contracts which are incidental to such business or are reasonably necessary in conducting it," or to make reasonable repairs, since Zanac's president stated that he specifically forbade such an expenditure unless it was an emergency. *See* Restatement 2d, Agency, § 73(a) & (b) (1958).

Nevertheless, even without express, apparent or inferred authority, Spears, as the general agent for a partially disclosed principal, may bind the principal under his inherent agency powers. *See* Restatement (Second) of Agency, §§ 8A, 161. The latter section states:

> A general agent for a disclosed or partially disclosed principal subjects his principal to liability for acts done on his account which usually accompany or are incidental to transactions which the agent is authorized to conduct if, although they are forbidden by the principal, the other party reasonably believes that the agent is authorized to do them and has no notice that he is not so authorized.

Georgia courts have used the terms "apparent," "incidental," "implied" and "inferred" authority, interchangeably, without regard to their distinctions as noted in the Restatement (Second). Because of these vagaries, it is difficult to formulate a general rule governing authority of a general agent to make contracts, except to say that Georgia statute and case law appear to be in accord with the Restatement, § 161, quoted above. In the present case we find there is sufficient evidence to support the trial court's conclusion that Spears had authority to enter into the contract and that same is binding on Zanac.

Note

What is the basis for the *Zanac, Inc. v. Frazier Neon Signs, Inc.* holding that Spears had inherent agency power to bind Zanac to the contract to repair the neon signs? If it *does not* arise from Spears' authority to solicit bids, does it arise from Spears' position as "assistant manager"? What other facts would you want to know before deciding whether it was reasonable for Frazier Neon Signs to believe Spears had authority to bind Zanac? If on one hot July day Spears ordered the installation of central air conditioning in the restaurant, would Zanac be liable for it? What if Spears instead ordered ten fans at a cost of $495?

3. Conclusion

Courts and commentators have developed various *doctrines* to explain the circumstances in which an agent will have the power to bind the principal by unauthorized acts. Bear in mind that the purpose of any doctrine is to rationalize the law, to organize it into a logically consistent framework. While doctrine seeks to *explain* the law, it is only an approximation; it is never a complete description.

While the Restatement explains power to bind by unauthorized acts using the concepts of apparent authority, estoppel to deny authority, and inherent agency power, many courts use only a single concept, "ostensible authority." Moreover, the Restatement categories themselves *overlap* in their application. Luckily, all four concepts make similar inquiries. First, did the third party with whom the agent dealt *believe* that the principal had consented to the agent binding the principal? Second, was that belief *reasonable* under the *circumstances*? Third, to what extent was the principal *responsible* for that belief?

In studying opinions discussing the power to bind by unauthorized acts, keep in mind the tendency of courts to use the Restatement categories, as well as ostensible authority, interchangeably. Think of the Restatement categories as a set of tools you can use to reach a result. Regardless of how the *court* analyzes the facts, try each of the Restatement categories to see how the facts fit them.

Chapter 3

Principal's Accountability for Notification to and Knowledge of the Agent

A. General Rules

E. Udolf, Inc. v. Aetna Casualty & Surety Company

214 Conn. 741, 573 A.2d 1211 (1990)

HULL, Associate Justice.

The sole issue in this appeal is whether the plaintiff, E. Udolf, Inc., was entitled to coverage under certain employee dishonesty insurance policies issued by the defendants, Aetna Casualty and Surety Company (Aetna) and Fire and Casualty Insurance Company of Connecticut (Fire and Casualty), for the misappropriation of monies by an employee of the plaintiff. The plaintiff notified the defendants of losses it had incurred as a result of an employee's dishonesty and sought from the defendants indemnification, plus interest, for those losses. Upon the defendants' refusals to pay its claim, the plaintiff instituted the present action. The matter was thereafter tried to the court and judgment was rendered in favor of the defendants. From this judgment the plaintiff appeals.

The underlying facts as found by the trial court are as follows. The plaintiff is a small corporation that operates a retail men's clothing store in the city of Hartford. During the relevant period, 1980 through 1983, the plaintiff employed between eight and ten employees. The only officer, director and shareholder of the plaintiff was Leonard Udolf, who was present in the store approximately 10 to 20 percent of the time. In his absence the store was run by Kenneth Auer, the store manager. Auer was the overseer of the store and was principally in charge of its operations in the absence of Leonard Udolf. He was expected, however, to report all relevant activities to Leonard Udolf.

During the years 1980 and 1981, Lynn Bjork, an employee of the plaintiff, misappropriated $6000 from the plaintiff. To effect the misappropriations, she substituted her personal checks for money generated by the plaintiff's sales, and then simply put these checks in her desk rather than depositing them into the plaintiff's account. In the spring of 1981, during one of Leonard Udolf's frequent absences from the store, Anna Shukis, the plaintiff's bookkeeper, discovered the misappropriations and immediately informed Auer of them. Auer and Shukis were expected to inform Leonard Udolf of activities such as Bjork's misappropriations. They, however, did not consult with Leonard Udolf, but rather agreed with one another to allow Bjork to repay the $6000 and remain employed by the plaintiff. Thereafter, Bjork repaid the $6000.

Beginning in late 1981, and continuing until February, 1983, Bjork again misappropriated monies from the plaintiff, totaling $48,715.08. These misappropriations were discovered in February, 1983, and Bjork was immediately fired by Auer on the direct order of Leonard Udolf.

Pursuant to employee dishonesty insurance policies that the plaintiff had purchased from Aetna and from Fire and Casualty, the plaintiff notified the two companies of the losses incurred as a result of Bjork's misappropriations. Both Aetna and Fire and Casualty refused to indemnify the plaintiff for those losses, claiming that the language of the policies excluded coverage for Bjork's actions. Aetna's refusal to pay was based on the following provision contained in section 7 of its policy:

> The coverage of Insuring Agreement I shall not apply to any Employee from and after the time that the Insured or any partner or officer thereof not in collusion with such Employee shall have knowledge or information that such Employee has committed any fraudulent or dishonest act in the service of the Insured or otherwise, whether such act be committed before or after the date of employment by the Insured.

Fire and Casualty's refusal was based on similar language contained in section 1(3) of its policy:

> Insurance hereunder shall be deemed cancelled as to any Employee immediately upon discovery by the Insured, or any partner or officer, of any fraudulent or dishonest act of such Employee.

The trial court concluded that, under the terms of the policies, the plaintiff was not entitled to recovery of the losses it had incurred as a result of Bjork's actions. The basis of the court's conclusion was its determination that the knowledge of Auer and Shukis concerning misappropriations committed by the plaintiff's employees was imputed to the plaintiff. The court thus reasoned that because the 1980-81 misappropriations by Bjork constituted "fraudulent or dishonest act[s]" within the scope of [the insurance policies], and because the plaintiff, by imputation of Auer's and Shukis' knowledge, became aware of those misappropriations no later than the summer of 1981, any subsequent losses caused by a "fraudulent or dishonest act" on the part of Bjork were excluded from coverage under the policies. In so concluding, the court rejected the plaintiff's claim that, because Auer and Shukis did not inform Leonard Udolf of Bjork's 1980-81 misappropriations, they were in collusion with Bjork. The court stated that while the failure of Auer and Shukis to notify Leonard Udolf may have been an act of poor judgment, it was not a fraudulent act and therefore was not collusive.

The plaintiff concedes that generally

> notice to, or knowledge of, an agent while acting within the scope of his authority and in reference to a matter over which his authority extends, is notice to, or knowledge of, the principal.

West Haven v. United States Fidelity & Guaranty Co., 174 Conn. 392, 395, 389 A.2d 741 (1978). As stated in the Restatement (Second) of Agency § 272

> a principal is affected by the knowledge of an agent concerning a matter as to which he acts within his power to bind the principal or upon which it is his duty to give the principal information.

The plaintiff argues, however, that this agency principle should not apply in the context of employee dishonesty insurance, citing as authority for its position *American Employers' Ins. Co. v. Cable,* 108 F.2d 225 (5th Cir. 1939), *Miami National Bank v. Pennsylvania Ins. Co.,* 314 F. Supp. 858 (S.D. Fla. 1970), *Phoenix Indemnity Co. v. Union Finance Co.,* 54 So. 2d 188 (Fla. 1951), and *Peurifoy v. Loyal,* 154 S.C. 267, 151 S.E. 579 (1930).

The trial court was unpersuaded by the plaintiff's argument and the cases on which it was based, and relied instead primarily on *Ritchie Grocer Co. v. Aetna Casualty & Surety Co.,* 426 F.2d 499 (8th Cir. 1970), in concluding that the knowledge of Auer and Shukis concerning Bjork's 1980-81 activities should be imputed to the plaintiff. The similarities between *Ritchie* and the instant case are striking. At issue in *Ritchie* was the same policy exclusion as in the present case.

The underlying facts involved in *Ritchie Grocer Co.* were as follows. Joseph Polk, the manager of a branch office of the plaintiff's wholesale grocery business, received an application for employment from Wayne Kemp. Prior to hiring Kemp, Polk inquired into Kemp's reputation for trustworthiness and discovered that several months earlier Kemp and two other boys had broken into a gas station and had stolen some tires and money. Notwithstanding that information, Polk hired Kemp as a truck driver for the plaintiff. During the eighteen months that Kemp was employed by the plaintiff, he misappropriated $17,486.20, for which the plaintiff made a claim under its fidelity policy. The insurance company defended on the grounds that Polk's knowledge of Kemp's prior "fraudulent or dishonest" act made him a known risk and excluded him from coverage under the policy's terms. The District Court held in favor of the insurance company on this ground and the Eighth Circuit Court of Appeals affirmed, reciting the general agency principle that knowledge of an agent acquired in the ordinary discharge of his duties for the corporation is generally to be imputed to the principal.

The trial court in the present case also relied on *Alfalfa Electric Cooperative, Inc. v. Travelers Indemnity Co.,* 376 F. Supp. 901 (W.D. Okla. 1973), as support for its decision to impute to the plaintiff the knowledge of Auer and Shukis. In *Alfalfa Electric Cooperative, Inc.,* the court imputed to an employer the knowledge of an office manager concerning prior fraudulent or dishonest acts of an employee.

The cases relied upon by the trial court and the cases cited by both the plaintiff and the defendants lack any meaningful analysis of the reasons that imputation was either appropriate or inappropriate under the facts of the particular cases. We conclude, however, that a proper analysis flows logically from the tension between the conflicting views presented by the plaintiff and the defendants. The plaintiff argues that the general rule imputing knowledge of an agent to a principal presumes the agent's loyalty in the performance of his duties. The corporation purchases fidelity insurance to protect itself from the risk that the employee will be disloyal. The plaintiff claims that it, therefore, would be "absurd" to hold that each employee so insured was an agent of the plaintiff whose duty it was to discover and report acts of dishonesty by other employees. Moreover, the plaintiff argues, if the neglect or reluctance of the insured's employees to report on one another relieved the insurance carrier of its liability, the corporation would be denied a remedy. The defendants' counterpoint is that, taken to its extreme, the plaintiff's contention would render "prior employee dishonesty" exclusions useless. Without employee imputation, the defendants argue, it would be impossible to charge an insured corporation with knowledge of an employee's prior wrongful actions.

The answer to this conundrum can be found in the cases relied upon by the trial court, although not explicitly articulated therein. We conclude that the knowledge of an employee may be imputed to an employer under an employee dishonesty insurance policy if the employee holds a position of management or control in the exercise of which a duty to report known dishonesty of a fellow employee can be found to exist either explicitly or by fair inference from a course of conduct.

On appeal, the plaintiff argues that the evidence presented at trial indicated various limitations on the responsibilities of Auer and Shukis that made imputation inappropriate. The trial court, however, concluded that Auer was principally in charge of operations during Leonard Udolf's absences from the store and that one of his responsibilities in that capacity was to report matters such as misappropriations to Leonard Udolf. The court further determined that Anna Shukis, the plaintiff's bookkeeper, was responsible for running the bookkeeping operation and that she likewise had a responsibility to report to Leonard Udolf any misappropriations that occurred in that department. The nature and extent of an agent's authority is a question of fact for the trier.

Bjork testified at trial that in 1980-81, Auer's position was that of "store manager." Although Auer testified at trial that he was only the "sales manager," this testimony was inconsistent with his prior deposition testimony in which Auer had claimed that he was in fact the "store manager." Further, while Auer stated that he did not have the authority to hire and fire employees in 1980-81, he did arrange with Bjork, without first consulting with Leonard Udolf, for repayment of the $6000 and then fired Bjork upon learning of the 1983 misappropriations. Auer's testimony also revealed that he was expected to report to Leonard Udolf everything that happened in the store. Finally, Leonard Udolf was present in the store only 10 to 20 percent of the time. Although Leonard Udolf claimed at trial that he was always in charge of the store, even while absent, this claim conflicted with his deposition testimony in which, in response to the question of "who was in charge of the operations in your absence," he answered: "Well I felt I had them in capable hands with Ken Auer on the floor and in the office with Ann Shukis and the other girls."

We conclude that the trial court's factual findings concerning the responsibilities and consequent duties of Auer and Shukis were supported by the evidence. Therefore, since the court found that the positions held by Auer and Shukis gave rise to a duty to report misappropriations to Leonard Udolf, the court's imputation to the plaintiff of Auer's and Shukis' knowledge concerning Bjork's 1980-81 actions was not error.

There is no error.

Notes

1. Restatement section 272 provides that the principal will be affected by the *knowledge* of an agent *either* (i) when the knowledge concerns a matter within the scope of the agent's power to bind the principal *or* (ii) when the agent has a duty to give the principal that information. Note, however, that a principal will *not* be affected

by an agent's knowledge concerning a matter outside the scope of the agent's *actual* authority, but within the agent's *apparent authority*, *unless* a third person has *relied* on the agent's apparent authority. Restatement § 273.

An agent has a duty to inform the principal of information learned by the agent that relates to the matters entrusted to the agent by the principal:

> An agent may have a duty to act upon, or to communicate to his principal information which [the agent] has received, although not specifically instructed to do so. The duty exists if [the agent] has notice of facts which, in view of [the agent's] relations with the principal, [the agent] should know may affect the desires of [the agent's] principal as to [the agent's] own conduct or the conduct of the principal or of another agent. [This] duty is inferred from [the agent's] position, just as authority is inferred. The extent of the duty depends upon the kind of work entrusted to [the agent], [the agent's] previous relations with the principal, and all the facts of the situation.

Restatement § 381 comment a.

2. As used in the Restatement, *knowledge* of a fact is limited to actual conscious awareness of it. *See* Restatement § 9 comment c. Persons have *notice* of a fact when they *know* it, have *reason to know* it, *should know* it, or have been *notified* of it. Restatement § 9(1). The rules regarding attributing to the principal an agent's *knowledge* also apply to the attribution of *notice*. Restatement §§ 9(3), 272 comment b.

3. Note that a principal will not necessarily be held responsible for an agent's knowledge for all purposes. For example, in *Sisk v. McPartland*, 267 Ore. 116, 515 P.2d 179 (1973), the trial court entered a default judgment against the defendant, Zelle, after striking Zelle's answer on account of her failure to appear at a deposition. Plaintiff had served Zelle's attorney, Griffith, with formal notice of the deposition, but Griffith was unable to inform Zelle of the deposition. The appellate court reversed the default judgment on the ground that a *willful* failure to appear was necessary to strike an answer:

> Even if we assume that defendant Zelle received proper notice of the deposition through service on her attorney, we do not believe that her failure to appear can properly be characterized as 'willful.' [A willful act is generally defined as one which '(proceeds) from a conscious motion of the will; voluntary' or is 'designed; intentional; not accidental or involuntary.' Black's Law Dictionary 1773 (rev. 4th ed. 1968).]
>
> The record suggests that defendant Zelle might have had actual knowledge of the lawsuit but nothing in the record suggests that she had actual knowledge of the deposition. According to an established principle of agency law, notice given an agent is attributable to the principal. [Restatement (Second) of Agency § 268.] Nevertheless, courts recognize the distinction between vicarious notice and notice based on actual knowledge when construing a statute or contract which imposes liability on the basis of actual knowledge only.
>
> > If the state of mind of a principal in a transaction is a factor, a notification by a third person giving information to an agent who does not communicate it to the principal does not operate with like effect as a similar notification given to the principal.
>
> Restatement (Second) of Agency § 268, Comment d.

> In many situations, in order for one to be responsible, it is necessary that the act should be done with knowledge in a subjective sense, and it is not sufficient that one has means of information.

Id. § 275, Comment b.

We believe that the requirement that the failure to attend the deposition be willful, indicates that the party must have actual notice of the deposition and not notice imputed from the knowledge of an agent attorney. The legislative aim is to discourage the deliberate obstruction of established discovery procedures. Only when the party has actual notice of the pending deposition can the subsequent failure to appear be accurately described in words such as 'willful,' 'conscious,' 'designed,' or 'intentional.' A failure to attend due to ignorance of the hearing is simply not a willful act. Since defendant Zelle's failure to attend the deposition was not willful, the trial court erred in striking her answer and placing her in default.

Dvoracek v. Gillies

363 N.W.2d 99 (Minn. App. 1985)

LANSING, Judge.

The tenant in this unlawful detainer action appeals from a judgment determining that the landlord is entitled to restitution of the premises because the lease term had expired. The trial court directed a verdict for the landlord at the close of evidence, finding as a matter of law that the tenant had given inadequate notice to renew the lease.

Stephen Gillies rented commercial space from Cleo Dvoracek at 3014 South Lyndale Avenue. Gillies does business as Gemini Service Center, an automobile and marine repair service. Dvoracek owns the adjoining premises and business, called Art Materials, Inc., at 3018 South Lyndale Avenue. She works there full-time and employs about 18 people.

The parties executed a lease that provided for a one-year term expiring May 31, 1984, with an option to renew for a two-year period and a right of first refusal for an additional two-year period. Paragraph 2.2 of the lease required the tenant to give the landlord a written renewal notice at least 60 days before the lease expired. In addition, paragraph 25 provided:

> Any notice required under this Lease shall be in writing, and shall be deemed to have been given if deposited in the United States mail, postage prepaid, certified or registered mail, return receipt requested, and addressed as follows:
>
> Landlord: Cleo Dvoracek
3018 Lyndale Avenue South
Minneapolis, MN 55408
>
> Tenant: Stephen Gillies
2645 Lyndale Avenue South
Minneapolis, MN 55408

Gillies testified that he hand-delivered all his rent checks to Dvoracek at Art Materials because it was right next door. If Dvoracek was not available, he left the checks with employees at the city desk there. Dvoracek admitted that Gillies had left rent checks with employees at the city desk in the past and that she had hand-delivered notices to him in the past.

Gillies testified that on the morning of March 16, 1984, he dictated a letter giving notice of his intent to renew the lease for two years. His secretary typed and notarized the letter at Gillies' office in his home at 2645 South Lyndale. They drove together to the common driveway between Art Materials and the Gemini Service Center. Gillies went into a nearby store to copy the letter, while his secretary waited in the car. When he returned he handed the copy to his secretary, put the original into an envelope, and went into Art Materials sometime around noon. He said he asked for Dvoracek and was told she was not available. He left the letter with an employee at the city desk and said, "Please see that Cleo gets this." He said the employee responded, "I certainly will," but he doesn't remember if the employee was a man or woman. The secretary, who had worked for Gillies for 15 years, testified to the same sequence of events.

Dvoracek and her employees who testified denied receiving the letter, although some employees who had worked that day did not testify. According to the employees' testimony, anyone working in the store that day could have attended the city desk over the lunch hour.

Dvoracek received a letter from Gillies on about May 1 asking her to repair the air conditioning before the summer. She responded with a letter from her attorney dated May 14, advising Gillies that she had received no notice of his intent to renew the lease and that the lease was to terminate on May 31. Gillies attempted to pay the June rent, but Dvoracek refused to accept it.

This unlawful detainer action was brought in June 1984. The trial court directed a verdict for the landlord at the close of evidence on the ground that, even assuming Gillies delivered the notice as he had testified, Dvoracek's employees were not her agents for purposes of receiving the renewal notice.

Gillies argues that the landlord's employees had either actual or apparent authority to accept the renewal notice and that the evidence presented at minimum a question for the jury. A notification given to an agent is notice to the principal if it is given to "an agent authorized to receive it" or to "an agent apparently authorized to receive it." *Distillers Distributing Co. v. Young,* 261 Minn. 549, 552, 113 N.W.2d 175, 177 (1962) (quoting Restatement (Second) of Agency § 268 (1957)). The existence of an agency relationship is a fact question for the jury.

The trial court relied on *Prendergast v. Searle,* 81 Minn. 291, 294, 84 N.W. 107, 109 (1900), in directing a verdict for the landlord. In *Prendergast* the court held that evidence should have been admitted tending to show that the tenant had mailed a notice to an agent of the landlord, because the agent had "the charge and management of his principal's business with reference to such tenancy."

The trial court determined that, even assuming Gillies delivered the letter to an Art Materials employee, the notice was inadequate because Dvoracek's employees were not agents "having the charge and management" of her rental property business. In *Prendergast* the agent did have the charge and management of the principal's rental business, but the case does not establish a rule of law that such agents are the only ones who may receive notices. Agency is a fact question. The question here is whether

Dvoracek's employees became her agents for the purpose of receiving Gillies' renewal notice.

The record shows that Gillies always hand-delivered his rent checks to either Dvoracek or her employees at Art Materials. Although Dvoracek testified that she had not expressly authorized her employees to accept hand-delivered correspondence from Gillies, she allowed the practice to continue. She never told Gillies not to leave correspondence at the city desk, and she never told the employees at the city desk not to accept deliveries for her. Furthermore, mail sent to Dvoracek at 3018 South Lyndale is delivered to the city desk.

Viewing the evidence in the light most favorable to Gillies, a jury could reasonably have concluded that Dvoracek had either impliedly authorized her employees to accept the notice or had consented to Gillies' practice of hand-delivering correspondence to them, so that he was justified in relying on them as her agents. We reverse and remand for another trial on this issue.

Notes

1. Be careful to distinguish *knowledge and notice*, on the one hand, and *notification*, on the other hand. As indicated in the notes following *E. Udolf, Inc. v. Aetna Casualty & Surety Company,* knowledge and notice involve responsibility for *awareness* of information. Notification is a formal act intended in itself to determine the rights of the parties, regardless of the degree of knowledge of the recipient. Restatement § 9(3) & comment f. In *Dvoracek,* for example, Gillies delivered his letter to Dvoracek's "city desk" for the purpose of exercising his option to renew the lease.

Unfortunately, the word "notice" can be used in two different contexts. Notice often refers to a person's responsibility for information because they know it or have *constructive knowledge of it* (reason to know it, should know it or receipt of a notification of it). *See* Restatement § 9(1). Notice is also used in the context of *notification.* In *Dvoracek*, for example, Gillies sent a "notice" of his intent to renew the lease. Similarly, in *Sisk v. McPartland*, the plaintiff gave the defendant's attorney "notice" of the deposition of the defendant. In reading cases dealing with notification and knowledge, students should be alert to whether the court is using the word "notice" in a notification or constructive knowledge sense.

2. *Dvoracek* did not involve the question of whether the notification resulted in constructive knowledge. Instead, the issue was whether the notification was *legally effective* to renew the lease. The question of the effectiveness of a notification to an agent is similar to the questions studied in chapter 2: did the notification *bind* the principal? As a result, the rules regarding notification are somewhat different from those regarding the attribution of knowledge and notice. For example, notification to an agent is notification to the principal if the agent was actually *or apparently* authorized to receive the notification. Restatement § 268. *Knowledge* that is only within an agent's apparent authority will not be *attributed* to the principal unless a third party relied on the appearance of authority. Restatement § 273.

3. The question of the effect of notification, knowledge, and notice is not limited to *principals and agents.* A *master* will be affected by notification to, or knowledge or notice of, a *servant* so long as the servant had a duty to act on or communicate the information or notification as a part of the servant's employment or apparent employment. Restatement § 283.

Davenport v. Correct Manufacturing Corp.

24 Ohio St. 3d 131, 493 N.E.2d 1331 (1986)

FACTS*

This case involves the appeal by Davenport from a summary judgment in favor of E.H.J. Skyworker Services, Inc. (Skyworker). Davenport alleged that he was injured when a "cherry picker" owned by his employer, Fisher, collapsed due to the failure of a defectively designed "rod end assembly." Davenport alleged, among other things, that before the accident Skyworker had repaired the cherry picker and had failed to warn Fisher that the rod end assembly was defective. Skyworker responded that it did not know of the defect and had no duty to discover it. The summary judgment record included a disputed statement that a representative of manufacturer of the cherry picker had told Herbert A. Van Dyke, an agent of Skyworker at the time of the repair, of the need to replace the defective part with a new one. Skyworker claimed it was not responsible for Van Dyke's knowledge because the alleged conversation with the manufacturer's representative had occurred *before* Van Dyke had become an agent of Skyworker.

The trial court granted summary judgment in favor of Skyworker. On appeal, the court of appeals reversed the summary judgment, but ruled that Skyworker could not be held accountable for the knowledge of an agent acquired prior to the time the agent became an agent. On appeal, the Ohio Supreme Court rendered the following opinion.

PER CURIAM

Because a number of disputed questions of material fact remain, we hold that the trial court improperly granted Skyworker's motion for summary judgment. These factual questions include: whether [Van Dyke] in fact knew of the danger; and whether any such knowledge was obtained after Skyworker [employed Van Dyke] and could therefore be imputed to the corporation.

We affirm the judgment of the court of appeals and remand the cause for further proceedings in the trial court.

WRIGHT, Justice [with Sweeney and Brown, JJ.], concurring in part and dissenting in part.

I agree with the majority that sufficient questions of material fact exist for Davenport to withstand a motion for summary judgment. I believe, however, that this court should go one step further and lay to rest the Ohio rule that prohibits courts from imputing to a corporation the knowledge of a corporate agent which was acquired before that agent was employed by the corporation.

The general rule is that relevant knowledge is imputed to the corporation or principal in such a situation. See Restatement of the Law 2d, Agency (1958), Section 276. The time when the knowledge is acquired should be relevant only to draw the appropriate inference as to the existence of knowledge. If the knowledge was acquired either before the agency relationship existed or while the agent was not acting for the purposes of the principal and the agent has forgotten the knowledge, the principal

---

* [Footnote by the editors.] The following description of the facts and procedural history was prepared by the editors and not by the court.

would not be held liable because the agent had no duty to the principal to remember it. *Id.*, Comment b. Likewise, the knowledge would not be imputed to the principal if the agent acquired it while acting in a position of confidentiality. Knowledge would be imputed only if it can reasonably be said to be present in the agent's mind while he was acting for the principal or if it was acquired so recently as to raise the presumption that he still retained it in his mind.

This general rule makes much more sense than the so-called Ohio rule. Herbert A. Van Dyke's post-[employment] actions in servicing Fisher's skyworker [cherry picker] would permit an inference that he was acting with previously acquired knowledge about such units.

A person often is employed by a corporation because of his specialized knowledge, obtained through either educational training or job experience. It is illogical to hold that the person does not have this knowledge for purposes of corporate liability. This court should overrule the court of appeals to the extent that it held that any knowledge acquired by Van Dyke before [employment by] Skyworker could not be imputed to the corporation for purposes of this case. On remand, Davenport should be required to establish that it would be reasonable to infer that Van Dyke knew of the dangerous condition of the rod-end assembly in the Fisher skyworker.

Notes

1. The dispute regarding whether the principal should be affected by the knowledge or notice of an agent where that knowledge or notice was acquired *casually* (outside of the agent's "employment") turns on the question of whether the agent should be expected to recall "extraneous" information. Certainly, an agent may no longer have knowledge—actual conscious awareness of the information—and should not automatically be expected to recall it (should not automatically have reason to know). On the other hand, if the agent does recall it, or reasonably should have recalled it, while acting with authority or with a duty to inform, the principal should be accountable for that information unless the information was confidential information the agent was not privileged to disclose.

2. This is another context in which the rules regarding *notification* differ from those regarding knowledge and notice. Because the issue in *notification* is whether the agent had *power to bind* the principal, a notification is effective *only* if the agent had such power *at the time the notification was received.* Restatement § 269.

B. Time from Which Notification or Knowledge Affects Principal

Biggs v. Terminal Railroad Association

110 Ill. App. 3d 709, 442 N.E.2d 1353 (1982)

KARNS, Presiding Justice:

Rodney Steven Biggs brought this action under the Federal Employers' Liability Act to recover damages for personal injuries sustained while employed as a track laborer for defendant, Terminal Railroad Association of St. Louis. Defendant appeals from the judgment entered in the circuit court of Madison County on a jury verdict in plaintiff's favor.

The testimony established that plaintiff and co-employee, Robert Parr, were track laborers and had been working for defendant 15 days on April 17, 1979. On that morning, plaintiff, Parr and 10 to 12 other employees reported for work at a shanty at the railroad yards. While in the shanty, plaintiff related to the men a dream he had the night before about Parr pouring "Cheerios" in the heating and air conditioning ducts of plaintiff's trailer. Plaintiff testified that some of the men laughed but that there was no other reaction to the story. At that time, Ron Gartner, the track foreman, told the men to get their tools and get to work. Plaintiff and Parr then walked to the tool shed. Plaintiff repeated the dream in the tool shed to Gartner at which time Parr asked Gartner if he (Parr) could beat-up plaintiff. Plaintiff further testified that Gartner responded by saying that he wanted to get out of the shed first. Gartner testified he responded by telling Parr and plaintiff to get to work. Gartner then left the shed. Plaintiff then testified that Parr hit him on the jaw. Subsequently, plaintiff went outside and began pulling spikes at the track. When Parr came out plaintiff said, in Gartner's presence, "[H]ow come you hit me?" Parr then began grabbing at plaintiff and plaintiff reacted by striking Parr with a railroad spike he had in his hand. The spike cut Parr's lip. Parr picked up a pick axe and threatened plaintiff but threw the axe down without striking plaintiff. Plaintiff testified he turned away, believing Parr was now in control of himself. At that point, plaintiff was struck on the head with a railroad spike by Parr.

Gartner testified that he saw nothing occur between plaintiff and Parr in the tool shed and that he was turned away from plaintiff and Parr outside at the track until after Parr's lip was cut. When Parr picked up the axe, Gartner told him to drop it and get to work. When Parr did so, Gartner testified that he then turned back to his work having no reason to suspect further trouble.

The principles of law in these cases are well established. A railroad, as any employer, may be held liable under the Act where the assault by the fellow employee may be said to be within the scope of his employment, but the employee acts negligently. Liability may also be predicated upon the direct negligence of the railroad in knowingly employing, or retaining in its employ, a person with a quarrelsome disposition and vicious propensities who might reasonably be said to be a threat to other employees while performing their jobs within the scope of their employment. (Restatement (Second) of Agency § 213 (1957).)

Initially, we note that plaintiff makes no claim that defendant is vicariously liable under the principles of respondeat superior, that is, negligent because Parr acted negligently while acting within the scope of his employment. Instead, plaintiff's claim is one of direct negligence.

Plaintiff alleged three separate acts of negligence: failure to protect plaintiff from Parr, failure to provide plaintiff with a reasonably safe place to work and retention of Parr in its employ although it knew or should have known Parr was an ill-tempered and vicious person.

The reported cases establish that before the railroad may be found negligent, it must have had prior notice of the assailant-employee's violent propensities. Without any notice, defendant could not be negligent by retaining Parr in its employ. And, it could not be negligent by failing to protect plaintiff or by failing to provide plaintiff with a safe place to work if it did not know of Parr's violent nature and thus could not foresee any harm to plaintiff.

It was not alleged, nor was there any evidence, that defendant was negligent in employing an employee with known vicious propensities. There was no evidence that Parr had ever been quarrelsome or a person of violent disposition. The only evidence of this kind was the attack on plaintiff and if defendant was negligent in retaining Parr in its employ, the only evidence of prior notice of Parr's vicious disposition was that brought to the attention of Gartner, the track foreman, on the morning of the incident.

A corporate defendant acts only through its officers and employees. We do not believe that this brief notice of Parr's violent manner, brought only to the attention of the track foreman, could be considered to be notice of the corporate defendant under these facts. The Restatement (Second) of Agency, § 213, comment d, states that an employee must have some antecedent reason to believe that the employee presents an undue risk of harm to others because of his vicious nature.

Both plaintiff and Gartner testified that Parr had not caused any previous trouble nor had Parr and plaintiff had any other conflicts. The incident on April 17 was an isolated, brief occurrence. It was uncontradicted that Gartner did not see Parr hit plaintiff in the tool shed. Thus, any notice defendant had of Parr's violent nature occurred as the events at the track took place. Although the witnesses did not give a specific timetable, the events at the track were characterized as occurring very quickly.

In addition to the briefness of the events, it was uncontradicted that Gartner did not see much of what occurred. He did not see Parr strike plaintiff in the tool shed. At the track he was turned away from plaintiff and Parr as he did his work. He did not see Parr grabbing and coming at plaintiff nor did he see plaintiff graze Parr's lip with the spike. Not until Parr raised the axe did Gartner see any trouble and Parr quickly dropped the axe at Gartner's request.

Although plaintiff claims Gartner did nothing to defuse the trouble between plaintiff and Parr, we are at a loss as to what Gartner could have done bearing in mind Gartner saw very little of a very brief occurrence. The one case that has considered the question of the duty of a supervisory employee in this situation has denied that a supervisory employee has a duty to anticipate and prevent the conduct of an employee, such as Parr, in this situation. *Atlantic Coast Line R. Co. v. Southwell* (1927), 275 U.S. 64, 48 S. Ct. 25, 72 L. Ed. 157.

Plaintiff relies on the decision in *Harrison v. Missouri Pacific R.R. Co.* (1963), 372 U.S. 248, 83 S. Ct. 690, 9 L. Ed. 2d 711. In that case plaintiff was assaulted by a fellow employee whom he accused of stealing a ballast fork. A jury awarded damages to plaintiff but the Illinois circuit court granted the railroad's motion for judgment notwithstanding the verdict. The appellate court affirmed, holding there was insufficient evidence that the railroad knew or should have known of the assailant's violent nature prior to the assault. (*Harrison v. Missouri Pac. R.R. Co.* (4th Dist. 1962), 35 Ill. App. 2d 66, 181 N.E.2d 737.) In a per curiam opinion, the United States Supreme Court found the evidence sufficient to sustain the jury verdict and reversed. The testimony established that when the assailant was assigned to plaintiff's crew, the roadmaster warned plaintiff about assailant, calling him a bad actor and a troublemaker. Plaintiff testified that he complained to the roadmaster several times about his assailant's misconduct prior to the assault. After plaintiff reported the assault, the roadmaster again said "I told you to watch out for him." The Supreme Court noted that the testimony was contradicted but that if believed by the jury it was sufficient evidence to support the railroad's notice of assailant's violent propensities.

We find the evidence of notice in *Harrison* quite different from the facts here. In *Harrison* the railroad's notice arose because plaintiff complained about the assailant several times and because the roadmaster knew of the assailant's vicious nature. Neither of those factors were present here.

Finding no negligence on the part of the defendant railroad, the trial court erred in denying defendant's motions for directed verdict and judgment notwithstanding the verdict. Accordingly, the judgment of the circuit court of Madison County is reversed.

Notes

1. "Knowledge is important only if, because of it, one can intelligently choose [one's] course of action." Restatement § 278 comment a. Thus, before a principal may be charged with an agent's knowledge or notice, the agent must have had *both* a reasonable time to communicate the information to the principal, Restatement § 278, and the principal must have had a reasonable opportunity to act on it. *Id.* comment a. In the case of organizations with many agents or servants a reasonable opportunity to communicate and act on the information means that there must be sufficient time for information to be filtered through the organization and into the hands of the agents or servants acting on behalf of the principal (master). This rule is embodied in the Uniform Commercial Code's rules regarding the attribution of notice and knowledge:

> Notice, knowledge or a notice or notification received by an organization is effective for a particular transaction from the time when it is brought to the attention of the individual conducting the transaction, *and in any event from the time when it would have been brought to his attention if the organization had exercised due diligence.* An organization exercises due diligence if it maintains reasonable routines for communicating significant information to the person conducting the transaction *and* there is reasonable compliance with the routines. Due diligence does not require an individual acting for the organization to communicate the information unless such communication is part of his regular duties or unless he has reason to know of the transaction and that the transaction would be materially affected by the information.

U.C.C. § 1-201(27) (Official Text 1990) (emphasis added).

2. This is another context in which the rules regarding notification vary from those regarding knowledge and notice. Because notification is a legal act intended to be effective in and of itself, notification to an authorized or apparently authorized agent is effective *immediately*. As to the informational aspects of a notification (recall that receipt of a notification is also *notice*), notice is also effective immediately. Restatement § 270. However, where the principal is *required to act* on account of the notification, the principal is allowed reasonable time for the agent to *communicate* the fact of notification, as well as reasonable time to *act* on the notification. *Id.* comment a.

C. Adverse Agents

LanChile Airlines v. Connecticut General Life Ins.

759 F. Supp. 811 (S.D. Fla. 1991)

MORENO, District Judge.

THIS MATTER is before the Court on defendant's, Connecticut General Life Insurance Company of North America ("CIGNA"), Motion for Summary Judgement.

In its most simplistic form, this case centers on the conduct of the two principals and their agents in the negotiation and performance of a contract for insurance. Plaintiff LanChile was represented by its agent, defendant Santiago Rodriguez. Defendant CIGNA was represented by its agent, defendant Michael Molina. Unbeknownst to the principals, Rodriguez and Molina were partners in defendants S & M Insurance Consultants, Inc.

Together, defendants Rodriguez and Molina arranged for CIGNA to provide group health insurance benefits to LanChile. LanChile paid for, and received, the insurance that it sought, at the price that it agreed upon, for over four years. LanChile made these payments to S & M, rather than directly to CIGNA.

The crux of this action concerns certain administrative/consulting fees received by S & M. LanChile asserts that the fee arrangement was undisclosed and that it was not until March 1989, over four years after the inception of the contract, that plaintiff allegedly discovered that the premiums it paid for health insurance included a service fee for S & M. CIGNA counters that LanChile was well aware, or at least should have been, of the fee arrangement at the time of the contract formation. The total amount paid as a fee to S & M over the four year period is approximately $279,000.

Beginning in March 1983, LanChile's insurance broker or agent-of-record for group health insurance was Santiago Rodriguez. As LanChile's agent, Rodriguez was charged with finding health insurance coverage for LanChile's employees, at a level of benefits and premium costs acceptable to LanChile.

In late 1983, LanChile, which was then insured by CIGNA, was informed that its insurance premiums would increase by approximately 46 percent for 1984. Juan Matus, LanChile's Head of Administration and Finance for North America, was responsible for obtaining group health insurance for LanChile's employees. Guillermo Goldberg, then General Manager for North America, was responsible for overseeing Mr. Matus, including the administration of LanChile's employee group health insurance. Goldberg and Matus instructed Rodriguez to procure comparable insurance coverage for LanChile's employees at a lower cost to LanChile than the projected 46 percent increase.

In 1983, Michael Molina became CIGNA's group insurance representative for LanChile. Molina, CIGNA's agent, and Rodriguez, LanChile's agent, were also principals and owners of S & M Insurance Consultants, Inc. In late 1983, Molina and Rodriguez proposed to LanChile an insurance plan that not only avoided the scheduled 46% increase in CIGNA's insurance premiums for 1984, but provided approximately a 5% decrease in LanChile's overall cost of insurance.

The plan provided for basic hospitalization coverage to be provided by Empire Blue Cross and Blue Shield of New York with a wraparound major medical plan underwritten by CIGNA. From January 1984 through March 1988, LanChile timely made all premium payments and enjoyed the insurance coverage they were entitled to pursuant to the Blue Cross and CIGNA insurance policies.

The definitive question in this lawsuit is which party must bear the financial responsibility for the fraudulent acts of an agent. While the general issue has been visited by numerous courts over the years, the Court has found little guidance for the case at bar which contains equally culpable agents representing both principals. CIGNA asks this Court to determine that, as a matter of law, it is less responsible for the acts of its agent than is LanChile for the same acts of its agent. The Court finds that this ultimate conclusion can only be reached upon resolution of numerous factual issues which are hotly contested. Such issues are, therefore, questions for the jury.

The [issue] for determination by the Court [is] whether the knowledge of defendant Rodriguez, as the agent for plaintiff LanChile, can be attributed to LanChile.

CIGNA asserts that each of LanChile's claims for relief necessarily relies on LanChile's contention that it was not informed of the administrative/consulting fees being charged by S & M. CIGNA alleges that LanChile's claims fail because it had actual, constructive and imputed knowledge of the fees it was paying to S & M for its services.

LanChile correctly notes that a court must not decide any factual issues it finds in the record. It is well-settled that under Florida law, a question of agency is reserved to the trier of fact when resolution of the issue depends on the inferences to be drawn from the facts adduced.

It is the most elementary hornbook law that this Court cannot resolve a factual dispute upon a motion for summary judgment as to whether LanChile had actual or constructive knowledge that it was paying S & M a fee for procuring insurance. Actual or constructive knowledge is a factual question; the existence or non-existence of this knowledge is the pivotal fact around which this case turns. Not so clear, however, is the issue of whether Rodriguez' knowledge may be imputed to LanChile.

Circumstances where knowledge may be imputed typically involve questions of law rather than fact. The general rule is that whatever knowledge an agent acquires within the scope of his authority is imputed to his principal.

However, knowledge and misconduct of an agent will not be imputed to a principal if an agent is "secretly acting adversely to the principal and entirely for his own or another's purposes." Restatement (Second) of Agency, § 282 (1958). The law does not then presume that the wrongdoer would perform his usual duty of disclosing all material facts regarding his action if such disclosure would reveal his fraud. Restatement, § 282(1).

The Restatement also provides that a principal will be held to the knowledge of an agent who acts adversely to the principal if: the agent enters into negotiations within the scope of his powers and the person with whom he deals reasonably believes him to be authorized to conduct the transaction; or, before he has changed his position, the principal knowingly retains a benefit through the act of the agent which otherwise he would not have received. Restatement, § 282(2)(b) and (c).

The threshold determination, then, is whether the agent was "acting adversely." The Restatement counsels that the mere fact that the agent's primary interests are not coincident with those of the principal does not prevent the latter from being affected by the knowledge of the agent if the agent is acting for the principal's interests. Restatement, § 282, comment c. This comment however does not offer sufficient guidance for the Court to make a legal determination as to whether Rodriguez was secretly acting adversely to LanChile and entirely for his own or S & M's purposes.

The Court is unable to determine as a matter of law, that Rodriguez' conduct in charging LanChile an amount that it had agreed to pay for insurance, but was in excess of the actual cost of the insurance, is adverse to LanChile. Similarly, the Court is not convinced that Rodriguez was acting entirely for his own or S & M's purposes. While Rodriguez retained a portion of the premiums paid by LanChile as an undisclosed fee, he did arrange the health insurance desired and received by LanChile. The Court concludes that these issues are factual determinations that can only be made by the jury.

In accordance with the foregoing, CIGNA's Motion for Summary Judgment is DENIED.

Notes

1. *Center v. Hampton Affiliates, Inc.*, 66 N.Y.2d 782, 497 N.Y.S.2d 898, 488 N.E.2d 828 (1985), involved the question of whether a corporation that had purchased certain shares of stock should be charged with the knowledge of its purchasing agent that the transfer to the corporation violated the rights of a third person:

> [The adverse agent] exception provides that when an agent is engaged in a scheme to defraud his principal, either for his own benefit or that of a third person, the presumption that knowledge held by the agent was disclosed to the principal fails because he cannot be presumed to have disclosed that which would expose and defeat his fraudulent purpose (Restatement [Second] of Agency § 282 [1]). To come within the exception, the agent must have totally abandoned his principal's interests and be acting entirely for his own or another's purposes. It cannot be invoked merely because he has a conflict of interest or because he is not acting primarily for his principal (*see* Restatement [Second] of Agency § 282[1] comment c). Defendants' moving papers contain only conclusory allegations that [the agent] was seriously conflicted throughout these transactions and tried to defraud the corporation. These allegations do not establish sufficient adversity as a matter of law to negate imputed knowledge to the corporation at the time it took delivery of the shares.

Often an agent will act on behalf of more than one principal at the same time. For example, in *Manley v. Ticor Title Insurance Co.*, 168 Ariz. 568, 816 P.2d 225 (1991), an escrow agent in a real estate transaction knew that a lien on the property had not been discharged. The court held that even though the escrow agent was a "dual agent" acting on behalf of both the buyer and the seller, the escrow agent was not an "adverse agent," and attributed the escrow agent's knowledge to the buyers.

2. Adverse agents are another context in which the rules regarding notification differ from those regarding knowledge and notice. Notification by a third person given to an agent acting adversely to the principal is effective unless the third person has *notice* the agent is acting adversely. Restatement § 271. Presumably, the basis for the difference in treatment is that in the case of notification, the third person is relying on the authority or apparent authority of the agent to act for the principal in receiving the notification.

3. One of the common exceptions to the adverse agent exception is the "sole actor doctrine." Restatement §§ 282(2)(b) & (c), referred to in *LanChile Airlines v. Connecticut General Life Ins.*, are the Restatement's formulation of the sole actor doctrine:

> The principal is affected by the knowledge of an agent who acts adversely to the principal:
>
> * * *
>
> (b) if the agent enters into negotiations within the scope of [the agent's] powers and the person with whom he reasonably believes [the agent] to be authorized to conduct the transaction; or
>
> (c) if, before [the principal] has changed position, the principal knowingly retains a benefit through the act of the agent which otherwise [the principal] would not have received.

The basis of the sole actor doctrine, or at least that part embodied in Restatement section 282(2)(c), is estoppel. The insureds in *LanChile Airlines* should not be permitted to keep (retain) the benefit of Rodriguez's conduct (coverage under the insurance policy) while at the same time avoiding responsibility for Rodriguez's knowledge at the time the insurance policy was procured. *See* Restatement § 282 comment h; *Mantanuska Valley Bank v. Arnold,* 116 F. Supp. 32 (D. Alaska 1953). In this respect, the sole actor doctrine is only a variant of the rule against partial ratifications (to be discussed in chapter 4).

Restatement section 282(2)(b), which charges the principal with the knowledge of a (sole) agent arising out of a transaction in which the agent deals with an innocent third party within the scope of the agent's powers to bind the principal, involves a somewhat different proposition. Consider, for example, illustration 7 to Restatement section 282:

> A is authorized by P to sell P's horse and to represent it as it is. A, intending to keep the proceeds from the sale and intending also to defraud the purchaser, sells the horse to T, representing the horse to be sound, although knowing the horse to be unsound. A absconds with the proceeds. P is bound by A's knowledge that the horse is unsound.

Clearly P has not retained the benefits of A's misrepresentation. If P is to be liable for the misrepresentation, it must be on the basis that A had *power to bind* P to the misrepresentation, either on the basis of apparent authority or because T reasonably believed the agent had authority to make the representation. *See* Restatement § 282 comment f.

State Farm Fire & Casualty Co. v. Sevier

272 Or. 278, 537 P.2d 88 (1975)

TONGUE, Justice.

This is an action by an insurance company for a declaratory judgment that it had "validly rescinded" a policy of automobile liability insurance because of misrepresentations by the insured in his application for the policy. The named defendants included not only the insured, but also the personal representative of a person killed in a subsequent accident with the insured before the policy was rescinded. The case was tried before the court, without a jury. Plaintiff appeals from an adverse judgment.

From 1961 to 1970 Kenneth Sevier had been at the Veterans Administration "Domiciliary" hospital in White City, near Medford, except for several months in California and occasional furloughs to his original home in Arkansas. During that entire period he had no Oregon driver's license, but he did have a California driver's license. In 1969 he was arrested and convicted in Oregon for driving under the influence of intoxicating liquor.

In December 1969 he returned to his "home town" in Arkansas. On May 29, 1970, having purchased an automobile, he went to see Jack Henderson, one of plaintiff's insurance agents. Henderson filled out an application for a policy of automobile insurance which included a question asking whether, during the past five years, the applicant had been convicted for traffic violations and a question asking whether his license to drive was ever suspended, revoked or refused.

Sevier testified that Henderson did not ask him those two questions. He also testified that he had known Henderson "for a long time" and that he told Henderson that he had been picked up and convicted for drunken driving in Oregon. He also testified that Henderson said "to Hell with it, maybe they'll never find it out"; that he did not know that Henderson put a "no" answer in the "box" for that question; and that he signed the application as filled out by Henderson.

Henderson testified that he asked both questions. He also admitted that Sevier told him that he had been stopped by the police for drinking and driving and given a "balloon" or "breathalyzer" test, but said that he had not been convicted for DUIL.

That application for insurance was then sent to plaintiff's office in Monroe, Louisiana, for consideration by its underwriting department. The application showed "no" answers to both questions and made no reference to the 1969 DUIL arrest and conviction in Oregon.

Plaintiff's underwriting department then had a "routine, general" investigation of Sevier made by the Retail Credit Company. That investigation included contacts at White City, apparently because his application indicated "physical or mental defects" or limitations and because of further information from Henderson that Sevier had been at the Veterans "Domiciliary" in White City for nine years. No request was made, however, for a "motor vehicle record check," as would have been done by Retail Credit as part of its investigation upon request.

Plaintiff's witness testified that if plaintiff had been informed by its agent Henderson that Sevier had been stopped for drinking and driving and had been required to take a test (as admitted by Henderson), "there is a good chance" that a motor vehicle check would have been requested. The same witness testified that if plaintiff had been informed by Henderson that Sevier had been convicted of DUIL it would not have issued the policy to Sevier.

In any event plaintiff issued a policy of automobile liability insurance to Sevier in Arkansas for a period of six months, effective July 7, 1970.

In September 1970 Sevier returned to White City. He was told by Henderson to re-apply for a policy in Oregon. According to plaintiff's witnesses, when a policyholder moves from another state to Oregon, a new application is then filled out and submitted to plaintiff's underwriting department, which then also has and reviews a file from the other state including the original application.

In November 1970, Sevier went to the office of one of plaintiff's agents in Medford, who filled out a new application. That agent considered his Arkansas policy to be "a policy that was in force" and that "all I was doing was taking a transfer on the policy that was already in force."

That application was then signed by Sevier and sent to plaintiff's Oregon underwriting department and a new policy was issued for an additional six months, effective January 7, 1971. According to plaintiff's witnesses, that policy was issued based on the new application and on the information in the "Arkansas file" with no additional investigation. Plaintiff's witnesses also testified, however, that if Henderson, the original agent, had made a notation on the file that Sevier had been stopped in Oregon for drinking they would have made a further investigation and that if it had appeared that Sevier had been convicted of DUIL the new policy would not have been issued and the original policy would have been rescinded.

On March 15, 1971, Sevier was involved in the accident in which Mr. Sutton was killed and his wife injured. Within approximately two weeks after the accident, plaintiff's Oregon underwriting department superintendent learned from its claims department that there was a "total loss," with "drinking involved," and of the previous DUIL conviction. On May 7, 1971, plaintiff called the Oregon Department of Motor Vehicles by telephone to confirm that conviction.

On July 7, 1971, more than three months after learning in late March from its claims department of Sevier's DUIL conviction of 1969 and more than one year after its agent Henderson was informed of that fact by Sevier, plaintiff sent a letter to Sevier enclosing a check for the amount of all premiums paid by him in both Arkansas and Oregon and rescinding the policy. The tender of that check was refused by Sevier.

On August 10, 1971, plaintiff filed a complaint in this action, alleging that the policy was issued in reliance upon misrepresentations by Sevier and seeking a declaratory judgment that it had "validly rescinded" the policy and that plaintiff had no liability under it for the death of Mr. Sutton or the injury to his wife. Defendants' answer to that complaint alleges, as an affirmative defense, that "plaintiff was negligent in failing to investigate the insured and therefore is estopped to rescind the policy because of alleged misrepresentations."

The trial court found that at the time of his original application the insured told plaintiff's agent in Arkansas that "he had lived in Oregon the previous nine years"; that "he had been charged for driving and drinking and had taken some type of test"; and that he had a "drinking conviction." The court found further that the plaintiff was negligent in that its agent "failed to note the information given to him by Sevier on the application concerning Sevier's being stopped for a drinking and driving charge"; in that it failed "to request a motor vehicle check in Oregon at the time of the Arkansas application, which would have disclosed that Sevier had been convicted" of DUIL; and in that it renewed "the policy in Oregon, relying upon its Arkansas application where there had been no motor vehicle check."

Based upon these findings the trial court concluded that "plaintiff had a duty to the public to make a reasonable investigation of the insurability of Sevier within a reasonable time after the issuance of the policy," and that its failure "to make such reasonable investigation" prohibits it "from rescinding the Sevier policy as to the claims of" the other defendants. As authority for that holding the trial court cited the decision by the California Supreme Court in *Barrera v. State Farm Mutual Au-*

tomobile Ins. Co., 71 Cal. 2d 659, 456 P.2d 674 (1969). In *Barrera* it was held, under somewhat similar facts, that an automobile insurance company has a duty to the public to make a reasonable investigation within a reasonable time after the issuance of a policy and that it cannot thereafter rescind a policy so as to deny its coverage to the claim of an injured person.

Plaintiff's primary contention on this appeal is that in Oregon the rights of an injured person are no greater than the rights of the insured, with the result that the failure of an insurance company to make a motor vehicle check or other investigation of the insured does not take away its right to rescind a policy for false representations by an insured "as to the claims" of an injured person, despite the holding to the contrary by the California court in *Barrera*.

Plaintiff also contends, in response to a request by this court for supplemental briefs, that the decision of the trial court in this case cannot properly be affirmed by application of the usual rule of contract law that a party to a contract who has knowledge of facts constituting grounds for rescission must do so promptly or lose the right to rescind. The reason why that rule does not apply in this case, according to the plaintiff, is that the knowledge of its agent that Sevier had been convicted of DUIL was not imputed to it by reason of collusion between Sevier and his agent, in that Sevier knew that the answers contained in the application for the policy were false and participated in the fraud.

The general rules of contract and agency law are well established to the effect that notice to an agent is notice to his principal; that a party who has notice of grounds for the rescission of a contract and who elects to rescind it must do so promptly or lose his right to rescind.

Consistent with these established rules, it has been held by other courts that an insurance company which has knowledge through one of its agents of the falsity of facts stated in an application for insurance and which nevertheless issues an insurance policy is either "estopped" from rescinding the policy based upon the alleged misrepresentation of such facts or cannot then establish that it acted in reliance upon such misrepresentations, as necessary for the rescission of a contract for misrepresentation.

In this case plaintiff, through its agent Henderson, acquired knowledge of the fact that Sevier had at least been stopped by the police for drinking and driving and had been given a "balloon" or "breathalyzer" test. Indeed, the trial court found that plaintiff's agent had knowledge of the fact that Sevier had been convicted for DUIL. As a corporation, plaintiff could act only through its agents and employees and once it acquired knowledge of that fact through one of its agents or employees plaintiff was chargeable with continued knowledge of that fact, regardless of whether or not its agent Henderson failed to make a written record of that fact or to convey that information to other agents or employees of the plaintiff.

It follows, in our opinion, that at the time that both the Arkansas policy and the Oregon "renewal" policy was issued plaintiff had knowledge of facts which constituted sufficient grounds for the rescission of both policies. It also follows, in our opinion, that if plaintiff desired to elect to rescind the Oregon policy it was required to do so promptly, and that in this case plaintiff did not undertake to rescind promptly, but did not do so until July 7, 1971, the date on which the Oregon policy expired by its terms. We hold that it was then too late to do so.

Because we decide this case upon these grounds we need not consider and decide the questions whether plaintiff, as an automobile liability insurance company, had a duty to the public, under the facts and circumstances of this case, to make a reasonable investigation of Sevier before it issued to him a policy of automobile liability insurance and whether the plaintiff was negligent, under the facts and circumstances of this case, in that it failed to make such an investigation.

For the same reasons, we need not decide whether to adopt the rule adopted by the California Supreme Court in *Barrera* as apparently adopted by the trial court as the basis for its decision and as strongly urged by the defendants on this appeal.

Plaintiff vigorously contends that the knowledge of its agent of Sevier's DUIL conviction was not imputed to it because of alleged collusion between its agent and Sevier to withhold knowledge of that fact from it.

Plaintiff's claim of collusion is based upon testimony that Sevier was given an opportunity to read the application before signing it and knew that the answers in the application as filled in by plaintiff's agent were false and upon the further testimony that, according to Sevier, when he told plaintiff's agent of his DUIL conviction the agent said "to Hell with it, maybe they'll never find it out."

The evidence was conflicting on both of these points. Plaintiff's agent denied that he said "to Hell with it, maybe they'll never find out." He also testified that he was not sure whether or not Sevier read the application before signing it. At the time of his deposition Sevier said that he knew that the agent wrote down false answers in the application before he signed it, but on trial he testified that he did not know what answers the agent wrote down.

[W]e hold that for the purposes of this case the knowledge of plaintiff's agent that Sevier had been convicted of DUIL was imputed to the plaintiff.

There may be good reasons why, in litigation between an insurance company and an insured who has acted in collusion with an agent of the company in concealing facts from it, there should be an exception to the general rule that knowledge to the agent of the company is to be imputed to it. The reason for that result in such cases is not so much that the knowledge of the agent was not imputed to the principal, but that a participant in a fraud should not be permitted to profit from his own fraud. Such reasons, however, have no proper application in litigation between an automobile insurance company and an innocent person who was injured by the negligence of the insured. The cases cited by plaintiff, all from other jurisdictions, either involve litigation between the insurer and insured or do not discuss the question whether a different rule should apply in cases involving innocent third parties.

The rule that knowledge of an agent is to be imputed to his principal, regardless of actual knowledge by the principal, is a rule based upon considerations of public policy to the effect that one who selects an agent and delegates authority to him should incur the risks of the agent's infidelity or want of diligence rather than innocent third persons. Those reasons of public policy are not present in cases involving litigation between a principal and a third party who has acted in collusion with the agent. When, however, as in this case, the injured party is one who did not act in collusion with the agent, those same reasons of public policy are present.

A rule in automobile insurance cases under which knowledge of an agent is imputed to his principal in cases involving third persons injured in automobile accidents, despite possible collusion between the insured and the insurance agent, would not encourage fraud, as suggested by the plaintiff. On the contrary, it provides no inducement for the insured to enter into a fraudulent scheme with the agent of the insurance company for the reason that if collusion is proven the insurer, after satisfying the injured person's claim, may prosecute a cause of action against the insured for fraud or, in an action brought by the insured, defend on the ground of collusion. Instead, this rule should encourage the insurer to select and to supervise its agents with greater care.

For these reasons we hold that when Sevier told plaintiff's agent of his DUIL conviction, knowledge of that fact was imputed to the plaintiff insurance company for the purposes of this case.

For all of the reasons stated above, and finding no error, we affirm the judgment of the trial court.

O'CONNELL, Chief Justice ([with Denecke and Holman, JJ.], dissenting).

The majority holds that an injured third party may recover on a policy of insurance even though the insured would not be allowed to enforce the policy. In so doing, it introduces much confusion into the law of agency and, although purporting to avoid the question, effectively adopts the reasoning and effect in *Barrera* which rejects the fundamental principles of the law of contract. The opinion of the majority is not supported either by logic or any of our prior cases on the subject.

The point the majority fails to note is that the rights of one injured through the negligence of the insured are derivative of the rights of the insured. The third party, however innocent, has no right to recover from the insurer unless there is a duty to pay the losses of the insured growing out of a valid contract of insurance or a duty to the public "at large." Since the majority does not deem it necessary to follow *Barrera* in recognizing such a duty to the public, it must explain how the third party may recover on a contract of insurance to which it is not a party or an intended beneficiary and which is rendered voidable as to the insured through his misrepresentations of a material fact. This the majority does not do.

It is clear that plaintiff is entitled to rescind the contract as to Sevier, its insured. Defendants contend that Henderson's knowledge, which was admittedly not transmitted to plaintiff's underwriters, should be imputed to plaintiff. The general rule of imputation of knowledge or notice is well settled:

> The corporation is affected or charged with knowledge of all material facts of which its officer or agent receives notice or acquires knowledge while acting in the course of his employment and within the scope of his authority, even though the officer or agent does not in fact communicate his knowledge to the corporation through its other officers or agents.

This general rule is subject to an exception, however, which is applicable to the facts of this case. The knowledge or notice of the agent is not imputed to the principal when the person knows the agent is acting adversely to the interests of the principal. In the present case, Sevier testified that when he told Henderson of his arrest for DUIL, Henderson stated, "to Hell with it, maybe they'll never find out." Thus, even by his own testimony, there can be no reasonable room for doubt that Sevier knew that Henderson was not going to convey the information to plaintiff. Therefore, Henderson's knowledge cannot be imputed to plaintiff.

It is, perhaps, the majority's position that the policy that "one who selects an agent and delegates authority to him should incur the risks of the agent's infidelity or want of diligence rather than innocent third persons," should be extended to protect one in the position of defendant Sutton. The problems with such approach, if intended by the majority, are insurmountable. Defendant Sutton's damages were not caused, in any reasonable sense, by the misfeasance of plaintiff's agent. She cannot have relied upon the presence of insurance in sharing the road with Sevier, since insurance is not a pre-condition for driving in Oregon. Moreover, even if a theory of causation could be constructed, there is no finding that plaintiff was negligent in hiring or retaining the services of Henderson, nor is there any basis apparent in the record for such a finding. Nor does the majority purport to make a principal strictly liable for the breaches of fiduciary duty of an agent.

I am forced to conclude, therefore, that the majority's position is supportable only on the basis of the imposition of a newly created duty on insurers to investigate the representations of applicants for automobile liability insurance based upon some theory of strict liability, even though the majorty [sic] purports to avoid consideration of this question. Therefore, I would hold that plaintiff was entitled to rescind the policy and is not liable to either defendant.

Notes

1. Was Henderson acting as an adverse agent? Had Henderson completely abandoned State Farm's interests so as to act entirely for Sevier's purposes? Would your answer change if Henderson had authority or apparent authority to determine what information was required to be reported on the application?

2. Is the underlying issue in *State Farm Fire & Casualty Co. v. Sevier* the effectiveness of Sevier's *notification* to the agent, or is it the effect of the agent's (Henderson's) *knowledge*? Should that make any difference in how the case should be analyzed?

3. The *Sevier* trial court ruled that State Farm owed a duty to persons who might be injured by one of its insured drivers. Under Restatement section 282(2)(a), the existence of such a duty would make the adverse agent rule inapplicable:

> The principal is affected by the knowledge of an agent who acts adversely to the principal if the failure of the agent to act upon or to reveal the information results in a violation of a contractual or relational duty of the principal to a person harmed thereby[.]

4. On appeal, the *Sevier* majority claimed it could resolve the case without relying on any duty on the part of State Farm owed to the victim. Wholly apart from the soundness of the majority's reasoning on the agency law issue, note that the trial court's formulation of State Farm's duty was quite broad. State Farm's duty was not limited to a duty to act on any information obtained in the application process. Instead, the trial court imposed a *general* duty to *investigate* the driving record of applicants for insurance. The majority clearly was reluctant to reach the question of whether State Farm owed any duty *at all*, much less grapple with the question of the *scope* of any such duty.

5. The *Sevier* dissent argues that in the absence of any duty owed by State Farm, the victim's rights *under the policy* are *derivative* of those of the insured. Regardless of whether we are talking about knowledge or notification, *Sevier* has no rights against

State Farm (why?). If the victim has no contractual rights against State Farm, and if State Farm (and the agent, Henderson) were not *negligent* because neither owed any duty to the victim, why does equity require that the victim recover from State Farm?

The *Sevier* majority relied solely on the principle that, as between the principal and an innocent third party (the victim), the principal should bear the risk of the agent's misconduct. Based on the materials in chapter 2, do you agree with the proposition that the principal is *per se* responsible for all actions of an agent? For example, is a principal always bound by an agent's unauthorized actions? If not, what is the basis for holding the principal liable?

Consider again the differences in the Restatement's treatment of an agent's *knowledge* and a *notification* given to an agent. Notification to an agent *apparently* (but not actually) authorized to receive it is effective against the principal. Restatement § 268(1)(a), (b). On the other hand, an agent's *knowledge* concerning matters within the agent's apparent (but not actual) authority *only* affects the principal where a third party has *relied* on the appearance of authority. Restatement § 273. Similarly, while the adverse agent rule applies to the adverse agent's knowledge, it applies to a *notification only* where the third party had *notice* the agent was acting adversely to the principal. *Compare* Restatement § 282(1) (knowledge) *with* Restatement § 271 (notification).

Given that the only time the question of knowledge or notification will come up is when there is a (presumably) innocent third person, what does the *Sevier* majority's reasoning do to the adverse agent rule?

Chapter 4

Ratification of Unauthorized Transactions

Like the doctrines of apparent authority, estoppel to deny agency power and inherent agency power, the doctrine of ratification arises out of the risk of unintended dealings inherent in the use of agents in the marketplace. Even where an agent dealing with a third party has acted outside the scope of the agent's power to bind the principal, the principal may nevertheless be bound if the principal ratifies the agent's act.

A. Affirmance

Botticello v. Stefanovicz

177 Conn. 22, 411 A.2d 16 (1979)

PETERS, Associate Justice.

The defendants, Mary and Walter Stefanovicz (hereinafter "Mary" and "Walter") in 1943 acquired as tenants in common a farm situated in the towns of Colchester and Lebanon. In the fall of 1965, the plaintiff, Anthony Botticello, became interested in the property. When he first visited the farm, Walter advised him that the asking price was $100,000. The following January, the plaintiff again visited the farm and made a counteroffer of $75,000. At that time, Mary stated that there was "no way" she could sell it for that amount. Ultimately the plaintiff and Walter agreed upon a price of $85,000 for a lease with an option to purchase; during these negotiations, Mary stated that she would not sell the property for less than that amount.

The informal agreement was finalized with the assistance of counsel for both Walter and the plaintiff. The agreement was drawn up by Walter's attorney after consultation with Walter and the plaintiff; it was then sent to, and modified by, the plaintiff's attorney. The agreement was signed by Walter and by the plaintiff. Neither the plaintiff nor his attorney, nor Walter's attorney, was then aware of the fact that Walter did not own the property outright. The plaintiff, although a successful businessman with considerable experience in real estate never requested his attorney to do a title search of any kind, and consequently no title search was done. Walter never represented to the plaintiff or the plaintiff's attorney, or to his own attorney, that he was acting for his wife, as her agent. Mary's part ownership came to light in 1968, when a third party sought an easement over the land in question.

Shortly after the execution of the lease and option-to-purchase agreement, the plaintiff took possession of the property. He made substantial improvements on the property and, in 1971, properly exercised his option to purchase. When the defendants refused to honor the option agreement, the plaintiff commenced the present action against both Mary and Walter, seeking specific performance, possession of the premises, and damages.

The trial court found the issues for the plaintiff and ordered a specific performance of the option-to-purchase agreement. In their appeal, the defendants [claim] that Mary was never a party to the agreement, and its terms may therefore not be enforced [as] to her.

The plaintiff alleged, and the trial court agreed, that although Mary was not a party to the lease and option-to-purchase agreement, its terms were nonetheless binding upon her because Walter acted as her authorized agent in the negotiations, discussions, and execution of the written agreement. The defendants have attacked several findings of fact and conclusions of law, claiming that the underlying facts and applicable law do not support the court's conclusion of agency.

Marital status cannot in and of itself prove the agency relationship. Nor does the fact that the defendants owned the land jointly make one the agent for the other. Moreover, the fact that one spouse tends more to business matters than the other does not, absent other evidence of agreement or authorization, constitute the delegation of power as to an agent. [I]t is clear that the facts found by the court fail to support its conclusion that Walter acted as Mary's authorized agent, and the conclusion therefore cannot stand.

The plaintiff argues, alternatively, that even if no agency relationship existed at the time the agreement was signed, Mary was bound by the contract executed by her husband because she ratified its terms by her subsequent conduct. The trial court accepted this alternative argument as well, concluding that Mary had ratified the agreement by receiving and accepting payments from the plaintiff, and by acquiescing in his substantial improvements to the farm.

Ratification is defined as "the affirmance by a person of a prior act which did not bind him but which was done or professedly done on his account." Restatement (Second), Agency § 82 (1958). Ratification requires "acceptance of the results of the act with an *intent* to ratify, and with *full knowledge of all the material circumstances.*" *Ansonia v. Cooper*, 64 Conn. 536, 544, 30 A. 760, 762 (1894) (emphasis added).

The [trial court] finding neither indicates an intent by Mary to ratify the agreement, nor establishes her knowledge of all the material circumstances surrounding the deal. At most, Mary observed the plaintiff occupying and improving the land, received rental payments from the plaintiff from time to time, knew that he had an interest in the property, and knew that the use, occupancy, and rentals were pursuant to a written agreement she had not signed. None of these facts is sufficient to support the conclusion that Mary ratified the agreement and thus bound herself to its terms. It is undisputed that Walter had the power to lease his own undivided one-half interest in the property; and the facts found by the trial court could be referable to that fact alone. Moreover, the fact that the rental payments were used for "family" purposes indicates nothing more than one spouse providing for the other.

The plaintiff makes the further argument that Mary ratified the agreement simply by receiving its benefits and by failing to repudiate it. *See* Restatement (Second), Agency § 98 (1958). The plaintiff fails to recognize that before the receipt of benefits may constitute ratification, the other requisites for ratification must first be present. "Thus if the original transaction was not purported to be done on account of the principal, the fact that the principal receives its proceeds does not make him a party to it." Restatement (Second), Agency § 98, comment f (1958). Since Walter at no time purported to be acting on his wife's behalf, as is essential to effective subsequent ratification, Mary is not bound by the terms of the agreement, and specific performance cannot be ordered as to her.

Our conclusion that there can be no recovery against Mary is not dispositive of the rights that the plaintiff may have against Walter. A person who contracts to convey full title to real property is not himself excused from performance, or immune from liability for breach, because of his inability to convey more than an undivided half interest in the property.

We turn now to the question of relief. In view of our holding that Mary never authorized her husband to act as her agent for any purpose connected with the lease and option-to-purchase agreement, recovery against her is precluded. As to Walter, the fact that his ownership was restricted to an undivided one-half interest in no way limited his capacity to contract. He contracted to convey full title and for breach of that contract he may be held liable. The facts of the case are sufficient to furnish a basis for relief to the plaintiff by specific performance or by damages.

Since no third parties are here involved, the form of relief to be accorded must take into account the plaintiff's preference as well as the court's own discretion, "depending upon the equities of the case and based on reason and sound judgment."

There is error as to the judgment against the defendant Mary Stefanovicz; the judgment as to her is set aside and the case remanded with direction to render judgment in her favor. As to the defendant Walter Stefanovicz, there is error only as to the remedy ordered. The judgment as to him is set aside and the case remanded for a new trial limited to the form of relief.

Notes

1. May an undisclosed or partially disclosed principal ratify an unauthorized act? Under the Restatement, a person (the "ratifier") only has the right to ratify the act of another (the "actor") where (i) the actor purported to act as an agent, section 85, and (ii) the actor either identified the ratifier as the principal or intended to act on account of the ratifier, sections 85 comment c & 87. Note that this prevents a stranger from intervening to take advantage of a good deal. Despite these limitations on the power to ratify an unauthorized transaction, nothing prevents the would-be ratifier from entering into a *separate, new contract* with the third party. *See* Restatement § 104.

2. Under the Restatement, a principal may "affirm" a transaction either by *electing* to be bound or by *conduct*. §83. As indicated in *Botticello*, one type of conduct constituting an affirmance is the knowing *acceptance* by the principal of *benefits* from the transaction. Note, however, that for an implied affirmance by conduct, the conduct must be such that it can only be justified if the principal is electing to affirm the transaction (why?). Restatement § 83. For acceptance of benefits to constitute affirmance, the principal must have no claim to the accepted benefits other than through or under the transaction in question. Restatement § 98. How did the *Botticello* court apply this principle?

3. A ratifier may elect to avoid an affirmance if at the time of the affirmance the ratifier was ignorant of any material fact involved in the affirmed transaction. *See* Restatement § 91. Material facts are those which

> substantially affect the existence or extent of the obligations involved in the transaction, as distinguished from those which affect the values or inducements involved in the transaction.

If the ratifier does not have *actual knowledge* of material facts, but only *reason to know* them, then the ratifier may avoid the affirmance. Restatement § 91 comment c.

Suppose that Allen, purporting to represent Paula but without authority or power to bind, leases Paula's farm to Terry for a term of five years. Allen tells Paula what he has done, but does not tell her the term of the lease. Without inquiring as to the lease term, Paula demands, and accepts from Terry, the security deposit and first month's rent. In view of Paula's willful ignorance of the lease term, may Paula avoid the lease after she learns the term is five years? Did Paula know enough facts that she should have investigated before affirming instead of blundering ahead heedless of her ignorance? Under Restatement 91 & comment e, Paula may be found to have *assumed the risk* of proceeding with only generalized knowledge of the circumstances. Would it make any difference if the terms of similar farm leases customarily range between three and five years? One to two years? *See* Restatement § 91 comment e, illustration 15.

4. In order to ratify, a principal must have been able to undertake the transaction both at the earlier time when the agent acted and at the later time of the act of ratification. Thus, for example, a principal cannot ratify a transaction which the principal could not have entered into *at the time the agent acted. See, e.g., Zottman v. City and County of San Francisco,* 20 Cal. 96 (1862) (transaction could not legally have been entered into). In addition, a principal cannot ratify a transaction which the principal does not have the authority to enter *at the time of the attempted ratification. See, e.g., Taslich v. Industrial Commission,* 71 Utah 33, 262 P. 281 (1927) (statutory period for action by principal had elapsed before ratification of timely but unauthorized action by the agent).

5. Note that ratification of prior unauthorized acts can form the basis for a claim of *apparent authority*. Suppose an agent enters into an unauthorized transaction which the principal ratifies without indicating to the third party that the agent had acted without authority. Suppose further that the same third party again deals with the agent, and the agent again exceeds authority in a similar fashion. The principal may be bound to the second contract on the basis of the apparent authority created by the manifestation to the third party that the agent had authority to deal. *See, e.g., Lewis v. Cable,* 107 F. Supp. 196 (W.D. Pa. 1952). Would it make a difference in the outcome if at the time of ratifying the first transaction the principal advised the third party of the lack of authority of the agent regarding the first transaction?

Rakestraw v. Rodrigues

104 Cal. Rptr. 57, 500 P.2d 1401 (Cal. 1972)

WRIGHT, Chief Justice.

Sherwood T. Rodrigues (Rodrigues) appeals from a judgment upon a jury verdict for $30,000 in favor of Joyce Rakestraw (Joyce). His claimed liability arises out of involvement in a transaction whereby Joyce's name was forged on a promissory note and a deed of trust in order to obtain funds for a business venture of her then husband William Rakestraw (William), who was also a cross-defendant.

The action was initiated by Acme Financial Corporation (Acme) and Security Title Insurance Company (Security) to enforce payment of a $75,000 promissory note bearing Joyce's purported signature which in fact had been forged and which was secured by a deed of trust (also forged) covering property owned by her. Joyce, Robert Ellinghouse (Ellinghouse), who affixed the notarial acknowledgment on the deed of trust and Agricultural Insurance Company (Agricultural) as surety on Ellinghouse's bond as a notary public, were named defendants. Joyce asserted the forgeries as a defense to the action and cross-complained against Rodrigues and William.

Joyce entered into a stipulated judgment with Acme and Security by which she agreed to be bound by the note and deed of trust. Joyce's cross-complaint against Rodrigues and William proceeded to trial and resulted in a jury verdict in her favor. Rodrigues' motion for judgment notwithstanding the verdict was denied, as were motions for a new trial. Rodrigues and William appealed from the judgment.

In late 1964 Joyce discussed with William the possibility of using her separate improved real property in Woodside as collateral for a loan to provide capital for the operation of a supermarket. On January 28, 1965, Joyce executed but did not deliver a promissory note in the amount of $40,000 and, as security for the obligation, a deed of trust on her Woodside property. Although at that time she expected to obtain a loan, the transaction was never completed. Joyce thereafter withdrew her consent to the use of her Woodside property as collateral. William, however, signed Joyce's name to both a promissory note for $75,000 in favor of Acme and a deed of trust on her Woodside property securing the loan. The signature on the deed of trust was notarized by Ellinghouse on February 18, 1965. Although Rodrigues, an auditor and a close friend and business associate of William, denied any participation in the execution and notarization of the deed of trust, the evidence supports implied findings that he told Ellinghouse he had seen Joyce sign the document and requested Ellinghouse to attest that she had acknowledged the execution of the instrument.

William took the forged documents to Acme and arranged for the loan. A check was drawn by Acme payable to William and Joyce which she endorsed without realizing that she was purportedly liable on the note or that her property had purportedly been encumbered. The major portion of the proceeds of the loan was used to satisfy obligations incurred in connection with a supermarket which was owned and operated by the William Rakestraw Co., Inc. (the corporation).

Joyce concedes that within a few days after she endorsed the check she learned of the forgeries. Later in conversations with her husband and others she claimed that she was the owner of the supermarket since her property had been used as security to finance it. She also demanded that stock in the corporation be issued to her. William, however, refused to issue or transfer any stock to her and initially refused to permit her to take any active role in the operation of the business.

Shortly after the discovery of the forgeries Joyce consulted an attorney who advised her to report the matter to the trustee designated in the deed of trust. Joyce, however, did not follow this advice and sought no remedy until three years later when both the business and her marriage had failed and the complaint had been filed by Acme and Security. Notwithstanding the position first taken by William he later permitted Joyce to take an active role in the affairs of the corporation during a period of time before its ultimate failure. Although she denied at trial that she managed the business she did testify that she went to the market "every single day" and she further testified that one of the primary reasons why she did not take more timely action to challenge the forgeries was her belief that she had an equitable interest in the corporation.

Joyce benefited financially through corporate operations made possible by the loan. Approximately $1,000 from an account of the corporation was applied toward a loan previously obtained by Joyce which was also secured by a deed of trust covering her Woodside property, and the corporation paid $3,612.50 in taxes on the parcel. In addition, William's paychecks from the corporation were deposited in a joint account standing in the names of William and Joyce and all payments applied on the Acme loan (totaling $36,250) were made by the corporation. Pursuant to the stipulated judgment, Joyce paid Acme the balance of $38,750. The jury impliedly found that she received benefits made possible by the loan in the sum of $8,750 and, accordingly, awarded her $30,000 compensatory damages on her cross-complaint. Rodrigues asserts that because Joyce ratified the forgeries he is relieved from any liability in damages to her.

The issues we deal with involve the application of traditional principles of agency law. Two basic rules are involved: (1) ratification by a person of an act purportedly done on his behalf not only creates the relationship of principal and agent but also constitutes approval by the ratifier of the purported agent's act, relieving such agent of liability to the ratifier for the act; and (2) forgeries can be ratified thereby relieving the wrongdoer agent of liability to the principal.

The first rule is embodied in Civil Code section 2307 which provides: "An agency may be created, and an authority may be conferred, by a precedent authorization *or a subsequent ratification.*" (Italics added.) Ratification is the voluntary election by a person to adopt in some manner as his own an act which was purportedly done on his behalf by another person, the effect of which, as to some or all persons, is to treat the act as if originally authorized by him. A purported agent's act may be adopted expressly or it may be adopted by implication based on conduct of the purported principal from which an intention to consent to or adopt the act may be fairly inferred, including conduct which is "inconsistent with any reasonable intention on his part, other than that he intended approving and adopting it." It is essential, however, that the act of adoption be truly voluntary in character. Moreover, there can be no adoption if the act, although voluntary, is done only because the purported principal is obligated to minimize his losses caused by the agent's wrongful act or because of duress or misrepresentation by the agent.

Generally, the effect of a ratification is that the authority which is given to the purported agent relates back to the time when he performed the act. Since he is considered to be an agent with authority at the time he performed the act, he does not incur liability for acts done within the scope of that authority.

As to the second rule here involved, it is well settled in California "that a principal may ratify the forgery of his signature by his agent." We conclude that the ratification of an act of forgery by one held out to be a principal creates an agency relationship between such person and the purported agent and relieves the agent of civil liability to the principal which otherwise would result from the fact that he acted independently and without authority.

We now turn to the facts of this case. Joyce concedes that she became aware of the forgeries within a few days after she had endorsed the check from Acme and thereafter consulted an attorney in connection therewith. Accordingly, the requirement of knowledge of the material facts essential to voluntary ratification is satisfied. The doctrine of exoneration by ratification, however, "is limited, so far as the agent is concerned, to those cases where there remains with the principal, after his first complete knowledge of the transaction, the power to rescind, and failing so to do he is properly charged with full acceptance of all the responsibilities of the contract, even to the exoneration of his agent, because, with the ability to rescind, if he rescinded, the transaction would be at an end and nobody would be injured." Here it is clear that Joyce elected not to rescind at a time when she was fully informed and had power to do so and had been advised of her rights.

It was not until three years after discovery of the forgeries, and then only when a complaint was filed against her, that Joyce sought relief. Her conduct during the interim period has been previously set forth and is revealing. When both her marriage and the business failed she formally asserted for the first time a claim for wrongdoing against her former husband and Rodrigues. It thus appears as a matter of law that Joyce affirmatively endorsed the fraudulent acts of William and Rodrigues in anticipation of benefits to be gained, and sought to negate her endorsement thereof only when benefits failed to materialize as anticipated.

Joyce contends that her approval of the transaction and acceptance of benefits was involuntary because at the time she discovered the forgeries she could not rescind the transaction by returning the proceeds of the loan as they had already been expended. There is no merit in this contention. Whether or not she was in a position to return the proceeds of the loan, she could have disavowed the transaction and relieved herself of potential liability by informing Acme and Security of the forgeries. At the time of discovery she had done nothing to preclude her from asserting that the signatures were not hers. Had she then repudiated the forgeries, her failure to take action to force the corporation to make restitution of the proceeds of the loan would not have validated the forged signatures.

Joyce also contends that there can be no ratification of Rodrigues' acts since such ratification had to be in writing. Civil Code section 2310, a codification of the "equal dignities" doctrine, provides: "A ratification can be made only in the manner that would have been necessary to confer an original authority for the act ratified, or where an oral authorization would suffice, by accepting or retaining the benefit of the act, with notice thereof." Since authorization to bind a principal to a deed of trust must be in writing (Civ. Code, § 2309) and because her consent to or adoption of the fraudulent acts was not in writing, Joyce argues that there has been no valid ratification.

Joyce's liability, however, arises from the promissory note; the deed of trust only secured the note. An agent's authority to execute a promissory note need not be in writing and, accordingly, Joyce's ratification of the note likewise need not have been in writing. Her ratification of the transaction in part, moreover, constituted a ratification of the entire transaction including acts by Rodrigues.

Finally, Civil Code section 2310 was not intended to apply to a ratification as between a principal and agent. In [*Sunset-Sternau Food Co. v. Bonzi,* (1964) 60 Cal. 2d 834, 36 Cal. Rptr. 741, 389 P.2d 133] we held that Civil Code section 2309, requiring that authorization for a contract required in law to be in writing must also be in writing, was not intended to apply [in disputes] between an agent and principal. The decision's rationale applies with equal force to Civil Code section 2310. That section, therefore, is inapplicable as between the principal and the agent, and thus inapplicable in the present case.

As Joyce's ratification of the fraudulent transaction relieved Rodrigues of liability to her as a matter of law, the trial judge improperly denied his motion for judgment notwithstanding the verdict. The judgment insofar as it relates to Rodrigues is therefore reversed and the cause remanded with directions to enter judgment in his favor.

Notes

1. Joyce endorsed the check representing the proceeds of the challenged loan. That would seem to be an affirmance in and of itself. If that is the case, why is the remainder of the opinion necessary? In any event, note that a ratifier may also impliedly affirm a transaction by *retaining* (as opposed to *accepting*) benefits arising out of the transaction. Restatement § 99.

2. In order for the principal to be held to have ratified due to knowingly accepting or retaining benefits of an unauthorized transaction, must the benefit be actual? Would only a potential for gain be sufficient?

3. The holdings of *Rakestraw v. Rodriguez* and *Sunset-Sternau Food Co. v. Bonzi* (cited in *Rakestraw*) regarding the application of the equal dignities doctrine are limited to disputes between the principal and the agent. As between the principal and *third persons*, the California statute requires equal dignities in the appointment of the agent. In any event, note that where the agent's *authorization* requires certain formalities, the *ratification* must use the same formalities. Restatement § 93(2) & comment.

3 A'S Towing Co. v. P & A Well Service, Inc.

642 F.2d 756 (5th Cir. 1981)

TATE, Circuit Judge:

Chevron appeals from a judgment holding it liable in damages for its cancellation of a service contract.

In December of 1975, Chevron U.S.A., Inc. (Chevron) hired P & A Well Service, Inc. (P & A) to plug and abandon a Chevron well located in the Louisiana coastal waters of Breton Sound. The contract provided that P & A would complete the work within sixty days and would receive $28,900 and the rights to the tubing recovered from the well.

Work commenced in early March of 1976. In late March, equipment problems led the parties to agree to a different method of plugging the well. During the ensuing delay period, rough weather damaged a P & A barge, forcing P & A to withdraw from the well site on April 5, 1976, to obtain repairs.

On April 9, 1976, P & A's president, Edward Estis, telephoned Chevron's Algiers office and was told by an unidentified individual that the Breton Sound contract was cancelled, and that P & A should not return to complete its work at that site. In reliance upon that order, P & A did not return to the Breton Sound well. On June 26, 1976, Chevron sent a letter to P & A cancelling the Breton Sound contract, and in August of 1976, Chevron itself plugged and abandoned that well.

On August 10, 1976, P & A sent an invoice billing Chevron for costs incurred in its attempt to complete the Breton Sound contract, including the salvage value of the unrecovered tubing. This litigation was precipitated when 3 A's Towing Company brought suit against P & A to recover sums due under certain towing contracts. P & A filed a third party demand against Chevron to recover the towing charges incurred in connection with the Breton Sound contract and in addition the lost profit resulting from Chevron's cancellation.

Following a bench trial, the district court concluded that since P & A had not forfeited its right to perform as of June 25, 1976, Chevron's letter cancellation of that date without first putting P & A in default constituted a violation of the contract, and that in any event, Chevron had attempted to cancel the contract during the telephone conversation on April 9, 1976. Accordingly, the district court held that P & A was entitled to recover the profit it would have made had it been permitted to complete its performance, and entered judgment in favor of P & A in the amount of $77,980, with interest and costs.

Chevron does not dispute on this appeal that the April 9 telephone conversation did in fact occur. Chevron argues, rather, that since the unidentified individual who purported to cancel the contract was without authority—express, implied, or apparent—to act for Chevron in that regard, the cancellation cannot legally be imputed to Chevron.

The law and jurisprudence of Louisiana clearly establish that the unauthorized act of one purporting to bind a corporation may be implicitly ratified by the corporate principal through the knowing acquiescence of those having the authority, so long as the unauthorized act is not violative of the corporate charter, state law, or public policy. Such ratification has retroactive effect and is equivalent to prior authority. A ratification may be held to have occurred when corporate personnel with the authority to bind the corporation acquire, or are charged with, knowledge of the unauthorized act and fail to repudiate it within a reasonable period of time. Although the acceptance of benefits by a corporation may evidence ratification, the cited decisions do not hold such to be a requirement for ratification of an act by a corporate employee repudiating a corporate obligation.[3]

---

3. Chevron incidentally suggests that a corporation cannot be held to have ratified the unauthorized act of its agent under circumstances such as these unless it had full knowledge of the act and received and accepted the benefits incurring to it from the act. Chevron thus appears to argue that since no benefits accrued to it from the cancellation of the contract on April 9, it cannot be held to have tacitly ratified it.

We disagree.

[T]he general rule that a ratification occurs when personnel with the authority to bind the corporation acquire knowledge of the unauthorized act and thereafter fail to repudiate it within a reasonable period of time is particularly applicable where the delay in repudiating is a long one, where the failure to repudiate is accompanied by acts indicating approval of the unauthorized act—such as receiving and retaining the benefits accruing from it—or where the circumstances call for a quick repudiation. There is no *requirement* that some measurable benefit inure to the corporate principal from the unauthorized act.

To be sure, where the unauthorized act consists of the making of a contract that purports to bind a corporate principal, there is no more telling indication of the principal's ratification or approval of that act than its receipt and retention of the contracted-for benefits. But not all unauthorized acts involve the potential flow of some measurable benefit or consideration from a third party to the principal. In such cases, the principal's ratification or approval of the

We find sufficient evidence in this record to support a conclusion that Chevron acquiesced in the April 9 telephone cancellation of the Breton Sound contract, thereby implicitly ratifying it and adopting it as an act of the corporation.

The Breton Sound contract was negotiated for Chevron by E.J. Morgan, a staff engineer in Chevron's Algiers office. The contract was signed in Morgan's office. All subsequent discussions of the contract were with Morgan, or with his replacements, C.R. Block and Richard Gist. Virtually all of P & A's dealings with Chevron in connection with the Breton Sound well were conducted over Morgan's telephone. It was Morgan who represented Chevron in altering the procedure to be used in plugging the well and who agreed on Chevron's behalf to supply the mud for the new procedure.

On April 8, 1976, a call was placed to the home of P & A's president, Edward Estis, and a message was left requesting Estis to return the call. The number given was later determined to be that of James Isonhood, E.J. Morgan's immediate inferior, in Chevron's Algiers office. On April 9, 1976, Estis returned the call to the designated number and received no answer. He then called E.J. Morgan's number and spoke to the now-unknown individual who purported to cancel the Breton Sound contract.

Francis R. Daigle, the person who was second in rank at the Algiers office and E.J. Morgan's immediate supervisor, testified that he was aware of the fact and the substance of the April 9 telephone conversation. That testimony was at least suggestive of a more general awareness throughout the Algiers office.

Despite that awareness, and despite numerous subsequent contacts between Chevron personnel and P & A personnel, neither Daigle nor any other Chevron employee ever repudiated that conversation, requested P & A to resume its operations on the Breton Sound well, or even inquired into P & A's continued absence from the well site. Chevron took no action in the ensuing weeks that was in any way inconsistent with a cancellation by telephone on April 9. The record shows that telephone cancellation with a follow-up letter of cancellation was an accepted practice in contracts of this sort; and indeed, on June 25, 1976, Chevron notified P & A by letter that it considered the contract cancelled, and thereafter rendered performance by P & A impossible by plugging and abandoning the Breton Sound well with its own resources in August of that year.

Under these facts, we find ample support for a conclusion that Chevron ratified the telephone cancellation by acquiescing in it, and therefore find it unnecessary to determine whether Chevron could likewise be bound by the cancellation under theories of actual or apparent authority. Chevron personnel with the authority to bind the corporation had knowledge of the telephone cancellation and failed to repudiate it within a reasonable period of time. We therefore find no error in the district court's conclusion that *Chevron* had attempted to cancel the Breton Sound contract by telephone on April 9, 1976.

AFFIRMED.

Note

Under the Restatement, silence or a failure to act indicates affirmance "under such circumstances that, according to the ordinary experience and habits of men, one would naturally be expected to speak [or act] if he did not consent." Section 94 comment a. In determining whether the circumstances are such as to imply an af-

---

repudiation must obviously be manifested in terms other than the receipt of contracted-for benefits.

firmance, recall that under Restatement section 83, implied affirmance requires that the affirming conduct must be justifiable only if the ratifier was electing to affirm the transaction.

Should it make any difference if the claimed affirmance relates to an act of a stranger, as opposed to an *actual* agent exceeding the scope of his or her power to bind?

B. Knowledge of Agents

Estate of Sawyer v. Crowell

559 A.2d 687 (Vt. 1989)

GIBSON, Justice.

Defendant, Charles E. Crowell, appeals a decision of the Chittenden Superior Court ordering him to pay the sum of $50,000 to the plaintiff, the Estate of Thomas C. Sawyer (Estate), an estate administered under the jurisdiction of the Chittenden Probate Court. Attorney John Durrance served as administrator of the Estate from the death of Thomas Sawyer in 1980 until March of 1982. The superior court determined that defendant materially breached an agreement between the parties and was liable as a result.

In 1980, defendant co-founded the Vermont Real Estate Investment Trust (VREIT). The stated purpose of VREIT was to provide a vehicle for investments in Vermont real estate ventures. Defendant ran VREIT single-handedly as its president from its creation until January of 1982. This case arises out of the alleged misuse of money entrusted by the Estate to the defendant for investment during 1981.

In February of 1981, attorney Durrance contacted defendant to discuss investing $50,000 of the Estate's funds in high-grade commercial paper. On February 11, 1981, the two met and agreed that defendant would invest the $50,000 in six-month commercial paper through Crowell, England & Co., of which defendant was the sole principal. Mr. Durrance stressed that the money was to be invested conservatively in a national corporation and ruled out VREIT as an investment. On March 5, 1981, defendant purchased commercial paper issued by the Ford Motor Credit Corporation with a maturity date of August 12, 1981.

On August 12, 1981, defendant and Mr. Durrance met on the street and discussed the reinvestment of the Estate's funds. Mr. Durrance told defendant that he wanted to reinvest the money, including interest, for a shorter period of time in order to ensure that the proceeds would be available at the end of the year—the anticipated date of the closing of the Estate. Mr. Durrance asked defendant to reinvest the funds in high-grade commercial paper for thirty days with a continuous rollover. He did not, however, specify a particular investment. Defendant subsequently invested the funds in VREIT.

In mid-October, Mr. Durrance asked his secretary to inquire about the requirements for withdrawing the Estate's money from its investment with defendant. By letter dated October 14, 1981, the secretary asked defendant how to continue the investment and the procedure for withdrawal of funds. Defendant responded by letter dated October 15, 1981, addressed only to the secretary, that three days' written notice was required for withdrawal of the funds. Defendant also included in the letter the information that the funds were invested in VREIT commercial paper.

Upon receipt of this response, the secretary informed Mr. Durrance of the notice requirement for fund withdrawal, but did not discuss with him the fact that defendant had invested the money in VREIT. Instead, she placed the letter in the file.

On December 31, 1981, after learning that funds belonging to another client had been invested in VREIT and that VREIT was having difficulty returning them, Mr. Durrance consulted the Estate file and found the October 15th letter. He immediately contacted defendant and demanded the return of the Estate's funds. Shortly thereafter, but before any money was returned to the Estate, VREIT filed a petition in bankruptcy.

The superior court concluded that the deposit of the Estate's funds in VREIT constituted a material breach of the agreement under which defendant had undertaken to invest the Estate's money. The court ordered that the Estate recover the $50,000 from defendant, less any amount recovered in bankruptcy, plus interest at 15% from August 12, 1981 (the date of the breach).

[Defendant] argues that the October 15th letter from defendant to Mr. Durrance's secretary constituted notice to Mr. Durrance of the funds' investment in VREIT, and that by not acting at such time to disaffirm the investment, Mr. Durrance ratified it.

Defendant argues that he is not liable for any breach, contending that where financial investments are concerned, a customer is deemed to have ratified a wrongful investment upon his failure to repudiate it promptly after he becomes chargeable with knowledge thereof. In support, he urges us to accept his conclusion that Mr. Durrance was chargeable with knowing the funds were invested in VREIT when his secretary received the October 15th letter. Because Mr. Durrance was then chargeable with the knowledge, the argument proceeds, his failure to repudiate the VREIT investment at that time constituted ratification of it.

As a general rule, the knowledge of an agent acting within the scope of his or her authority is chargeable to the principal, regardless of whether that knowledge is actually communicated.[2] Thus, in order for Mr. Durrance to be chargeable with knowledge of the VREIT investment on October 15th, it was necessary for defendant to establish that it was within the scope of the secretary's authority to obtain that information. This, defendant, failed to do.

Although the trial court did not directly address the issue in terms of "scope of authority," it clearly found that with respect to the correspondence of October 14-15, the secretary's authority did not extend to inquiring where the Estate's funds were invested:

---

2. Defendant bases part of his argument on the contention that the secretary's authority was "apparent" if not truly "actual." His reliance on this distinction is misplaced, however. Actual authority is that conveyed by the principal directly to the agent, while apparent authority is the scope of an agent's authority manifested by the principal to a third party, not the agent. Restatement (Second) of Agency §§ 7 and 8 (1958). Thus, although the secretary's actions in writing the letter and requesting information might "reasonably appear" to defendant to be actions done within her scope of authority, he offered no evidence to prove that her authority to do more than inquire as to how to continue the investment and withdraw funds was communicated to him by Mr. Durrance, the principal.

> No confirmation [of the reinvestment] was sent by Crowell to Durrance, and Durrance did not ask for any. [Durrance] had asked his secretary simply to obtain specific information, and she had done so to the extent of his inquiry.

Finding of fact No. 14. The court then concluded:

> Durrance did not ask his secretary to inquire where the funds had been invested. His only inquiry was how to continue the investment and how long it would take to withdraw the funds. Durrance had neither actual notice of the VREIT investment nor constructive notice of the breach.

The existence and extent of an agent's authority is a question of fact. There is no evidence in the record that the secretary knew the money should not have been invested in VREIT, or that there was any restriction on its investment. Without such knowledge, she had no reason to bring that information to Mr. Durrance's attention. As defendant has made no showing that the secretary had any authority extending beyond the inquiry contained in her letter, the court's finding is not clearly erroneous, and we will not disturb it here. Since the secretary's knowledge of the VREIT investment did not arise within the scope of her authority, Mr. Durrance cannot be charged with such knowledge.

Defendant next argues that by doing nothing from October 15 until December 31, Mr. Durrance ratified the contents of the October 15th letter to the secretary. This argument is premised on the doctrine of ratification, under which a principal may affirm a prior action by an agent which did not bind the principal but was purportedly done on his or her account, with the ratification "relating back" to the time of the actual act. *See* Restatement (Second) of Agency § 82. It is clear that if Mr. Durrance ratified his secretary's actions in obtaining the additional information, he would be chargeable with that knowledge as of October 15.

Defendant argues, in essence, that Mr. Durrance's silence after the October 15th letter was received in his office amounted to a ratification of its contents. While we accept the proposition that in certain circumstances it is possible for silence to be construed as an affirmance resulting in ratification, see Restatement (Second) of Agency § 94 comment a, we do not reach that conclusion here. Affirmance alone will not necessarily bind a principal who acts upon incomplete or inaccurate information. The law is clear that for ratification of an unauthorized act to occur so as to bind the principal, he or she must have *actual knowledge* of the material facts being adopted at the time affirmance occurs. Absent such knowledge, an affirmance may be avoided upon the principal's learning the material facts. Restatement (Second) of Agency § 91.

In this case, the court concluded that Mr. Durrance had neither actual nor constructive knowledge of the VREIT investment at the time his secretary received the October 15th letter. As defendant has not met his burden of showing that this conclusion was not supported by the findings of fact, there is no error. Since Mr. Durrance moved promptly to disaffirm the wrongful investment as soon as he received actual notice of it on December 31 (a fact not disputed by defendant), we conclude that he thereby avoided whatever affirmance of the breach which could have arisen from his earlier silence.

Affirmed.

Note

Earlier in this chapter we discussed the right of a ratifier who did not know all the material facts to avoid the affirmance. Suppose that the ratifier's *agent* did know all such facts. May the ratifier still avoid the affirmance? As indicated in *3 A's Towing Co. v. P & A Well Service, Inc.* and *Estate of Sawyer v. Crowell*, the general rules holding a principal accountable for the knowledge of an agent apply in a ratification context to prevent the ratifier from avoiding the affirmance. Note, however, that the principal will *not* be charged with an agent's knowledge of facts relating to the agent's *own unauthorized acts*. Restatement §§ 91 comment c, 280.

C. Partial Ratifications

Many transactions entered into by agents or purported agents on behalf of principals will be of some degree of complexity. There may be multiple provisions of written agreements, or there may be multiple segments of transactions (such as the negotiation, execution, performance, and enforcement components of contracts). Even these components may be further subdivided. Should a principal be allowed to select among the parts of a transaction, to ratify certain portions, and to disaffirm others?

Navrides v. Zurich Insurance Co.

5 Cal. 3d 698, 488 P.2d 637 (1971)

SULLIVAN, Justice.

In this action against defendant insurance company arising out of the compromise of a personal injury claim made with the company by plaintiff's attorney without her consent, we must decide whether defendant was discharged from liability where its settlement draft after delivery to the attorney was cashed on plaintiff's forged endorsement and the proceeds of the draft appropriated.

On February 19, 1962, plaintiff Audrey Navrides was injured on the premises of one Crancer who was insured by defendant Zurich Insurance Company (Zurich). She employed an attorney, Robert S. Forsyth, who filed an action for damages on her behalf. Forsyth negotiated with Zurich a compromise settlement of plaintiff's claim for $9,000. Plaintiff rejected the compromise but Forsyth represented to Zurich that she had approved. Zurich then delivered to Forsyth for signature a release of all claims, a request for the dismissal of the pending action and a draft dated September 22, 1964 in the sum of $9,000 payable to "Audrey R. Navrides and Robert S. Forsyth, her attorney." Forsyth retained the draft and returned to Zurich the release purportedly signed by plaintiff, together with the request for dismissal. The latter document was thereupon filed and the action dismissed.

On September 25, 1964, the settlement draft, bearing the purported endorsements of plaintiff and Forsyth, was cashed at the Bank of America and eventually charged to Zurich's account with the Continental Bank. Plaintiff's signature on the release and her endorsement on the draft were forgeries. She received no money from the settlement. About a year later, plaintiff discovered that her personal injury action had been dismissed and that the above settlement draft had been delivered to her attorney. She was unable to effect any recovery from the latter.

On December 14, 1965 plaintiff commenced this action against Zurich and the Bank of America.[1]

Plaintiff's first stated cause of action against Zurich alleged in substance that the latter for a valuable consideration drew, executed and delivered the draft to plaintiff, that the draft was wrongfully paid by the Bank of America on a forged endorsement, that Zurich "has not paid said check, nor any part thereof to plaintiff, and by reason of said fact, there has been a failure of consideration" and that defendant owed plaintiff the sum of $9,000. The trial court essentially found that all of the material allegations of the first cause of action were true, that plaintiff did not affix, or authorize anyone to affix, her signature to the draft, and that she was not estopped from asserting that she neither signed nor authorized an endorsement of the draft. From these facts the court concluded simply that (1) plaintiff's signature was a forgery and (2) that Zurich owed plaintiff $9,000 plus interest. Judgment was entered accordingly.

The trial court's conclusion that plaintiff's signature on the draft was a forgery is amply supported by the findings and the evidence. Unfortunately, however, the court nowhere indicates any legal theory explaining its leap from its findings and first conclusion of law to its second conclusion that Zurich owed plaintiff $9,000 plus interest. It is a fair assumption that the trial judge concluded that the forged endorsement was wholly inoperative and that as a consequence Zurich still owed plaintiff $9,000.

Although Forsyth clearly had no authority, express or implied, to compromise plaintiff's claim, the record before us establishes as a matter of law that plaintiff, by bringing the instant action against Zurich for the $9,000, ratified the settlement. As we shall explain, by so doing she necessarily approved Zurich's delivery of the draft to Forsyth and the latter's delivery to Zurich of the release (on which her signature had been forged) and the request for the dismissal of her action.

It is well settled that a client may ratify the unauthorized actions of his attorney, that a principal may ratify the forgery of his signature by his agent, and that a principal may ratify the unauthorized act of an agent by bringing suit based thereon.

By virtue of such ratification, there then existed between plaintiff and Zurich a *valid* compromise agreement which was fully performed on the part of plaintiff by Forsyth's delivery of the release and dismissal to Zurich. The true and indeed only tenable theory of plaintiff's action thus emerges: that Zurich owes her $9,000 under the settlement agreement and that she had not been paid. Indeed at oral argument plaintiff's present counsel conceded that by bringing suit against Zurich she had ratified the settlement and was seeking to enforce it. However, inherent in the ratification of the settlement is ratification of Forsyth's authority to settle the claim, which necessarily includes authority to receive and collect the payment of the settlement on behalf of plaintiff.

---

1. Apparently plaintiff made no attempt to set aside the unauthorized dismissal of her personal injury action. We need not speculate as to the probable success of any such proceedings had they been undertaken. Nevertheless we observe that the law is well settled that an attorney must be specifically authorized to settle and compromise a claim, that merely on the basis of his employment he has no implied or ostensible authority to bind his client to a compromise settlement of pending litigation and that clearly he has no authority pursuant to an unauthorized settlement to enter a dismissal with prejudice.

Unfortunately for plaintiff, she cannot stop at this point. She must reckon with the elementary rule of agency law that a principal is not allowed to ratify the unauthorized acts of an agent to the extent that they are beneficial, and disavow them to the extent that they are damaging. If a principal ratifies part of a transaction, he is deemed to ratify the whole of it. Rest. 2d Agency, § 96. The reason for the rule is obvious. Ratification is approval of a transaction that has already taken place. Accordingly the principal has the power to approve the transaction only as it in fact occurred, not to reconstruct it to suit his present needs. As the court said in *Gift v. Ahrnke* (1951), 107 Cal. App. 2d 614, 623, 237 P.2d 706, 710, "A principal 'cannot split the agency transaction into separate parts, and take the benefits without the burden.' " In the instant case plaintiff, by ratifying Forsyth's settlement of her pending action for damages for personal injuries, necessarily ratified the entire transaction between Forsyth and Zurich, including Forsyth's receipt of the settlement draft.

We, therefore, turn to consider whether Zurich's delivery of the draft to Forsyth discharged the insurance company from all liability to plaintiff, notwithstanding the fact that the draft was subsequently cashed on plaintiff's forged endorsement and its proceeds converted. We begin by adverting to established principles of agency dealing with the authority of agents to receive payment.

An attorney has authority "To receive money claimed by his client in an action or proceeding during the pendency thereof and upon payment thereof, and not otherwise, to discharge the claim." (Code Civ. Proc. § 283, subd. 2.) This statute, enacted in 1872, codifies the well-established proposition of law that an attorney who has authority to settle or collect a claim also has authority to receive payment in money and that such payment to the attorney discharges the claim, even if the attorney absconds with the money.

However, the mere giving of a check payable to the agent does not constitute payment. "A check is never a payment of the debt for which it is given until the check itself is paid or otherwise discharged, unless expressly agreed to be taken in payment." But once the check is paid, the payment of the underlying debt which was theretofore conditional becomes absolute and relates back to the date of the delivery of the check.

The foregoing authorities support the now-settled rule that where an agent authorized to collect a debt owing to his principal accepts in lieu of cash a valid check *payable to the agent*, the debtor is discharged upon payment of the check, although the agent absconds with the proceeds, since payment to the agent is equivalent to payment to the principal.

Section 178(2) [of the Restatement of Agency 2d] provides: "If an agent who is authorized to receive a check payable to the principal as conditional payment forges the principal's endorsement to such a check, the maker is relieved of liability to the principal if the drawee bank pays the check and charges the amount to the maker."

Upon application of the foregoing rule of agency we conclude that there is no basis in the record before us upon which to sustain the judgment.

The judgment is reversed.

Notes

1. The general rule against partial ratification does not apply to situations involving distinct transactions or separate acts. Restatement 96 comment b. For example, in *Navrides v. Zurich Insurance Co.*, although the attorney had *power to bind* Navrides by his forgery of Navrides's signature, that forgery was a separate act *and was not*

ratified by Navrides's ratification of the settlement. *See* Restatement 96 comment b, illustration 6. Whether Navrides has ratified the forgery is important in light of the "relation back" doctrine and the rule discussed in *Rakestraw v. Rodrigues*, earlier in this chapter, that a principal's ratification of an agent's unauthorized act "exonerates" the agent as against the principal.

2. Suppose Thief steals a truckload of bricks from Brick Company, then purports to act as its agent in selling the stolen bricks to Third Party. Suppose further that Thief, purporting to act as Brick Company's servant in delivering the bricks, runs over and injures Pedestrian while delivering the bricks. Assuming Brick Company knows all the facts and sues Third Party to collect payment for the bricks, would it also be ratifying the tort under the "no partial ratifications" doctrine? Is the delivery independent from the ratified sale? Is the tort independent from the delivery? *See* chapter 7 for a fuller discussion of the topic of ratification of torts.

Chapter 5

Termination of the Agent's Authority

A. Voluntary Terminations

Zukaitis v. Aetna Casualty & Surety Co.

195 Neb. 59, 236 N.W.2d 819 (1975)

BLUE, District Judge.

This is an action for a declaratory judgment brought to determine whether defendant-appellee, the Aetna Casualty and Surety Company, is obligated under its professional liability insurance policy to defend plaintiff-appellant, Raymond R. Zukaitis, in a medical malpractice suit.

Raymond R. Zukaitis was a physician practicing medicine in Douglas County, Nebraska. Aetna issued Dr. Zukaitis a policy of professional liability insurance through its agent, the Ed Larsen Insurance Agency, Inc. This policy was for a period from August 31, 1969, to August 31, 1970.

On August 7, 1971, Dr. Zukaitis received a written notification of a claim for malpractice which allegedly occurred on September 27, 1969. On August 10, 1971, Dr. Zukaitis telephoned the Ed Larsen Insurance Agency. At the request of the agency the written claim was forwarded to it by Dr. Zukaitis. This was received on August 11, 1971, and was erroneously referred to the St. Paul Fire and Marine Insurance Company on that date by the agency.

Dr. Zukaitis was insured with St. Paul Fire and Marine Insurance Company from August 31, 1970, to August 31, 1971. But on the date of the alleged malpractice, he was insured with Aetna. Apparently without notice to Dr. Zukaitis, the agency contract between Ed Larsen Insurance Agency and Aetna had been canceled effective August 1, 1970. At the time the agency placed Dr. Zukaitis' insurance with St. Paul.

On November 22, 1971, a malpractice action was brought against Dr. Zukaitis based on the alleged malpractice of September 27, 1969. Attorneys for St. Paul undertook the defense of the lawsuit. On January 25, 1974, St. Paul discovered that it was not the insurance carrier for Dr. Zukaitis on September 27, 1969, the date of the alleged malpractice, and advised Aetna of this at that time. Dr. Zukaitis was also advised of this, and the attorney retained for St. Paul to represent Dr. Zukaitis withdrew. Dr. Zukaitis made demand upon Aetna on May 28, 1974, for it to undertake the defense of Dr. Zukaitis, but this demand was refused.

Dr. Zukaitis retained his own attorney to represent him in the malpractice case. A motion for summary judgment was filed by Dr. Zukaitis in that case, which motion was sustained. This action for a declaratory judgment against Aetna therefore resolved itself into an effort to recover attorney's fees and costs. The District Court found for Aetna.

Aetna contends that it is relieved from its obligation to Dr. Zukaitis since notice was not given as required by paragraph 4(b) of the policy which provides: "If claim is made or suit is brought against the insured, the insured shall immediately forward to the company every demand, notice, summons or other process received by him or his representative."

Dr. Zukaitis contends that under the circumstances, notice to Aetna was given within a reasonable period in that the agent who wrote the policy was given notice.

This court has previously construed provisions of insurance policies similar to the one here. In *Keene Coop. Grain & Supply Co. v. Farmers Union Ind. Mut. Ins. Co.*, 177 Neb. 287, 128 N.W.2d 773, it is stated:

> The word 'immediate' in referring to the notice required in an insurance policy means with reasonable celerity, with reasonable and proper diligence, and what is a reasonable time depends upon all the facts and circumstances of each particular case.

Ordinarily notice to a soliciting agent who countersigns and issues policies of insurance is notice to the insurance company. Restatement, Agency 2d, § 127. This is also true even if the agent forwards the notice to the wrong company. At 44 Am. Jur. 2d, Insurance, § 1468 p. 336, it is stated:

> Also, an insured who has promptly given notice of an accident to the general agent that issued the policy, and has also promptly delivered process to him, has been held not required to do anything further, although in each instance the agent by mistake forwarded the papers to the wrong company.

The question then is whether this is true after the agency contract between the insurance company and the agent has been terminated as it was in this case. To answer this, it is necessary to refer to the general law of agency.

The rule is that a revocation of the agent's authority does not become effective as between the principal and third persons until they receive notice of the termination.

Here, Dr. Zukaitis did what most reasonable persons would do in the situation; he notified the agent who sold him the policy. There is no evidence that notice of the termination was sent to him or that he knew the agency contract had been canceled.

It is stated in 3 Couch on Insurance 2d, § 26:50, p. 513:

> When the insurer terminates the agency contract, it is its duty to notify third persons, such as the insureds with whom the agent dealt, and inform them of such termination. If it does not so notify and such third persons or insureds deal with the agent without notice or knowledge of the termination, and in reliance on the apparently continuing authority of the agent, the insurer is bound by the acts of the former agent.

The following appears in 3 Couch on Insurance 2d, § 26:50, p. 515:

> The principle of the carrying over of the authority of an agent after termination with respect to third persons having no notice or knowledge thereof has been applied so as to bind the insurer when the third person dealt with the

apparent agent by contracting with him, or by forwarding or delivering to him suit papers and proofs of loss.

A case involving similar facts as the case presented here is *Yannuzzi v. United States Cas. Co.*, 19 N.J. 210, 115 A.2d 557. The insureds in that case were sued as the result of an accident which occurred on December 9, 1951. After insureds were served with the suit papers on October 16, 1952, they forwarded them to the agent who sold them an automobile accident insurance policy. The agency forwarded the suit papers to the wrong insurance company. The agency contract had been terminated effective January 1, 1952. The insurance company claimed the insureds did not comply with a condition of the policy requiring them to immediately forward to insurer every summons or other process. The New Jersey Supreme Court held that the insureds complied with this provision when they sent the suit papers to the agent from whom insureds had received the policy even though the agency relationship had been terminated. The New Jersey Court set out the following applicable statement from *Southern Life Ins. Co. v. McCain*, 96 U.S. 84, 24 L. Ed. 653:

> No company can be allowed to hold out another as its agent, and then disavow responsibility for his acts. After it has appointed an agent in a particular business, parties dealing with him in that business have a right to rely upon the continuance of his authority, until in some way informed of its revocation.

We conclude that under the facts and circumstances of this case, the notice given by the plaintiff to the agent of the defendant constitutes notice to the defendant and would obligate defendant to carry out the terms of its insurance contract with plaintiff. The District Court was in error when it determined to the contrary.

Notes

1. The principal may at any time *revoke* his or her consent to action on his or her behalf by the agent. Restatement § 118 & comments a & b. The authority of an agent to act for the principal terminates when the principal "manifests" to the agent that the principal no longer consents, *or* when the agent has *notice* the principal no longer consents. Restatement § 119. The agent will have notice when the agent knows, has reason to know, should know, or has been given a notification, of the principal's lack of consent. Restatement §§ 9(1) & 134. Recall that the agent will be affected by notice to the *agent's* agents under the principles discussed in chapter 3.

The agent may in a similar manner *renounce* the agency and withdraw his or her consent to act on behalf of the principal. Restatement §§ 118, 119, & 134.

2. Termination of the agent's authority terminates all power of the agent to affect the principal's legal relations, except apparent authority and emergency authority. Restatement § 124A. The extent of the agent's remaining *apparent authority* depends on the attendant circumstances, including the nature of the agency.

3. *Lingering Apparent Authority of General Agents.* As indicated in *Zukaitis v. Aetna Casualty & Surety Co.*, a *general* agent continues to have *apparent authority* to bind the (former) principal to a third person *despite* a voluntary termination of the agency relationship until such time as the third person has *notice* of the termination. Restatement § 127. That is, apparent authority continues until the third person (or the appropriate agent of the third person) knows, has reason to know, should know, or has been given a notification of the termination. Restatement § 135.

Notification *by publication* in a newspaper of general circulation in the place where the agency had regularly been carried on is effective to terminate the (former) general agent's apparent authority as to all third persons *except* certain limited classes of persons. Restatement § 136(3). Notification by publication is *not* effective where:

> (a) the third person had previously extended or received *credit* to or from the principal through the general agent;
>
> (b) the third person had "specially accredited" the agent to the third person (a principal specially accredits an agent by inviting a third person to deal with the agent, *cf.* Restatement § 128 comment a);
>
> (c) the principal should have known that the agent had already begun to deal with the third person; or
>
> (d) where the principal has entrusted the agent with an "indicia of authority" (a power of attorney or other writing given to the agent for the purpose of evidencing the agent's authority, Restatement § 130).

Restatement § 136(2). Why should notification by publication be required for the above classes of third persons, but not as to other kinds of third persons?

4. *Lingering Apparent Authority of Special Agents.* Where the agent has *not* been held out as a general agent, the agent generally has *no* lingering apparent authority. Restatement § 132. A special agent will have lingering apparent authority *only* where

> (a) the principal has specially accredited the agent to the third person;
>
> (b) the principal has *notice* that the agent has begun to deal with the third person; or
>
> (c) the principal has entrusted the agent with an indicia of authority.

Restatement § 132. Why should special and general agents be treated differently? Given that it would be next to impossible to notify all persons who might rely on the agent's possession of an indicia of authority, how can the principal cut off the (former) agent's apparent authority?

5. Suppose Husband had established a credit account at Department Store to which Wife was authorized to charge purchases. Husband decides that Wife is spending too much money, and informs Department Store not to extend further credit to her, but does not tell Wife this. Wife charges further merchandise to the account, and Department Store demands payment from Husband.

Recall that an agent continues to have (actual) authority to bind the principal until such time as the agent has notice that the principal no longer consents to action by the agent. May Department Store, which had notice that Husband no longer consented to Wife acting on his behalf, hold Husband responsible under Wife's actual authority?

One well-known Canadian case concluded that Department Store could hold Principal liable. *Robert Simpson Co. v. Godson*, 1 D.L.R. 454 (Can. 1937). *But see* Restatement § 125 comment c (while the agent has authority to bind the principal, third persons with notice of the principal's lack of consent can acquire no rights against the principal).

6. Because the authority of an agent to act on behalf of the principal is based on the principal's consent for the agent so to act, the agent's authority to act sometimes

terminates *by implication*. Implied terminations arise when the agent should realize that, in light of intervening events, the principal would no longer consent to action by the agent if the principal knew of the events. For example, the occurrence of the following events (among others) may call into question the continued consent of the principal:

(a) A change in value of the subject matter of the agency or a change in business conditions, Restatement § 109;

(b) the loss or destruction of the subject matter of the agency or the termination of the principal's interest in it, Restatement § 110;

(c) a change of law of which the agent has notice and which causes the execution of his or her authority to be illegal, or which otherwise materially changes the effect of its execution, Restatement § 116;

(d) the bankruptcy or substantial impairment of the assets or credit of the agent or the principal of which the agent has notice, Restatement §§ 113, 114; and

(e) the outbreak of war of which the agent has notice, Restatement § 115.

B. Terminations by Operation of Law

1. Death

Estate of Krempasky

501 A.2d 681 (Pa. Super. 1985)

WATKINS, Judge:

This case comes to us on appeal from the Court of Common Pleas of Cambria County and involves the issue as to whether a valid joint tenancy with the right of survivorship was created in certain certificates of deposit prior to a decedent's death.

The decedent, Elizabeth Krempasky, died on June 8, 1979 at 2:45 P.M. while a patient at a hospital. She was 82 years of age at the time of her death. She died of heart failure and cardiovascular disease. In her will she devised the residue of her estate to her niece, Lydia Elizabeth Vrablova Wanamaker, who was also appointed executrix. The decedent had four bank certificates of deposit worth $5,000 each which she kept in a metal box at her home. The executrix testified at trial that the certificates of deposit were not found in the metal box after decedent's death. Upon further inquiry the executrix discovered that the name of Anna A. Parana had been added to the four certificates on the very day of her death. The executrix then filed a petition requesting that the certificates of deposit be ordered returned to the estate as estate property. After hearing, the court below denied the petition and directed a verdict in favor of Parana. After exceptions to the order were dismissed by the court below, the executrix took the instant appeal.

[T]he name of Anna A. Parana was added to the instruments by the bank on the very day of the decedent's death. The name was added pursuant to an authorization form containing the decedent's signature and brought to the bank by Anna Parana. Anna Parana had also prepared the authorization forms. A bank official testified that

Anna Parana had brought the form to the bank in the "late afternoon," "about 3 o'clock" on the date of the decedent's death and the name of Anna Parana was added to the instrument between 3:00 P.M. and 4:00 P.M. when the bank closed. However, the testimony also revealed that the decedent died on June 8, 1979 at 2:45 P.M. Thus, when the addition of the other name to the certificates took place the decedent was dead.

> It is well established as the general rule that the death of the principal operates, as an instantaneous and absolute revocation of the agent's authority or power, unless the agency is coupled with an interest. Hence, any act done by the agent, as such, after the principal's death will not affect the estate of the latter.

3 Am. Jur. 2d 453 § 51. It is well settled that the death of the principal puts an end to the agency and terminates the agent's authority to act for the principal unless the agency is coupled with an interest. In our case the decedent died before [the agent] created the joint tenancy. Anna Parana had no interest in the certificates of deposit at the time of the decedent's death. Thus, her death terminated both Parana's and the bank's authority to change the account. For that reason we agree with the appellant's contention that the four certificates of deposit belong to the decedent's estate.

Notes

1. At common law, death terminates *all* power of the agent to bind the principal, both authority and *apparent authority*, *without notice* to either the agent *or* the third person dealing with the agent. Restatement §§ 120 & comment c, 124A comment a; *cf.* Restatement § 133. Comment a to Restatement section 120 gives the rationale for this rule:

> Agency is a personal relation, necessarily ending with the death of the principal; the former principal is no longer a legal person with whom there can be legal relations. One cannot act on behalf of a non-existent person.

2. The common law rule terminating without notice all power of the agent to act on behalf of a dead principal puts agents in a double bind. So long as the principal lives, the agent is under a duty to act on behalf of the principal. An agent without notice of the principal's death will believe he or she is still required to act. Because the agent will no longer be able to bind the principal (*or his or her estate*), the agent contracting with a third person will breach his or her implied *warranty* of authority under Restatement section 329. Other than by refusing to consent to an agency relationship, how may the agent protect himself or herself against the death of the principal?

3. The harshness of the common law rule regarding the effect of the principal's death on an agent's power to bind a principal has been criticized, even by the Restatement. Restatement § 120 comment a. Later in this chapter we will discuss *statutory modifications* of the common law rule.

4. When does death occur?

> From ancient times down to the recent past it was clear that, when the respiration and heart stopped, the brain would die in a few minutes; so the obvious criterion of no heart beat as synonymous with death was sufficiently accurate. In those times the heart was considered to be the central organ of the body; it is not

> surprising that its failure marked the onset of death. This is no longer valid when modern resuscitative and supportive measures are used. These improved activities can now restore "life" as judged by the ancient standards of persistent respiration and continuing heart beat. This can be the case even where there is not the remotest possibility of an individual recovering consciousness following massive brain damage.

Ad Hoc Committee of the Harvard Medical School, "A Definition of Irreversible Coma," 205 J. A.M.A. 337, 339 (1968). *See also In re Quinlan*, 70 N.J. 10, 355 A.2d 647, 656, *cert. denied* 429 U.S. 922 (1976) ("Developments in medical technology have obfuscated the use of the traditional definition of death").

2. Incapacity

Campbell v. United States

657 F.2d 1174 (Ct. Cl. 1981)

FRIEDMAN, Chief Judge:

This is another chapter in the continuing saga of attempts by the Internal Revenue Service to limit the use of "flower bonds" to pay federal estate taxes. Flower bonds are United States Treasury bonds that were issued a number of years ago at interest rates substantially below current ones and therefore sell significantly below par, but that may be redeemed at par before maturity to pay federal estate taxes.

The bonds were purchased for the decedent soon after he became comatose and shortly before he died, pursuant to a power of attorney executed several years earlier. The government contends that the power of attorney lapsed when the decedent became comatose, that the purchase of the bonds on his behalf was ineffective, and that the decedent therefore was not the "owner" of the bonds when he died which, under the governing regulation, is a condition to the early redemption of the flower bonds at par to pay estate taxes.

In 1965, the decedent, Lionel L. Campbell ("Campbell"), while in good health, gave his son ("Campbell Junior") "a full and universal power of attorney" authorizing Campbell Junior "to do any and every act, and exercise any and every power" that Campbell could do or exercise through any other person. On December 9, 1976, Campbell, then 73 years old, was "stricken with a cerebral hemorrhage, and became permanently and irreversibly mentally incompetent, remaining so until his death." He died 24 days later on January 2, 1977.

On December 10, the day after Campbell was stricken, Campbell Junior purchased, at a substantial discount and with Campbell's funds, a United States Treasury bond, in the face amount of $200,000, bearing interest at 3½ percent per annum, and maturing on November 15, 1998. In purchasing the bond, Campbell Junior intended to act as agent and attorney for his father, although he was fully aware of his father's medical condition.

The only question before us is whether the bonds were actually owned by Campbell at his death. The government contends that when Campbell became "permanently and irreversibly mentally incompetent" following his stroke, the effect was to terminate Campbell Junior's "authority to act on decedent's behalf in effecting a bond purchase." Under the government's theory, therefore, Campbell Junior's purchase of the bond for his father was ineffective.

A preliminary question is whether state or federal law determines whether Campbell Junior's power of attorney terminated when his father became comatose. Plaintiff urges that state law governs; the government invokes federal law. We conclude that we should look to Texas law to decide the question.

Although there is no Texas authority dealing with this specific question, Texas law indicates that Texas courts would hold that when Campbell became comatose, the power of attorney did not immediately terminate but rather continued effective for some brief period, subject to disaffirmance by Campbell's executrix after his death. This is also the view of most of the federal courts that have considered the question under the laws of other states.

It is settled in Texas that when a principal is adjudicated insane, the authority of his agent to act for him is terminated. In *Jensen v. Kisro*, 547 S.W.2d 65 (Tex. Civ. App. 1977), the court refused to hold that a power of attorney, pursuant to which the decedent's stock had been sold shortly after she entered a hospital in a "disabled" condition and while she was "very, very sick" had been terminated, since these two circumstances "cannot be held to establish that on (the date of the conveyance) she lacked the mental capacity to sell the stock." *Id.* [at] 67.

The government relies heavily upon the Restatement (Second) of Agency. Section 122(1) of the Restatement states:

> Except as stated in the caveat, the loss of capacity by the principal has the same effect upon the authority of the agent during the period of incapacity as has the principal's death.

The caveat states that

> (t)he Institute expresses no opinion as to the effect of the principal's temporary incapacity due to a mental disease.

The comments add little to defining temporary incapacity:

> (T)he agent of one who becomes mentally incompetent to act on his own account or to appoint an agent does not necessarily lose authority to act for the principal. Very brief periods of insanity caused by temporary mental or physical illness of the principal do not destroy the power of a previously appointed agent to act in his behalf. The matter is too amorphous for a statement of a definite rule.

Comment on Caveat.

In refusing to accept the Restatement as a basis for holding in a flower bond case that under New York law a power of attorney was terminated when the decedent became comatose shortly before the bonds were purchased, the Second Circuit pointed out in [*United States v. Manny*, 645 F.2d 163, 168 (2d Cir. 1981)]:

> The difficulty with the Restatement analysis is that at the time of acting the agent cannot tell whether the incapacity will be temporary or permanent. [D]ecedents could have recovered from their comatose conditions and survived. We are persuaded that the Restatement provisions are best construed as depriving agents of capacity only where the incapacity of their principals is known to be permanent from the outset; mental or physical incapacity which does not preclude

recovery should render the interim acts of the agent voidable rather than void. This reading is wholly consistent with the weight of New York cases in point and preserves the salutary principle that those temporarily unable to act for themselves should be able to benefit from favorable acts which their agents take during their incapacity.

In *Manny*, which involved two consolidated cases similar to the present case, the court held that in both cases the disability resulting from the decedent's comatose state rendered the purchase of flower bonds voidable and not void and that since the executors had not rejected the purchase by the agent, the decedent was the owner of the bonds when he died. In one of the cases the bonds were purchased 10 days after the decedent lapsed into a coma; he died 8 days after the purchase. In the other case the bonds were purchased 5 days after a stroke rendered the decedent semi-comatose, disoriented, and confused; he died 3 days after the purchase. Those two cases are strikingly similar to the present case, in which the bonds were purchased the day after Campbell became comatose, and Campbell died 24 days after the purchase.

We agree with the reasoning of *Manny* and follow it. Although *Manny* dealt with New York rather than Texas law, there is no reason to think that the two states would reach different conclusions on this issue.

The government stresses the stipulation in the present case that when Campbell suffered his stroke and became comatose, he "became permanently and irreversibly mentally incompetent, remaining so until his death." When Campbell suffered his stroke, however, his son could not then have been certain that his father's incapacity was permanent. Here, as was the case when the bonds were purchased in *Manny*, Campbell Junior, when he purchased the bond one day after his father's stroke, could not know whether incapacity would be permanent or only temporary.

The government points to a Texas statute providing that a power of attorney does not terminate upon the "disability or incompetence of the principal" if the power "contains the words 'this power of attorney shall not terminate on disability of the principal' or similar words showing the intent of the principal that the power shall not terminate on his disability." Tex. Prob. Code Ann. art. 36A (Vernon) (1980). The inference the government draws from this provision, however, that without such words the power terminates upon disability does not follow.

On its face the statute merely provides a method by which a principal may enable his agent to continue to act for him even after the principal has become disabled. The statute does not provide that without such language, the power immediately terminates if the principal becomes comatose. The government relies solely upon the language of the statute. Standing alone, this statute does not outweigh the arguments previously set forth that support the conclusion we have reached.

Thus, under Texas law, Campbell Junior's purchase of the bond for his father, like any other contract or conveyance executed on behalf of a person lacking mental capacity, was a voidable and not a void act. Upon Campbell's death, only Campbell's heirs, devisees, or personal representatives could have disaffirmed the purchase. The government would not have the power to disaffirm the flower bond purchase.

Since Campbell's estate did not repudiate the purchase and, in fact, ratified it by submitting the bond for early redemption, the purchase remained valid and enforceable. Consequently, under Texas law, Campbell was the owner of the bond at his death.

In so holding, we decide only this case, in which the bond was purchased the day after the decedent became comatose and less than 4 weeks before he died. We express no opinion on whether the result would be the same if the purchase was not made until a substantial time after the decedent became comatose, during which period a guardian could have been appointed, or if the decedent survived the purchase for an extended time.

The plaintiff is entitled to recover. Because we hold that the government is required to redeem at par the portion of the flower bond necessary to pay the estate tax, plaintiff is entitled to recover damages it suffered as a result of the government's refusal to redeem the bond. The case is remanded to the Trial Division to determine the amount of such damages.

Notes

1. The principal's loss of capacity also terminates by operation of law all power of the agent to act on behalf of the principal. Restatement § 122. As indicated in *Campbell v. United States,* incapacity raises even more questions than does death. If temporary loss of capacity does not *necessarily* terminate agency power, how does an agent know whether the incapacity is temporary or permanent? Moreover, short of a declaration by a court, the question of *when* the principal has become incapacitated is far from certain:

> [M]ental disease causing insanity has no definite boundary at which a person loses capacity. Thus, one may have capacity to make a will without having capacity to conduct an intricate business transaction. Even where there is a pronounced mental incompetency, there may be ratification of previously executed transactions during lucid intervals. The matter is too amorphous for a statement of a definite rule.

Restatement § 122 comment d.

2. What happens to the affairs of someone suffering from an extended lack of capacity, such as a coma? The traditional response is for a court to declare the person incompetent and to appoint a guardian of both the incompetent and the incompetent's estate. At common law there is no non-judicial alternative. Even though a (previously executed) general power of attorney could be invaluable in just this context, the common law rule terminates the power of attorney just when it is needed most. Here again, the result has been changed by statutory modification of the common law rule (see below).

3. In addition to the death or incapacity of the principal, a number of other occurrences will terminate by operation of law an agent's power to act on behalf of the principal: (i) the impossibility of performing the agency, Restatement § 124, and (ii) the death or incapacity of the *agent*, Restatement §§ 121, 122.

3. Statutory Responses

1. Survival of Powers under Written Powers of Attorney. Under section 4 of the Uniform Durable Power of Attorney Act (1979), the death or incapacity of a principal who has executed a *written power of attorney* does not revoke or terminate either

> (i) the *authority* of agent without knowledge of the principal's death or incapacity to act under the power of attorney *or*

(ii) the *apparent authority* of the agent as to third persons without knowledge of the principal's death or incapacity.

Note that where the third person, but not the agent, knows of the death or incapacity, we have a situation similar to that in *Robert Simpson Co. v. Godson* (discussed earlier in this chapter). The Uniform Durable Power of Attorney Act has been adopted in 27 jurisdictions.

2. General Survival of All Agency Powers. Under section 2356 of the California Civil Code (1985), both authority and apparent authority continue until the agent and third person, respectively, know of the death or incapacity of the principal.

3. Durable (General) Powers of Attorney. A majority of states have statutes authorizing *durable powers of attorney* to survive the incapacity or disability of the principal. *E.g.*, UNIF. DURABLE POWER OF ATTORNEY ACT § 2 (1984). A durable power of attorney is a written power of attorney that *expressly provides* that the power will not be affected by the subsequent disability or incapacity of the principal. *Id.* § 1.

As discussed in chapter 2, the utility of general powers of attorney is limited by problems of defining the scope of the power. Unless specifically granted by the power, an act by the agent/attorney-in-fact *outside* the ordinary course of business may not be effective.

4. Durable Health-Care Powers of Attorney. One highly uncertain question at common law is the power of an agent/attorney-in-fact to make *health-care* decisions on behalf of a comatose principal, especially decisions to refuse medical treatment, life support, or even food and water. As a part of the "Living Will" movement, many states have adopted statutes authorizing *durable health-care* powers of attorney under which a person may appoint a health-care agent to make such decisions on his or her behalf when he or she no longer has the capacity to make them. *E.g.*, TEX. CIV. PRACTICE & REMEDIES CODE §§ 135.001-135.018 (Vernon's Supp. 1992). Generally, at the time a durable health-care power of attorney is executed, the principal also executes a "Living Will"—a directive indicating his or her wishes regarding the continuance of medical treatment, life support, food, and water. *Id.* §§ 135.012.

C. Irrevocable Agencies

1. Voluntary Terminations

Lee v. O'Brien

21 Md. App. 165, 319 A.2d 614 (1974)

POWERS, Judge.

The death on 16 February 1969 of Letitia N. Lee terminated her rights as beneficiary in a farm of some 193 acres in Howard County conveyed in trust by her mother in 1914. Upon Mrs. Lee's death it became the duty of Mercantile-Safe Deposit & Trust Company, the trustee, to have the property appraised by two or more disinterested and qualified persons, and to offer it at private sale, at 90% of the appraised value, to each of Mrs. Lee's children, one by one, in the order of their age.

The four surviving children of Mrs. Lee were three daughters—Hannah Lee Sharp, Laura L. O'Brien, and Neville Lee Worthington, and one son—M. L. Dawson Lee, Jr. After the trustee made the offer to Mrs. Sharp, all four children joined in requesting the trustee to convey the property to all of them as tenants in common, each to own an undivided one fourth interest. The trustee concluded that such a conveyance would be a proper exercise of its trust responsibilities, and agreed to the request.

Simultaneously with the conveyance, the four children entered into an agreement, dated 9 July 1969, to which the trust company was also a party. The agreement was recorded with the deed among the Land Records of Howard County. Subsections 6(b) and 6(c) are as follows:

> (b) That by this agreement said parties and their respective spouses do hereby constitute, nominate and appoint Hannah Lee Sharp of Montgomery County, Maryland (one of the parties hereto) to be their true, sufficient, and lawful attorney, for them and in their name, place and stead, to grant and convey the property described in said deed of May 18, 1914, as a whole or in parcels, from time to time; and she shall have the sole right and authority to determine, when to sell and convey, to whom to sell and convey and at what price and upon what terms to sell and convey. Such sale or sales may be to such person or persons or to any body corporate, its successors and assigns as she shall determine.
>
> (c) That in the event the said Hannah Lee Sharp shall die before having disposed of all of said property in accordance with the power and authority hereby conferred upon her, the parties hereto do hereby constitute, nominate and appoint Laura L. O'Brien, of Baltimore County, State of Maryland, one of the parties hereto, to be their true, sufficient and lawful attorney to act for them, in the place and stead of the said Hannah Lee Sharp then deceased, with the same powers, duties and authority as herein conferred upon the said Hannah Lee Sharp.

The agreement provided that all expenses in connection with the transfer of title and expenses accruing on the property as a whole, such as taxes and insurance, would be borne equally by the four children, and that they would participate equally in the net proceeds derived from any sale or sales of the property.

Hannah died in December, 1971. The succeeding events, as stated in appellant's brief and agreed to by appellees as reasonably accurate and correct, were:

> [I]n June 1972, Perkins (Counsel for Laura and for Hannah's estate) forwarded to Dawson's counsel a firm contract for the purchase of the property by Urban Systems Development Corporation (USDC), which was prepared for the signatures of Dawson, Laura, George T. Sharp and the Sharp Estate as the sellers. At this time Perkins requested that Dawson indicate, among other things, whether or not the price (approximately $550,000) was acceptable. On July 13, 1972, Dawson's counsel informed Perkins that the offer was not acceptable to Dawson, and Perkins asked what counter-offer Dawson would make and consider to be an acceptable price. Dawson's counsel informed Perkins that Dawson was not desirous of making or suggesting any counter-offer, as the price was not 'in the ballpark.'
>
> By letter dated August 15, 1972, Perkins presented to Dawson's counsel a revised agreement of sale with USDC still listing Dawson individually as one of

the sellers, with the same purchase price as the initial agreement. On August 24, 1972, Dawson's counsel informed Perkins that since (the) purchase price had not changed, the offer was still unacceptable. During this conversation, Perkins made no mention of the existence of a third purported agreement of sale dated August 23, 1972. With a letter dated August 25, a copy of this Agreement was received from Perkins by Dawson's counsel by mail on August 28, 1972, which was the first knowledge of said agreement by Dawson or his counsel. This Agreement was signed by Laura individually and as attorney in fact for Dawson, by George T. Sharp individually and as Personal Representative of the Estate of Hannah. The purchase price was still the same as that set forth in the preceding proposed agreements. On August 28th, counsel for Dawson notified Perkins as counsel for all other parties 'seller' that Dawson did not believe that the agreement of August 23, 1972 was binding upon him.

In his complaint Dawson prayed that the court declare whether the designation of Laura as attorney-in-fact was terminated prior to the contract with Urban Systems and whether her execution of it was in derogation of his rights; [and] that Laura be enjoined from acting further as attorney-in-fact and Urban Systems be enjoined from acting in any manner in respect to its purported interest under the contract.

On 23 July 1973 the chancellor filed an opinion and decree declaring 'that the agreement of July 9, 1969 is a valid subsisting agreement and now in full force and effect and binding upon the Plaintiff [and entering a summary judgment in favor of the defendant].

The appeal before us was taken from that decree. In his brief appellant presents these questions: Was the power of attorney granted in the Agreement of July 9, 1969 revocable by Appellant? Has the Agreement of July 9, 1969 terminated, thus terminating the designation of Appellee, Laura L. O'Brien, as attorney in fact?

The agreement which created the agency or power of attorney in Hannah, and upon her death, in Laura, was silent both as to expiration and as to revocation. Therefore it continued in effect among the parties until lawfully terminated by breach, by action of a party, by agreement of the parties, by operation of law, or by accomplishment of its purpose.

In *Attrill v. Patterson*, 58 Md. 226 (1882), Attrill owned a majority stock interest in a corporation chartered in Louisiana to furnish gas service in New Orleans. Its franchise claims conflicted with those of the New Orleans Gas Light Company. Attrill asked Patterson to go to New Orleans to negotiate a compromise with the other company. He said, 'if there is a good negotiation effected, you shall have $50,000.00.' Patterson negotiated for a period of three to four months, but failed to effect a compromise. Attrill terminated Patterson's services, engaged counsel, and filed suit. Attrill's company prevailed in its franchise claims, after which Attrill and others, without any participation by Patterson, dictated the terms of a merger of the two companies.

Patterson sued Attrill for $50,000.00 plus interest, claiming that Attrill could not discharge him without paying him. The court said:

> It may be laid down, as a general rule, that an agent's authority to act for a principal, is always revocable at the will of the principal; and may at any time be put an end to by withdrawing the authority; unless the authority be coupled

with an interest; or has been conferred on the agent for a valuable compensation moving from him to the principal.

What constitutes an authority coupled with an interest, the decisions without exception, are agreed about. In *Hunt v. Rousmanier*, [8 Wheat. 174], Chief Justice Marshall says, it 'is an interest in the thing itself on which the power is to be exercised, and not an interest in that which is to be produced by the exercise of the power.'

The same rule is now the doctrine of all the text books.

In *Smith v. Dare*, 89 Md. 47, 42 A. 909 (1899), the owners of a farm appointed Smith as agent to attend the farm, collect rents when due, and refund same to the owners, after deducting such money as is necessary for the benefit of the farm, but 'not to advance any rents before due, except when absolutely convenient.' Smith advanced the owners more than the net rents he collected from the tenant. The owners revoked the power of attorney, and conveyed the farm to another, in trust. Smith filed suit for the appointment of a receiver to collect the rents, and apply them on account of the sums he had advanced. In discussing the nature of Smith's agency the Court of Appeals said:

> There is no implication to be found anywhere in the contract that his authority, or any part of it, was conferred upon him as a security for indebtedness due to him or thereafter to become due him from the Dares, or that he paid anything for his agency or for any of the powers that were conferred on him. This case, therefore, falls within the principles laid down in *Hunt v. Rousmanier* and in *Attrill v. Patterson*.

In *Howard v. Street*, 125 Md. 289, 93 A. 923 (1915), the Court of Appeals reaffirmed the law as stated in *Attrill v. Patterson* and *Smith v. Dare*. In *Piper v. Wells*, 175 Md. 326, 2 A.2d 28 (1938), dealing with a real estate brokerage contract, clearly not coupled with an interest, the Court of Appeals recognized the power of a principal to revoke an agency, though not necessarily the right to do so without incurring liability.

In Mechem's Law of Agency, Second ed. § 570, the author describes two kinds of interests which may be coupled with an agency to make it irrevocable. One is,

> An interest, not amounting to a property or estate in the thing itself, but still an interest in the existence of the power or authority to act with reference to it, not for the purpose of earning a commission by the exercise of the power, but because the agent has parted with value, or incurred liability, or assumed obligations, at the principal's request or with his consent, looking to the exercise of the power as the means of reimbursement, indemnity or protection.

The other is,

> An interest or estate in the thing itself, concerning which the power is to be exercised, arising from an assignment, pledge or lien created by the principal, coupled with which is the power to deal with the thing itself in order to make the assignment, pledge or lien effectual.

The author goes on to say, in § 571,

> The(y) differ from each other only in the fact that, in the latter, the agent has an estate or interest in the subject matter of the power, while in the former

his interest is rather in his right to exercise the power over the thing, in order to make it available for the security or protection contemplated.

In the facts of the case under consideration, each of the four children of Letitia N. Lee became the owner of an undivided one fourth interest in the property. The power given in the agreement to Hannah, and later to Laura, neither enhanced nor diminished the share of the agent, or of any principal. As far as Dawson was concerned, the subject matter of the power he granted to the agent was his one fourth share in the property. The agent received no interest in that subject matter. There was no valuable compensation moving from the agent to Dawson in return for which the power was conferred on the agent. There was no liability incurred, or obligation assumed by the agent which required the security of the power as a means of reimbursement, indemnity, or protection.

In short, the agreement among the four children surely created an agency, but not an agency coupled with an interest, nor one given for valuable compensation moving from the agent to the principal, nor one given to secure to the agent reimbursement for liabilities incurred or obligations assumed. The agency was not irrevocable. Restatement of Agency 2d says, in § 118:

> Authority terminates if the principal or the agent manifests to the other dissent to its continuance.

Comment b. under § 118 says:

> The principal has power to revoke and the agent has power to renounce, although doing so is in violation of a contract between the parties and although the authority is expressed to be irrevocable.

We hold that as between Dawson as the principal and Laura as the agent, Dawson revoked Laura's authority when he rejected the first contract she submitted. That rejection clearly manifested to Laura his dissent to the continuance of her sole right and authority to determine at what price and upon what terms to sell and convey Dawson's property. The filing of this suit by Dawson, asking that Laura be enjoined from acting further as his attorney in fact is, to say the least, another manifestation that he dissented to the continuance of her authority.

In our view of the law, Dawson had revoked Laura's authority to sell his share of the property, and the court erred in holding to the contrary.

Decree reversed, and remanded for passage of a decree in accordance with this opinion.

Notes

1. Because the principal entrusts the agent with the power to bind him or her, the principal generally has the power to revoke at any time the agent's power to act on his or her behalf. Even where the principal and the agent have agreed that the agency would be irrevocable, or where the exercise of the power to revoke would otherwise violate a contract between the principal and the agent, the principal retains the power to revoke at will. Restatement § 118 comment b. The principal might well be liable in *damages* for revoking the agency in violation of the contract, but the principal nevertheless could revoke the agency.

As indicated in *Lee v. O'Brien*, the only agency powers that were irrevocable *by voluntary act* were (i) powers coupled with an interest in the subject matter of the power, and (ii) powers given for consideration or as security.

2. *Powers Coupled with an Interest.* An agent's power was coupled with an interest, and thus irrevocable, only where the agent had a *separate* interest in the subject matter of the power that arose *independently* of the agency power. An interest only in the *proceeds*, or the result of the exercise of the power, was insufficient. A typical example would be a creditor with a *mortgage or other lien* on Blackacre to secure repayment of debt, and who is also given a *power to sell* Blackacre on default (without a power of sale, the creditor would have to go to court to have the mortgage foreclosed).

In *Lee v. O'Brien,* the agent and all the principals owned interests in the property, yet the court held that the power of sale was *not* irrevocable. What did the court view as the *subject matter* of the power of sale?

3. *Powers Given for Consideration or as Security*. As the opinion in *Lee v. O'Brien* indicates, a power given for consideration or as security may not be revoked by the principal's voluntary act. Restatement section 138 defines a power given as security as a power

> created in the form of an agency authority, but held for the benefit of the power holder or a third person and given to secure the performance of a duty or to protect a title, either legal or equitable, such power being given when the duty or title is created or given for consideration.

For example, if Debtor gives Creditor a power to sell Blackacre, but Creditor has no lien or other interest in Blackacre, other than the power to sell it on default, Creditor's power would *not* be coupled with an interest, but *would* be a power given for consideration or as security. Thus, Debtor could not *by voluntary act* revoke Creditor's power of sale.

Recall the circumstances under which the *Lee v. O'Brien* power of sale was given. The property was the corpus of trust of which Letitia N. Lee was the beneficiary. On the death of Letitia, the terms of the trust required the trustee to offer to sell the property serially to each of the children, starting with the oldest. Hanna was the oldest, and the trustee first offered the property to her. At that point the children agreed to take undivided interests in the property, with Hanna, and then Laura (presumably the next oldest), to have the power to sell all their shares in the property. If the *quid pro quo* for Hanna's agreement to give up her prior right to purchase the property was the agreement by the others giving her the power to sell the entire property, was the power of sale given for consideration?

2. Terminations by Death of Principal

Fidelity Bank v. Gorson

296 Pa. Super. 1, 442 A.2d 265 (1982)

CAVANAUGH, Judge.

These cases involve appeals from court orders upon petitions to open and strike judgments which were entered upon a promissory note by The Fidelity Bank against S. Marshall Gorson, The Estate of Joseph N. Gorson and Harry F. Glazer, individually and trading as Gorson Enterprises. The note was an unsecured demand note in the amount of three million dollars dated May 23, 1978. It contained a provision empowering Fidelity to confess judgment against the maker at any time before or after maturity. A confession of judgment was entered on the note on January 11, 1980. [T]he executors of the Estate of Joseph N. Gorson, who had been a maker of the note but had deceased, filed petitions to strike the judgment. The court denied the petitions.

Joseph N. Gorson was one of the makers of the judgment noted dated May 23, 1978. He died on February 4, 1979. Judgment was entered against the Estate on January 11, 1980. This appeal is from the refusal of the lower court to strike judgment on a demand note after the death of the maker. On close analysis we are unable to accept Fidelity's conclusion that the cases distinguish between situations where the right to confess judgment is contingent upon a default which occurs after the maker's death, and the right to enter judgment on a note (as here) not contingent upon a default, and that they permit the entry of judgment in the latter situation. A reading of the cases does not make such a distinction cognizable under Pennsylvania law. Rather, the cases indicate that the maker's demise terminates the warrant of attorney to confess judgment. It is true that the early case of *Webb v. Wiltbank*, 1 Clark 324, 2 Pa. L.J. 303 (1842) is cited by the lower court as support for the principle that the death of the maker does not void the warrant to confess. However, this authority is merely a brief summary of a lower court decision and in light of later pronouncements by the Pennsylvania Supreme Court is of doubtful authority.

It is also true that the validity of the "death voids warranty" principle has been questioned. In *Brennan v. Ennis*, 219 Pa. Super. 291, 280 A.2d 605 (1971), the court stated:

> Cases citing the general rule that judgment cannot be entered by confession after the maker's death have done so without discussion of any underlying rationale. And recent cases have placed possible reasons for the rule in question. *See Mid-City Federal Savings and Loan Ass'n of Phila. v. Allen*, 413 Pa. 174, 196 A.2d 294 (1964); Restatement of Agency 2d, §§ 138, 139(1)(d).

Indeed, in *Mid-City Federal* cited by the *Brennan* decision as one of the cases questioning the authority of the no entry of judgment after the maker's death line of cases, Justice Eagen wrote in a case involving mental incompetency of the maker:

> A power of attorney to confess judgment for a proper consideration is security to the creditor, is coupled with an interest and is irrevocable. The entry of the judgment is not a new act of the debtor, but is a legal result beyond his control. Lunacy will not revoke a power of attorney to confess judgment, which was valid when executed.

From this it is argued that the proper rule is that an irrevocable power which was validly granted and which requires no further occurrence to become operative does not terminate upon the grantor's death or incompetence. It is contended that while the authority in a note that permits confession of judgment after a default might expire on the death of the maker, the authority in a note which, as here, permits the entry of judgment at any time does not.

Despite the report of the early *Wiltbank* case and the question raised in *Brennan* we hold that it is the law of Pennsylvania that the death of the maker revokes the warrant to confess judgment even for the purposes of security and even if the warrant is not contingent upon a default under the obligation. In so holding we are persuaded by the following line of cases which support our conclusion.

In *Lanning v. Pawson*, 38 Pa. 480, 486 (1861), it was held that:

> It was manifestly very proper to strike off the judgment that had been entered on the warrant of attorney, on the fact being found that the defendant was dead before it was entered.

In *Stucker v. Shumaker*, 290 Pa. 348, 351, 139 A. 114 (1927), it was stated that:

> The warrant to confess lost its efficacy when the maker died.

Nor can we accept Fidelity's claim that even if the death of the maker prevents the holder from executing on the note, that entry of judgment for security purposes only is permissible. We do not find this distinction to be supported by the cases. Rather, the language of our Supreme Court is absolute. In *Strucker v. Shumaker*, the court stated "the warrant to confess lost its efficiency when the maker died."

The order of the lower court is reversed and the judgment entered in favor of Fidelity Bank against the Estate of Joseph N. Gorson, Deceased, is ordered stricken.

SPAETH, Judge, dissenting:

Professor Seavey noted in his article, Termination by Death of Proprietary Powers of Attorney, 31 Yale Law Journal 283, 286 (1921), that

> [t]he first case in the United States raising the question of the termination of [an agency] power by death of the grantor was that of *Bergen v. Bennett* in which Chancellor Kent held that a power of sale in a mortgage was a "power coupled with an interest" and was not affected by the death of the mortgagor. It was *Hunt v. Rousmanier's Administrators*, however, which proved to be the foundation of later American cases.

In *Hunt v. Rousmanier's Administrators*, 8 Wheat. 174, 5 L. Ed. 589 (1823), Rousmanier had given Hunt a power of attorney to sell certain vessels as security for the repayment of a loan. Rousmanier died insolvent without having repaid the loan. [The ships were at sea at that time. Hunt took possession of them on their return and offered the intestate's interest in them for sale. The defendants objected.] When Hunt sued to recover, Rousmanier's administrator demurred. The lower court sustained the demurrer. Although Chief Justice Marshall reversed the order of the lower court and remanded the case for argument on the issue of mutual mistake, he outlined the law of agency as applied to a power of attorney held as security for a debt:

> This instrument contains no words of conveyance or of assignment, but is a simple power to sell and convey. As the power of one man to act for another depends on the will and license of that other, the power ceases when the will, or this permission, is withdrawn. The general rule, therefore, is, that a letter of attorney may, at that time, be revoked by the party who makes it; and is revoked by his death. But this general rule, which results from the nature of the act, has sustained some modification. Where a letter of attorney forms a part of a contract, and is a security for money, or for the performance of any act which is deemed valuable, it is generally made irrevocable in terms, or if not so, is deemed irrevocable in law. Although a letter of attorney depends, from its nature, on the will

of the person making it, and may, in general, be recalled at his will, yet, if he binds himself for a consideration, in terms, or by the nature of his contract, not to change his will, the law will not permit him to change it. Rousmanier, therefore, could not, during his life, by any act of his own, have revoked this letter of attorney. But does it retain its efficacy after his death? We think it does not. We think it well settled, that a power of attorney, though irrevocable during the life of the party, becomes extinct by his death.

The legal reason of the rule is a plain one. It seems founded on the presumption that the substitute acts by virtue of the authority of his principal, existing at the time the act is performed; and on the manner in which he must execute his authority, as stated in *Coombes*' case. In that case it was resolved that "when any has authority as attorney to do any act, he ought to do it in his name who gave the authority." The reason of this resolution is obvious. The title can, regularly, pass out of the person in whom it is vested, only by a conveyance in his own name; and this cannot be executed by another for him, when it could not, in law, be executed by himself. A conveyance in the name of a person who was dead at the time, would be a manifest absurdity.

This general rule, that a power ceases with the life of the person giving it, admits of one exception. If a power be coupled with an "interest," it survives the person giving it, and may be executed after his death.

As this proposition is laid down too positively in the books to be controverted, it becomes necessary to inquire what is meant by the expression, "a power coupled with an interest." Is it an interest in the subject on which the power is to be exercised, or is it an interest in that which is produced by the exercise of the power? We hold it to be clear that the interest which can protect a power after the death of a person who creates it, must be an interest in the thing itself. In other words, the power must be engrafted on an estate in the thing.

[T]he substantial basis of the opinion of the court on this point, is found in the legal reason of the principle. The interest or title in the thing being vested in the person who gives the power, remains in him, unless it be conveyed with the power, and can pass out of him only by a regular act in his own name. The act of the substitute, therefore, which, in such a case, is the act of the principal, to be legally effectual, must be in his name, must be such an act as the principal himself would be capable of performing, and which would be valid if performed by him. Such a power necessarily ceases with the life of the person making it. But if the interest, or estate, passes with the power, and vests in the person by whom the power is to be exercised, such person acts in his own name. The estate, being in him, passes from him by a conveyance in his own name. He is no longer a substitute, acting in the place and name of another, but is a principal acting in his own name, in pursuance of powers which limit his estate. The legal reason which limits power to the life of the person giving it, exists no longer, and the rule ceases with the reason on which it is founded. The intention of the instrument may be effected without violating any legal principle.

Finding that "the power given in this case is a naked power of attorney, not coupled with an interest," the Chief Justice concluded that Hunt's interest did not survive the death of Rousmanier. Thus Hunt lost his position as a secured party despite the parties' undisputed intention to the contrary.

Since 1823, when *Hunt v. Rousmanier's Administrators* was decided, many courts "have seen the equity of the situation and have attempted to avoid the consequences of Marshall's opinion."

> The result has been great confusion: The courts are not at all clear, save in England, as to what constitutes a power coupled with an interest. In many cases the American courts have used "power coupled with an interest" as meaning a contractual power. When a square determination as to the termination of the power by death has been presented, there are a variety of holdings. Thus where a legal title to real estate is given to a power holder, it is everywhere held that the title survives. Where there is a legal lien upon real property, it would seem that the existence of the lien should be held to create an interest and make the power nonterminable. But some of the courts, finding that the power of sale can not be exercised in the name of the mortgagee, hold that the power terminates with the death of the mortgagor. Where there is less than a lien, the courts have generally held that the power does not survive upon the ground that the power can not be exercised in the name of a dead man.

Seavey, supra at 297.

This confusion is apparent in the Pennsylvania cases. While many cases accord with the majority's view, others have held the power of attorney to survive the grantor's death. In *Key's Estate*, 137 Pa. 565, 20 A. 710 (1890), Daniel Keys died after having executed a power of attorney to his sister authorizing her to collect the proceeds from a real estate sale and to keep so much of the money as necessary to repay a debt he owed her. Upholding the power, the Court stated:

> The manifest purpose of Daniel Keys was to specifically appropriate so much of his share in his brother's estate as was necessary to pay the indebtedness therein mentioned; and, to that end, he invested his sister with full authority to receive the money that was coming to him from the land that was then about being sold, and credit the same on account of that indebtedness. There is nothing in the evidence to indicate any other intention. The land referred to in that and subsequent letters is undoubtedly the same that was shortly afterwards sold under the proceedings in partition, and the money in court is part of the proceeds of that sale. What, then, was the effect of the power of attorney and accompanying letter, both of which appear to have been delivered to appellant at the same time? Without pausing to inquire what is necessary to constitute a power coupled with an interest, and wherein it differs from a specific appropriation of property, or the proceeds thereof, to the payment of a particular debt, or for any other special purposes, we are of opinion that the power of attorney and letter above quoted operated as an equitable assignment to appellant of so much of Daniel Keys's interest in the estate of his brother John as would be sufficient to pay the indebtedness of $250, and interest, specified in the letter. To that extent, appellant thereby acquired a vested right to the purchase money raised by the sale in partition, and that right was not divested by the subsequent death of Daniel Keys in April, 1887.

For cases upholding a power of attorney after the grantor's death where the grantor had delivered to the holder the property securing the debt, *see Fisher v. New York & Middle Coal Field R. & Coal Co.*, 31 Wkly. Notes Cas. 502 (1892), and *Droste's Estate*, 9 Wkly. Notes Cas. 224 (1880).

The present case is of course distinguishable from such cases. Fidelity Bank was neither equitably assigned nor given possession of specific property as security for the debt. But such requirements seem archaic. Fidelity's power of attorney was "coupled with an interest" insofar as its exercise was to benefit the holder and not the creator. Had Fidelity taken control of property sufficient to secure its three million dollar debt, it is unlikely that Gorson Enterprises could have been maintained as a going business. The effect of the majority opinion is to interfere with, if not make unavailable, a sensible commercial device.

The American Law Institute's treatment of the problem of irrevocable agency reflects such commercial considerations. Instead of defining when a power is "coupled with an interest," Restatement (Second) Agency emphasizes the concept of security. Section 138 provides:

> § 138. Definition
>
> A power given as security is a power to affect the legal relations of another, created in the form of an agency authority, but held for the benefit of the power holder or a third person and given to secure the performance of a duty or to protect a title, either legal or equitable, such power being given when the duty or title is created or given for consideration.

Section 139 defines the circumstances in which a power given as security may be terminated:

> § 139. Termination of Powers Given as Security
>
> (1) Unless otherwise agreed, a power given as security is not terminated by:
>
> (a) revocation by the creator of the power;
>
> (b) surrender by the holder of the power, if he holds for the benefit of another;
>
> (c) the loss of capacity during the lifetime of either the creator of the power or the holder of the power; or
>
> (d) the death of the holder of the power, or, if the power is given as security for a duty which does not terminate at the death of the creator of the power, by his death.
>
> (2) A power given as security is terminated by its surrender by the beneficiary, if of full capacity; or by the happening of events which, by its terms, discharges the obligations secured by it, or which makes its execution illegal or impossible.

In the Comment to Section 139 it is said:

> d. Death. If the power holder dies, a court of equity will direct the exercise of the power for the benefit of the beneficiary. If the creator of the power dies and the power is given to secure the performance of a duty not terminated by the death of the power giver, the power survives.

Among the illustrations to the Section are the following:

> 5. P sells shares in a corporation to A and delivers to A his share certificate, and a power of attorney to transfer the shares upon the books of the corporation. P dies before the shares are transferred upon the books. A's power to make the transfer is not terminated.

6. P borrows money from A and as security gives A a power, in case of P's default in payment, to collect a debt owned by T to P and to pay himself out of the proceeds. A's power to collect the debt is not affected by the death of P.

7. P borrows money from A, and as security in case of nonpayment, gives A a power of attorney to take and sell certain ships belonging to P, then at sea. P makes default in payment, and A takes possession of the ships in pursuance of the power. P dies. A can now sell the ships, notwithstanding P's death.

This formulation of the law first appeared in Preliminary Draft #54, which was issued by the American Institute of Law in 1932 (Professor Seavey acting as Reporter). The draft was accompanied by an explanatory Note to the Council, which stated:

Note to the Council: This Section is a departure from the corresponding Sections in the Second Tentative Draft (§§ 233, 234 and 235) in that it states that a power given for security is not terminated by the death of the power giver. These Sections were written in light of the case of *Hunt v. Rousmanier*, 8 Wheat. 174 [5 L. Ed. 589] (1823). The American courts have professed to follow the authority of this case but have distinguished the cases involving the point so that it may be fairly said that today in substantially all situations in which a power has been given, the death of the giver of the power does not terminate it. The only cases in which it can be said to have any remaining validity are those where the power is given in reference to land and in which the court finds that it was not intended to give either an equitable interest in the land or a lien upon it. The cases holding that the power terminates upon the death of the giver are almost all fifty years old or more, and the rule does not accord with the modern idea that one having a power in regard to something has an interest in it. It may fairly be said therefore that with the change of view in regard to the creation of an interest in things, in every case where a power of this sort is created, the rule as stated satisfies the requirement of Marshall in *Hunt v. Rousmanier*, that in order to survive a power must be coupled with an interest. The views of the Reporter upon this matter were expressed in 31 Yale Law Journal 283 (1922). The more recent case of *Mulloney v. Black*, 244 Mass. 391 [138 N.E. 584] (1923) is typical since, although citing *Hunt v. Rousmanier*, it held that a power to appropriate money due the power giver was not terminated by his death. The original sections purported to follow *Hunt v. Rousmanier* but a critical examination of them shows that their meaning is substantially similar to that of the present Section. It appears to the Reporter that it will serve the profession better to state frankly that the law as to these powers has become consistent with the law of contracts and property.

In my opinion, the American Law Institute has stated the better rule, and we should adopt it. I acknowledge that doing so would be inconsistent with some cases. But it would be consistent with others, and would bring our law up-to-date by recognizing the practical considerations of the commercial world.

As to the Estate of Joseph N. Gorson, the order of the lower court should be affirmed.

Notes

1. As stated in the extract from *Hunt v. Rousmanier's Administrators* (set forth in the *Fidelity Bank v. Gorson* dissent), at common law *only* powers coupled with an interest survived the death of the principal. Although powers given for consideration or as security could not be revoked by *voluntary act* of the principal, such powers

were revoked by the *death* of the principal unless they were *also* coupled with an interest in the subject matter.

2. The question of whether powers given for consideration or as security should survive the death of the principal is one in which the Restatement did not *restate* existing law, but tried to *reform* it. Under Restatement section 139, a power given as security *not only* is irrevocable *by voluntary act*, but *also* is not revoked by the principal's *death*, regardless of whether the power is coupled with an interest. As indicated by the extract from the Reporter's Notes (set forth in the *Fidelity Bank v. Gorson* dissent), the Reporter's position was that the common law rule had been so eroded by the willingness of courts to find equitable titles or liens in the power-holder as to retain no meaning.

Consider, for example, the case of *Chrysler v. Blozic*, 267 Mich. 497, 255 N.W. 399 (1934). Steve Blozic was insured under a group life and disability insurance policy, with Frank Blozic as his named beneficiary. Blozic came down with tuberculosis and was hospitalized in County's hospital. Blozic executed a power of attorney appointing County as his agent to collect all sums due him under his insurance policy and to apply them to repay the expenses of his hospitalization. Blozic died before a *disability claim* could be filed on his behalf. Both Frank Blozic (the named beneficiary) and the County submitted claims for the insurance benefits. Because at the time of the assignment Blozic was already entitled to disability benefits under the policy, the court held that the power of attorney amounted to a "crude" assignment of those benefits, so that it survived Blozic's death. Is *Chrysler v. Blozic* consistent with *Hunt v. Rousmanier's Administrators*?

3. As *Fidelity Bank v. Gorson* indicates, the common law rule that only powers coupled with an interest survive the death of the principal largely retains its vitality; like Mark Twain, the reports of its death have been exaggerated.

Chapter 6

Fiduciary Duties of Agents and Employees

Fiduciary relationships are not limited to trustee-beneficiary relationships. Webster's Third New International Dictionary (1971) defines a "fiduciary relation" as "the relation existing where one person reposes confidence, faith & reliance in another whose aid, advice or protection is sought in some matter." Because an agent is entrusted with the power of acting on behalf of the principal, an agency is a fiduciary relationship. Restatement § 1. Similarly, a servant is a fiduciary of the master and subject to the same duties as an agent. Restatement § 429. In addition, fiduciary relationships arise in a wide variety of other contexts. Attorneys, partners, corporate officers, and directors all act in fiduciary capacities and are subject to fiduciary duties. However, the nature and extent of the duties to which any particular fiduciary are subject are "determined by the terms of the agreement between the parties [and] interpreted in light of the circumstances." Restatement § 376.

A. Duty of Care

Maricopa Partnerships, Inc. v. Petyak

790 P.2d 279 (Ariz. App. 1989)

HATHAWAY, Judge.

Edward and Jane Doe Petyak (appellants) appeal from a judgment in the amount of $29,800 entered in favor of The Maricopa Partnerships, Inc. (appellee), following a jury verdict. The sole issue on appeal is whether the trial court's instruction on the agency theory was an incorrect statement of the law constituting reversible error.

Appellant Edward Petyak, an American Airlines pilot, was also engaged in importing and reselling luxury cars. He met with appellee in the spring of 1985. Following a discussion of specifications, they orally agreed that appellant would locate and import a new Jaguar automobile for appellee. On June 4, 1985, appellee gave appellant a $2,500 check as a down payment. The vehicle was to be imported from Europe and delivered to appellee after completion of modifications to meet U.S. regulations.

There were delays in importing the Jaguar over a six-month period of time. Appellant advised appellee of the problems and indicated it might be another three to four months before the Jaguar would arrive, if at all.

Appellant apparently advised that he had seen newspaper ads in Dallas showing Jaguars available at similar prices. It is disputed whether appellee or appellant initially suggested pursuing the Dallas ads instead of waiting to import directly from Europe. It is undisputed that appellant agreed to look into the Dallas ads on behalf of appellee.

Appellant visited the Dallas dealership, Gerimco, and found a vehicle meeting appellee's specifications. He telephoned appellee from the dealership and negotiated the price and modifications between appellee and the dealer over the phone. It was agreed at that time that the purchase price would be $29,800, including modifications. Appellee and appellant agreed that Gerimco would ship the car to appellee in Phoenix. Appellant agreed to write his personal check for the purchase price and within several days appellee delivered a check to appellant for the purchase price, less the $2,500 deposit already paid. No profit to appellant was contemplated under these terms.

Appellant's cancelled check to Gerimco for $29,800 was admitted in evidence. Appellee's testimony both on direct and cross-examination was that the dealer, Gerimco, not appellant, was to deliver the car to Phoenix. The Jaguar never arrived in Phoenix. Upon inquiry, appellant learned that the dealer absconded with the money and the Texas bank which held the lien on the Jaguar repossessed it. Appellee demanded a refund of the purchase price which appellant refused to pay. Appellee then filed suit and following a three-day trial, the case went to the jury on two theories. Under the first theory, appellee alleged breach of a sales contract. Under the second, appellee alleged that appellant breached an agency agreement. The jury was instructed on both theories. On the agency issue, the court instructed:

> In deciding that issue, you must decide the extent of the agent's duties to the principal as determined by the terms of the agreement between the parties, interpreted in the light of the circumstances under which it was made. The plaintiff has the burden of proving the terms of the agency agreement.
>
> If the agent fails to accomplish what he agreed to achieve, there is a breach [of] contractual duty and the agent is liable to the principal for actual damages caused by the breach.
>
> You are to determine the terms of the agency agreement if you find the parties had a relationship of principal and agent.

During the settling of jury instructions, appellant's counsel objected to the refusal to give an instruction stating that before the jury could find breach of an agency agreement it would have to find that the agent failed to exercise reasonable care and skill in carrying out his duties. Following deliberation, the jury returned a general verdict in favor of appellee, finding damages of $29,800.

Appellants argue that the trial court erroneously instructed the jury on the law of agency. On review, we will consider as a whole the jury instructions given to determine whether the challenged instruction misled the jury as to the proper rule of law. They contend the instructions given resulted in strict liability if the jury found any breach, regardless of the circumstances. Under the instructions given, they reason that the jury would have to find against appellants on an agency theory if it found appellee did not receive the Jaguar (an already agreed fact) because it had no instructions regarding the reasonableness of the performance rendered.

Appellee responds that the trial court simply instructed the jury that appellee had the burden of establishing the existence of the agency contract, a breach by the appellant, and the resulting damages. Further, appellee contends the law does not require proof of the elements of a negligence claim in order to prove a breach of contract claim. Appellee cites Restatement (Second) of Agency, § 379, comment a, and § 400 (1958), as support.

In the absence of prior decisions to the contrary, we will follow the Restatement of the Law whenever applicable. Agency is both a consensual and a fiduciary relationship. Restatement (Second) of Agency, [§§ 376-431]. This creates a duty upon the agent to act in good faith and according to the terms of the agency agreement. The inherent nature of the agency relationship imposes a fiduciary duty upon the agent to act according to the terms of the agency agreement. We believe that Restatement (Second) of Agency, § 377 clarifies the law regarding the present issue before us. This section states that one who makes a contract with another to perform services as an agent for him is subject to a duty to act according to his promise. Comment a indicates the agent's liability and defenses for a breach of contract are according to those stated in the Restatement of Contracts and as set forth in the Restatement (Second) of Agency at §§ 399-431. Comment b explains that

> [u]nder ordinary circumstances, the promise to act as an agent is interpreted as being a promise only to make reasonable efforts to accomplish the directed results. If so interpreted, the promisor is not liable unless he fails to make such efforts as he reasonably can.

Therefore, a threshold finding would require the jury to consider whether the agent acted reasonably in executing the duties spelled out in the agency agreement.

Appellee argues that under Restatement (Second) of Agency, § 400 controls and appellant could have asserted any contract defenses excusing his performance, but failed to do so. Appellee contends the jury was properly instructed regarding liability for breach of the agency contract.

We believe that determining whether an agent has violated a duty owed to his principal does not depend upon that agent asserting a contract defense. We note that in the illustrations cited following § 400, each example finds liability only after the agent has negligently failed to perform. We read this to mean the agent has a duty to act with reasonable care and skill.

We find the instructions to the jury deficient in not informing the jury that the agent's liability was predicated upon a finding that the agent breached its duty to act with reasonable care and skill. We reverse and remand for further proceedings consistent with this opinion.

Note

The general duty of care of a *paid agent* is easy to state:

> Unless otherwise agreed, a paid agent is subject to a duty to the principal to act with standard care and with the skill which is standard in the locality for the kind of work which [the agent] is employed to perform and, in addition, to exercise any special skill that [the agent] has.

Restatement § 479(1). The problem, of course, is in *applying* the duty of care.

One perennially controversial subject is the standard by which to measure the conduct of a fiduciary entrusted with complex matters involving discretion and judgment. What happens when the fiduciary's exercise of judgment leads to a loss? On the one hand, no fiduciary has perfect foresight and perfect knowledge; even an ordinarily skillful, competent, and careful fiduciary will make decisions that will *seem* improper in the harsh glare of hindsight. No fiduciary should be made into a *guarantor* or *insurer* of a favorable result. *See* Restatement § 379 comment c. On the other hand, if a duty of care is to have any meaningful substantive content, a fiduciary *should* be held accountable for a failure to act with ordinary skill, competence, and care.

One response to this problem is the "*business judgment rule*" applied in evaluating the decisions of a corporate officer or director:

> A director or officer who makes a business judgment in good faith fulfills his duty [of care] if:
>
> (1) he is not interested in the subject of his business judgment;
>
> (2) he is informed with respect to the subject of his business judgment to the extent he reasonably believes necessary; and
>
> (3) he rationally believes that his business judgment is in the best interests of the corporation.

AMERICAN LAW INSTITUTE, PRINCIPLES OF CORPORATE GOVERNANCE § 4.01(c) (Tent. Draft No. 11, 1991). Contrast the business judgment rule with the following proposed statement of a *partner*'s duty of care:

> A partner owes a duty of care to the partnership and the other partners to act in the conduct of the business of the partnership in a manner that does not constitute gross negligence or willful misconduct. An error in judgment or a failure to use ordinary care is not gross negligence.

Revised Uniform Partnership Act § 4.04(e) (Draft dated March 3, 1992) ("RUPA"). Does either ALI section 4.01(c) or RUPA section 4.04(e) swing the balance too far in the favor of the fiduciary?

B. Duty of Loyalty—Generally

One of the fundamental principles of agency law is the agent's or other fiduciary's duty of loyalty. Unless the principal agrees otherwise, an agent must act exclusively for the benefit of the principal in all matters connected with the agency. Restatement § 387. The fiduciary relationship is a very special one in the eyes of the law. Where a principal selects an agent, thereby placing trust and confidence in the agent's integrity and ability, the law thereafter during the term of the agency holds the agent accountable as measured against the highest standard of loyalty. Perhaps the most famous and eloquent summary of the nature of a fiduciary's duty of loyalty is by Judge Cardozo in *Meinhard v. Salmon,* 249 N.Y. 458, 164 N.E. 545 (1928):

> Joint adventurers, like copartners, owe to one another the duty of finest loyalty while the enterprise continues. Many forms of conduct permissible in a workaday world for those acting at arm's length are forbidden to those bound by fiduciary ties. Not honesty alone but the punctilio of an honor most sensitive is the standard of behavior. There has developed a tradition about this standard that is unbending and inveterate. Uncompromising rigidity has been the attitude of courts of equity.

1. Dealing with the Principal as an Adverse Party

Desfosses v. Notis

333 A.2d 83 (Me. 1975)

DELAHANTY, Justice.

The Superior Court entered a judgment of $15,377.92 in favor of plaintiff Robert Desfosses in his action for deceit and breach of fiduciary duty against defendant Steve A. Notis. The Superior Court awarded defendant a real estate broker's commission of $1,547.46 based on defendant's role in selling certain real estate to plaintiff. Defendant appeals from the judgment entered against him; plaintiff cross-appeals from the award of a broker's commission to defendant.

Plaintiff owned and operated a close corporation engaged in selling mobile homes and developing mobile home parks. In May 1969 plaintiff employed defendant, a licensed real estate broker in the State of Maine, to assist generally in the work of the company, with the special assignment of acquiring land for development as mobile home parks. From May through August 1969 defendant received a weekly salary of $125 for his work.

During May and June of 1969 plaintiff requested defendant in the course of his employment to negotiate for plaintiff the purchase of a tract of land suitable for the company to develop as a mobile home park. When defendant related that the land in question was available, plaintiff requested defendant to purchase the land as a straw man, in the course of employment, and then to convey the land to plaintiff.

During the period when defendant was negotiating for the purchase of the land, he repeatedly told plaintiff that the land would cost $32,400 although defendant knew the land could be purchased for $15,474.62. Defendant made these false statements for the purpose of inducing plaintiff to deliver to him the sum of $32,400. Relying on defendant's false statement as to the cost of the land, plaintiff delivered $32,400 to defendant, it being plaintiff's intention to deliver only the money necessary to make the purchase. On June 23, 1969, using plaintiff's money, defendant paid the owner of the land $14,474.62 to close the sale; defendant took title in his own name and promptly conveyed the land to plaintiff and plaintiff's wife. After paying out the sum necessary to complete the purchase of the land, defendant retained the balance of the $32,400 which the plaintiff had given him.

[I]t would appear that in November 1968, prior to his commencing to serve the plaintiff, defendant had entered into a separate agreement, under a bond for a deed, to purchase the land in question from its owner. Pursuant to this agreement defendant had participated in a deposit of $1,000. Thus, at the time when defendant was negotiating the purchase of the land for plaintiff, the contemplated purchase was to be achieved by effectuating defendant's own bond for a deed agreement, although defendant did not inform plaintiff of the existence or operation of the bond for a deed. Thus, the $32,400 extracted from plaintiff was applied to the sum of $14,474.62 due in order to close the bond for a deed agreement. But the actual and total price which defendant paid for the land was $15,474.62.

Defendant mainly argues that if he sold to his principal property in which he, defendant, had an ownership interest before the commencement of his agency, and if the principal chose to keep the property, the principal cannot compel the agent to refund the difference between the price paid by the principal in excess of the cost of the property to the agent. We must look to the legal relations of the parties and the duties they owed each other; then we can properly establish the extent of the remedies the law provides, and whether the conduct of the defendant warranted the relief granted by the Superior Court.

Defendant was not entitled to receive a real estate broker's commission for his role in transferring the land in question to plaintiff. Defendant never claimed such a commission as part of his case; there is no basis in the record for concluding that defendant acted as a real estate broker on behalf of any of the parties concerned. The Superior Court erred in awarding the commission gratuitously. We sustain plaintiff's cross-appeal on this issue.

On the facts as found by the Superior Court, we hold the legal relation between plaintiff and defendant to be that of principal and agent. Agency is the fiduciary relation which results from the manifestation of consent by one person to another that the other shall act on his behalf and subject to his control, and consent by the other so to act. Here, the parties agreed that the defendant was to seek out property to advance plaintiff's business purposes, the defendant's endeavors were subject to plaintiff's control and approval, and that defendant consented to act on plaintiff's behalf for the purposes of the agency, and accepted salary and other emoluments in doing so.

An agent is a fiduciary with respect to matters within the scope of his agency. Restatement (Second) of Agency § 13 (1957). No principle of law is better settled than that which requires the agent in all his dealings concerning the matter of his agency to act with utmost faith and loyalty and disclose all facts within his knowledge which bear materially upon his principal's interest. An agent acting for the purchaser of land, whether by appointment or as a volunteer, must see that he meets fairly and squarely the responsibility of his position and does not take any advantage, either for his own gain or to the injury of the person whom he represents. The agent's fiduciary duties to his principal may be broadly phrased as duties of service and obedience, and duties of loyalty. Here, plaintiff has satisfactorily established numerous breaches by defendant of his fiduciary duties, to wit: failure to fully disclose material facts; misrepresentations of matters within the scope of the agency; false inducements to obtain money from the principal; and misuse and wrongful retention of funds peculated by defendant from his principal. A fiduciary who commits a breach of his duty as fiduciary is guilty of tortious conduct and the beneficiary can obtain redress either at law or in equity for the harm done.

Here, plaintiff claims that he is damaged to the extent that defendant retained moneys given to him in excess of what was required to properly accomplish the agency. Defendant contends that plaintiff is at most entitled to a remedy in the form of recision [sic]; that plaintiff may receive back all of the money given to defendant if plaintiff will rescind the bargain and reconvey the land in question to defendant.

Even if we concede for the sake of argument that defendant's interest in the bond for a deed arrangement antedated the inception of the agency relation, we do not think plaintiff's remedy must be restricted on that account. Defendant urges that although he did not disclose his antecedent, independent interest in the land, plaintiff is without remedy unless he wants to rescind the sale altogether. The shortcoming of defendant's argument is that it fails to consider an additional aspect of the defendant's wrongful conduct, that defendant used plaintiff's money to complete defendant's own purchase of the property under the bond for a deed. Whatever the nature of defendant's antecedent interest in the property, his acquisition of the property was an indubitable incident of the agency. An agent who, in violation of his duty to his principal, uses for his own purposes or those of a third person assets of the principal's business is subject to liability to the principal for the value of the use. Restatement (Second) of Agency, § 404. If an agent has received a benefit as a result of violating his duty of loyalty, the principal is entitled to recover from him what he has so received, its value, or its proceeds, and also the amount of damage thereby caused. *Id.* § 407. Here, defendant applied his principal's assets in such a way as to obtain the land for his principal by using only a portion of the assets entrusted to him. On these facts it is unacceptable to suggest that defendant may retain his ill-gotten gains, originally entrusted to purchase the very same land. We think the above principles of the Restatement mandate a clear and decisive result. Defendant has misapplied his principal's assets, using them for his own benefit and manifestly violating his fiduciary duty of loyalty and fair dealing. He is liable to his principal for secret profits, in this case moneys wrongfully retained after the purpose of the agency was accomplished.

In simpler days, this Court has reached similar conclusions. When a principal gave an agent $80 to purchase a certain horse and instructed the agent to pay no more than the sum, and less if possible, it was held that the agent was not at liberty to make a profit for himself in the transaction. Thus, when the agent represented to his principal that the purchase had consumed the whole $80—though the agent had in fact paid only $72.50—it was further held that the sum remaining in the agent's hands was the money of his principal, which could be recovered in a proper action. *Bunker v. Miles,* 30 Me. 431, 432-33 (1849). There was no suggestion in *Bunker* that the principal was obliged to return the horse in order to recover the funds given to the agent.[1] Rather the principal was entitled to retain the benefit of the agent's acting within the scope of his agency, while also recovering the excess money which the agent had duplicitously and wrongfully arrogated.

We hold that plaintiff may retain the land and sue the agent to recover his profits, in this case money of the principal wrongfully retained by the agent. Whether plaintiff's remedy is viewed as an accounting of a fiduciary in equity or the recovery of damages at law is not material to our view of the case. On these facts, the exact and unfailing measure of plaintiff's damage is the difference between the sum entrusted to defendant, and the contract purchase price actually paid by defendant to acquire the property in his own name prior to the transfer to plaintiff in accordance with the agency relation. At that point the defendant had acquired the power to perfect his fiduciary obligation, and plaintiff is entitled to the full benefit of his agent's rightful duties. Defendant owed plaintiff a fiduciary obligation; defendant bought the land in his own name under a contract for $15,474.62; he conveyed the land to his principal, who had given him $32,400 to make the purchase. Defendant must now answer for the $16,925.38, together with interest and costs.

Appeal denied. Cross-appeal sustained.

---

1. It may be of interest to mention that according to the headnotes in the *Bunker* case, the agent had acquired a contractual interest in the horse in his own behalf before he entered into an agency relation with his principal and received his principal's funds.

Notes

1. Restatement sections 389 and 390 set forth the duties of an agent dealing with the principal as an adverse party:

§ 389. Acting as Adverse Party without Principal's Consent

Unless otherwise agreed, an agent is subject to a duty not to deal with his principal as an adverse party in a transaction connected with [the agent's] agency without the principal's knowledge.

§ 390. Acting as an Adverse Party with Principal's Consent

An agent who, to the knowledge of the principal, acts on [the agent's] own account in a transaction in which [the agent] is employed has a duty to deal fairly with the principal and to disclose to him all facts which the agent knows or should know would reasonably affect the principal's judgment, unless the principal has manifested to the agent that [the principal] knows such facts or that [the principal] does not care to know them.

2. Presumably the principal in *Desfosses* believed at the time of contracting that the land was worth $32,400. If that is so, why should the principal be entitled to keep the land *and* get a refund on thc purchase price?

2. Representing Adverse Parties or Conflicting Interests

Rogers v. Robson, Masters, Ryan, Brumund & Belom

81 Ill. 2d 201, 407 N.E.2d 47 (1980)

CHIEF JUSTICE GOLDENHERSH:

Plaintiff, James D. Rogers, M.D. appealed from the judgment of the circuit court of Will County entered in favor of defendants, Robson, Masters, Ryan, Brumund and Belom, upon allowance of their motion for summary judgment. The appellate court reversed and remanded, and we allowed defendants' petition for leave to appeal.

In plaintiff's complaint, filed pro se, it is alleged that he had been named as a party defendant in an action alleging that a post-operative wound infection was due to the negligence and carelessness of the plaintiff and his codefendants; that discovery depositions taken by defendants, the attorneys employed by plaintiff's insurance company, showed that there was no negligence on the part of plaintiff; that despite that fact and contrary to plaintiff's wishes and instructions conveyed to the defendants, a settlement was negotiated in the malpractice action. The complaint alleged damages suffered by plaintiff.

Defendants' motion for summary judgment shows that at the time of the alleged negligent acts out of which the malpractice action arose plaintiff was insured by Employer's Fire Insurance Company, and that defendants negotiated a settlement with the plaintiff in the malpractice action and, upon execution of a covenant not to sue, paid $1,250 and effected dismissal of the action as to plaintiff. The policy under which plaintiff was insured provided that the written consent of a former insured was not required before the insurer made any settlement of any claim or suit "even if such claim or suit was made, preferred or alleged while such former insured was an insured under this policy."

In an affidavit filed in opposition to the motion for summary judgment plaintiff stated that during the pendency of the malpractice action he repeatedly informed one of the partners in the defendant law firm that he would not consent to the settlement of the action, that he was assured that the action would be defended, and that at no time was he advised that defendants intended to settle the malpractice suit.

The circuit court allowed defendants' motion for summary judgment and plaintiff appealed. In reversing, the appellate court held that under the terms of the policy plaintiff's insurer was authorized to settle the medical malpractice action without plaintiff's consent. It held, however, that when defendants became aware that a settlement was imminent and that plaintiff did not wish the case settled, a conflict arose which prevented their continuing to represent both plaintiff and the insurer without a full and frank disclosure of the circumstances. The appellate court held that defendants, having continued to represent both plaintiff and the insurer without the requisite disclosure, breached their duty to plaintiff and would be liable to him for any loss caused by the lack of disclosure.

Defendants contend that they did not breach an independent duty owed to plaintiff; that because the insurer was authorized to settle the malpractice litigation without plaintiff's consent, no conflict of interest arose between the parties to the insurance contract; and that the alleged conflict upon which the majority of the appellate court rests was not argued by plaintiff. They argue, too, that plaintiff suffered no damage as a proximate result of the alleged failure to advise him of the impending settlement. *Amici curiae,* the Illinois Defense Counsel and Illinois State Bar Association, argue that the appellate court erred in implying that proof of a violation of the canons or disciplinary rules of the American Bar Association Code of Professional Responsibility established a per se basis for imposing liability on an attorney in a malpractice action.

It is plaintiff's position that the appellate court correctly reversed the circuit court judgment for the reason that there is presented a genuine issue of material fact. He argues that it was the duty of defendants to inform him of the intent to settle and that his consent to the settlement was required.

Although defendants were employed by the insurer, plaintiff, as well as the insurer, was their client and was entitled to a full disclosure of the intent to settle the litigation without his consent and contrary to his express instructions. Defendants' duty to make such disclosure stemmed from their attorney-client relationship with plaintiff and was not affected by the extent of the insurer's authority to settle without plaintiff's consent. We need not and therefore do not consider the question whether plaintiff's insurance carrier was authorized to settle the malpractice action without his consent.

Further, since no disclosure was made and plaintiff was not given the opportunity to elect what course to pursue, we need not speculate what recourse, if any, plaintiff had under the terms of the insurance policy. Nor need we reach the question whether plaintiff can prove damages which are the proximate result of the breach of the duty to make a full disclosure of the conflict between defendants' two clients. It cannot be determined from this record what damages, if any, plaintiff can prove. We decide only that this record does not preclude the possibility that some damage to plaintiff may have flowed from defendants' alleged failure to make the requisite disclosure.

The record does not show that there is no genuine issue as to any material fact and the judgment of the appellate court is affirmed.

Notes

1. During the term of the agency, an agent may not, without the informed consent of the principal, act on behalf of persons whose interests conflict with those of the principal. The agent may not act on behalf of an adverse party in a transaction connected with the agency. Restatement § 391. In addition, the agent is prohibited from acting on behalf of any third person whose interests conflict with those of the principal, even if the third person is not engaging in a transaction with the principal. Restatement § 394.

2. In *Rogers*, if the insurance company was right in its interpretation of the policy, how has the attorney damaged the client?

3. What should the attorney in *Rogers* have done when instructed by the insurance company to settle without the insured's consent?

3. Duty to Account for Profits

Cook County v. Barrett

36 Ill. App. 3d 623, 344 N.E.2d 540 (1975)

DEMPSEY, Justice.

The County of Cook filed a complaint and an amended complaint in chancery against former County Clerk, Edward J. Barrett, seeking the declaration of a constructive trust and an accounting for bribes allegedly received by him while he held office. Also named as defendants were the sureties on Barrett's official bond, the Fidelity and Deposit Company of Maryland and the United States Fidelity and Guaranty Company. The defendants filed motions to strike which were granted. In dismissing the action the chancellor ruled that:

> a cause of action of this kind, by a public body to recover a bribe or kickback paid to one of its officers or employees or agents, as a matter of law cannot be maintained.

The amended complaint was composed of three counts. The County represented that Barrett served as the elected Clerk of Cook County from 1956 through 1970, a position of trust imposing obligations to faithfully perform the duties of office in the interest of the people of Cook County and not for the incumbent's personal gain. His salary for the position was fixed by law and was to be his "only compensation for services rendered in the capacity of county clerk, or any other capacity." Throughout the period of Barrett's tenure, the County Board of Commissioners at various times purchased and rented voting machines for use in elections. The board acted on the basis of contracts and proposals submitted and recommended by Barrett. By virtue of his office and influence with the board, his recommendations were "tantamount to the acceptance" of the proposals tendered by him. During this same time, he was also charged with the responsibility to care for voting machines in County custody which included the discretion to award contracts of insurance on the machines.

Count I charged that Barrett abused his position of trust by employing it to seek secret personal gains from the Shoup Voting Machine Corporation, in that he caused Shoup "to secretly pay him money that constituted fees and/or allowances and/or bribes," as a consequence of which the County paid considerably more money for the voting machines purchased and rented from Shoup than it would have otherwise. It is alleged that these payments form Shoup to Barrett amounted to approximately $180,000 for the years 1967-1970 but were unknown for previous years and a detailed accounting was needed to determine the exact figure for the entire period covered by the complaint. The plaintiff prayed that Barrett be declared a constructive trustee for the citizens and taxpayers of the County for the amounts received by him from Shoup, and that he be required to account to the County for those sums.

Count II also prayed for a declaration of constructive trust and for an accounting, but arose from a different group of transactions. The remedy was invoked to recover secret payments received by Barrett from Arthur Gallagher & Company, an insurance agency, in connection with his award of insurance contracts on County voting machines to companies represented by Gallagher. As in the first count, it was alleged that the amount of these payments for the period 1956 to 1967 was completely unknown, that it had been approximated for 1967 to 1970 at $6,000, but that a detailed accounting was necessary to discover the exact figure by which the defendant had been unjustly enriched.

Both in that motion and in his brief on appeal, Barrett has suggested numerous reasons why the County cannot recover from him. He contends that the County is entitled only to fees and allowances which are legally collected, that to allow recovery by a public body of bribes or kickbacks paid to its officers would be against public policy; that the County alleged no damage and suffered none, that no money moved from the County to him, that if any money was paid it was paid by Shoup and Gallagher not by the County, and that since no money moved out of the County treasury it could not have been depleted; that the complaint did not allege that he had been unjustly enriched at the expense of the County or that in the absence of bribery the County would have paid less for voting machines or insurance.

A constructive trust arises not by any agreement or understanding of the parties but by operation of law and is imposed upon grounds of public policy, to prevent a person from holding for his own benefit that which he has gained by reason of a special trust or confidence reposed in him by an innocent party. Stated most succinctly, the purpose of the remedy is to prevent unjust enrichment.

The particular circumstances in which equity will impress a constructive trust are "as numberless as the modes by which property may be obtained through bad faith and unconscientious acts." The barriers to its effective operation are few. The form of the property claim determines nothing, since a constructive trust will extend to reach real and personal property, choses in action and funds of money. To make out a case a plaintiff must allege facts which disclose either actual or constructive fraud or an abuse of a confidential relationship. It is the latter situation with which this case is concerned.

At all times and for all the transactions pertinent to the complaint Barrett was the fiduciary of the people of Cook County. As an elected public official he held a position of the highest public trust. In the transactions with Shoup and Gallagher, Barrett acted as the County's agent, negotiating terms of purchase and recommending County action. An agent is fiduciary to his principal and the relation is treated generally the same, and with virtually the same strictness, as that of trustee and beneficiary.

In deciding this appeal, it is not necessary to locate the perimeters of the fiduciary obligations due the public from their elected officials. It is sufficient to recognize that, when such an official acts as agent for the public body in business transactions, he owes to his principal duties of loyalty and good faith at least equal to those required of a private fiduciary in like circumstances. The obligations of a person who occupies that latter category are such that he must not place himself in a position which is adverse to that of his principal during the continuance of the agency.

> "[A]n agent should not unite his personal and his representative characters in the same transaction; and equity will not permit him to be exposed to the temptation, or brought into a situation where his own personal interests conflict with the interests of his principal and with the duties which he owes to his principal." 3 Pomeroy's Equity Jurisprudence (5th Ed.) sec. 959, p. 819.

The remedy for breach of this duty is simple and salutary. Since a fiduciary is bound to act solely for the benefit of his principal, equity will intervene to prevent him from accruing any advantage—however innocently—from transactions conducted in behalf of the principal. So, when a fiduciary, who has acted for his beneficiary or principal, receives a gift, or bonus or commission from a party with whom he has transacted business, that benefit may be recovered from him by the beneficiary of the fiduciary relationship. In *Janes v. First Fed. Sav. & Loan Ass'n*[, 57 Ill. 2d 398, 312 N.E.2d 605,] it was alleged that the defendant lending bank procured title insurance for its borrower on mortgaged property and charged the borrower the full price of that insurance, but subsequently received and retained a ten percent rebate from the title insurance company. The reviewing court ruled that under such facts the bank held the rebate upon a constructive trust for the borrower as beneficiary in the absence of the borrower's express contrary authorization. The court quoted approvingly from the American Law Institute restatements of the law of restitution and agency. The Restatement of Restitution, section 197, states:

> Sec. 197. BONUS OR COMMISSION RECEIVED BY FIDUCIARY
>
> Where a fiduciary in violation of his duty to the beneficiary receives or retains a bonus or commission or other profit, he holds what he receives upon a constructive trust for the beneficiary.
>
> Comment a. Bribes and commissions. The rule stated in this Section is applicable not only where the fiduciary receives something in the nature of a bribe given him by a third person in order to induce him to violate his duty as fiduciary, but also where something is given to him and received by him in good faith, if it was received for an act done by him in connection with the performance of his duties as fiduciary. Thus, if a trustee, or corporate officer, or an agent entrusted with the management of property insures the property in a company of which he is an agent, and he receives from the company a commission for placing the insurance, he is accountable for the commission so received and holds it upon a constructive trust for his beneficiary.
>
> [Comment] c. Where no harm to beneficiary. The rule stated in this Section is applicable although the profit received by the fiduciary is not at the expense of the beneficiary. Thus, where an agent to purchase property for his principal acts properly in making the purchase but subsequently receives a bonus from the seller, he holds the money received upon a constructive trust for his principal. The rule stated in this Section is not based on harm done to the beneficiary in

> the particular case, but rests upon a broad principle of preventing a conflict of opposing interests in the minds of fiduciaries, whose duty is to act solely for the benefit of their beneficiaries.

The Restatement (second) of Agency, section 388, states:

> Sec. 388. DUTY TO ACCOUNT FOR PROFITS ARISING OUT OF EMPLOYMENT.
>
> Unless otherwise agreed, an agent who makes a profit in connection with transactions conducted by him on behalf of the principal is under a duty to give such profit to the principal.
>
> Comment a. Ordinarily, the agent's primary function is to make profits for the principal, and his duty to account includes accounting for any unexpected and incidental accretions whether or not received in violation of duty. Thus, an agent who, without the knowledge of the principal, receives something in connection with, or because of, a transaction conducted for the principal, has a duty to pay this to the principal even though otherwise he has acted with perfect fairness to the principal and violates no duty of loyalty in receiving the amount.

Despite the dearth of Illinois law on the subject, there is no logical reason why the remedy should not be extended to public officers in appropriate cases, the same as it would reach private trustees, employees and agents. Indeed, such application is no novelty. *United States v. Carter* (1910), 217 U.S. 286, 30 S. Ct. 515, 54 L. Ed. 769. The facts of *United States v. Carter* are especially illustrative. In that case the defendant, a captain in the Army Corps of Engineers, served as officer in charge of a vast public works project. His position carried with it large discretion, and numerous options were reserved to him as the government's agent in devising projects, drafting specifications, supervising and accepting work. It was alleged that he exercised this discretion uniformly to create profits for certain contractors at the expense of the United States and received in return secret cash payments exceeding $500,000. The Supreme Court decided that Carter had violated his fiduciary duty to the government and that he therefore held the secret payments in trust for the United States. Proof of the particular methods by which he had augmented the contractors' profits or the effectiveness of those methods was deemed immaterial to the government's case.

Barrett attempts to distinguish *Carter* as a suit in which the government paid inflated prices and traced the inflated sums into the hands of its employee, but this distinction is refuted by the court's own language:

> It is immaterial whether the complainant was able to show any specific abuse of discretion, or whether it was able to show that it had suffered any actual loss by fraud or otherwise. It would be a dangerous precedent to lay down as law that unless some affirmative fraud or loss can be shown, the agent may hold on to any secret benefit he may be able to make out of his agency. The larger interests of public justice will not tolerate, under any circumstances, that a public official shall retain any profit or advantage which he may realize through the acquirement of an interest in conflict with his fidelity as an agent.

A constructive trust is not an action for "recovery" or compensation under any theory of contract or tort. It is a strict equitable doctrine applied to cure a fiduciary's breach of his duty of loyalty by erasing the source of his conflict of interest, and transferring it to the innocent beneficiary. Bad faith is not an essential element of disloyalty and good faith is no defense to the charge. Courts are not interested in a fiduciary's particular motive for accepting a payment or gift, but rather with the general effect of such payments or gifts.

The allegations in Count I and Count II stated a cause of action for breach of a fiduciary duty and for a constructive trust, and they should not have been dismissed. The judgment is reversed and the cause is remanded.

Note

A principal whose agent has violated a fiduciary duty has a range of available remedies, including:

(1) an action to recover damages for any loss caused the principal by the breach of duty, Restatement § 401; and

(2) an action for a constructive trust on any property received by the agent in violation of the duty of loyalty, or the value or proceeds of such property, Restatement § 403; and

(3) an action to recover the value of the use of any of the principal's property used by the agent for the agent's own purposes, Restatement § 404.

C. Duty of Loyalty— Competing with the Principal

1. During the Agency Relationship

A central aspect of the duty of loyalty is the duty of an agent not to compete with the principal as to the subject matter of the agency. Restatement § 393. The duty not to compete without consent is so well understood that in most cases, the issue is not whether the duty was violated, but the appropriate measure of damages.

Monotronics Corp. v. Baylor

107 Ill. App. 3d 14, 436 N.E.2d 1062 (1982)

LINDBERG, Justice:

Monotronics Corporation, a small closely-held corporation and two principals of that corporation, John S. Archer and Howard L. Plante, brought suit against Gary D. Baylor, a third principal who had served as the corporation president. In their complaint for injunctive relief and monetary damages, plaintiff alleged (1) that Baylor had breached his fiduciary duty to the corporation by engaging in a competing business; (2) that Baylor had used the services of Monotronics employees in the conduct of his competing business without reimbursing Monotronics.

Following a bench trial, the court found that defendant had, in fact, breached his fiduciary duty to Monotronics by engaging in a competing business and entered judgment against him in the amount of $4,019, his gross profit realized from the competing venture; granted defendant's claim for $1,000 back salary.

On appeal, the plaintiffs raised four issues. These are: (1) whether the trial court properly calculated the damages awarded to plaintiffs as a result of Baylor's breach;

(2) whether as a matter of law, the finding that defendant had breached his fiduciary duty necessitated forfeiture of all compensation owing defendant for the period of the breach.

Plaintiff contends that the trial court erred in entering a judgment which fixed damages for Baylor's breach of fiduciary duty in the amount of the gross profit Baylor realized as a result of his breach. The plaintiff maintains that the Illinois Supreme Court's decision in *Vendo Company v. Stoner* (1974), 58 Ill. 2d 289, 321 N.E.2d 1, cert. denied (1975), 420 U.S. 975, 95 S. Ct. 1398, 43 L. Ed. 2d 655, requires that damages for such a breach reflect the amount of profits lost to the corporation. In *Vendo*, an employer brought suit against a former officer/director alleging a violation of fiduciary duty by virtue of that officer's efforts to develop a machine which would be competitive with the older, less satisfactory model produced by the plaintiff corporation. On appeal, it was the plaintiff-corporation's position that damages should be granted in the amount of profits which it would have realized had it owned the new machine. Defendant maintained that plaintiff could recover only those lost profits attributable to the fact that the products made by plaintiff had to compete with the new machine. The supreme court adopted the former standard, noting the existence of two "limiting factors." First, the court stated that the loss of profits is not a matter ordinarily susceptible of highly detailed direct proof. Thus the court held, inferential proof should be admissible to establish the amount of damages. The second limiting factor noted by the court is that the assessment of damages by a trial court sitting without a jury will not be set aside unless it is manifestly erroneous.

In this case we find that the ruling of the trial court was not manifestly erroneous, was supported by substantial evidence, and further, is in harmony with the ruling set forth in *Vendo Company v. Stoner*.

Plaintiffs in their brief argue that the award made by the court should include, at minimum: (1) the amount of time defendant spent on his business while being paid by Monotronics; (2) the amount of time spent by Monotronics employees in defendant's business; (3) profits earned by defendant from his competing business; and, (4) sales lost to Monotronics as a result of defendant's competing business.

Little evidence was presented on these points by the plaintiffs at trial. The record indicates that at the time when plaintiffs claim injury due to the fact that defendant was not concentrating on Monotronics business, sales rose, principally due to the efforts of Baylor, 29% in 1978 and 34% in 1979. Evidence was also adduced which indicated that Baylor was the chief sales officer and that the other principals had historically devoted their energies to nonselling activities. Plaintiffs make no references to the record which established that it suffered damages in excess of the amount of the trial court's award. Further, the trial court noted that the witnesses presented by plaintiffs were long-time employees or relatives of the plaintiffs and that their testimony indicated a fairly strong bias against and hostility toward Baylor.

Plaintiff next contends that, as a matter of law, the finding that defendant has breached his fiduciary duty must result in complete forfeiture of all compensation paid or owing to him for the time of the breach. Plaintiffs seek to have the court order disgorgement of all payments made to defendant during the period of the breach.

Plaintiffs rely principally upon *Vendo Company v. Stoner* and *ABC TransNational Transport v. Aeronautics Forwarders, Inc.* (1980), 90 Ill. App. 3d 817, 413 N.E.2d 1299, for the proposition that as a matter of law the defendant must disgorge any and all compensation paid to him during the period of the breach of his fiduciary duty. Although an order dictating full forfeiture was affirmed in that case we find no such ruling in *Vendo*. Rather, in that case the supreme court rejected arguments that the existence of an employment contract precluded such relief and that forfeiture of salary in addition to an award of lost profits resulted in an improper double recovery.

In *ABC*, the appellate court did, as plaintiff contends, overturn a trial court's attempt to "apportion" a forfeiture. In that case, the trial court ordered a defendant found to be in breach of his fiduciary duty to disgorge only one-third of the compensation paid him during the breach, in recognition of that portion of his services which were, in the court's opinion, "properly" rendered. The appellate court modified the award and forced the defendant to pay back the full amount. The court held that:

> Under the law of this State it has long been recognized that 'an agent is entitled to compensation only on a due and faithful performance of all his duties to his principal.' In applying this rule it makes no difference whether the result of the agent's conduct is injurious to the principal or not, as the misconduct of the agent affects the contract from consideration of *public policy* rather than of injury to the principal.

Plaintiffs place great weight upon this language.

We note several crucial factual distinctions between *ABC Trans National Transport v. Aeronautics Forwarders, Inc.*, and the case before us. In *ABC*, the evidence clearly established that the defendant had conspired to bring about a massive personnel walkout and customer defection to a competing firm. The court in *ABC* insisted upon full forfeiture because defendant's willful participation in a conspiracy to steal employees and accounts rendered his performance as an agent incomplete. In the instant case, the evidence supports the trial court's conclusion that Baylor continued to work diligently for the plaintiff corporation, while forming an independent company which competed to some extent with Monotronics. Further, the evidence adduced at trial tended to show that plaintiffs had acquiesced in Baylor's competitive activity. No such acquiescence was apparent in *ABC*.

Finally, and we think most importantly, the record before us establishes that the plaintiffs benefitted substantially from Baylor's performance of his duties during the period of his breach. Due primarily to his efforts, Monotronics sales rose and along with them, the incomes of the plaintiff principals. This factor was utterly lacking in *ABC*, and ritualistic application of that rule would produce an extremely harsh and unjust result in this case.

In its order, the trial court made reference to "equitable principles"which worked to prevent an order of complete forfeiture in this case. Other jurisdictions have recognized the need for flexibility in their applications of the forfeiture rule. For instance, in *Richardson v. Blue Grass Mining Co.* (E.D. Ky. 1939), 29 F. Supp. 658, aff'd (6th Cir. 1942), 127 F.2d 291, cert. denied (1942), 317 U.S. 639, 63 S. Ct. 30, 87 L. Ed. 515, the court found that the defendants had breached their fiduciary duties by diverting corporate funds and property to their own use. While acknowledging the general rule that such a breach will result in a forfeiture of the right to compensation, the court noted that the rule was not so rigid as to leave no room for the exercise of judicial discretion by a court of equity. The court refused to order full forfeiture noting that the defendants had served the corporation efficiently and had materially contributed to the success of the enterprise.

The trial court in this case was confronted with a complicated and highly acrimonious "business divorce." In addition to being supported by the evidence contained in the record, the order entered by the circuit court of DuPage County was fair and evenhanded. Accordingly, we affirm.

Notes

1. The right of Monotronics Corp. to recover Baylor's profits from competing with the principal despite the lack of demonstrable damages from the competition is largely an application of the basic principles of agency law discussed in *Desfosses v. Notis* and *Cook County v. Barrett.*

2. The more interesting question is whether the agent must "disgorge" all compensation paid during the period in which the agent was violating the duty of loyalty. Recall that the principal of a disloyal agent is entitled not only to damages for any loss caused by the disloyalty, but also to all the agent's profits from the disloyalty. If that is the case, on what basis, if any, should the agent *also* forfeit all compensation earned in the service of the principal?

2. Post-Termination Competition

Prudential Insurance Company v. Crouch

606 F. Supp. 464 (S.D. Ind. 1985)

DILLIN, District Judge.

The plaintiff, Prudential Insurance Company of America (Prudential), seeks relief in this cause of action against the defendant, Gregory M. Crouch (Crouch), in the form of a declaratory judgment, injunctive relief and damages. Prudential alleges that following Crouch's resignation from Prudential, he breached an implied covenant of good faith and breached an alleged fiduciary duty to Prudential in causing the termination of certain whole life insurance policies sold or serviced by him while a Prudential agent.

Crouch was employed by Prudential as a District Agent, selling Prudential life insurance policies exclusively, from August 9, 1974 to August 17, 1984. While a Prudential agent, Crouch developed a substantial clientele and upon his resignation, Crouch took with him a list of his client's names and addresses. This client list included Prudential policyholders whose policies were purchased through Crouch or were serviced by Crouch. Crouch returned all other property which may have belonged to Prudential at the time of his resignation.

On August 16, 1984, Crouch became a Career Agent employed by State Mutual Life Assurance Company and its wholly owned subsidiary SMA Life Assurance Company (SMA). Crouch solicited and sold insurance on behalf of SMA to his former Prudential clients. In some instances Crouch encouraged his clients to terminate their Prudential whole life insurance policies if they had a surrender value. In other instances, Crouch encouraged his clients to allow their Prudential policies to lapse by failing to pay premiums as they fell due so they could then purchase insurance through SMA.

At the time of the hearing on Prudential's motion for a preliminary injunction, Crouch had succeeded in replacing approximately fifty Prudential policies with SMA policies.

Briefly, Crouch received compensation in the form of commissions on insurance policies he sold and serviced.

Upon termination of the agent's employment with Prudential, no further commissions are paid even though premiums subsequently may be received under those policies.

Neither the Agent's Agreement nor the Collective Bargaining Agreement expressly prohibits Prudential agents from engaging in replacement activities or otherwise soliciting or selling insurance to Prudential policyholders following termination of their employment with Prudential. Crouch's Agent's Agreement contains only the following provisions respecting his duties to Prudential following termination of employment:

> Sec. 7(a) That upon termination of this Agreement either by myself or the Company, or at any other time upon request by the Company, I will immediately submit said books and records for an inspection and accounting, to be made in accordance with the rules of the Company then in force.
>
> (b) That all books, records, and supplies furnished to me by the Company shall be the property of the Company; and that, upon the termination of this Agreement, I will hand over said books, records, and supplies to a proper representative of the Company.

Although Crouch returned Prudential's property upon termination of his employment, Crouch took with him the names and addresses of his clients. Crouch's client list contained no other information except names and addresses.

Prudential makes no claim against Crouch under Section 7, above, and does not seek to enjoin Crouch from using the client list in selling additional insurance to his former Prudential clients. Rather, Prudential seeks to prevent Crouch from inducing or endeavoring to induce his former clients to cancel their Prudential policies or to allow them to lapse by nonpayment of premiums in order that Prudential policies may be replaced by other insurance policies sold by or through Crouch's employment. Prudential argues that during Crouch's employment, Crouch made an implied promise of good faith and became subject to a fiduciary duty to Prudential and that these obligations survived the termination of the employment relationship to proscribe Crouch's replacement activities.

Alternatively, Prudential relies upon the general rule of agency law that every agent owes a fiduciary duty to his principal to act with good faith and loyalty in furtherance of the principal's interests. This fiduciary duty precludes the agent from engaging in conduct dealing with the subject matter of the agency for his own benefit or in derogation of the interests of his principal. Upon termination of the agency, the fiduciary duty generally no longer applies and the former agent may compete with his former principal. Nevertheless, it is universally recognized that the agent, following termination of the agency, may not use trade secrets or other confidential information acquired during the agency in a manner which is detrimental to the principal's interests in the subject matter of the agency. Additionally, an agent is bound by his fiduciary relationship to refrain from interfering with the principal's ability to accomplish the purpose of the agency. *Trice v. Comstock*, 121 Fed. 620 (8th Cir. 1903).

This latter principle, although stated in broad language by the court in *Trice*, has been narrowly applied. The duty of an employee to a former employer must be considered alongside the common-law right of an employee to compete against his former employer. The continuing duty described in *Trice* does not abrogate the right to compete, even "steal" clients following termination of employment. Rather, the rule in *Trice* is applied only to prohibit an employee from completing transactions, which the employee negotiated during his employment, for his own benefit following termination of employment. This application of the rule in *Trice* is consistent with the law in Indiana which recognizes the right to compete against one's former employer absent contractual or statutory restrictions.

In the present case, therefore, the "purpose of the agency" must be viewed in terms of the "transactions" which Crouch was employed to complete on behalf of Prudential. Crouch was employed to sell and service insurance policies so that Prudential would receive the premiums thereunder. With respect to each insurance policy sold or serviced by Crouch, the "purpose of the agency" or the "transaction" was completed when the premium was paid to Prudential. Each sale of a new policy or renewal of an existing policy is represented by the payment of a premium and constitutes a separate transaction. Under the continuing fiduciary duty owed by Crouch to Prudential, therefore, Crouch is prohibited from negotiating any sale (either original sale or renewal) of a life insurance policy during his employment with Prudential and then completing that sale after his resignation by receiving the premium payment for his own or his new employer's benefit.

Again, consistent with the common-law right to compete against one's former employer, Crouch is otherwise free to engage in replacement activities after termination of his employment which may include inducing his former clients to allow their Prudential policies to lapse.

For the foregoing reasons, therefore, Prudential is not entitled to injunctive relief and its motion for a preliminary injunction will be denied.

Note

Fiduciary duties arise out of certain relationships, such as the agency relationship. It follows that most such duties, including most aspects of the duty of loyalty, must necessarily terminate when the relationship terminates. Thus, in *Prudential Insurance Co.*, the agent was no longer, in the absence of an agreement to the contrary, prohibited from competing with the principal. *See* Restatement § 396(a).

3. Duties with Respect to Principal's Confidential Information

ABKCO Music, Inc. v. Harrisongs Music, Ltd.

722 F.2d 988 (2d Cir. 1983)

PIERCE, Circuit Judge:

Background

A. *Events Leading to Liability Trial*

On February 10, 1971, Bright Tunes Music Corporation (Bright Tunes), then copyright holder of the song "He's So Fine," composed by Ronald Mack, brought this copyright infringement action against former member of the musical group "The Beatles" George Harrison, and also against related entities ("Harrison Interests"),[1] alleging that the Harrison composition "My Sweet Lord" ("MSL") infringed the Ronald Mack composition "He's So Fine" ("HSF").

When this action was commenced, the business affairs of The Beatles, including Harrison Interests, were handled by ABKCO Music, Inc. (ABKCO) and Allen B. Klein, its President and "moving spirit."[3] ABKCO was Harrison's business manager during the initial stages of the copyright liability action herein, at which time the litigation was handled for Harrison by ABKCO's General Counsel.

The following events preceded the instant appeal. Shortly after this action was commenced in February, 1971, Klein (representing Harrisongs Music, Inc. and George Harrison) met with Seymour Barash (President and major stockholder of Bright Tunes) to discuss possible settlement of this lawsuit.[4] Thus, in 1971, Klein was acting on behalf of Harrison Interests in an effort to settle this copyright infringement claim brought by Bright Tunes, although no settlement resulted.

Subsequent to the Klein-Barash meeting, Bright Tunes went into "judicial dissolution proceedings." This infringement action was placed on the district court's suspense calendar on March 3, 1972, and was resumed by Bright Tunes (in receivership) in early 1973. Also in early 1973 (March 31), ABKCO's management contract with The Beatles expired. Bitter and protracted litigation ensued between The Beatles and ABKCO over the winding down of management affairs—a dispute that ended in 1977 with The Beatles paying ABKCO $4.2 million in settlement.

There is some disagreement as to whether further settlement negotiations took place between Harrison Interests and Bright Tunes between 1973 and mid-1975. It appears undisputed, however, that Harrison Interests' attorney at least initiated settlement talks in the late summer of 1975; that in the period October 1975 through

1. Suit was brought against Harrisongs Music. Ltd. (Harrison's English company), Harrisongs Music, Inc. (Harrison's American company), Apple Records Inc.

3. References to "ABKCO" or to "Klein" are to include ABKCO Music, Inc., its parent ABKCO Industries, Inc., and Allen B. Klein. [ABKCO]

4. At this meeting Klein suggested purchasing the entire Bright Tunes catalogue (which included HSF) as a means of resolving the lawsuit, although apparently no precise dollar amount was mentioned. At the same time, Klein informed Barash that Harrison was unwilling to admit to copyright infringement.

February 1976, settlement discussions took place between Bright Tunes' counsel and counsel for Harrison Interests regarding settlement of this infringement action (an offer by Harrison Interests based on United States royalties); and that those discussions were in the 50%/50% or 60%/40% range. These discussions culminated in a $148,000 offer by Harrison Interests in January of 1976 (representing 40% of the United States royalties).

At about the same time (1975), apparently unknown to George Harrison, Klein had been negotiating with Bright Tunes to purchase all of Bright Tunes' stock. That such negotiations were taking place was confirmed as early as October 30, 1975, in a letter from Seymour Barash (Bright Tunes' former President) to Howard Sheldon (Bright Tunes' Receiver), in which Barash reported that there had been an offer from Klein for a substantial sum of money. The same letter observed that "[Klein] would not be interested in purchasing all of the stock of Bright Tunes if there was any doubt as to the outcome of this litigation."

In late November 1975, Klein (on behalf of ABKCO) offered to pay Bright Tunes $100,000 for a call on all Bright Tunes' stock, exercisable for an additional $160,000 upon a judicial determination as to copyright infringement. In connection with this offer, Klein furnished to Bright Tunes three schedules summarizing the following financial information concerning "My Sweet Lord:" (1) domestic royalty income of Harrisongs Music, Inc. on MSL; (2) an updated version of that first schedule; and (3) Klein's own estimated value of the copyright, including an estimate of foreign royalties (performance and mechanical) and his assessment of the total worldwide future earnings.

Barash considered the Klein offer only a starting point. He thought that a value of $600,000 was more accurate and recommended a $200,000 call, based on a $600,000 gross sales price. Also in December 1975, Barash noted, in a letter to counsel for the Peter Maurice Co., that Harrison Interests' counsel had never furnished a certified statement of worldwide royalties of MSL, but that Bright Tunes had been given that information by Klein.

Shortly thereafter, on January 19, 1976, Barash informed Howard Sheldon (Bright Tunes' Receiver) of the Klein offer and of the Bright Tunes stockholders' unanimous decision to reject it. Barash noted that "[s]ince Mr. Klein is in a position to know the true earnings of 'My Sweet Lord,' his offer should give all of us an indication of the true value of this copyright and litigation." Sheldon responded in a letter dated January 21, 1976, noting that Harrison's attorneys were informed that no settlement would be considered by Bright Tunes until total sales of MSL were determined after appropriate figures were checked.

On January 30, 1976, the eve of the liability trial, a meeting was held by Bright Tunes' attorney for all of Bright Tunes' stockholders (or their counsel) and representatives of Ronald Mack. The purpose of the meeting was to present Bright Tunes with an offer by Harrison Interests of $148,000, representing 40% of the writers' and publishers' royalties earned in the United States (but without relinquishment by Harrison of the MSL copyright). At the time, Bright Tunes' attorney regarded the offer as "a good one." The Harrison offer was not accepted, however. Bright Tunes raised its demand from 50% of the United States royalties, to 75% worldwide, plus surrender of the MSL copyright. The parties were unable to reach agreement and the matter proceeded to trial.

B. *Liability Trial and Events Thereafter*

A three-day bench trial on liability was held before Judge Owen on February 23-25, 1976. On August 31, 1976 (amended September 1, 1976), the district judge rendered a decision for the plaintiff as to liability, based on his finding that "My Sweet Lord" was substantially similar to "He's So Fine" and that Harrison had had access to the latter. The issue of damages and other relief was scheduled for trial at a later date.

Following the liability trial, Klein, still acting for ABKCO, continued to discuss with Bright Tunes the purchase of the rights to HSF. During 1977, no serious settlement discussions were held between Bright Tunes and Harrison Interests. Indeed, the record indicates that throughout 1977 Bright Tunes did not authorize its attorneys to give Harrison a specific settlement figure. By November 30, 1977, Bright Tunes' counsel noted that Klein had made an offer on behalf of ABKCO that "far exceeds any proposal that has been made by the defendants."[6]

On February 8, 1978, another settlement meeting took place, but no agreement was reached at that meeting. Although it appears that everyone present felt that the case should be settled, it also appears that there were no further settlement discussions between Harrison Interests and Bright Tunes subsequent to that date. The Bright Tunes negotiations with ABKCO, however, culminated on April 13, 1978, in a purchase by ABKCO of the HSF copyright, the United States infringement claim herein, and the worldwide rights to HSF, for $587,000, an amount more than twice the original Klein (ABKCO) offer. This purchase was made known to George Harrison by Klein himself in April or May of 1978. Harrison "was a bit amazed to find out" about the purchase.

C. *Damages Proceedings*

On July 17, 1978, ABKCO adopted Bright Tunes' complaint and was substituted as the sole party plaintiff in this action. In May 1979, Harrison Interests obtained leave to assert affirmative defenses and counterclaims against Klein and ABKCO for alleged breaches of fiduciary duty relating to the negotiation for and purchase of the Bright Tunes properties.[8] An eight-day bench trial was held on damages and counterclaims between August 27 and October 15, 1979.

The damages decision was filed on February 19, 1981. Having determined that the damages amounted to $1,599,987, the district judge held that ABKCO's conduct over the 1975-78 period limited its recovery, substantially because of the manner in

---

6. In a letter dated November 30, 1977 from Bright Tunes' counsel to the attorney for the estate of composer Ronald Mack, Tenenbaum and Sheldon, Klein's offer was set forth in detail: acquisition of the rights to HSF, including Bright Tunes' damages claim against Harrison Interests herein, in exchange for (1) payment of $150,000 to the estate of Ronald Mack (ten-year annuity of $15,000 per year); (2) payment to Bright Tunes' Receiver of $350,000 [plus an amount for legal fees].

8. Specifically, Harrison Interests alleges that the following conduct by Klein and ABKCO constituted such breaches of duty: (1) clandestine interference with Harrison Interests' settlement efforts; (2) covert furnishing of MSL financial data to Bright Tunes in connection with ABKCO's own efforts to obtain the HSF copyright; (3) covert furnishing to Bright Tunes of Klein's personal estimates of MSL financial expectations; (4) sideswitching in the present litigation; (5) use of information acquired as a fiduciary in prosecuting this action after the purchase of HSF; and (6) use of confidential information to compete with Harrison Interests and wrongful appropriation of an opportunity rightfully belonging to Harrison Interests.

which ABKCO had become a plaintiff in this case. Particularly "troublesome" to the court was "Klein's covert intrusion into the settlement negotiation picture in late 1975 and early 1976 immediately preceding the trial on the merits." 508 F. Supp. at 802. He found, *inter alia,* that Klein's status as Harrison's former business manager gave special credence to ABKCO's offers to Bright Tunes and made Bright Tunes less willing to settle with Harrison Interests either before or after the liability trial. Moreover, the court found that in the course of negotiating with Bright Tunes in 1975-76, Klein "covertly furnished" Bright Tunes with certain financial information about MSL which he obtained while in Harrison's employ as business manager. The foregoing conduct, in the court's view, amounted to a breach of ABKCO's fiduciary duty to Harrison. The court held that although it was not clear that "but for" ABKCO's conduct Harrison Interests and Bright Tunes would have settled, he found that good faith negotiations had been in progress between the parties and Klein's intrusion made their success less likely, since ABKCO's offer in January 1976 was viewed by Bright Tunes as an "insider's disclosure of the value of the case." Consequently, the district judge directed that ABKCO hold the "fruits of its acquisition" from Bright Tunes in trust for Harrison Interests, to be transferred to Harrison Interests by ABKCO upon payment by Harrison Interests of $587,000 plus interest from the date of acquisition.

ABKCO's Arguments on Appeal

[ABKCO argues on appeal that it] did not breach its fiduciary duty to Harrison because (a) no confidential information was improperly passed from ABKCO to Bright Tunes during the negotiations to purchase HSF, and (b) there was no causal relationship between ABKCO's actions and Harrison Interests' failure to obtain settlement.

A. *Breach of Fiduciary Duty*

There is no doubt but that the relationship between Harrison and ABKCO prior to the termination of the management agreement in 1973 was that of principal and agent, and that the relationship was fiduciary in nature. The rule applicable to our present inquiry is that an agent has a duty "not to use confidential knowledge acquired in his employment in competition with his principal." *Byrne v. Barrett,* 268 N.Y. 199, 206, 197 N.E. 217, 218 (1935). This duty "exists as well after the employment is terminated as during its continuance." *Id.*; *see also* Restatement (Second) of Agency § 396 (1958). On the other hand, use of information based on general business knowledge or gleaned from general business experience is not covered by the rule, and the former agent is permitted to compete with his former principal in reliance on such general publicly available information. Restatement (Second) of Agency § 395 comment b (1958). The principal issue before us is whether the district court committed clear error in concluding that Klein (hence, ABKCO) improperly used confidential information, gained as Harrison's former agent, in negotiating for the purchase of Bright Tunes' stock (including HSF) in 1975-76.

One aspect of this inquiry concerns the nature of three documents—schedules of MSL earnings—which Klein furnished to Bright Tunes in connection with the 1975-76 negotiations. Although the district judge did not make a specific finding as to whether each of these schedules was confidential, he determined that Bright Tunes at that time was not entitled to the information. It appears that the first of the three schedules may have been previously turned over to Bright Tunes by Harrison. The two additional schedules which Klein gave to Bright Tunes (the detailed updating of royalty information and Klein's personal estimate of the value of MSL and future earnings) appear not to have been made available to Bright Tunes by Harrison. Moreover, it appears that at least some of the past royalty information was confidential. The evidence presented herein is not at all convincing that the information imparted to Bright Tunes by Klein was publicly available.

Another aspect of the breach of duty issue concerns the timing and nature of Klein's entry into the negotiation picture and the manner in which he became a plaintiff in this action. In our view, the record supports the position that Bright Tunes very likely gave special credence to Klein's position as an offeror because of his status as Harrison's former business manager and prior coordinator of the defense of this lawsuit. *See, e.g.*, letter from Barash to Sheldon, dated January 19, 1976 ("Since Mr. Klein is in a position to know the true earnings of My Sweet Lord, his offer should give all of us an indication of the true value of this copyright and litigation."). To a significant extent, that favorable bargaining position necessarily was achieved because Klein, as business manager, had intimate knowledge of the financial affairs of his client. Klein himself acknowledged at trial that his offers to Bright Tunes were based, at least in part, on knowledge he had acquired as Harrison's business manager.

Under the circumstances of this case, where there was sufficient evidence to support the district judge's finding that confidential information passed hands, or, at least, was utilized in a manner inconsistent with the duty of a former fiduciary at a time when this litigation was still pending, we conclude that the district judge did not err in holding that ABKCO had breached its duty to Harrison.

We find this case analogous to those "where an employee, with the use of information acquired through his former employment relationship, completes, for his own benefit, a transaction originally undertaken on the former employer's behalf." *Group Association Plans, Inc. v. Colquhoun*, 466 F.2d 469, 474 (D.C. Cir. 1972). In this case, Klein had commenced a purchase transaction with Bright Tunes in 1971 on behalf of Harrison, which he pursued on his own account after the termination of his fiduciary relationship with Harrison. While the initial attempt to purchase Bright Tunes' catalogue was several years removed from the eventual purchase on ABKCO's own account, we are not of the view that such a fact rendered ABKCO unfettered in the later negotiations. Indeed, Klein pursued the later discussions armed with the intimate knowledge not only of Harrison's business affairs, but of the value of this lawsuit—and at a time when this action was still pending. Taking all of these circumstances together, we agree that appellant's conduct during the period 1975-78 did not meet the standard required of him as a former fiduciary.

In so concluding, we do not purport to establish a general "appearance of impropriety" rule with respect to the artist/manager relationship. That strict standard—reserved principally for the legal profession—would probably not suit the realities of the business world. The facts of this case otherwise permit the conclusion reached herein. Indeed, as Judge Owen noted in his Memorandum and Order of May 7, 1979 (permitting Harrison Interests to assert counterclaims), "The fact situation presented is novel in the extreme. Restated in simplest form, it amounts to the purchase by a business manager of a known claim against his former client where, the right to the claim having been established, all that remains to be done is to assess the monetary award." We find these facts not only novel, but unique. Indeed, the purchase, which rendered Harrison and ABKCO adversaries, occurred in the context of a lawsuit in which ABKCO had been the prior protector of Harrison's interests. Thus, although not wholly analogous to the side-switching cases involving attorneys and their former clients, this fact situation creates clear questions of impropriety. On the unique facts presented herein, we certainly cannot say that Judge Owen's findings and conclusions were clearly erroneous or not in accord with applicable law.

Appellant ABKCO also contends that even if there was a breach of duty, such breach should not limit ABKCO's recovery for copyright infringement because ABKCO's conduct did not cause the Bright Tunes/Harrison settlement negotiations to fail. Appellant urges, in essence, that a finding of breach of fiduciary duty by an agent, to be actionable, must be found to have been the proximate cause of injury to the principal. We do not accept appellant's proffered causation standard. An action for breach of fiduciary duty is a prophylactic rule intended to remove all incentive to breach—not simply to compensate for damages in the event of a breach. Having found that ABKCO's conduct constituted a breach of fiduciary duty, the district judge was not required to find a "but for" relationship between ABKCO's conduct and lack of success of Harrison Interests' settlement efforts.

[On] the facts herein, we agree that a constructive trust on the "fruits" of ABKCO's acquisition was a proper remedy.

[We] affirm, with modification,* the decisions of the district court, and remand [for further proceedings] consistent with this opinion.

Notes

1. During the term of the agency, the agent may not use or communicate confidential information belonging to the principal "in competition with or to the injury of the principal, on [the agent's] own account or on behalf of another." Restatement § 395. The agent's duty regarding confidential information—trade secrets and customer lists—is one of the few duties that survive termination of the agency relationship. Restatement § 396(b).

2. An agent may compete with the principal *after* termination of the relationship. The issue in most post-termination competition cases is whether the agent in competing used confidential information proprietary to the principal or only "general information concerning the method of business of the principal and the names of customers retained in [the agent's] memory." Restatement § 396(b).

---

* [Note by the editors.] In an omitted portion of the opinion, the court modified the scope of the constructive trust on grounds not affecting the included portion of the opinion.

Chapter 7

Liability of the Master for Acts of the Servant

A. Scope

1. Introduction

Up until now, we have focused largely on contractual issues, on the *agent's* ability to *bind* the *principal* by acts within his or her actual or apparent authority. We now turn our attention to the liability of the principal for the *incidental torts* committed by the agent in course of carrying out the agency. As a general rule, a person is *not* liable for the incidental torts of an agent *unless* (i) the agent was also a *servant* and (ii) the tortious acts were committed in the servant's *scope of employment*. Restatement § 219(1).

> A servant is defined as a person employed to perform personal service for another in his affairs, and who, in respect to his physical movements in the performance of the service is subject to the other's control or right to control, while an agent is defined as a person who represents another in contractual negotiations or transactions akin thereto. The reason assigned for the importance of making the distinction is that an agent who is not at the same time acting as servant cannot ordinarily make his principal liable for incidental negligence in connection with the means incidentally employed to accomplish the work intrusted to his care.

Stockwell v. Morris, 46 Wyo. 1, 22 P.2d 189, 191 (1933). A principal who has employed a servant is called a "*master*." Restatement § 2(1).

Where the principal has not reserved the right to control the agent's physical conduct, the agent is *not* a servant, but only an *independent contractor*, and the principal generally will not be liable for the agent's incidental torts.

This chapter focuses on the liability of the master, and of the servant, for the servant's torts.

Chapter 8 deals with independent contractors. Which agents are independent contractors, and which are servants? Chapter 8 deals at length with the many *exceptions* to the rule of employer non-liability for the torts of the independent contractor, including the doctrine of *apparent authority* or *estoppel*:

> One who represents that another is his servant *or other agent* and thereby causes a third person justifiably to rely on the care or skill of such apparent agent is subject to liability for harm caused by the lack of care or skill of the one appearing to be a servant or other agent *as if he were such*.

Restatement § 267 (emphasis added).

For example, suppose that the gasoline tank of your car is leaking, and you take the car to the mechanic at the nearby "Chevron" gasoline station. The mechanic negligently repairs the leak, and the car explodes. When you sue Chevron U.S.A., Inc., for negligence, you discover that the local "Chevron" gasoline station is owned and operated by one of your neighbors as an independent contractor. The only connection with Chevron is that the station *sells* "Chevron" brand gasoline. Assuming the car was negligently repaired, is Chevron U.S.A., Inc., liable for that negligence? In *Chevron U.S.A., Inc. v. Lesch,* 570 A.2d 840 (Md. 1990), the court held that Chevron had taken no action to induce the plaintiff to rely on the care and skill of the station owner-operator. Even though the station used the name and colors of Chevron, it was "common knowledge" that many gasoline stations are independently owned, so the plaintiff could not have reasonably believed that Chevron was endorsing the quality of anything other than the gasoline itself.

2. Related Doctrines

The basis of *respondeat superior* liability is the master's ability to *control* the servant's conduct. The existence of control is also relevant in determining whether the relationship of persons other than masters and servants is such that one should be responsible for the acts of the other. For example, suppose two persons *share* control, and one of them is negligent. Even though the *second* person is not liable for the act of the other under the doctrine *respondeat superior* (*neither* was the "master" of the other), the second may be liable under the *joint enterprise* doctrine.

For example, in *Howard v. Zimmerman*, 120 Kan. 77, 242 P. 131 (1926), the defendant was a minor. He and Orville Higbee were in the habit of taking automobile journeys together for pleasure. On a Sunday evening, they went to the defendant's father and asked together for one of his cars to take two girls automobile riding. Defendant and Higbee took turns driving. After dark, Higbee was driving too fast, and failed to see the horsedrawn buggy in which the plaintiff and his family were riding, and the two vehicles collided. Defendant was held responsible for Higbee's negligence:

> The basis of liability of one associate in a joint enterprise for the tort of another is equal privilege to control the method and means of accomplishing the common design. If the means employed is an instrumentality, the negligent use of which inflicts injury, the associate whom the law regards as participating in the actor's conduct must have had equal control over its use. This control, however, need not have extended to actual manipulation at the time injury was inflicted. It is sufficient that at the beginning of the enterprise, or as it progressed, or at any time before the tortious event, the associate possessed equal authority to prescribe conditions of use. In this instance, the enterprise was a joint one. [N]either boy was a guest of the other nor a mere passenger while the other was driving. Each had equal authority to say [where] they should go and to say [who] should drive or whether they should alternate more frequently at the wheel. Each had equal authority to decide how much time should be spent at [their destination] and when they should get back [home]. Each had equal authority over the manipulation of the instrumentality by which the undertaking was to be

accomplished and, as a matter necessarily involved, had equal authority regarding speed.

The joint enterprise doctrine originated as a plaintiff's theory. Today it is predominantly a *defendant's* theory used in automobile accident cases to impute a driver's negligence to the plaintiff passenger in the same vehicle.

Although many of the early joint enterprise cases involved social outings, such as that in *Howard v. Zimmerman*, over time courts began to limit the doctrine's application to commercial settings. *See, e.g., Shoemaker v. Whistler's Estate*, 513 S.W.2d 10 (Tex. 1974). A commercial joint enterprise is sometimes called a *joint venture*, a form of business organization similar to a partnership (see chapter 11).

B. Master's Liability for Own Negligence

Evans v. Morsell

284 Md. 160, 395 A.2d 480 (1978)

ELDRIDGE, Judge.

We issued a writ of certiorari in this case in order to consider the principles applicable to an action against an employer based upon the alleged negligent hiring or retention of an employee.

The plaintiff Joseph Evans brought this action for compensatory and punitive damages for personal injuries which he sustained as a result of being shot by a bartender in a tavern owned by the defendant. The plaintiff alleged in his declaration that he entered the defendant's establishment "as a customer and invitee," that he was acting in a peaceful manner when he was "maliciously shot with a twelve gauge shotgun" by the bartender, Jessie Hopkins, and that the defendant "knew or should have known of the vicious propensities" of his employee Hopkins because of the latter's "past record of criminal assaults." The plaintiff went on to assert that the defendant tavern owner breached his duty to the plaintiff, a customer, "by employing a person of the character of Jessie Hopkins, in a sensitive position as that of bartender, and permitting him access to a dangerous weapon." The case was tried before a jury in the Superior Court of Baltimore City, and, at the close of all of the evidence, the trial judge granted the defendant's motion for a directed verdict.

The plaintiff testified that on the evening of April 27, 1973, he entered the defendant's tavern, went to the bar, and asked the bartender Hopkins for some beer. According to plaintiff, he was refused service by the bartender, and later by the defendant owner, on the ground that previously he had allegedly brought beer into the bar from someplace else. After being denied service, the plaintiff talked a while with some other customers and then left the tavern. Later that evening, the plaintiff came back to the tavern and, as he testified:

> I was snapping my fingers to the music. When I look up the bartender is aiming a shotgun at me. So I just stood there. Then he got a wild look in his face so I threw my arm across my head and started spinning and I got hit in my arm and got hit in my stomach, and I ran to the door. When I reached for the door that's when he shot me in my upper thighs and leg.

The bartender Hopkins was later convicted of assault and sentenced to twelve years' imprisonment.

The plaintiff testified that he did nothing to provoke the bartender and that he never had any arguments with him, although Hopkins "had a few words with me the day before." The plaintiff also testified that he was a regular patron of the defendant's tavern and that he had seen Hopkins "drunk and arguing with other customers" on several occasions before this. However, he did not testify to any facts indicating that the owner was present on such occasions or had any knowledge of his employee's arguing with other customers.

The evidence further showed that the defendant had purchased the tavern in November 1972, and had hired Hopkins as a bartender in December 1972. At that time, Hopkins had a significant criminal record, with several convictions for assault—all in the 1950's and 1960's. The defendant was not aware of this, and made no inquiry of Hopkins concerning a possible criminal record.

Hopkins had worked for the prior owner of the tavern for eighteen months as a bartender. The prior owner testified that Hopkins, although he would occasionally "go on a drunk," never got drunk in the tavern, was a "good worker," was "honest" and had never assaulted anyone or had fights with anyone in the tavern. The former owner of the tavern also testified that when he sold the business to the defendant, the defendant inquired about previous employees, and the witness recommended Hopkins as a good worker and a person whom the defendant should employ. Additionally, the former owner testified that he had been in the tavern business for about ten years, that he had known other tavern owners in the area, and that there was no practice among the owners to inquire concerning the possible criminal records of persons who were applying for positions of bartenders.

The defendant testified that he had been a Baltimore City police officer for seventeen years before leaving the police force and purchasing the tavern in November 1972. While he was a police officer, he had known Mr. Hopkins and never had any difficulty with him. The defendant confirmed that before employing Hopkins, he had inquired of the former owner of the tavern, and the former owner told him that Hopkins was a "good worker." Additionally, the defendant testified that between the time that he had hired Hopkins and the shooting on April 27, 1973, he was aware of no fights with customers or any other actions by the bartender that would lead him to believe that such a shooting might take place. The defendant kept the shotgun in a back room directly behind the bar because he kept a large amount of cash on hand for check cashing purposes.

Finally, the records supervisor in the Central Records Division of the Baltimore City Police Department testified that in 1972, if an employer wanted the criminal record of an employee or prospective employee, the employer could not get it himself, but he could require the employee or prospective employee to obtain it. If he did, the Police Department would furnish the employee or prospective employee with a certified copy of his criminal record or a letter stating that he did not have a criminal record.

The plaintiff argues here, as he did below, that under circumstances such as existed in this case, the defendant breached a duty to the plaintiff by not inquiring about Hopkin's criminal record before hiring the bartender.[2]

---

2. Both in the trial court and in this Court, the plaintiff's contention has been that the

Long ago this Court recognized, prior to the enactment of the Worker's Compensation Act and in the somewhat different context of an employee injured by the alleged negligence of a drunken co-worker, that in hiring and retaining someone, an employer owes a duty to his other employees and to the general public to use reasonable care. Judge McSherry thus stated for the Court in *Norfolk and Western Railroad Co. v. Hoover*, 79 Md. 253, 262, 29 A. 994 (1894):

> But he owes to each of his servants the duty of using reasonable care and caution in the selection of competent fellow-servants, and in the retention in his service of none but those who are. If he does not perform this duty, and an injury is occasioned by the negligence of an incompetent or careless servant, the master is responsible to the injured employee, not for the mere negligent act or omission of the incompetent or careless servant, but for his own negligence in not discharging his own duty towards the injured servant. As this negligence of the master must be proved, it may be proved like any other fact, either by direct evidence or by the proof of circumstances from which its existence may, as a conclusion of fact, be fairly and reasonably inferred. That drunkenness on the part of a railroad employee renders him an incompetent servant will scarcely be disputed; nor can it be questioned *that a master who knowingly employs such a servant, or who, knowing his habits, retains him in his service, would be guilty of a reckless and wanton breach of duty, not only to the public, but to every employee in his service.*

(Emphasis supplied). The Court went on to point out that there is a rebuttable presumption that an employer uses due care in hiring an employee, and that this presumption may of course be overcome by direct or circumstantial evidence. The Court also indicated that the employer's failure to make a proper inquiry may under some circumstances constitute negligence itself.

Similar principles have been applied by the court in cases like the one at bar, involving intentional torts committed by employees or other agents upon members of the public. A critical standard here is whether the employer knew or should have known that the individual was potentially dangerous. As stated by the Supreme Court of New York, Appellate Division, in *Vanderhule v. Berinstein*, 285 App. Div. 290, 136 N.Y.S.2d 95, 100 (1954):

> The ultimate duty of the defendants, for a breach of which the defendants could be held liable, was the duty to refrain from hiring or retaining anyone whom they knew or, in the exercise of reasonable care, they should have known was potentially dangerous.

And as pointed out by the court in *Fleming v. Bronfin*, 80 A.2d 915, 917 (D.C. Mun. App. 1951):

---

defendant himself was negligent in hiring and retaining the bartender. At no time has the plaintiff suggested that the defendant might be vicariously liable under the doctrine of respondeat superior. Consequently, we do not consider such possibility, and cases dealing with the respondeat superior liability of an employer for the intentional torts of his employee committed in the scope of employment are not here applicable.

Similarly, the plaintiff has not relied upon the doctrine of negligent entrustment with respect to the shotgun, although plaintiff does point to the presence of the shotgun as one of the circumstances which allegedly imposed the duty on the defendant to inquire about the bartender's criminal record.

> One dealing with the public is bound to use reasonable care to select employees competent and fit for the work assigned to them and to refrain from retaining the services of an unfit employee. When an employer neglects this duty and as a result injury is occasioned to a third person, the employer may be liable even though the injury was brought about by the willful act of the employee beyond the scope of his employment. This principle has been applied in a variety of cases dealing with innkeepers, carriers, stores, apartment houses, and other business.

See also Restatement of Agency 2d, § 213, Comment d.[3]

Where an employee is expected to come into contact with the public, which is obviously the situation concerning a bartender, it has been held that the employer must make some reasonable inquiry before hiring or retaining the employee to ascertain his fitness, or the employer must otherwise have some basis for believing that he can rely on the employee. The nature and extent of the inquiry that is needed will naturally vary with the circumstances.

However, the majority of courts flatly reject the contention of the plaintiff in the present case, namely that where an employee is to regularly deal with the public, an inquiry into a possible criminal record is required. On the contrary, the cases hold if the employer makes adequate inquiry or otherwise has a sufficient basis to rely on the employee, there is no need to inquire about a possible criminal record.[4]

We agree with the cases holding that an employer ordinarily has no duty to inquire concerning the possible criminal record of a prospective employee. It may today be quite difficult to obtain criminal records. In addition, when one has completed a criminal sentence or has been paroled, the employer to some extent is entitled to rely upon the determination of the government's criminal justice system that the individual is ready to again become an active member of society.[5] Furthermore, it would impose a significant burden upon employers, as well as upon unemployed prospective employees, if an employer had to regularly investigate the possible criminal background of applicants for employment.

Applying the foregoing principles to the instant case, we agree with the defendant that the motion for a directed verdict was properly granted. There was no evidence whatever that the defendant knew or should have known that the bartender Hopkins was potentially dangerous. The defendant did inquire about Hopkins before employing

---

3. Although most cases dealing with negligent hiring or retention involved employees, the applicable principles appear to be the same regardless of whether the employer hires an employee or an independent contractor to deal with his customers. *Bennett v. T & F Distributing Co.*, 117 N.J. Super. 439, 285 A.2d 59 (1971).

4. Furthermore, even where the employer knows of a criminal record and still hires the employee, this does not automatically make out a prima facie case of negligent hiring. Instead, it depends upon the nature of the criminal record and the surrounding circumstances. *Argonne Apartment House Co. v. Garrison*, 59 App. D.C. 370, 42 F.2d 605, 608 (1930) (prior conviction for intoxication did not put employer on notice that the employee might be dishonest); *Strawder v. Harrall*, 251 So. 2d 514, 518 (La. App. 1971) (employer's knowledge that employee was on parole from the penitentiary was not sufficient to render it negligent to hire employee as a service station attendant); *Bradley v. Stevens*, 329 Mich. 556, 46 N.W.2d 382, 385 (1951) (knowledge by service station owner that employee was convicted of nonsupport was insufficient to put employer on notice that employee might attack female customer).

5. There are limits to this idea, however, depending upon the sensitivity of the position, the nature of the past criminal conduct, and the surrounding circumstances.

him, asking the former owner of the tavern who had been Hopkins' employer for eighteen months. The former owner recommended Hopkins to the defendant, telling him that he was a "good worker" and that he would employ him. Moreover, the defendant himself in his prior capacity as a police officer knew Hopkins as a bartender and had no difficulty with him. The only basis for a jury issue advocated by the plaintiff, both in the trial court and this Court, is the plaintiff's contention that in every case like the instant one, the employer must inquire concerning the possible criminal record of a prospective employee. However, as previously discussed, we cannot accept such a proposition.

JUDGMENT OF THE SUPERIOR COURT OF BALTIMORE CITY AFFIRMED.

Notes

1. Suppose that in *Evans v. Morsell* the owner of the bar (Morsell) had known that Hopkins had a criminal record of violent assaults. Would Morsell then have been negligent in hiring Hopkins as a bartender?

2. Assume Morsell *was* negligent in hiring Hopkins, and thus liable to Evans for Hopkins' assault. Would Morsell be liable *solely* because of Hopkins' act? Would Morsell's negligence be the *proximate cause* of Evans' injuries, given Hopkins' intentional tort?

3. In addition to exercising care in the selection of servants, the master must also exercise care in instructing, supervising, and controlling the agent. Restatement § 213.

4. As noted in *Norfolk & Western RR Co. v. Hoover* (discussed in *Evans v. Morsell*), a master negligent in employing (or retaining), supervising, or controlling an intoxicated servant may be liable for the servant's negligence or reckless conduct in the scope of the servant's employment. May the master be liable for the operation by the servant of a motor vehicle while intoxicated where the servant is *not* acting in the scope of employment? Consider the facts in the controversial case of *Clark v. Otis Engineering Corp.*, 633 S.W.2d 538 (Tex. App. 1982), *aff'd* 668 S.W.2d 307 (Tex. 1983). During the evening shift at the Otis plant, Matheson, one of Otis' workers, became too intoxicated to operate the machinery. Instead of sending Matheson to the company nursing station to sober up, Matheson's supervisor not only told Matheson to go home, he escorted Matheson to the company parking lot and poured him into his car (he did ask if Matheson could make it home). On the way home, Matheson had an accident in which Matheson and three other persons were killed. The autopsy revealed that Matheson's blood alcohol level was 0.268%. A wrongful death action was brought against Otis, alleging that it was negligent in its handling of the situation.

The trial court entered summary judgment in favor of Otis, and the Texas Court of Appeals reversed:

> In ordinary circumstances, a person has no duty to use care to control the conduct of a third person in order to prevent that person from causing harm to others unless there exists between the actor and the third person some special relation which imposes such a duty. Restatement (Second) of Torts § 315 (1965). The bare relation of employer-employee is not one which in itself imposes such a duty unless the employee is upon the employer's premises or using his chattel, and the employer has the required knowledge of ability and necessity for controlling the employee. Restatement (Second) of Torts § 317 (1965). Nevertheless,

such a relation may arise when a person takes charge of a third person whom he knows or should know is likely to cause harm to others if not controlled. Restatement (Second) of Torts § 319 (1965).

One of the earliest cases to apply this principle is *Missouri, K. & T. Ry. Co. of Texas v. Wood*, [95 Tex. 223, 66 S.W. 449 (1901),] where our Supreme Court held that a railroad company which negligently allowed an employee suffering from smallpox to escape from quarantine was liable to others who were exposed to the disease by coming into contact with him after his escape. Other cases have applied the general rule to an infirmary which negligently allowed a crazed and drunken inmate to escape from his room and injure another inmate, *University of Louisville v. Hammock*, [127 Ky. 564, 106 S.W. 219 (1907),] and where the superintendent of a state insane asylum negligently paroled an inmate who later destroyed the plaintiff's property by burning it, *Austin W. Jones Co. v. State*, [122 Me. 214, 119 A. 577 (1923)].

Otis argues that there is no evidence raising a fact issue as to whether it took or attempted to take control of Matheson on the occasion in question. Matheson was so intoxicated that he was practically helpless. His supervisor found it necessary to take him off duty before his work shift ended in order to protect him from his machine on which he was working. He was ordered to go home prior to the end of his shift, and the supervisor accompanied him to the parking lot to begin his ill-fated attempt to reach home by driving on the heavily traveled highway. Viewing these facts and the other summary judgment evidence most favorably to the appellants, we find them sufficient to raise a genuine issue of fact on the question of whether Otis, through its agents and employees, took charge or attempted to take charge of Matheson at the time of these events.

There is also sufficient summary judgment evidence raising fact issues as to negligence and proximate cause. Matheson's extreme intoxication on the occasion was well known to his supervisor and his fellow workers. They knew that he was not in a condition to drive safely. They had a nurse's station available where ill or disabled employees could be taken and cared for, yet they accompanied him to the parking lot and, it may be inferred, sent him out on the highway. Mr. Roy testified that he feared Matheson might have a collision, and when he heard of the wreck he immediately suspected that Matheson was involved. There is no summary judgment evidence that Matheson's intoxication actually caused the collision, but Otis did not attempt to negate that fact in its summary judgment motion, so if fact issues were raised on the other essential elements of the Clarks' cause of action, Otis failed to carry its burden to sustain a summary judgment.

Cases relied upon by Otis, such as *Pilgrim v. Fortune Drilling Co., Inc.*[, 653 F.2d 982 (5th Cir. 1981),] are clearly distinguishable. In *Pilgrim*, for example, where the claim of negligence was based on the employer's failure to prevent exhausted employees from driving long distances to their homes, there was no evidence of an assumption of any degree of control over the employee by the employer, there was no evidence that the employee was obviously incapacitated, the employee's work shift had terminated, and he had voluntarily left the premises.

We are not to be understood as holding that in ordinary circumstances an employer is responsible for the acts of his employees while they are off duty, off premises, and not using company facilities. The contrary is the case, even if the employer knows of a dangerous condition involving the employee. But where the employer-employee relationship exists and there is action on the part of the employer amounting to an assumption of some control over the employee who is likely to be dangerous to others, that special relation recognized by the Restatement in § 319 arises, which may in a proper case impose a duty of reasonable care and the resulting liability if that duty is breached.

The decisions have thus far applied the rule of control only where there has been a type of institutional custody of the dangerous person, but we do not believe the rule should necessarily be restricted to that type of case. Rather, we think its application should depend upon the facts of each case, evaluated upon a consideration of the defendant's ability, opportunity and duty to act, and the reasonable foreseeability of the consequences of a failure to act.

The issue is not Otis' failure to control Matheson's conduct on the highway; it is the failure to control him before he got on the highway. In fact, it may be said that appellants' case here is not merely that of a failure to exercise reasonable care to restrain Matheson; the evidence can be construed to show an element of affirmative action in Otis' sending from its premises onto a crowded highway a person so dangerous to himself and others. It has been held that when such affirmative action is involved, liability may be imposed even though there is no relationship between the defendant and the dangerous person.

Obviously, we are not holding that the evidence establishes the Clarks' cause of action. It may or may not do so in a trial of the case. We simply conclude that, viewed most favorably to their position, material issues of fact have been raised which preclude summary judgment.

The Texas Supreme Court affirmed the holding of the Court of Appeals:

[W]hen, because of an employee's incapacity, an employer exercises control over the employee, the employer has the duty to take such action as a reasonably prudent employer under the same or similar circumstances would take to prevent the employee from causing an unreasonable risk of harm to others. Such a duty may be analogized to cases in which a defendant can exercise some measure of control over a dangerous person when there is a recognizable great danger of harm to third persons. *See, e.g., Restatement (Second) of Torts, § 319.* Additionally, we adopt the rule from cases in this Restatement area that the duty of the employer is not an absolute duty to insure safety, but requires only reasonable care.

5. As noted by the *Evans v. Morsell* court (in footnote 3), the employer of an independent contractor must also exercise care in selecting, instructing, and supervising the independent contractor. *See Redinger v. Living, Inc.* in chapter 8, "Independent Contractors."

C. Master's Liability without Fault (Respondeat Superior)

Why should a master be held responsible for torts of a servant when the master was not himself or herself negligent in selecting, supervising, or controlling the servant? Consider the following extract from *Fruit v. Schreiner*, 502 P.2d 133, 139-40 (Alaska 1972):

The origins of the principle whereby an employer may be held vicariously liable for the injuries wrought by his employee are in dispute. Justice Holmes traces the concept to Roman law while Wigmore finds it to be of Germanic origin. The doctrine emerged in English law in the 17th Century. Initially a master was held liable for those acts which he commanded or to which he expressly assented. This was expanded to include acts by implied command or authority and eventually to acts within the scope of employment. The modern theory evolved with the growth of England's industry and commerce.

A truly imaginative variety of rationale have been advanced by courts and glossators in justification of this imposition of liability on employers. Among the suggestions are the employer's duty to hire and maintain a responsible staff of employees, to "control" the activities of his employees and thus to insist upon appropriate safety measures; the belief that the employer should pay for the inherent risks which result from hiring others to carry on his business; the observation that the employer most often has easier access to evidence of the facts surrounding the injury; and the metaphysical identification of the employer and employee as a single "persona" jointly liable for the injury which occurred in the context of the business.

Baty more cynically states: "In hard fact, the reason for the employers' liability is the damages are taken from a deep pocket."

The two theories which carry the greatest weight in contemporary legal thought are respectively, the "control" theory which finds liability whenever the act of the employee was committed with the implied authority, acquiescence or subsequent ratification of the employer, and the "enterprise" theory which finds liability whenever the enterprise of the employer would have benefitted by the context of the act of the employee but for the unfortunate injury.

Since we are dealing with vicarious liability, justification may not be found[ed] on theories involving the employer's personal fault such as his failure to exercise proper control over the activities of his employees or his failure to take proper precautions in firing or hiring them. Lack of care on the employer's part would subject him to direct liability without the necessity of involving respondeat superior.

1. Scope of Employment

Regardless of the *rationale* for imposing liability on the master for *some* torts of the servant, the law must identify those risks properly allocable to the master. The *scope of employment* doctrine is the primary test used to allocate the risks of servant misconduct.

Thompson v. United States

504 F. Supp. 1087 (D.S.D. 1980)

DONALD J. PORTER, District Judge.

The facts of this case are dismayingly simple. On July 12, 1975, Benjamin Kitteaux was a CETA trainee employed by the Crow Creek Sioux Tribe as a police officer. On that day, while Kitteaux was on duty, he entered the police station of the Bureau of

Indian Affairs (BIA), United States Department of the Interior, where the tribal police were headquartered, drew his gun, and pointed it at Tommy Thompson. Kitteaux then put the gun down alongside his holster, and in a simulation of a "fast draw," pulled the gun up again. This appears to have been a frequent practice of his. This time, however, the gun fired, the bullet struck Thompson in the chest, and Thompson died.

Slightly more than one month later, on August 25, 1975, Kitteaux came before this Court, and on his plea of guilty, was convicted of involuntary manslaughter.

An administrative claim for damages resulting from Thompson's death was filed with the Department of the Interior, and was denied. Thereafter, suit was filed against the United States under the Federal Tort Claims Act.

It is not enough to show that a particular individual was an employee of the United States at the time an accident occurred; a plaintiff must also show that at the time of the injury, the employee was "acting within the scope of his office or employment." This must be determined by the law of the state where the act occurred.

The law of South Dakota on this point is reasonably clear. The employer-master is liable for

> the acts of the servant, within the general scope of his employment, while engaged in his master's business, and *done with [sic] a view to the furtherance of that business and the master's interest even though the acts be done wantonly and wilfully.*

Skow v. Steele, 49 N.W.2d 24 (S.D. 1951).

In *Skow*, for example, the facts were that defendant had sent his brother onto the farm defendant rented to plaintiff to supervise the shelling of corn. Plaintiff protested, and defendant's brother assaulted plaintiff. Upholding the jury verdict against the defendant employer, the court stated that whether the assault occurred in the scope of the employee's office was an issue for the finder of fact:

> This is so because the servant's motive is usually a material issue. Thus in this case the real question presented is whether [the servant] committed the assault as a result of his desire to [carry out the master's business], or whether he assaulted plaintiff simply to effect some purpose of his own.

Can it be said that Kitteaux was acting within the scope of his employment when Thompson was killed? Kitteaux was on duty at the time, within the confines of the BIA police station, armed with his BIA-issued gun. This leaves the question of his *motive* in leveling his gun at Thompson, which *Skow* indicates is particularly one for the finder of fact. To reach a determination of this matter, one must consider the context in which the act took place.

Kitteaux was a recently hired police trainee. As a part of his training as a policeman, he was given firearms training by a Special Agent of the FBI, David Powers. This training includes, as Powers testified, extensive instruction of "quick draw." Given this background, and the circumstances with which Kitteaux was surrounded on the day the shooting occurred, the Court must draw the inference that, though tragically misguided, Kitteaux's motive in pulling his gun up and pointing it at Thompson was to practice and perfect his police firearms techniques. In this unfortunate way, Kitteaux evidently intended to improve himself as a policeman, and to thereby carry out his employer's business. It could not be contended that if a similar accident had occurred on a firearms range, in the course of firearms practice by a government employee, the United States would not be liable. Simply because the situs of the practice is moved from a range to the interior of a BIA police station, the result is not changed.

Defendant complains that such behavior was strictly forbidden. Whether it was forbidden or not does not allow defendant to escape liability, for the law is plain that an "act may be within the scope of employment even though forbidden or done in a forbidden manner." As Prosser said, if a master could escape liability by ordering his servant to act carefully, few employers could ever be held liable.

> If the other factors involved indicate that the forbidden conduct is merely the servant's own way of accomplishing an authorized purpose, the master cannot escape responsibility no matter how specific, detailed and emphatic his orders may have been to the contrary.

Prosser, Torts, 461 (4th ed. 1971). As made clear before, Kitteaux's "practice" on Thompson was Kitteaux's way of perfecting his mastery of his gun, a goal which Power's testimony shows was highly desired, even if Kitteaux's way of doing it may have been forbidden. It is thus the ruling of this Court that the shooting which took Tommy Thompson's life occurred in the scope of Benjamin Kitteaux's office as a federal employee.

[This Court therefore holds that defendant is liable in the amount of $35,000 for pecuniary damages resulting from this death.]

Notes

1. Restatement section 228 sets forth the general test for determining whether a servant's act is within the scope of employment:

> (1) Conduct of a servant is within the scope of employment if, *but only if*:
>
> (a) it is of the kind he is employed to perform;
>
> (b) it occurs substantially within the authorized time and space limits;
>
> (c) it is actuated, *at least in part,* by a purpose to serve the master; and
>
> (d) if force is used by the servant against another, the use of force is *not un*expectable by the master.
>
> (2) Conduct of a servant is not within the scope of employment if it is different in kind from that authorized, far beyond the authorized time or space limits, or *too little actuated* by a purpose to serve the master.

(emphasis added). Restatement section 229 elaborates on the general test as follows:

> (1) To be within the scope of the employment, conduct must be of the same general nature as that authorized, or incidental to the conduct authorized.
>
> (2) In determining whether or not the conduct, *although not authorized,* is nevertheless so similar to or incidental to the conduct authorized as to be within the scope of employment, the following matters of fact are to be considered:
>
> (a) whether or not the act is one commonly done by such servants;
>
> (b) the time, place and purpose of the act;

(c) the previous relations between the master and the servant;

(d) the extent to which the business of the master is apportioned between different servants;

(e) whether or not the act is outside the enterprise of the master or, if within the enterprise, has not been entrusted to the servant; . . .

(i) the extent of departure from the normal method of accomplishing an authorized result; and

(j) whether or not the act is seriously criminal.

(emphasis added).

2. In *Thompson v. United States,* Kitteaux was not motivated *solely* by a desire to serve the master. Why did that not make any difference in the result? Should it have?

3. Servants have considerable leeway before their acts will be considered outside the scope of employment. Some of the cases refer to those deviations from the "straight and narrow" that do *not* take the servant outside the scope of employment as "mere *detours*." Similarly, where the servant's conduct is "different in kind from that authorized, far beyond the authorized time and place limits, or too little actuated by a purpose to serve the master," Restatement § 228(2), and thus *outside* the scope of employment, the courts characterize the conduct as involving a "frolic." Students should be careful to note that "detour" and "frolic" are only *labels* attached to *conclusions* that the servant's conduct is, or is not, within the scope of employment; they are *not substitutes* for analysis.

4. In *Thompson v. United States,* the government was held liable *despite* the fact that Kitteaux violated an *express policy* prohibiting police officers from drawing their weapons in the station house. *Accord* Restatement § 230 ("An act, although forbidden, or done in a forbidden manner, may be within the scope of employment."). If masters cannot limit their *respondeat superior* exposure by exercising care in instructing and supervising their servants, is there *any* way they can limit their liability in respondeat superior?

Henderson v. AT&T Information Systems

552 A.2d 935 (Md. App. 1989)

KARWACKI, Judge.

On October 17, 1986, appellant Michael E. Henderson filed a complaint against Daniel Zuckerman seeking damages for injuries arising out of a January 11, 1986 motor vehicle accident. His original complaint was amended on December 18, 1986 to assert that Zuckerman's employer, AT&T Information Systems, Inc. (AT&T), the appellee, was vicariously liable for Zuckerman's negligence. Carmen Crews, a passenger in Henderson's vehicle at the time of the accident, intervened in the action as a co-plaintiff on June 22, 1987 and joins Henderson as an appellant in the case before this Court.

At the hearing on the summary judgment motion, Judge Ward ruled, as a matter of law, that AT&T's employee, Zuckerman, was not acting within the scope of his employment at the time of the motor vehicle accident and, therefore, that AT&T was not vicariously liable.

Since this is an appeal from an order granting appellee summary judgment, we shall review the evidence before the hearing judge in a light most favorable to the appellants and resolve all inferences from that evidence in their favor.

In the early afternoon of January 11, 1986, the appellants were traveling in a southbound direction on Interstate Route 95 (JFK Highway). Due to the abrupt loss of a wheel the 1979 Dodge van in which they were traveling came to a complete stop in the center southbound lane of the highway. Henderson exited the vehicle to search for the wheel, while Crews remained in the van. While Henderson was looking in the rear of the vehicle for emergency flares to display, he and the disabled van were struck from behind by an automobile which Zuckerman was driving in a southbound direction on I-95. As a result of the accident Henderson sustained severe injuries including the loss of both legs.

Mr. Zuckerman was en route from New Jersey to Virginia at the time of the accident. He owned the 1976 AMC Hornet he was operating.

Zuckerman became employed by AT&T in March of 1985. Under the terms of his employment, Zuckerman was to work at appellee's Homdel, New Jersey location, as a software engineer, until the fall of 1985 when he was to participate in AT&T's Graduate Study Program, One Year on Campus (OYOC). As a participant in the OYOC program, Zuckerman would become a full time resident student at an approved graduate institution for one year. Zuckerman was given a list of AT&T approved colleges from which to choose in applying for graduate school. Zuckerman ultimately decided to attend the University of Virginia. Mr. Ritacco, Zuckerman's supervisor at AT&T, approved Zuckerman's selection and agreed that Zuckerman would begin his studies in January of 1986.

AT&T, pursuant to the OYOC program, advanced 100% of all tuition and fees for Zuckerman's course of study at the University of Virginia. Zuckerman was compensated at 60% of his regular salary while attending school. In the event Zuckerman did not complete his course of study he was subject to termination of employment by AT&T. If he successfully completed his course of study at the University of Virginia, Zuckerman would receive a salary increase from AT&T when he returned to work, reflecting his additional education.

Zuckerman worked at AT&T's Homdel location through Friday, January 10, 1986. He left New Jersey to drive to Charlottesville, Virginia on Saturday, January 11, 1986. Classes began on Tuesday, January 14, 1986. Zuckerman elected to drive his own vehicle and was being reimbursed 21 cents per mile by AT&T. Zuckerman had the option of flying, or taking any mode of transportation he chose, to get to the University of Virginia. Zuckerman's household belongings were relocated at AT&T's expense.

In AT&T's OYOC Relocation Policy Manual specific rules were set out for the reimbursement of travel expenses. The maximum reimbursable mileage from Homdel to Charlottesville was estimated at 320 miles and Zuckerman was allowed one day to make the trip. AT&T would pay for three meals and one night's lodging for this trip. If Zuckerman chose to deviate from this guideline, he would not be reimbursed for any additional expenses. Zuckerman was required to fill out an en route trip expense log for submission to AT&T.

Under the doctrine of respondeat superior, an employer is vicariously liable for the negligent acts of its employee if those acts are committed within the scope of employment. To be within the scope of employment the conduct of the employee must be

> of a kind the actor is employed to perform, occur during a period not unreasonably disconnected from the authorized period of employment, in a locality not unreasonably distant from the authorized area, and actuated at least in part by a purpose to serve the master.

A. & P. Co. v. Noppenberger, 171 Md. 378, 390, 189 A. 434 (1937), quoting the Restatement (Second) of Agency § 229 (1958). In short, the test for determining if an employee is acting within the scope of employment is "whether the servant was advancing his master's interests in doing what he did at the time he did it." *Rusnack v. Giant Food, Inc.*, 26 Md. App. 250, 261-65, 337 A.2d 445 (1975), *cert. denied*, 275 Md. 755 (1975).

In *Henkelmann v. Metropolitan Life Insurance Co.*, 180 Md. 591, 599, 26 A.2d 418 (1942), the Court of Appeals discussed respondeat superior liability with respect to the use of automobiles. The Court stated:

> In recent years, on account of the extensive use of the motor vehicle with its accompanying dangers, the courts have realized that a strict application of the doctrine of respondeat superior in the modern commercial world would result in great injustice. It is now held by the great weight of authority that a master will not be held responsible for negligent operation of a servant's automobile, even though engaged at the time in furthering the master's business unless the master expressly or impliedly consents to the use of the automobile, and had the right to control the servant in its operation, or else the use of the automobile was of such vital importance in furthering the master's business that his control over it might reasonably be inferred.

In *Henkelmann*, the employee was an insurance salesman who was involved in an automobile accident on his way, in his own vehicle, to his assigned "territory." A car was not necessary to the performance of his duties and the employer had never consented to or authorized the use of a personal vehicle either to travel to or from the assigned area or while working within it. The Court of Appeals held that the insurance company was not vicariously liable for the negligence of its salesman under these circumstances.

The general rule is that, absent special circumstances, an employer will not be vicariously liable for the negligent conduct of his employee occurring while the employee is traveling to or from work. It is essentially the employee's own responsibility to get to and from work. Restatement (Second) of Agency § 229, comment d (1958). Appellants recognize this general rule but argue that it is not applicable to the instant case. Zuckerman, they contend, was not merely traveling to work on January 11, 1986; he was relocating at the specific direction of AT&T. Appellants argue that there was sufficient evidence of AT&T's consent to the use of Zuckerman's personal automobile and AT&T's control of the operation of the automobile to create vicarious liability for its employee's negligent operation of said automobile. The hearing judge disagreed and held that *Dhanraj v. Potomac Electric Power Co.*, [305 Md. 623, 506 A.2d 224 (1986)] was dispositive.

In *Dhanraj*, a PEPCO employee, while driving his own vehicle, was involved in an automobile accident while traveling to an employer endorsed six-week training located some distance from both his home and from his ordinary work place. The employee was given a travel allowance in order to attend these classes, but was not told what means of transportation to utilize. Further, the employee was not compensated for his travel time. His work day began when he reached the training facility and ended when he departed. The plaintiff sued PEPCO, alleging respondeat superior liability. The hearing judge entered summary judgment in favor of PEPCO; we affirmed, as did the Court of Appeals. In upholding the summary judgment, the Court of Appeals concluded that:

> [I]f Sandy [PEPCO's employee] was negligent as alleged, PEPCO was not vicariously liable for his tortious conduct under the doctrine of respondeat superior. PEPCO did not expressly or impliedly consent to the use of the automobile; it had no right to control Sandy in its operation, and the use of the automobile was not of such vital importance in furthering PEPCO's business that the control over it might reasonably be inferred.

Appellants attempt to distinguish *Dhanraj* from the instant case, asserting that:

1. AT&T required Zuckerman to drive his personal vehicle to the University of Virginia.
2. AT&T consented to Zuckerman's use of his personal vehicle as the means of transportation to the University of Virginia.
3. AT&T specifically controlled the use of Zuckerman's vehicle during his trip to the University of Virginia.
4. AT&T considered and recognized Zuckerman's injuries as having been incurred on a company related business trip and paid Zuckerman full benefits and salary during the time he was recuperating.

We are not persuaded.

Appellants contend that AT&T required Zuckerman to drive his own vehicle to graduate school. They suggest that since the OYOC Policy Manual stated that AT&T would not pay for the relocation of Zuckerman's automobile, he was required to drive it to Virginia. We do not agree. In several letters addressed to Mr. Zuckerman and in various provisions of the OYOC policy Manual, it is clearly stated that Zuckerman was entitled to choose his manner of transportation to Virginia. He would be reimbursed for "air or surface transportation" whichever he chose. When Zuckerman visited the University of Virginia in November of 1985, for an "exploratory trip," he flew to Charlottesville at AT&T's expense.

Whereas it seems that Zuckerman reviewed the OYOC Manual and discussed his travel plans with his supervisor, Mr. Ritacco, the final decision to drive to Virginia was his. While it did not matter to AT&T if Zuckerman had the use of his car at school, it obviously benefitted Zuckerman to have his own vehicle for transportation while living away from home for a year.

Appellants next attempt to distinguish *Dhanraj* from the instant case on the basis of consent. In *Dhanraj* the employee was given a travel allowance to use however he chose to do so. Here, since Zuckerman was given a specific amount of money per mile, appellants argue that AT&T knew he was driving and consented to the use of his personal automobile. Appellants cite *Regal Laundry Co. v. Abell Co.*, 163 Md. 525, 163 A. 845 (1933) as dispositive of this issue.

The tort-feasor in *Regal* was a newspaper reporter who was assigned to cover a political campaign. The accident in question occurred while the reporter was en route, in his own vehicle, from a political event in Salisbury, which he covered for the newspaper, to his office in Baltimore, where he was to receive further assignments. The Court of Appeals reversed a judgment, entered upon a directed verdict in favor of the newspaper, on the ground that the employer knew the reporter was using his own automobile in carrying out assignments and agreed to reimburse him for that expense. *Regal* was distinguished, by this Court, from the facts in *Dhanraj* because the newspaper employee was "on the job" at the time of the accident. It was his regular job to travel from place to place to cover newsworthy events. Such was not the situation in *Dhanraj* and is not in the instant case.

In *L.M.T. Steel Products v. Peirson*, 47 Md. App. 633, 425 A.2d 242 (1981), cert. denied, 290 Md. 717 (1981), an employee was driving his vehicle, during working hours, from a job site to a telephone booth to make a job related telephone call when the accident occurred. The jury's verdict against the employer was upheld. This Court agreed that the evidence was legally sufficient to show the employer's implied consent to the use of the automobile in furtherance of its interests. Later, in distinguishing *L.M.T. Steel Products v. Peirson*, we stated that

> unlike the incident in the case sub judice, the happening in L.M.T. occurred while the employee was en route on a clear business purpose during working hours.

Zuckerman was not "on the job" at the time of the accident. Further, he was not hired by AT&T for a position that required any amount of driving. This was a one time journey which Zuckerman agreed to make at his convenience, on a Saturday morning. Unlike the PEPCO employee in *Dhanraj*, Zuckerman was a salaried employee. That does not mean, however, that Zuckerman was being compensated for his time traveling to Virginia. While at graduate school Zuckerman was to be paid to pursue a course of study which hopefully would benefit AT&T in the future. That was the business purpose Zuckerman was executing, not driving his car for the benefit of AT&T.

Assuming arguendo that AT&T impliedly or expressly consented to the use by Zuckerman of his personal automobile, Henderson's argument fails the *Henkelmann* and *Dhanraj* tests on the basis of control. As stated supra, for an employer to be liable for its employee's negligence in an automobile accident, the employer must have had

> the right to control the servant in its [the vehicle's] operation, or else the use of the automobile was of such vital importance in furthering the master's business that his control over it might reasonably be inferred.

Appellants argue that AT&T specifically controlled Zuckerman's use of his car by requiring him to follow the most direct route from New Jersey to Virginia. This contention is not borne out by Zuckerman's deposition testimony upon which appellants rely. When questioned about his route to Virginia, Zuckerman replied,

> the mileage had been established for me and I was following a route which most people by looking at a map would follow. If you draw a line, that's roughly how you go.

The fact that Zuckerman was given a specified amount for reimbursable mileage does not mean that AT&T required him to travel a certain route. Zuckerman could have taken any route he chose and would have been reimbursed the same amount by AT&T.

Last, appellants contend that AT&T should be held vicariously liable since it considered Zuckerman's accident an "on the job" injury and paid him salary and benefits while he was recuperating. Here, appellants confuse questions of scope of employment for purposes of workers' compensation with those pertaining to third party negligence actions. In *Dhanraj v. Potomac Elec. Power Co.*, the Court of Appeals refused to resort to cases construing the Workers' Compensation Act to determine the applicability of the doctrine of respondeat superior to the facts in that case. Likewise in other jurisdictions it has been held that the analysis of scope of employment for workers' compensation purposes is not apposite to the analysis of scope of employment for establishing liability under respondeat superior.

In *Dinkins* [*v. Farley*, 434 N.Y.S.2d 325, 329, 106 Misc. 2d 593 (1980)], an employee of Xerox Corporation was driving a borrowed car to night school graduate courses when he was involved in an accident. The employee was attending night school pursuant to a tuition aid program provided by Xerox. The plaintiff sued the driver of the automobile (the student-employee), the vehicle owner and Xerox. In granting Xerox summary judgment, the court stated:

> If Xerox could be held liable in this case under respondeat superior, other circumstances come to mind which would also appear to impose liability upon it. For example, if Victor Farley [employee] carelessly handled volatile materials in a chemistry class and another student were injured or property were destroyed, Xerox could be held responsible. If Xerox is responsible for what an employee does on his way to class, why would it not be equally responsible for what an employee does in class? Or, if educational sabbaticals funded by scholarship grants under the same aid program were encouraged by Xerox, it could be responsible for injuries caused by one of its employees during such a sabbatical driving to or from class at a university hundreds of miles away from the plant.

Further, in discussing whether a workers' compensation analysis should be applied the court held:

> To obtain compensation benefits all that an employee need do is establish that his injury was caused by an activity related to his job. However, respondeat superior mandates that the employee be either under the control of the employer at the time of the injury or that he could have been. Whereas qualifying for workers' compensation benefits requires only that the injury occur out of and in the course of employment, recovery under the doctrine of respondeat superior necessitates that the employee be acting in the scope of his employment, a much narrower test.

We hold that whether Zuckerman was paid workers' compensation benefits for the injuries he suffered in the accident is immaterial to the issue of AT&T's vicarious liability for his negligence.

JUDGMENT AFFIRMED.

Notes

1. One exception to the rule of master non-liability for the torts of servants traveling to and from work is the so-called "*special errand*" rule. Where the servant performs a "special errand" on behalf of the master that would otherwise have required a separate trip by another servant, the servant will be deemed to be acting within the scope of employment (why?). *E.g., Faul v. Jelco*, 122 Ariz. 490, 595 P.2d 1035 (1979) (facts not sufficient to invoke special errand exception).

2. In *Henderson v. AT&T Information Systems,* the court distinguished between the respondeat superior concept of *scope* of employment and the *workers' compensation* concept of *course* of employment, and refused to apply workers' compensation cases in a respondeat superior context. Why?

3. Where the servant is employed at a job site *remote* from his or her regular residence, the question of the master's responsibility for the servant's negligent torts while traveling to and from work becomes especially acute. The majority of courts that have considered this issue have applied the basic "coming & going" rationale as articulated in *Henderson v. AT&T Information Systems*: (i) the servant is furthering his or her own interests (the servant's personal arrangements do not concern the master); and (ii) the master still has no express or implied control over the servant's conduct. *E.g., Faul v. Jelco, Inc.,* 122 Ariz. 490, 595 P.2d 1035 (1979); *Pilgrim v. Fortune Drilling*, 653 F.2d 982 (5th Cir. 1981).

In *Hinman v. Westinghouse Electric Co.,* 2 Cal. 3d 956, 88 Cal. Rptr. 188, 471 P.2d 988 (1970), the California Supreme Court held the master liable where the master had not only compensated the employee for travel expenses, but also for travel *time.* Although the fact that the master is paying for the servant for his or her time while commuting may imply that the master has the right to *control* the servant's conduct while commuting, *see Luth v. Rogers & Babler Construction Co.,* 507 P.2d 761 (Alaska 1973), the California Supreme Court did not primarily rely on that. Instead, the court reasoned that the master, by *benefiting* from distant labor markets, had *increased the risk* to the public, so should bear the cost of resulting injuries. In so doing, the court changed the California justification for respondeat superior from a *control* theory to an *enterprise liability* theory.

4. Under Restatement section 239

> [a] master is not liable for injuries caused by the negligence of a servant in the use of an instrumentality which [is] of a substantially different kind from that authorized as a means of performing the master's service, or over the use of which the master is to have no right of control.

Is Restatement section 239 consistent with the principles embodied in Restatement sections 228 and 229? On what basis should the master avoid liability under the circumstances described in Restatement section 239?

Sage Club v. Hunt

638 P.2d 161 (Wyo. 1981)

BROWN, Justice.

Appellant, The Sage Club, appeals a judgment entered against it in a lawsuit arising out of an altercation between a bartender employed at the club, Mr. Thyfault, and a customer, appellee David Leland Hunt. The trial court entered a default judgment against Mr. Thyfault and held The Sage Club liable under the theories of respondeat superior and negligence in continuing to employ Mr. Thyfault. Appellant asserts that it cannot be held liable for the intentional tort of its employee because the tort was personal to Mr. Thyfault and was not within the scope of employment.

A dispute took place over money which appellee had left on the bar. Appellee thought that someone, supposedly Thyfault, had taken more money than he was entitled to take for his drinks. Mr. Thyfault undoubtedly resented the insinuation, so he jumped over the bar and attacked appellee. Thyfault hit appellee in the face, breaking his nose and inflicting other bruises, and then threw appellee down the stairs, reinjuring his back.

This court has held that an employer may be held liable for the negligent acts of an employee acting within the scope of employment. We have not, however, had occasion to rule on whether an employer may be held responsible for the intentional tort of an employee. The majority rule, in fact the universally accepted rule, holds employers liable for the intentional torts of employees committed within the scope of employment. Prosser, Law of Torts, § 70, p. 464 (4th ed., 1971). The rule is a matter of economic and social policy, based both on the fact that the employer has the right to control the employee's actions and that the employer can best bear the loss as a cost of doing business. The Restatement (Second), Agency 2d § 245 (1958), phrases the rule as:

> A master is subject to liability for the intended tortious harm by a servant to the person or things of another by an act done in connection with the servant's employment, although the act was unauthorized, if the act was not unexpectable in view of the duties of the servant.

We agree with the accepted rule and hold that an employer may be held liable for the intentional tort of an employee if the employee is acting within the scope of employment.

Appellant here contends that Mr. Thyfault was not acting within the scope of employment because the altercation which took place was a personal one between Thyfault and appellee. The question of whether an employee is acting within the scope of employment is one for the trier of fact, in this case the trial court, and becomes a question of law when only one reasonable inference can be drawn about the question from the evidence. We think the evidence here was sufficient to show that Thyfault was acting within the scope of employment when he attacked appellee. We said in *Combined Insurance Co. of America v. Sinclair*, [584 P.2d 1034, 1041 (Wyo. 1978),] that in general the servant's conduct is within the scope of his employment,

> if it is of the kind which he was employed to perform, occurs substantially within the authorized limit of time and space, and is actuated, at least in part, by a purpose to serve the master,

citing Prosser, Law of Torts, p. 461 (4th ed.). Here, Mr. Thyfault's duties included collecting money for drinks, and he lost his temper over that matter. His duties also included keeping order in the bar and removing disruptive customers, which Thyfault apparently tried to do by pushing appellee down the stairs.

Appellant relies on *Lombardy v. Stees*, 132 Colo. 570, 290 P.2d 1110 (1956), for the proposition that since the assault was purely personal, it was not within the scope of employment. In that case, however, the evidence showed that the only express instruction to the bartender was that if anyone got too much to drink he was not to be served further. The bartender there had no authority to act as a bouncer; Thyfault did, and his employment was of such a nature as to contemplate the use of force. Indeed, the owner of The Sage Club testified that Thyfault sometimes had to remove people from the club on a daily basis.

In addition to the facts set out in *Combined Insurance Co. of America v. Sinclair*, an important factor in deciding a principal's liability for his agent's intentional torts is whether "the use of force is not unexpectable by the master." Restatement (Second), Agency 2d § 228(1)(d) (1958). Where the nature of the employment is such that the master must contemplate the use of force by the servant, the master will be held liable for the willful act of the servant even though he had no knowledge that the act would take place. The employer need not have foreseen the precise act or exact manner of injury as long as the general type of conduct may have been reasonably expected. Some who frequent grogshops are not the most docile members of society. Where an employee is serving in this type of environment as a bartender, the master is usually responsible if the employee loses his temper and willfully injures a patron because the result is foreseeable in view of the servant's job.

This court will therefore not indulge in nice distinctions to determine whether the excessive force was motivated by personal reasons. It is appellant's misfortune to have hired a quarrelsome and violent bartender who in turn attacked a plaintiff experienced at collecting on injury claims. Appellant evidently allowed Thyfault to use force at his discretion, and he was performing work of the kind he was employed to perform. The assault occurred within the authorized limits of time and space and was motivated, at least partially, by a desire to serve the Sage Club. Appellant is consequently vicariously liable to Mr. Hunt under the doctrine of respondeat superior.

Affirmed.

Notes

1. Under Restatement section 245, intentional torts are not *per se* outside the scope of employment, so long as the tort was "not unexpectable" in view of the servant's duties. Is that the same as saying the tort must have been expectable, that is, *foreseeable*?

2. The case of *Manning v. Grimsley*, 643 F.2d 20 (1st Cir. 1981), involved an intentional tort committed during a professional baseball game at Fenway Park in Boston between the Baltimore Orioles and the Boston Red Sox. Ross Grimsley, a Baltimore pitcher, was warming up in the right field bullpen. Some spectators, including the plaintiff, were seated behind a wire mesh fence in bleachers next to the bullpen. The spectators continuously heckled Grimsley. Several times Grimsley looked directly at the hecklers. Later, Grimsley's catcher left his catching position and was walking over to the bench. Grimsley faced the bleachers and wound up or stretched as though to pitch in the direction of the bullpen plate, but threw the ball at more than 80 miles an hour directly toward the hecklers in the bleachers. The ball passed through the wire mesh fence and hit the plaintiff.

The trial court's directed verdict in favor of Baltimore was reversed on appeal. The appellate court held that Grimsley's intentional tort was within the scope of his employment:

> [W]here a plaintiff seeks to recover damages from an employer for injuries resulting from an employee's assault [w]hat must be shown is that the employee's assault was in response to the plaintiff's *conduct* which was *presently interfering with the employee's ability to perform his duties successfully*. This interference may be in the form of an *affirmative attempt to prevent an employee from carrying out his assignments*.

Miller v. Federated Department Stores, Inc., 364 Mass. 340, 349-350, 304 N.E.2d 573 (1973). (Emphasis added.)

The Baltimore [Orioles contend] that the heckling from the bleachers constituted words which annoyed or insulted Grimsley and did not constitute "conduct" and that those words did not "presently" interfere with his ability to perform his duties successfully so as to make his employer liable for his assault in response thereto.

Our analysis of the *Miller* case leads us to reject the contention. There a porter, whose duties consisted of cleaning the floors and emptying the trash cars in Filene's basement store, slapped a customer who had annoyed or insulted him by a remark that "If you would say 'excuse me,' people could get out of your way." The Massachusetts Supreme Judicial Court held that while the employee "may have been annoyed or insulted by" the customer's remark, "that circumstance alone does not justify imposition of liability on" the employer.

Miller's holding that a critical comment by a customer to an employee did not in the circumstances constitute "conduct" interfering with the employee's performance of his work is obviously distinguishable from the case at bar. Constant heckling by fans at a baseball park would be, within the meaning of *Miller*, conduct. The jury could reasonably have found that such conduct had either the affirmative purpose to rattle or the effect of rattling the employee so that he could not perform his duties successfully. Moreover, the jury could reasonably have found that Grimsley's assault was not a mere retaliation for past annoyance, but a response to continuing conduct which was "presently interfering" with his ability to pitch in the game if called upon to play. Therefore, the battery count against the Baltimore Club should have been submitted to the jury.

Is *Manning v. Grimsley* consistent with *The Sage Club v. Hunt*? Was Grimsley's assault motivated at least in part by a purpose to serve the master?

3. *Noah v. Ziehl*, 759 S.W.2d 905 (Mo. App. 1988), involved an intentional tort committed by Overton, a "doorman" and bouncer at a nightclub. Noah had spent almost three hours at the club, during which time he and a friend had consumed at least two pitchers of beer. There was disputed testimony that earlier in the evening, the club manager had broken up a fight between Overton and Noah in which Overton had come out much the worse and swearing that he would "get back" at Noah. As Noah was leaving the club, he "patted [a woman] on her behind end to get her going." As it turned out, the woman was Overton's girlfriend. Overton became enraged. Although the facts were disputed, apparently Overton grabbed Noah by the hair, and they struggled out of the club and into the parking lot. At one point, Overton stuck his fingers "up to his knuckles" into Noah's eye sockets, and may have beat Noah's head against a wall several times. Noah ended up on the ground, with Overton on top of him and beating at his head. Eventually, Overton pulled a "buck knife," and stabbed Noah several times.

The jury's verdict against the owner of the club was reversed on appeal:

> Whether or not an employee's use of force is within the scope of his employment is dependent on many factors. Of primary importance are the nature of the principal's business, whether or not the employment will bring the employee into contact with the public and the likelihood that the employment will involve the use of force and whether or not the employee acts from a personal motive. In *Wellman v. Pacer Oil Co.*, [504 S.W.2d 55 (Mo. 1973),] our Supreme Court held that an employer was not responsible for the personal act of a gas station attendant who shot a customer. The Supreme Court concluded that the actions of the employee were so outrageous and criminal—so excessively violent as to be totally without reason or responsibility—and hence "must be said, as a matter of law, not to be within the scope of employment." [*Id.*] at 58.
>
> Similarly, in *Henderson v. Laclede Radio, Inc.*, [506 S.W.d 434 (Mo. 1974)], the Supreme Court held that a salesman for a radio station committed an outrageous and unforeseeable act when he made an unprovoked attack on plaintiff and kicked plaintiff's leg with sufficient force to fracture a bone, when trying to collect a bill.
>
> The doctrines in *Wellman* and *Henderson*, although framed in terms of outrageous conduct or unexpected results, are part and parcel of the principle that when conduct of an employee exceeds the scope of employment and are done, not in furtherance of the employer's business, but to gratify the employee's feelings of resentment or revenge, the conduct is outside the scope of his employment.
>
> The fact that we deal here with a liquor establishment and Overton was a "doorman" or "bouncer" does not, under the facts here, affect our conclusion. It is true that the nature of the duties of a "bouncer" often affect the vicarious liability of the employer. By the nature of the business and the nature of the employment an employer cannot object if [a bouncer] vigorously acts in furtherance of his employer's business. It is a job calling more for force than finesse; if a jury finds that more force was used than the situation quite warranted, it seems neither unlikely nor unreasonable that such a happening will be considered one of the risks of the saloon business and that the tort will be treated as committed in the [scope] of employment.
>
> But, under the facts here, we believe that Overton's conduct in assaulting Noah exceeded the scope of employment. The conduct of Overton outside the tavern exceeded reasonable bounds and was excessively violent and not to be expected by his employer. Neither was such conduct at the time in furtherance of the employer's business. Overton admitted he sought "revenge," that he "lost complete control" and that he did some "pretty crude things" to Noah.
>
> We hold that the conduct of Overton exceeded the scope of his employment, in that his conduct was not, at the time, in furtherance of his employer's business.
>
> We reverse the judgment with directions to enter judgment in favor of [the owner of the nightclub].

Compare the holding in *Noah v. Ziehl* with Restatement section 245 comment f:

> *Servant actuated by personal motives.* The liability of a master for the use of force by a servant is not prevented by the fact that a servant acts in part because of a personal motive, such as revenge. The master, however, is relieved from liability under the rule stated in this Section if the servant has not intent to act on his master's behalf, although the events from which the tortious act follows arise while the servant is acting in the employment and the servant becomes angry because of them. The fact that the servant acts in an outrageous manner or inflicts punishment out of all proportion to the necessities of his master's business is evidence indicating that the servant has departed from the scope of employment in performing the act.

Do you agree with the holding in *Noah v. Ziehl* that Overton's act was outside the scope of employment *as a matter of law*?

If you had represented the owner of the nightclub, would you have been satisfied with a jury instruction outlining the *general principles* used to determine whether an act is within the scope of employment?

4. Once a servant has departed from the scope of employment, has he or she abandoned it forever or can he or she reenter the employment? The seminal case on the reentry doctrine—the resumption of employment—is *Fiocco v. Carver*, 234 N.Y. 219, 137 N.E. 309 (1922). The defendants sent a truckload of merchandise from Manhattan to Staten Island. After making the delivery, their driver was to bring the truck back to their garage on the west side of the city. Instead, he went to the east side to visit his mother. A neighborhood carnival was in progress in the street, and a crowd of boys dressed in fantastic costumes asked the driver for a ride on his truck. He agreed and made a tour of the district with them on board. When the driver stopped the truck in front of a poolroom and left it momentarily, the plaintiff child climbed on board the truck. The driver told the boys to get off the truck, but before the plaintiff could reach the ground, the driver started the truck, and plaintiff's foot was drawn into the wheel. Even though the driver said that his purpose then was to go back to the garage, the court held he had not reentered the scope of employment:

> At the time of the accident, the truck was crowded with boys, whom the driver was taking on a frolic. They filled not only its body but the roof and side and box. All we can find from the driver's testimony is a suggestion that the servant had at last made up his mind to put an end to his wanderings and return to the garage. He was still far away from the point at which he had first strayed from the path of duty, but his thoughts were homeward bound. Is this enough, in view of all the circumstances, to put him back in the sphere of service?
>
> We have refused to limit ourselves by tests that are merely mechanical or formal. Location in time and space are circumstances that may guide the judgment but will not be sufficient to control it, divorced from other circumstances that may characterize the intent of the transaction. The dominant purpose must be proved to be the performance of the master's business. Until then, there can be no resumption of a relation that has been broken and suspended. The field of duty, once forsaken, is not to be reentered by acts evincing a divided loyalty and thus continuing the offense. Many of the illicit incidents of the tour about the neighborhood persisted. The company of merrymakers was still swarming about the truck. Add to this that the truck was still far away from the route that it would have traveled if the servant had followed the line of duty from the beginning.

Division more substantial must be shown before a relation, once ignored and abandoned, will be renewed and reestablished.

2. Abuse of Position

Suppose a servant acts for purely personal reasons and without any purpose to serve the master. Under traditional analysis, such acts will be *outside* the scope of the servant's employment. Suppose further that the servant's employment *facilitated* the misconduct, but that the master was not negligent in selecting, retaining, supervising, or controlling the servant. How should the law allocate the risk of such misconduct? May the master nevertheless be liable without fault under respondeat superior?

Entente Mineral Co. v. Parker

956 F. 2d 524 (5th Cir. 1992)

THORNBERRY, Circuit Judge:

This is an appeal from a directed verdict. The defendant-appellee law firm was sued for vicarious liability. The district court directed a verdict in favor of the firm, concluding as a matter of law that the jury could not find vicarious liability. The plaintiff-appellant, Entente, appeals the district court's directed verdict.

In February 1987, H.B. Sneed ("Sneed"), a petroleum landman employed by Entente Mineral Company ("Entente"), negotiated with McKinley Young ("Young") to purchase one-half of Young's royalty interest in certain property. On February 23, Young and Sneed orally agreed that Entente would purchase one-half of Young's interest for $25,000. Sneed then presented a $25,000 draft and a royalty deed to Young. Young, who does not read well if at all, stated that he wanted his banker, Bruce Edwards ("Edwards")[,] to review the deed to ensure that it accurately reflected the terms of the oral agreement. Young and Sneed took the deed to Edwards, who suggested that Young's attorneys at the firm of Barrett, Barrett, Barrett, and Patton ("the firm") review the deed. Edwards telephoned Derek Parker, a partner in the firm, and arranged for Sneed and Young to meet with Parker.

That afternoon, Sneed and Young drove to the firm and met with Parker. Parker reviewed the deed and told Young that the deed reflected the terms and conditions of the oral agreement. He also advised Young that before signing the deed, he should have a title search performed to guarantee that he owned a one-sixteenth royalty, the one-half of one-sixteenth that he intended to sell to Entente and the one-half of one-sixteenth that he intended to retain. Young then asked Parker to perform the title search. Parker instructed Sneed and Young to return the next day at one o'clock p.m. to close the deal. Sneed left the royalty deed and the $25,000 draft with Parker.

After Sneed and Young left the firm, Parker telephoned his brother, who was an oil and gas lease and royalty speculator. Parker asked his brother whether he knew about a well being drilled on Young's property. After doing some research, Parker's brother informed him that the well looked promising and that he would provide financing to Parker if he attempted to purchase the royalty from Young. Parker's brother suggested offering Young $30,000 for the one-half royalty. Parker replied that he did not want to pay $30,000 and that he could probably buy it for $27,000. Later that day, Parker asked his partner Pat Barrett, Jr. whether he thought there was anything wrong with a lawyer's purchasing mineral interests from a client, and Barrett replied that he did not see anything wrong with it.

The following morning, Parker called Edwards and told him that he knew of someone who could make Young a better offer. He asked Edwards to have Young contact him. Young returned Parker's call and the two agreed to meet that afternoon at Edwards's bank. Once at the bank, Parker informed Young that he wanted to purchase the one-half royalty for $27,000. Young agreed, and they executed the same deed that Sneed had prepared except that Parker's name appeared in the Grantee blank.

When Sneed arrived at the firm, prepared to close the sale, he was informed that Young had received a better offer for the one-half royalty. Sneed asked who purchased the one-half royalty but was not given an answer. Eventually, Sneed discovered from the officially recorded deed that Parker had purchased the one-half royalty.

Entente sued Parker and the firm in federal district court based on diversity jurisdiction. Entente asserted that Parker's actions constituted tortious interference with business relations and contract in violation of Mississippi law, and that the firm was vicariously liable for Parker's tortious conduct. The court held a jury trial. At the close of Entente's evidence, the firm moved for a directed verdict on the ground that Parker's purchase of the royalty was not within the scope of his employment, and hence, the firm could not be vicariously liable for any tort he may have committed in purchasing the royalty. The district court concluded that Parker had not been acting within the scope of his employment when he purchased the royalty and granted the firm's motion for directed verdict. Entente now appeals the district court's grant of the firm's motion for directed verdict.

Mississippi law applies in this diversity case. Accordingly, the law firm's vicarious liability for Parker's conduct is assessed under agency principles.

Section 219 of the Restatement (Second) of Agency discusses the circumstances in which a master is liable for the torts of his servant. Subsection (1) of § 219 provides that a master is vicariously liable for the torts of his servant that are committed within the scope of employment. Restatement (Second) of Agency § 219(1) (1958). Section 228 of the Restatement requires that, in order to be within the scope of employment, the [servant's] conduct must be actuated, at least in part, by a purpose to serve the master.

Subsection (2) of § 219 lists four situations in which conduct that fails to satisfy the "within the scope of employment" test found in § 228, may still provide a basis for imposing vicarious liability. Subsection (2) provides in part that

> A master is not subject to liability for the torts of his servants acting outside the scope of employment, unless:
>
> * * *
>
> (d) the servant purported to act or to speak on behalf of the principal and there was reliance upon apparent authority, or he was aided in accomplishing the tort by the existence of the agency relation.

Thus, under the Restatement, a [master] is liable for the torts of his [servant] if the [servant] commits the tort while acting within the scope of his employment as defined by § 228, or if § 219(2) applies. The situations listed in § 219(2) are not necessarily exceptions to the scope of employment doctrine, but rather situations in which courts have decided to impose liability on the principal or employer even if the agent's conduct does not meet all of the traditional "within the scope of employment" criteria.

Section 261 is an extension of § 219(2)(d), and states that

> A principal who puts a servant or other agent in a position which enables the agent, while apparently acting within his authority, to commit a fraud upon third persons is subject to liability to such third persons for the fraud.

Comment a to § 261 states that

> The principal is subject to liability under the rule stated in this section although he is entirely innocent, has received no benefit from the transaction, and as stated in Section 262, although the agent acted solely for his own purposes.

Unlike § 228, § 261 assesses vicarious liability even though the agent[/servant's] conduct was not actuated by a purpose to serve the principal[/master]. Although Mississippi case law has not expressly differentiated between the two types of vicarious liability found in § 219(1) and § 219(2) of the Restatement, the distinction is implicit.[2] Hence, cases imposing liability under the theory embraced by § 219(1) and defined in § 228, require the agent's conduct to be for the principal's purposes; while other cases, under the theory embodied in §§ 219(2)(d) and 261, allow liability even when an agent acts solely for his own purposes.

Recognizing the distinction between the types of liability, we first address whether Parker's purchase of the royalty was within the scope of his employment as defined by § 228, and second, whether the firm can be held liable under the theory delineated in § 261.

1. *Was Parker's Conduct Within the Scope of His Employment?*

The district court concluded that Parker's purchase of the royalty from Young was an "abandonment of employment" and, therefore, not within the scope of his employment with the firm. Entente does not dispute that the firm is not in the business of buying minerals or that the firm received no gain from Parker's purchase of the royalty. Instead, Entente asserts that the district court improperly focused on the last event, the purchase itself, and that if the transaction is viewed in the proper context, Parker's conduct satisfies each element of § 228.

In essence, Entente contends that Parker purchased the royalty while acting as Young's attorney, and was motivated by the firm's purposes both when he agreed to meet with Young, a longstanding client, and when he agreed to perform the title search. Entente maintains that Parker's conduct, from the time he agreed to meet with Young to the time he purchased the royalty, is only one series of conduct that cannot be separated into distinct acts; in Entente's words, Parker's "legal engagement could not be turned on and off."

Entente would have us hold that once Parker began representing Young pursuant to the firm's purposes, no deviation from the firm's purpose could take him outside the scope of his employment. Such a holding would violate the well established rule

---

2. Entente, however, conflates the two theories, arguing that it is not necessary that Parker's acts be for the firm's benefit to be within the scope of his employment under § 228, but citing *Billups Petroleum Co. v. Hardin's Bakeries Corp.*, 217 Miss. 24, 63 So. 2d 543 (1953), a case in which the theory of liability is of the type embodied in § 219(2)(d).

that if an employee who is delegated to perform certain work for his employer steps or turns aside from his master's work or business to serve some purpose of his own, not connected with the employer's business, or, as it is often expressed, deviates or departs from his work to accomplish some purpose of his own not connected with his employment—goes on a "frolic of his own"—the relation of master and servant is thereby temporarily suspended, and the master is not liable for his acts during the period of such suspension. As the "abandonment of employment" doctrine is entrenched in the law of vicarious liability, we conclude, as the district court did, that the proper inquiry is whether, at the time of the purchase, Parker was acting within the scope of his employment.

There is no dispute that Parker purchased the royalty for himself and was acting in his own interest, not in the interest of the firm. There is also no dispute that the firm did not receive any benefit from Parker's purchase of the royalty. In fact, Young was never billed by Parker or the firm. In order to satisfy the § 228 definition of "within the scope of employment," Parker's conduct must have been motivated, at least in part, by a desire to serve the firm. It is undisputed that Parker was motivated only by a desire to serve himself when he purchased the royalty. Viewing the conduct from the proper perspective, as a matter of law, Parker could not have been acting within the scope of his employment when he purchased the royalty interest.

2. *Did the Agency Relationship Aid Parker in Committing Allegedly Tortious Acts, Within the Meaning of §§ 219(2)(d) and 261?*

Entente claims that two cases, *Billups Petroleum Co. v. Hardin's Bakeries Corp.*, 217 Miss. 24, 63 So. 2d 543 (1953), and *Napp v. Liberty National Life Insurance Co.*, 248 Miss. 320, 159 So. 2d 164 (1963), support its argument that conduct need not be motivated by any desire to serve a master in order to be within the scope of a servant's employment. As discussed above, Entente's argument conflates two theories of liability.[4] We examine the *Billups* and *Napp* cases, however, to determine whether the type of liability anticipated by § 261 exists in this case. After a careful examination of the cases and the underlying theories of liability, we find that as a matter of law, the liability described in §§ 219(2)(d) and 261 does not exist in this case.

In *Billups*, a salesman for Hardin's Bakeries overcharged Billups for bread over a period of several months, and kept the excess for himself. The Mississippi Supreme Court held Hardin's Bakeries vicariously liable for its agent's fraud, stating that

> [t]he Principal is liable to third persons for injuries resulting from the fraud and deceit of his agent if such is within the scope of the agent's authority. Acts of fraud by the agent, committed in the course or scope of his employment, are binding on the principal, even though the principal did not know of or authorize the commission of the fraudulent acts, and although he derives no benefit from the success of the fraud, and the agent committed it for his own benefit.

Contrary to some of the language in the *Billups* case, the principal's liability is based on the theory embodied in §§ 219(2)(d) and 261 of the Restatement, rather than traditional "scope of employment" liability contained in § 219(1). The four cases the *Billups* court discusses in support of its holding evidence that the court imposed

4. Although the holding of the *Billups* case is framed in "scope of employment" language, upon close examination, the underlying theory of liability is that expressed in § 219(2)(d) of the Restatement. *See* RESTATEMENT (SECOND) OF AGENCY § 219 cmt. e (1958).

§ 219(2)(d) liability. Each of the four cases involves fraud by an agent upon the principal's customer. Each case involved a situation in which the principal delegated to the agent the power to perform a certain task, such as collect monies for the principal. In each case, the agent acted for his own purposes, but the fraud transpired as part of the very duty that the principal authorized the agent to perform. Because the customers had a relationship with the principal that induced the customers to rely on the principal's agent, and the agent defrauded the customers in the performance of the duty entrusted to him by the principal, the agent was "aided in accomplishing the tort by the existence of the agency relation." Restatement (Second) of Agency, § 219(2)(d) (1958).

In *Napp*, the insurance company's agent defrauded a beneficiary by painstakingly convincing her that her husband's policy had lapsed before his death, but that the insurance company would pay half of the benefit she otherwise would have been due. In fact, the policy had not lapsed, and when the agent delivered a check for the full amount of the benefit to the beneficiary, he told her that the check had been made out for the incorrect amount, and that she would have to give half of it back to him to return to the company. He induced her to sign a receipt for the full amount and he kept one half of the money for himself. The court found that even though this conduct was not within the scope of the agent's employment contract, the company elected to have the agent deliver the check, and "could not delegate to one certain duties and then deny agency because the written contract between them limited his activities to other matters." Thus, as in *Billups*, the fraud in *Napp* transpired as part of the very duty that the agent was authorized to perform for the principal and customer.

Entente contends that, just as in *Billups* and *Napp*, Parker was aided in purchasing the royalty by the existence of his agency relationship with the firm. Entente advances that but for his employment at the firm, Parker never would have met Young and never would have had the opportunity to purchase the royalty; yet, but-for causation is irrelevant in this case. The proper inquiry for determining vicarious liability of a principal whose agent defrauds the principal's customer is the relationship between the principal and the customer. In *Billups*, the four cases it discusses, and *Napp*, the principal had a relationship with the customer and the customer was defrauded by the principal's agent. The courts reasoned that a principal who provides his agent with the tools or position necessary to perpetrate a fraud on the principal's customers should be held responsible to the innocent customers who relied on the agent. In this case, there was no relationship between the firm and Entente that could be imputed to the firm's agent. It is undisputed that neither Parker nor the firm represented Entente. The premise underlying § 219(2)(d) and § 261 liability, a relationship between the principal and an innocent third party, is absent in this case. Therefore, as a matter of law, the firm could not have been held vicariously liable for Parker's acts.

We AFFIRM the verdict directed by the district court.

Note

The most frequent application of Restatement section 219(2)(d) is in situations to which Restatement section 261 applies. A servant acting within the scope of his or her apparent authority defrauds a third person (such as by receiving property) solely for personal reasons. Even though the servant acted *outside* the scope of employment, the master will be held liable because the master put the servant in a position where third parties would rely on the servant's apparent authority. May Restatement section 219(2)(d) be applied in different contexts?

McCalla v. Ellis

180 Mich. App. 372, 446 N.W.2d 904 (1989)

HOOD, Presiding Judge.

Following a jury trial in Washtenaw Circuit Court, defendant Electrolux Corporation was found liable to plaintiff in the amount of $186,000 for sexual harassment resulting in employment discrimination in violation of the Civil Rights Act.

Richard Ellis was a supervisor formerly employed by Electrolux. Plaintiff McCalla had been hired by Ellis to sell vacuum cleaners door-to-door. McCalla brought her claim under the Civil Rights Act based on her allegation that Ellis had forced her to have sexual intercourse with him.

Defendant's first issue is that the trial court should have ordered entry of judgment notwithstanding the verdict or, in the alternative, a new trial. Defendant challenges both the legal basis for plaintiff's claim and the sufficiency of the evidence to support that claim.

The Civil Rights Act, like Title VII of the federal Civil Rights Act, prohibits employers from discriminating against a person on the basis of sex with respect to "a term, condition or privilege of employment." M.C.L. § 37.2202; M.S.A. § 3.548(202); 42 U.S.C. § 2000e-2(a)(1). In Michigan, discrimination on the basis of sex has been further defined by statute to include "sexual harassment which means unwelcome sexual advances, requests for sexual favors, and other verbal or physical conduct or communication of a sexual nature." M.C.L. § 37.2103(h); M.S.A. § 3.548(103)(h). The statute includes such activities when:

> (i) Submission to such conduct or communication is made a term or condition either explicitly or implicitly to obtain employment.
>
> (ii) Submission to or rejection of such conduct or communication by an individual is used as a factor in decisions affecting such individual's employment.
>
> (iii) Such conduct or communication has the purpose or effect of substantially interfering with an individual's employment or creating an intimidating, hostile, or offensive employment environment.

M.C.L. § 37.2103(h)(i), (ii) and (iii); M.S.A. § 3.548(103)(h)(i), (ii) and (iii). This language parallels that found in the EEOC guidelines regarding sexual harassment and Title VII.

[T]he burden is then on plaintiff to show a nexus between the [unwelcome sexual] conduct and her employment situation. In this case plaintiff sought to do so by showing the existence of quid pro quo sexual harassment.

Both Civil Rights Act and Title VII provide relief for two basic types of sexual harassment: (1) quid pro quo sexual harassment; and (2) sexual harassment which results from a hostile or offensive work environment.

The parties have not provided, and we are not aware of, any Michigan authority applying the quid pro quo theory as such. However, in *Langlois [v. McDonald's Restaurants*, 149 Mich. App. 309, 385 N.W.2d 778 (1986),] a hostile environment case, the Court recognized the elements of a quid pro quo claim as set forth by the federal court in *Henson v. City of Dundee*, 682 F.2d 897 (CA 11, 1982). While this Court is not bound by federal precedent based on Title VII, those precedents analogous to questions presented under the Civil Rights Act are highly persuasive and will be considered.

The five elements of a quid pro quo claim as set forth in *Henson* are:

(1) The employee belongs to a protected group.
(2) The employee was subject to unwelcome sexual harassment.
(3) The harassment complained of was based upon sex.
(4) The employee's reaction to harassment complained of affected tangible aspects of the employee's compensation, terms, conditions, or privileges of employment.
(5) Respondeat superior.

(Emphasis changed.) Defendant argues that elements 4 and 5 are not met in this case because the requisite nexus between the harassment and her employment is missing and because Ellis was not acting as defendant's agent when the sexual conduct occurred.

The fourth element is established where the employee in a supervisory position encourages or demands sexual favors in return for some employment benefit. As noted in *Henson*, the harassment may be express or implied. It may be evidenced by a single incident. The classical example of quid pro quo harassment is the situation in which the plaintiff is fired because of a refusal to succumb to sexual demands. Where an employee involuntarily resigns in order to escape an employment situation made intolerable because of sexual harassment, the termination of employment is considered a constructive discharge or firing.

As to the respondeat superior element, defendant argues that it could not be liable because it did not authorize Ellis to rape the plaintiff and because it had no notice of Ellis' sexual proclivity prior to the incident.

The Civil Rights Act defines "employer" to include "an agent." M.C.L. § 37.2201(a); M.S.A. § 3.548(201)(a). Defendant does not contest that Ellis was an agent at least to the extent that he was in its employ as a supervisor with authority to make employment decisions.

Under the Restatement (Second) of Agency, § 219(2)(d), an employer may be liable for its employee's actions where the employee "was aided in accomplishing the tort by the existence of the agency relation[ship]." Even if the act is not within the scope of his employment and the employee is acting entirely for his own benefit, the employer may be liable where the employee exercises the authority actually delegated to him by his employer in acting so as to affect the employment status of subordinates. Where it is the employer's delegation of authority that empowered the supervisor to act, the employer can be found liable. As noted in *Horn v. Duke Homes*, 755 F.2d 599, 605 (CA 7, 1985):

> It could be argued that because [the plant superintendent] Haas was not authorized to discriminate on the basis of sex and because his sexual proclivities were wholly unconnected to the well-being of the employer, he was acting outside the scope of his employment. On the other hand, by delegating power to Haas the "employer" and Haas essentially merged; as long as the tort complained of

was caused by the exercise of this supervisory power, Haas should be deemed as acting within the scope of his employment, and the employer should be held liable for the tort.

As to defendant's claim of lack of notice, if this were a hostile environment claim, employers are not always automatically liable for sexual harassment by their supervisors. *Meritor Savings Bank, FSB v. Vinson*, 477 U.S. 57, 72, 106 S. Ct. 2399, 2408, 91 L. Ed. 2d 49 (1986). However, in the quid pro quo claim, the federal courts have imposed strict liability on the employer even absent proof that higher management knew or should have known of the sexual harassment. The reason for imposing strict liability in a quid pro quo case was set forth in *Henson*:

> In such a case, the supervisor relies upon his apparent or actual authority to extort sexual consideration from an employee. Therein lies the quid pro quo. In that case the supervisor uses the means furnished to him by the employer to accomplish the prohibited purpose. He acts within the scope of his actual or apparent authority to "hire, fire, discipline or promote." Because the supervisor is acting within at least the apparent scope of the authority entrusted to him by the employer when he makes employment decisions, his conduct can fairly be imputed to the source of his authority.

Therefore, in this case, plaintiff must show that she left her employment because the sexual conduct of her supervisor, acting within at least the apparent scope of his authority, either expressly or impliedly affected her employment status or benefits to the extent that unwelcome sexual harassment can be shown to exist.

At trial, plaintiff testified that in the early evening of September 1, 1979, a Saturday, she was called at home by Ellis, her supervisor, and asked to come to the office to sign some contracts. Plaintiff had completed her first week with Electrolux, observing others in the field and attending meetings. She had terminated her prior employment to take the job at Electrolux. Plaintiff understood that the papers were necessary for her to receive a paycheck. She also understood that her pay was based on commissions and that she had not yet made a sale.

A company representative testified that sales commissions were given to new people when they are learning the job in order to provide them with a paycheck during this learning period. Ellis testified that he usually told new hires that they would be getting some money to see them through the first week and that he might have told plaintiff this. On cross-examination, he agreed that when he called plaintiff and offered her the chance to sign the contracts and make some money that he knew she would probably come to the office. He estimated that the contracts involved commissions of $250-$300.

According to plaintiff's testimony, when she arrived at the office, Ellis was alone. As she signed the papers, she felt Ellis breathing down the back of her neck. As she turned to leave, Ellis ordered her to remove her clothes. Plaintiff testified that she was terrified and that after she removed her clothes, Ellis ordered her to have at least four separate acts of intercourse. Following the episode, Ellis told plaintiff that if she "stuck with him, I'd have no worries."

Ellis testified that he did not force plaintiff to have sex and that he believed that plaintiff had signalled during the prior week that she was sexually available. He denied breathing down her neck and testified that there was only one act of intercourse. He testified that he would have given plaintiff the commissions in any event because he had told her that he would "pay her so much money the first week anyhow."

Plaintiff testified that she did not return to Electrolux after the assault as a result of the incident.

The parties do not dispute that plaintiff came to the office in response to Ellis' call in order to complete the paperwork necessary for her to receive a paycheck. Contemporaneously with the sexual assault, Ellis told plaintiff that if she stuck with him she would have no problems. Based on the situation, plaintiff could reasonably assume this meant more sexual contact, which would be a factor in decisions affecting or interfering with her employment. Viewing the record in light of the relevant law, we find there was a sufficient factual basis for the jury's verdict.

Our review does not indicate that the court erred in denying defendant's motions for a new trial or for judgment notwithstanding the verdict.

With the exception of the damages issue which is remanded for further proceedings, the jury's verdict is affirmed. This Court does not retain jurisdiction.

Notes

1. The application of Restatement section 219(2)(d) to quid pro quo sexual harassment depends on the servant's abuse of the authority given the servant by the master. In *Hirschfeld v. New Mexico Corrections Dept.*, 916 F.2d 572 (10th Cir. 1990), Galvan made sexual advances to Hirschfeld at the workplace. Although Galvan was a fellow worker, Galvan was not Hirschfeld's supervisor. The court of appeals affirmed the district court holding that the master, the New Mexico Corrections Department, was not liable under Title VII for sexual harassment:

> The district court held that:
>
> > Section 219(2)(d) properly imputes an employee's actions to the employer whose delegation of authority empowered the agent to undertake them. Here, Galvan did not purport to act on behalf of the institution by his inappropriate actions towards the plaintiff. The only conceivable way Galvan was aided by the agency relationship in the accomplishment of the tort is that he would not have been there but for his job. This is too broad a reading of 219(2)(d). The second half of 219[(2)](d) which reads "or is aided in accomplishing the tort by the existence of the agency relation,["] must be read in [the] context of what immediately precedes it.
>
> We agree. Plaintiff presented no evidence suggesting that Galvan had any supervisory authority over plaintiff's position whatsoever. Although Galvan had [limited] authority over security guards, there was no evidence indicating that Galvan ever invoked that authority in order to facilitate his harassment of plaintiff.

2. In *Hirschfeld v. New Mexico Corrections Dept.*, the court of appeals, citing Restatement section 219(2)(*b*), adopted the rule that the employer (master) will only be liable for "hostile work environment" sexual harassment based on the employer's own negligence or recklessness.

> Employer negligence in this context is defined as "failing to remedy or prevent a hostile or offensive work environment of which management level employees knew, or in the exercise of reasonable care should have known."

The steps that the employer (acting through its management level employees) should take to discharge its duty of reasonable care in assuring that the workplace is not a hostile or offensive work environment is beyond the scope of this course.

Stropes v. Heritage House Children's Ctr.

547 N.E.2d 244 (Ind. 1989)

DeBRULER, Justice.

Fourteen-year-old David Stropes was the victim of cerebral palsy and severe mental retardation. He had the mental capacity of a five-month-old infant and was without the verbal and motor skills necessary to perform or assist in even the simplest tasks associated with his own sustenance or sanitation. David had been placed at the Heritage House Children's Center of Shelbyville, Inc. (Heritage), as a ward of the Marion County Welfare Department to assure his maintenance, security, and well-being.

Robert Griffin, a nurse's aide employed by Heritage, was expected to feed, bathe, and change the bedding and clothing of residents, including David Stropes, as well as to monitor their comfort and safety. To fulfill these duties, Griffin was required to minister to residents in their beds, remove their clothing, and touch and handle their bodies. During his 11:00 p.m. to 7:00 a.m. shift on February 28, 1986, Griffin entered David's room to change the boy's bedding and clothes for the day. After Griffin stripped off the sheets, he [sexually assaulted him]. Griffin stopped the assault when David made a sound indicating that he was in pain, then finished changing the boy's clothes. This incident was seen and reported by another Heritage employee, and Griffin ultimately was charged with and pleaded guilty to criminal deviate conduct, a Class B felony, and child molesting, a Class C felony.

David Stropes, by his next friend, Pamela Taylor, filed a complaint against Heritage and Griffin which asked for compensation and punitive damages and which was based in part on a claim that Heritage was responsible for acts committed by Griffin while on duty. Heritage moved for summary judgment on that claim, arguing that this sexual assault was outside the scope of Griffin's employment and that, therefore, Heritage could not be held liable under the doctrine of respondeat superior. The trial court granted that motion with no accompanying findings of fact or conclusions of law on May 29, 1987. On July 20, 1987, the trial court modified its initial order by adding the following conclusion of law:

> That the act of committing a sexual assault was[,] as a matter of law, outside the scope of Robert Griffin's employment and, as a result, plaintiff cannot recover against The Heritage House, Inc. based upon a theory of respondeat superior.

[T]he Court of Appeals affirmed the decision of the trial court in an unpublished opinion.

The question presented for our review is whether, as a matter of law, Heritage may be subject to liability for its employee's wrongful acts under the doctrine of respondeat superior as traditionally applied.

Respondeat superior imposes liability, where none would otherwise exist, on an employer for the wrongful acts of his employee which are committed within the scope of employment. The Court of Appeals has stated, "In order to be within the scope of employment the employee must be in the 'service of the employer.' " *Shelby v. Truck & Bus Group Div. of GMC* (1989), Ind. App., 533 N.E.2d 1296, 1298. Acts for which the employer is not responsible are those done "on the employee's own initiative," "with no intention to perform it as part of or incident to the service for which he is employed." However, an employee's wrongful act may still fall within the scope of his employment if his purpose was, to an appreciable extent, to further his employer's business, even if the act was predominantly motivated by an intention to benefit the employee himself. Two cases decided under Indiana law have held employers liable for criminal acts of their employees, despite the fact that the crimes were committed to benefit the employee, because the criminal acts originated in activities so closely associated with the employment relationship as to fall within its scope.

In *Gomez v. Adams*, 462 N.E.2d 212, a security officer employed by a private security agency arrested Adams and confiscated his personal identification. The agency's officers were authorized "to request, receive and retain personal identification while investigating disturbances or in effecting arrests," and to retain confiscated items until turning them over to the agency office, which was to be done as soon as practicable. Officers were not authorized to retain items for their personal use. This officer kept Adams confiscated identification past the end of his shift and later used it to cash a check to which he had forged Adams' name. Adams sued the security agency under the doctrine of respondeat superior for damages arising from the conversion of his identification and the forgery of his signature. The jury found for Adams and awarded him $80,000 in compensatory and punitive damages.

Although the Court of Appeals reversed the judgment, the security agency was not totally freed from liability. The Court found that the forgery was, as a matter of law, outside the scope of the officer's employment because it was "divorced in time, place, and purpose from [the officer's] employment duties" and because the only connection between the forgery and the employer was that the officer "was enabled to commit the act by virtue of his confiscation of Adams' papers while performing his duties as a security officer." The security agency did not escape liability for the conversion, however, because "[t]here was sufficient evidence for the jury to reasonably conclude that [the officer] was within the scope of his employment when he converted the check-cashing card to his own use." In reaching its decision, the Court of Appeals distinguished *Eagle Machine Co., Inc. v. American Dist. Telegraph Co.* (1957), 127 Ind. App. 403, 140 N.E.2d 756, where a business which sold and provided maintenance service for alarm systems was held not to be liable under respondeat superior for thefts committed by its employees against one of its customers. The Court stated:

> In *Eagle Machine*, the duties of the employees did not include confiscation or retention of property, nor were the employees authorized to handle business property or inventory with the exception of the alarm system. Furthermore, the nature of their acts were [sic] entirely different than the service for which they were employed, and were motivated entirely by personal interests rather than the employer's interest. *Eagle Machine* is inapplicable to the instant case because [the officer's] actions were, at least for a time, authorized by his employer, related to the service for which he was employed, and motivated to an extent by [the agency's] interests.

The Seventh Circuit Court of Appeals, sitting in diversity, relied on *Gomez* to decide a respondeat superior claim in *Tippecanoe Beverages v. S.A. El Aguila Brewing*

Co., 833 F.2d 633 (7th Cir. 1987) (Posner, J.). The Seventh Circuit affirmed a judgment against El Aguila based on the conversion by one of its employees of a cashier's check given by Tippecanoe Beverages in payment for a shipment of beer. The Court found that a reasonable jury could find that the employee had acted to further, "to an appreciable extent, his master's business," analogizing the facts at hand to those in *Gomez*:

> [S]ince it was [the officer's] job to take Adams' personal effects for safekeeping during the scuffle and subsequent arrest, "the confiscation was undertaken in furtherance of [his employer's] business." Likewise here, whatever [El Aguila's employee] had in mind when he received payment from [Tippecanoe Beverages] for the beer, the transaction was within the scope of [his] authority.

It is significant that neither of these cases was dismissed on summary judgment. Both factual episodes involved authorized acts unquestionably within the scope of employment, the confiscation of identification pursuant to arrest and the acceptance of money given in payment for goods, and unauthorized acts unquestionably outside the scope of employment, the criminal conversion of items rightfully received, yet the employers were not automatically shielded from liability. The plaintiffs sought to impose liability under respondeat superior for crimes clearly committed ultimately to benefit the employee rather than the employer, yet the doctrine did not insulate the employer from subjection to trial. Instead, both cases went to the jury for a determination of whether the employees acted to further, "to an appreciable extent, his master's business."

The question of employer liability under respondeat superior here should have gone [to] trial as it did in *Gomez* and *El Aguila*. Like the employees in those cases, Heritage's employee committed some acts unquestionably within the scope of his employment. Griffin began the episode by performing a fully authorized act, stripping the sheets from David's bed prior to changing the bedding. He was also authorized to undress David Stropes and to touch his genitals and other parts of his body when bathing him and changing his clothes. Had David been distressed or frightened, the nurse's aide could have appropriately offered comfort and assurance by a pat or a caress; had he been violent or resistant, Griffin could have used appropriate physical force to restrain him. Griffin also ended the episode with a fully authorized act, dressing David for the day. Like the conversions committed by the *Gomez* and *El Aguila* employees, it is beyond question that the abuse David suffered at Griffin's hands was unauthorized by Heritage and committed for Griffin's own gratification.

The fact that this was a sexual assault is not per se determinative of the scope of employment question. A blanket rule holding all sexual attacks outside the scope of employment as a matter of law because they satisfy the perpetrators' personal desires would draw an unprincipled distinction between such assaults and other types of crimes which employees may commit in response to other personal motivations, such as anger or financial pressures. Rather, the nature of the wrongful act should be a consideration in the assessment of whether and to what extent Griffin's acts fell within the scope of his employment such that Heritage should be held accountable.

Rape and sexual abuse constitute arguably the most egregious instances of wrongful acts which an employee could commit on the job and lend themselves to arguably the most instinctive conclusion that such acts could never be within the scope of one's employment, yet other courts have recognized that the resolution of the question does not turn on the type of act committed or on the perpetrator's emotional baggage accompanying the attack. Rather, these courts indicate that the focus must be on how the employment relates to the context in which the commission of the wrongful act arose. The Minnesota Supreme Court has gone so far as to say that "the employee's motivation should not be a consideration" at all in determining the imposition of liability. *Marston v. Minneapolis Clinic of Psychiatry* (1982), Minn., 329 N.W.2d 306, 311. There, a mental health facility was held liable under respondeat superior for sexual improprieties committed by one of its doctors who exploited the physical or emotional access to two patients afforded by their association through the clinic. The Court stated,

> [I]t is both unrealistic and artificial to determine at which point the [acts] leave the sphere of the employer's business and become motivated by personal animosity—or an improper, personal benefit.

In *Lyon v. Carey*, 533 F.2d 649 (D.C. Cir. 1976), a customer was raped by a delivery man following an argument over the terms of the delivery. The scope of employment question was found to be

> a question of fact for the trier of fact, rather than a question of law for the court, whether the assault stemmed from purely and solely personal sources or arose out of the conduct of the employer's business.

The Court stated that cases of this sort

> are decided on the basis that a master is liable for an assault *arising out of*, and committed *in the course of* the employment, even though it is accompanied by or motivated in part by emotions of passion, savagery or personal revenge,

(emphasis in original), and found that it was the jury's job to determine whether the assault was "the result of only propinquity and lust" or whether it "stemmed from job-related sources."

A jury presented with the facts of this case might find that Robert Griffin acted to an appreciable extent to further his master's business, that his actions were, "at least for a time, authorized by his employer, related to the service for which he was employed, and motivated to an extent by [his employer's] interests," and that, therefore, his wrongful acts fell within the scope of his employment and Heritage should be accountable. Conversely, a jury might find that Griffin's acts were so "divorced in time, place and purpose" from his employment duties as to preclude the imposition of liability on his employer. The nature of the acts were, at the very least, sufficiently associated with Griffin's authorized duties to escape dismissal on summary judgment. The trial court's entry of judgment for Heritage on that motion is therefore reversed.

The opinion of the Court of Appeals is vacated, the trial court is reversed, and this cause is remanded with instructions to grant David's motion to proceed to trial on all claims in a manner not inconsistent with this opinion.

Notes

1. In *Stropes v. Heritage House Children's Ctr.*, the court, in holding there was a question of fact as to whether the sexual assault was within the scope of employment, relied in part on language from *Marston v. Minneapolis Clinic of Psychiatry* to the effect that the traditional focus on a servant's motives or purpose was "both unrealistic

and artificial." The court also relied on *Gomez v. Adams* and *Tippecanoe Beverages v. S.A. El Aguila Brewing Co.*, both of which involved employee conversion of property they were authorized to receive on behalf of their employer. In *Entente Mineral Co. v. Parker*, Judge Thornberry pointed out that the Restatement section 219(2)(d) liability is often "conflated" with Restatement section 219(1) scope of employment liability. Does the *Stropes v. Heritage House Children's Ctr.* opinion make the same error?

2. *Mary M. v. City of Los Angeles,* 54 Cal. 3d 202, 285 Cal. Rptr. 99, 814 P.2d 1341 (1991), involved the responsibility of the City of Los Angeles for a police officer's criminal rape of a woman the officer had detained. About 2:30 a.m., Sergeant Schroyer of the Los Angeles Police Department stopped Mary M. for erratic driving. Schroyer was in uniform, wore a badge and a gun, and was driving a marked black-and-white police car. When Mary M. did not do well on a field sobriety test, she began to cry, and pleaded with Schroyer not to arrest her. Schroyer ordered her to get in the police car, and drove her home. When they arrived, Schroyer told her that he expected "payment" for taking her home instead of to jail. She tried to run away, but Schroyer threw her on the couch. She screamed, but Schroyer put his hand over her mouth and threatened to take her to jail. At that point, she stopped struggling, and Schroyer raped her.

At trial, the jury found that Sergeant Schroyer was acting within the scope of his employment. On appeal, the court of appeals reversed, holding that Schroyer's conduct was, as a matter of law, outside the scope of his employment:

> [Schroyer's rape of Mary M. was] an independent, self-serving pursuit wholly personally motivated and unrelated to his law enforcement duties.

Mary M. v. City of Los Angeles, 246 Cal. Rptr. 487 (App. 1988). The California Supreme Court reversed the court of appeals. Although the court couched its analysis in terms of scope of employment, and did not even cite Restatement section 219(2)(d), its ruling focused on the officer's abuse of his authority as a police officer:

> [S]ociety has granted police officers extraordinary power and authority over its citizenry. An officer who detains an individual is acting as the official representative of the state, with all of its coercive power. As visible symbols of that power, an officer is given a distinctively marked car, a uniform, a badge, and a gun. As one court commented,
>
> > police officers [exercise] the most awesome and dangerous power that a democratic state possesses with respect to its residents—the power to use lawful force to arrest and detain them.
>
> (*Policeman's Benev. Ass'n of N.J. v. Washington Tp.* (3rd Cir. 1988) '850 F.2d 133, 141.) Inherent in this formidable power is the potential for abuse. The cost resulting from misuse of that power should be borne by the community, because of the substantial benefits that the community derives from the lawful exercise of police power.
>
> The City nevertheless maintains that a police officer who commits rape while on duty can never be acting within the scope of his employment because the conduct is so unusual that to impose liability on the officer's employer in that instance would be unfair.
>
> As noted previously, society has granted police officers great power and control over criminal suspects. Officers may detain such persons at gunpoint,

place them in handcuffs, remove them from their residences, order them into police cars and, in some circumstances, may even use deadly force. The law permits police officers to ensure their own safety by frisking persons they have detained, thereby subjecting detainees to a form of nonconsensual touching ordinarily deemed highly offensive in our society. In view of the considerable power and authority that police officers possess, it is neither startling nor unexpected that on occasion an officer will misuse that authority by engaging in assaultive conduct. The precise circumstances of the assault need not be anticipated, so long as the risk is one that is reasonably foreseeable. Sexual assaults by police officers are fortunately uncommon; nevertheless, the risk of such tortious conduct is broadly incidental to the enterprise of law enforcement, and thus liability for such acts may appropriately be imposed on the employing public entity.

Here, Sergeant Schroyer was acting within the scope of his employment when he detained plaintiff for erratic driving, when he ordered her to get out of her car and to perform a field sobriety test, and when he ordered her to get in his police car. Then, misusing his authority as a law enforcement officer, he drove her to her home, where he raped her. When plaintiff attempted to resist Sergeant Schroyer's criminal conduct, he continued to assert his authority by threatening to take her to jail. Viewing the transaction as a whole, it cannot be said that, as a matter of law, Sergeant Schroyer was acting outside the scope of his employment when he raped plaintiff.

[W]e hold that when, as in this case, a police officer on duty misuses his official authority by raping a woman whom he has detained, the public entity that employs him can be held vicariously liable. This does not mean that, as a matter of law, the public employer is vicariously liable whenever an on-duty officer commits a sexual assault. Rather, this is a question of fact for the jury. In this case, plaintiff presented evidence that would support the conclusion that the rape arose from misuse of official authority. Sergeant Schroyer detained plaintiff when he was on duty, in uniform, and armed. He accomplished the detention by activating the red lights on his patrol car. Taking advantage of his authority and control as a law enforcement officer, he ordered plaintiff into his car and transported her to her home, where he threw her on a couch. When plaintiff screamed, Sergeant Schroyer again resorted to his authority and control as a police officer by threatening to take her to jail. Based on these facts, the jury could reasonably conclude that Sergeant Schroyer was acting in the [scope] of his employment when he sexually assaulted plaintiff.

Our society has entrusted police officers with enforcing its laws and ensuring the safety of the lives and property of its members. In carrying out these important responsibilities, the police act with the authority of the state. When police officers on duty misuse that formidable power to commit sexual assaults, the public employer must be held accountable for their actions. " 'It is, after all, the state which puts the officer in a position to employ force and which benefits from its use.' " (*Thomas v. Johnson* (D.D.C. 1968) 295 F. Supp. 1025, 1032, quoting Jaffe, *Suits Against Governments and Officers: Damage Actions* (1963) 77 Harv. L. Rev. 209, 229.)

3. In another portion of the opinion in *Stropes v. Heritage House Children's Ctr.*, the court held that Heritage House owed its patients a "non-delegable duty to provide protection and care" similar to that imposed on common carriers. *See also*

Restatement § 219(2)(*c*). As will be discussed in the next chapter, the existence of a non-delegable duty of care is also a basis for holding the employer of an independent contractor liable for the latter's torts.

3. Ratification of Torts and Crimes

Although it may seem incredible, a master may ratify a tort committed by a non-servant or a servant acting outside the scope of employment. Restatement § 218. For the most part, the principles developed in chapter 4, including the partial ratification rule, also apply to the ratification of torts.

For example, in *Dempsey v. Chambers*, 154 Mass. 330, 28 N.E. 279 (1891), Patrick Dempsey sued James Chambers for McCullock's negligence in unloading coal ordered by the plaintiff from the defendant. McCullock, who was not Chambers' servant, undertook to deliver the coal without his knowledge. While he was delivering the coal, McCullock broke a pane of glass in the window of the plaintiff's building. Afterward, with full knowledge of the accident and of McCullock's delivery of the coal, Chambers billed Dempsey for the coal.

> The earliest instance of liability by ratification in the English law was where a man retained property acquired through the wrongful act of another. If we assume that an alleged principal, by adopting an act that was unlawful when done, can make the act lawful, it follows that he adopts at his peril and is liable if it should turn out that his previous command would not have justified the act. It has never been doubted that a person's subsequent agreement to a trespass done in his name and for his benefit amounts to a command so far as to make him answerable. Doubts have been expressed about whether this doctrine applied to a case of a bare personal tort. If a man assaulted another in the street out of his own head, it would seem rather strong to say that if he merely called himself my servant and I afterward assented, our mere words, without more, would make me a party to the assault. Perhaps the application of the doctrine would be avoided on the ground that the facts did not show an act done for the defendant's benefit.
>
> But the language generally used by judges and text writers and the decisions we have been able to find are broad enough to cover a case like the present one where the ratification is established. The ratification was not directed specifically to McCullock's trespass, and that act was not for the defendant's benefit if taken by itself, but it was so connected with McCullock's employment that the defendant would have been liable as master if McCullock really had been his servant when delivering the coal. The defendant's ratification of the employment established the relation of master and servant from the beginning, with all its incidents, including the anomalous liability for his negligent acts. The ratification goes to the relation and establishes it ab initio. The relation existing, the master is answerable for torts he has not ratified specifically, just as he is for those he has not committed, and as he may be for those he has expressly forbidden.

Even where a servant acts *within* the scope of employment, ratification may be important in determining whether the master should be liable for *punitive damages*. Under Restatement section 217C, punitive damages (assuming that they are otherwise appropriate) may be imposed on a master or principal on account of a servant's or agent's wrongful act,

> if, but *only* if:
>
> (a) the principal authorized the doing and the manner of the act, or
>
> (b) the agent was unfit and the principal was reckless in employing him, or
>
> (c) the agent was employed in a managerial capacity and was acting in the scope of employment, or
>
> (d) the principal or a managerial agent of the principal *ratified* or approved the act.

(emphasis added).

4. Liability to Passengers

Pierson v. United States

527 F.2d 459 (9th Cir. 1975)

SNEED, Circuit Judge:

This case comes to us on an appeal from an order of the district court granting the motion of the United States for summary judgment against Mrs. Pierson in her suit under the Federal Tort Claims Act, 28 U.S.C. § 1346 (1970).

The facts are somewhat unusual. In brief, plaintiff's husband, Douglas Pierson, was killed in the crash of a United States Army aircraft on August 6, 1969 in the State of Washington. Mr. Pierson was then employed as a biologist by the State of Washington and was involved in radio-tracking elk on the Olympic Peninsula. We assume, without deciding, that this endeavor, although partially federally funded, was for all relevant purposes a state project.

In the early part of August 1969, Dr. Wendell Dodge, a United States Department of the Interior research biologist working for the Bureau of Sport Fisheries and Wildlife, made a request of Major Leo Schmitz, the standardization and training officer at Gray Army Air Field in Washington, for the use of a military aircraft. The aircraft was to be used in radio-tracking porcupines in the same general area where Pierson was radio-tracking elk. Major Schmitz obtained approval for this request from Dodge's supervisors, but not from his own, and authorized the use of a military aircraft in the project. It is undisputed that such authorization violated a number of Department of the Army and Department of Defense regulations. It will be assumed that Major Schmitz had no actual authority to authorize the flight, although apparently he did not realize this.

One porcupine tracking mission was flown on August 4, 1969. A second had been planned for August 8, but was changed to August 6 upon Pierson's request to Dodge to allow the plane to be used for the state elk tracking project. The rescheduling was apparently done without the knowledge of Major Schmitz. During the August 6 flight the aircraft crashed, killing all three occupants: the Army pilot, Pierson, and a telemetry expert who was employed by Mr. Dodge's agency. The flight request forms filled out by the pilot for the fatal flight misidentified the passengers as Department of the Army civilians ["D/A Civ."].

The Government in its brief offers three arguments to support an affirmance of the grant of summary judgment. The first argument turns on the apparent authority of Major Schmitz to authorize the use of military aircraft by employees of a state agency.

The Government argues that Major Schmitz had no apparent authority because he had no actual authority and because the United States had taken no action which could induce Pierson to believe that there was authority in Schmitz to allow a state employee to use the aircraft for an official state project not related to military affairs. The leading Washington case on apparent authority holds that the apparent authority of an agent can only be inferred from acts of the principal and not from acts of the agent. *Lamb v. General Associates, Inc.*, 60 Wash. 2d 623, 374 P.2d 677 (1962). *Lamb* goes on to state that:

> [t]he burden of establishing agency rests upon the one who asserts it. Facts and circumstances are sufficient to establish apparent authority only when a person exercising ordinary prudence, acting in good faith and conversant with business practices and customs, would be misled thereby, and such person has given due regard to such other circumstances as would cause a person of ordinary prudence to make further inquiry.
>
> A principal may be estopped to deny that his agent possesses the authority he assumes to exercise, where the principal knowingly causes or permits him so to act as to justify a third person of ordinary, careful, and prudent business habits to believe that he possesses the authority exercised, and avails himself of the benefit of the agent's acts.

The question here, then, is whether under this state law standard the United States established that no issue of material fact as to apparent authority exists and no inference from the facts is possible which would establish apparent authority.

The actions of the principal upon which an inference of apparent authority can be based need not be explicit individual communications to the party alleging apparent authority. In *Walker v. Pacific Mobile Homes, Inc.*, 68 Wash. 2d 347, 413 P.2d 3 (1966) the question was the apparent authority of a mobile home salesman to take a consignment of the plaintiff's trailer on behalf of his employer in a situation in which it was clear that there was no actual authority. In finding apparent authority the Washington Supreme Court relied on the general appearance of authority which the dealer had given the salesman by placing him on a lot labeled with the dealer's name in circumstances where there was no reason for an ordinary man of prudence to believe that the salesman did not have full power to deal in trailers—including the power to take consignments. There had been no specific representation made by the dealer with respect to consignments.[1] In the case before us, Major Schmitz did have actual au-

---

1. "The salesman's solitary presence in the company office and about the lot on several occasions, among numerous trailers on display, beneath a sign conspicuously proclaiming the whole to be an enterprise of Pacific Mobile Homes, Inc., and his towing plaintiff's trailer to the trailer lot and putting it on display there, allowed a person of ordinary business prudence to reasonably assume that the salesman had authority from Pacific Mobile Homes, Inc. to buy,

thority over the assignment and use of the aircraft which crashed when it was used for normal military training operations. Pierson knew that Schmitz had allowed Dodge to use an aircraft. According to the affidavit of Schmitz, his superiors knew of this use and did not prohibit it. The fact of the flight on August 4 and the failure to prohibit future flights is conduct by the principal (the U.S.) which would tend to establish that Schmitz had apparent authority to authorize *non-Department of Defense federal employees* to use military aircraft for a plainly non-military purpose. Hence, the issue narrows to the question of whether a reasonable and prudent man would have seen the difference between being a *non-Department of Defense federal employee* and a *state government employee* as important to the authority of Major Schmitz to allow the aircraft to be used. We cannot say that this distinction between Pierson and Dodge was enough to negate the apparent authority of Schmitz as a matter of law. The programs the two men were working on were very similar. The line between Defense Department employees and all other government employees seems to us to be, on its face, at least as significant as the federal/non-federal line. Pierson had good reason to believe the former line was not a restriction on Schmitz's power. He had no good reason to think that the latter distinction was a restriction on Schmitz.[2]

Pierson apparently had no contact with Schmitz. He worked through Dodge who in turn contacted the Army for the rescheduling of the flight. If Pierson knew that Schmitz was not contacted, or had reason to believe that he was not, then the apparent authority of Schmitz is irrelevant. However, this is a factual question which cannot be resolved on the present record.

In short, we find none of the arguments put forth for summary judgment convincing. The Order is reversed and the cause remanded.

---

sell, receive and deliver trailers for cash, on credit, consignment or in exchange. Then, too, the salesman's untrammeled access to and use of his principal's letterhead, stationery and business forms, and his seeming control of the office and lot, fortify the idea of apparent authority."

2. The Washington cases cited by the Government involving unauthorized passengers are clearly distinguishable from this case. All three involved instances in which plaintiff was invited by an employee of defendant to ride on a part of a vehicle plainly and obviously not designed to transport passengers. The Washington Supreme Court, without using the label, dealt with the cases in terms of the plaintiff assuming the risk of riding in an obviously unsafe place. *McQueen v. People's Store Co.*, 97 Wash. 387, 166 P. 626 (1917) (woman invited to ride on running board of truck); *Gruber v. Cater Transfer Co.*, 96 Wash. 544, 165 P. 491 (1917) (plaintiff invited to ride on back of moving truck); *Fischer v. Columbia & P. S. R. R.*, 52 Wash. 462, 100 P. 1005 (1909) (plaintiff invited to ride on locomotive engine). No such issue is presented in this case.

Section 242 of the Restatement (Second) of Agency (1957) cited by the Government, simply is not dispositive of the case. Section 242 states:

> A master is not subject to liability for the conduct of a servant towards a person harmed as a result of accepting or soliciting from the servant an invitation, *not binding upon the master*, to enter or remain upon the master's premises or vehicle, although the conduct which immediately causes the harm is within the scope of the servant's employment. (emphasis supplied).

The italicized phrase states a premise which is the very question at issue. The comments to this section state that it applies to a servant who, "without authority or apparent authority to do so, permits or invites persons to ride on [the master's vehicle]." In this case apparent authority is an issue, not an assumption.

Note

One issue that frequently arises in respondeat superior cases involves the liability of the master to *passengers*. These cases do not necessarily involve questions of scope of employment. For example, in *Pierson v. United States*, the pilot was clearly acting within the scope of his employment for the government. Instead, the question is whether the master owed any *duty* of care to the passenger. That turns on whether the passenger was a *trespasser* or an invitee/licensee. That status turns on whether the person inviting the passenger to ride in the vehicle had authority or apparent authority to do so. Restatement § 242.

D. Liability of Servant for Own Tort

Wheeler v. Frito-Lay, Inc.

743 F. Supp. 483 (S.D. Miss. 1990)

BARBOUR, Chief Judge.

This case is before the Court pursuant to Rule 72(a) of the Federal Rules of Civil Procedure on the Application of the Plaintiff to Review the Order of the United States Magistrate denying the Plaintiff's Motion to remand the case to the Circuit Court of Hinds County, Mississippi.

Plaintiff, a Mississippi resident, seeks to recover damages which he allegedly sustained in a collision between his automobile and a truck driven by Defendant Siler, also a Mississippi resident, and owned by Defendant Frito-Lay, a non-resident corporation. Frito-Lay does not dispute that Siler was acting within the scope of his employment at the time of the accident. The complaint alleges that Defendant Siler's negligence was a proximate cause of the injury to Plaintiff and that Defendant Frito-Lay is liable for the acts of its employee Siler under the doctrine of respondeat superior. Plaintiff's complaint prays for a joint and several judgment against both Defendants.

Defendants Frito-Lay and Siler filed a notice of removal to federal court from the Hinds County, Mississippi Circuit Court, alleging that Siler had been fraudulently joined in the suit since the complaint asked for a joint and several judgment against both Defendants and did not ask for an individual judgment against Siler. Plaintiff filed a motion to remand for lack of complete diversity. The Magistrate denied Plaintiff's motion to remand to state court.

Where removal of an action from state to federal court is sought, the party seeking removal must establish a basis for federal jurisdiction. *B., Inc. v. Miller Brewing Co.*, 663 F.2d 545, 549 (5th Cir. 1981). However, the removal of cases in which the federal court may have had original jurisdiction on the basis of diversity of citizenship is subject to limitation, and

> [a]ny civil action of which the district courts have original jurisdiction founded on a claim [of diversity of citizenship] shall be removable only if none of the parties in interest properly joined and served as defendants is a citizen of the State in which such action is brought.

28 U.S.C. § 1441(b). Thus, for removal to be proper in this case, it must be established that Siler was a fraudulently joined defendant so that his presence does not defeat diversity of citizenship jurisdiction or bring the limitation of § 1441(b) into play.

In establishing that a defendant to the action has been fraudulently joined, the removing party must show that there has been fraud in the pleading of jurisdictional facts or that there is no possibility that the plaintiff would be able to establish a claim against the allegedly improper party in a state court proceeding. There is no allegation in the instant case that Plaintiff is guilty of fraudulently pleading jurisdictional facts. Therefore, this action was properly removed to federal court only if Plaintiff would not be able to establish a claim against Defendant Siler in a state court action.

Whether a case is removable, and implicitly whether it states a cognizable claim against a defendant, is determined by reference to the allegations made in the original pleadings. The court must then evaluate those allegations in the light most favorable to the party opposing removal, resolving all contested issues of fact and law in favor of that party.

In determining if the facts alleged by the pleadings set forth a cognizable claim against the allegedly improper party, the United States Court of Appeals for the Fifth Circuit has set forth the following standard:

> If, having assumed all of the facts set forth by the plaintiff to be true and having resolved all uncertainties as to state substantive law against the defendants, the district court should find that there is no possibility of a valid cause of action being set forth against the in-state defendant(s), only then can it be said that there has been a "fraudulent joinder." However, if there is even a possibility that a state court would find a cause of action stated against any one of the named in-state defendants on the facts alleged by the plaintiff, then the federal court may find that the in-state defendants have been properly joined, that there is incomplete diversity, and that the case must be remanded to the state courts.

B., Inc., 663 F.2d at 550. Thus, applying the above standard, this court must determine whether Plaintiff has stated a claim, recognized under the laws of Mississippi, against Defendant Siler.

Defendant Frito-Lay asserts that, because Plaintiff has cast his claim in terms of the employer-employee relationship, the doctrine of respondeat superior, and has asked for a joint and several judgment against both Defendants, Siler would not be held individually liable for any of the complained of acts and has therefore been fraudulently joined in the complaint in order to defeat diversity.

Under the mandate of *Erie*, the substantive law to be applied in this case is that of Mississippi. The law of Mississippi does impute to the employer the negligence of an employee if such acts occur within the scope of employment. Where such employee negligence is imputed to the employer under the doctrine of respondeat superior, the employer may be held liable. *Granquist v. Crystal Springs Lumber Co.*, 190 Miss. 572, 1 So. 2d 216, 218 (1941). However, the fact that a judgment may be entered against an employer does not absolve the employee of liability for his acts; rather, the doctrine of respondeat superior operates to establish a joint and several liability between both the employer and the employee. While the liability of an employee under respondeat superior may not be individual in the sense that the employee is the only party responsible for the payment of any judgment, the employee nevertheless remains liable for the total amount of any judgment, though such liability will be joint and several with his employer.

In *Southern Mississippi Planning & Development District v. Robertson*, 660 F. Supp. 1057 (S.D. Miss. 1986), the court considered whether the doctrine of respondeat superior absolved corporate employees of liability for allegedly tortious conduct that took place within the scope of their employment. Noting that

> an agent or other employee, merely because of this relationship as an agent or an employee, or because of the additional fact that he has acted at the direction or command of his employer, cannot escape or exonerate himself from liability to a third person for his own negligence,

the court concluded that employees remain individually liable for torts of their own commission despite the fact that employers may also become primarily liable through respondeat superior.

Under the rationale expressed in these cases, the Court cannot conclude that Plaintiff would be unable to assert a claim for relief against Defendant Siler in a state court proceeding merely on the basis of the respondeat superior doctrine. While that doctrine may be used to establish liability on the part of the employer, it does not operate to relieve the employee of liability, and thus, Plaintiff may be able to obtain relief against Defendant Siler in addition to any relief that may be obtained against Defendant Frito-Lay.

Defendant Frito-Lay has asserted that the laws of agency pertaining to acts of a disclosed principal should be applied in this case. Defendant relies on the case of *Gray v. United States Fidelity & Guaranty*, [646 F. Supp. 27 (S.D. Miss. 1986)], wherein the court considered the propriety of removal in a suit brought by a Mississippi resident against a nonresident insurance corporation and its Mississippi agent for breach of contract, gross negligence, and bad faith handling of a claim. Noting that an agent for a disclosed principal incurs no personal liability for a breach of duty or contract between the disclosed principal and a third party, the court found that no cause of action had been stated against an agent where the third party had brought a suit for breach of contract and there were no allegations that the agent acted outside of the scope of his agency. However, where a third party was able to establish separate, tortious conduct by the agent, the agent could be held personally liable. Since the agent was not a party to the insurance contract in question, and since the complaint did not allege any tortious acts by the agent outside of the scope of his employment, no claim for relief had been stated against the agent and removal of the case to federal court was proper.

The facts of *Gray* are distinguishable from the facts of the instant case and therefore preclude this Court from applying the rationale of that decision. The *Gray* suit involved claims that rely on a contractual relationship between the parties: breach of contract, bad faith performance of contractual duties, and grossly negligent performance of contractual duties. In the context of contractual duties, the "disclosed principal" rule does apply, and the agent does not incur personal liability to third parties for acts within the scope of his employment. Conversely, the instant case deals with a tort allegedly committed by the employee. Defendant Siler will remain personally liable for such tortious conduct even if it occurred within the scope of his employment. The application of respondeat superior does not alter this result.

In light of the above cited authority, this Court finds that there is a possibility that a state court could determine that a cause of action has been stated against Defendant Siler. Therefore, he has not been fraudulently joined in this suit. Because Defendant Siler is a proper party to this suit, complete diversity does not exist between Plaintiff and all Defendants, and this Court is without jurisdiction to hear the case.

Accordingly, this cause will be remanded to the Circuit Court for the First Judicial District of Hinds County, Mississippi for further proceedings.

Note

Because the master and the servant are jointly and severally liable to a third person injured by the servant's tort, the doctrine of *election of remedies* studied in chapter 1 does not apply. For example, in *Orrock v. Crouse Realtors, Inc.,* 823 S.W.2d 40 (Mo. App. 1991), the plaintiff (Orrock) sued Crouse for breach of contract and misrepresentation based on a misrepresentation by Crouse's agent (Flynn) in the sale of Crouse's property to Orrock. In a previous suit, Orrock had obtained a default judgment against Flynn, the agent. The trial court entered a summary judgment in favor of Crouse on the grounds that Orrock had elected to proceed against the agent, so was precluded from pursuing Crouse as principal. On appeal, the summary judgment was reversed as to the *misrepresentation* cause of action (but not the breach of contract cause of action):

> The applicable rule is that if there is an election to pursue one of two inconsistent theories, mere entry of a judgment bars suit on the second theory. However, if there is an election between two consistent theories, only satisfaction of a judgment bars proceedings under the second theory.
>
> This case does not involve an election of inconsistent theories. The test of inconsistency is that one theory must allege what the other denies, or that the theory must be repugnant to the other. The plaintiff obtained judgment against the agent and now bring [sic] suit against the principal under the same theories of law. Under these principles it is clear that
>
> > [A] person injured by the act of an agent for which the principal is liable can bring separate actions against either one.
>
> Seavey, *Agency* § 95, p. 170 (1964 Hornbook Edition).

Fireman's Fund American Insurance Cos. v. Turner

260 Ore. 30, 488 P.2d 429 (1971)

TONGUE, Justice.

This is an action for indemnity brought by the insurer of an employer against an employee. The purpose of the action is to recover from insurer of the employee the defense costs and amount paid by the insurer of the employer in satisfaction of a judgment against both employer and employee in favor of a third party injured by an automobile owned by the employee and negligently driven by him in the course of his employment. Plaintiff appeals from a judgment in favor of defendant as entered by the court, sitting without a jury.

Plaintiff issued to Oregon Sign & Neon Corporation (Oregon Sign) a policy of liability insurance with limits for personal injury in the sum of $100,000. That policy covered Oregon Sign against liability arising from the operation of vehicles owned by certain employees, including defendant, but did not cover the employees against liability. The policy also contained a subrogation clause in general form, under which plaintiff, as the insurer, was subrogated to the rights of Oregon Sign in the event that plaintiff, as its insurer, made payments under the terms of the policy.

Defendant was the manager of Oregon Sign and carried his own liability under a policy with limits of $10,000 for injury to one person. He was paid a monthly "car allowance" by Oregon Sign for expenses incurred in the operation of his car for business purposes.

While operating his automobile in the course of his employer's business defendant rear-ended another automobile. The party injured in that accident brought an action for personal injuries and recovered judgment in the sum of $9,177.23 and $75 in costs against both Oregon Sign and defendant, based solely on the doctrine of respondeat superior, without claim of negligence by it as employer.

Plaintiff insurer paid $7,401.76 in satisfaction of that judgment (or 10/11th of that judgment), and expended an additional $1,186 in defending the action. Defendant's insurer contributed the balance (or 1/11th), in satisfaction of that same judgment.

The trial court made the following additional finding of fact:

> That the negligence of Robert S. Turner was established at the trial of the cause, and that the Court having heard evidence on the nature of the accident and the conduct of the defendant at the time of said accident finds that the accident resulted from inadvertence [sic] and a mistake of judgment on the part of Robert S. Turner, but that Robert S. Turner at the time of the accident was rendering good and faithful service to his employer.

The trial court also made the following conclusions of law:

> That no recovery may be had by an employer against an employee even though such employee is guilty of negligence constituting mere inadvertence [sic] or mistake where the employee is at the time complained of rendering good and faithful service to his employer.
>
> That plaintiff's action may not be maintained because it is against public policy to permit subrogation of a personal injury award.
>
> That each carrier having discharged its pro rata share of the judgment, and each having received a premium therefor no recovery can be had by the one against the other.

Plaintiff, as appellant, contends that it has long been recognized at common law and by most courts, including this court, that an employer held vicariously liable to a third person injured by the negligence of an employee, without negligence on the part of the employer, may seek indemnity against the employee.[3]

Defendant, while recognizing the authorities cited by plaintiff, contends that "considerations of public policy [are] of greater importance than recognition of an out-dated rule of law exercised without regard to its effect." Thus, defendant contends that Oregon Sign, as an employer, knew that it was inevitable that defendant in driving from 24,000 to 36,000 miles each year would have an accident; that defendant obtained insurance coverage to protect it against such accidents and that where, as in this case, there was no drinking or gross negligence, but no more than "mere inadvertent negligence which was within the contemplation of the parties," the em-

---

3. Restatement (Second) Agency (1958) § 401, comment d; Restatement, Restitution (1937) § 96, comment a.

ployer should not, as a matter of public policy, be entitled to "pass the economic loss off on to the employee when it is foreseeable at the outset."

We may agree that this contention may have considerable merit as a matter of abstract justice, depending upon the circumstances of the particular case. Indeed, the common law rule of indemnity by an employer against his employees has been strongly criticized for much the same reasons. Defendant has cited no cases, however, in which the courts have undertaken to abolish that rule by judicial decision, and perhaps for good reason.

The "fault concept"—that all persons should be held responsible for the consequences of their wrongful acts, including "inadvertent negligence"—while subject to criticism, is still firmly established as the foundation of tort liability. Exceptions to and modifications of that rule, such as the requirement of gross negligence, rather than simple negligence, as the basis for liability of the driver of an automobile to a guest passenger have usually been adopted as the result of statute, rather than court decision. And while the legislatures, rather than the courts, are ordinarily considered to have the primary responsibility for changes in the law for reasons of public policy, legislation which undertakes to relieve persons from responsibility for their wrongful acts is also usually subject to strong criticism. (Witness the current controversy over proposals for "no-fault" insurance legislation.)

It has been contended that to permit employers to seek such indemnity against their employees would "thwart efficient loss distribution in pursuit of perfecting the fault principle" and that "if this doctrine were carried to its logical conclusion most of our accident loss would ultimately be paid for by the operators of machines or other workmen."

In considering this contention, however, it must be kept in mind that, as a practical matter, few employers seek to exercise such a right of indemnity against their individual employees, and for three good reasons: (a) the adverse effect upon employee morale; (b) the inability of most employees to pay such indemnity; and (c) the opposition of unions. And while in cases involving automobile accidents the insurers of employers may not be inhibited by these considerations, most employees today also carry automobile liability insurance, as in this case. In addition, in this case, defendant was paid a monthly "car allowance" to cover the cost of expenses incurred in the operation of his car for business purposes. This, of course, raises the problem of the exercise by the insurer of an employer of its rights of subrogation and the problem of whether the insurance companies for both employer and employee should contribute to the loss in a case such as this, as considered separately below.

It must also be kept in mind that the rule of vicarious liability of employers, although a court-made rule, is a rule under which persons injured by the wrongful acts of employees may seek recovery against the employer as the one best able to pay and to distribute the resulting loss—all in the absence of any negligence or "fault" on part of the employer. Thus, it is contended, and with some merit, that if such liability without fault is imposed on the employer, it is not contrary to public policy to permit him to seek indemnity against the person at fault, despite the fact that such person may be his employee.

In any event, it is our view that the right of an employer held vicariously liable to a third person injured by the wrongful act of an employee to seek indemnity against the employee is too well established to be abolished at this time by decision of this court as contrary to public policy, at least under the facts and circumstances of this case.

Defendant next contends that even assuming such a right of indemnity, the basis for such a right is the employment contract, with the servant's act being a breach of an implied condition of that contract, and that the extent of the duty of the employee under his contract of employment is "to render faithful service to the employer." Thus, it is contended that the employee should not be held liable to the employer for "mere inadvertent negligence," or "mistake of judgment," so long as he was "rendering good and faithful service to his employer," as found by the trial court in this case. Defendant also contends that "this modern view is accepted in the cases interpreting the Federal Tort Claims Act where indemnity against the negligent employee by the United States is not permitted."

Although many of the authorities speak of the basis for the employer's right of indemnity in terms of a breach by the employee of an implied condition of his employment contract, most authorities recognize a much broader basis for that right, to the effect that any person who, without fault, becomes liable for the wrongful conduct of another is entitled to indemnity against the other and that this extends to all wrongful conduct, including ordinary negligence ("mere inadvertence" or "mistake of judgment").

In any event, the duty of an agent or employee is usually considered to include not only a duty to render "faithful" service, but also a duty to exercise reasonable care in the performance of his duties. Accordingly, and whether the right of an employer to seek indemnity from an employee is to be considered as a right based upon tort or upon implied contract, we hold, in accordance with what we believe to be the weight of authority, as well as our previous decisions, that such a right includes the right to seek indemnity from liability resulting from any and all "wrongful acts" by employees, including ordinary negligence.

[T]he judgment of the trial court must be reversed and the case remanded for proceedings not inconsistent with this opinion.

Note

If the master *ratifies* the servant's wrongful act, would the master be entitled to indemnification from the servant? Does *Rakestraw v. Rodriguez*, discussed in chapter 4, bear on this question?

Yates v. New South Pizza, Ltd.

412 S.E.2d 666 (N.C. 1992)

FRYE, Justice.

On 5 September 1985, plaintiff was a passenger in an automobile owned by Franklin Hobert Simmons and operated by Lisa Dawn Simmons. Donald Lee Powell, a delivery person for defendant, New South Pizza, Ltd., d/b/a Domino's Pizza, ran a stop sign and collided with the Simmons car. As a result of the collision, plaintiff suffered injuries to his head and right wrist, and permanent damage to his left hip. On 26 August 1987, plaintiff executed a covenant not to sue Powell or his insurer in exchange for $25,000 consideration, the amount of coverage under Powell's insurance policy. The covenant expressly reserved all rights to proceed against defendant, Powell's employer, and reads in relevant part:

> It is understood that [plaintiff] contends there are joint tortfeasors in this matter; to wit, Donald Lee Powell and Domino's Pizza, Inc., said joint tortfeasor relationship arising out of the servant-master relationship and [plaintiff] expressly reserves and maintains his right to pursue any and all claims against Domino's Pizza, Inc. arising out of the incident and that [plaintiff] agrees only not to sue Donald Lee Powell and INA/Action, his vehicular insurance carrier.

The issue before this Court is whether an injured plaintiff is entitled to proceed against an employer on the theory of respondeat superior after having executed, for valuable consideration, a covenant not to sue the negligent employee or his insurer.

At trial, the employer (defendant) admitted that the employee (Powell) was acting within the scope of his employment when the collision occurred but denied that Powell was negligent in causing the collision. Defendant also moved for summary judgment, arguing that the settlement between plaintiff and Powell operated to release defendant from liability as a matter of law. The trial court granted the motion. The Court of Appeals affirmed the trial court, concluding that the covenant not to sue released any claim against defendant under the doctrine of respondeat superior. The court further held that when there is a right of indemnity from another tort-feasor, the Uniform Contribution Among Tort-feasors Act, N.C.G.S. § 1B-1, et seq. (the Act),[1] does not apply.

Plaintiff contends that the Court of Appeals erred in holding that the Act does not apply to the present case. Plaintiff argues that the plain language of the Act includes employer-employee liability, and thus a covenant not to sue the employee does not release the employer pursuant to section 1B-4 of the Act. Defendant contends that the Act is irrelevant to the disposition of this case because, inter alia, an employer is not a tort-feasor within the meaning of the Act.

We agree with plaintiff that section 1B-4 of the Act controls the disposition of this case. Section 1B-4 of the Act provides:

> When a release or a covenant not to sue or not to enforce judgment is given in good faith to one or more persons liable in tort for the same injury or the same wrongful death:
>
> (1) It does not discharge any of the other tort-feasors from liability for the injury or wrongful death unless its terms so provide; but it reduces the claim against the others to the extent of any amount stipulated by the release or the covenant, or in the amount of the consideration paid for it, whichever is the greater; and,
>
> (2) It discharges the tort-feasor to whom it is given from all liability for contribution to any other tort-feasor.

The question of whether this provision applies to vicarious liability in the master-servant context is one of first impression for this Court. Other courts, as noted by the Court of Appeals, have not been uniform in interpreting this provision of the

---

1. The Uniform Contribution Among Tort-feasors Act was originally promulgated in 1939 by the National Conference of Commissioners on Uniform State Laws. It was revised in 1955. North Carolina adopted the 1955 version in 1967.

Uniform Act. We agree with those courts which have held that this provision does apply to liability that has been vicariously derived. See, e.g., *Alaska Airlines v. Sweat*, 568 P.2d 916, 929 (Alaska 1977) (release of independent contractor negligently performing licensed common carrier's nondelegable duty does not release carrier); *Brady v. Prairie Material Sales, Inc.*, 190 Ill. App. 3d 571, 583, 546 N.E.2d 802, 810 (2d Dist. 1989), appeal denied, 129 Ill. 2d 561, 550 N.E.2d 553 (1990) ("Since the servant who acts negligently is obviously a person liable in tort, it is reasonable to conclude that the liability of the master, although derivative, is still a form of liability in tort as that term is used in the Contribution Act, and an employer is also a "tortfeasor" as that term is used in the Contribution Act."); [and citing 6 more cases]; *contra, e.g., Mamalis v. Atlas Van Lines, Inc.*, 364 Pa. Super. 360, 528 A.2d 198, aff'd, 522 Pa. 214, 560 A.2d 1380 (1989) (interpreting the 1939 version of the Act); *Craven v. Lawson*, 534 S.W.2d 653 (Tenn. 1976). We hold, therefore, that section 1B-4 applies to master-servant vicarious liability, and that on the facts of this case, the covenant not to sue the employee does not release defendant-employer from liability.

We recognize that at common law this Court held that the release of or covenant not to sue the servant also served to release the master. *Smith v. R.R.*, 151 N.C. 479, 66 S.E. 435 (1909). Since the decision in *Smith*, our legislature has adopted the Uniform Contribution Among Tort-feasors Act. The question becomes, therefore, whether the Act changes this holding in *Smith*. Defendant argues that the Act is not applicable to the present situation because a vicariously liable master is not a wrongdoer and therefore not a "tort-feasor." Although defendant's argument finds support in our case law prior to the adoption of the Uniform Act, we believe the Act broadens the definition of "tort-feasor" to encompass a vicariously liable master. Stated differently, *for purposes of this Act*, a "tort-feasor" is one who is liable in tort.

An analysis of the 1939 Act and its 1955 revision supports our conclusion. The 1939 Act defined "joint tort-feasors" broadly:

> For the purposes of this chapter[,] the term 'joint tort-feasors' means two or more persons jointly or severally liable in tort for the same injury to person or property, whether or not judgment has been recovered against all or some of them.

This language clearly includes master-servant vicarious liability. Although this definition was omitted from the 1955 Act,[2] we believe the 1955 Act is consistent with this broad definition. For example, section 1B-1(a) provides as follows:

> Except as otherwise provided in this Article, where two or more persons become jointly or severally liable in tort for the same injury to person or property or for the same wrongful death, there is a right of contribution among them even though judgment has not been recovered against any or all of them.

2. The term "joint tort-feasor" and its definition were not included in the 1955 version of the Act because the term "joint tort-feasor" in the 1939 Act led to confusion:

> The term 'joint tort-feasors' was not used in the Uniform Act in order to avoid confusion in those jurisdictions where persons who act independently, and not in concert, cannot always be joined as defendants.

The term "joint tort-feasor" was replaced with "tort-feasor." Neither the 1955 Uniform Act nor the North Carolina statute defines "tort-feasor."

More importantly, as we have noted, section 1B-4 provides that when a release or covenant not to sue is given in good faith "to one of two or more persons liable in tort for the same injury or the same wrongful death," it does not discharge "any of the other tort-feasors from liability." Clearly, both the master and the servant are "persons liable in tort for the same injury," and "tort-feasors" as used in this provision refers to those persons liable in tort. We therefore hold that the provisions of N.C.G.S. § 1B-4 apply to situations involving master-servant vicarious liability, such as in the instant case.

Defendant also suggests that section 1B-1(f) of the Act excludes indemnity actions. We disagree. Section 1B-1(f) reads:

> This Article does not impair any right of indemnity under existing law. Where one tort-feasor is entitled to indemnity from another, the right of the indemnity obligee is for indemnity and not contribution, and the indemnity obligor is not entitled to contribution from the obligee for any portion of his indemnity obligation.

We agree with the Supreme Court of Nevada that nothing in this provision precludes application of the Act to situations involving vicarious liability. *Van Cleave [v. Gamboni Construction Co.]*, 101 Nev. at 529, 706 P.2d at 848. The provision

> simply states that the vicariously liable employer would have a right to indemnity, rather than contribution. This provision merely provides that no contribution exists where indemnity exists.

In its opinion, the Court of Appeals noted that because a right of indemnity remains against a servant who has settled with the injured party, the servant effectively gains nothing. Thus, the underlying policy of the statute to encourage settlements is undermined. We do not agree. Although the Court of Appeals is correct that the servant remains liable to the master, in practice the master may elect not to seek indemnification. This is especially true in cases such as this one where the servant's settlement was for the entire amount of his insurance coverage. Given that the master may choose not to seek indemnity from his servant, who in many cases may be judgment proof, the servant's settlement with the injured party fulfills the underlying policy of the Act.

REVERSED AND REMANDED.

MEYER, J., dissenting [with Exum, C.J., and Whichard, J.]:

The majority errs when it concludes that N.C.G.S. § 1B-4 (governing contribution among tort-feasors) controls the outcome here. Traditional tools of statutory construction require that the principles of common law, rather than the statute, dictate the outcome in this case.

As an initial matter, the majority misconstrues the plain language and intent of N.C.G.S. § 1B-4, concluding that "the Act broadens the definition of 'tort-feasor' to encompass a vicariously liable master." When technical terms or terms of art are used in a statute, they are presumed to have been used with their technical meaning in mind. Where the language of a statute is clear and unambiguous, there is no room for judicial construction, and the Court must give the language its plain and definite meaning and resist temptation to interpolate or superimpose provisions and limitations not contained therein.

Such should be the case with respect to the term "tort-feasor" as used in N.C.G.S. § 1B-4. "Tort-feasor" is defined as "[a] wrongdoer, an individual or business that *commits or is guilty of a tort.*" Black's Law Dictionary 1489 (6th ed. 1990) (emphasis added). This Court has evinced an identical view. "To make persons joint tort feasors they must actively participate in the act which causes the injury." *Brown v. Louisburg*, 126 N.C. 701, 703, 36 S.E. 166, 167 (1900).

In short, the majority's conclusion that a vicariously liable defendant is a "tort-feasor" exists in stark contrast to North Carolina law as it has existed for over ninety years as well as in contrast to the law of many other states. The conclusion that New South Pizza, an employer derivatively liable under only the doctrine of respondeat superior, is a "tort-feasor" blurs the significant distinction between vicarious and joint liability and is completely unsupportable given our understanding of that term.

Similarly, the majority errs in its construction of N.C.G.S. § 1B-4 when it infers from the structure of the statute itself that the legislature intended those merely vicariously liable to be "liable in tort" and thus joint "tort-feasors." While the statute's prefatory sentence speaks of "one or more persons liable in tort," the succeeding sub-paragraphs speak with particularity of "other tort-feasors," "the tort-feasor," and "any other tort-feasor." As the majority itself concedes, the term "tort-feasor" is not defined in the Act. Nevertheless, the majority states that necessarily

> both the master and the servant are 'persons liable in tort for the same injury,' and 'tort-feasors' as used in [the Act] refers to those persons liable in tort.

On this basis, the majority concludes that under N.C.G.S. § 1B-4, a master, wholly lacking in active involvement in the alleged tort, is a "tort-feasor" and therefore remains liable notwithstanding the release from liability of the directly culpable servant.

Furthermore the majority is wrong when it states that its interpretation serves the policy and ends of N.C.G.S. § 1B-4. The Uniform Act was enacted to serve two purposes. First, it was intended to "distribute the burden of responsibility equitably among those who are jointly liable and thus avoid the injustice often resulting under the common law." Unif. Contribution Among Tortfeasors Act, 12 U.L.A. commissioners' prefatory note (1955 rev.), at 59 (1975). Second, the Act was designed to encourage settlements.

The majority's decision to impose liability on a vicariously liable principal when the agent has been discharged from liability promotes neither of these goals. The avowed interest in avoiding injustice is already well served by N.C.G.S. § 1B-1(f), which provides that the Act "does not impair any right of indemnity under existing law." Moreover, under the majority's view, incentives for settlement will be lessened: even if a servant and plaintiff enter into a covenant not to sue, the servant remains potentially liable as an indemnitor. The majority's cavalier assertion that "in practice the master may elect not to seek indemnification" is unconvincing not only as an empirical matter, but also given the explicit policy goals of the Act itself.

Chapter 8

Liability for Acts of Independent Contractors

A. Non-Liability for Acts of Independent Contractors

Kane Furniture Corp. v. Miranda

506 So. 2d 1061 (Fla. App. 1987)

RYDER, Acting Chief Judge.

Kane is a furniture store which also sells carpeting. Kane sold its carpet installation business to Perrone in 1975, and since that time, Kane has provided carpet installation services through Perrone's installation business (known as Service) as well as through other independent carpet installers.

For the past ten years, however, Perrone has been the principal carpet installer at Kane's St. Petersburg store. Initially, Kane put Perrone on a two-week probationary period during which Kane inspected Perrone's work to determine that Perrone was qualified. Thereafter, Perrone was given a small work area from which to assign installation jobs. Perrone hired other independent carpet installers, such as Kraus, to complete jobs which he could not perform.

On the morning of Saturday, August 6, 1983, Perrone assigned Kraus two installation jobs from Kane. Kraus completed the installation called for by the jobs around noon. Thereafter, Kraus, in his own truck, drove to a bar with his helper, Kevin Carleton, as a passenger. After drinking for approximately four hours, Kraus attempted to drive Carleton to Kane's warehouse parking lot in order that Carleton could retrieve his car. On the way to the parking lot, Kraus, traveling at a speed in excess of 50 m.p.h., ran a stop sign and collided broadside with the Miranda vehicle. Dr. Miranda's wife, Zenaida Quintos-Miranda, a passenger in the Miranda vehicle, died in a hospital soon after the accident.

This consolidated appeal arose from a wrongful death action which Dr. Romulo Miranda brought against Kane Furniture Corporation and Joseph P. Perrone for the death of Zenaida Quintos-Miranda. Kane appeals from the trial court's final summary judgment finding that Perrone was Kane's employee and that Kraus was Kane's subemployee. Kane appeals the jury verdict finding that Kraus was acting within the scope of his employment at the time of that accident. Kane also appeals the jury verdict award of 2.3 million dollars to Dr. Miranda.

In *Cantor v. Cochran,* 184 So. 2d 173 (Fla. 1966), the Supreme Court of Florida approved the test set out in Restatement (Second) of Agency § 220[(2)] (1958) for determining whether one is an employee or independent contractor:

In determining whether one acting for another is a servant or an independent contractor, the following matters of fact, among others, are considered:

(a) the extent of control which, by the agreement, the master may exercise over the details of the work;

(b) whether or not the one employed is engaged in a distinct occupation or business;

(c) the kind of occupation, with reference to whether, in the locality, the work is usually done under the direction of the employer or by a specialist without supervision;

(d) the skill required in the particular occupation;

(e) whether the employer or the workman supplies the instrumentalities, tools, and the place of work for the person doing the work;

(f) the length of time for which the person is employed;

(g) the method of payment, whether by the time or by the job;

(h) whether or not the work is a part of the regular business of the employer;

(i) whether or not the parties believe they are creating the relationship of master and servant; and

(j) whether the principal is or is not in business.

Upon applying the Restatement test to the facts before us, we come to the conclusion that Perrone and Kraus were independent contractors, not employees.

(a) *The extent of control which, by the agreement, the master may exercise over the details of the work.*

It has been said that the extent of control is the most important factor in determining whether a person is an independent contractor or an employee. The right of control as to the mode of doing the work is the principal consideration. If a person is subject to the control or direction of another as to his results only, he is an independent contractor; if he is subject to control as to the means used to achieve the results, he is an employee.

For instance, in *Miami Herald Publishing Co. v. Kendall*, 88 So. 2d 276 (Fla. 1956), the court found that a newspaper carrier was an independent contractor and not an employee. In that case, the Miami Herald had entered into a contract with a newspaper carrier to distribute the Miami Herald within a set territory. The contract among other things provided that the carrier was an independent contractor and that the Miami Herald could not control his method of distributing or handling the newspaper. The contract defined the newscarrier's obligations: he was to furnish the names of new subscribers; to pay money collected to the appellant within a certain time; to present within forty-eight hours claims for shortages in papers; to call to appellant's attention within six days errors in statements; to handle the Miami Herald exclusively; to keep in confidence the names of subscribers; to select a substitute in the event he was unable to make his deliveries and be "responsible" for the substitute; to bear all costs of enforcing the contract; to give bond for his faithful performance of the agreement; to acquaint any successor with the route and list of subscribers; to secure delivery of papers in good condition; and to undertake to increase the number of subscribers.

The Miami Herald set the retail price of the papers and was often the recipient of customer complaints about unsatisfactory delivery of the paper. The Miami Herald, however, did not supervise delivery of the papers. Rather, the court found that the newspaper boy, while making his deliveries, "was acting alone and was a specialist, at least to the extent of following his route, remembering the addresses of subscribers who were in good standing, and collecting and properly accounting for funds coming into his hands." The newsboy was accountable for papers the publisher delivered to him whether or not he collected from the subscriber. The court stated that "we do not doubt that distribution of newspapers is a part of the regular business of the publisher but there is no reason that this cannot be done by independent contractors."

In *T & T Communications* [*v. Dept. of Labor*, 460 So. 2d 996 (Fla. App. 1984)], the court found cable installers to be independent contractors primarily because the company's only concern was with the final product or result. Although the cable installers agreed with the cable company to complete the cable installations pursuant to the cable company's plans and specifications, the installers themselves determined the method by which to accomplish the installation. The court stated that further indicia that they were independent contractors were:

> The fact that cable installers are normally unsupervised[,] are skilled tradesmen[,] provide their own tools and transportation[,] are not employed for any length of time, are paid per installation, and receive no vacation and fringe benefits.

In the instant case, although Kane's salesmen diagrammed the installation layout plan, the carpet installers, Perrone and Kraus, had unbridled discretion in the physical performance of their tasks. Perrone did not report to anyone at Kane and had absolute discretion in contracting out installation jobs. The only instructions Kane gave Perrone were that he and the other carpet installers should be neatly attired and not intoxicated while on the job. Kane also instructed Perrone on customer satisfaction.

Once the carpet installer got the job, he was on his own. He performed his work completely without Kane's supervision or any other involvement. Upon completion of his task, the installer was free to go where he pleased: to another job or, unfortunately, to the local bar.

(b) *Whether or not the one employed is engaged in a distinct occupation or business.*

Carpet installing can be viewed as a distinct occupation. Perrone and Kraus each had their own independent installation businesses. Perrone performed his services through a company which he purchased from Kane in 1975. Kraus performed his services through his own company, Mike's Carpet Service.

(c) *The kind of occupation with reference to whether, in the locality, the work is usually done under the direction of the employer or by a specialist without supervision.*

Carpet installers are skilled workers who routinely perform without supervision. Perrone and Kraus performed work which emanated through Kane sales on an "as needed" basis. Both performed without Kane's supervision. Each was responsible for his own work. Kraus guaranteed his work for one year. Each, personally, was responsible for replacing carpeting he lost or damaged.

(d) *The skill required in the particular occupation.*

Testimony at trial indicated that carpet installers are required to complete an apprenticeship in order to acquire the necessary skill to perform installation. As was aforementioned, Perrone also underwent a two-week probationary period at Kane.

(e) *Whether the employer or the workman supplies the instrumentalities, tools, and the place of work for the person doing the work.*

Perrone and Kraus supplied their own installation equipment: knives, kickers, seaming irons, etc. They owned and insured their own trucks for work. Kane did not reimburse them for mileage and other expenses, such as gasoline.

While Kane supplied Perrone with a small space and telephone from which to assign installation jobs, such accommodations did not make Perrone Kane's employee.

(f) *The length of time for which the person is employed.*

Again, Perrone and Kraus worked for Kane on an "as needed" basis. The time spent on each job varied in length. The installation jobs were assigned on an "A.M. job or P.M. job." Neither was obligated to work exclusively for Kane. Kane was not obligated to use only Perrone and Kraus.

(g) *The method of payment, whether by time or by job.*

While Kane determined the amount Perrone was paid, Perrone was paid strictly on a per yard basis. Kane made its checks out to Perrone's company. Perrone, in turn, paid Kraus and the other installers to whom he had assigned jobs.

Independent contractors are normally paid "per installation" rather than "by time." For instance, in *VIP Tours* [*v. Dept. of Labor*, 449 So. 2d 1307 (Fla. App. 1984)] a tour company was not deemed employer of tour guides using company vehicles who worked on a per job basis. In *T & T Communications*, cable splicers were found to be independent contractors where they were not employed for any length of time, were paid per installation and received no vacation or fringe benefits.

(h) *Whether or not the work is part of the regular business of the employer.*

Kane is engaged in the retail furniture business. As a part of that business, Kane also sells carpeting and advertises installation as included in the purchase price. This is the only factor favoring the conclusion that Perrone and Kraus are employees. With all the other factors pointing to the conclusion that they are independent contractors, this factor alone is insufficient to sustain a holding that they are employees.

(i) *Whether or not the parties believe they are creating the relation of master and servant.*

The parties' intent and course of dealing are important factors in determining their legal status. Clearly, the parties believed they were entering into an independent contractor relationship. Perrone and Kraus paid taxes as the owners of independent carpet installation businesses. Kane did not withhold social security or income taxes. Kane filed a Form "1099" for Perrone which is the IRS tax form a company files for nonemployees. A person who is responsible for paying all taxes due has been found to be an independent contractor.

Both Perrone and Kraus were free to accept or reject Kane's work. Perrone and Kraus were also able to work for companies in addition to Kane. Kane was not obligated to use Perrone or Kraus exclusively and, in fact, did not. Both Perrone and Kraus could hire their own employees.

Neither Perrone nor Kraus had employment agreements with Kane. Neither enjoyed the usual amenities associated with an employment relationship: fringe benefits, health care insurance, unemployment compensation, worker's compensation and paid vacations or holidays.

(j) *Whether the principal is or is not in business.*

We concur in Mr. Justice Grimes' opinion in *D.O. Creasman* [*Electronics v. Dept. of Labor*, 458 So. 2d 894 (Fla. App. 1984)] that "the relevance of this factor is obscure, but for what it is worth, appellant is in business."

Measured against the Restatement criteria, we hold that Perrone and Kraus are independent contractors.

[W]e reverse and set aside the verdict entered herein, vacate the summary final judgment and remand the matter to the trial court with instructions to enter summary judgment for Kane finding that Perrone and Kraus are independent contractors.

Pamperin v. Trinity Memorial Hospital

144 Wis. 2d 188, 423 N.W.2d 848 (1988)

CALLOW, Justice.

This is a review of an unpublished decision of the court of appeals which affirmed an order of the circuit court dismissing Trinity Memorial Hospital from [an] action brought by Clarence Pamperin to recover damages for the alleged negligence arising out of the care and treatment provided to Pamperin following his admission to Trinity's emergency room. Pamperin argues that Trinity should be liable for the negligence of a radiologist, practicing medicine at Trinity.

Because this case comes to us following motions for summary judgment, the facts before us on review are limited. In essence, they are that on January 3, 1982, Pamperin fell and injured his leg. He was thereafter taken to the emergency room at Trinity where he was examined by Dr. Ronald Schulgit. During the examination, Schulgit requested X-rays be taken of Pamperin's lower right leg. Schulgit read the X-ray, determined there was a minor ankle fracture, splinted the fracture, and then sent Pamperin home.

The next day the X-rays were read at Trinity by Dr. Boex, a radiologist. Boex also determined there was a minor ankle fracture. However, both Boex and Schulgit failed to observe that the X-rays also revealed a comminuted fracture of the proximal tibia at the knee.

[A]t the time Boex read the X-rays, he was an employee of Lakeview Radiologists, S.C. According to Boex, Lakeview is a service corporation which contracted with Trinity to provide diagnostic radiology for Trinity. Under the terms of the contract, Lakeview is to provide twenty-four hour radiological services. Trinity is to provide the physical facilities, equipment, and staff. Although Lakeview is, under the contract, prohibited from engaging in any activity which will impair its ability to provide adequate radiological services, Lakeview is not prohibited from maintaining a separate practice. However, according to Boex, Lakeview provides radiological services only to Trinity.

On May 27, 1986, Pamperin commenced [an] action in the circuit court against Trinity and Schulgit. In the complaint, Pamperin alleged that Trinity and Schulgit were negligent in the care and treatment rendered to Pamperin. Pamperin moved for summary judgment requesting an order that Trinity was vicariously liable for the negligence of Boex.

On October 27, 1986, the circuit court issued a decision granting summary judgment dismissing the malpractice action against Trinity. In reaching this conclusion, the court first held that Boex was an independent contractor. Next, the court noted that, in this case, because there was no allegation that Trinity was negligent in failing to check the credentials of Lakeview, whether the hospital was liable was "a question of agency." However, because the only type of agency relationship which would impose liability was a master-servant agency relationship, Trinity could not be liable for the acts of Boex, an independent contractor.

Pamperin appealed, and the court of appeals affirmed the circuit court's order.

We begin our review by considering Pamperin's assertion that Trinity is responsible for the negligence of Boex under the doctrine of respondeat superior. Essentially, Pamperin contends that Trinity has substantial control over Lakeview and that because of Trinity's retention of control over Lakeview, Boex—as an employee of Lakeview—is a servant of Trinity.

Under the doctrine of respondeat superior, a master is subject to liability for the tortious acts of his or her servant [committed within the scope of employment]. A servant is one who is

> employed to perform service for another in his affairs and who, with respect to his *physical conduct* in the performance of the service, is subject to the other's control or right to control.

Arsand v. City of Franklin, 83 Wis. 2d 40, 45-46, 264 N.W.2d 579 (1978) (emphasis in original). The right to control is the dominant test in determining whether an individual is a servant. However, other factors are considered, including the place of work, the time of the employment, the method of payment, the nature of the business or occupation, which party furnishes the instrumentalities or tools, the intent of the parties to the contract, and the right of summary discharge of employees.

Looking first at the element of control, we conclude that Trinity does not exercise any control over the manner in which Lakeview's radiological services are provided. The very nature of a radiologist's function requires the exercise of independent professional judgment. Accordingly, a hospital is not in a position to, and generally does not, exercise control over a radiologist's performance of his or her professional activities. Although Trinity does require that the Lakeview radiologists be members of Trinity's staff, and although Trinity retains a limited ability to monitor the quality of the care which Lakeview provides, Trinity does not reserve the right of control over the specific techniques employed by the Lakeview radiologists.

Other factors also indicate that Lakeview is not Trinity's servant. Lakeview and Trinity maintain separate offices. Each is responsible for billing and collecting for the costs associated with the particular service each provides. Consistent with this responsibility, Lakeview has final authority in establishing its fees. In addition, Lakeview is required to provide its own malpractice insurance. Finally, Lakeview is not prohibited from serving other hospitals or patients.

The factors listed by Pamperin, including Trinity's right to request review of Lakeview's performance, Trinity's ability to review procedures adopted by Lakeview, its power to approve Lakeview's appointment of a director of the radiology department, as well as the requirement that the Lakeview radiologists be members of Trinity's staff, do not compel the conclusion that Lakeview is Trinity's servant. A number of these factors focus on maintaining professional standards; they do not indicate that a master-servant relationship exists. Other factors noted by Pamperin, particularly the requirement that the Lakeview radiologists be members of Trinity's staff and subject to the hospital's approval, are imposed by statute. In addition, factors which indicate a master-servant relationship, e.g., a fixed monthly salary and withholding of taxes and social security, are not present in this case. The limited control which Trinity has reserved over Lakeview's providing radiological services does not transform Lakeview's relationship with Trinity into a master-servant relationship. Under the facts of this case, we hold, as a matter of law, that Lakeview—and thus Boex—is not Trinity's servant, i.e., Lakeview is an independent contractor. [T]he doctrine of respondeat superior is not applicable in the present case.

Notes

1. An independent contractor is one who is hired to perform physical services or to accomplish a specified task without being subject to the detailed control of the employer:

> An independent contractor is a person who contracts with another to do something for him but who is not controlled by the other nor subject to the other's right to control with respect to his physical conduct in the performance of the undertaking. He may or may not be an agent.

Restatement § 2(3). Even an "employee" may be viewed as an independent contractor, rather than a servant, for tort liability purposes. Although he or she may be an agent for purposes of contract accountability of the employer, he or she may not be a servant but an independent contractor.

2. Often, the independent contractor's business is distinct from that of the employer, and in these settings, the independent contractors will be most readily identifiable. Thus, when a merchant hires a painter to paint his or her store, hails a taxicab, or retains a private detective to investigate a competitor, the merchant has employed an independent contractor. So long as the merchant does not exercise too much control over the manner in which the painter, the cab driver, or the detective performs his or her duties, the merchant will be insulated from liability for torts committed by the painter, the cab driver, or the detective.

3. The question of whether one is an employee or an independent contractor may arise in contexts other than tort liability situations. For instance, an employer may prefer to have some individuals characterized as independent contractors to avoid liability for federal employment taxes that must be paid where employees are involved. Consider the following case. Avis Rent-A-Car System Inc., a national car rental business, paid "car shuttlers" to drive cars from one Avis station to another in order to adjust local inventories to meet demand. Car shuttlers were ordinarily servicemen, housewives, and others who were not regularly or permanently employed by Avis and who were recruited informally without interviews or training. A standard form contract was signed by the parties on each occasion of a shuttle which provided that the driver would deliver the car to a designated place at a designated time for the stated fee, that the car would remain in the same condition as when it was received by the

driver, that the car was not to be used for any purpose other than transport to the Avis station, and "that this contract in no way constitutes the contractor as an agent or employee" of Avis. The drivers did not wear Avis uniforms like other Avis employees and did not participate in the Avis employment benefit program. Furthermore, Avis did not pay federal employment taxes on the car shuttlers. Were the car shuttlers employees or independent contractors of Avis? See *Avis Rent-A-Car Sys. Inc. v. United States*, 503 F.2d 423 (2d Cir. 1974).

B. Exceptions

1. Apparent Authority/Estoppel

Pamperin v. Trinity Memorial Hospital

144 Wis.2d 188, 423 N.W.2d 848 (1988)

CALLOW, Justice.

[Re-read the facts presented earlier.]

Under the facts of this case, we hold, as a matter of law, that Lakeview—and thus Boex—is not Trinity's servant, i.e., Lakeview is an independent contractor

We turn next to Pamperin's assertion that Trinity should be liable for Boex's acts under the doctrine of apparent authority.[5] According to Pamperin, hospitals—by holding themselves out as the providers of complete medical care—should be held liable for the acts of physicians who are employees of, or appear to be employees of, the hospital. Trinity, on the other hand, argues that a hospital's liability should be limited to that stemming from negligence in selecting a physician and from the negligence of a physician who is an employee of the hospital. According to Trinity, to impose liability when the treating physician is not a servant and the hospital has not been negligent in selecting the physician would make a hospital liable for all acts of negligence occurring within the "four walls" of the hospital.

Under apparent authority, a principal may be held liable for the acts of one who reasonably appears to a third person, through acts by the principal or acts by the agent if the principal had knowledge of those acts and acquiesced in them, to be authorized to act as an agent for the principal. For liability to exist, three elements must be present:

> (1) Acts by the agent or principal justifying belief in the agency;
> (2) knowledge thereof by the party sought to be held; [and]
> (3) reliance thereon by the plaintiff, consistent with ordinary care and prudence.

[*Schaefer v. Dudarenke,* 89 Wis. 2d 483, 489-90, 278 N.W.2d 844 (1979).]

Although we have recognized the doctrine of apparent authority in other contexts, this is the first time we have been called upon to apply this doctrine to impose liability

---

5. Pamperin, in arguing that liability should be imposed, refers to the doctrine under which liability is sought as apparent/ostensible agency. To be consistent with our prior cases imposing liability under this doctrine, we shall refer to the theory of liability as apparent authority.

on a hospital for the negligence of hospital physicians who are independent contractors. Other jurisdictions, however, have imposed liability under apparent authority upon hospitals for the negligence of physicians who are independent contractors.

The courts adopting apparent authority have noted a number of reasons why the doctrine of apparent authority should be applied to suits against hospitals. In *Hardy v. Brantley,* 471 So. 2d 358, 371 (Miss. 1985), the court held that a hospital may be liable under apparent authority for the negligence of an emergency room doctor who failed to properly diagnose and treat a patient who came to the emergency room for treatment of severe abdominal pain. The court reasoned that hospitals were no longer the providers solely of the physical facilities where physicians practice their professions. According to the court, hospitals hold themselves out to the public as offering and rendering quality health care services. In so doing, they act through persons whose services are engaged by the hospitals. Because the hospitals stood to profit from the acts of those hired to provide medical care, the court concluded that it would be anomalous for the hospitals to escape liability if those same individuals delivered care below minimally acceptable standards.

The court further stressed that "patients often seek emergency care and treatment from the hospital, not from any particular physician. The patient entering the hospital emergency room seldom knows the name of the physician who will treat him." Accordingly, the court concluded that, where the hospital holds itself out as the provider of care and the patient looks to the hospital for care and treatment, the hospital should be estopped from denying responsibility.

The New Jersey Superior Court, in holding that a hospital may be liable for the negligence of physicians providing emergency room treatment, noted that imposing liability was particularly appropriate when examined in terms of the reasonable expectations of the public. *Arthur* [*v. St. Peters Hospital*, 169 N.J. Super. 575, 583, 405 A.2d 443 (1979)]. According to the court,

> generally people who seek medical help through the emergency room facilities of modern-day hospitals are unaware of the status of the various professionals working there. Absent a situation where the patient is directed by his own physician or where the patient makes an independent selection as to which physicians he will use while there, it is the reputation of the hospital itself upon which he would rely.

Similarly, in *Paintsville* [*Hospital Co. v. Rose*, 683 S.W.2d 255, 258 (Ky. 1985)], the court looked at the perceptions of the patients in deciding whether to apply the doctrine of apparent authority to lawsuits against hospitals. After noting that patients in emergency rooms are generally unaware of the employment status of the various professionals working in an emergency room, the court concluded that "it is unreasonable to put a duty on the patient to inquire of each person who treats him whether he is an employee or independent contractor of the hospital." Accordingly, the court held that apparent authority could be used to hold a hospital liable for the negligence of its emergency room personnel.

We further note that those courts imposing liability have frequently looked to two sections of the Restatements—Restatement (Second) of Torts sec. 429 (1965), and Restatement (Second) of Agency sec. 267 (1958). Under [Restatement (Second) of Torts] sec. 429,

> [o]ne who employs an independent contractor to perform services for another which are accepted in the reasonable belief that the services are being rendered by the employer or by his servants, is subject to liability for physical harm caused by the negligence of the contractor in supplying such services, to the same extent as though the employer were supplying them himself or by his servants.

Furthermore, [Restatement (Second) of Agency] sec. 267 provides,

> [o]ne who represents that another is his servant or other agent and thereby causes a third person justifiably to rely upon the care or skill of such apparent agent is subject to liability to the third person for harm caused by the lack of care or skill of the one appearing to be a servant or other agent as if he were such.

Relying upon either or both of these sections, courts have held that where an individual enters a hospital and receives care from a physician who is an independent contractor, liability may be imposed on the hospital if the individual receiving care has reasonably relied upon the hospital's representation that the treating physician was the servant or agent of the hospital.

Having previously recognized the doctrine of apparent authority in other contexts, we agree with the decisions from other jurisdictions that the doctrine of apparent authority should also be available in suits brought against hospitals for a physician's negligence in providing emergency room care.[6] As we noted in [*Johnson v. Misericordia Community Hospital*, 99 Wis. 2d 708, 724, 301 N.W.2d 156 (1981)]:

> The concept that a hospital does not undertake to treat patients, does not undertake to act through its doctors and nurses, but only procures them to act solely upon their own responsibility, no longer reflects the facts. The complex manner of operation of the modern-day medical institution clearly demonstrates that they furnish far more than mere facilities for treatment. Certainly, the person who avails himself of our modern 'hospital facilities' expects that the hospital staff will do all it reasonably can to cure him and does not anticipate that its nurses, doctors and other employees will be acting solely on their own responsibility.

Consistent with this concept of the modern-day hospital facilities, a patient who is unaware that the person providing treatment is not the employee or agent[7] of the hospital should have a right to look to the hospital in seeking compensation for any negligence in providing emergency room care. The fact that, unbeknownst to the patient, the physician was an independent contractor should not prohibit a patient from seeking compensation from the hospital which offers the emergency room care.

---

6. Trinity also argues that the doctrine of apparent authority is inapplicable except in contract cases. However, we have recognized previously that under sec. 429 of the Restatement (Second) of Torts (1965), tort liability can be imposed on a principal for the acts of an independent contractor. *See Brooks v. Hayes*, 133 Wis. 2d 228, 248-49, 395 N.W.2d 167 (1986).

7. In holding a hospital liable for the acts of one perceived to be an agent, we do not retreat from our holding in *Arsand v. City of Franklin*, 83 Wis. 2d 40, 264 N.W.2d 579 (1978), that the liability attaches only where the agent is an agent/servant as opposed to an agent/independent contractor. If a patient knows, or should have known, that the person treating him or her is an agent/independent contractor, then there will be no liability under the doctrine of apparent authority.

Accordingly, we hold that, unless the patient knows, or should have known, that the provider of health care is an independent contractor, a hospital can be held liable under the doctrine of apparent authority for the negligent acts of the physicians retained by the hospital to provide emergency room care, irrespective of the fact that the person who committed the negligent act was an independent contractor. The elements of apparent authority are equally applicable when the action involves a tort claim brought against a hospital for negligence in providing emergency room care. For a hospital to be liable under the doctrine of apparent authority, a plaintiff must show that:

> (1) the hospital, or its agent, acted in a manner which would lead a reasonable person to conclude that the individual who was alleged to be negligent was an employee or agent of the hospital;
>
> (2) where the acts of the agent create the appearance of authority, the plaintiff must also prove that the hospital had knowledge of and acquiesced in them; and
>
> (3) the plaintiff acted in reliance upon the conduct of the hospital or its agent, consistent with ordinary care and prudence.

Trinity's concern—that applying the doctrine of apparent authority to hold a hospital liable for the negligence of an independent contractor would make a hospital liable for all acts of negligence within the hospital—is without foundation. The rule we adopt today applies only where the patient looks to the hospital as the provider of health care, and the hospital selects the physicians and its staff. Where a patient seeks care from a physician who then uses the hospital facilities, the hospital would not be liable under the doctrine of apparent authority.

In addition, Trinity's reliance upon *Misericordia*, as defining the areas in which a hospital may be liable, is misplaced. In *Misericordia*, we did not consider the question of whether a hospital could be liable for the acts of its independent contractors under the doctrine of apparent authority. Thus our holding in *Misericordia* does not preclude our conclusion that a hospital can also be liable under the doctrine of apparent authority for the negligence of independent contractors.

Some question has been raised in the present case concerning (1) what a plaintiff must show to prove acts by the hospital sufficient to lead a reasonable person to conclude that the alleged negligent individual was an employee of the hospital, and (2) what must be shown to prove reliance. In answering these concerns, we find the decisions of other jurisdictions instructive.

The cases from other jurisdictions indicate that the first element of apparent authority—acts by the hospital or agent justifying belief in an agency relationship—can be proven without an express representation by the hospital that the individual alleged to be negligent is an employee. Many courts have concluded that a hospital, by providing emergency room care and by failing to advise patients that they were being treated by the hospital's agent and not its employee, has created an appearance that the hospital's agents, not independent contractors, will provide medical care to those who enter the hospital.

The rationale underlying these cases is that generally people who seek medical help through the emergency room facilities of modern-day hospitals are unaware of the status of the various professionals working there. Unless the patient is in some manner put on notice of the independent status, it would be natural for the patient to assume that these people are employees of the hospital. [W]e conclude that, if Pamperin proves that Trinity held itself out as a provider of emergency room care without informing Pamperin that the care was provided by independent contractors, Pamperin has satisfied the first requirement for proving liability under the doctrine of apparent authority.

Although not raised by the parties, we note that the second element of apparent authority—in those cases where the acts of the agent create the appearance of authority, knowledge of and acquiescence in those acts by the principal must be proven—is not at issue in this case because it is not the acts of the agent of the principal which created the appearance of authority. It is the acts of Trinity (the principal) which allegedly justified Pamperin's belief that an agency relationship existed.

We turn next to the third element of apparent authority—proof that the patient relied upon the acts of the hospital or its agent. In determining that a plaintiff acted in reliance upon the conduct of the hospital or its agent, courts have focused on the patient's reliance upon the hospital, through its staff, to provide medical care. They have not focused on the patient's reliance upon care from a particular physician. Courts have uniformly recognized that, except when the patient enters a hospital intending to receive care from a specific physician while in the hospital, it is the reputation of the hospital itself upon which a patient relies.

In *Grewe* [*v. Mt. Clemens Hospital*, 404 Mich. 240, 251, 273 N.W.2d 429 (1978)] the court stated that,

> [i]n our view, the critical question is whether the plaintiff, at the time of his admission to the hospital, was looking to the hospital for treatment of his physical ailments or merely viewed the hospital as the situs where his physician would treat him for his problems.

Moreover, it has been recognized that the doctor-hospital relationship is unique because a patient, in seeking medical assistance from a hospital, in fact relies upon the staff as part of the hospital. According to the court in *Stewart* [*v. Midani*, 525 F. Supp. 843, 851 (N.D. Ga. 1981)], by its very nature a hospital represents that it is the hospital, through its employees, which provides care to the sick and injured.

We agree with these decisions that the critical distinction is whether the plaintiff is seeking care from the hospital itself or whether the plaintiff is looking to the hospital merely as a place for his or her personal physician to provide medical care. Except for one who seeks care from a specific physician, if a person voluntarily enters a hospital without objecting to his or her admission to the hospital, then that person is seeking care from the hospital itself. An individual who seeks care from a hospital itself, as opposed to care from his or her personal physician, accepts care from the hospital in reliance upon the fact that complete emergency room care—from blood testing to radiological readings to the endless medical support services—will be provided by the hospital through its staff. We therefore hold that, if Pamperin proves that he relied upon the hospital to provide complete emergency room care, rather than upon a specific physician, Pamperin has met his burden of proving reliance under apparent authority.

The decision of the court of appeals is reversed, and the cause is remanded to the circuit court for proceedings consistent with this opinion.

STEINMETZ, Justice [with BABLITCH, J.], dissenting:

As to the third element—reasonable reliance on the apparent agency by the plaintiff—the majority misconstrues the meaning and applicability of this element altogether. The majority improperly focuses, as did the courts in the cases cited by the majority, on whether the plaintiff relied *on the reputation of the hospital.* This focus is misplaced; under the doctrine of apparent authority, which is basically a theory of agency by estoppel, the question is whether a patient reasonably relied on the apparent agency relationship, not whether reliance was placed on the reputation of the hospital.

Furthermore, patients rarely, if ever, elect to receive emergency medical care at a particular hospital based on the contractual arrangement between the hospital and staff physicians. Most probably, a hospital is typically chosen on the basis of the geographic proximity of the emergency room to the injury, condition or accident. Contrary to the suggestion implicit in the majority opinion, a person needing emergency care does not exercise deliberate and informed choice or "shop around" for emergency medical care services. Nor is the decision likely ever to be made based upon the employment structure contained within the hospital. More often than not, the receiving hospital is chosen by the driver of the emergency vehicle or private care conveyance and the primary concern of all involved is to get to the closest hospital as quickly as possible. The reputation of the hospital is likely only rarely considered; rather, its convenience is the greatest consideration in the patient's mind, assuming the patient is even conscious at the time. In this case, there is nothing in the record to show that it was the plaintiff who selected Trinity Hospital for treatment. The majority states the plaintiff was taken to Trinity, not that he selected Trinity. Furthermore, the majority's broad definition of "seeking care from the hospital," i.e., where "a person voluntarily enters a hospital without objecting to his or her admission to the hospital," is simplistically unrealistic in the context of emergency room admissions. Webster defines "emergency" as "an unforeseen combination of circumstances or the resulting state that calls for immediate action[,] a sudden bodily alteration such as is likely to require immediate medical attention (as a ruptured appendix or surgical shock)." Webster's Third New International Dictionary (1967). Faced with a medical emergency which oftentimes requires immediate treatment, a person cannot be held to have made a truly voluntary or meaningful choice of a hospital simply because he or she did not object to the facility. This Hobson's Choice is merely a self-serving method of creating the element of reliance where it does not in reality exist.

Under the doctrine of apparent authority as this court has consistently applied the theory, the real issue here is whether Pamperin could have reasonably relied on the alleged acts of Trinity or Dr. Boex to justify Pamperin's belief that an agency relationship existed. However, in the context of this case, there is not a factual basis to examine this issue. Because Pamperin was not even aware of the existence of Dr. Boex until after the statute of limitations passed, he cannot under any stretch of the imagination be said to have "relied" on anything with respect to this physician. Without even knowing the man existed, Pamperin could not have formed a belief regarding Dr. Boex's relationship to the hospital, much less relied on that belief. If Pamperin sought instead to hold Trinity liable for Dr. Schulgit's negligence, there might be a factual basis, if not a legal basis, to make an apparent authority claim. That is, assuming the first two elements of apparent authority were satisfied, a factual issue might arise as to whether Pamperin justifiably believed Dr. Schulgit was an agent of the hospital and relied on that belief when Dr. Schulgit treated him. Here, however, the patient was discharged before Dr. Boex entered the picture, and the radiologist's existence was not known to Pamperin until more than two years had passed. Thus, there is not a factual basis under which an apparent authority claim can be meaningfully discussed.

Furthermore, despite the apparent limitation of hospital liability to "negligent acts of the physicians retained by the hospital to provide emergency room care," the majority would permit liability in this case, even though Dr. Boex was not retained by the hospital to provide emergency room care. Dr. Boex was an employee of Lakeview Corporation, an independent contractor who contracted with Trinity to provide all radiologic services, whether the need for these services originated in the emergency room or from another department of the hospital. The distinction between independent contractors providing emergency room care and those working elsewhere in the hospital not only appears to emanate from an artificial and arbitrary line, but it does not appear to have been followed in this case.

Finally, the majority opinion raises more questions than it answers. For example, where an unconscious patient is conveyed to an emergency room, is the reliance element negated? Does a public or private ambulance conveyance become an agent for the hospital for liability purposes if the ambulance driver rather than the patient selects the hospital?

In sum, under the majority's decision, the concept of reliance within an apparent agency context is strained to the breaking point. The majority has, in effect, rewritten the contractual relationship between Trinity and Dr. Boex and has converted the radiologist's role for liability purposes from an independent contractor to an agent of the hospital. This conversion effectively renders the hospital liable for any activity occurring within its four walls with the possible exception of visitors' behavior, unless, of course, the hospital can avoid liability altogether by merely strategically scattering a few signs at the emergency room door and within the hospital describing the employment relationship of various medical departments to the hospital and the legal effect thereof.

Notes

1. Consider Justice Steinmetz's arguments in his *Pamperin* dissent regarding the nature of a patient's "choice" of an emergency room. To what extent would the *Pamperin* majority consider that such arguments actually *support* its reasoning?

2. How would *Pamperin* apply to the following situation? Patient goes to Surgeon to arrange a surgery. Surgeon selects Hospital as the place where the surgery will be performed. Assuming Surgeon and Hospital are independent contractors, will Hospital be liable for the negligence of Surgeon? If during the operation anesthesia was negligently administered by Anesthesiologist, an independent contractor chosen and supplied by Hospital, will Hospital be liable for the negligence of Anesthesiologist?

2. Intended Actions

King v. Loessin

572 S.W.2d 87 (Tex. Civ. App. 1978)

COLEMAN, Chief Justice.

The question is whether the action of a purported agent is chargeable to the defendant where the purported agent is the employee of a corporation who was employed to do investigative work for the defendant.

Delcer King, appellant, contracted with Smith Protective Services, Inc. to investigate a number of his competitors in the equipment business. Smith's employee, Thompson, along with another employee burglarized the offices of appellee in order to obtain certain sales invoices. Appellee sued Smith Protective Services, Inc., Cal Meyers, the investigations manager for Smith, and appellant, King, for damages incurred as a result of the alleged break-in.

It is undisputed that Thompson entered the premises of Loessin without permission of Loessin and removed certain items. The appellant contends that the plaintiff failed to prove that Thompson was an agent of King at the time of the trespass and that he was acting within the course and scope of his employment.

A contract between King and Smith Protective Services, Inc., is in evidence. It reflects that King contracted with Smith to conduct certain investigative services and agreed that the services would be performed by licensed investigators if required by law.

There was testimony that Mr. King told Mr. Meyers, who was acting for Smith Protective Services, Inc. that he desired an investigation of tool thefts and sabotage at his John Deere Tractor Agency and certain other matters. In particular, he wanted to determine who was selling parts to a competitor "at a [lower] cost than what was the normal rule within his area." Mr. Meyers testified that King explained to him what was required in order to satisfy the John Deere people that someone was infringing upon his region. Meyers stated that King told him that the only thing that would satisfy the John Deere people would be an invoice showing a 20% discount and that he wanted to secure one of those invoices. "He didn't particularly care how he went about getting it and said money was no object."

Mr. Meyers testified that while Mr. King did not specifically discuss a violation of the law in connection with the investigation, he did stipulate that he didn't particularly care how he went about getting the information he needed. Mr. Meyers hoped that his employees would not exceed the law because they had been warned not to, but he stated that he had given Mr. Jerry Dolly permission to discuss the matter with Mr. King. Mr. Meyers stated that he told Mr. King that if anything criminal came up he was going to have to bear the burden if he was going to coach the Smith investigators.

Mr. Thompson was a Smith employee before the contract with King was executed. Thompson took his instructions from Meyers. Mr. Thompson testified that he went with Jerry Dolly to see Delcer King and that Dolly did all the talking. He didn't hear Mr. King say anything about committing a burglary. Mr. Dolly gave him his instructions. Thompson admitted that he burglarized the Loessin Implement Company located in Weimar, Colorado County, Texas. He reported to Mr. Meyers after he "pulled the burglary." Meyers paid him for "conducting such burglary" with a Smith Protective Services, Inc. payroll check.

There is nothing in the testimony of Mr. King which would support the conclusion that he had any right to control Smith as to the method or means by which the work contracted for was to be accomplished. There is no testimony that King in fact instructed either Meyers, Thompson, or Dolly concerning the methods to be used in conducting the investigations.

A crucial question for determination is whether Smith Protective Services, Inc. was an independent contractor or whether the corporation and its employees had the status of agents or employees of King. The written agreement merely provides that Smith Protective Services, Inc. will be compensated at the rate of $20 per hour plus expenses for its investigative services. It does not specify the services to be rendered.

An employer is not responsible for the acts or omissions of an independent contractor and his subcontractors or servants, committed in the prosecution of work that is not in itself unlawful or attended with danger to others. The doctrine of respondeat superior has no application.

A person who contracts with another to perform a service unlawful in itself, even as an independent contractor, is responsible in damages for injury which might result from the performance of that service.

There is evidence which will support an implied fact finding of contemplated illegal activity on the part of Smith Protective Services, Inc. in conducting the investigation and of authorizing such activity if necessary to the successful completion of the investigation. This fact will be presumed found in support of the trial court's judgment. Under such circumstances the employer would not be insulated from liability by reason of the fact that the person perpetrating the offense might otherwise enjoy the status of an independent contractor.

Notes

1. A person who directs another to take an action is subject to liability for the consequences

> result[ing] from his directions [to the same extent] as he would be [liable] for his own personal conduct if, with knowledge of the conditions, he intends the conduct, or if he intends its consequences.

Restatement § 212.

2. May an employer of an independent contractor be held accountable for the tort of the independent contractor on the theory of ratification? In *Braud v. Theriot*, 170 So. 2d 679 (La. App. 1964), the defendant employed Chitty, who appeared to be an independent contractor, to fill a bayou that ran between the defendant's and the plaintiff's land and to substitute a drainage ditch five to six feet deep. Without the plaintiff's permission, Chitty went on the plaintiff's land and dug the ditch, which was later determined to encroach on the plaintiff's land to a depth of three to ten feet and for a length of twenty-two feet.

> Defendant paid Chitty for the work done by him subsequent to the completion of the undertaking, without protesting the agent's violation of any authority to perform the excavation in the manner in which it was done, and

certainly this must be regarded as a condonation of the agent's action. Accordingly, we are of the opinion Defendant is liable for the damages sustained by Plaintiff because of the trespass committed by Defendant through his agent, Chitty.

3. Direct Negligence

Redinger v. Living, Inc.

689 S.W.2d 415 (Tex. 1985)

CAMPBELL, Justice.

Louis Redinger sued Living, Inc., the general contractor, and Bobby Baird, an independent contractor, for damages resulting from an injury to Redinger's finger. The trial court rendered judgment for Redinger based on jury findings that Baird and Living, Inc. [were each] negligent. The court of appeals reversed and remanded for a new trial.

Living, Inc. was the general contractor on the building construction site. Bobby Baird was the dirt hauling subcontractor, and Redinger was an employee of a plumbing subcontractor. David Yargo, the superintendent for Living, Inc., was preparing the site for a subcontractor to pour concrete. When the concrete trucks arrived, piles of dirt placed by Baird blocked the route to the work area. Yargo ordered Baird to move the dirt. As he was moving the dirt, the box blade of his tractor crushed Redinger's left index finger.

[T]he jury found that Living, Inc. was negligent in allowing Bobby Baird to operate his tractor while Louis Redinger and others were working in the area and also for failing to warn.

Living, Inc. contends the court of appeals erred in failing to render judgment that Redinger take nothing against it because Living, Inc., a general contractor, does not have a duty to Redinger, an employee of a subcontractor.

We will first consider whether a general contractor has a duty to a subcontractor's employee, and, if so, whether there is evidence in this case that the duty was breached. An owner or occupier of land has a duty to use reasonable care to keep the premises under his control in a safe condition. A general contractor on a construction site, who is in control of the premises, is charged with the same duty as an owner or occupier. This duty to keep the premises in a safe condition may subject the general contractor to direct liability for negligence.

The general rule is that an owner or occupier does not have a duty to see that an independent contractor performs work in a safe manner. However, when the general contractor exercises some control over a subcontractor's work he may be liable unless he exercises reasonable care in supervising the subcontractor's activity. We adopt the rule enunciated in the Restatement (Second) of Torts:

> One who entrusts work to an independent contractor, but who retains the control of any part of the work, is subject to liability for physical harm to others for whose safety the employer owes a duty to exercise reasonable care, which is caused by his failure to exercise his control with reasonable care.

Restatement (Second) of Torts § 414 (1977).

This rule applies when the employer retains some control over the manner in which the independent contractor's work is performed, but does not retain the degree of control which would subject him to liability as a master. Restatement (Second) of Torts § 414, comment a (1965). The employer's role must be more than a general right to order the work to start or stop, to inspect progress or receive reports. *Id.*, comment c.

> He may retain only the power to direct the order in which the work shall be done, or to forbid its being done in a manner likely to be dangerous to himself or others. Such a supervisory control may not subject him to liability under the principles of Agency, but he may be liable under the rule stated in this Section unless he exercises his supervisory control with reasonable care so as to prevent the work which he has ordered to be done from causing injury to others.

Id., comment a.

There is evidence that Living, Inc. retained the power to direct the order in which the work was to be done and to forbid the work being done in a dangerous manner. When the concrete trucks arrived at the site, Yargo ordered Baird to immediately move the dirt to another location. Yargo exercised supervisory control by coordinating the work performed by two subcontractors. Living, Inc. owed a duty to Redinger to exercise this supervisory control in a reasonable manner.

There is evidence that Living, Inc. negligently exercised this control. The dirt was located within one to five feet of an area where Redinger and employees of other subcontractors were working. While Baird was moving the dirt, his back-hoe operated within one to five feet of Redinger and the other workers. There is evidence to support the jury finding that Living, Inc. was negligent in allowing Bobby Baird to operate his tractor while Redinger was working in the area and in failing to warn Redinger. We agree with the court of appeals that Living, Inc. owed a duty to Redinger to exercise reasonable care.

We affirm the judgment of the trial court.

Note

An employer of an independent contractor not only must exercise care in the supervision of the independent contractor, the employer must also exercise care in the *selection* of the independent contractor where the work involves the risk of harm to others. Restatement § 213(b). *See also Wilson v. Good Humor* and the following notes, later in this chapter.

4. Non-Delegable Duties

Under Restatement (Second) of Agency section 214

> A master or other principal who is under a duty to provide protection for or to have care used to protect others or their property and who confides the performance of such duty to a servant *or other person* is subject to liability to others for harm caused to them by the failure of such agent to perform the duty.

See also Restatement (Second) of Agency section 251(a) (principal "subject to liability for physical harm caused by the negligence of a servant or non-servant agent in the performance of an act which the principal is under a duty to have performed with care").

The *law of agency* does not impose any "non-delegable duties." Rather, such duties arise either by contract or by the law of torts.

a. Occupier's Duty to Invitees

Lipman Wolfe & Co. v. Teeples & Thatcher, Inc.

268 Or. 578, 522 P.2d 467 (1974)

DENECKE, Justice.

This is an action for indemnity in which the jury found for plaintiff against both defendants. The trial court, notwithstanding the verdict for plaintiff, vacated the judgment against both defendants. Plaintiff appeals.

Plaintiff Lipman's operates a large retail department store in Portland. Plaintiff contracted with Teeples & Thatcher to perform over a period of several years certain remodeling in the store. As part of the remodeling, Teeples subcontracted with Artcraft Linoleum to lay floor tile in certain areas of the store. On March 13, 1967, Artcraft was laying tile in front of the elevators on the seventh floor. A customer fell and was injured when she stepped in a slippery substance spread on the floor by Artcraft in preparation for laying tile. The jury could have found Artcraft and Teeples had failed to place or maintain any or adequate barriers around the area in which Artcraft was working. There were no contractual provisions between the parties relating to protecting customers from dangers caused by the remodeling.

The customer sued Lipman's who tendered the defense of the action to Teeples and Artcraft. The tender was refused and Lipman's then settled with the customer and brought this action to recover the amount paid in settlement together with its attorney fees and expenses.

Fulton Ins. v. White Motor Corp., 261 Or. 206, 493 P.2d 138 (1972), states the elements that a party must prove to obtain indemnity. They are: (1) that the plaintiff seeking indemnity has discharged a legal obligation owed to a third party; (2) that the defendants against whom indemnity is sought are also liable to such third party; and (3) that as between plaintiff and defendants, the obligation ought to be discharged by the latter.

The key question is whether the obligation to the injured customer ought to be discharged ultimately by the contractors or by Lipman's. The answer to this question may depend upon the nature of the liability of Lipman's to its customer. Is Lipman's liable to its customer because of Lipman's own negligence or is Lipman's liable vicariously because of the negligence of the independent contractor, Teeples, and its subcontractor?

Probably the case was submitted to the jury both on the basis that Lipman's was personally negligent for failing to protect its customer, and on the basis that Lipman's was liable to its customers because of the negligence of Teeples and Artcraft. Both defendants in their cross-appeals contend that the trial court erred in submitting the case on the basis of Lipman's vicarious liability.

The parties have assumed, and we believe correctly, that Teeples was an independent contractor and Lipman's was its employer. It is not necessary to determine the overall relationship of Teeples to Artcraft as we have already decided that there was evidence that Teeples had a duty to erect barricades to protect customers from dangers created by the remodeling and it was liable to the customer either for failing to personally perform that duty or for Artcraft's failure.

We have never decided the basis for a storekeeper's liability or that of any other possessor of land for injuries to a customer caused by a condition negligently created by an independent contractor employed by the storekeeper.

Other courts and writers have placed a storekeeper's liability in these circumstances upon two different bases—personal liability for failing to supervise the work of the independent contractor and vicarious liability for the negligence of the independent contractor. Some decisions seemingly have relied upon a combination of the two without distinguishing between them.

We are surprised at the confusion existing in this small corner of the law. Harper and James write of the confusion thusly:

> As to invitees, some cases proceed on the reasoning that the land occupier's duty is nondelegable, so that he will be held vicariously for the contractor's negligence at least where that results in an unreasonably dangerous condition of the premises. Other cases rest liability on the occupier's own duty to supervise, inspect, etc. work done or operations carried out by the independent contractor. Many opinions draw on both lines of reasoning without apparently realizing the distinctions between them.

2 Harper and James, Law of Torts, 1407 n. 51, § 26.11 (1956).

We have concluded that the most logical and desirable basis for liability is the vicarious basis: that is, to apply the doctrine of respondeat superior and hold the storekeeper liable for the negligence of the contractor. We reach this conclusion for several reasons. The storekeeper, of course, has the duty to have its premises in a reasonably safe condition for the reception of its customers. The storekeeper is liable for the negligence of its own employees who fail to keep the store in a reasonably safe condition. When a contractor is brought in to remodel or repair and the store permits customers to continue to enter the premises the danger to customers increases. Under such circumstances it would be inconsistent to hold that a storekeeper can escape liability by asserting that the increased danger to its customers was created by an independent contractor and, therefore, the storekeeper is not liable.

In addition to vicarious liability being imposed because of the duty of a storekeeper to keep its premises in a safe condition for its customers another accepted principle points to adopting vicarious liability. In *Gordon Creek Tree Farms v. Layne*, 230 Or. 204, 220, 368 P.2d 737, 741 (1962), we stated this principle as follows:

> It is well settled that an employer who orders work to be performed from which, in the natural course of things, injurious consequences must be expected to arise unless means are adopted by which such consequences may be prevented, is bound to see that necessary precautions are taken to prevent injury and such person can not by employing some other person relieve himself of his liability to do what is necessary to prevent the work from becoming wrongful.

Another reason why we prefer the doctrine of vicarious liability is that placing a duty upon a storekeeper to closely supervise its remodeling contractor appears to us to be unrealistic. Unless the business or the particular project is large enough to employ one or more persons whose exclusive duties are to supervise the work, the contractor is usually in a better position to protect the storekeeper's customers. The testimony in this case was that the employees of Artcraft worked so fast that the barricade had to be practically a rolling barricade. If the storekeeper had a duty to supervise, the storekeeper would have to employ a person whose sole duties were to constantly inspect the tile layer's work to be certain that the successive barricades were adequate.

Having established that the basis of Lipman's liability is the negligence of the two defendants we necessarily must conclude that Lipman's is entitled to indemnity from the defendants:

> A party held responsible by reason of his vicarious liability for the negligence of another, such as a servant or independent contractor, can recover indemnity from the servant or independent contractor.

The trial court erred in setting aside the verdict for plaintiff. Reversed with instructions to enter judgment for plaintiff.

b. Work Requiring Special Precautions against Inherent Dangers

Wilson v. Good Humor Corp.

757 F.2d 1293 (D.C. Cir. 1985)

WALD, Circuit Judge:

This appeal involves a wrongful death action brought by Willis and Rosita Wilson against the Good Humor Corporation ("Good Humor") and David A. Williams for the death of their three-year-old daughter Tomikia. Tomikia died from injuries sustained when she was struck by an automobile while attempting to cross the street in order to purchase ice cream from a Good Humor truck allegedly operated by Williams. At the close of the plaintiffs' case, the district court directed verdicts in favor of both Williams and Good Humor. The court ruled that the plaintiffs had not adequately identified Williams as the vendor involved in the accident and that they had failed to submit evidence upon which Good Humor could be held vicariously or directly liable for the acts or omissions of its vendor.

Good Humor has been engaged in the street sale of ice cream products in the Washington metropolitan area for well over 35 years. Until 1980, Good Humor maintained a traditional employer-employee relationship with its salespeople: it owned and maintained its ice cream trucks and it employed drivers to vend its products. During this period, Good Humor recognized that curbside sales of ice cream created special hazards for its customers, especially children. Accordingly, the company conducted an extensive safety program that included on-site safety training, weekly safety bulletins, periodic slide shows, and the circulation of a general safety manual. Good Humor employees were admonished, among other things, to refrain from selling in locations which would require customers to cross busy roadways and, in any event, to assist children in crossing the street.

Prior to the 1980 season, however, Good Humor substantially altered its business format and purported to establish its vendors as "independent contractors." Under this new modus operandi, vendors "purchased" their trucks from Good Humor, with the aid of Good Humor financing, and entered into a "vendor's agreement" authorizing them to sell Good Humor products which they bought wholesale from Good Humor. The vendors could sell ice cream at any price and at any location, they were not on the company payroll, and Good Humor did not supervise their day-to-day activities. Good Humor scuttled its entire safety program when it adopted this independent contractor format.

On June 9, 1981, Williams purchased a Good Humor truck and entered into a vendor's agreement. On June 29, 1981, a Good Humor vendor alleged to be the individual named in this lawsuit parked his Good Humor truck on the 4500 block of Benning Road in the northeast section of Washington—after dark at approximately 9:00 p.m.—and began to solicit customers by ringing the distinctive Good Humor jingle bells. Benning Road is a heavily-trafficked thoroughfare, probably servicing more vehicles than any street in the neighborhood.

That evening, plaintiff Rosita Wilson and her daughter Tomikia were visiting Rosita's aunt, who lived across the street from the parked Good Humor truck. While Rosita Williams telephoned her husband, she left Tomikia in the care of two nieces. When the Good Humor vendor announced his arrival by ringing his distinctive bells, the nieces obtained ice cream money and proceeded across Benning Road. Unbeknownst to them, Tomikia followed, and, as she attempted to cross the street, several children apparently began shouting at her to return to the curb. When she tried to do so, she was struck by a car driven by Dominic Aluisi.

On November 22, 1983, the case against Williams and Good Humor went to trial. The plaintiffs sought to prove that Williams was liable for Tomikia's death under ordinary negligence principles. They sought recovery from Good Humor under theories of direct negligence and under several exceptions to the general rule that employers are not vicariously liable for the torts of their independent contractors.

The general rule in the District of Columbia is that an employer of an independent contractor is not liable for physical harm caused by the acts or omissions of the contractor. Restatement (Second) of Torts § 409 (1965). This independent contractor rule, however, bristles with a series of long-standing exceptions specifying certain conditions under which employers can be held vicariously or directly liable for the torts of their contractors. Both the rule and its exceptions are derived from the same underlying policies. The general rule encompasses the notion that employers should not be held responsible for activities they do not control and, in many instances, lack the knowledge and resources to direct. The exceptions, in the main, reflect special situations where the employer is in the best position to identify, minimize and administer the risks involved in the contractor's activities.

The plaintiffs argue that Good Humor's street vending operation falls within one of the most important exceptions to the general rule of non-liability because it involves a "peculiar risk" or an "inherent danger" to Good Humor customers, especially children. See, e.g., Restatement 2d §§ 413, 427. The district court ruled that Good Humor could not be found liable under the "inherent danger" exception because the selling of ice cream, as such, is not a generically dangerous activity that creates risks to others notwithstanding reasonable precautions.

We believe that the district court based its rejection of the inherent danger doctrine on too narrow a view of both the doctrine and its rationale as articulated in local law and elsewhere. In particular, we conclude that the plaintiffs should be able to go to the jury on the theory that Good Humor knew or had special reasons to know that its street vending operation was likely to create, under particular circumstances, a peculiar risk to children absent special precautions, and did absolutely nothing to minimize or even warn its vendors of that risk.

The District of Columbia unmistakably recognizes an exception to the general rule of non-liability when an employer engages an independent contractor to perform "inherently dangerous" work. In our view, these cases can reasonably be read to suggest that two distinct types of independent contractor activity can bring an employer within this exception. As the district court recognized, the doctrine quite clearly applies to *generically* hazardous activities—work that regardless of the skill with which it is undertaken, poses a danger to others. Yet local law also suggests that this exception applies when an employer has reason to know that his independent contractor is likely, *under particular circumstances,* to endanger others absent reasonable precautions. As this court has noted, "[d]anger is a relative term. Inherently dangerous may be defined as 'unusually hazardous.' However, it is also a relative term *depending on the entire situation under examination.*" *Vale* [*v. Bonnett,* 191 F.2d 334, 338 (D.C. Cir. 1951)] (emphasis added).

The Restatement of Torts, in turn, explicitly indicates that an employer can be found liable under either this circumstance-specific application of the inherent danger exception or under a distinct, but intimately related, "peculiar risk" exception to the general rule of nonliability. Under the Restatement's inherent danger doctrine, for example,

> [o]ne who employs an independent contractor to do work involving a special danger to others which the employer knows or has reason to know to be inherent in or normal to the work, *or which he contemplates or has reason to contemplate when making the contract,* is subject to liability for physical harm caused to such others by the contractor's failure to take reasonable precautions against such danger.

Restatement 2d § 427 (emphasis added). The comments to this section, moreover, make clear that the inherent danger exception is *not* limited to generically hazardous work.

> The rule stated in this Section is commonly expressed by the courts in terms of liability of the employer for negligence of the contractor in doing work which is "inherently" or "intrinsically" dangerous. It is not, however, necessary to the employer's liability that the work be of a kind which cannot be done without a risk of harm to them, or that it be of a kind which involves a high degree of risk of such harm, or that the risk be one of very serious harm, such as death or serious bodily injury. It is sufficient that *work of any kind* involves risk, *recognizable in advance*, of physical harm to others which is inherent in the work itself, *or normally to be expected in the ordinary course of the usual or prescribed way of doing it, or that the employer has special reason to contemplate such a risk under the particular circumstances under which the work is to be done.*

Id. comment b (emphasis added).

Section 413 of the Restatement supports direct liability if the employer has reason to know that the independent contractor's work is likely to create a peculiar risk to others absent special precautions and if the employer takes no steps to minimize that risk by contract or otherwise.

> One who employs an independent contractor to do work which the employer should recognize as likely to create, during its progress, a peculiar unreasonable risk of physical harm to others unless special precautions are taken is subject to liability for physical harm caused to them by the absence of such precautions if the employer
>
> (a) fails to provide in the contract that the contractor shall take such precautions, or
>
> (b) fails to exercise reasonable care to provide in some other manner for the taking of such precautions.

Restatement 2d § 413. The Restatement defines a "peculiar risk" as a risk "peculiar to the work to be done, and arising out of its character, or *out of the place where it is to be done,* against which a reasonable [person] would recognize the necessity of taking special precautions." *Id.* § 413 comment b (emphasis added).

The peculiar risk doctrine, then, also depends on the fact that the employer knew or had special reason to know that, absent special precautions, an independent contractor's activities were likely to create a particular risk to others in the specific circumstances under which the work is normally done. Many jurisdictions, in turn, have applied section 413 of the Restatement where, as here, the employer failed in any way to guard against known peculiar risks. While the District of Columbia courts have not faced the question of whether to adopt or reject section 413, we believe that there are sufficient indications in local law to suggest that they would apply some version of the peculiar risk doctrine to the circumstances of this case. In particular, we predict that local courts would permit a jury to find Good Humor liable in this case under the circumstance-specific exception to the general rule of non-liability codified in the peculiar risk doctrine of section 413.

[W]e note that Good Humor's relationship with its vendors presents a rather unusual factual situation. In the typical independent contractor scenario, an individual or a business hires a contractor to carry out a relatively discrete, one-shot activity outside the general scope of the employer's enterprise. In that context, insulating the employer from tort liability continues to have some appeal: the contractor, not the employer, is rightly held responsible for recognizing when her activities are likely to create risks to others and for exercising reasonable care to avoid those risks. The employer normally does not control the manner in which the task is performed, is not in the best position to take safety precautions, and ordinarily lacks the special knowledge necessary to recognize that the contractor's work will likely create peculiar risks to others absent special precautions.

None of these factors characterizes Good Humor's relationship with its "independent contractor" vendors. Good Humor vendors are engaged to perform the bulk of Good Humor's business, and Good Humor undoubtedly contemplates that they will do so through the curbside sale of Good Humor products from "Good Humor" trucks. The vendors do not possess any special experience or knowledge concerning the risks peculiar to their task. Good Humor, by contrast, has special and detailed knowledge of the peculiar risks to children involved in its operation and is in the best position to ensure reasonable safety awareness. Despite its concededly extensive knowledge of those risks, moreover, Good Humor has apparently *chosen* to disclaim responsibility for warning its vendors or for taking any precautions whatsoever against the known and specific dangers to children who purchase ice cream from their vendors.

The Restatement indicates that employer liability is especially reasonable in this context where an independent contractor is engaged to perform an integral aspect of the employer's business and the employer has special knowledge and experience concerning the work to be performed.

> [In applying the peculiar risk exception to the general rule of non-liability,] the extent of the employer's knowledge and experience in the field of work to be done is to be taken into account; and an inexperienced widow[er] employing a contractor to build a house is not expected to have the same information, or to make the same inquiries, as to whether the work to be done is likely to create a peculiar risk of physical harm to others, or to require special precautions, as is a real estate development company employing a contractor to build the same house.

Restatement 2d § 413 comment f; see also *Mackey v. Campbell Constr. Co.*, 101 Cal. App. 3d 774, 779, 162 Cal. Rptr. 64, 68 (1980) ("[In applying section 413], the *extent* of the knowledge of the employer in the field of work is to be taken into account, *i.e.*, the more extensive his knowledge and experience, the more applicable the rule."). The Restatement likewise suggests that the peculiar risk exception is especially relevant where, as here, the risk is one which the employer should recognize as likely to arise in the course of the particular method which the employer knows the contractor will adopt. See Restatement 2d § 413 comments b, f.

We emphasize that our limited holding here is predicated on the somewhat unusual circumstances surrounding Good Humor's recent conversion to an independent contractor operation, its detailed knowledge of the special risks to children involved in curbside ice cream vending, and its refusal to take any steps aimed at ensuring that special precautions were taken to guard against those risks. In particular, our holding does not mean that an employer such as Good Humor is forever "locked" into liability for the negligence of its contractors as a result of its previous experience in a field of business. A finding of liability under the peculiar risk doctrine or the circumstance-specific component of the inherent danger doctrine must be supported by evidence that, at the time the contractor was hired, the employer knew or had special reason to know of the specific risks likely to arise from the manner in which the contractor performed his assigned risk. Because the plaintiffs provided ample evidence that Good Humor possessed comprehensive knowledge of the special risks to children involved in the street vending of ice cream products when it hired its independent contractor vendors, we need not determine when an employer's prior experience in a field of business alone constitutes sufficient knowledge of the peculiar risks involved. Accordingly, we hold *only* that, under the circumstances of this case, Good Humor cannot insulate itself from liability in its own field of business when it engaged vendors to sell Good Humor products from the curbside, knew or had special reason to know of the risks to children inherent in its operation, and flatly refused to take *any* steps designed to minimize those risks, including warning its vendors. Under these circumstances, we conclude that the plaintiffs are entitled to a jury determination on Good Humor's liability under the peculiar risk doctrine.

[W]e affirm the directed verdict in favor of David Williams and we affirm the directed verdict in favor of Good Humor on the actual control, apparent agency and negligent selection theories. We conclude, however, that the plaintiffs are entitled to a jury determination of Good Humor's liability under the inherent danger or peculiar risk exceptions to the general rule that employers are not liable for the torts of independent contractors. We therefore reverse the directed verdict in favor of Good Humor on that issue and remand this case for a new trial limited to the question of whether Good Humor should be found liable under the peculiar risk or inherent danger doctrines.

Notes

1. How does the Restatement (Second) of Torts section 413, duty of an employer of an independent contractor for work involving inherent dangers or peculiar risks, differ from the general duty of care of all employers of independent contractor under Restatement (Second) of Torts section 411?

2. Suppose that Good Humor exercises reasonable care and trains its vendors in the special precautions necessary to avoid the risk of harm to children crossing streets to buy ice cream. Suppose further that one of its vendors negligently fails to observe such precautions. Would Good Humor be liable under Restatement (Second) of Torts section 413? Under section 427?

3. What determines whether a risk is "normal" or "peculiar," and thus imposing on the employer of the independent contractor a non-delegable duty to provide precautions?

> This Section is concerned with special risks, peculiar to the work to be done, and arising out of its character, or out of the place where it is to be done, against which a reasonable man would recognize the necessity of taking special precautions. The situation is one in which a risk is created which is *not a normal, routine matter of customary human activity,* such as driving an automobile, but is rather a special danger to those in the vicinity, arising out of the particular situation created, and calling for special precautions. *"Peculiar" does not mean that the risk must be one which is abnormal to the type of work to be done, or that it must be an abnormally great risk. It has reference only to a special, recognizable danger arising out of the work itself.*

Restatement (Second) of Torts § 413 comment b (emphasis added).

> A "peculiar" risk is a risk differing from the common risks to which persons in general are commonly subjected by the ordinary forms of negligence which are usual in the community. It must involve some special hazard resulting from the nature of the work done, which calls for special precautions. Thus, if a contractor is employed to transport the employer's goods by truck over the public highway, the employer is not liable for the contractor's failure to inspect brakes on his truck, or for his driving in excess of the speed limit, because the risk is in no way a peculiar one, and only an ordinary precaution is called for. But if the contractor is employed to transport giant logs weighing several tons over the highway, the employer will be subject to liability for the contractor's failure to take special precautions to anchor them on his trucks.

Restatement (Second) of Torts § 416 comment d.

4. Work that is not inherently dangerous, or does not inherently require special precautions, may *become* such because of the way the independent contractor performs

it. If the employer knows how the independent contractor will perform the work, Restatement (Second) of Torts sections 413, 416, and 427 will apply. *E.g.*, Restatement (Second) of Torts § 416, comment e.

> [O]rdinary hauling by a truck is not inherently dangerous; and therefore a shipper is under no duty to ascertain whether the motor carrier has complied with the motor vehicle laws or to inquire into the nature and adequacy of his equipment.
>
> [A]lthough a truck may not in itself be considered a dangerous instrumentality, its operation in hauling by a drunk driver is an inherently dangerous undertaking. It should be analogous that the hauling of wheat on wet pavement in an overloaded tractor-trailer which has no speedometer, defective brakes, deficient springs, threadbare tires, and which evidence revealed to be in such poor mechanical condition that it would be unsafe to drive if unloaded, may likewise be an inherently dangerous undertaking.

Hudgens v. Cook Industries, Inc., 521 P.2d 813 (Okla. 1974).

Brandt v. Missouri Pacific Railroad Co.

787 S.W.2d 781 (Mo. App. 1990)

KAROHL, Judge.

Kenneth Brandt sued defendants for personal injuries he suffered while working as an employee of C.E. Jarrell & Associates. Jarrell & Associates contracted with defendants, owners and occupiers of a twenty-two story office building, to install gas boilers to convert the heating system. He alleged performance of the contract necessarily involved an inherently dangerous activity. Two trial judges determined the activity which caused Brandt's injuries was not inherently dangerous. Each judge found "the undisputed facts of the present case constitute mere negligence which could have been prevented by routine precautions of a kind that a careful contractor would be expected to take." Both judges granted summary judgment for some of the defendants.

Brandt concedes that as a general rule one who contracts with an independent contractor is not liable for the negligent acts of the independent contractor. He relies on an exception to the general rule, the inherent danger doctrine.

Our task in the present case is not confined to determining whether the facts developed during discovery would support submitting plaintiff's theory of liability. Liability was alleged on the theory that an employer has a non-delegable duty imposed by law where performance of the contract necessarily involves inherently dangerous activity. Brandt's appeal is from summary judgments in favor of defendants. He claims the trial courts erred in granting summary judgments because application of the inherently dangerous doctrine depends upon questions of fact which remain in dispute. Summary judgment is proper only if summary judgment facts developed in discovery, together with affidavits, show there is no genuine issue as to any material fact and that defendants are entitled to judgment as a matter of law.

The parties agreed that defendants owned, operated, managed, leased or controlled a twenty-two story office building in downtown St. Louis. Defendant, Missouri Pacific Railroad Company, as lessee of Bakewell Corporation, contracted with Jarrell

& Associates to install a flue pipe from the basement to the top of the building. Jarrell & Associates was prepared to use its pipe-threading machine as a hoist to lower the flue pipe into an existing duct in the building. Three employees of Jarrell & Associates, including plaintiff, were on the roof of the building preparing to test the hoist. The machine rested on a tripod. When plaintiff activated the machine as part of the test the machine lurched. One of the three legs struck his hip. It threw him up and across the roof. He landed ten feet away on his neck and shoulder. The tripod legs were not secured in any way. It was the intention of Jarrell & Associates to use the pipe-threading machine as a hoist to lower sections of pipe from the roof down through existing duct work and to lower employees in a swing seat in a similar manner to make connections of the sections of pipe. The parties do not dispute any of these facts.

The question in the present appeal narrows to whether on the above undisputed facts both trial courts could determine, as a matter of law, Brandt was injured performing work which was not inherently dangerous. If, at the time of the injury, Brandt was performing work from a position of safety and the casualty could have been avoided by ordinary care in the performance of his duties then the decision was available as a matter of law. Under the circumstances it is irrelevant to the application of the inherently dangerous doctrine that Brandt was working on a tall building, that there was a hole from the basement to the roof thirty-six inches in diameter, that materials had been delivered to the roof by helicopter, and Jarrell & Associates intended to lower materials from the roof to the basement with a pipe-threading machine used as a hoist. These are the facts which Brandt contends remain in dispute and from which a trier of fact could determine the activity was inherently dangerous. However, the unsecured tripod could have caused the same events if activated at ground level. Brandt did not fall off the roof. He did not fall down the airshaft. He was not injured by a helicopter. If the use of the pipe-threading machine as a hoist was a dangerous misuse, the fact remains it was not being used as a hoist at the time of casualty. The negligence and sole cause of injury was failure to secure the legs. The event was one which occurred under conditions not inherently dangerous.

Work is not inherently dangerous unless it started with danger and required preventive care to make safety [sic]. Under the present facts the work Brandt was performing, testing the hoist, started with safety and required negligence to make danger. If the legs of the tripod had been secured Brandt would not have been injured. Defendants may have anticipated inherent danger in lowering employees of an independent contractor down through duct work. There may have been a duty arising from anticipation of such danger to insure use of a safer method for such activity. However, Brandt was not injured under these circumstances. Defendants are not liable under the doctrine for failing to anticipate that the legs of the tripod would not be secured before the machine was tested. The doctrine is not applicable merely because some of the work under the contract includes inherently dangerous activity. On undisputed facts the particular activity being performed at the time of the injury was not inherently dangerous. The doctrine as an exception to the general rules does not apply as a matter of law.

We affirm.

Notes

1. The doctrine applied in *Brandt* is the collateral risk or collateral negligence doctrine, under which a non-negligent employer is *not* liable for an independent contractor's negligence where

> (a) the [independent] contractor's negligence consists solely in the improper manner in which he does the work, and
>
> (b) [the independent contractor's conduct] creates a risk of harm *which is not inherent in or normal to the work*, and
>
> (c) the employer had no reason to contemplate the contractor's negligence when the contract was made.

Restatement (Second) of Torts § 426 (emphasis added). By definition, if a risk is not inherent in the work, then Restatement (Second) of Torts sections 413 and 416 and 427 do not impose a non-delegable duty on the employer. The fact that the work may have involved some *other* risk that required special precautions is irrelevant.

2. The plaintiff in *Brandt* was an employee of the independent contractor employed to do the work. Whether the special precaution/inherent danger doctrines of Restatement (Second) of Torts sections 413, 416, and 427 can be applied to hold an employer of an independent contractor liable to the employees of the independent contractor is a matter of some debate. The problem arises because the negligent independent contractor generally will *not* be liable to its own employees. Assuming a *workers' compensation* regime applies *and* that the independent contractor provided workers' compensation insurance, that insurance is the employee's *sole* remedy *as against the independent contractor* (but not as against others). If *no* workers' compensation regime is in place, an employee is deemed *at common law* to have *assumed* risks *inherent* to the work. *See* chapter 10, "Workers' Compensation."

In either case, the issue is whether the employee should be able to proceed against the employer of the independent contractor. If the employer had undertaken the assigned task directly, it would have been similarly insulated from liability. *See Wagner v. Continental Casualty Co.*, 143 Wis. 2d 379, 421 N.W.2d 835 (1987). Unfortunately, many of the cases do not confront the issue directly, but instead apply the inherent danger/special precaution doctrine in a distorted manner. Such cases hold that *because* the risk was *inherent* in the work, it was *not* a *peculiar* risk requiring *special* precautions. *E.g.*, *Micheletto v. State*, 798 P.2d 989 (Mont. 1990). This reasoning seems to harken back to the assumption of the risk doctrine. As discussed in *Wilson v. Good Humor*, the basis of the inherent danger/special precaution rule is that the employer has a non-delegable duty as to risks inherent in the work that require special precautions. Consider the following statement by Justice Hunt, dissenting in *Micheletto v. State*, 798 P.2d 989 (Mont. 1990) (Hunt, J., dissenting):

> [F]or the reasons stated in my dissent in *Kemp v. Bechtel Constr. Co.*, 221 Mont. 519, 528-34, 720 P.2d 270, 276-80 (1986), I must dissent from the Majority's conclusion that trenching is not an inherently dangerous activity.
>
> Trenching is precisely the type of inherently dangerous activity envisioned by the Restatement (Second) of Torts §§ 416 and 427 (1977). By its very nature, trenching is "likely to create during its progress a peculiar risk of physical harm to others unless special precautions are taken." Restatement [(Second) of Torts] § 416. Further, trenching involves "a special danger to others which the employer

knows or has reason to know to be inherent in or normal to the work." Restatement [(Second) of Torts] § 427. The danger inherent in or normal to trenching is exactly the type that appears in the present case—the risk that an excavation might collapse upon and injure an individual inside the trench.

The Majority apparently believes that trenching is not inherently dangerous because "standard" precautions, rather than "special" precautions, can be taken to prevent or lessen the perils of excavating. However, as I noted in my dissent in *Kemp*, the special precautions contemplated by the Restatement are precautions specially designed to counter the peculiar risks inherent in the activity, not extraordinary precautions. Indeed, the safeguards that may be taken to prevent the dangers inherent in trenching are "ordinary in the sense that a reasonably cautious contractor would take them." What makes the precautions "special" in trenching is that they are needed to lessen the dangers inherent in or normal to the activity.

The Majority confuses the idea of "standard" precautions with the idea of "standard" activity, *i.e.*, activity that is not inherently dangerous. The fact that "standard" rather than extraordinary safeguards may counter the risks inherent in trenching does not mean that trenching itself is "standard" activity.

Chapter 9

Borrowed Servant Doctrine

A. Liability of Special Employer

A common situation in commercial settings is the presence of two or more employers. For example, contractors undertaking construction projects often bring in "subcontractors" to help with the work. The construction sites are busy places, filled with the employees of the contractor and with the employees of the various subcontractors. The contractor, through its servants, directs and coordinates the activities of all the subcontractors. Thus, both parties are involved in the continued direction and supervision of the work. If the servant of one of the subcontractors causes a tort loss to a plaintiff, will the contractor be liable to the injured person? The contractor will argue it is not liable because the subcontractor was an *independent contractor*. If the plaintiff loses on the independent contractor issue, plaintiff may then argue that the contractor should be liable on the basis that it had "borrowed" the subcontractor's servant.

In cases discussing the "borrowed servant doctrine," the original and regular employer of the servant—the subcontractor in the above scenario—is called the "general employer." The party found to have borrowed the servant—possibly the contractor in the above scenario—is called the "special employer."

Paoli v. Dave Hall, Inc.

462 A.2d 1094 (Del. Super. 1983)

O'HARA, Judge.

Cross-motions for summary judgment have been advanced by defendant Dave Hall, Inc. ("Hall") and defendants Donald F. Deaven, Inc. ("Deaven") and William C. Zern ("Zern"). The issues upon which the parties seek summary adjudication concern 1) whether Zern, a crane operator in the service of equipment owner Deaven and leased by him to general contractor Hall to operate said crane, was, in fact, a "loaned employee" of the latter during the incident giving rise to this lawsuit, and 2) whether Deaven and Zern are entitled to indemnity from Hall in the event liability for negligence is assessed against them.

The underlying action is one for personal injuries arising in the following manner. In accordance with a contract entered into with E.I. DuPont de Nemours & Company, Hall was in the progress of constructing a pharmacological laboratory in Newark, Delaware. In order to complete the roof of said structure, Hall leased from Deaven a crane to lift prefabricated, triangular shaped trusses onto the perimeter walls. Deaven likewise supplied an operator, Zern, to the job site to man this equipment. In undertaking this construction procedure, Zern placed the trusses along the length of the building's concrete walls, with each truss braced and connected to the adjacent truss.

Midway through this procedure, Hall's foreman instructed Zern to begin depositing plywood bundles on the trusses. The first bundle was placed thereupon without incident; the second, however, was not, and as a result the trusses toppled over and the walls of the building collapsed, injuring plaintiff Dominick A. Paoli, Sr., who was thrown from the scaffolding on which he was standing.[2]

At this juncture there is a factual dispute as to what precisely occurred during placement of the second bundle of trusses to cause the structure to collapse. Zern explained the incident as follows:

> The bundles were on the outside of the building. I was signaled to pick the bundle up and send it up to the roof, which I did. I got it up to the roof in the position they wanted. They wanted me to lower it on the roof. I lowered it on the roof. And they held me there. I—the bundle was on the roof completely, but I still had the majority of the weight. And at that point they wasn't ready for me to release the full load yet; so I locked the crane in position and waited. They gave me the signal to let it down; I let it down. And I am not sure exactly who was the man unhooking. I released it. He gave me a signal to release it. I give him the weight. He reached up to unhook me. And that's when the trusses fell. So I seen movement, I picked back up on the load, I thought maybe he would hang on to the load. And the building fell. I swung back over, let the plywood down and that was it.

Earl Bowman, a Hall employee who witnessed the event, offered a different account of Zern's actions:

> He started to let it down. It got closer to the truss so it looked like he was letting it down and then at the last minute he swung it to the south but at this time it was close enough to the trusses where it must—to come down on this teeter-totter a bit and come down and hit a couple trusses and bounced against them.

The evidence is similarly controverted with respect to Zern's reliance on hand signals from the Hall employees.

On their motion for summary judgment, defendants Deaven and Zern seek to have any liability for negligence assessed against Zern imputed to Hall under the borrowed-servant or loaned employee doctrine. The proper inquiry in determining whether the doctrine is applicable appears in *Richardson v. John T. Hardy & Sons, Inc.*, Del. Supr. 182 A.2d 901 (1962):

> Whether or not a loaned employee becomes the employee of the one whose immediate purpose he serves is always a question of fact, and depends upon whether or not his relationship to the specific employer has the usual elements of the employer-employee status. Fundamentally, it is not important whether or not he remains the employee of the general employer as to matters generally. What is important to determine is, with respect to the alleged negligent act in question, whether or not he was acting in the business of and under the direction of the general or the specific employer. This is almost always determined by which

2. At the time of the accident, plaintiff was an employee of John W. Walker Construction Co., a sub-contractor of defendant Hall.

> employer has the right to control and direct his activities in the performance of the act allegedly causing the injury, and whose work is being performed.

Furthermore, in the instant case, Hall directs the Court's inquiry to the presumption that an owner of heavy rented equipment, who supplies to the lessor an operator therefor, retains control over the actual operation of the equipment, and in the actual operation thereof, the operator remains the employee of the owner. *Brittingham v. American Dredging Company*, Del. Supr., 262 A.2d 255 (1970).

Although both *Richardson* and *Brittingham* involved the lease of heavy equipment, the above cited presumption was conclusive in neither case; in *Richardson* it did not even attach since the Court found that the negligence charged was not an act of actual operation of the machine. Specifically, *Richardson* involved an action against the lessor of a backhoe for injuries sustained by the lessee's foreman when the side wall of a trench collapsed on him. The Court therein ruled that the alleged negligence of the machine's operator in piling the dirt too close to the trench was not imputable to the lessor, who had furnished [the] operator and paid his wages, where 1) the operator was instructed where and how deep to dig the ditch by the foreman; 2) the foreman staked out the ditch for the operator's guidance; and 3) the foreman directed the operator on which side of the trench to pile the dirt removed. This conclusion was dictated by the fact that the negligence cited was not an act of actual operation of the machine, but rather the act of piling the dirt too close to the mouth of the trench.

The *Brittingham* case, on the other hand, did involve negligent operation of the heavy rental equipment itself. However, *Brittingham* was not an action *against* a lessor for his operator's negligence, but rather a suit brought *by* the owner/lessor against the lessee dredging company for damage to a bulldozer by imputing the operator's alleged negligence to the lessee, presumably under the borrowed servant doctrine. While the Court therein acknowledged the presumption against the owner/lessor of equipment, it further cited evidential considerations which support the presumption as well as those tending to defeat it:

> The evidence in the case at bar is that the plaintiff selected the operator of the machine, retained the right to discharge him, retained the right to determine and supervise the method of operating the machine, paid the operator's wages, and paid for the upkeep and maintenance of the machine. The evidence further shows that defendant could not, and did not, attempt to control the actual operation of the machine; could not discharge the operator but only complain to plaintiff about him and had no responsibility for the upkeep and care of the machine.

Inasmuch as the authority of the lessee therein was limited to instructing the operator as to the area in which he was desired to work and the result he was to accomplish, the *Brittingham* Court declined to impute the operator's negligence to lessee under the borrowed servant doctrine.

Thus, under *Richardson* and *Brittingham*, this Court's inquiry reduces itself to whether the negligence charged involved actual operation of Deaven's crane, in which case there is a presumption that Zern remained the owner's employee for purposes of liability, or some other attendant act involving the control or discretion of Hall or his crew, thereby imputing liability to the lessee under the borrowed servant doctrine. At this juncture, the Court notes that plaintiffs allege that Zern was negligent as follows:

(a) In operating the crane to lift bundles of plywood sheets from the ground to the level of the then height of the partially constructed building, he allowed one or more of said bundles each weighing approximately 1,500 pounds to drag across and strike trusses which had been installed as part of the construction of said building causing the trusses to topple over and push out the walls of the building;

(b) By placing the bundles of plywood in a concentrated portion of the building resulting in the overloading of the trusses.

The first act articulated above suggests that the negligence occurred in the actual operation of the equipment. However, the latter basis of liability, involving placement of the bundles, indicates negligence in the exercise of judgment or discretion. Moreover there is evidence of record that the placing of plywood bundles was determined by Hall's crew and that operator Zern performed said act at their direction, a situation factually analogous to *Richardson.*

The parties admit that there is a factual dispute as to how the incident occurred; however, Hall asserts that the only material fact is that Zern alone controlled the actual operation of the machine. With that contention the Court does not agree, noting that said fact was not dispositive in *Richardson.*

In sum, the applicability of the borrowed servant doctrine with respect to defendant Zern is an issue ripe for jury determination. Under no circumstances will summary judgment be granted when there is a reasonable indication that a material fact is in dispute.

Notes

1. If, as *Paoli v. Dave Hall, Inc.* indicates, borrowed servant questions depend on the presence or absence of the customary indicators of the master-servant relation, are the factors studied in chapter 8, "Liability for Acts of Independent Contractors," relevant here?

2. In *Progressive Construction v. Indiana & Michigan Electric,* 533 N.E.2d 1279 (Ind. App. 1989), the court set forth the following general tests to determine the liability of the special employer for the negligent acts (there, a collision) of a borrowed servant:

> [T]hree related analyses have been developed:
>
> (1) the "whose business" test which seeks to discern whether the tortfeasor was furthering the business of the special or general employer at the time of the collision;
>
> (2) the "control" test which attempts to determine which employer had the right to control the specific act in question; and
>
> (3) the "scope of business" test which attempts to determine if the work being done by the servant is within the scope of the business of the special employer.

3. In *Wilson v. McCullough,* 180 Ga. App. 579, 349 S.E.2d 751 (1986), Herndon owned a bulldozer and employed Flowers to operate it. McCullough, a nearby landowner, asked Flowers to do some work on a ditch. Herndon gave Flowers permission to do the work, but charged McCullough $200. While Flowers was working, Mc-

Cullough came by and asked him to knock down a tree also. When Flowers knocked down the tree, it fell into a nearby road and into Wilson's path. Wilson sued McCullough, claiming he had borrowed Flowers as his servant. The trial court entered summary judgement in favor of McCullough, which was upheld on appeal:

> McCullough gave Flowers no instructions with regard to the method or manner he was to use to complete the task, and McCullough exercised no control over when or how Flowers did the work. McCullough was not present when Flowers chose to do the job and when the tree fell.
>
> As noted by the trial court, it was undisputed that Flowers was regularly employed by Herndon. It is clear that Flowers was not a borrowed servant. [McCullough] in no way directed the time, manner, or method Flowers was to use in accomplishing the task at hand. Since, at the time of the injury, Flowers was not subject to McCullough's orders and control and was not liable to be discharged by him for misconduct or disobedience to orders, Flowers was not McCullough's servant.
>
> Rather than a servant, Flowers was more like an independent contractor, one who carried on an independent business and who contracted with McCullough to perform services, answerable only for the result and not under McCullough's control as to time, method, or manner of doing the work.

4. Why would a general employer *both* rent equipment to a third person *and* supply an operator to run the equipment? Suppose the third person instructs the operator to use the equipment in a manner that the operator knows is dangerous. Would the general employer expect the servant to ignore the orders? Should it make any difference whether the general employer is in the *business* of renting equipment/operator teams? *See* Restatement § 227 comment c.

5. As indicated in *Paoli v. Dave Hall, Inc.*, even where the putative special employer is found *not* to have borrowed the general employer's servant, the "special employer" may be liable for his or her *own* negligence in selecting, retaining, or supervising the servant.

Parker v. Vanderbilt University

767 S.W.2d 412 (Tenn. App. 1988)

CANTRELL, Judge.

This is a medical malpractice action against multiple defendants. Plaintiff Richard O. Parker emerged from surgery with severe brain damage and has since remained in a coma.

During the evening of June 17, 1984, plaintiff Richard O. Parker was shot in the back with a small caliber handgun as he tried to escape from an armed robber. He was taken to Nashville General Hospital, a hospital operated by the Metropolitan Government of Nashville and Davidson County.

The surgical staff at Nashville General was furnished by Vanderbilt University under a contract with the Metropolitan Government. On the evening in question, Drs. Powell, Kreuger, Alexander and Peacock were on duty in the operating room at General. Sandra Conner, a nurse anesthetist employed by the Metropolitan Government, and Rebecca Murphy, a student nurse anesthetist at the Middle Tennessee School of Anesthesia, provided the anesthesia services in the operation room. Dr. Ildefonso Alcantara headed the department of anesthesia services for General, but he was not present at the hospital on the evening of June 17, 1984.

At the time of his admission, Mr. Parker was able to walk and his vital signs were stable. After an examination in the emergency room, Mr. Parker was taken to the operating room for surgery.

After Mr. Parker was sedated and given oxygen by mask for approximately five minutes, Ms. Murphy inserted an endotracheal tube into Mr. Parker's throat. The tube was to supply oxygen to Mr. Parker during the operation. The complaint alleges that the tube entered Mr. Parker's esophagus rather than his trachea and he was therefore deprived of oxygen for approximately twelve minutes. Within five minutes, Mr. Parker's blood pressure and heart rate dropped dramatically. His abdomen had been opened and the surgical team noticed that his blood was dark and his stomach distended. As his heart rate continued to drop, the anesthetists administered atropine and bicarbonate and one of the surgeons started pressing Mr. Parker's chest to restore circulation. Ms. Conner removed the endotracheal tube and replaced it with another. At approximately the same time, one of the surgeons opened Mr. Parker's chest and started heart massage. Within seven minutes after Mr. Parker's heart rate began to fall, his blood pressure and heart rate were restored. However, during the twelve minute period when his lungs were deprived of oxygen, he suffered severe brain damage.

Mr. Parker, through his next of kin and limited guardian, filed an action against Nashville General Hospital, the Metropolitan Government of Nashville and Davidson County, Vanderbilt University, five Vanderbilt doctors, Sandra Conner, Rebecca Murphy, Middle Tennessee School of Anesthesia, Inc. and Dr. Alcantara.

On October 8, 1986, the trial court dismissed Dr. Alcantara on a motion for summary judgment. The plaintiffs voluntarily dismissed one of the Vanderbilt doctors and, on June 9, 1987, the trial judge dismissed Vanderbilt University and the remaining Vanderbilt doctors on a motion for summary judgment. The plaintiffs then voluntarily dismissed the remaining defendants. An order to that effect was entered by the trial judge on July 29, 1987.

The cause of action asserted by the plaintiffs is described in the complaint as follows:

> As a result of the careless placement of the endotracheal tube and/or failure to recognize the problem and correct it for so long a period of time, Richard O. Parker suffered profound irreversible brain damage.

Thus, the plaintiffs allege two acts of negligence: the first is the misplacement of the tube, and the second is the failure to recognize the problem and to take prompt action to correct it.

The parties disagree as to whether the endotracheal tube was actually misplaced. Although the record in this court does not show that the tube was misplaced, that is one inference to be drawn from the proof on file.

As to all the appellees (Dr. Alcantara, Vanderbilt University, Drs. Powell, Kreuger, Alexander, and Peacock), their responsibility for the misplacement of the tube must result from some theory of vicarious liability. We will deal with that aspect of the case first.

One legal theory by which vicarious liability has been placed on a surgeon is the so-called "Captain of the Ship Doctrine." The analogy was first used in the case of *McConnell v. Williams*, 361 Pa. 355, 65 A.2d 243 (1949), where the court said,

> He [the surgeon] is in the same complete charge of those who are present and assisting him as is the captain of a ship over all on board.

Taken to the extreme, this logic would impose absolute liability on a surgeon for the negligent acts of every person connected with the surgery. However, the facts and holding of *McConnell* do not seem to indicate the beginning of a revolution. The court simply held that there was a factual question for the jury as to whether, under familiar agency principles, the obstetrician could be vicariously liable for the negligence of an assisting intern.

In later cases, the Pennsylvania courts relied on the Captain of the Ship Doctrine to expand the liability of surgeons to acts of subordinates occurring outside of the operating room. But, in more recent cases, the courts in Pennsylvania have redefined the doctrine so that, now, it more nearly resembles the "borrowed servant" concept. In *Collins* [*v. Hand*, 431 Pa. 378, 246 A.2d 398 (1968)], the court said:

> The crucial test in determining whether an employee furnished to another becomes a servant of the one to whom he is loaned is whether he passes under the latter's right of control with regard not only to the work to be done but also as to the manner of performing it.

With the concept taking on so many shades of meaning in the state of its origin, it is not surprising that other states have had difficulty in defining it. While referring to the doctrine in several cases, the Tennessee courts have not attempted to formulate a definition. In two unreported cases, the Western Section of the Court of Appeals has rejected the Captain of the Ship Doctrine after failing to find its precise meaning.

We are of the opinion that the use of the term "Captain of the Ship" with respect to the liability of a surgeon for the negligent acts of others in or around the operating room is unnecessarily confusing and should be avoided. We think the surgeon's liability for the acts of others should rest on the more familiar concepts of master and servant; "[o]perating surgeons and hospitals are subject to the principles of agency law which apply to others." *Sparger v. Worley Hospital, Inc.*, 547 S.W.2d 582, 585 (Tex. 1977).

Under Tennessee law, a master is liable for his servant's negligence solely on the doctrine of respondeat superior. That doctrine is based upon the principle "that the wrong of the [servant] is the wrong of his employer." To hold the master liable, it must be established "that the servant shall have been on the superior's business, acting within the scope of his employment."

When does a master-servant relationship exist? The Tennessee cases indicate that

> the right to control the 'result' is not determinative of the existence of the relation of master and servant, but the actual control of means and method is.

Thus, one test employed to determine whether a person is a servant of another involves an inspection of the amount of control exerted over the "means and method" of the work of the putative servant.

An employee of one employer may become the servant of another. The test to determine whether an employee is a loaned servant of another employer was set out in *Gaston v. Sharpe*, 179 Tenn. 609, 168 S.W.2d 784 (1943). In *Gaston*, the court said:

> [A] servant at a particular time may remain under the control of his general employer for some purposes and yet be under the control of a special employer for others. Likewise it sometimes happens that a particular work in which the servant is engaged may be properly considered as the work or business of both the general employer and the special employer.
>
> The question is difficult. It is considered at some length in Restatement of Agency, § 227. We take the following from [the] Restatement as a satisfactory rule:
>
> > Since the question of liability is always raised because of some specific act done, the important question is not whether or not he remains the servant of the general employer as to matters generally, but whether or not, as to the act in question, he is acting in the business of and under the direction of one or the other. It is not conclusive that in practice he would be likely to obey the directions of the general employer in case of conflict of orders. The question is as to whether it is understood between him and his employers that he is to remain in the allegiance of the first as to a specific act, or is to be employed in the business of and subject to the direction of the temporary employer as to the details of such act. This is a question of fact in each case.

There were four doctors present in the operating room on the night of Mr. Parker's operation. All four were receiving their surgical training through the Vanderbilt University residency program. Dr. Powell was the chief resident in surgery at General. He was in charge of and directed the surgical procedures involving Mr. Parker. Dr. Kreuger, the senior resident in surgery, performed the operation. Drs. Alexander and Peacock assisted the chief resident and the senior resident.

The student nurse, Ms. Murphy, conducted the insertion of the endotracheal tube. She was working under the supervision of Ms. Conner, a certified registered nurse anesthetist. Ms. Murphy was a registered nurse also and a student at Middle Tennessee School of Anesthesia. She had hospital privileges to administer anesthesia and was paid by General for her work. She had performed fifty-two intubations prior to the night in question.

Ms. Murphy and Ms. Conner were working under protocols developed by Dr. Alcantara, the chief of anesthesiology at General. The protocols authorized the anesthetist to administer anesthesia to surgical patients in Dr. Alcantara's absence. In part, the protocol provided:

> A nurse anesthetist shall administer anesthesia to a patient in accordance with the general standard principles of anesthesiology to the best of his/her knowledge and belief, and along the guidelines of the anesthesia services of the Department of Anesthesia, and as directed and/or advised by the anesthesiologist-in-charge, if any.
>
> The attending physician/surgeon's preference in the way of anesthesia will be honored provided the preferred way of anesthesia is generally compatible with the guideline of the Department of Anesthesia, and the general standard principles of anesthesiology. Otherwise, the nurse anesthetist will proceed with his/her own chosed [sic] way of anesthesia.

> A nurse anesthetist will never be forced to administer anesthesia to a patient against his/her own will based upon a reasonable rationale except that, by the discretion of the attending physician/surgeon with full responsibility, the situation is such that an immediate surgical intervention with anesthesia is warranted regardless of the consequences. In case an anesthesiologist is not available for the above matter, the nurse anesthetist will either follow the attending physician/surgeon's decision or withdraw from the case by his/her own judgment with the exception of an emergency case.

A nurse anesthetist is a highly trained specialist acquiring skills in the course of his or her training that a surgeon does not possess. In this case, the nurse anesthetists were assigned by General Hospital according to a call schedule developed and implemented by the hospital. The surgeons did not select the drugs used to put the patient to sleep nor did they oversee or direct the procedures used by the nurse anesthetists.

If we are correct in the conclusions we have reached in regard to the application of the Captain of the Ship Doctrine, a surgeon is responsible for the negligence of third persons only when those persons are the servants of the surgeon and engaged in the surgeon's business.

Under the general principles we have discussed, the question in this case is whether the surgeon exercised control over the means and method of the nurse anesthetists. This is a question of fact. If the essential facts are undisputed, however, and the movant shows that he is entitled to judgment as a matter of law, summary judgment is proper.

In this case, we are of the opinion that the undisputed facts in the record show that the nurse anesthetists were not the servants of the doctors in the operating room. The doctors did not select the individuals involved in the administration of the anesthesia. They were selected in accordance with the policy of General Hospital. The drugs and procedures used by the nurse anesthetists were governed by hospital policy. The protocol under which the nurse anesthetists operated provided that the administration of anesthesia would be governed by standard principles of the anesthesiology department of the hospital. Any direction by the surgeon would be honored only so long as it was compatible with the guidelines of the Department of Anesthesia. If the two conflicted, the nurse anesthetist must withdraw from the case (except in an emergency).

The plaintiffs rely on the testimony of Dr. Alcantara that in his absence the nurse anesthetist is under the direct control of the surgeon. This conclusion is confirmed by the protocol. Nurse Conner also testified that she considered herself under the direction of the doctors present at the surgery. Ms. Murphy stated that she believed that the doctors could control her actions. However, these statements refer to the general chain of command in the operating room—to the right to control the result, and not to the actual control over the means and method of administering the anesthesia. There is no testimony in this record that the surgeons in the operating room had power over the means and method of inserting the endotracheal tube.

Recent cases from other jurisdictions recognize the distinction we have drawn in this case. In *Fortson v. McNamara*, 508 So. 2d 35 (Fla. 1987), the court said:

> While we agree that a surgical nurse, under the direct supervision of the surgeon, who acts according to the surgeon's specific directions, is certainly the servant

> of the surgeon, we are not willing to place a nurse anesthetist in this category, particularly where there is no showing that the surgeon directed the procedures to be utilized by the nurse anesthetist or had a genuine opportunity to alter the course of events.

In *Kemalyan v. Henderson*, 45 Wash. 2d 693, 277 P.2d 372 (1954), the court held that a surgeon was not liable as the master of an anesthetist where the anesthetist

> knew considerably more about administering an anesthetic than he did, and he left completely to her discretion the administration of the ether to the plaintiff.

We conclude that the nurse anesthetists in this case were not servants of the surgeons.

The judgment of the court below is affirmed and the cause is remanded to the Circuit Court of Davidson County for any further necessary proceedings.

Notes

1. The question of when a medical professional is another's servant is difficult at best. The Captain of the Ship Doctrine resolves those problems by holding the surgeon *per se* liable for negligent acts occurring during an operation. Is there a difference between the position of the surgeon in *Parker v. Vanderbilt University* and that of the hospital in *Pamperin v. Trinity Memorial Hospital* (discussed in chapter 8, "Liability for Acts of Independent Contractors")?

2. The Captain of the Ship Doctrine has largely been rejected in favor of the application of general borrowed servant analysis. *See* Price, *The Sinking of the "Captain of the Ship": Reexamining the Vicarious Liability of an Operating Surgeon for the Negligence of Assisting Hospital Personnel*, 10 J. LEGAL MED. 323 (1989).

B. Liability of the General Employer

Up until now, we have seen the borrowed servant doctrine used as a *sword* by the plaintiff to impose on the special employer liability for the acts of the borrowed servant. The borrowed servant doctrine often is used as a *shield* to protect the *general* employer from liability.

Jefferson Smurfit Corp. v. JBS, Inc.

546 So. 2d 30 (Fla. App. 1989)

SHIVERS, Judge.

Jefferson Smurfit Corporation (Smurfit) appeals the summary judgments against it on its action in negligence.

Smurfit is in the business of manufacturing corrugated boxes. Smurfit contacted Handi-Man Industrial Temporary Help Service (Handi-Man), which is in the business of providing temporary labor, and requested four temporary workers. Handi-Man did not provide a supervisor and did not supervise any of the work performed by the workers. David Lott, the general manager at Handi-Man, stated in an affidavit that Smurfit had the right to (1) control the work assignments, (2) terminate the employment of the workers with or without cause, and (3) establish work hours, breaks, and lunches. He also stated that Handi-Man pays the workers $3.35 an hour for every hour Smurfit assigned and then Handi-Man bills Smurfit for those hours at $5.50 per hour.

When the four workers arrived at Smurfit on April 7, Mr. Holton, the floor supervisor, gave them some brooms and told them to sweep up around the outside of a nearby warehouse. Mr. Holton stated upon deposition that he instructed the men that they were not to smoke inside any building. He stated that after the workers began their tasks, he checked on them about every two hours or so.

Later that morning, the nearby warehouse where two of the workers were working caught fire. Holton said that one of the employees told him that Vincent Singleton had thrown down a cigarette or a match in some of the boxes and then had run off.

After a hearing, summary final judgment was entered in favor of Handi-Man on the negligence count. The court found that

> Vincent Singleton, who allegedly negligently discarded a cigarette causing the destruction by fire of Jefferson Smurfit warehouse and its contents, was the borrowed employee of Jefferson Smurfit.

The question presented by this case is whether the borrowed servant doctrine applies to a borrowing employer as a matter of law when a borrowing employer seeks damages from a temporary labor service resulting from the tortious acts of a worker supplied by the temporary labor service.

In applying the borrowed servant doctrine to attach liability under the theories of respondeat superior and vicarious liability, the Florida Supreme Court held in *Postal Telegraph and Cable Co. v. Doyle*, 123 Fla. 695, 167 So. 358 (1936) that

> [i]t is competent for a principal to loan or farm out his servant to a third party, and if such third party has complete dominion over the servant, and directs his conduct at all times, he will be held responsible for his derelictions even though the principal is paying his salary; but this rule does not hold good if the principal in any way withholds control over him.

Smurfit asserts that it did not have complete dominion over Singleton because Handi-Man chose Singleton for the job, paid Singleton, and could have pulled Singleton off the job. It asserts that Handi-Man hired Singleton and Smurfit hired Handi-Man to provide a service.

> It sometimes happens that one wishes a certain work to be done for his benefit and neither has persons in his [employ] who can do it nor is willing to take such persons into his general service. He may then enter into an agreement with another. If that other furnishes him with the men to do the work and places them under his exclusive control in the performance of it, those men become *pro hac vice* servants of him to whom they are furnished. But, on the other hand, one may prefer to enter into an agreement with another that that other, for a consideration, shall himself perform the work through servants of his own selection, retaining the direction and control of them. In the first case, he to whom the workmen are furnished is responsible for their negligence in the conduct of the work, because the work is his work and they are for the time his workmen. In the second case, he who agrees to furnish the completed work through servants

> over whom he retains control is responsible for their negligence in the conduct of it, because, though it is done for the ultimate benefit of the other, it is still, in its doing, his own work. To determine whether a given case falls within the one class or the other we must inquire whose is the work being performed—a question which is usually answered by ascertaining who has the power to control and direct the servants in the performance of their work.

Standard Oil Co. v. Anderson, 212 U.S. 215, 221, 29 S. Ct. 252, 254, 53 L. Ed. 480, 483 (1909). In this [sic] case Standard Oil contracted with a stevedore to load a ship and it provided the stevedore with some of the equipment and the winchman to do so. The winchman was in the general employ of Standard Oil which hired him, paid him, and could discharge him. A gangman and others were employed by the stevedore. The Court found that the winchman, who negligently failed to observe a gangman's signals in the lowering of oil cases into a ship's hold, was the rightful employee of Standard Oil under the facts of the case. The Court stated that the winchman's obedience with the gangman's signals was more a cooperation with one large, general task than it was evidence of subordination to the stevedore's gangman. The Court concluded that

> the mere fact that a servant is sent to do work pointed out to him by a person who has made a bargain with his master does not make him that person's servant; more than that is necessary to take him out of the relation established by the only contract which he has made, and to make him a voluntary subject of a new sovereign.

Though *Standard Oil* is not directly controlling on the instant issue, its instruction guides our conclusion that the question of whether Singleton was under the control and direction of Smurfit, for purposes of applying the borrowed servant doctrine to immunize Handi-Man, was a question that presented a material issue of fact which cannot be disposed of by summary judgment.

REVERSED and REMANDED.

Notes

1. Would the result in *Jefferson Smurfit Corp. v. JBS, Inc.*, have been different if Singleton (the Handi-Man temporary worker) had negligently injured a third person while working at Smurfit? Could Singleton's act be within the scope of employment of *both* Smurfit and Handi-Man?

2. In *Jefferson Smurfit Corp. v. JBS, Inc.*, the court indicates that the special employer must have assumed *complete* control over the borrowed servant before *either* the special employer will become liable *or* the general employer will be relieved of liability. Is that consistent with *Paoli v. Dave Hall, Inc.*, and *Parker v. Vanderbilt University*?

3. In *Charles v. Barrett*, 233 N.Y. 127, 137 N.E. 199 (1922), Steinhauser, who was in the trucking business, leased Adams Express Company, the defendant, a van and a driver ("chauffeur"). Adams Express loaded the van and sealed it at the point of departure and unsealed and unloaded it at the point of destination. While the chauffeur was driving the van in between, the van struck and killed the plaintiff's son. The court held that truck and driver were not borrowed servants, but remained in the general employer's service:

> In between the point of departure and destination, the truck remained in the charge of the chauffeur without interference or supervision. There was no such change of masters as would relieve Steinhauser of liability if the driver of the van had broken the seals and stolen the contents. By the same token, there was no such change as to relieve liability for other torts committed in the conduct of the enterprise. Where to go and when to go could be determined for the driver by [Adam Express'] commands. The duty of going carefully, for the safety of the van as well as for that of wayfares, remained a duty to the master at whose hands he had received possession. Neither the contract nor its performance shows a change of control so radical as to disturb that duty or its incidence. The rule now is that as long as the employee is furthering the business of his general employer by the service rendered to another, there will be no inference of a new relation unless command has been surrendered and no inference of its surrender from the mere fact of its division.

4. Is it possible for the general and special employers to *share* control of a single servant, so that *both* can be held liable for the servant's tort within the scope of both employments?

Strait v. Hale Construction Co.

26 Cal. App. 3d 941, 103 Cal. Rptr. 487 (1972)

KERRIGAN, Associate Justice.

Two lawsuits were filed against three defendants as a result of a collision between a tractor (earthmover) and a truck on September 6, 1966, at the intersection of Route 115 and Allbright Street in the County of Imperial. The truck driver (Oliver Strait) was seriously injured in the collision and sued to recover damages for his injuries. The truck owner (Topham & Sons, a corporation) sued for the property damage to its truck. The earthmover was owned by a farmer (William E. Young, Jr.) and was being operated by his employee (Miguel Hurtado). Young had let the tractor and the operator (Hurtado) to a road construction firm (Hale Construction Company, as co-partnership). At the time of the accident, the road builder (Hale) was converting Allbright Street from a dirt road to a paved street.

The two actions against the farmer, the tractor operator and road builder (Young, Hurtado and Hale) were consolidated for trial. The jury awarded the truck driver $225,700 and the truck owner $8,603 against all defendants. This appeal ensued.

The crucial problem involves the vicarious liability, if any, of the general employer (Young) and the special employer (Hale) for the negligence of the borrowed servant (Hurtado). The general employer claims that the court erred in instructing the jury as a matter of law that he was liable for the loaned servant's negligence. The special employer claims that the trial court erred in denying its motions for nonsuit, directed verdict and judgment notwithstanding the verdict and in leaving the issue of vicarious liability to the jury.

Hale Construction Company is a firm specializing in road and airport work. It entered into a contract with the County of Imperial and the federal government to do the work on Allbright Street. The job consisted of preparing Allbright Street for eventual hardtop surfacing. This required excavating dirt from some areas and building-up other areas which, in turn, required the use of earthmoving machines commonly called rigs.

After the road firm undertook the Allbright Street job, it found it was falling behind in its work schedule. Hale was under a completion deadline with a penalty of $100 per day. Initially, Hale had the use of 3 John Deere 50-10 tractors (earthmovers or rigs). One was owned by Hale and operated by its own employee. The other two were rented, with the operators being provided by the equipment owners. Someone told Hale that Young owned a 50-10 tractor. To accelerate construction, Hale contacted Young about letting the rig with an operator.

Young is a farmer living near Calipatria in Imperial County. He uses the earthmover in connection with his extensive farming operations. He had never leased out the rig or operator prior to being contacted by the road builder. Inasmuch as the machine was not then being utilized in farming operations, he agreed to rent the rig and supply Hurtado as the operator for $18 an hour. Young was to pay Hurtado $5 an hour to operate the rig from the $18 hourly rental.

In addition to a construction superintendent, the Allbright Street job was under the direct supervision of Raymond Hale, a general partner and officer of Hale Construction Company. Hale had a grade checker located at the place where the dirt was to be removed by the various tractor operators, as well as a dump boy at the site where the dirt was to be deposited by them. The grade checker would tell the rig operators where to cut and how deep to cut and the dump boy instructed them where and how to deposit the removed dirt. In removing and dumping the earth, it was necessary for the rigs to cross Route 115—a through highway—where it intersects with Allbright. Entrances to the highway on both sides of Allbright were posted with stop signs. In hauling dirt from a removal point west of the intersection to the dumpsite at a point east of the intersection, Hurtado collided with the truck being driven by Strait and owned by Topham & Sons which was proceeding north on Route 115.

Turning to the legal aspects of the two lawsuits, cases involving the application of the *loaned servant rule* have not always been uniform in the results obtained. This observation is not new or novel. In 1928, an illustrious jurist came to the same conclusion when he wrote: "The law that defines or seeks to define the distinction between general and special employers is beset with distinctions so delicate that chaos is the consequence. No lawyer can say with assurance in any given situation when one employment ends and the other begins. The wrong choice of defendants is often made, with instances, all too many, in which justice has miscarried." Cardozo, A Ministry of Justice, [1921] 35 Harv. L. Rev. 113, 121. The passage of time has not eliminated the confusion. Courts have refused to attempt to differentiate and harmonize the case law on the grounds that to do so would merely add to the confusion; for the most part, the decisions have been characterized as irreconcilable.

The difficulty in determining the issue as to whether the general employer or the special employer, or both, should be liable for the tort of the loaned servant arose out of the test governing its application. In determining the vicarious liability issue, the courts have uniformly applied the *test of control*, i.e., which employer had actual control or the right of control—the power to direct the borrowed servant in the details of the work at the time the tort occurred? In adopting the control theory and in weighing the elements of control, courts were inexorably driven to the expedience of making and accepting disparate refinements, ethereal in substance and revolting in reason, in order to reach any semblance of reconciliation of the results flowing from the borrowed servant cases.

As in other jurisdictions, California courts applied the control test with varying results. In 1922, it was held that when a master (general employer) hires out under a rental agreement the services of his employee (loaned servant) for the operation of an instrumentality owned by the master, together with the use of the instrumentality, without relinquishing to the hirer (special employer) the power to discharge such servant, the legal presumption is that, although the hirer directs the servant where to go and what to do in the performance of the work, the servant who is the operator of the instrumentality employed in the doing of the work, remains, in the absence of an agreement to the contrary, the servant of the general employer insofar as concerns the manner and method of operating the instrumentality, and the general employer is solely liable for the servant's negligence in the operation of such instrumentality. *Billig v. Southern Pacific Co.*, 189 Cal. 477, 485-486, 209 P. 241. In accord are other authorities holding that if the special employer does not have power to discharge the servant even though he directs the servant where to go and what to do in performance of the work, the servant, as operator of the instrumentality employed in the doing of the work, remains the employee of the general employer, with the latter being responsible under the doctrine of respondeat superior for the servant's negligence.

Conversely, the proposition has been propounded that an employee may be the general servant of one person and may be hired to another for a special service, and when he is subject wholly to the direction and control of the special employer, the latter, not the general employer, is liable for the borrowed servant's negligence; but to escape liability for the negligence of a servant whose services have been rented or hired to another, the general employer must resign full control of the servant for the time being. In those cases where the special employer may be liable, the paramount consideration is whether the alleged special employer exercises control of the details of the work; such control strongly supports an inference that a special employment exists. If one employer hires out either the services of his employee to another employer or rents an instrumentality and an employee to operate it, the second or special employer may become temporarily liable for his tortious actions under the "borrowed servant" rule.

With the development of the borrowed servant doctrine, another line of cases appeared suggesting that instead of imposing liability solely on the general employer or only on the special employer, a third alternative should be considered, to wit, both could be held liable. Under these authorities, the control factor was still utilized as the primary test in determining vicarious liability. A general and special employer may both be held liable for the employee's negligence where each had some power, not necessarily complete, of direction and control; the control need not be exercised; it is deemed sufficient if the right to direct the details of the work existed. Where, at the time of the accident, both the general and the special employer exerted some measure of control over the employee, both may be held liable for the employee's negligence.

Consequently, three possible results have flowed from the application of the control test in the borrowed servant cases: (1) liability of the general employer; (2) liability of the special employer; and (3) liability of both employers.

Capably recognizing the inconsistencies in the decisions resulting from the application of the control test in the loaned servant cases, Young (general employer) claims that the trial court committed serious error in ruling, as a matter of law, that he was responsible for Hurtado's negligence. Young predicates his claim of error on the evidence indicating that he did not exercise any control over Hurtado on the Allbright Street job and, in fact, never visited the job or gave the rig operator any instructions or directions whatsoever, except to follow Hale's orders. Similarly, Hale (special employer) claims that its firm did not exercise any significant control over Hurtado so as to be vicariously responsible for his tort. In support of its argument, Hale contends that the essential element of control is the right to discharge the employee, as contrasted with the giving of mere information or general signals as to where the instrumentality should be used, and that it did not have the right to fire Hurtado.

Turning first to Hale's contention, the paving firm relies on *Billig v. Southern Pacific Co.*, and its progeny, holding that where a special employer does not enjoy the right to discharge the borrowed servant, only the general employer is liable for his negligence. While the *Billig* court held that the special employer was not liable under the doctrine of respondeat superior, in doing so, it utilized the following language:

> [T]he application of the doctrine of respondeat superior in any given case depends upon the power of control which the superior possesses, and which for the protection of third persons he is required to exercise, over the conduct and activities of his subordinates. Consequently the doctrine has application only in cases where the power of control exists, and such power does not exist in a situation where the special employer has no voice in the selection or retention of the negligent subordinate.

In answer to Hale's argument to the effect that it did not possess the power to discharge Hurtado and that its checker and dump boy merely gave him signals or directions as to where to remove the dirt and where to deposit it, it should be emphasized that if the ultimate determination of liability in borrowed servant cases is controlled by the doctrine of respondeat superior, then the policy considerations underlying respondeat superior must also be examined.

As early as 1947, the California Supreme Court defined the public policy factors underlying an employer's vicarious liability in the following terms:

> The principle justification for the application of the doctrine of respondeat superior in any case is the fact that the employer may spread the risk through insurance and carry the cost thereof as part of his costs of doing business.

Johnston v. Long, 30 Cal. 2d 54, 64, 181 P.2d 645, 651. Twenty-three years later, the same court amplified the policy factors underlying the doctrine imposing liability without fault in *Hinman v. Westinghouse Elec. Co.*, 2 Cal. 3d 956, 959-960, 471 P.2d 988, in the following language:

> Although earlier authorities sought to justify the respondeat superior doctrine on such theories as 'control' by the master of the servant, the master's 'privilege' in being permitted to employ another, the third party's innocence in comparison to the master's selection of the servant, or the master's 'deep pocket' to pay for the loss, 'the modern justification for vicarious liability is a rule of policy, a deliberate allocation of a risk. The losses caused by the torts of employees, which as a practical matter are sure to occur in the conduct of the employer's enterprise, are placed upon that enterprise itself, as a required cost

of doing business. They are placed upon the employer because, having engaged in an enterprise which will, on the basis of past experience, involve harm to others through the torts of employees, and sought to profit by it, it is just that he, rather than the innocent injured plaintiff, should bear them; and because he is better able to absorb them, and to distribute them, through prices, rates or liability insurance, to the public, and so to shift them to society, to the community at large.'

In an expert critique, a legal source points out why the control justification for liability should be discarded in the dual employer situation just as it has been abandoned in the single employer situation. In the case of a borrowed servant, both the general employer and special employer share control; while the general employer can fire the employee, the special employer can dismiss him from the particular job; while the general employer can direct the borrowed servant in the general use of the instrumentality, the special employer directs him on the particular aspects of the job at hand; control is thus actually split and it is a test without meaning. *Borrowed Servants and the Theory of Enterprise Liability*, [1967] 76 Yale L.J. 807; *see also* Smith, *Scope of the Business: The Borrowed Servant Problem*, [1940] 38 Mich. L. Rev. 1222, 1228-31.

Liability in borrowed servant cases involves the exact public policy considerations found in sole employer cases. Liability should be on the persons or firms which can best insure against the risk, which can best guard against the risk, which can most accurately predict the cost of the risk and allocate the cost directly to the consumers, thus reflecting in its prices the enterprise's true cost of doing business.

Control, then, at least in the narrow sense suggested by Hale, is not dispositive of this case. The theory having greater integrity in respondeat superior cases is allocation of risk.

In light of the policy factors underlying respondeat superior, it is inconceivable that Hale should escape liability. A special employment relationship with Hurtado was conclusively established. Obviously, the resurfacing work being accomplished was within the regular scope of Hale's business. Hale was to profit from this job. Hale understood the risks inherent in construction work and was in a position to guard against, and insure against, such risks. Consequently, Hale was not at all prejudiced by the trial court's ruling allowing the question of its liability to go to the jury. To the contrary, the court could have instructed the jury, in view of the foregoing policy factors, that the road builder was vicariously liable for Hurtado's negligence as a matter of law.

Finally, Young (general employer) urges that the trial court committed prejudicial error in ruling as a matter of law that Hurtado was his agent at the time of the accident. He contends the facts of the case are susceptible to more than one inference as to the relationship between him [*sic*] and Hurtado, and the agency issue therefore required jury resolution.

For an employer to be vicariously liable for the negligent acts of his servant, the servant must have been acting within the scope of his duties. Young seems to contend that when Hurtado was working for Hale, he was not necessarily working for Young. But as Young concedes, an employee can have more than one employer, both of whom may be simultaneously liable for a negligent act of the employee.

This is just such a case, Young owned the tractor and was profiting from the renting of the rig, as well as Hurtado's employment with Hale. Young reserved the right to dismiss Hurtado. This analysis of Young's liability does not contradict the earlier discussion holding Hale liable despite previous case law that may not have held Hale liable. In those cases the court held the general employer liable as a matter of law. The language questioned previously in those cases does not bear on that issue, but whether the special employer should also be liable. Their holdings as to the general employer's initial liability are sound.

Young urges he should not be liable to the plaintiffs inasmuch as he is not in the business of renting heavy equipment and furnishing an operator. But the policy factors heretofore discussed weigh as heavily on Young as on Hale. While Young is a farmer and not directly engaged in letting construction equipment and providing an operator, his agriculture venture can be equated with any other enterprise engaged in business for profit. Farming in California can be big business. Tractors are driven on highways frequently and infrequently in agriculture production. One cannot expect to put a $25,000 rig and driver to work on a public highway—a place fraught with danger—without incurring liability for the operator's negligence. If Young did not feel he had sufficient control of the working conditions or sufficient knowledge of the construction business to guard against the risks, he could have contracted for specific indemnity or obtained the appropriate liability insurance.

In conclusion, it should be parenthetically noted that Hale (special employer) and Young (general employer) have filed cross-complaints against the other based on implied indemnity. In any future trial, the joint tortfeasors will then be accorded the opportunity to show, on equitable principles, why the other should be held primarily liable for Hurtado's negligence. In this connection, Young argues that Hale should have had a flagman on duty to warn drivers on Route 115 of the construction work being done on Allbright Street and of the heavy equipment crossing the main highway, or a flagman to direct the rig operator's crossing the highway, and that the failure to provide a flagman was the actual and proximate cause of this accident. Assuming, without deciding, that Hale had such a duty or assuming that even if Hale had no such duty, Young will have an opportunity to establish in his action for indemnity that Hale was primarily responsible for the injuries and damages incurred by the plaintiffs herein, particularly in view of the evidence indicating Young played a passive role in the events culminating in plaintiffs' damages. However, the merits of the indemnity actions are not before us and patently cannot be resolved in this appeal.

The judgment is affirmed.

Notes

1. In *DePratt v. Sergio,* 102 Wis. 2d 141, 306 N.W.2d 62 (1981), the court addressed the question of whether borrowed servant liability should necessarily be an either-or question, with only *one* of the general and the special employers liable:

> Under the borrowed servant rule, the borrowing master, not the loaning master, is liable for the negligent acts of a loaned servant if the loaned servant becomes the servant of the borrowing master. This result is reached even though the loaned servant remains in the employ of the loaning master and is acting within the scope of his employment with the loaning master. Thus when a servant

is loaned, either the loaning master or the borrowing master, not both masters, will be held vicariously liable for the servant's tort.

[T]he circuit court concluded that the [servant] had become the employee of [the borrowing employer], so that only [the borrowing employer] bore liability for the [servant's] negligent conduct.

On appeal from an order and a portion of the judgment the court of appeals affirmed. We granted review to decide an issue not specifically presented to the circuit court or to the court of appeals: Should Wisconsin abandon the borrowed servant rule and adopt the concept of dual liability. Under the dual liability approach, which the plaintiff urges us to adopt, both the borrowing employer and the loaning employer may be held liable in tort to a third party who sustains injuries caused by the negligence of the loaned employee when the loaning employer retains broad control over the loaned employee (such as the right to discharge the employee) and the borrowing employer has control over the details of the loaned employee's work.

The plaintiff attacks the borrowed servant rule on two grounds: first, that the borrowed servant rule is theoretically unsound, i.e., that an underlying premise of the borrowed servant rule is difficult to apply.

The plaintiff contends that the borrowed servant rule is premised on the concept that the master who has control over the servant and derives benefit from the servant should be exclusively liable for the negligent acts of the loaned servant. This premise, that one master can thus be selected to be exclusively liable for the torts of the servant, is weak because both the borrowing and loaning masters have some control over the servant; the loaned servant acts within the scope of employment of both masters; and both masters derive some benefit from the servant's work. Calling our attention to this weakness, the plaintiff asserts that justice and common sense indicate that an equitable system for allocating responsibility and liability between the two masters should replace the current rule imposing exclusive liability on one of the masters. Under the entrepreneur or enterprise theory of liability both employers should be responsible to the injured party because both exercise a degree of control, both profit from the employee's conduct, and both are capable of planning for and transferring the losses incurred. Under the dual liability approach the injured party, for whom the doctrine of respondeat superior was designed, would enjoy greater assurance of recovery.

The plaintiff further contends that the borrowed servant rule is difficult to apply. The plaintiff argues that when the tests to determine whether a loaned servant becomes the servant of the borrowing master are applied to particular fact situations, the results are not predictable or consistent. We acknowledge that this criticism is well founded. We have said that while the tests or rule to determine whether a loaned employee retains employment with his original employer or becomes the employee of the borrowing employer

> are readily comprehensible, when applied to specific factual situations, the distinctions are sometimes slight and the decisions well-nigh irreconcilable.

We concede that the traditional borrowed servant rule has deficiencies in theory and in application. We conclude, however, that the dual liability approach, although having some merit, does not offer a simple and easily applicable alternative to the borrowed servant rule, and we decline to substitute it for the present rule. If we were to adopt the dual liability approach as explained and urged by the plaintiff, the courts would have to decide when each employer retained sufficient control—or when each employer retained sufficient indicia of the master-servant relation—to subject that employer to liability for the negligent conduct of the loaned employee. Similarly courts would have to decide how responsibility and liability should be allocated to each employer. One way of allocating responsibility and liability between the employers is on the basis of their degree of control over the employee's conduct. This dual liability control test might prove similar to the borrowed servant control test used now to determine which employer is exclusively liable.

We have found no support nor have we been furnished any authority to suggest that the dual liability approach would afford greater certainty or precision in its application than the current approach. It appears that the preferred replacement would create a new area of uncertainty in the law and might force a change in business practices of borrowing and loaning employers, the purchase of additional insurance, and the negotiation of indemnity agreements. Also the dual liability approach might, instead of diminishing unfairness, add unfairness in an already troubled area. For example, if we were to adopt the dual liability approach in the instant case and view both [the loaning and the borrowing employers] as liable to the injured plaintiff for the tort of the [servant], [the loaning employer] would have to pay the entire judgment. [The borrowing employer's] liability to the injured plaintiff, an employee of [the borrowing employer], is limited to worker's compensation benefit; [the loaning employer] could not require contribution from [the borrowing employer] even if [the borrowing employer] was substantially more at fault than [the loaning employer]. Until a more satisfactory solution is developed as to the liability of the borrowing and loaning employers for the torts of a loaned employee than the broadly stated dual liability approach urged by the plaintiff, we decline to abandon the borrowed servant rule which, although troublesome, has been followed by this court for many years.

Decision of the court of appeals affirmed.

2. In the cases so far considered, the courts have focused on the question of which possible employer had *actual control* of the servant's acts at the time of the tort. Is the master's responsibility in respondeat superior for the torts of the servant committed within the scope of employment based on the master's control or the master's *right* of control? May both the general and the special employers have the right to control the borrowed servant's conduct?

City of Somerset v. Hart

549 S.W.2d 814 (Ky. 1977)

LUKOWSKY, Justice.

This is an appeal by the Hospital and its alter ego, the City, from their share of a $28,144.38 malpractice judgment in favor of Hart. The verdict of the jury apportioned the recovery forty percent or $11,257.75 against the operating surgeon and sixty percent or $16,886.63 against the Hospital and the City. The surgeon has paid his share and gone forth rejoicing.

In July of 1970 Hart was afflicted with a kidney stone. Surgery was indicated and Hart was admitted to the Hospital.

Hart was taken to the operating room and given a general anesthetic. The surgeon opened his abdomen and exposed the ureter and bladder. After the stone was removed, the surgeon closed. This is the first time Hart had undergone abdominal surgery.

Hart's hospital recuperation was uneventful. He was seen by his surgeon post-operatively at four and six weeks and discharged. On each occasion he complained of pain and was told that this was not abnormal. For about three months the pain remitted and then it exacerbated. In August of 1971 he was referred to another surgeon who examined him and took x-rays. The x-rays revealed a bladder stone from which a scalpel blade protruded. A second major operation was performed and the stone and blade were removed.

Obviously, the part of the Hospital in the first operation becomes the subject of scrutiny.

The Hospital supplied the operating room and staffed it with a supervisor, a scrub nurse and a circulating nurse. This staff was selected, paid and generally supervised by the Hospital. The staff was required to set up the room, lay out the instruments, including scalpels with blades attached, hand instruments to the surgeon and generally assist him during the operation. The operating surgeon was authorized to supervise and direct the staff in the operating room.

The Hospital supplied the instruments in the form of an instrument pack. This pack is a set of instruments of a type and number prescribed by the Hospital sufficient to perform the operation scheduled by the surgeon. The packs are assembled by employees of the Hospital. The rules of the Hospital do not require that the number of instruments be verified by their operating room staff by either a preoperation or preclosing instrument count. However, the Hospital does require its operating room staff to make a post operation count at the time the instruments are cleaned, to keep count of the number of scalpel blades used and to report any deficiency. No such report was made here either to the hospital administration or the operating surgeon.

The only assignment of error by the Hospital worthy of discussion is that the operating room staff are the borrowed servants of the surgeon and that the Hospital as their general employer is not liable for their negligence. Hart's response to this assignment of error is that there is distinction between administrative and medical acts, that the Hospital is the master in regard to administrative and medical acts, that the surgeon is the master in regard to medical acts, and that the failure to account for a scalpel blade is an administrative omission chargeable to the Hospital. The parties rely on a plethora of cases, most of which are discussed in an annotation, "Liability of Hospital for Negligence of Nurse Assisting Operating Surgeon," 29 A.L.R.3d 1065 (1970). We find both submissions to be superficial.

The borrowed servant doctrine frequently rears its head in malpractice cases primarily because of the relationship between hospital employees and attending staff physicians and surgeons. In few other areas where the doctrine of respondeat superior may be potentially applicable is the issue of control as crucial or as difficult to resolve as it is in many of the doctor-hospital relationships. Although hospital employees are primarily servants of the hospital and not of the doctor the familiar rule of agency law that a servant may serve two masters simultaneously, and at times only momentarily, comes into play when interns, nurses or other hospital personnel assist a physician or surgeon as he treats a patient. Restatement of Agency 2d, Secs. 226, 227 (1957).

A dangerous tendency exhibited in some of the borrowed servant malpractice cases is to blindly hold that because a nurse or other hospital employee was lent to a physician or surgeon so as to render him liable under the doctrine of respondeat superior for the employee's negligence, the hospital by reason of the loan necessarily ceased to be liable. Sometimes, even though the question may be left to the jury as to which was liable, doctor or hospital, the assumption is clearly that only one of them could have been liable because the hospital employee could not simultaneously have been the servant of both. This is to ignore the legal principle that a person may be the servant of two masters, not joint employers, at one time as to one act, if the service to one does not involve the abandonment of the service to the other. Restatement of Agency, 2d, Sec. 226 (1957).

Frequently, if not most often, the hospital nurse or other employee who is temporarily lent to the physician or surgeon, in every realistic sense continues to carry on her hospital duties. Her work is of mutual interest to both of two employers, the physician or surgeon and the hospital, and is performed to effect their common purpose. The doctrine of respondeat superior is therefore equally applicable to both employers.

The failure of courts to more generally perceive this is probably due to an unarticulated feeling that it would be unjust to impose liability on the hospital where the nurse has only obeyed the orders of her superior, the physician or surgeon. We recognize that the nurse's duty to obey such orders exculpates her and her hospital employer from responsibility for the results of the competent execution of the orders, unless the orders are so obviously improper that the ordinarily prudent nurse would not obey them. When exculpation is the result, it is so because the nurse's obedience to the orders does not constitute negligence, and consequently, there is no basis for vicarious liability of the hospital. This is far different from a general and uncritical elimination of the hospital's liability under the doctrine of respondeat superior solely because the nurse or other employee was lent to the physician or surgeon.

It is beyond cavil in this case that the accurate accounting for scalpel blades is "of mutual interest to both" the surgeon and the hospital, that such an accounting "effects their common purpose," i.e., the cure of the patient, and that the surgeon issued no orders to the operating room staff in regard to the accounting for scalpel blades which conflicted with those of the Hospital. Consequently, the operating room staff acted as servants of both the surgeon and the hospital as a matter of law.

The judgment is affirmed.

Notes

1. Courts are increasingly applying Restatement section 226, especially in the hospital context. *See* Reuter, *Toward a More Realistic and Consistent Use of Respondeat Superior in the Hospital,* 29 St. Louis U.L.J. 601 (1985).

2. Restatement section 226 has also been applied in other contexts. *Consider, for example*, *Gordon v. S.M. Byers Motor Car Co.*, 309 Pa. 453, 164 A. 334 (1932). Hazlett, a wholesale and retail seller of gasoline, was interested in buying a used truck from Byers Company. Byers Company lent the truck and a driver, Lewis, to Hazlett for one week to demonstrate that the truck would do Hazlett's work. The truck was

equipped with three gasoline tanks, which were loaded with gasoline for delivery to a customer. Lewis began unloading the gasoline even though there was an open fire nearby. Some gasoline overflowed and then exploded, killing plaintiff's husband. The court held that both Byers Company and Hazlett were liable for Lewis' negligence:

> While manipulating the mechanism on the truck, Lewis was acting in the course of his employment and instructions, actual or implied, from Byers Company as part of the demonstration of the performance of the truck. In his efforts to deliver the gasoline to Hazlett's customer, he was carrying out Hazlett's instructions. Thus, Lewis, in the sale service of Byers Company as demonstrator, was transferred to the service of Hazlett to also do his work as directed by him. The employment involved a double service. Hazlett testified that he had direction and control over Lewis only for the delivery of the gasoline. While demonstrating the truck, Lewis was assisting in making a sale of the truck for the Byers Company. He was acting for both parties according to their common understanding; the power of control as to one part of his work was in Byers Company and, so to the other part, in Hazlett.
>
> The next question is whether Lewis's acts that resulted in the explosion were performed on behalf of both? Was he acting pursuant to directions from each? He was promoting the interest of Byers Company in manipulating the machinery on the truck to cause the gasoline to flow, for obviously, if the mechanism on the truck would not discharge the load, Hazlett would not wish to purchase the truck. Lewis was also complying with specific instructions in delivering the gasoline. The Byers Company controlled Lewis as demonstrator for the purpose of selling the truck, and Hazlett controlled him in delivering the gasoline. While breach of Lewis's duty to either alone would not have involved the other in responsibility for damage, he was negligent in doing an act for the account of both; they are joint tortfeasors.

Chapter 10

Worker Safety and Compensation for Injuries

A. Concern for Worker Safety

The workplace is often a dangerous place. For many employees, they spend more of their waking hours at work than anywhere else. In terms of shear likelihood of injury over time, the odds of sustaining a work-related accident or illness are substantial. In this age of chemical technology, work-related disease is a serious concern. Then, too, some kinds of employment and workplaces are commonly understood to involve risks—such as factory, construction, police, fire, and demolition work.

The human suffering and the direct and indirect costs of work-related injuries and occupational diseases in the United States are staggering. Ultimately, everyone pays the costs of these injuries and occupational diseases. Due to worker injuries and diseases and to the recoveries therefor, business expenses increase and/or insurance premiums rise. Businesses pass the costs along to the customers. Work accidents, injuries, and diseases may cause delays in completion of projects and thereby cause additional costs of time and increased prices. Where workers are injured or rendered ill and where they must seek public medical and financial assistance, taxpayers suffer the consequences. Employers, employees, and government need to be vigilant about worker safety.

Daugherty v. Pfizer, Inc.

588 F. Supp. 716 (S.D. Ill. 1983)

BEATTY, District Judge.

The plaintiff, William Daugherty, brought this action pursuant to the Illinois Structural Work Act, Ill. Rev. Stats. Ch. 48, Sec. 60-69 (1981), for injuries suffered when he fell from the top of a ladder while painting a "dirty liquor storage tank" owned by the defendant, Pfizer, Inc.

At the time of his injury, the plaintiff was a 36 year old journeyman high steel painter employed by the Bazan Painting Company. Pursuant to a contract entered into between his employer and the defendant for the scraping and painting of two such storage tanks, the plaintiff and another employee of Bazan, Christopher Reynolds, were sent to the defendant's facility. The tanks in question were structures of a cylindrical nature more than 30 feet high. A 32 foot aluminum extension ladder and airless spray gun were provided by Bazan to do the job. To paint the tanks the plaintiff was required to ascend the ladder to a height of 25 feet with spray gun in hand and air hoses trailing behind to a paint pot below. Mr. Reynolds was to hold the base of the ladder, fill the paint pot, assist with the air hoses and check the tanks for spots the plaintiff had missed. Prior to beginning the work, the plaintiff specifically questioned his superiors at Bazan concerning the safety of employing the ladder for this type of job. The plaintiff was nonetheless instructed to use the ladder.

The plaintiff and Mr. Reynolds then scraped and painted the tanks in the manner they were instructed. They were not tying the ladder off to the top of the tank. Several times a day, the defendant's project engineer, Bernie Bosse, inspected the work being done by Bazan. Bosse admitted he had observed the plaintiff and Reynolds employing the aluminum extension ladder in the manner described. Mr. Bosse testified that he did not instruct the painters to tie the ladder off to the top of the tank.

On the third day of the job, February 21, 1981, the plaintiff fell to the ground from the top of the ladder, a distance of approximately 25 feet. Mr. Reynolds testified that just prior to the plaintiff's fall, they had moved the ladder to a new position, the plaintiff had ascended the ladder with Reynolds holding it and the plaintiff had commenced spraying the tank. Reynolds then moved away from the ladder to attend the paint pot. As a result of the fall, the plaintiff fractured bones in his foot, heel, leg, hip, hand and wrist.

The contract between Bazan and the defendant provided that the painting was to be done under the supervision of the defendant's project engineer. The contract required Bazan to comply with Pfizer plant safety rules and specified that the defendant's project engineer would provide those rules to all outside employees upon their initial entry into the plant. Those rules included a provision that all portable ladders must be tied off at the top. The defendant's project engineer could not recall giving a copy of these rules to any Bazan personnel. Incredibly, Mr. Bosse admitted he was not even aware of the rule provision concerning the tying off of portable ladders.

This case graphically illustrates the need for and the purposes served by the Illinois Structural Work Act. The set of circumstances surrounding this plaintiff's fall dramatizes just how worker safety can succumb to the economic pressures of the competitive bidding market place. This particular project was described by a Bazan employee as a "loss leader." That is, Bazan intentionally submitted a contract bid price which was less than the actual costs it would incur in the scraping and painting of the tanks. Such a strategy was pursued in an effort to acquaint Pfizer with the services Bazan Painters could provide and thereby ideally lead to the award of future contracts with Pfizer.

Safety precautions obviously increase the costs incurred in any project. Actually requiring the painters in this case to tie their portable ladder off at the top of the tank or to employ alternative methods such as scaffolding, staging or cherry pickers to reach the elevated work would have significantly raised the costs of this project. An executive of Bazan Painting testified that just tying off the ladders would have doubled the cost of this job. Such additional costs may well have precluded Bazan from pursuing such a "loss leader" strategy. In any event, the manner in which these painters were instructed to employ the ladder was indeed the most cost effective way for Bazan to do the job. Sadly, as is evidenced by the plaintiff's fall, it was also the most hazardous for the painters.

The objective of the Illinois Structural Work Act is to deter injuries to individuals engaged in certain dangerous and extra hazardous occupations which require them to be on or make use of scaffolds, ladders and other like contrivances employed in and about the erection, repair, alteration, removal or painting of any house, building, bridge, viaduct or other structure. To promote job safety in these situations the Act imposes financial responsibility upon persons having charge of the work being done for personal injuries suffered by such workers as the result of a wilful violation of the Act. In other words, the Act seeks to expose all the various entities involved in certain designated activities to potential financial liability for workers' injuries in order to promote their concern and participation in job site safety. The Act additionally reflects a recognition of the inherent limitations that the Illinois Workers' Compensation system has in advancing worker safety.

An owner who solicits competitive bids for an undertaking involving the designated activities is in a peculiarly influential position from the inception of such a project to insure worker safety. The owner is the only party in the competitive bidding situation that can truly insure that the bids received do adequately reflect the additional costs that job site safety requires. An owner cannot be allowed to gain financially by accepting a bid which has sacrificed safety to economic considerations. The threat of potential liability for worker injuries that the Illinois Structural Work Act provides is an incentive needed to counteract market place pressures imposed upon safety precautions. The owner's primary concern is to secure the construction of a specified building or project at the lowest possible price and it is to this end that competitive bidding is employed. By placing such downward pressures on the price that a contractor must bid to obtain the contract, the owner may well be encouraging the contractor to cut corners in the area of worker safety. As noted above, the tying off of ladders, setting up proper staging or scaffolding and other safety precautions take time and are expensive.

The usual construction contract calls for the work to be done in a "safe and workmanlike manner." The owner cannot through his architect or inspectors insist on compliance with high standards of workmanship and materials and then subsequently be allowed to disclaim responsibility for worker injuries resulting from the low standards of safety being employed. Always, the owner will get only what he pays for. Absent the sanctions of the Structural Work Act, the owner has little if any economic interest in the extent to which the contractor safeguards the life and limb of the construction worker.

This Court finds that the defendant was in charge of the work being done within the meaning of the Illinois Structural Work Act. There is ample evidence in the record supporting this conclusion based on factors traditionally considered such as contractual right to control by the owner, job site inspection by the owner, actual control of the project by him and his reservation of the right to stop ongoing work at the site. However, this Court believes that because an owner utilizing competitive bidding is in sole control of the purse strings of a project and thereby has actual control of the safety standards employed on a job site, such an owner should be held in charge of the work being done as a matter of law. As noted above, the owner in such situations is in a peculiarly influential position from the start of a project to insure worker safety and is truly the only party that can make certain that the bids submitted do reflect adequately the additional costs that safety requires. Adding these considerations to the other factors traditionally looked to in determining whether a party is in charge of the work being done can only further the proclaimed purposes of the Structural Work Act.

The evidence presented at trial conclusively establishes that at the time of his fall the plaintiff was engaged in an activity within the scope of the Structural Work Act and that the defendant, Pfizer, Inc., was one of the persons having charge of the work being done. Further, this Court finds that the plaintiff's fall from the ladder and the injuries he sustained are a direct result of a wilful violation of the Structural Work Act by Pfizer, Inc. On the issue of liability under the Illinois Structural Work Act, this Court accordingly finds for the plaintiff, William Daugherty, and against the defendant, Pfizer, Inc.

On the issue of damages, it is evident from the plaintiff's testimony and the medical evidence that the plaintiff has sustained a massive and permanent injury as a result of his fall. The Court was able to observe the plaintiff during the trial and it was apparent that he could not sit without discomfort and that he walked with a pronounced limp and obvious pain. Plaintiff's treating orthopedic physician indicated that plaintiff is permanently unemployable in any type of work. That testimony also indicated plaintiff suffered a severe emotional problem as a result of his disability and pain. Because of the hazardous nature of this employment his current rate of pay, if working, would be $16.12 per hour, plus insurance and retirement benefits. Plaintiff's wife testified that her husband, prior to his accident, was a positive person who enjoyed baseball, jogging, and other types of sports, as well as being a "handy" person around the home. She further testified that he is now extremely depressed and sleeps about 16 hours a day. She stated that he is unable to perform any useful activity around the house.

It is apparent to the Court that the plaintiff's massive injuries prevent him from ever again engaging in the same type of work that he was performing at the time of his injury and further, that the persistent pain and virtual loss of the use of his right hand makes him nearly unemployable for most types of gainful occupation. The plaintiff's capacity to earn has been permanently and very nearly totally impaired.

The Court finds that the testimony that predicts the present cash value of the plaintiff's future wage loss in light of a probable retirement age of 65 and a probable future wage increase of 6% is more likely correct than the figures which are based on an 8% increase and retirement at age 70. However, the Court's observations of the construction industry brings it to the conclusion that most people in plaintiff's hazardous occupation of high steel painting, and probably plaintiff, as they become older, no longer desire to go high and forfeit the premium pay associated with that extrahazardous employment. For this probability, the Court will reduce the figure of $458,994, which reflects the present cash value of the plaintiff's future lost wages, by 10%. The Court further finds that in the future the plaintiff probably will engage in some type of minimal employment and further reduces the figure of $458,944 by an additional 10%, reflecting this likelihood. The Court, therefore, finds the present cash value of plaintiff's future wage loss to be the sum of $367,195. The Court further finds that plaintiff's wage loss and proven medical expenses amounts to $56,980. The Court finds that just compensation for plaintiff's past and future pain and suffering amounts to $100,000 and that damages for disability and disfigurement are assessed in an amount of $100,000. Accordingly, the Court enters judgment for the plaintiff and against the defendant and assesses damages in the sum of $624,175 plus taxable costs.

Wagner v. Continental Casualty Co.

143 Wis. 2d 379, 421 N.W.2d 835 (1987)

STEINMETZ, Justice.

The circuit court awarded Robert J. Wagner, the plaintiff, damages for injuries sustained when he fell through the roof of a building owned by Harold H. Klein and Randy Klein, the defendants.

This case comes to us on certification by the court of appeals to determine under what circumstances an employee who has received worker's compensation benefits from his employer, an independent contractor, may maintain a tort action against the independent contractor's employer.

We conclude that an employee of an independent contractor is precluded from receiving worker's compensation benefits from the independent contractor and also maintaining a tort action against the person who employs the independent contractor, the principal employer or general contractor, unless the principal employer is affirmatively negligent with respect to the employee.

The material facts in this case are undisputed. The defendants, Harold H. and Randy Klein, hired Vince Kobida (Kobida), an independent contractor, to demolish a dilapidated factory on their land. Defendants are partners in the Klein Land Company, which is a holding company involved in real estate development. The defendants also are shareholders in Klein Industrial Company, Incorporated, a salvage company specializing in scrap iron.

Once the defendants decided to demolish the building, Randy Klein searched the yellow pages for a contractor to perform the work. Kobida heard the defendants were taking bids and so he submitted one. Randy Klein received three oral bids and awarded the contract to Kobida, the lowest bidder. The defendants did not supervise the demolition nor exercise any control over the activities.

The one-page contract stated simply that Kobida would abide by all government regulations, would hold the defendants harmless for injuries and damages arising from the project, and would provide the necessary insurance, including worker's compensation.

Kobida started in the wrecking business in 1936 but had not demolished a building in more than 25 years. For the past 20 years, he acted as an unpaid consultant to various wrecking firms. When Kobida was hired, he had no equipment or employees with which to perform the demolition. He did, however, acquire equipment and hire personnel after the job was undertaken.

Randy Klein did not investigate Kobida's qualifications. He did not inquire whether Kobida was a member of the National Association of Demolition Contractors, an organization of persons involved in demolition which compiles a safety manual for demolition and provides safety information to those in the field. He did not inquire whether Kobida had the proper equipment, nor did he call any references.

Among the several workers hired by Kobida to undertake the demolition project was the plaintiff, Robert J. Wagner, a 20-year-old with no experience in demolition. At the time of the injury, Wagner and a co-worker were working on the roof of the factory at least 40 feet above the ground. The roof was riddled with holes. As the plaintiff and his co-worker rolled a heavy steel tripod off the roof, the plaintiff caught his glove on the tripod. Wagner was thrown into the air and fell through the roof to the ground, sustaining permanent injury to his left foot.

The plaintiff received worker's compensation benefits from Kobida, his employer. Wagner then filed this tort action, seeking additional recovery from the defendants who employed Kobida under the theories that the demolition work was nondelegable because it was inherently dangerous and that defendants negligently hired the independent contractor.

At trial, the plaintiff's expert witness testified that without safety precautions the conditions on the roof were inherently dangerous. The expert stated that a competent contractor would have used a crane to remove the roof. He testified that a person who hires an independent contractor to perform demolition work should check the contractor's background and make sure the contractor has the proper equipment.

The jury, by special verdict, concluded that the demolition work constituted an inherently dangerous activity and that the Kleins had negligently hired the independent contractor, Kobida. Additionally, the jury attributed 24 percent negligence to the Kleins, 71 percent to Kobida and 5 percent to Wagner and awarded Wagner $481,750.58 in damages. The Kleins were held liable for 95 percent of the damages.

The issues in this case, i.e., the scope of duty owed by an owner or general contractor to a subcontractor's employees, present questions of law. Accordingly, this court undertakes an independent review of the issues, without giving deference to the trial court.

Section 102.03(2), Stats.,[1] provides that the employee's right to recover worker's compensation benefits shall be the employee's exclusive remedy against the employer. This section does not, however, preclude an employee from suing a person who is not his or her employer. Section 102.29(1)[2] provides that an employee's claim for worker's compensation against the employer shall not affect the employee's right to bring an action in tort against "any other party." The defendants in this case are not the plaintiff's employer.

Wisconsin follows the general rule that a principal employer is not liable to others for the torts of independent contractors. Plaintiff asserts that this court has previously recognized two exceptions to this general rule to hold a principal employer responsible to an independent contractor's employee. First, a principal employer may be liable to the independent contractor's employee for injuries caused by the principal employer's affirmative act of negligence. Second, a principal employer may be held vicariously

---

1. Sec. 102.03(2), Stats., provides in pertinent part: "102.03 Conditions of liability.... (2) Where such conditions exist the right to the recovery of compensation under this chapter shall be the exclusive remedy against the employer, any other employee of the same employer and worker's compensation insurance carrier...."

2. Sec. 102.29(1), Stats., provides in part as follows: "102.29 Third party liability. (1) The making of a claim for compensation against an employer or compensation insurer for the injury or death of an employee shall not affect the right of the employee, the employee's personal representative, or other person entitled to bring action, to make claim or maintain an action in tort against any other party for such injury or death, hereinafter referred to as a 3rd party; nor shall the making of a claim by any such person against a 3rd party for damages by reason of an injury to which §§ 102.03 to 102.64 are applicable, or the adjustment of any such claim, affect the right of the injured employee or the employee's dependents to recover compensation. ..."

liable for the negligence of an independent contractor when the contractor's employee is injured while performing inherently dangerous activities.

Defendants agree that under *Barth* [*v. Downey Co., Inc.*, 71 Wis.2d 775, 239 N.W.2d 92 (1976)], an employee of an independent contractor may recover from a principal employer for affirmative acts of negligence. However, they claim that any negligence involved in hiring Kobida constituted an act of omission insufficient to rise to the level of an affirmative act.

In *Barth*, the plaintiff was employed by an independent contractor who had contracted with a general contractor to remove heating and ventilation ducts from the Milwaukee Arena. The plaintiff was injured when a piece of equipment fell to the ground. He then sued the general contractor for his injuries. In discussing the issue of general contractor's negligence as it pertained to the claims of the employee of the independent contractor, the court stated the case was an action based:

> '[U]pon common-law failure to exercise ordinary care toward an employee to whom, under the circumstances, a duty was owed.' Liability of a general contractor to the employee of a subcontractor, like the liability of a corporate officer as a coemployee, would have to depend or derive from 'affirmative acts' of negligence. This court said of a suit against a corporate officer: 'Clearly something extra is needed over and beyond the duty owed the employer.' In the claim against a corporate officer or supervisor employee that 'something extra' is an affirmative act which increased the risk of injury. In a third-party action against a general contractor brought by an employee of a subcontractor, there would need to be the same 'something extra,' an affirmative act of negligence that increased the risk of injury.

In *Snider* [*v. Northern States Power Co.*, 81 Wis. 2d 224, 260 N.W.2d 260 (1977)], this court affirmed the principle enunciated in *Barth* stating that a third-party action brought by a subcontractor's employee against a general contractor would have to be predicated upon affirmative acts of negligence that increased the risk of injury.

In the present case, the jury found that the Kleins negligently selected the independent contractor to perform the demolition work. The question then becomes whether this negligent hiring was an act of commission constituting an affirmative act of negligence or whether it was an act of omission which does not rise to the level of an affirmative act.

The distinction between acts or omissions—between "misfeasance" and "nonfeasance," while not always clear, has long been examined in the common law of negligence in order to determine the existence of a duty. Prosser & Keeton, The Law of Torts, sec. 56, p. 373 (1984).

> The reason for the distinction may be said to lie in the fact that by 'misfeasance' the defendant has created a new risk of harm to the plaintiff, while by 'nonfeasance' he has at least made his situation no worse, and has merely failed to benefit him by interfering in his affairs.

In the case at bar, the defendants failed to check the credentials of the independent contractor or make other inquiries. This failure cannot be seen as active misconduct constituting an affirmative act; rather, it was a "passive inaction or a failure to take steps to protect" the plaintiff from harm. Accordingly, we hold as a matter of law that the plaintiff could not recover from defendants on this basis; negligent hiring does not by itself constitute an affirmative act of negligence upon which the liability of a principal employer to a contractor's employee can be based. Stated another way, a principal employer or general contractor owes no duty to an independent contractor's employee to carefully select the independent contractor.

Turning to the second claim, we examine the liability of the principal employer to an independent contractor's employee for injuries sustained while performing inherently dangerous activities.

Plaintiff relies heavily on various sections of the Restatement (Second) of Torts to support his claim that an employee of an independent contractor can recover from a principal employer for injuries sustained while performing inherently dangerous work. Sections 413 and 416 (dealing with work creating "a peculiar risk of physical harm to others" absent special precautions), and sec. 427 (dealing with inherently dangerous work) impose vicarious liability on a principal employer for the negligence of the independent contractor. Section 413 makes the principal employer liable where he or she fails to take special precautions against the danger by specifying for them in the contract or otherwise exercising reasonable care. Sections 416 and 427 impute the independent contractor's negligence to the principal employer irrespective of whether the employer is himself or herself at fault on the basis that the dangerous activities involved give rise to a nondelegable duty.

> They arise in situations in which, for reasons of policy, the employer is not permitted to shift the responsibility for the proper conduct of the work to the contractor.

Plaintiff argues that these sections were adopted in Wisconsin with respect to employees of independent contractors in *Snider v. Northern States Power Co.*, 81 Wis. 2d 224, 260 N.W.2d 260. In *Snider*, the plaintiff was an employee of an independent contractor engaged in electrical construction work in a nuclear generating plant. Snider sued the plant owner, the principal employer, after sustaining injuries from a fall of 90 inches while installing a sheet metal cabinet. Snider claimed, inter alia, that the work of an electrician in the construction of a nuclear power plant was "extra-hazardous."

This court stated in *Snider* that "[a]ssuming that the work in which Snider was engaged was extra-hazardous, a nondelegable duty was imposed upon Northern States Power." The court found that as a matter of law "the risk to which Snider was exposed was not related to the hazards that would be experienced in working with high voltage or working at unusual heights. The hazard here was one which could be encountered typically in the work of any construction worker."

Snider cited in dicta secs. 413, 416 and 427 of the Restatement and discussed the peculiar risks associated with inherently dangerous or extrahazardous activities. While the dicta in *Snider* did not specifically differentiate between activities that are "inherently dangerous" and those that are "extrahazardous," this distinction was not necessary in that case because, as the court pointed out, the claimed negligence of the principal employer was not related to either inherently dangerous or extra-hazardous work. However, we clarify the use of those terms in this case. We do not regard an activity which is inherently dangerous because of the absence of special precautions to be synonymous with an activity that is extrahazardous. A person engaged in an activity of the first type, i.e., one that is inherently dangerous without special precautions, can take steps to minimize the risk of injury. Examples include general construction, demolition, and excavation.

By contrast, an activity that is said to be extrahazardous, or abnormally dangerous, is one in which the risk of harm remains unreasonably high no matter how carefully it is undertaken. Examples would include transporting nuclear waste or working with toxic gases. Although the *Snider* briefs reveal that the parties discussed inherently dangerous circumstances, the plaintiff in *Snider* was in essence making a claim of the second type, i.e., that the work was so extrahazardous that responsibility could not be delegated to an independent contractor.

While *Snider* may lend support to the claim of an independent contractor's employee engaged in extrahazardous or abnormally dangerous activities, it cannot be seen as supporting the claim in the present case. It is not exactly clear on what precise basis Wagner claims the work he performed was inherently dangerous; however, he has not advanced the argument that the work involved activity so intrinsically dangerous that the risks could not have been minimized.

Instead, Wagner asks us to read *Snider* as holding that an employee of an independent contractor states a cause of action against the principal employer for injuries sustained while engaged in activities which are inherently dangerous because of the absence of special precautions. That is, plaintiff asks us to apply secs. 413, 416 and 427 of the Restatement to employees of independent contractors. This we decline to do.

The defendants are, on the other hand, advocating that we overrule *Snider* insofar as that case may be interpreted as recognizing that an employee of an independent contractor engaged in inherently dangerous work may maintain a common law tort action against the principal employer. The defendants urge that this court hold that employees of an independent contractor should be barred from maintaining a tort action against the principal employer even when the work is inherently dangerous. They argue that the principal employer should be liable under secs. 413, 416 and 427 of the Restatement for injuries incurred during inherently dangerous work only to non-employees.

The drafters of secs. 413, 416 and 427 of the Restatement (Second) of Torts purposely avoided deciding whether a principal employer is liable in tort for the injuries to an employee of an independent contractor as well as to third parties injured by the independent contractor negligently performing inherently dangerous work. All of the illustrations in secs. 413, 416 and 427 of the Restatement relate to third parties. None involves an employee. Thus, the defendants reason that the drafters of the Restatement did not intend to permit employees of the independent contractor to recover from the principal employer for injuries the employee sustained while performing inherently dangerous work.

The history of secs. 413, 416 and 427 casts some light on the issue of whether employees of independent contractors are covered under those sections. In an early tentative draft (Tentative Draft No. 7, 1962), a special note to Chapter 15 stated that a principal employer's liability to "others" injured because an independent contractor was negligent in performing inherently dangerous work was not generally viewed as extending to employees of the independent contractor because the employees receive worker's compensation and the principal employer indirectly pays for the worker's compensation in the contract price. The note states in pertinent part:

> [T]he workman's recovery is now, with relatively few exceptions, regulated by workmen's compensation acts, the theory of which is that the insurance out of which the compensation is to be paid is to be carried by the workman's own employer, and of course premiums are to be calculated on that basis. While the workmen's compensation acts not infrequently provide for third-party liability, it has not been regarded as necessary to impose such liability upon one who hires the contractor, since it is to be expected that the cost of the workmen's compensation insurance will be included by the contractor in his contract price for the work, and so will in any case ultimately be borne by the defendant who hires him.

The special note is not, however, included in the final version of the Restatement. Indeed, there is no reference in the Restatement to employees. Courts have disagreed regarding the significance to be attached to the drafters' omission of the note. Compare *Eutsler v. United States*, 376 F.2d 634, 636 (10th Cir. 1967) (citing the note as "persuasive authority" of the drafters' intent to limit the principal employer's liability to third persons only) with *Sloan v. Atlantic Richfield Co.*, 552 P.2d 157, 160 (Alaska 1976) (noting that the drafters' decision not to include this note in their final draft might well indicate that the drafters disagreed about the ability of employees to recover in tort).

According to the Proceedings of the American Law Institute, the special note was apparently omitted to avoid making any statement—one way or the other—about the principal employer's liability to employees of independent contractors. Dean Prosser, the reporter of the Restatement, explained to the members of the Institute that the issue of the principal employer's liability is so closely tied to each state's worker's compensation act and rules on third party liability that it appeared undesirable, if not impossible, to say anything at all in the Restatement about the extent of the principal employer's liability to employees of independent contractors. Thus, the drafters apparently took a "strictly neutral position" on the issue of the principal employer's liability to independent contractor's employees.

Courts across the country have disagreed about whether principal employers should be liable to injured employees of independent contractors negligently performing inherently dangerous work. Several courts have allowed an employee to maintain tort actions against a principal employer for injuries the employee sustained while performing inherently dangerous work. These courts acknowledge that a principal employer is not ordinarily liable to the employee of the independent contractor performing inherently dangerous work for the negligence of the independent contractor. They recognize that the principal employer has relinquished control to the independent contractor, and that the independent contractor is in the best position to weigh the costs and benefits of various precautions against the costs and probability of an injury.

These courts conclude, however, that where the principal employer contracts out a job which is inherently dangerous, there is special reason to place some responsibility for safety precautions on the principal employer. The principal employer is likely to know that the work is inherently dangerous, and imposing liability on the principal employer is justified as a means of encouraging the principal employer to take steps to prevent injury. Thus, these courts have concluded that public policy demands that tort liability be imposed on a principal employer for injuries to the employees of independent contractors engaged in inherently dangerous work.

Other courts, distinguishing employees of independent contractors from other persons, have held that the principal employer is not liable in a tort action for personal injuries sustained by an employee of an independent contractor performing inherently dangerous work. The decisions declining to hold the principal employer liable in tort to an injured employee employ one of four reasons.

One reason is that the principal employer should be subject to the same liability when the work is performed by employees of an independent contractor as when the work is performed by the principal employer's own employees. If the principal employer uses his own employees, he is subject to worker's compensation payments, not tort liability. If the principal employer incurs tort liability when he hires an independent contractor, the principal employer would, for reasons of cost, prefer to use his own employees, who may be inexperienced, rather than employ an independent contractor skilled in the task. Thus, several courts conclude that to impose tort liability on the principal employer would have unfavorable consequences to the principal employer, the independent contractor, the employees and the public. These courts therefore immunize the principal employer from tort liability.

A second reason some courts offer for not imposing liability on the principal employer is that injured employees of an independent contractor do not require compensation through the tort system because they receive compensation for their injuries through worker's compensation benefits. A primary purpose of imposing tort liability is to assure compensation to an injured person. A third party who is injured may be assured compensation only if he or she is able to sue both the independent contractor and the principal employer. Because the employee of the independent contractor is guaranteed recovery through worker's compensation, these courts conclude that permitting an employee to recover in a tort action and to receive worker's compensation results in an unjustifiable windfall.

A third reason given for not imposing tort liability on the principal employer is that employees should bear part of the risk of injury. Employees possess some knowledge regarding the work; they agree to perform the work and may to some extent be able to protect themselves against any danger. In contrast, third parties should not bear the risk of injury; their proximity to the work-related danger is coincidental; they are probably unaware of the danger; and they are unable to protect themselves.

A fourth reason some courts give for not imposing tort liability on a principal employer is that the principal employer has already indirectly compensated the employee for the injuries. According to these courts, the cost of worker's compensation is built into the cost of the contract. These courts recognize that the underlying purpose for imposing tort liability on a principal employer for the torts of an independent contractor engaged in inherently dangerous work is to insure that the principal employer does not escape liability. A principal employer who can escape tort liability is less apt to use due care to prevent harm. Furthermore, if a principal employer escapes liability, no financially responsible person may be available to compensate the injured party.

The courts which immunize principal employers from tort liability on this fourth ground are persuaded that principal employers do not actually escape liability when employees are precluded from maintaining tort actions. They assert that the principal employer has already assumed financial responsibility for injuries to the employees, because the contract price between the principal employer and the independent contractor includes a payment for worker's compensation coverage. The employee has a remedy for the injury—worker's compensation—for which the principal employer has indirectly paid. Because the principal employer indirectly pays for worker's compensation, the principal employer has an incentive to assure that the independent contractor takes safety precautions and that the injured party is compensated.

This reasoning was employed by the Seventh Circuit Court of Appeals in *Anderson v. Marathon Petroleum Co.*, 801 F.2d 936, 941 (7th Cir. 1986), a case cited by the court of appeals in its certification memorandum. In *Anderson*, the defendant, Marathon Petroleum Co., hired an independent contractor to sandblast the inside of Marathon Petroleum's storage tanks. Anderson, an employee of the independent contractor, died of silicosis. The representative of the deceased employee presented evidence that sandblasting in a confined space produces silicon dust, which, if inhaled over a long period of time, causes silicosis and that the independent contractor did not take adequate precautions against the silicon dust. Further evidence was presented to show that Marathon Petroleum's supervisory personnel did nothing to encourage the independent contractor to protect his employees better.

The *Anderson* court reasoned that the injured employee, unlike the injured non-employee, is compensated for the risks of employment by a combination of wages, benefits and entitlement to worker's compensation. The court further reasoned that the principal employer pays for the employee's package of wages, benefits or entitlements indirectly through the contract price which includes the labor costs. According to the court, the principal employer does not escape liability for injury to the employee; the principal employer pays for any injury through the contract price; and the principal employer has an incentive to provide a safe environment to reduce its contract costs and its contingent liability for worker's compensation.

We are persuaded by the policy considerations advanced in these cases and today join the majority of jurisdictions that refuse to hold a principal employer vicariously liable to the independent contractor's employee for the torts of the contractor while performing inherently dangerous work. We are convinced that the vicarious liability exception cannot apply to employees of independent contractors involved in work which is inherently dangerous without special precautions. Any other holding would circumvent the bedrock principles of Wisconsin worker's compensation law.

Under our worker's compensation scheme, the guaranteed payment without regard to fault of either the employee or the employer (in this type of case, the independent contractor) of a certain, albeit lesser sum of money justifies drawing narrow exceptions to the general nonliability rule protecting principal employers. We decline to expand this exception on a vicarious liability theory where the work involved activities characterized as inherently dangerous because special precautions were not taken. Consistent with our prior holdings, something more than omissions or vicarious liability on this basis is necessary to support a claim against a principal employer.

Our holding in this case is not meant to affect in any way the rights of third parties to the employment situation against a principal employer. Nor do we hold that under no circumstances may a principal employer be held vicariously liable to the employee of an independent contractor where the work is classified as abnormally dangerous or extrahazardous, rather than inherently dangerous absent special precautions, as here.

Plaintiff does not argue that demolition is extrahazardous or abnormally dangerous. Although it is not exactly clear for what precise reasons plaintiff claimed that the work was inherently dangerous, it appears Wagner argued that improper equipment was used and special precautions were not taken.

In any event, the question of whether an activity is extrahazardous should not have been submitted to the jury in the first instance. We recognize that standard jury instructions exist on this issue and that trial courts in prior cases have treated the question as one of fact. However, the issue of whether an activity is extrahazardous presents a question of law for the court to decide. We hold as a matter of law that the activities in the present case were not abnormally dangerous or extrahazardous.

We also find as a matter of law that the owners/employers, Kleins, committed no affirmative negligence increasing the risk of injury to the plaintiff; there was no affirmative negligence in hiring the independent contractor, the plaintiff's employer. We hold no tort liability has been established against the defendants.

The judgment of the circuit court for Milwaukee County is reversed.

SHIRLEY S. ABRAHAMSON, Justice ([with HEFFERNAN, C.J., and BABLITCH, J.] dissenting).

I dissent because I conclude that the decision in this case contravenes our prior case law and the policies underlying tort law and worker's compensation law. I would affirm the jury's verdict and the judgment of the circuit court.

Precedent supports the conclusion that the principal employer may be liable in tort for injuries sustained by the employee of an independent contractor performing inherently dangerous work. In *Snider v. Northern States Power Co.*, 81 Wis.2d 224, 260 N.W.2d 260 (1977), this court recognized that a principal employer is liable in tort to an employee of an independent contractor who sustains injuries because the independent contractor negligently performed inherently dangerous work. *Snider* was a vicarious liability case. If principal employers are vicariously liable to an injured employee for the negligence of the independent contractor, it follows that principal employers are liable to an injured employee for their own negligence. The court today overrules *Snider* by reinterpreting it.

The court's conclusion that the principal employers in this case are not liable to the injured employee rests on decisions in other jurisdictions holding that principal employers are not vicariously liable to employees of an independent contractor for the negligence of the independent contractor. Reliance on these vicarious liability decisions is misplaced.

First, the question in this case is whether principal employers should be liable in tort for their own negligence, not whether they should be vicariously liable to injured employees of an independent contractor for the independent contractor's negligence. Thus the vicarious liability cases exonerating principal employers from liability are inapposite. Second, the vicarious liability cases rest on the premise that the principal employers used due care in selecting the independent contractor who negligently performed the inherently dangerous work. In *Anderson v. Marathon Petroleum Co.*, 801 F.2d 936, 941-942 (7th Cir. 1986), a vicarious liability case upon which the majority relies, the federal court of appeals expressly stated that it was not addressing a case in which the principal employer negligently hired the independent contractor. The implication of *Anderson* and other vicarious liability decisions is that different considerations come into play when principal employers fail to use due care in selecting the independent contractor to do inherently dangerous work. In this case, unlike the vicarious liability cases, the principal employers did not use due care.

Third, the courts exonerating principal employers from vicarious liability reason that tort law should not discourage principal employers from employing skilled independent contractors to do inherently dangerous work. Courts have concluded that immunizing principal employers from vicarious liability to injured employees of an independent contractor for the negligence of the independent contractor would allow principal employers to decide whether to use their own employees or to hire an independent contractor for inherently dangerous work on the merits of the decision without regard to concerns about tort liability to an injured employee.

If the goal is to encourage principal employers to use a skilled independent contractor to do inherently dangerous work, then principal employers should not enjoy tort immunity when, as in this case, they are negligent in hiring the independent contractor to do inherently dangerous work. When the work is inherently dangerous, public safety requires at a minimum that principal employers be held liable for injury caused by their negligence in hiring the independent contractor.

The majority opinion sends the message that principal employers may negligently hire an incompetent independent contractor to perform inherently dangerous work and escape tort responsibility for injuries their negligent hiring causes to an employee of the independent contractor. This result contravenes our prior case law and the policies underlying tort law and worker's compensation law.

Note

A collateral issue involves the loss suffered by an *employer* when an employee is injured by some third party.

> [T]he precise issue raised by the demurrer is whether an employer can maintain a cause of action against a tort-feasor for loss of profits directly resulting from an injury to a key employee who, while on his employer's business, was injured through the negligence of the tort-feasor. It appears that there have been no Connecticut cases dealing with this specific question.
>
> The theory under which the claim in issue is made is found in the early English common law. The common-law rule was based on the concept that the servant had a chattel relationship to the master and therefore any injury to the chattel was an injury to a property interest of the master, thus giving rise to an action by the master against the responsible party. The historical development of this sort of action from the Middle Ages to the present was fully discussed by the English Court of Appeal in *Inland Revenue Commissioners v. Hambrook*, [1956] 2 QB 64. See note, 57 A.L.R.2d 802. It was the conclusion of the English court that the action should be confined, as originally conceived, to the situation where the injured employee can be regarded as a member of the master's household. The court held that the doctrine was an anomaly which does not fit in with the principles of law as now understood and that it should not be extended beyond the master and household servant situations.
>
> The authorities in the field seem to agree generally on the principle that if an employee is intentionally harmed, the employer may recover from the wrongdoer for the loss caused him because of his being deprived of the employee's

services, but that the employer cannot recover if the injury is inflicted through mere negligence.

There have been relatively few recent decisions on this issue. Those that have considered the question are in accord with the authorities mentioned above. In *Snow v. West*, 250 Or. 114, 117, 440 P.2d 864, 865, where a recovery by the employer was denied, the court said:

> We have examined the American cases cited by the parties and cited in the various texts and articles upon the subject and we have found no decision of the highest court of any jurisdiction holding that an employer can recover for profit lost because of a negligent injury to an ordinary employee. 'To be actionable an interference must be a knowing and not an inadvertent or incidental invasion of plaintiff's contractual interests.' The tortfeasor should be held responsible for the natural and probable consequences of his wrong. To protect a contractual interest from negligent interference would place an undue burden on freedom of action and could impose a severe penalty on one guilty of mere negligence.

Steele v. J & S Metals, Inc., 32 Conn. Supp. 17, 335 A.2d 628 (1974). (Accord *Hartridge v. State Farm Mut. Auto Ins. Co.*, 86 Wis. 2d 1, 271 N.W.2d 598, 601 (1978).)

B. Common Law v. Workers' Compensation Recovery

1. Common Law

a. Contributory Negligence and Assumption of Risk

Before the advent of special statutes to give employees a remedy for work-related injuries, the injured employees faced the choices of either bearing the costs of their injuries themselves or attempting to mount common law legal actions against their employers. If workers sued, they often faced the likelihood that employers would assert one or both of the closely related defenses of contributory negligence and assumption of risk.

Borth v. Borth

112 Kan. 494, 561 P.2d 408 (1977)

MILLER, Justice.

This is a civil action for damages based upon a claim of personal injuries sustained by the plaintiff when he was charged and struck by a cow belonging to the defendant. The jury returned a verdict for the plaintiff for $9,500.

The defendant, Clark Borth, is an adult son of the plaintiff, Dan Borth. Clark raises Charolais cattle. On January 26, 1971, Clark was vaccinating, castrating and dehorning cattle. He employed Larry Myers, Cecil Brookshire, Steve Kruse, Wayne Lundstrom, and the plaintiff to help him. About 50 head of cattle were placed in a large holding pen or corral. The cattle were herded singly from the corral into a long chute, at the far end of which was a "squeeze chute" where each animal was held while it was being treated. Myers, Brookshire, Kruse and plaintiff were in the pen where they kept the cattle moving and caused them to enter the chute as needed. Wayne Lundstrom was helping on the chute. The defendant and a veterinarian, Dr. V.D. Lundstrom, were up at the squeeze chute where they worked on each animal. The activity was carried on without incident until it came to the last cow in the corral. Suddenly and without warning, the animal turned and charged toward the plaintiff. The other men in the corral climbed over the fence and escaped; the cow struck the plaintiff in the lower back and threw him over the fence, causing him to sustain serious injuries.

[T]he defendant contends that the trial court erred in failing to direct a verdict and in failing to enter judgment for the defendant notwithstanding the verdict on the basis that the evidence and the reasonable inferences created by it when viewed in a light most favorable to the plaintiff, showed as a matter of law that plaintiff was guilty of assumption of risk and/or contributory negligence which was a proximate cause of his injuries.

The doctrine of assumption of risk is still viable in Kansas though its application is limited to cases such as this where a master-servant relationship is involved. We turn first to our recent decisions in master-servant cases involving the doctrine. *Mechtley v. Price*, 217 Kan. 344, 536 P.2d 1385, was an action by a farm employee against his employers to recover for personal injuries when an unshod horse he was riding stumbled and fell. We there said:

> Assumption of risk, in the law of master and servant, is a phrase commonly used to describe a term or condition in the contract of employment, either express or implied from the circumstances of the employment, by which the employee agrees that certain dangers of injury, while he is engaged in the service for which he is hired, shall be at the risk of the employee. Assumption of risk generally bars recovery by an employee who knows of the danger in a situation but nevertheless voluntarily exposes himself to that danger. In *Kleppe v. Prawl*, 181 Kan. 590, 313 P.2d 227, 63 ALR2d 175, we said:
>
> > '[A]ssumption of risk arises through implied contract of assuming the risk of a known danger; the essence of it is venturousness; it implies intentional exposure to a known danger; it embraces a mental state of willingness; it pertains to the preliminary conduct of getting into a dangerous employment or relation; it means voluntarily incurring the risk of an accident, which may not occur, and which the person assuming the risk may be careful to avoid; it defeats recovery because it is a previous abandonment of the right to complain if an accident occurs.'

Uhlrig v. Shortt, 194 Kan. 68, 397 P.2d 321, was an action by a farm hand against his employer to recover damages for the loss of an eye. The injury occurred while the parties were filling a silo. We said:

> The employer is not to be held liable for an injury to an employee simply because of danger which was inherent in the employment, whether in the place of employment or the cause of the danger inherent in the tools, machinery or appliances with which the work must be performed. A master is not an insurer against injuries which his servants may incur in the discharge of their duties.

> Generally an employer will not be held liable if he . . . conducts his business in a manner conforming to the usage of others engaged in the same business under similar circumstances. In 35 Am. Jur., Master and Servant, § 299, pp. 722, 723, in considering the risk assumed, the rule is stated thus:
>
> > 'The injuries for which an employee is barred from recovery by virtue of the doctrine of assumption of risk include but, according to the general accepted statement, do not extend beyond those which result from the "ordinary" risks of the employment or such as are "incident" thereto. An assumption of risk merely by virtue of the contract of employment embraces such perils, hazards, and dangers as are ordinarily and normally incident to or a part of the employment in question and of which the employee has knowledge, actual or implied, or of which it may be said that he is presumed to know. Under the head of "ordinary risks" are classed all those dangers or perils ordinarily incident to the conduct of the particular business in which the employee engages—those which exist after the employer has done everything that he is bound to do for the purpose of securing the safety of his employees. The term includes not merely those dangers which are obvious and open, but also those risks which, while not visible, are nevertheless a natural incident of the employment. The employee does not, however, merely by accepting employment, assume the risks which are not usually and ordinarily incident to that employment. As thus restricted, the doctrine rests on the thought that the employee, upon entering the employment of the master, assumes all the risks that are ordinarily and usually incident to the service upon which he enters, and if he is injured solely by reason of these perils he is not entitled to recover.'

In *Blackmore v. Auer*, 187 Kan. 434, 357 P.2d 765, where a farm laborer was injured while loading baled hay, we said:

> The assumption of the usual risks of an employment is not ordinarily a jury question. It is a matter of law. It is only where the risk is or may be unusual that a jury question can arise; and even in such cases, if the risk though unusual is obvious, such as an ordinarily prudent man could appreciate and understand, the workman who persists in the employment assumes the risk of it.

Wayne Lundstrom testified that every one of the men that were there that day was an experienced cattleman. He said that in his opinion any cattleman knows that when you get down to one or two animals left in the big pen and the others have been moved through, you had better watch those animals because they are very nervous and may try anything.

Dr. V.D. Lundstrom has been in McPherson County for twenty-four years and has worked with Dan on numerous occasions. He has worked on Dan's cattle, performing routine procedures, castrating and dehorning; he considers Dan Borth a knowledgeable, experienced cattleman. When you are separating cattle, the last animal or few animals are going to be the most unruly of all. Everybody who works around cattle knows this. A few minutes before the accident happened, the animal that charged Dan was identified by someone as an unruly animal. He heard someone say "watch out for him." The witness saw that the animal tended to be unruly. From that time on, an experienced cattleman should have been on guard for his own safety.

Dan Borth testified that he was 64 years of age and always had a few cattle on the farm, sometimes only four, and after he got into Herefords, perhaps thirty at the most.

The record is abundantly clear that Dan Borth has had a lifetime of experience working around cattle. He has owned, handled, and cared for them. He has previously done the same type of work that he was doing at the time of injury. He knew of the risk he was taking in the cattle pen, and he knew that a particular risk arose when but one animal remained in the pen, after the others had been separated out.

He could have refused to work under the attendant conditions, or he could have secured and used a metal or wood panel for his protection. He did neither. He knew what the facilities were when he went to Clark's place on the day of the accident, having been there perhaps three times before.

The evidence is undisputed that the facilities at Clark Borth's farm were average for the community, and that they were fit for the purposes for which they were being used. The operation was being carried on in a way familiar to cattlemen of the area, and as one stated, it "is what the ordinary, reasonable and prudent cattleman does." The risk of injury by the cattle is clearly one that arises out of the activity being carried on, and one that is open and apparent. While the extent of the injuries sustained by plaintiff is regrettable, and no doubt greater than is usual, it cannot be said that the type of injury is unusual. It is a type of injury ordinarily and normally incident to the employment. There was an obvious risk of harm to the men working in the corral.

We hold that Dan Borth assumed the risk of his employment as a matter of law. The trial court therefore erred in failing to sustain defendant's motion for a directed verdict, and for judgment notwithstanding the verdict.

OWSLEY, Justice, dissenting.

I cannot agree with the portion of the majority opinion which holds that the plaintiff is precluded from recovery for his damages because he assumed the risk of injury as a matter of law. In *Railroad Co. v. Morris*, 76 Kan. 836, 93 P. 153, this court established the rule which has been frequently quoted in master and servant cases, stating:

> Where a master orders a servant into a situation of danger, and in obeying the command the servant in [*sic*] injured, he will not be charged with contributory negligence or with an assumption of the risk, unless the danger was so glaring that no prudent man would have encountered it, even under such orders, provided he acts with reasonable prudence in executing such orders.

Defendant ordered plaintiff to "go in there [the pen] and keep them milling around. Never stop. Just keep them moving." Thus plaintiff should not be charged with an assumption of risk unless the danger he faced was "so glaring that no prudent man would have encountered it." While the evidence indicated plaintiff had been around cattle most of his life, it also revealed he had never worked cattle in a holding pen. Furthermore, he had been told by defendant and defendant's wife that their cattle were docile and like pets. The animals, to plaintiff's observation, had never demonstrated any skittishness or hostility until the cow charged plaintiff and threw him over the fence. It wasn't until after the accident that he learned Charolais cattle were generally more skittish than other livestock. These factors, coupled with the fact two other men went into the pen with plaintiff to move the cattle, create an issue which should be resolved by a jury.

b. Fellow-Servant Rule

The fellow-servant doctrine is another common-law defense that developed to reduce claims against employers in the early period of industrialization. Accordingly, an employer was not liable for an injury of an employee if it was inflicted by a fellow employee; the injured employee had to proceed against the tortfeasor employee.

Buckley v. City of New York

56 N.Y.2d 300, 437 N.E.2d 1088 (1982)

GABRIELLI, Judge.

Each of the cases involved in these appeals presents the question of whether the fellow-servant rule continues to apply in New York. In each case an employee of the City of New York, who was injured through the negligence of a coemployee, brought an action against the municipality. In *Buckley v. City of New York*, 81 A.D.2d 1044, 439 N.Y.S.2d 785, a police officer was accidentally shot in the leg when a gun being loaded by a fellow officer discharged in the station house locker room; and in *Lawrence v. City of New York*, 82 A.D.2d 485, 447 N.Y.S.2d 506, a fire fighter was seriously injured when a fellow fire fighter threw a smoldering couch from the second story window of a fire-damaged building and struck the plaintiff while he was standing in the yard. In each case the plaintiff secured a jury verdict of liability against the city on a theory of vicarious liability and the city's motion to dismiss the complaint on the basis of the fellow-servant rule was denied. The Appellate Division has affirmed the judgments in both instances and leave has been granted to appeal to this court.

Under the rule of respondeat superior, an employer will be liable to third parties for torts of an employee committed within the scope of his employment.

By virtue of the fellow-servant rule, however, if an employee is injured by a fellow employee in the workplace he will have no recourse against the employer in respondeat superior. Succinctly stated, the rule provides that "where a servant is injured through the negligence or fault of a fellow servant, engaged in a common business and employment, and the master is himself free from fault, the master is not responsible for the injury."

The fellow-servant rule had its origin in England in 1837 *(Priestly v. Fowler*, 3 M & W [Messon & Welsby's Ex. Ch. Rep.] 1, 150 Eng. Rep. 1030) and was adopted in the United States shortly afterward (*Murray v. South Carolina R.R. Co.*, 1 Mc.Mul.[L. Rep.] 385; Prosser, Torts [4th ed.], § 80, p.528). The rationales attributed to the rule are varied; the most convincing is that the rule promotes the safety of the public and of the workers by encouraging each employee to be watchful of the conduct of others for his own protection. It has also been suggested that the rule was based upon the notion that an employee assumes the risk of negligence on the part of his fellow servants or, more fundamentally, that the rule simply reflected a 19th century bias by the courts in favor of business. The theoretical underpinning of this rule have, to a large extent, been discredited in recent years. Logically, there appears to be little reason for denying an employee the right which a third party possesses to recover from the employer in respondeat superior, since for one thing, in both instances the employer might have avoided the injury by selection of more careful employees. Moreover, the class of persons most frequently endangered by the negligence of an employee—his fellow workers—should not, without compelling reason, be denied a remedy accorded to the general public.

The over-all effect of the fellow-servant rule was drastically curtailed by the advent of workers' compensation legislation, for the rule, involving injuries sustained in the course of one's employment, provides no defense to a demand for this remedy. Nevertheless, the rule has not yet been completely obliterated since there are some areas of employment, such as those involved in the present appeal where the Workers' Compensation Law does not apply.

In *Poniatowski v. City of New York*, [14 N.Y.2d 76, 198 N.E.2d 237, 248 N.Y.S.2d 849], our court signaled the beginning of the end of the fellow-servant rule in New York. There, a police officer was injured in a motor vehicle accident through the negligence of a fellow officer. Although the plaintiff's cause was sustained in our court on the basis of a statute which obviated the necessity of directly confronting the fellow-servant rule, we referred to this rule in passing by stating that

> [t]he inherent injustice of a rule which denies a person, free of fault, the right to recover for injuries sustained through the negligence of another over whose conduct he has no control merely because of the fortuitous circumstance that the other is a fellow officer is manifest. This may well suggest the desirability of abolishing the rule but we leave decision of that question to the future. It is sufficient at this time to decide only that we should not extend it into an area in which it has not previously been applied.

Today we are presented with the question left open in *Poniatowski*—whether the fellow-servant rule is to survive in New York. The rule had its birth in the 19th century, was severely crippled with the advent of workers' compensation, and was dealt an almost fatal blow in this State in *Poniatowski*. Today, in rejecting this rule entirely, we inter its remains.

In constructing its argument for retention of the fellow-servant rule, the defendant city has largely abandoned the rationales originally underpinning the rule and, instead, the city asserts that the rule should be retained primarily because it has enjoyed a lengthy tenure in our jurisprudence. While the longevity of a rule of law requires that its re-examination be given careful scrutiny, it does not demand that its effect be given permanence. The continued vitality of a rule of law should depend heavily upon its continuing practicality and the demands of justice, rather than upon its mere tradition. Although the policy of stare decisis is not to be lightly cast aside, this court has previously noted that

> [i]t was intended, not to effect a 'petrifying rigidity,' but to assure the justice that flows from certainty and stability. If, instead, adherence to precedent offers not justice but unfairness, not certainty but doubt and confusion, it loses its right to survive, and no principle constrains us to follow it.

Furthermore, we make it abundantly clear that we do not subscribe to the view that the abolition of the fellow-servant rule is strictly a matter for legislative attention. The fellow-servant rule originated as a matter of decisional law, and it remains subject to judicial re-examination.

The fellow-servant rule serves no continuing valid purpose in New York, but instead merely works an unjustifiable hardship upon individuals injured in the workplace, and we must thus conclude that the fellow-servant rule is no longer to be followed in New York.

Note

With the adoption of workers' compensation statutes, contributory negligence, assumption of risk, and the fellow-servant doctrine have been rendered inapplicable in cases covered by those statutes because workers' compensation is basically a no-fault system. An injured employee's exclusive remedy is under workers' compensation whether the injury was caused by the employer or a fellow employee (but the employee retains the right to pursue recovery under the common law against other parties who cause or contribute to the injury). Thus, today, these defense doctrines (including comparative negligence) apply to those areas outside the purview of the workers' compensation statutes.

2. Workers' Compensation

Not surprisingly with the advent of mechanization in business and commerce came a significant amount of injury to workers. The reasons were plentiful—unsafe working conditions, long hours on the job, employees inexperienced with machinery, child workers, lack of safety consciousness, and so on. We were lucky to have equipment at all, let alone machinery with any safety features.

Predictably, the system insulated employers (business) against claims by workers for compensation for their injuries. After all, if the substantial numbers of workers who were injured at work had been able to collect from their employers, it would have bankrupt business, and the Industrial Revolution would have been short lived. But the system was simply too harsh on injured employees. Depending upon whose statistics are accepted, somewhere between about 75% and 95% of all workers injured at their jobs received no compensation of any kind.

Again, the reasons for those numbers were plentiful. Injured workers in order to pursue recovery would have to sue (or threaten to sue) their employers for the negligence of the employers (if any). But those were the days before any degree of protection of at-will employees, so that workers who were still able to work and who sued or threatened suit could expect to be fired from their jobs. In order to succeed against their employers, workers would have to be able to prevail in negligence actions, so that they would have to be free of contributory negligence and assumption of risk. Both of those doctrines were complete bars to recovery. The injuries to the workers could not have been inflicted by a co-worker (the fellow-servant rule was also a complete bar to recovery). Moreover, few injured employees would have the financial resources to mount a full-scale legal action and to await the time for recovery.

Because of the harshness of the system to workers suffering work-related accidents, a legislative compromise was struck with the adoption at both the state and federal levels of workers' compensation statutes.

> Workers' compensation laws in the United States and California had their genesis in the inability of the 19th century common law remedies to cope with modern industrialization and its inherent unfairness to injured workers. Implicit

> therefrom is the concept that workers' compensation statutes relate generally to the legal status or relationship between employer and employee.

Bell v. Industrial Vangas, Inc., 30 Cal. 3d 268, 637 P.2d 266, 271 (1981). The statutes cover most, though not all, employment settings in the United States. All states have some form of workers' compensation statutes, and there are major variations from state to state. More than 90 percent of all employees are covered by workers' compensation programs. Under these statutes, which are to be liberally construed to effectuate their remedial purpose, a partial recovery schedule is established to permit employees to be compensated for injuries and illnesses sustained in the course of and arising out of their employment.

While almost all employees are permitted to recover for their suffering, they are not allowed to recover fully. Thus, the compromise is that both sides give up something—employers give up their freedom from accountability, and employees give up their right to full compensation. Although employees are entitled to receive compensation for medical expenses and a portion of their lost income, they are not generally entitled to recover for pain and suffering or for punitive damages.

Workers' compensation is a no-fault system. That is, regardless of whether the worker's injury is caused by the negligence of the employer, the worker, a co-employee, or someone else, the injury is compensable—as long as the individual is an employee injured in the course of and arising out of the employment.

Once it is determined that an employee is covered by the workers' compensation statute, the workers' compensation recovery is the exclusive remedy available to the employee against the employer (and co-employees). There can be no common law recovery against the employer (or co-employees). Of course, the injured employee can still proceed against parties other than the employer (and co-employees) on a common law action for causing the worker's injury.

Notes

1. The workers' compensation statutes establish a system of state supervision. A state agency, often an Industrial Commission or Workers' Compensation Board, administers the program. The agency prescribes and provides a process for workers to file claims when they are injured and, in those instances in which employers deny the claims for compensation, to have their cases heard and decided.

2. Employers have basically two choices of how to pay for the claims of workers injured due to work-related accident or illness. Employers can self-insure, or they can purchase workers' compensation insurance. In either case, employers tend to resist paying compensation claims because it is one more cost of business that they would prefer to avoid.

a. Employee v. Independent Contractor v. Borrowed Servant

In order for one to be covered by the workers' compensation statutory scheme, one must qualify as an *employee*. Thus, for instance, an employer would not ordinarily be required to compensate an injured worker who was the employer's independent contractor or who had been borrowed by some other employer, because such a worker would not be the employer's employee.

Thompson v. Travelers Indemnity Co.

789 S.W.2d 277 (Tex. 1990)

PHILLIPS, Chief Justice.

The sole issue for our determination is whether Petitioner, Tommy Thompson ("Thompson"), a jockey, was as a matter of law an employee of a race track at the time he was injured immediately after a horse race, prior to dismount. Thompson was injured when he was thrown from his mount at Manor Downs, a member track of the American Quarter Horse Association ("AQHA"). The trial court, sitting without a jury, denied Thompson's workers' compensation claim, holding that he was not an employee of Manor Downs. The court of appeals affirmed in an opinion rejecting Thompson's contention that, as a matter of law, he was an employee of Manor Downs.

The test to determine whether a worker is an employee or an independent contractor is whether the employer has the right to control the progress, details, and methods of operations of the employee's work. This same test applies whether the claim arises at common law or under workers' compensation. The employer must control not merely the end sought to be accomplished, but also the means and details of its accomplishment as well. Examples of the type of control normally exercised by an employer include when and where to begin and stop work, the regularity of hours, the amount of time spent on particular aspects of the work, the tools and appliances used to perform the work, and the physical method or manner of accomplishing the end result.

On the day of his injury, Thompson was a jockey in a daily pool of jockeys, available for selection by horse owners who had not already hired a jockey for a particular race. In one of the races, an owner selected Thompson to ride, and during the ride Thompson was injured. Thompson argues that Manor Downs was his employer at the time of his injury as it exercised control over the "pool jockeys" by: 1) requiring them to be licensed in compliance with the AQHA; 2) monitoring every jockey prior to, during and after a race; 3) explaining the AQHA riding rules to the jockeys before the race; 4) requiring them to report to the track one hour before the first race of the day for weight verification and other preliminary matters; 5) paying $40 per race (less $5 for accident insurance) to each jockey, which was a mount fee collected from each owner or trainer; 6) providing a saddle towel and helmet cover to identify and differentiate contestants; and 7) fining jockeys or revoking their Manor Downs licenses upon violation of the AQHA racing rules.

These circumstances do not establish, as a matter of law, an employer-employee relationship. We hold there is some evidence in the record to support the judgment of the trial court.

The evidence in the record to support the judgment demonstrates that the owner or trainer, not the track, controlled the progress, details and methods of Thompson's work. Owners and trainers, not Manor Downs, pay the $40 mount fee, which is collected by the track and subsequently disbursed to the jockeys. Jockeys are free, without restrictions by the track, to negotiate an additional purse with the owner or trainer, usually in the event of a successful race. Owners or trainers, not Manor Downs, give instructions on strategy and tactics to the jockeys.

There is some evidence in the record to support the trial court's findings that Manor Downs does not prevent jockeys from racing at other tracks on any given day, does not require a jockey to remain at the track for the entire day and does not require a jockey to ride any particular horse. Finally, it does not withhold taxes or social security from any jockey's pay. In short, Manor Downs does not exercise the control over a jockey indicative of, as a matter of law, an employer-employee relationship.

We have found no other case in Texas involving the employment status of jockeys. In most of the cases outside Texas that have examined this issue, the jockey has been determined not to be an employee of the track at which he or she rides. See *Haggard v. Industrial Commission*, 71 Ariz. 91, 223 P.2d 915 (1950) (jockeys are not employees of track at which they race); *Munday v. Churchill Downs, Inc*, 600 S.W.2d 487 (Ky. Ct. App. 1980) (freelance jockey who solicited mounts and was paid through track without tax or social security deductions was not an employee of track); *Biger v. Erwin*, 57 N.J. 95, 270 A.2d 12 (1970) (jockey is employee of the horse owner); *Drillon v. Industrial Accident Comm'n*, 17 Cal. 2d 346, 110 P.2d 64 (1941) (jockey is employee of horse owner); *Simmons v. Kansas City Jockey Club*, 334 Mo. 99, 66 S.W.2d 119 (1933) (jockey not an employee of track); *Pierce v. Bowen*, 247 N.Y. 305, 160 N.E. 379 (1928) (jockey is employee of horse owner); but cf. *Wolf v. Louisiana State Racing Comm'n*, 545 So. 2d 976 (La. 1989) (worker's compensation was afforded to jockeys who raced at a track, but no discussion of employment status of jockey).

We therefore hold that the evidence does not conclusively establish that, as a matter of law, Thompson was an employee of Manor Downs. The judgment of the court of appeals is affirmed.

Rensing v. Indiana State University

444 N.E.2d 1170 (Ind. 1983)

HUNTER, Justice.

The plaintiff-appellant, Fred W. Rensing, was a varsity football player at Indiana State University who suffered an injury on April 24, 1976, during the team's spring football practice which left him a quadriplegic. Rensing filed a claim with the Industrial Board of Indiana (Industrial Board) seeking recovery under workmen's compensation for permanent total disability as well as medical and hospital expenses incurred due to the injury. The Industrial Board rejected his claim finding that an employer-employee relationship did not exist between Rensing and the Trustees and, therefore, he was not entitled to benefits under the Workmen's Compensation Act, Ind. Code § 22-3-2-2 et seq. The Court of Appeals reversed the decision of the Industrial Board on the basis that Rensing was an "employee" for pay within the meaning of the statute and his employment by the Trustees was also within the coverage of the statute.

The facts established before the Industrial Board were summarized by the Court of Appeals:

> The undisputed testimony reveals the Trustees, through their agent Thomas Harp (the University's Head Football Coach), offered Rensing a scholarship or 'educational grant' to play football at the University. In essence, the financial aid agreement, which was renewable each year for a total of four years provided that in return for Rensing's active participation in football competition he would receive free tuition, room, board, laboratory fees, a book allowance, tutoring

and a limited number of football tickets per game for family and friends. The 'agreement' provided, inter alia, the aid would continue even if Rensing suffered an injury during supervised play which would make it inadvisable, in the opinion of the doctor-director of the student health service, 'to continue to participate,' although in that event the University would require other assistance to the extent of his ability. It is not contested the monetary value of this assistance to Rensing for the 1975-76 academic year was $2,374, and that the 'scholarship' was in effect when Rensing's injuries occurred. During the 1975 football season, Rensing participated on the University's football team. In the spring of 1976 he partook in the team's annual three week spring practice when, on April 24, he was injured while he tackled a teammate during a punting drill. The specific injury suffered by Rensing was a fractured dislocation of the cervical spine at the level of 4-5 vertebrae. Rensing's initial treatment consisted of traction and eventually a spinal fusion. During this period he developed pneumonia for which he had to have a tracheostomy. Eventually, Rensing was transferred to the Rehabilitation Department of the Barnes Hospital complex in St. Louis. According to Rensing's doctor, Rensing's paralysis was caused by the April 24, 1976 football injury leaving him 95-100% disabled.

Rensing's appeal to the Industrial Board was originally heard by a Hearing Member who found that Rensing had

> failed to sustain his burden in establishing the necessary relationship of employer and employee within the meaning of the Indiana Workmen's Compensation Act,

and rejected his claim. The Full Industrial Board adopted the Hearing Member's finding and decision; then this decision was reversed by the Court of Appeals. [T]he Trustees argue that there was no contract of hire in this case and that a student who accepts an athletic "grant-in-aid" from the University does not become an "employee" of the University within the definition of "employee" under the Workmen's Compensation Act. On the other hand, Rensing maintains that his agreement to play football in return for financial assistance did amount to a contract of employment.

Here, the facts concerning the injury are undisputed. The contested issue is whether the requisite employer-employee relationship existed between Rensing and the Trustees so as to bring him under the coverage of our Workmen's Compensation Act. Both the Industrial Board and the Court of Appeals correctly noted that the workmen's compensation laws are to be liberally construed.

With this proposition as a starting point, the specific facts of this case must be analyzed to determine whether Rensing and the Trustees come within the definitions of "employee" and "employer" found in the statute, and specifically whether there did exist a contract of employment. Ind. Code § 22-3-1 defines the terms "employee" and "employer" as follows:

> (a) 'Employer' includes the state and any political subdivision, any municipal corporation within the state, any individual, firm, association or corporation or the receiver or trustee of the same, or the legal representatives of a deceased person, using the services of another for pay.
>
> (b) The term 'employee' means every person, including a minor, in the service of another, under any contract of hire or apprenticeship, written or implied,

> except one whose employment is both casual and not in the usual course of the trade, business, occupation or profession of the employer.

It is clear that while a determination of the existence of an employee-employer relationship is a complex matter involving many factors, the primary consideration is that there was an intent that a contract of employment, either express or implied, did exist. In other words, there must be a mutual belief that an employer-employee relationship did exist. It is evident from the documents which formed the agreement in this case that there was no intent to enter into an employee-employer relationship at the time the parties entered into the agreement.

In this case, the National Collegiate Athletic Association's (NCAA) constitution and bylaws were incorporated by reference into the agreements. A fundamental policy of the NCAA, which is stated in its constitution, is that intercollegiate sports be viewed as part of the educational system and are clearly distinguished from the professional sports business. The NCAA has strict rules against "taking pay" for sports or sporting activities. Any student who does accept pay is ineligible for further play at an NCAA member school in the sport for which he takes pay. Furthermore, an institution cannot, in any way, condition financial aid on a student's ability as an athlete. The fundamental concerns behind the policies of the NCAA are that intercollegiate athletics must be maintained as a part of the educational program and student-athletes are integral parts of the institution's student body. An athlete receiving financial aid is still first and foremost a student. All of these NCAA requirements designed to prohibit student-athletes from receiving pay for participation in their sport were incorporated into the financial aid agreements Rensing and his parents signed.

Furthermore, there is evidence that the financial aid which Rensing received was not considered by the parties involved to be pay or income. Rensing was given free tuition, room, board, laboratory fees and a book allowance. These benefits were not considered to be "pay" by the University or by the NCAA since they did not affect Rensing's or the University's eligibility status under NCAA rules. Rensing did not consider the benefits as income as he did not report them for income tax purposes. The Internal Revenue Service has ruled that scholarship recipients are not taxed on their scholarship proceeds and there is no distinction made between athletic and academic scholarships.

As far as scholarships are concerned, we find that our Indiana General Assembly clearly has recognized a distinction between the power to award financial aid to students and the power to hire employees since the former power was specifically granted to the Boards of Trustees of state educational institutions with the specific limitation that the award be reasonably related to the educational purposes and objectives of the institution and in the best interests of the institution and the state.

Furthermore, we find that Ind. Code § 22-4-6-2 is not applicable to scholarship benefits. In that statute, which deals with contributions by employers to unemployment insurance, employers are directed to include

> all individuals attending an established school who, in lieu of remuneration for such services, receive either meals, lodging, books, tuition or other education facilities.

Here, Rensing was not working at a regular job for the University. The scholarship benefits he received were not given him in lieu of pay for remuneration for his services in playing football any more than academic scholarship benefits were given to other students for their high scores on tests or class assignments. Rather, in both cases, the students received benefits based upon their past demonstrated ability in various areas to enable them to pursue opportunities for higher education as well as to further progress in their own fields of endeavor.

In addition to finding that the University, the NCAA, the IRS and Rensing, himself, did not consider the scholarship benefits to be income, we also agree with Judge Young's conclusion that Rensing was not "in the service of" the University. As Judge Young stated:

> Furthermore, I do not believe that Rensing was 'in the service of' the Trustees. Rensing's participation in football may well have benefitted the university in a very general way. That does not mean that Rensing was in the service of the Trustees. If a student wins a Rhodes scholarship or if the debate team wins a national award that undoubtedly benefits the school, but does not mean that the student and the team are in the service of the school. Rensing performed no duties that would place him in the service of the university.

Courts in other jurisdictions have generally found that such individuals as student athletes, student leaders in student government associations and student resident-hall assistants are not "employees" for purposes of workmen's compensation laws unless they are also employed in a university job in addition to receiving scholarship benefits. *Marshall v. Regis Educational Corp.* (10th Cir. 1981), 666 F.2d 1324; *Bobilin v. Board of Education* (D. Hawaii 1975), 403 F.Supp. 1095.

All of the above facts show that in this case, Rensing did not receive "pay" for playing football at the University within the meaning of the Workmen's Compensation Act; therefore, an essential element of the employer-employee relationship was missing in addition to the lack of intent. Furthermore, under the applicable rules of the NCAA, Rensing's benefits could not be reduced or withdrawn because of his athletic ability or his contribution to the team's success. Thus, the ordinary employer's right to discharge on the basis of performance was also missing. While there was an agreement between Rensing and the Trustees which established certain obligations for both parties, the agreement was not a contract of employment. Since at least three important factors indicative of an employee-employer relationship are absent in this case, we find it is not necessary to consider other factors which may or may not be present.

The Judgment and determination of the Industrial Board are affirmed.

b. Injury Arising Out Of and In the Course of Employment

The workers' compensation laws generally require that, in order for a worker to recover for a work-related accident or illness, the injury must arise out of the employment and occur in the course of the employment.

Cary Fire Protection District v. Industrial Commission

211 Ill. App. 3d 20, 569 N.E.2d 1338 (1991)

Justice WOODWARD:

Claimant, Paul Anderson, a volunteer fireman employed by the Cary Fire Protection District (District), filed a claim for benefits against the District after he was injured while participating in a "water fight" sponsored by the Cary Fireman's Association (Association). The arbitrator awarded benefits. The Industrial Commission (Commission) reversed the decision of the arbitrator. On review, the circuit court of McHenry County set aside the decision of the Commission and reinstated the decision of the arbitrator awarding benefits to the claimant.

Claimant testified that he is employed by the District as a volunteer fireman, his primary duty being that of engineer, which means he operates the pump unit to supply water to a fire scene. He has a classification as a fire fighter 2, which required him to obtain a certain number of hours in credited courses. There is also continuous training through the District on "drill nights," which are held once per month. Drill nights provided training in specific areas, such as breathing apparatus, ladder climbing or other aspects of fire service work. Seminars to provide information on fire scene work are also provided. Firehose handling training would take place on Lake Julian two or three times per year. The training sessions or practices would consist of shooting water at barrels. According to claimant, the fire fighters would organize as teams and make a game of it.

Claimant testified that the Association differed from the District in that the Association was made up of the fire fighters in the District, as well as retired fire fighters. The Association was an incorporated organization that had a separate financial system from that of the District. While the District financed the equipment and maintained equipment for use in the District, the Association provided funds for expenditures not allocated for by the District.

Claimant testified further that on September 11, 1982, he participated in a water fight tournament at the McHenry County fairgrounds. He was participating as a member of the District team. Each team in the tournament got a hose and tried to push a barrel past the other team within two minutes of the referee's command. Claimant's team that day consisted of four men who worked with claimant in the District and one man from the Woodstock rural fire department. Claimant's position was nearest to the nozzle. During the match with Woodstock, claimant injured his right leg. Claimant described how he was injured as follows:

> I was anticipating the barrel coming over the wire and across the Court and when it did I anticipated that movement, pulling the line with me and trying to match with that barrel going across the Court and at the end of my push, an extension of my leg, my leg snapped over.

According to claimant, while he was participating in the tournament, he wore a helmet, coat and boots which were furnished to him by the District. He also wore a team shirt, which was paid for by the District. The other equipment, such as hoses, nozzles, engines, etc., was provided by the host team, as were the referees. The equipment used in the water fight tournament was identical to that used to fight a fire. There is a 10-pound difference in the water pressure used due to the different size tip on the hose nozzle.

The Association sponsored such tournament two times per year at Cary. Teams from several of the surrounding counties were invited to participate. About 12 to 15 Cary firemen participated in the water fight, although the whole department would turn out for the tournament. The Association paid for insurance to cover the spectators. Refreshments were paid for by the Association. No admission fee was charged, though donations could be made, and the donated funds were used to pay expenses for the tournament, and any extra funds would be kept by the Association. A practice was held prior to the tournament at Lake Julian. The Association provided the equipment, and almost everyone from the fire department participated. It was claimant's understanding that if the practice was held on a drill night, there was insurance coverage for the practice. Each member of the Association was given 10 tickets to sell. Ticket sales earned the Association approximately $350.

Claimant testified further that participating in water fights benefitted him in that he was better able to handle the water hose in actual fire fighting and acquired feeling of camaraderie with the other fire fighters that enable them to function as a team while fighting fires. Water fighting also built up his physical stamina. Mishandling a fire hose can severely injure both persons and property. Contact with firemen from other counties during the tournament aids in situations where different departments are fighting a common fire.

On cross-examination, claimant testified that he was never ordered or compelled by the District to participate in water fighting tournaments. He pays yearly dues of $20 for membership in the Association, which amount is not reimbursed by the District. Claimant did receive water hose training through the District. Claimant further testified that the Association sponsored parties, a Christmas party, a turkey raffle and drawings. The Association also made donations to charity such as the fire victims' fund.

Randall Ray Schlottman testified that he was employed as a fire fighter by the District for several years beginning 1974-75. While he was employed by the District, he participated in the monthly training sessions held by the Association. The only hands-on training utilizing the fire hoses under pressure was the water fights. According to Schlottman, about three-quarters of the men in the Association participated at one time or another in the water fights. The techniques and equipment used in the water fights were the same as were used in fire fighting. In Schlottman's opinion, participation in the water fights benefitted him as it enabled him to know the capabilities of his fellow fire fighters. It was also a good morale booster. Schlottman explained that a mishandled fire hose could cause serious injuries.

On cross-examination, Schlottman testified that participating in the water fighting tournament was voluntary.

Ernest Carlson testified that he is employed by the District as a fire fighter and has been for the past 10 years. His training on the fire hose consisted of participating in the water fights. The equipment and the techniques for water fighting are the same as they are for fire fighting. He had some training as an engineer. The engineer's duties are in some cases the same in water fighting as they are fire fighting. He felt that water fighting was a good training procedure because there was no training like actually handling the hose. Water fighting had given him experience in drafting water quickly, and he had trained a few firemen himself on using the engine through water fighting. He recalled one occasion on which the fire chief had said they were going to have a water fight so as to familiarize the new men with the department how to handle the fire hose.

Clifford Anderson, father of the claimant, testified that he has been a volunteer fireman with the District since 1946. He presently held the position of assistant chief. He participated in water fights from 1946 until three or four years before the arbitration hearing. The equipment and the techniques in water fighting and fire fighting are similar.

Anderson testified that the water fights were held to attract people to activities, such as carnivals, festivals or benefits the Association was working on. Anderson would pass out tickets to each fireman and had information about water fight meets and tournaments printed in newspapers.

According to Anderson, participating in water fights gave individual firemen improved ability to handle and patrol the fire hoses. It also assisted the engineers in drafting and pumping operations. On the whole, water fighting made better firemen.

The arbitrator concluded that claimant's injury arose out of and in the course of his employment. The arbitrator based his conclusions on the fact that all of the claimant's witnesses believed that water fighting was a useful training device "because hose handling techniques were developed and honed, team work was encouraged and morale uplifted." The arbitrator also relied on the fact that the fire chief, who was designated president of the Association, was responsible for training of the firemen and had in essence utilized the Association "as an instrument of his training and education program for the fire fighters."

On review, the Commission reversed the decision of the arbitrator. The Commission found that

> notwithstanding that the event [water fighting] might have enhanced the skills of participating fire fighters and the activity was similar to that engaged in at District training drills, [claimant] was injured while voluntarily engaging in a recreational program.

The claimant appealed the Commission's decision to the circuit court of McHenry County. The circuit court set aside the Commission's decision and reinstated the decision of the arbitrator. The circuit court found that the Commission's decision denying benefits was against the manifest weight of the evidence because the evidence supported the arbitrator's finding that the claimant was engaged in a training activity rather than a recreational activity as the Commission had found. The District appeals from the decision of the circuit court.

The sole issue on appeal is whether the decision of the Commission is against the manifest weight of the evidence.

Section 11 of the Workers' Compensation Act (Act) (III. Rev. Stat. 1981, ch. 48, par. 138.11) provides in pertinent part as follows:

> Accidental injuries incurred while participating in voluntary recreational programs including but not limited to athletic events, parties and picnics do not arise out of and in the course of the employment even though the employer pays some or all of the cost thereof. This exclusion shall not apply in the event that the injured employee was ordered or assigned by his employer to participate in the program.

It is undisputed that claimant voluntarily participated in the water fighting event in which he was injured. The issue to be resolved here is whether claimant was engaged in a "recreational" program which, under section 11 of the Act, would bar him from receiving compensation for his injury. The term "recreational program" has not previously been defined by our case law nor is it defined in the Act.

The issue presented by this case is whether the claimant was participating in a voluntary recreational activity or program. The determination of this issue presents a factual question. It is undisputed that the claimant was not ordered to participate in the tournament; accordingly, his participation was voluntary. The portion of section 11 of the Act previously set forth clearly excludes voluntary recreational programs even if the employer pays some or all of the cost thereof. Here, the employer paid none of the cost and did not order or assign the claimant to participate in the program or event in which the claimant was injured. There was evidence that the District and Association were separate entities although sharing many of the same members. The Association rather than the District sponsored the water fighting event. The fire fighters were not compensated for participating in these tournaments.

We are of the opinion that the record in this case supports the Commission's finding that, by participating in the water fighting tournament, claimant was engaged in a voluntary recreational activity. Such a determination by the Commission is not against the manifest weight of the evidence. We are bound by the Commission's finding that the claimant was participating in a voluntary recreational activity when he was injured. Thus, the circuit court of McHenry County erred in setting aside the decision of the Commission.

Eckis v. Sea World Corp.

64 Cal. App. 3d 1, 134 Cal. Rptr. 183 (1976)

AULT, Presiding Justice.

Defendants Sea World and Kent Burgess have appealed from a judgment entered on a jury verdict awarding Anne E. Eckis $75,000 in compensatory damages. Plaintiff had sought both compensatory and punitive damages for personal injuries she sustained while riding "Shamu the Whale," framing her complaint on three theories: fraud, negligence, and liability for an animal with vicious or dangerous propensities.

The day plaintiff filed her action in the superior court (April 18, 1972) she also filed an application for benefits with the Workers' Compensation Appeals Board (WCAB). Sea World moved for summary judgment in the superior court action, contending plaintiff was an employee and that her exclusive remedy was with the WCAB. [T]he superior court denied its motion for summary judgment.

The major issue raised on appeal is the contention there was no substantial evidence to support the jury's finding that plaintiff's injuries did not occur in the course of her employment by Sea World.

When injured on April 19, 1971, plaintiff Anne E. Eckis, then 22 years old, was a full-time employee of Sea World. First hired by Sea World in 1967, she had worked variously as ticket sales girl, receptionist, in the accounting department, and in 1970 became the secretary for Kent Burgess, the director of Sea World's animal training department. From then on her job title was secretary, and that is what she considered herself to be, although from time to time she did other tasks at Burgess' request, such as taking the water temperature, doing research, and running errands. She worked five days a week, for which she was paid a salary of $450 per month. When first hired, plaintiff, like all other Sea World employees, had signed an authorization for reproduction of her physical likeness. Plaintiff was also an excellent swimmer, with some scuba diving experience, and had occasionally worked as a model, sometimes for pay.

In April 1971 Gail MacLaughlin, Sea World's public relations director, and Kent Burgess asked plaintiff if she would like to ride Shamu, the killer whale, in a bikini for some publicity pictures for Sea World. Although the ride was not made a condition of her keeping her job, plaintiff eagerly agreed, thinking it would be exciting. Although warned in general terms that the ride involved dangers and aware that she might fall off, plaintiff was confident of her swimming ability and anxious to do it. She had never heard of whales pushing riders around.

Burgess had been responsible for training Shamu ever since Sea World first acquired the animal. He knew Shamu was conditioned to being ridden only by persons wearing wetsuits, and that Shamu had in the past attacked persons who attempted to ride her in an ordinary bathing suit. In addition, Burgess had read training records which showed Shamu had been behaving erratically since early March 1971. This information he did not disclose to plaintiff.

Plaintiff was trained for the ride by Sea World trainers in the tank at Sea World during normal office working hours. First she practiced riding Kilroy, a smaller, more docile whale, while wearing a bathing suit. During her one practice session on Shamu, she wore a wetsuit, fell off, but swam to the edge of the tank without incident.

On April 19 plaintiff became apprehensive for the first time when one of Sea World's trainers said he was not going to watch her ride Shamu because it was "really dangerous." Plaintiff then went to Burgess and told him of her concern. He told her not to worry, said there was nothing to be concerned about, and that the ride was "as safe as it could be." Thus reassured, plaintiff, wearing a bikini Sea World had paid for, then took three rides on Shamu. During the second ride one of the trainers noticed Shamu's tail was fluttering, a sign the animal was upset. During the third ride plaintiff fell off when Shamu refused to obey a signal. Shamu then bit her on her legs and hips and held her in the tank until she could be rescued.

Plaintiff suffered 18 to 20 wounds which required from 100 to 200 stitches and left permanent scars. She was hospitalized five days and out of work several weeks. She also suffered some psychological disturbance. Sea World paid all her medical expenses and continued to pay her salary as usual during this period.

When an employee's injuries are compensable under the Workers' Compensation Act, the right of the employee to recover the benefits provided by the Act is his exclusive remedy against the employer.

Under Section 3600, with exceptions not applicable here, liability of the employer to pay compensation under the Act, "in lieu of any other liability whatsoever," attaches:

(b) Where, at the time of the injury, the employee is performing service growing out of and incidental to his employment and is acting within the course of his employment, [and]

(c) Where the injury is proximately caused by the employment, either with or without negligence.

The provisions of the Act must be "liberally construed by the courts with the purpose of extending their benefits for the protection of persons injured in the course of their employment."(§ 3202)

It has been uniformly held that the rule requiring a liberal construction of the Act in favor of its applicability applies in civil suits as well as in compensation proceedings.

> The rule [of liberal construction of the Act in favor of its applicability] is not altered because a plaintiff believes that he can establish negligence on the part of his employer and brings a civil suit for damages. If the injury falls within the scope of the act, a proceeding thereunder constitutes his exclusive remedy.

(*Freire v. Matson Navigation Co.*, 19 Cal. 2d 8, 10, 118 P.2d 809, 810.)

Where a reasonable doubt exists as to whether an act of an employee is contemplated by the employment, or as to whether an injury occurred in the course of the employment, section 3202 requires courts to resolve the doubt against the right of the employee to sue for civil damages and in favor of the applicability of the Compensation Act.

> Though it may be more opportunistic for a particular plaintiff to seek to circumscribe the purview of compensation coverage because of his immediate interest and advantage, the courts must be vigilant to preserve the spirit of the act and to prevent a distortion of its purposes. That the question before us in this case arises out of litigation prosecuted in the superior court is all the more reason for care lest rules of doubtful validity, out of harmony with the objectives of the Act, be formulated.

(*Scott v. Pacific Coast Borax Co.*, 140 Cal. App. 2d 173, 178, 294 P.2d 1039, 1043.)

Whether an employee's injury arose out of and in the course of his employment is generally a question of fact to be determined in the light of the circumstances of the particular case. Like other issues relating to causation, however, when the facts are undisputed and all point in the same direction, resolution of the question becomes a matter of law.

Governed by these legal principles, we examine the evidence to determine whether it supports the finding plaintiff was not acting within the course and scope of her employment at Sea World when she sustained her injuries.

The undisputed evidence shows: at the time she was injured plaintiff was an employee of Sea World; she was injured on the employer's premises during what were her regular working hours; she was injured while engaging in an activity which her employer had requested her to perform and for which it had provided her with the training and the means to perform; in riding Shamu the Whale for publicity pictures, plaintiff was not engaged in an activity which was personal to her, but rather one which was related to, furthered, and benefitted the business of her employer.

Despite this formidable array of factors which indicate her injuries did arise out of and occurred in the course and scope of her employment[,] plaintiff maintains substantial evidence supports the special finding to the contrary. She premises her position on the claim she was hired to be a secretary, not to ride a whale. Since her injuries were unrelated to the secretarial duties she was originally hired to perform, she argues her employment "had nothing whatsoever to do with her injury" and that her case does not come within the purview of the Compensation Act. Because of the highly unusual circumstances under which she was injured, she maintains the rules and formulas traditionally used to determine whether injuries have arisen out of or occurred in the course of employment are neither applicable nor helpful.

These arguments are without merit. The right to compensation is not limited to those cases where the injury occurs while the employee is performing the classical duties for which he was originally hired. Far less than a direct request by the employer operates to bring an injury-causing activity within the provisions of the Compensation Act. For example, in *Lizama v. Workmen's Comp. Appeals Bd.*, 40 Cal. App. 3d 363, 115 Cal. Rptr. 267, the employee was injured on the employer's premises after he had clocked out from work while using a table saw to construct a bench to sit on at lunch time. Although his assigned duties did not include use of the saw and he had never used it before, the injury was held compensable because the employer had expressly or impliedly permitted such use of equipment. At page 370, 115 Cal. Rptr. at page 271, the court stated:

> Textwriters have long proposed and California courts have applied a 'quantum' theory of work-connection; that seems peculiarly appropriate for application here. The theory merges the 'course of employment' and 'arising out of employment' tests, but does not dispense with a minimum 'quantum of work-connection.' There were at least these connections between petitioner's injury and his employment: the accident occurred on the employer's premises when petitioner was using the employer's equipment while constructing a bench for his personal comfort to be used on the employer's premises; and the employer expressly or impliedly permitted petitioner to use its equipment.

It would be wholly incongruous and completely at variance with the long declared purposes and policies of the Worker's Compensation Law to say that an employee who sustained injuries under the circumstances of this case is not entitled to the benefits of the Workers' Compensation Act. Since her injuries fall within the scope of the Act, a proceeding under it constitutes plaintiff's exclusive remedy. The concluding remarks of the court in *Scott v. Pacific Coast Borax Co.*, supra, are appropriate here.

> We are cognizant of the fact the plaintiff, believing himself without fault, regards it to his decided advantage to maintain an action for damages against his employer rather than to receive an award of workmen's compensation. But in deciding whether an injury is compensable, we must disregard completely the question of fault and be mindful that the rules we lay down in this particular case must be salutary and consonant with the spirit and purpose of the Compensation Act, since they will govern other cases where the Act will provide the worker disabled by industrial injury with his sole remedy. Inasmuch as this state is committed to the view that the Workmen's Compensation Act must be liberally construed in favor of coverage for the employee and jurisdiction in the commission and since the facts adduced show there existed a concurrence of the conditions of section 3600 of the Labor code, the trial court correctly ruled that the commission was the exclusive tribunal for the prosecution of plaintiff's rights.

The special finding of the jury is not supported by the evidence. Since the disputed evidence established that plaintiff's injuries were compensable under the Worker's Compensation Act, the trial court should have granted Sea World's motion for the judgment notwithstanding the verdict.

Note

While the workers' compensation issue of whether an employee was "in the course of employment" at the time of injury and the vicarious liability issue in third party tort cases of whether the servant was "in the scope of employment" at the time the tort was committed sound similar and are similarly analyzed, there is a major difference. Workers' compensation statutes are to be liberally construed. As was said in *Stockwell v. Morris*, 46 Wyo. 1, 22 P.2d 189, 192 (1933), "[T]here is, perhaps, in [workers' compensation] cases manifest a tendency toward a liberal construction in favor of a claimant under such laws." Thus, courts have resisted the efforts of plaintiffs in third party tort cases to utilize by analogy the workers' compensation cases as authority (those cases would tend to find an employee/servant to be within the course of employment and, thus, within the scope of employment).

c. Exclusivity of Remedy

Cuffe v. Sanders Construction Co., Inc.

748 P.2d 328 (Alaska 1988)

BURKE, Justice.

This case involves the exclusive remedy provision of the Alaska Workers' Compensation Act, AS 23.30.055. The superior court granted a directed verdict against plaintiff Thomas W. Cuffe.

In April, 1982, Thomas Cuffe was employed as a journeyman ironworker and certified welder by Griffard Steel Company (GSC). GSC was the erecting ironwork subcontractor in the construction of the "Butler building" on the North Slope. The general contractor on the project was Sanders Construction Company, Inc. (SCC). On April 24, 1982, a forklift operated by Rick Sanders hit a building support, dislodging an unsecured beam which fell and injured Cuffe. Cuffe brought suit for damages against Sanders and SCC, alleging that Sanders' negligence in the operation of the forklift caused his injuries. Sanders' employment status at the time of the accident is hotly disputed. Cuffe contends that Sanders was acting in his capacity as president and project manager for SCC at the time of the accident; Sanders asserts that he was employed solely as a forklift driver for GSC and was, thus, a "fellow employee" of Sanders, protected from suit by the exclusive remedy provision of the Workers' Compensation Act.

The case proceeded to trial where, at the close of plaintiff's case-in-chief, the trial court granted defendants' motion for directed verdict as to both Sanders and SCC. The court ruled that (1) Sanders was Cuffe's "fellow employee" at the time of the accident and, thus, immune from suit, under the exclusive remedy provisions of the Workers' Compensation Act; and (2) the evidence introduced by plaintiff failed to establish that SCC had "retained control" over GSC's operations sufficient to subject it to liability for injury to GSC's employee.

In reviewing the grant of a directed verdict, our role is to determine whether the evidence and all reasonable inferences which may be drawn therefrom, viewed in the light most favorable to the nonmoving party, is such that reasonable jurors could not differ in their judgment. Thus, we must first determine whether the trial court was correct in concluding that, after viewing plaintiff's evidence, no reasonable juror could differ regarding Sanders' status as Cuffe's "fellow employee" at the time of the accident.

Cuffe contends that the trial court erred in granting a directed verdict in this case because the evidence in question is susceptible to competing inferences. He further argues that it was per se error for the trial court to grant a directed verdict at the close of plaintiff's case-in-chief, insomuch as this constitutes an impermissible shifting of the burden of proof regarding Sanders' coemployee defense.

The evidence at trial established that, at the time of the accident, Sanders was operating a forklift which was being used to complete the ironwork assembly job for which GSC had contracted. There was also evidence suggesting that, while operating the forklift, Sanders was in fact taking his direction from the GSC foreman. On the other hand, Cuffe testified at trial that Sanders had personally represented to him that Sanders was "the project manager" for SCC on the job and that he (Sanders) could "do anything [he] want[ed]" on the work site, including operate a forklift for GSC.

Sanders contends that the foregoing evidence, even when viewed in the light most favorable to Cuffe, can reasonably lead the trier of fact to only one of two possible conclusions: Either Sanders was solely in the employment of GSC at the time he drove the forklift, or he was in the employ of both GSC and SCC at that time. In either case, Sanders asserts, he is protected by the exclusive remedy provisions of AS 23.30.055, which prohibits tort suits against a worker's "fellow employees" concerning job-related injuries.

Our prior decisions have recognized that an employee may be employed simultaneously by two or more employers while performing a given employment function. Where the employee is performing services for the mutual benefit of both employers at the time of the accident, we think that such simultaneous employment would logically carry with it the statutory immunity afforded coemployees under the Workers' Compensation Act.[4] Before an employee may avail himself of such immunity, however, he must, at minimum, offer evidence sufficient to establish that such mutual employment in fact existed at the time of the accident for which the immunity is sought. Since it is axiomatic that the employer/employee relationship can only be created by contract, such evidence must be sufficient to establish the existence of an express or implied employment agreement between the parties. In the case at bar, such evidence is notably absent.

In *Selid* [*Construction v. Guarantee Insurance*, 355 P.2d 389 (Alaska 1960)] we examined the question of whether the mere performance of duties at the direction of one other than one's employer was sufficient to create a new or additional employment relationship. We concluded that it was not, stating:

> Once created, the [employment] relationship cannot be changed to substitute another employer without the employee's consent. The employee must have understood and agreed before there can be any transfer to another employer. Where the employee commences to serve another at the direction of his employer, no new relationship is necessarily created. He may simply be performing his duty to the employer who gave the order. Even though his actions may be controlled by the new master, no new relationship is created in the absence of an express or implied contract between the employee and the new master.

In the case at bar, the fact that Sanders received direction from the GSC foreman while operating the forklift does not, of itself, evidence an agreement between Sanders

4. Where an employee is performing services for each employer separately, the employment might be deemed "dual," rather than "joint," and the extent of the employee's immunity would depend upon the severability of the employee's activities at the time of the accident... see generally 1C A. Larson, The Law of Workmen's Compensation § 48.41 (1986).

and GSC that Sanders was to be considered a GSC employee. On the contrary, Sanders may well have been driving the forklift at the behest of SCC and in furtherance of that company's interest. In any case, we believe that reasonable jurors could differ on the question. Consequently, we reverse the trial court's ruling as to Sanders.

SCC is correct in pointing out that we have adopted the "retained control" theory of recovery, as set forth in Restatement (Second) of Torts § 414 (1965),[7] for determining liability in certain general contractor/subcontractor contexts. This theory does not, however, constitute a blanket immunity from suit for general contractors as to all injuries sustained by employees of their respective subcontractors. As we explained more fully in *Moloso v. State*, 644 P.2d 205, 210 (Alaska 1982) (emphasis added):

> In general, the employer of an independent contractor owes no duty to the independent contractor's employees to protect them from the negligence of the employees' own master. On the other hand, the employer of the independent contractor does owe to these servants the duty to avoid endangering them *by the employer's own negligent actions or omissions.*

We expanded on this later point:

> Section 414 [of the Restatement] is sometimes referred to as an "exception" to the general rule that the employer of an independent contractor is not liable for injuries sustained by the employees of that independent contractor. Calling it an "exception," however, appears to be nothing more than a circuitous route around the simple rule that anyone, including an employer of an independent contractor, may be held liable for his or her own negligence.

Thus, when a general contractor injures a subcontractor's employee by his own affirmative act of negligence, the general contractor remains liable without regard to the extent of his control over the subcontractor's work. Accordingly, if, as Cuffe contends, Sanders was an employee of SCC acting within the course and scope of his employment at the time he was operating the forklift, Sanders' acts are attributable to SCC under standard respondeat superior principles. SCC would remain responsible for those negligent acts, notwithstanding the degree of control which it exercised over GSC, and notwithstanding the fact that Sanders may also have been acting as an employee of GSC. Because SCC's liability, if any, depends upon whether Sanders was acting within the scope of his employment as a servant of SCC at the time of the accident, a directed verdict prior to jury determination of this question was erroneous.[9]

The judgment of the superior court granting a directed verdict in favor of defendants Sanders and SCC is REVERSED, and the case is REMANDED for further proceedings consistent with this opinion.

---

7. Restatement (Second) of Torts § 414 provides in pertinent part: "One who entrusts work to an independent contractor, but who retains control of any part of the work, is subject to liability for physical harm to others for whose safety the employer owes a duty to exercise reasonable care, which is caused by his failure to exercise his control with reasonable care."

9. We note that if Sanders was acting within the scope of his employment for both masters at the time of the accident, the fact of his immunity should not affect the liability of SCC. *Marsh v. Tilley Steel*, 26 Cal. 3d 486, 606 P.2d 355, 360-62 (1980). Whether Sanders would be liable to SCC in an action for indemnity is a question we need not resolve at this time.

Halifax Paving v. Scott & Jobalia Construction

565 So. 2d 1346 (Fla. 1990)

KOGAN, Judge.

While working on a construction site in Volusia County, Scott & Jobalia Construction Co. ("S & J") borrowed a crane and its operator from Halifax Paving, Inc. There was no oral or written lease and no rent or other compensation was paid. The crane was loaned purely as a matter of courtesy. Although the crane operator was solely an employee of Halifax, his activities nevertheless were controlled by S & J workers through the use of hand signals. During work, a pipe fell from the sling attached to the crane and injured one of S & J's workers, named Grier.

Grier recovered workers' compensation from S & J, and then filed suit against Halifax as owner of the crane. Halifax, through its insurance carrier, United States Fidelity & Guaranty, settled Grier's claim for $67,500. Halifax then sued S & J for common law indemnity, contending that any active negligence was attributable to S & J. The jury concluded that the crane operator was a "borrowed servant" and returned a verdict for Halifax.

On appeal, the Fifth District [Court of Appeals] reversed. It concluded that the owner of a dangerous instrumentality loaned for use on a job site fell within the scope of the worker's compensation immunity enjoyed by the employer. As a result, the exclusive remedy available to Grier was worker's compensation and no tort action or resulting claim for indemnity was proper.

Florida law long has recognized the "borrowed servant" rule. See *Postal Telegraph & Cable Co. v. Doyle*, 123 Fla. 695, 167 So. 358 (1936). Under this rule, one who borrows and exercises control over the servant or worker of another in effect assumes all liability for the activities of the borrowed servant or worker.

We believe the record contains substantial competent evidence to show that the crane operator became a "borrowed servant" within the definition of that term provided in *Shelby Mutual Insurance Co. v. Aetna Insurance Co.*, 246 So. 2d 98, 101 (Fla. 1971).

Similarly, this Court established in *Smith v. Ryder Truck Rentals, Inc.*, 182 So. 2d 422 (Fla. 1966), that a worker injured by a leased dangerous instrumentality operated by a fellow worker is limited to no more recovery than that permitted by the worker's compensation statutes. The central rationale of *Smith* is that leased equipment used on a job site in effect has become the working tool of the employer. Thus, the exclusivity principle of worker's compensation comes to bear.

We see no reason why a different result should obtain in the present case. The only relevant differences between this case and *Smith* are that the dangerous instrumentality in this instance was informally borrowed, not leased, and the operator of this instrumentality was a borrowed servant, not a fellow servant. We agree with the Fifth District that these differences are not sufficient to justify a different result than that in *Smith*.

Indeed, the central policies of worker's compensation are to provide employees with a swift and adequate means of compensation for injury, and to insulate employers from potentially bankrupting tort liability for work-place accidents. Both of these policies are best advanced by the rule adopted by the district court below. In this case, the crane that injured Grier in effect had become one of the work-place tools of Grier's employer. The one who operated the crane did so under the direction of S & J and its agents or employees, thus justifying the jury below in concluding that the crane operator was a borrowed servant. There is no allegation that any undisclosed defect in the crane resulted in the injury or that Halifax in any other way was responsible for a negligent act that proximately led to Grier's injury. We acknowledge, as Halifax notes, that more recent conceptions of worker's compensation have cast into doubt at least some of the rationale of *Smith*. Halifax correctly notes, for instance, that we made the following observation in *Employers Insurance of Wausau v. Abernathy*, 442 So. 2d 953, 954 (Fla. 1983):

> The justification for limiting liability or granting immunity is the substitution of something else in its place, a quid pro quo. The duty to provide worker's compensation benefits supplants tort liability to those injured on the job. *If the duty to provide such coverage does not exist, then one has no reason to expect immunity from wrongdoings committed against a third party.*

(emphasis added). However, we believe that the last sentence of this quotation is fully in accord with the central premise of *Smith* and with the result we reach today.

The point of both *Smith* and our opinion here is that, while the third party certainly had no duty to provide worker's compensation to the injured party, neither did the third party in any logical sense contribute to the work-place injury that actually occurred. In both logic and fairness, the injury here and in *Smith* was work-place injury occurring as a result of a dangerous instrumentality in the control of the employer. This conclusion is only underscored by the fact that the jury below agreed with Halifax that any active negligence was attributable to S & J. When this is the case, the exclusive remedy is worker's compensation.

Note

Recovery under workers' compensation is not the exclusive remedy against an employer where the dual-capacity doctrine applies. Where the employer occupies a second capacity amounting to a distinct and separate legal persona with attendant legal obligations unrelated to those of employer, the employee may seek redress in a civil suit against the employer based on the obligations arising from the second function. For example, in *Duprey v. Shane*, 39 Cal. 2d 781, 249 P.2d 8 (1952), a nurse sustained a work-related injury while she was employed by a chiropractor. The chiropractor undertook personally to treat the nurse for her injury and did so negligently. The court upheld a recovery in an action for malpractice, reasoning that the chiropractor was acting as the attending doctor rather than as employer. What other dual capacities of employers would qualify under the dual-capacity doctrine?

J.M.F. v. Emerson

768 S.W.2d 579 (Mo. App. 1989)

GARY M. GAERTNER, Judge.

Plaintiff-appellant J.M.F. appeals from trial court's order dismissing her negligence action against her employer, defendant-respondent Hematology Oncology Consultants, Inc. (hereinafter employer), and its president, defendant-respondent Dr. William A. Emerson, M.D. Appellant alleged that Dr. Emerson negligently directed appellant to draw blood from an AIDS patient. Appellant alleged that her employer was negligent for failing to provide safe instruments to perform the task assigned to her. The trial court dismissed appellant's action for failure to state a claim upon which relief could be granted.

Appellant began working for employer in January 1986.[1] On April 7, 1987, appellant was directed by Dr. Emerson to draw a blood sample from a patient who was infected with Acquired Immune Deficiency Syndrome (AIDS). Dr. Emerson instructed appellant to use a lancet in performing this task. After appellant finished drawing the blood, appellant, Dr. Emerson and a nurse allegedly became involved in a disagreement regarding disposal of the instrument that was used to draw the blood. The disagreement allegedly caused confusion during appellant's collection of the instrument thereby causing her to cut her finger with the instrument which had just been used to draw blood from the AIDS patient.

Appellant filed her action alleging that Dr. Emerson was negligent in that he knew appellant was not trained to draw blood from an AIDS patient. Appellant further alleged that Dr. Emerson and a registered nurse were both in the examination room with appellant and the AIDS patient, were both trained to handle an AIDS patient, but Dr. Emerson nevertheless directed appellant to draw the blood. Appellant also alleged that Dr. Emerson was negligent in instructing appellant to use a lancet instead of a syringe to obtain the blood sample, in that using a syringe would have been a safer method. Appellant also asserted that Dr. Emerson was negligent in initiating the disagreement with appellant, causing confusion at the time she was in the process of collecting and disposing of the equipment. Appellant asserted that Dr. Emerson's negligent acts caused her to cut her finger thereby exposing her to the AIDS virus. Appellant stated that she does not know and will not know for an indeterminate amount of time whether she is contaminated with the AIDS virus.

Respondents filed motions to dismiss arguing that appellant's claim was barred by the Workers' Compensation Law and that said action otherwise failed to state a claim upon which relief could be granted. The trial court ruled that appellant failed to state a claim and dismissed her action. On appeal appellant first urges that Dr. Emerson was a supervisory employee who committed misfeasance. Appellant asserts, therefore, that her action is not precluded by the Workers' Compensation Law.

The law regarding the liability of an employee to a fellow employee injured during the course of her employment was fully set forth in *State ex rel. Badami v. Gaertner*, 630 S.W.2d 175 (Mo. App., E.D. 1982) (en banc). An employer is immune from common-law liability for a breach of its duty to provide a reasonably safe place to work. Likewise an employee chosen to implement that duty enjoys the same immunity for mere failure to discharge that duty. In *Badami*, this court established that in order to state a claim against a supervisory employee, the injured employee must allege something more than the general failure to fulfill the general duty of supervision and safety. The *Badami* court did not enumerate what acts would constitute actionable negligence, but rather suggested a case by case approach. The question before us is whether the acts of respondent Emerson constitute that "something extra" as set forth in *Badami*.

---

1. Appellant states in her petition that she was hired as a receptionist/secretary. The injury report filed by respondent Hematology with the Division of Workers' Compensation listed appellant as a medical assistant.

The court more recently addressed this question in *Craft v. Scaman*, 715 S.W.2d 531 (Mo. App., 1986). In *Craft*, the employee-plaintiff was employed at a fireworks factory owned by a Missouri corporation. The defendant, president of the company and supervisor of the factory, negligently applied friction to a spinning reel of fuse while attempting to assist the employee with a malfunction of the equipment. A flash fire ensued that injured plaintiff. We held

> that the 'something extra' required to impose tort liability upon a corporate officer includes any affirmative act, taken while the officer is acting outside the scope of the employer's responsibility, that breaches a personal duty of care the officer owes to a fellow employee.

In *Craft* the defendant had stepped out of his supervisory role and into the role of a co-employee.

But in the case before us, plaintiff has failed to allege anything other than a breach by defendant of his duty of proper supervision owed to the corporation. Appellant sets forth four allegedly negligent acts committed by Dr. Emerson. First, Dr. Emerson knew that appellant was inadequately trained as to the handling of blood samples from an AIDS patient but nevertheless directed her to draw blood from an AIDS patient. Second, Dr. Emerson did not appoint himself or an available registered nurse to draw blood from the AIDS patient. Third, Dr. Emerson instructed appellant to use instruments that were not proper and safe for performing the blood drawing task. Fourth, Dr. Emerson initiated a discussion regarding the disposal of the instruments used to draw the blood sample which allegedly confused appellant at the time she was disposing of said instruments. We believe each of these acts was within Dr. Emerson's duty of safe and proper supervision which was owed to his employer, respondent Hematology Oncology Consultants, Inc. Thus, appellant has failed to plead actionable negligence.

Having found no error, we affirm the trial court's dismissal of appellant's action.

KAROHL, J., dissents.

d. Employers' Intentional Torts

Among the many other issues confronted in the workers' compensation context is the question of whether intentional torts committed by employers are compensable exclusively under the statutes, or whether employees who suffer injury or ailment due to intentional wrongdoing by employers may look to the common law for compensation (including sums for pain, suffering, and exemplary damages).

Sitzman v. Schumaker

718 P.2d 657 (Mont. 1986)

HARRISON, Justice.

This is an appeal from a summary judgment of the District Court.

The plaintiff, James Sitzman, worked for the defendant, Jake Shumaker, performing general ranch labor. The two men did not get along. Shumaker often called Sitzman a "son-of-a-bitch" and "idiot." Sitzman did not respond to these names at first, but eventually began shouting back.

The day Sitzman was injured, he and Shumaker were working together. Shumaker asked Sitzman if the calf feeders were full. Sitzman responded by telling Shumaker that the first one was half full, the second about three-quarters full, and the third one was about two-thirds full. Shumaker exploded, saying "I believe you, you god damn idiot. Can't you just say 'yes' or 'no'?" Later in the morning, Shumaker asked Sitzman if he wanted to work on the tractor, Sitzman responded, "Yeah, sure, no problem. Let's go to work on it." Shumaker again exploded, saying, "you god damn son-of-a-bitch. Why can't you just say 'yes' or 'no'?" When Sitzman replied, "Don't call me an s.o.b.," Shumaker walked over to him and struck him several times in the face. Sitzman pushed Shumaker to the ground. Shumaker then picked up a four-foot length of two-inch pipe and held it over his head. Sitzman asked Shumaker not to hit him, and turned to walk away. Shumaker hit Sitzman on the back of the head and when Sitzman turned to protect himself, hit him on the front of the head, knocking him to the ground, unconscious. Sitzman suffered severe injuries, including a fractured skull. The extensive head injuries have altered the course of his life.

Sitzman applied for and was granted temporary total disability wage and medical benefits under the Workers' Compensation Act. He brought this action in the District Court to recover damages caused by Shumaker's attack. His wife, Barbara, brought an action for loss of consortium, society, support, comfort and companionship of her husband due to his injuries. Shumaker moved for summary judgment.

Judgment was granted in both actions for the stated reason that because of Sitzman's application for and receipt of Workers' Compensation benefits, their remedies were exclusive to the Workers' Compensation Act. Upon stipulation of the parties the Sitzmans' actions were consolidated for purpose of appeal.

The issue presented for review by Sitzman is whether receipt of Workers' Compensation benefits by them results in an election pursuant to § 39-71-411, MCA, thereby barring them from a common law tort action against employer Shumaker.

Ordinarily, when an employee is injured in the work place due to negligence or accident, his remedy is exclusive to the Workers' Compensation Act. Common law damages are not available for injuries negligently or accidentally inflicted by an employer. Negligence claims should be dismissed on this ground. Such are not the facts in this case—Sitzman's injuries are not the result of negligence or accident.

The question then becomes whether there is a permissible exception for the tort inflicted by Shumaker upon Sitzman.

This Court has said:

> The "intentional harm" which removes an employer from the protection of the exclusivity clause of the Workers' Compensation Act is such harm as is maliciously and specifically directed at an employee out of which such specific intentional harm the employee receives injuries as a proximate result.

There is evidence that Sitzman suffered intentional harm maliciously and specifically directed at him by Shumaker. It is not reasonable to suppose the legislature intended to give statutory protection in the form of immunity from suit to an employer who hits his employee in carrying out his employment duties.

The egregiousness of these circumstances removes the exclusivity bar for an employee. In a manner similar to injury by a fellow employee, § 39-71-413, MCA, where the legislature provided for coverage from an intentional injury, under the facts of this case, we provide for such coverage where the injury is by the employer.

There are sound policy reasons for reaching this decision. The purpose of the Workers' Compensation Act is to protect both the employer and the employee by incorporating a quid pro quo for negligent acts by the employer. The employer is given immunity from suit by an employee who is injured on the job in return for relinquishing his common law defenses. The employee is assured of compensation for his injuries, but forgoes legal recourse against his employer. To allow an employer to personally commit an assault and battery upon an employee and hide behind the exclusivity clause of the Workers' Compensation Act is to disregard the purpose of the Act. Other employers would have to pay for his protection. In effect, he would have bought the right to hit his employees. That is not a quid pro quo. The law does not allow a wrongdoer to benefit from his wrongs.

Consequently we hold that a narrow exception to the exclusiveness of the compensation remedy exists where the employer personally commits an assault and battery upon an employee.

The summary judgment is reversed and the case is remanded for trial consistent with the findings of this Court.

Meerbrey v. Marshall Field & Co.

189 Ill. App. 3d 1085, 545 N.E.2d 952 (1989)

Justice BUCKLEY.

Kenneth A. Meerbrey (plaintiff) brought suit against defendants Marshall Field & Company (Marshall Field) and its agent, Tim Marcolini (Marcolini), for damages for false imprisonment, false arrest, and malicious prosecution. The circuit court granted defendants' motion to dismiss Marshall Field from counts II through V of plaintiff's second-amended complaint.

Marshall Field employed plaintiff as a cashier and Marcolini as a security guard. On January 19, 1985, Marcolini interviewed plaintiff at work regarding the theft of approximately $600 from Marshall Field. During this interview, plaintiff signed a restitution form and promissory note acknowledging his theft and, under the terms of the restitution form, thereafter reimbursed Marshall Field $500.

On February 12, 1985, plaintiff returned to Marshall Field's premises and demanded his payroll check for past earnings. Rochella Davis, an agent of Marshall Field, informed plaintiff that he was forbidden to enter the premises and twice requested him to leave. After plaintiff failed to vacate the premises, he was arrested by the Chicago Police Department pursuant to Davis' sworn complaint.

Subsequently, plaintiff filed suit against Marshall Field and Marcolini alleging various causes of action. Count II of plaintiff's complaint alleges that Marshall Field and Marcolini falsely imprisoned plaintiff on January 19, 1985, while counts III through V assert claims against Marshall Field and Marcolini alleging false imprisonment, false arrest, and malicious prosecution stemming from the February 12, 1985 events.

Addressing first the circuit court's dismissal of Marshall Field from counts II through V of plaintiff's complaint, the court found that the exclusivity provisions of the Workers' Compensation Act (the Act) (Ill. Rev. Stat. 1987, Ch. 48, par. 138.5(a)) barred plaintiff's common law cause of action. The exclusive remedy provided for in section 5(a) of the Act reads in pertinent part, as follows:

> No common law or statutory right to recover damages from the employer or the agents or employees of [the employer] for injury or death sustained by any employee while engaged in the line of his duty as such employee, other than the compensation herein provided, is available to any employee who is covered by the provisions of this Act.

Through this provision, the Act establishes a system of liability without fault. It abolishes traditional common law defenses available to the employer in exchange for the prohibition against common law suits by employees. The exclusive remedy provision

> is part of the quid pro quo in which the sacrifices and gains of employees and employers are to some extent put in balance, for, while the employer assumes a new liability without fault, he is relieved of the prospect of large damage verdicts.

2A A. Larson, The Law of Workmen's Compensation § 65.11 (1988).

Plaintiff contends that the above exclusivity provisions do not apply to the case at bar. Specifically, as to Marshall Field, plaintiff argues that he is not barred by the exclusivity provision contained in the Act because Marcolini's acts were intentional. Plaintiff's contention is without merit.

Courts have held under the Act that to escape the bar of exclusivity provisions and to recover against persons covered under the Act, plaintiff is required

> to prove either that the injury (1) was not accidental, (2) did not arise from his or her employment, (3) was not received during the course of employment, or (4) was noncompensable under the Act.

In issue here is whether plaintiff's injury was "accidental" within the meaning of the Act to bar the common law action against Marshall Field. *Collier* and *Jablonski* hold that although the injuries inflicted by a fellow employee may be intentional from the wrongdoer's standpoint, they are compensable under the Act because the injury is "accidental" from the employee's/injured party's point of view—that is, despite the obvious fact that the injury was intentionally inflicted, an employee's injuries will not be held to be noncompensable under the Act due to the intentions of the co-employee. Common law causes of action, however, will be sustained against an employer for the intentional tort of his employee against a fellow employee where the employer has committed, commanded or expressly authorized the intentional act. A plaintiff under these circumstances apparently is required to allege that the employee was the alter ego of the employer in order to state a common law cause of action.

Plaintiff's complaint here does not allege that Marcolini was the alter ego of Marshall Field or that Marshall Field committed, commanded or expressly authorized Marcolini's acts, even after plaintiff was afforded the opportunity to amend his complaint to this effect. Plaintiff merely alleged that Marcolini was an agent of Marshall Field. Therefore, since no allegations exist that Marshall Field committed, commanded or expressly authorized the intentional conduct of its employee, the injury here is "accidental" within the meaning of the Act and plaintiff's common law cause of action against Marshall Field is barred.

Notes

1. If it is determined that an intentional injury by an employer to an employee is compensable outside of the workers' compensation law, then what constitutes an *intentional* tort? Does wilful and wanton misconduct qualify as intentional action? What about gross negligence?

2. May an employee injured by an employer's intentional misconduct recover first under workers' compensation, and then pursue a common law action for the same intentional tort? Or, does the filing of the workers' compensation claim amount to an election to seek only workers' compensation (a waiver of the common-law cause)?

3. Where the basis for the employee's injury is merely gross negligence or wilful and wanton conduct, would the filing first of a workers' compensation claim constitute evidence of the employee's real belief that the employer's conduct was not truly intentional?

e. Extent of Injury and Recovery

Workers generally are to be compensated for accidental injuries or illnesses caused in whole or part by the employment, including coverage for the aggravation of pre-existing conditions. Workers are entitled to recover the reasonably required costs of medical care (including rehabilitative services) and to recover for disability benefits. Such disabilities may be either temporary or permanent in nature, and the laws distinguish these. For instances of permanent disability, there can also sometimes be recovery for scarring and disfigurement. Death benefits are available.

But, the benefits for lost time from employment due to temporary or permanent disability represent only a percentage of a worker's weekly wages to a maximum level or a maximum number of weeks of compensation. Of course, disability may be partial or total.

Jackson Township Volunteer Fire Co. v. W.C.A.B.

594 A.2d 826 (Pa. Cmwlth. 1991)

KELLY, Judge.

The Jackson Township Volunteer Fire Company (fire company) appeals an order of the Workmen's Compensation Appeal Board (Board) which affirmed the order of the referee directing the fire company and/or its insurer to pay, pursuant to The Pennsylvania Workmen's Compensation Act (Act), medical costs incurred by Patrick Wallet (Wallet) for a series of shots and blood tests required by his occupational exposure to acquired immune deficiency syndrome (AIDS) and hepatitis B viruses.

Wallet was a volunteer for the Ambulance Association, a division of the fire company, when he responded to a call involving a fatal auto accident on July 7, 1988.[2]

---

2. Section 601 of the Act provides in pertinent part as follows:

(a) In addition to those persons included within the definition of the word 'employee' as defined in section 104, 'employee' shall also include:

(1) members of volunteer fire departments or volunteer fire companies.

(2) all members of volunteer ambulance corps of the various municipalities.

(3) all members of volunteer rescue and life-saving squads of the various municipalities.

The victim was pronounced dead at the scene of the accident. In the process of assisting at the scene, helping other volunteers remove the victim from his car and transporting the victim's bodily remains to a nearby funeral home, Wallet got some of the victim's blood and body fluids on his hands and shirt.

The victim was found to have had AIDS and was actively with the hepatitis B virus. Wallet testified that after leaving the funeral home, he and several other members of the ambulance crew cleaned the blood and other fluids from the stretcher and the back of the ambulance and scrubbed them both with bleach. They then responded to a brush fire. While on that call, Wallet was informed that Coroner John Barron wanted to see him at the hospital.

When Wallet arrived at the hospital, Barron and an unidentified physician at Conemaugh Valley Memorial Hospital informed him that arrangements had been made for him to receive tests for AIDS and hepatitis. Blood was drawn and as a precaution, Wallet received a series of injections to kill the hepatitis virus, had he contracted it. All tests came back negative.

The fire company and its insurer refused to pay for these medical services.[3] Wallet then filed a petition under the Act seeking only reimbursement for medical costs incurred. After a hearing on March 15, 1989, the referee found that Wallet's exposure to AIDS and hepatitis constituted an injury under the Act and directed the fire company and/or its insurer to pay for Wallet's tests and immunizations. The fire company appealed to the Board which affirmed the referee.

The issue presented here is whether the referee erred in finding that Wallet's occupational exposure to AIDS and hepatitis B is an "injury" under the Act, and in requiring the company to pay for the medical services provided to him. Section 306(c)(1) of the Act provides: "the employer shall provide payment for reasonable surgical and medical services when needed." Section 306(f)(4) limits compensation for medical services to situations where an "injury" has occurred. The fire company contends that Wallet was not injured and that if he was, he has not established that his injury was causally related to his work.

The term "injury" has been broadly defined to encompass all work-related harm including "any hurtful or damaging effect which may be suffered by anyone." *Pawlosky v. Workmen's Compensation Appeal Board*, 514 Pa. 450, 525 A.2d 1204 (1987). Wallet claims that his injury was the risk of infection.

It is uncontroverted that Wallet was exposed to the blood and bodily fluids of an individual with AIDS and hepatitis B. His exposure prompted both the coroner and a physician at the hospital to arrange for testing and precautionary measures to be taken in the form of tests and shots. It is also clear that Wallet, who was only sixteen years old at the time of this incident, has not pursued his claim for medical expenses in bad faith. He reasonably relied on the advice/directive of the coroner and a physician who recommended and arranged for diagnostic testing and a series of preventative inoculations for hepatitis B. Wallet has not claimed an ongoing disability, nor does he seek compensation for mental anguish or distress; he simply seeks reimbursement for the necessary medical expenses incurred for his work-related exposure to two highly contagious and deadly diseases.

---

3. Wallet's claim petition indicates that he incurred expenses totalling $1,554.06 for necessary medical services.

As we have often stated, the Act is remedial in nature and intended to benefit the worker, and its provisions should be liberally construed to effectuate its humanitarian objective. This purpose would surely be thwarted should benefits be denied here, particularly considering that Wallet was injured while performing the humanitarian services of an ambulance crew volunteer.[5]

Therefore, we hold that persons exposed to a serious risk of contracting a disease which is commonly known to be highly contagious/infectious and potentially deadly, have been "injured" for the purpose of receiving compensation under the Act. This conclusion is based on careful consideration of factors, such as the seriousness and immediacy of the risk created by exposure, as well as the reasonableness of the services sought and rendered. In this case, the actions and advice of the coroner and a physician clearly indicate that Wallet's exposure created a real, immediate, and serious risk of infection. The seriousness of Wallet's exposure is also evidenced by the urgency with which the recommended testing and precautionary treatment was pursued. These medical directives are consistent with a strong public policy in favor of restricting the spread of such serious and deadly contagious/infectious diseases as AIDS and hepatitis.

The fire company analogizes this case to a coal miner's pneumoconiosis case to imply that by granting compensation in this case, we will open the flood gates to litigation of claims involving employees who incur unwarranted and unreasonable medical expenses. The fire company hypothesizes that because exposure to coal dust may cause debilitating occupational lung diseases and even death, an employee might report to a doctor for diagnostic testing after each shift, then seek compensation for such expenses. However, this case is clearly distinguishable from a coal miner's pneumoconiosis case, and our holding it not nearly so broad.

We know of no cases in which a single incidence of exposure to coal dust has resulted in pneumoconiosis or death. The same cannot be said for AIDS and hepatitis, diseases so contagious and deadly that a person may contract them after being exposed only once. In addition, Wallet's expenses were not unwarranted nor unreasonable and, in fact, were incurred pursuant to the directives of health care professionals. Furthermore, as discussed above, only those persons exposed to a real and serious risk of contracting highly contagious/infectious and potentially deadly diseases are entitled to compensation.

Finally, the fire company argues that even if Wallet has suffered an "injury," he has failed to establish through unequivocal medical testimony that his injury was causally related to his work. However, unequivocal medical testimony is only required when the causal connection between one's injury and his work is not obvious. A review of the testimony in this case clearly reveals that Wallet's injury was obviously related to his work. In addition, because the fire company failed to object to Wallet's account of the diagnosis and treatment, his testimony was probative and sufficient to support the referee's decision.

Accordingly, we affirm the order of the Board.

---

5. Our refusal to compensate such individuals for reasonable medical expenses incurred would have an undesirable chilling effect on both volunteerism and the willingness of all health professionals to treat AIDS and hepatitis patients.

Notes

1. Workers' compensation benefits are not taxable as income to injured workers.

2. Workers' compensation laws ordinarily place a cap (and perhaps other limitations) on lawyers' fees for the pursuit of workers' cases against employers. In Illinois, for example, attorneys may as a general rule charge not more than 20% of the sum recovered for an injured worker. The reason for the limitation is the substantial likelihood that some amount of recovery will be achieved in a workers' compensation case (due to the liberal policy of compensating injured employees).

3. In earlier days, an injured worker who sought compensation from an employer could be discharged from employment where the worker was an at-will employee. However, under the workers' compensation laws and under the common law of wrongful discharge and retaliatory discharge, employees who seek compensation for injuries are generally protected from being fired for that reason.

4. The workers' compensation system is definitely a partial recovery system (consistent with the political compromise achieved to permit adoption of such laws in the first place). According to the 1990 regulations in effect in Illinois, for instance, when a worker suffers permanent partial disability due to 100% loss of use of certain listed body parts, the worker is entitled to recovery of a prescribed number of weeks of compensation at the worker's established salary or wage. Here is part of the schedule of benefits:

Body Part	*Weeks Paid*
Thumb	70
Index Finger	40
2nd Finger	35
3rd Finger	25
4th Finger	20
Hand	190
Arm	235
Foot	155
Leg	200
Great Toe	35
Other Toe	12

The schedule of injuries is far more extensive and detailed. As examples, a finger or toe might be amputated, and the level of recovery will depend upon how much of the appendage or limb is lost. If the loss is below the first joint, then there can be recovery for only one-half of the number of weeks listed above.

Chapter 11

Partnerships: Nature and Formation

A. Formation of Partnerships

Section 6 of the Uniform Partnership Act ("UPA") defines a partnership as "an association of two or more persons to carry on as co-owners a business for profit." Unlike a corporation or a limited partnership, formalities are not necessary to create a partnership. While the informality of a partnership is one of the chief advantages of the partnership form of doing business, persons involved in a business relationship sometimes discover that they have become partners without realizing it. Becoming a partner has significant implications: not only are all partners liable for partnership obligations [UPA § 15], but all partners must bear a share of partnership losses [UPA § 18(a)].

Dalton v. Austin

432 A.2d 774 (Me. 1981)

NICHOLS, Justice.

The Plaintiff, Emily Dalton, appeals from a judgment for the Defendant, Whitney W. Austin, Sr., entered by the Superior Court in Penobscot County after a jury-waived trial on her complaint for conversion of certain financial contributions she had made to a business in Bangor known as The Small Change Restaurant, of which Austin was originally the sole proprietor.

In March of 1974, the Plaintiff and Defendant reached an oral agreement concerning the business, the exact terms of which were the subject of conflicting testimony at trial. The Plaintiff, who had prior experience in the restaurant business, testified that she and the Defendant agreed to be equal partners in the restaurant and that, in consideration of certain financial contributions she was to make to the business, the Defendant agreed to incorporate the business, turn those business assets to which he had title over to the corporation, and distribute stock to the Plaintiff and himself. It appears, however, that the Plaintiff did not expect the business to be incorporated until after she became involved in its operation.

The Defendant testified that he and the Plaintiff agreed to become partners and that in consideration for being made a partner, the Plaintiff initially contributed her automobile to the business. The Defendant's understanding of the agreement differed from the Plaintiff's, however, in that he did not recall promising to turn assets over to the corporation, or to have stock issued and distributed. Rather, his testimony suggests that the agreement contemplated that the Plaintiff would ultimately purchase the restaurant, thus leaving him "free and clear" of the business, a circumstance the Defendant desired for reasons of health and overwork. In response to questions posed by opposing counsel as to whether the Defendant agreed to transfer assets in his name to the corporation and distribute stock to the Plaintiff, the Defendant testified that he did not remember or understand that arrangement but thought the heart of the agreement to be the Plaintiff's ultimate purchase of the entire business.

After the agreement was made, the Defendant no longer took an active part in management of the restaurant; the Plaintiff, on the other hand, operated the business on a day-to-day basis for several months. In the months that she managed the restaurant, the Plaintiff made major financial contributions to the business totalling $18,214.89. She made these contributions by directly paying the debts and operating expenses of the business. The Defendant testified that he had no knowledge of the nature or extent of her payments on behalf of the business and that he never personally received them.

Under the Plaintiff's management, business income declined dramatically. After operating the business for several months, the Plaintiff finally asked the Defendant to distribute the stock and transfer the assets. The record does not disclose whether the business was ever incorporated. Stock, however, was never distributed, and the Defendant's testimony suggests that ownership of business-related assets was never transferred to a corporation. Instead, a closing date for sale of the restaurant to the Plaintiff was set. On the advice of her attorneys, however, she ultimately refused to purchase the business from the Defendant and he eventually closed the business when its management totally failed. Thereafter, he made several attempts to lease profitably the business and finally sold it to a lessee. The proceeds from the sale, according to the Defendant's testimony, were used to pay mortgagees and creditors whose claims apparently exceeded the gain from the sale. The Defendant claims to have paid the balance out of personal funds.

At trial, after testimony by the two parties was heard, the presiding justice found for the Defendant. The justice specifically found that the parties were partners and that their original agreement created a partnership. From that finding, he concluded that neither party had a cause of action for restitution or conversion. In response to the request of the Plaintiff's counsel for a specific finding on whether an agreement existed between the parties in which the Defendant was obliged to transfer assets to the corporation and distribute stock, the court declined to rule on the specifics of any such agreement. Rather, the court limited its ruling to finding generally that a partnership agreement existed and that any controversy over the business arising out of the partnership was properly the subject of an action for an accounting between partners.

On appeal here, the Plaintiff contends the Superior Court erred in finding a partnership and in concluding that an action for conversion or money had and received was inappropriate.

We must uphold the Superior Court's conclusion that a partnership existed if competent evidence exists on the record to support that legal conclusion.

The Plaintiff argues that the Superior Court erred in concluding a partnership existed because no evidence of co-ownership or sharing of profits appears on the record.

Under the Uniform Partnership Act, which Maine adopted in 1973, as under the common law, the existence of a partnership is an inference of law based on established facts. Under the Act, a partnership is defined as "an association of 2 or more persons to carry on as co-owners a business for profit" [UPA § 6].

Evidence relevant to the existence of a partnership includes evidence of a voluntary contract between two persons to place their money, effects, labor, and skill, or some or all of them, in lawful commerce or business with the understanding that a community of profits will be shared. No one factor is alone determinative of the existence of a partnership, but the record before us supports the finding of the Superior Court.

While the specifics of the agreement were in dispute, evidence of an agreement between the parties existed. That agreement clearly related to operation of a business. Assets used in the business and capital contributions to the business were made by both parties. They consistently testified that both regarded themselves as partners. Finally, the Plaintiff actively managed the business for several months.

The Plaintiff contends, nevertheless, that there is no evidence of co-ownership or a sharing of profits. Under the Uniform Act, the concept of co-ownership does not necessarily mean joint title to all business assets. Rather, as the commentary to the Uniform Act suggests, the right to participate in control of the business is the essence of co-ownership. *See* Official Comment, UPA § 6.[1] Contrary to this Plaintiff's contention, then, the record sufficiently supports the existence of co-ownership inasmuch as it reveals that she actively managed the business for several months without the supervision of the Defendant. While the record is devoid of evidence that the parties shared profits, sharing is not required if, as the evidence shows in this case, the agreement itself implies that the parties contemplated the sharing of profits. In the case before us evidence of actual sharing of profits was naturally absent, given the financial straits of the business.

We conclude that the Superior Court did not err in concluding that Austin and Dalton were engaged in a partnership.

The Plaintiff also argues that the Defendant is liable to her for conversion under theories of unjust enrichment or quasi-contract. The record before us indicates that the basis of Plaintiff's claim is intimately related to partnership affairs. Moreover, the record is replete with confusion and ambiguity concerning the winding up of the partnership as well as the manner in which the partnership property was ultimately liquidated. These circumstances both suggest the prudence of settling the dispute between these two litigants in one comprehensive proceeding for an account and provide adequate support for the finding below that an independent action was inappropriate.

We conclude that there was no error when the Superior Court entered judgment for the Defendant.

---

1. The draftsman of the Model Act noted in the Comment following section 6:

> The definition asserts that the associates are "co-owners" of the business. This distinguishes a partnership from an agency—an association of principal and agent. A business is a series of acts directed toward an end. Ownership involves the power of ultimate control. To state that partners are co-owners of a business is to state that they each have the power of ultimate control.

Chariton Feed & Grain, Inc. v. Harder

369 N.W.2d 777 (Iowa 1985)

REYNOLDSON, Chief Justice.

We granted further review in this appeal to determine whether trial court erred in holding a landlord under the usual stock-share lease liable to a livestock feed supplier on the theories of partnership, agency and unjust enrichment. The court of appeals split three to three, hence the trial court's decision stood affirmed by operation of law.

Most of the facts developed at trial were undisputed. Defendant Isaac Harder, employed as an engineer in a Texas aircraft factory, purchased a 308-acre Marion County farm on contract in 1974. For reasons detailed later, it was unfortunate that he executed a routine fifty-fifty crop-share lease with defendant Carl Davidson,[2] to commence March 1, 1977. It was still more unfortunate that he executed a stock-share lease with Davidson for a term commencing March 1, 1978. As it turned out, the most Harder received for a $30,000 payment to Davidson for livestock was, according to Davidson, "maybe a few sheep."

There seems to be no dispute that the stock-share lease was prepared by Davidson, or by someone else at his direction. Although inartfully drawn in some respects, it appears to be the ordinary farm lease commonly employed in Iowa for situations in which the landlord and tenant share interests and expenses not only in the crops but also in the livestock. The instrument was entitled "Farm Lease," and consistently referred to the parties as "Landlord" and "Tenant." The tenant was to pay the landlord "½ of the receipts from all farm products sold." There is an itemization of the expenses to be shared, including feed. Other identified expenses were to be the separate obligations of the landlord and of the tenant. Especially relevant to the issues in this appeal are two paragraphs of the lease:

> 11. The Tenant shall have full management control, including but not limited to, when to sell the goods, where to sell the goods, to whom to sell the goods, what feed to buy, where to buy the feed, and how much feed to buy.
>
> 12. Tenant shall use the proper farming methods in the management of said farm.

No joint bank account was established. This left the problem of when and in what manner Harder was to pay his share of the joint expenses. Consistent with his contractual management role, Davidson bought feed from various firms. There is no evidence Harder ever exercised any control over where the feed was purchased, the amount, or the price. He did receive some of the bills and part of the time these accounts were placed in Harder's name. Sometimes Harder sent the feed expense money to Davidson, sometimes directly to the seller. Later, and long before any of the feed involved in this controversy was sold, Davidson—again exercising his contractual right to manage the operation—unilaterally started to purchase all feed in his own name and thereafter sought reimbursement from Harder for one-half. Davidson testified the parties understood that he was then going to take the responsibility for paying the feed bills.

---

2. Davidson's wife and business entity also were named defendants. For simplicity, we shall refer to them as "Davidson."

The feed furnished by plaintiff Chariton Feed and Grain, Inc. (Chariton Feed), was fed to livestock in which Harder thought he had a one-half interest but which, in fact, Davidson brought to the farm through leases and other arrangements with third parties. On the occasions when Harder visited the farm he always was led to believe all the livestock he saw there was subject to the stock-share lease arrangement. There is no dispute that Davidson consistently lied to and misled Harder, and the stock-share lease agreement never functioned as contemplated by the written agreement. Harder lived in Texas and traveled about 750 to 800 miles to Iowa once or twice a year, when, of course, he would check on his substantial farm investment. At intervals Davidson sent him reports and accounts, usually showing expenses that exceeded the receipts. Davidson could not remember sending Harder any money.

The feed Davidson purchased from Chariton Feed was purchased in his own name during the period May 18, 1979 to June 21, 1980. The payments Davidson did make were on his personal checks, variously styled "Davidson's Holstein and Angus Farms" and "3-D Farms" (after his wife's name, Dorothy Darlene Davidson). Paul Umbenhower, manager and owner of Chariton Feed, testified Davidson led him to believe that he, Davidson, owned all the cattle on the Harder farm. The account was in Davidson's name alone. Umbenhower looked to Davidson alone for payment. There is no evidence Chariton Feed had any knowledge of an alleged interest of Harder in the livestock until all the feed had been purchased and Davidson was being pursued for payment.

In January 1981 Umbenhower placed a telephone call to Harder in Texas. The former testified at trial that, "I asked Mr. Harder if he was the one that was in partnership with Mr. Carl Davidson and he said, yes, he was." Harder denied he ever indicated to anyone he was a partner of Davidson in the farming operation. He testified concerning this conversation:

> Q. All right. Just tell us as best you recall what he said to you and what you said to him.
>
> A. He asked me if I owned half the cattle up in Iowa and at the time I thought I did and I did say, "Yes." Then he said that Carl had been charging feed to him and he owed a bill.
>
> Now, I don't remember whether he even told me the size and then he said that, you know, he never indicated I owed anything, didn't even ask me that. But he said he was going to take some action against Carl and I am sure I said, "Okay."

Trial court adopted Umbenhower's version of this conversation. The court further found that Harder in this telephone exchange "admitted liability for the feed purchased on account by Davidson from Chariton Feed & Grain, Inc." Even Chariton Feed does not contend there was any evidence to support the latter finding.

Both Davidson and Harder testified that in making their second agreement they intended to make a stock-share lease, not a partnership. There is a substantial question left by this record whether Davidson even intended to comply with a stock-share lease. Further evidence of Davidson's actual and fraudulent intent during his association with Harder was supplied through the testimony of John Jensen, county supervisor for the Farmers Home Administration (F.H.A.) in Marion County. Davidson sought an operating loan from F.H.A. in February 1979. He presented Jensen with a crop-share lease upon which Harder's name had been forged, and claimed to own all the livestock on the farm.

The record reflects that at least by the fall of 1980 Davidson was in deep financial trouble, and his creditors, including Chariton Feed, were closing in. He sold numerous cattle belonging to other people. Before or during January 1981, Davidson abandoned the farm and any agreement he had with Harder was terminated.

It was at this point that Harder, seeking to salvage something, authorized his brother-in-law, who lived in Knoxville, to pick up and sell some of the stock remaining on the farm. On January 19, 1981, several butcher hogs and small pigs were sold at public auction for $1768.69 in Harder's name. An attempt on January 20, 1981, to sell 50 stock cows in which Harder thought he owned an interest was aborted when a third party claimed them. By January 24, 1981, the sheriff was on the farm with F.H.A.'s Jensen, Harder and several third persons. When various owners finished claiming their livestock, thirteen dairy cows remained. These were sold and F.H.A. paid Harder one-half of the proceeds.

The court, proceeding for the most part from the above facts, concluded a partnership existed. In reaching this determination it may not have had the benefit of several Iowa decisions because, as the trial ended, the court advised counsel that, "rather than to have you submit any briefs—and I think it is a question of law—I think I will ask the same effort that would go into preparing briefs go into preparation of proposed Findings and Conclusions." The court also found Harder liable on the basis of agency, and on the ground of "unjust enrichment or quantum meruit."

Iowa decisions have treated these livestock-share leases as *sui generis*, and generally hold they are leases and not partnerships in the absence of stipulations or evidence clearly manifesting a contrary purpose. Our view that the lease in issue is the sort of ordinary farm lease commonly seen in Iowa is supported in this record by F.H.A.'s Jensen, who testified such stock-share leases are more common in Marion County than crop-share leases. Thus we reexamine our long-standing common law with a careful concern for the impact on the great number of Iowans who will be affected.

Narrowing our focus to the first issue before us, what constitutes a partnership and whether a written instrument creates a partnership is a question of law for the court. *Florence v. Fox*, 193 Iowa 1174, 1178, 188 N.W.966, 967 (1922) ("[T]he construction of the contract was a question of law for the court, and it was for the court to determine whether it constituted a partnership contract, and was so intended by the parties."). If the facts are undisputed, it is for the judge to decide whether a partnership exists. Thus our analysis of this question should address the following subsumed issues:

(1) Does the written agreement between Harder and Davidson establish the elements essential to the creation of a partnership? This is a question of law and trial court's determination is not binding on us.

(2) Did Harder and Davidson conduct themselves as though they considered themselves a partnership, thereby supplying the essential elements of a partnership? This is a question of fact only if there is a dispute whether certain events occurred or if different inferences may be drawn from acts the parties agree occurred. If there are disputed facts in this case, then the issue becomes whether the facts, as found by

the trial court, constitute substantial evidence that the parties conducted themselves as partners.

In applying the above principles to these issues, however, due regard should be given to our historic treatment of these agricultural leases. We have held that it will not be presumed that the parties to such leases intended a partnership, in the absence of stipulations or evidence clearly manifesting such a purpose.

A leading Iowa decision is *Fox*. There the landlord provided the cows and was to receive one-half the milk and cream. Each party was to provide hogs, "share and share alike," and share in their increase. Each party was to own one-half the grain grown on the 120 acres leased. The parties were to share expenses of threshing and board of help, and both were to be informed of and have equal rights in the sale of stock and purchases of "stuff" for the farm. The court found the parties to stand in a tenant-landlord relationship, not a partnership. The court relied heavily upon the intention of the parties as expressed in the contract. The *Fox* court provided the public policy underlying its decision:

> If a partnership existed, it might be possible for the tenant, within the scope of the partnership, to purchase property and make the owner of the land responsible therefor in an amount largely in excess of the rent, and each might be responsible for the torts of the other committed within the scope of the agency. The courts hold quite generally that there are obvious reasons for holding that farm contracts or agricultural agreements, by which the owner of land contracts with another that such land shall be occupied and cultivated by the latter, each party furnishing a certain portion of the seed, implements, *and stock*, and that the products shall be divided at the end of a given term, or sold and the proceeds divided, shall not be construed as creating a partnership between the parties. Such agreements are common in this country, and are usually informal in their character, often resting in parol. In the *absence of stipulations or evidence clearly manifesting a contrary purpose, it will not be presumed that the parties to such an agreement intended to assume the important and intricate responsibility of partners, or to incur the inconveniences and dangers frequently incident to that relation.*

(Emphasis added.) *See Wilson v. Fleming*, 239 Iowa 718, 733, 31 N.W.2d 393, 401 (1948) (Agreement determined to be a stock-share lease, the court noting "[c]ourts are reluctant to construe an arrangement such as this between a farm owner and occupant as a partnership unless such relation is clearly shown.").

The only decision relating to leases from any jurisdiction found in trial court's decision is *Malvern Nat'l Bank v. Halliday*, 195 Iowa 734, 192 N.W. 843 (1923). In that case *both* the landlord and the tenant argued *in favor* of a finding of partnership. The written agreement referred frequently to "the firm." Of similar limited value here is the holding in *Miller v. Merritt*, 233 Iowa 230, 8 N.W.2d 726 (1943). The *Miller* agreement provided the business should be in the name of "Miller and Merritt Bros."; all receipts and disbursements should be made through a joint bank account in the name of Miller and Merritt; and both parties would cooperate fully in managing the "firm." The agreement contained copious references to "the firm," "partnership property" and "firm property." Quite predictably, the court found the arrangement to be a partnership, relying heavily on the intention of the parties.

Neither *Halliday* nor *Miller* modify our basic principle that a stock-share lease is not to be construed as a partnership in absence of clear evidence that the parties intended to create a partnership. It is noteworthy that in the Iowa decisions confronting the lease vis-a-vis partnership issue, this court has found the relationship between the parties to be a partnership only where the parties themselves expressly described their arrangement in those terms. The public policy articulated in *Fox*, quoted above, is supported in decisions from other jurisdictions including *Shrum v. Simpson*, 155 Ind. 160, 163, 57 N.E. 708, 709 (1900):

> There are obvious reasons for holding that farm contracts or agricultural agreements, by which the owner of land contracts with another that such lands shall be occupied and cultivated by the latter, each party furnishing a certain proportion of the seed, implements, and stock, and that the products shall be divided at the end of a given term, or sold and the proceeds divided, shall not be construed as creating a partnership between the parties. The parties to such agreements seldom contemplate anything more than a tenancy of the land, with provision for compensation to the landlord from the delity, labor, and skill of the tenant. There is no community of interest in the land, which is the principal thing in the agreement, and a division and several ownership of the crops and other products are usually provided for. While the custom of renting farm lands upon shares is general, the courts have seldom held that such agreements create partnerships between the owner of the land and the tenant.

As *Fox* and *Shrum* make clear, construing what essentially is a lease arrangement as a partnership exposes the parties to unwarranted and unexpected liability for conduct that he or she ordinarily is powerless to control or direct. The case before us is a vivid example. The $26,166.32 judgment charged against Harder could be only the beginning of successive judgments in favor of livestock owners and others Davidson defrauded, all without the knowledge of the unsuspecting Harder. Meanwhile, Davidson has insulated himself from liability by taking bankruptcy.

Against the backdrop of the above cases, we return to the two subsumed issues above identi ed.

Partnership Issue—The Written Agreement

The construction of a written contract, as already noted, is a question of law for the court. In construction of written contracts, the cardinal principle is that the intent of the parties must control; and except in cases of ambiguity, this is determined by what the contract itself says. An examination of the contract (exhibit two) in this case discloses that on its face it is the common stock-share lease. The elements of the landlord and tenant relationship are all patently present. Trial court makes no de nitive nding that exhibit two, on its face, is a partnership and not a lease. Nonetheless, our review relating to this law issue requires examination of this "Farm Lease" to determine whether it exhibits the elements required to create a partnership. These are (1) an association, i.e., an intent by the parties to associate as partners; (2) a business; (3) earning of pro ts; and (4) co-ownership of pro ts, property and control.

A. Intent to Associate.

In Iowa, intention to associate is "the crucial test" of partnership. Exhibit two shows no intent by the parties to associate as partners. On the contrary, it recites an express intention to create the relationship of landlord-tenant. The words "partner," "partnership," " rm," or any other term usually deemed to show such an intent to form a partnership appear nowhere in the document. On the other hand, the agreement is entitled "Farm Lease." The word "Landlord" is used sixteen times; the word "Tenant" twenty times. The parties are identi ed in no other way. Such language, employed by the parties in their contract, is important in discerning their intent.

B. A Business.

It is clear from exhibit two that the parties had a business purpose, as opposed to a patriotic, civic, religious, sports, or similar non-business purpose.

C. Earnings of Profits.

For the purposes of this analysis, this element adds nothing other than to reinforce the "business" requirement mentioned in the last paragraph.

D. Co-Ownership of Profits, Property and Control.

1. *Profits.*

Exhibit two contains no provision for the sharing of pro ts by Harder and Davidson. In paragraph two the lease requires that "[t]he Tenant shall pay to the Landlord ½ of the *receipts* from all farm products sold" (emphasis added). Paragraph four provides for the sharing of certain expenses. Reading these two provisions together, trial court inferred an agreement to share pro ts. This inference was the sole basis for the court's nding that the parties had a "community of interest" in pro ts.

Trial court's approach, of course, does not account for the requirement in the lease that each party individually assume certain expenses, which resulted in each showing a different level of pro t or loss generated out of the farm operation. For example, Harder's 1979 tax return disclosed a substantial farm loss; Davidson's a pro t of over $36,000.[3] Obviously, pro t and loss under this agreement could not be determined until each party deducted from his share of the gross receipts the expenses for which he individually was responsible. Thus, under exhibit two, Harder and Davidson did not "share pro ts."

Nor does exhibit two provide for the sharing of losses. Trial court inferred this, based upon the requirement that the parties share certain of the expenses, citing as authority 68 C.J.S. *Partnership* § 29(b)(2). The Iowa rule, however, is not the general rule stated in C.J.S. Our cases are in some disarray on this point, but stated most favorably to Chariton Feed, the Iowa rule is that an agreement to share losses may be inferred only where the partnership is established by other evidence.

Addressing the question of pro ts, trial court stated that "[i]n reaching its conclusion as to the existence of a partnership, the court notes [UPA Section 7(4)(b)] provides that the receipt by a person of a share of the pro ts of a business is prima facie evidence that he is a partner in the business." This conclusion does not take into account [UPA section 7(3)]:

> The sharing of gross returns does not of itself establish a partnership, whether or not the persons sharing them have a joint or common right or interest in any property from which the returns are derived.

Further, the statute referred to by trial court actually carries its own exception that further excludes this situation:

---

3. No partnership [tax] returns were led.

> The receipt by a person of a share of the profits of a business is prima-facie evidence that the person is a partner in the business, but no such inference shall be drawn if such profits were received in payment:
>
> b. As rent to a landlord.

[UPA § 7(4)(b)].

2. *Property.*

Exhibit two contemplated co-ownership of only part of the property used in the livestock operation, being the livestock and feeding equipment. That of course does not, of itself, establish a partnership.

3. *Control.*

Co-ownership of control, or a community of interest in the administration of the business, is a key element in determining the existence of a partnership.

Although obviously inartfully drawn, we find no ambiguity in the language of this "Farm Lease." Assuming trial court found it established a partnership we cannot agree with its conclusion of law. There remain for our review trial court's findings relating to the conduct of the parties, and its conclusion the parties created a partnership by their acts.

Partnership Issue—Conduct of the Parties

A. Intent to Associate.

We have noted that in Iowa the intent of the parties to associate as partners is "the crucial test." *Fox*, 193 Iowa at 1178. This is the most widely accepted test for determining whether a partnership exists.

At the outset we observe that if these parties had the intent to associate as partners, it was remarkable that no indication of that intent was included in the lease the parties signed to memorialize their agreement. A partnership can be formed only upon mutual consent of the parties and a meeting of the minds; the intention of one party alone cannot create the relation. It is clear that from the outset Davidson did not even intend to comply with the lease, let alone an unexpressed partnership understanding. The fact findings trial court adopted do not take into account Davidson's intent. A conclusion that Harder intended to associate as a partner is based upon two findings. The first was the court's selection of Umbenhower's version of the telephone call to Texas, rather than Harder's. In this version the latter, following all the relevant events, allegedly responded in the affirmative when asked if he was in partnership with Davidson. The second was Harder's efforts to sell livestock from the farm after Davidson had left the farm and their relationship had terminated. Trial court concluded "such control shows Harder believed himself to be more than a one-half owner of the livestock and a mere landlord."

Trial court's finding that Harder responded in the affirmative to the inquiry relating to a partnership is entitled to little weight on the scale of substantial evidence. Even in written instruments, the general rule is that "laymen misuse legal terms, and the fact they call each other partners is not conclusive if the essential elements of partnership are lacking in their relationship." When a party refers to himself or herself as a partner in the course of a conversation, courts are very reluctant to give the statement any weight at all.

Of similar inconsequential weight were Harder's desperate acts with respect to the livestock in which he thought he had an interest after Davidson departed the scene. No matter what arrangement Harder and Davidson had, the record af rmatively shows it had terminated at that point. Thus Harder's acts could neither be considered in furtherance of, nor in conformance with, a partnership association.

B. A Business.

There is no issue concerning this element, as it related to the acts of the parties.

C. Earnings of Profits.

Similarly, there is no issue relating to this element.

D. Co-Ownership of Profits, Property and Control.

1. *Profits.*

Trial court's decision reveals no nding that the parties, by their behavior, indicated an intention to share pro ts. Certainly the distinction between a contemplated sharing of gross receipts and a sharing of pro ts is commonly drawn and recognized as valid. [UPA § 7(3)].

2. *Property.*

Although the farm lease clearly provided for co-ownership of certain livestock and feeding equipment, Davidson's maneuvers largely avoided even this limited requirement. Trial testimony was undisputed that, as a result of Davidson's duplicity, Harder in fact never owned a one-half interest in livestock "other than a few sheep."

It is also important that the major assets utilized in this association—the real estate owned by Harder and the machinery owned by Davidson—were and remained the separate assets of the parties.

3. *Control.*

The main battleground at trial was the attempt to show that Harder, despite the lease provisions, exercised the requisite control of the business. Typically, testimony on this topic "concerns who gave instructions, hired and red employees, had the say on how money was spent, or made important business decisions. If one participated to a signi cant degree in these functions, he had suf cient control. If he did not, the normal result is no partnership." Crane and Bromberg § 14(d). The search for objective evidence of joint control of the business usually focuses on acts such as holding licenses, assuming a rm name, keeping books that show a capital account for each party, or ling federal partnership tax returns. None of these indicia, of course, were present here. Signi cantly, Kevin Sharp, the farmhand who helped Davidson, testi ed that he was Davidson's employee and had never met Harder.

Trial court relied on the following ndings in concluding Harder had the requisite control of the operations: feed accounts during an early period were put in Harder's name, thus enabling him to close the accounts had he become dissatis ed with the amount of feed or its cost; the parties corresponded or talked by telephone about once a month; Harder periodically visited the farm; Davidson furnished Harder a monthly accounting; and Harder sold hogs in his own name following Davidson's departure.

We already have discussed the feed account evidence. Had there been a joint bank account—one of the indicia of a partnership—other arrangements for Harder to pay the very substantial amounts Davidson was incurring in feeding other persons' livestock would have been unnecessary. As it happened, these bills, for a time, and some of Harder's bills for his separate expenses for building repair and improvement over a longer period of time, were sent directly to him. There was no modification of Davidson's right under the lease, to have sole control of "what feed to buy, where to buy the feed, and how much feed to buy," and there was undisputed evidence he consistently exercised that right. There is an inference Davidson thought Harder might be able to track his activities, thus causing Davidson to unilaterally terminate this procedure. Subsequently, Davidson purported to deduct Harder's share of the feed against milk and livestock sales, which Davidson of course received and controlled.

Regarding the telephone calls between Davidson and Harder, there again was no evidence Harder exercised or sought to exercise any control over the farming operations. When asked what was discussed during the telephone visits, Davidson testified:

> A. Sometimes he just wanted to know how things was at the farm weather-wise, crop-wise; a lot of times my wife's health.
>
> Q. Did he ever ask you anything about the livestock operation? A. Sometimes he might ask me how they was doing when I had some ready to go.

Harder's testimony was this:

> Q. And did you ever talk to him about it on the telephone like how do things look out on the farm or whatever? A. In maybe general appearance. You know, like I would ask Carl the same thing, like how do things look.

Harder obviously had a considerable stake in the Iowa farm and its improvements, in addition to the $30,000 he spent for the illusory livestock. It is understandable that he was interested in the progress of his investment, but there is nothing in the above evidence from which it could be concluded he was exercising any control. This is also the rational explanation for the once-or-twice-per-year visits Harder made to Iowa, where he also had relatives.

We already have discussed Harder's conduct with respect to the livestock after the lease terminated. There remains the "monthly" accounting that Davidson erratically sent Harder. Such accountings are not unusual in share lease arrangements, and do not signal an attempt to control the operation. Milk proceeds were received every month. Obviously the parties concluded Harder would receive his rent monthly, in the form of receipts, less joint expenses. That this apparently generated no money to Harder is not controlling on the issue under consideration. Harder was obligated to itemize and show his share of receipts and expenses on his income tax return, and required the information supplied by the "accounting." Again, there is no indication in the record Harder exercised control upon the basis of the information thus furnished.

None of the evidence, taken together, supplied substantial evidence for the court's conclusions that Harder exercised control of the farm operation or that the conduct of the parties disclosed their intent to associate as partners.

Finally, Chariton Feed concedes the weakness of its contentions when it states in its brief:

> The trial court undertook to decide the issue of the existence of a partnership, as to the Plaintiff [Chariton Feed] and Defendant [Harder], and did not purport to find whether the Defendant and Davidson were partners as to each other, since that issue was not before the trial court.

[UPA section 7(1)], however, expressly provides:

> Except as provided by [UPA section 16], persons who are not partners as to each other are not partners as to third persons.

[UPA section 16], referred to in the statute just quoted, concerns the situation in which a person is made liable by estoppel. That statute, of course, has no application here because Chariton Feed concedes it did not even know of the stock-share lease, let alone an alleged partnership, when it extended credit to Davidson for feed.

In summary, we hold trial court erred in concluding, if in fact it did, the written agreement between Harder and Davidson created a partnership. Similarly, we hold trial court's conclusion that Harder's conduct[5] otherwise furnished the requisite proof of the existence of a partnership was not supported by substantial evidence.

We vacate the court of appeals disposition, reverse the district court judgment and remand for judgment for defendant Harder.

P & M Cattle Co. v. Holler

559 P.2d 1019 (Wyo. 1977)

RAPER, Justice.

In the district court, the plaintiff-appellant, a partnership, sought and was denied recovery for losses incurred in 1974 under an alleged 'oral joint venture agreement' to purchase, lease and sell livestock.

[T]he only real issue is whether the parties to this appeal were parties to a joint venture or partnership agreement to share losses as well as profits from a cattle purchase, feed and sell operation.

In 1971, the defendant was looking for someone to pasture cattle on the defendant's land at $3.00 per head per month. One of two partners in the plaintiff partnership expressed an interest and invited defendant to talk. As a result, the following written agreement was entered into:

> 2-23-1971
>
> Contract—Rusty Holler (60 Bar Ranch) L. W. Maxfield and Bill Poage
>
> Rusty to furnish grass for est 100 yr st and 21 heifers—
>
> Maxfield & Poage to furnish money for cattle plus trucking & salt—and max of $300.00 per month for labor
>
> Rusty to take cattle around May 1st and cattle to be sold at a time this fall agreed upon by all parties involved
>
> Cost of cattle plus freight—salt and labor to be first cost
>
> Net money from sale of cattle less first cost to be split 50-50 between Rusty (½) and Maxfield and Poage (½) (death loss to be part of first cost)
>
> /s/ L. W. Maxfield
> /s/ Bill Poage
> LM
> /s/ Rusty Holler

---

5. Reference to any conduct of Davidson that would establish the existence of a partnership is conspicuously absent from the court's decision and from Chariton Feed's brief. Clearly, he was operating solely in his own behalf and had no intention to associate as a partner.

The 1971 agreement was orally renewed for the years 1972, 1973 and 1974. Plaintiff and defendant each realized substantial returns in the first three years but in 1974 there was not enough realized from the sale of cattle to pay first costs and a loss resulted. Plaintiff insists that the defendant is bound to pay it $44,500.00 representing one-half of the total cash loss in the sum of $89,000.00. The defendant personally expended first costs for expenses (salt) over and above the amount received from sale of cattle in sum of $3,967.76. Through an admitted error of defendant's counsel, along with a misunderstanding by defendant, only one-half of those expenses were claimed by defendant. When the error became apparent at or near the close of evidence, they elected not to amend the defendant's claim first made. The contract clearly states that plaintiff was to "furnish money for salt."

The parties never discussed nor is there any mention in the contract of what would happen if the cattle sold at a loss. Nor was any mention made of reimbursement or credit to the defendant for the value of his services and pasture or grass he contributed, in the event cattle sold at a loss.

A broad overview of the entire record suggests that this case involves only a contract in which plaintiff agreed to put up the money and defendant agreed to put up grazing land and grass, along with services, with a view to profit to both, each to bear their own losses. Before confirming that position, we must examine the law of joint ventures.

In Wyoming, a joint adventure partakes of the nature of a partnership and is governed substantially by the same rules of law, the principal distinction being that a joint adventure usually relates to a single transaction, though it may be continued over a period of years. Even though a joint adventure and a partnership are not identical, the relationship of co-adventurers is controlled largely by the law of partnership. A concise distinction between joint venture and partnership is drawn in 1 Cavitch, Business Organizations, s 13.05(2), pp. 677-678:

> It is apparent that the comparatively modern legal concept of joint adventure is intended to identify business ventures which, but for their limited scope and duration, would be partnerships. To date, however, there is no discernible legal difference between the two types of associations. As a result, the courts have held that the joint adventure is subject to the same rules of law which are applied to partnerships, especially when determining the rights of the parties *inter se*.

Since joint adventures, also frequently referred to as joint ventures, are a species of and governed by the law of partnerships, we must go to the Uniform Partnership Act. [UPA section 6] defines a partnership as follows: 'A partnership is an association of two or more persons to carry on as *co-owners* a business for profit.' (Emphasis added.) [UPA section 7] lays out the criteria for resolving the question as to whether a partnership obtains:

> In determining whether a partnership exists, these rules shall apply:
>
> (1) Except as provided by section 16 persons who are not partners as to each other are not partners as to third persons;
>
> (2) Joint tenancy, tenancy in common, tenancy by the entireties, joint property, common property, or part ownership does not of itself establish a partnership, whether such co-owners do or do not share any profits made by the use of the property;

(3) The sharing of gross returns does not of itself establish a partnership, whether or not the person sharing them have a joint or common right or interest in any property from which the returns are derived;

(4) The receipt by a person of a share of the profits of a business is prima facie evidence that he is a partner in the business, but no such inference shall be drawn if such profits were received in payment:

(a) As a debt by installments or otherwise,

(b) As wages of an employee or rent to a landlord,

(c) As an annuity to a widow or representative of a deceased partner,

(d) As an interest on a loan, though the amount of payment vary with the profits of the business,

(e) As the consideration for the sale of the good-will of a business or other property by installments or otherwise.

(Emphasis added.) As can be seen, an agreement to share profits is far from decisive that a partnership is intended.

As in any contractual relationship, the intent of the parties is controlling. The parties must intend to create the relationship of joint adventure or partnership. Superimposed upon the rule of intent, it is frequently held that where there is no express agreement to form a partnership, the question of whether such a relation exists must be gathered from the conduct, surrounding circumstances and the transactions between the parties. There is no automatic solution to the question of the existence of a partnership but it turns upon the facts and circumstances of association between the parties. No single fact may be stated as the complete and final test of a partnership. Even a written agreement, designating the parties as partners and providing for a sharing of the profits, is only evidential and not conclusive of the existence of a partnership.

In the case before us there was no express agreement to form a partnership. True, there was an agreement but nowhere in that document is there anywhere mentioned the term partnership. Nor is there anywhere mentioned any sharing of losses, which is normally concomitant with a sharing of profits in a partnership.[3] While [UPA section 7(4)] creates an inference, that inference is not conclusive.

We find in Wyoming two cases which reflect the usual holdings that division of profits has little significance by itself. In *Dunn v. Gilbert*, 1927, 36 Wyo. 249, 254 P. 121, it was held that the use of the expression 'fifty-fifty' and an understanding to split the profits do not necessarily mean a joint adventure but such expression must be construed in the light of surrounding facts and circumstances. In *State v. Bemis*, 1926, 34 Wyo. 218, 241, 242 P. 802, 809, the principal witness put up the money to

3. [UPA section 18] sets out a rule allowing for contribution to pay losses:

The rights and duties of the partners in relation to the partnership shall be determined, subject to any agreement between them, by the following rules:

(a) Each partner shall be repaid his contributions, whether by way of capital or advances to the partnership property and share equally in the profits and [surplus] remaining after all liabilities, including those to partners, are satisfied; and must contribute towards the losses, whether of capital or otherwise, sustained by the partnership according to his share in the profits. (Emphasis added.)

buy and pay shipping costs of a carload of apples. The defendant was to share in the profits by arranging their sale. They sold at a loss and defendant kept all the money. In a prosecution for embezzlement, the defendant claimed a right to retain the funds by reason of a partnership. This court spoke approvingly of the principle that when a business is limited to a single venture, there must be pretty clear evidence of an intent to create a partnership relationship and an understanding for division of profits may only be considered in connection with the whole transaction.

Since we cannot look at the face of the instrument here and determine whether there is a partnership, it is necessary that we examine into the complete relationship between plaintiff and defendant. We can in such a circumstance go outside its four corners to test the claim of a would-be partner and look at what the parties did and how they treated the arrangement between them. The contemporary construction of a contract by acts of the parties is entitled to serious consideration by the court whose duty it becomes to determine its meaning. The reason for that view rests in the fact that the parties are less liable to have been mistaken as to the meaning of their contract while harmonious relations existed and during that period a practical and real construction would be in effect reflective of their true intentions and not interpretations ventured during the heat of litigation.

In the first place, the agreement is not labeled a 'partnership agreement' nor is the term 'partnership' anywhere mentioned within its terms. The plaintiff was itself a partnership made up of two ranchers well acquainted with that arrangement, one of whom drew the contract. From its inception, then, none of the parties ever identified it as such. The part was conceived in an atmosphere created by defendant's desire to sell grass. The division of losses was never discussed between the parties until the plaintiff delivered the bad news to the defendant following fall cattle sales in 1974. No partnership federal income tax return in any of the years 1971-74 was prepared and submitted to the Internal Revenue Service of the United States. On the income tax returns made by the plaintiff during the period in question, the part of profits paid to the defendant was carried as a business expense listed as 'contract feeding.' The defendant included such payments on his individual income tax return as a sale of 'crops,' nor were the cattle grazed on his place by the defendant carried on defendant's income tax return livestock inventory. The livestock were carried on plaintiffs' partnership income tax returns. On the check given by plaintiff to defendant in 1973, for defendant's share of profits at the end of the season, it was shown as being for 'pasture.'

Within the framework of the Uniform Partnership Act, we find rules available to the trial judge to determine that there was no partnership. The division of profits was only a measure—a standard of payment by plaintiff to defendant in discharge of a debt for services and grass under [UPA section 7(4)(a)] or in payment to defendant for wages of an employee in caring for the cattle while on his ranch and rent to him as landlord for his pasture under [UPA section 7(4)(b)] or sale of grass as personal property under [UPA section 7(4)(e)] or through a combination of those lettered subsections for wages and rent or sale of property. We need not determine precisely what it was as long as outside the pale of partnership. We are satisfied that no partnership was intended. The agreement was only an apparatus to pay defendant for his grass and services and we return to its terms after reconnoitering the outer regions.

Whether or not there is a joint venture is a question of fact and preeminently one for the finder of fact. The trial judge found for the defendant and we see substantial evidence to support that result.

Affirmed.

Notes

1. Why do *Dalton v. Austin* and *Chariton Feed & Grain, Inc. v. Harder* not base more of their analysis on UPA section 7?

2. Persons who are *not* partners often share profits. Several of these kinds of non-partnership profit-sharing relationships are listed under UPA section 7(4). Courts evaluating a profit-sharing relationship to determine if there is a partnership often look to see if the parties are "acting like partners"—sharing control and losses.

Commentators frequently criticize this approach, arguing first that sharing of control and losses is a *consequence* of being partners, and not a condition of partner status. *See* UPA §§ 18(a), 18(e). Second, partners may delegate management, or allocate responsibility for losses, without ceasing to be partners.

What other factors could a court use in trying to decide if a share of profits was received as a partner, or in some other capacity?

3. For the past few years, the National Conference of Commissioners on Uniform State Laws ("NCCUSL") has been drafting a Revised Uniform Partnership Act ("RUPA"). It is expected that the RUPA will be finally adopted by the NCCUSL during its annual meeting in August 1992. The equivalent of UPA sections 6 and 7 is found in RUPA section 201.

4. As indicated in *P & M Cattle Co. v. Holler*, a joint venture is similar to—"in the nature of"—a partnership, but is not, strictly speaking, a partnership. Nevertheless, many courts apply partnership law, including the UPA, to joint ventures.

The formal difference is that a joint venture is formed for the purpose of carrying on a single transaction, rather than a series of transactions—a business. The modern joint venture is frequently a business venture between corporations. Until recently, there was some doubt as to whether corporations had the power to enter into partnerships, as opposed to joint ventures. *See* A. BROMBERG & L. RIBSTEIN, BROMBERG & RIBSTEIN ON PARTNERSHIP 2:23-26 (1988). As a result, may so-called joint ventures in fact operate over extended periods, and are indistinguishable from partnerships.

The common law test for a joint venture requires (1) a community of interest, (2) an agreement to share profits as principals, (3) an agreement to share losses, costs, and expenses, and (4) mutual rights of control. *E.g.*, *Brown v. Cole*, 155 Tex. 624, 291 S.W.2d 704 (1956). Many courts are reluctant to find a joint venture unless *all* the elements are present. In *P & M Cattle Co. v. Holler*, the court indicated that where a "business" is limited to a single venture, a finding of "partnership" would require "pretty clear evidence of an intent to create a partnership relationship." Do such requirements make sense in the context of a joint venture? As to continuing partnerships?

B. Partnership By Estoppel

Marszalk v. Van Volkenburg

24 Wash. App. 646, 604 P.2d 501 (1979)

WILLIAMS, Judge.

This action was brought by Stanley and Gretchen Marszalk against Donald C. Van Volkenburg to recover damages for the defective design and construction of two combined residential and commercial structures built on Camano Island in Island County. In an amended complaint, Ermie Alburas, alleged to be a copartner of Van Volkenburg, and the alleged copartnership, Van Volkenburg-Alburas Architects, were joined as party-defendants on the claim for defective design. Alburas and the copartnership moved for partial summary judgment dismissing them from the case. The motion was granted and the cause was then tried to the court without a jury resulting in a judgment in favor of Marszalk against Van Volkenburg. This appeal by Marszalk challenges the partial summary judgment dismissing Alburas and the copartnership.

The uncontradicted evidence before the trial court at the time the summary judgment was granted was that in 1969, Van Volkenburg and Alburas became general partners to practice architecture under the name "Van Volkenburg and Alburas." In 1975, the parties agreed to go their separate ways except for projects involving previous clients or public works. This agreement is evidenced by a written memorandum prepared January 10, 1975, but signed in May or June of 1977. In addition, there is evidence in affidavit form from Van Volkenburg and Alburas and in records of account showing that the partnership was restricted to former clients and public work after January, 1975. On June 23, 1977, the two parties signed a formal "Dissolution of General Partnership Agreement."

From 1969 until the June 23, 1977 agreement of dissolution, the firm name of Van Volkenburg and Alburas was carried on the sign at each of the architect's offices and listed in the regular and classified sections of the telephone directory. Marszalk and Alburas never met and Marszalk did not know of the existence of Alburas until after this action was commenced.

Marszalk's principal contention is that Alburas is responsible for Van Volkenburg's negligent work because of [UPA section 13] which reads:

> Partnership bound by partner's wrongful act. Where, by any wrongful act or omission of any partner acting in the ordinary course of the business of the partnership or with the authority of his copartners, loss or injury is caused to any person, not being a partner in the partnership, or any penalty is incurred, the partnership is liable therefor to the same extent as the partner so acting or omitting to act.

A non-acting partner such as Alburas would be bound under the rules of agency, if the acting partner, Van Volkenburg in this case, was acting within the scope of the partnership business. [UPA § 9]. Under the undisputed facts before the court, Van Volkenburg's actions in designing the structures for Marszalk were not "in the ordinary course of the business of the partnership"; therefore, Alburas is not responsible unless he may be bound upon some other theory.

Marszalk contends that Alburas is responsible for the judgment because the firm name was carried on the office signs and was listed in the telephone directory. This argument might be persuasive if Marszalk had relied upon the exhibition of the firm name in those ways. The rule, stated in *Lowenstein v. Whitelaw*, 178 Wash. 428, 431, 34 P.2d 1108, 1109 (1934), is that:

> One is liable to third persons as a partner only when a partnership actually exists, or when, by his conduct, he is estopped from denying it.

Unfortunately for Marszalk, he did not know of any connection between Van Volkenburg and Alburas and, hence, there is no estoppel.

The judgment is affirmed.

DORE, Judge (concurring).

The sole issue involved in the subject case is whether or not the Marszalk project was a partnership project of Van Volkenburg and Alburas or the project of Architect Van Volkenburg, an independent architect.

A key document, designated Exhibit "B" and attached to one of the affidavits, provided as follows:

> January 10, 1975
>
> It is hereby mutually agreed as an amendment to our partnership agreement that from the above date only those projects involving previous clients and/or public work will be a part of the partnership. All other work will be done by the individual acquiring the work without compensation or responsibility to the partnership. The partnership group insurance is to be continued for the partnership as a part of this amendment. Any separate business of either partner, architectural or otherwise, shall not be a part of the amended partnership and therefore neither partner shall be held liable for the other's separate business ventures.
>
> /s/ Donald C. Van Volkenburg /s/ Ermie C. Alburas

If this amendment to the partnership agreement of the two architects Van Volkenburg and Alburas was in existence prior to Marszalk's retaining architect Van Volkenburg, it follows that the Marszalk architectural project was not a partnership project but the separate project of Van Volkenburg. Both architects in their affidavits and depositions testified that the above memorandum was agreed to prior to January 10, 1975. However, they both also agree that such memorandum was not signed until January 10, 1977. These statements seem to raise some question as to whether or not the memorandum was in effect prior to the Marszalk architectural project.

The architectural drawings of Van Volkenburg, prior to the agreement of January 10, 1975, identified the partnership as Van Volkenburg and Alburas, Architects. Architectural drawings subsequent to January 10, 1975 identified only the individual architect Van Volkenburg. In the subject case the Marszalk building project plans set forth a logo in large print across the face of the drawing as "Architect Donald C. Van Volkenburg, A.I.A." To me this is conclusive evidence that the partnership logo had been changed to the logo of the individual architect meaning Marszalk was not a previous client. Clearly Marszalk was a "new" client and was not included in the continuation of the partnership of Van Volkenburg and Alburas.

I agree with the majority that the trial court correctly dismissed Alburas as a party defendant.

Volkman v. DP Associates

48 N.C. App. 155, 268 S.E.2d 265 (1980)

Plaintiffs brought suit alleging that they entered into a contract with DP Associates for construction advice in building a residence and that the contract was breached with damages resulting to them. Plaintiffs brought suit against DP Associates, which they alleged was a partnership, David L. McNamee and Philip E. Carroll as individuals, who were alleged to be partners in DP Associates. Before any answers were filed, interrogatories were served on plaintiffs by defendant Carroll. These interrogatories sought information on what basis plaintiffs made their claim that Carroll was a partner with McNamee in DP Associates.

Plaintiffs answered defendants' interrogatories indicating the following. At an early meeting in 1976, McNamee informed Mr. Volkman, who was authorized to act for his wife, that "he either had just commenced business, or was going into business with Philip E. Carroll." Subsequently, Mr. Volkman received correspondence from McNamee on DP Associates letterhead, and he assumed the "DP" was derived from the given names of the individual defendants, David and Philip. Prior to the signing of the contract, McNamee introduced Carroll to Mr. Volkman at the DP Associates' office where Carroll said, "I hope we'll be working together." Carroll identified McNamee as the person primarily concerned with Volkman's business with DP Associates but that he would also be available.

Mr. and Mrs. Volkman reviewed the written contract in the DP Associates office on 21 January 1977 with McNamee. McNamee suggested it might be advantageous to use a straight contractor's form to clearly identify DP Associates as acting as virtual general contractor. He then left the room saying, "I will ask Phil," and when he returned, he said they would use the contract with initialed modifications. After the signing of the contract but before construction of the house began, Mr. Volkman was in the office of DP Associates and again saw and conversed with Carroll who said to him in the course of the conversation, "I am happy that we will be working with you." During construction, Mr. Volkman visited the office of DP Associates on numerous occasions and saw Carroll there. During one visit, he expressed concern about construction delays to Carroll, who told him not to worry because McNamee would take care of it. Mr. and Mrs. Volkman have no documents tending to show a partnership existed. All money was paid to DP Associates. They never saw Carroll on the construction site and knew of no other construction supervised by Carroll. They understood they were purchasing Carroll's services and construction expertise through DP Associates.

Carroll moved for summary judgment on the basis that the pleadings, affidavits and answers to interrogatories showed that Carroll was not a partner in DP Associates. An affidavit by McNamee supporting the motion for summary judgment states that McNamee is not and never has been in partnership with Carroll and that Carroll received no income, profits, salary or other remuneration from the Volkman job.

The trial court entered an order dismissing Carroll as a party defendant because no issue was raised as to whether Carroll was a partner in DP Associates. Plaintiffs appeal.

VAUGHN, Judge.

The question raised on this appeal is not whether plaintiffs proved that Carroll was a partner. That burden will be upon plaintiffs when they go to trial. The question is whether defendant carried his burden of showing there was no genuine issue as to whether Carroll was a partner. The answers to the interrogatories indicate that there is at least a question as to whether Carroll was a partner. If at trial plaintiffs are unable to prove a partnership in fact, they may be able to show that Carroll should be held as a partner by estoppel or under the agency theory of apparent authority.

The Uniform Partnership Act as adopted in this State provides that "[t]he law of estoppel shall apply." [UPA § 4(2).] The essentials of equitable estoppel or estoppel *in pais* are a representation, either by words or conduct, made to another, who reasonably believing the representation to be true, relies upon it, with the result that he changes his position to his detriment. "[I]t is essential that the party estopped shall have made a representation by words or acts and that someone shall have acted on the faith of this representation in such a way that he cannot without damage withdraw from the transaction." 2 Williston, Sales § 312 (rev. ed. 1948).

As well as making the "law of estoppel" expressly applicable to partnerships, the Uniform Partnership Act as adopted in this State sets forth in more detail the conditions for liability as a partner by estoppel in [UPA section 16] which provides:

> Partner by estoppel—(a) When a person, by words spoken or written, by conduct, or by contract, represents himself, or consents to another representing him to anyone, as a partner in an existing partnership or with one or more persons not actual partners, he is liable to any such person to whom such representation has been made, who has, on faith of such representation, given credit to the actual or apparent partnership, and if he has made such representation or consented to its being made in a public manner, he is liable to such person, whether the representation has or has not been made or communicated to such person so giving credit by or with the knowledge of the apparent partner making the representation or consenting to its being made.
>
> (1) When a partnership liability results, he is liable as though he were an actual member of the partnership.
>
> (2) When no partnership liability results, he is liable jointly with the other persons, if any, so consenting to the contract or representation as to incur liability, otherwise separately.

Liability by estoppel may result either from defendant Carroll's representation of himself as a partner "by words spoken or written" or "by conduct" or defendant Carroll's "consent" to such a representation by another. The pleadings and answers to interrogatories of Mr. and Mrs. Volkman indicate they may be able to show that Carroll by his oral statements to them and conduct in their presence and by his consent to the representations of McNamee to the Volkmans, some of which were in the presence of Carroll, represented himself as a partner and should be estopped to deny such association. They may be able to show further they relied upon these representations not knowing them to be false and that based upon the representations of Carroll and McNamee, the Volkmans changed their position and were thereby damaged. Defendant has failed to show that there can be no question of fact on the issue of partnership by estoppel.

In addition to an estoppel theory of liability, Carroll may be liable under apparent or ostensible authority, a theory of agency law applicable to partnerships. [UPA § 4(3).] There is virtually no difference between estoppel and apparent authority. Both depend on reliance by a third person on a communication from the principal to the extent that the difference may be merely semantic. Despite its title, "Partner by Estoppel," [UPA section 16] "provides for a form of liability more akin to that of apparent authority than to estoppel." Painter, *Partnership by Estoppel*, 16 Vand. L.J. 327, 347 (1963). If this view is taken, the liability of the person seeking to deny partner status is not based on estoppel to deny agency or authority but on the objective theory of contract law, *i.e.*, a person should be bound by his words and conduct. Thus, when Carroll told Mr. Volkman, "I am happy that we will be working with you" and conducted himself as he did in the DP Associates office in the presence of Mr. Volkman, the trier of facts may find he was indicating a willingness to be bound by the statements and acts of McNamee, that Carroll held himself out as a partner of McNamee in DP Associates, that McNamee had apparent authority to act for Carroll and that the Volkmans reasonably relied upon this holding out. If so, he is bound as if he directly dealt with the Volkmans.

It was error for the trial court to grant summary judgment for defendant Carroll. Defendant has not conclusively shown that plaintiffs cannot possibly prove a claim against him because of an estoppel to deny the liability or because of his holding out to the Volkmans of apparent authority in McNamee to act in his behalf as a partner.

Reversed and Remanded.

Notes

1. Why does *Volkman* apply general principles of estoppel and apparent authority *via* UPA section 4 instead of applying only UPA Section 16?

2. Note that under UPA section 16, a holding out of a person as a partner may occur in two different contexts. First, there may not be any existing partnership. For example, suppose that a recent law school graduate, Brawny, holds out Savvy as a partner. Savvy then borrows money from Moneybags, who thinks she is lending to Brawny and Savvy as partners. Second, a person may be held out as a partner in an existing partnership. For example, suppose that Lynch and Burnham are partners in the investment banking business, and that Savvy is held out as their partner. Savvy borrows from Moneybags, who thinks she is lending to the Lynch and Burnham partnership.

In the first example (Brawny and Savvy), no partnership obligation can result, because there is no partnership. Instead, Brawny and Savvy (assuming both consented to the holding out) would be jointly liable. UPA § 16(2).

The second example is more complicated. If both Lynch and Burnham (all the partners) consented to the holding out, the debt to Moneybags would be a *partnership liability*. If only one partner, Lynch, consented, then Lynch and Savvy would be jointly liable, but the debt would *not* be a partnership obligation. Whether a partnership liability has resulted will have great effect on the rights of Moneybags. As will be discussed in chapter 15, "Partnerships and Property," only partnership creditors may attach partnership property. If no partnership liability resulted, then Moneybags may only go against the individual property of Lynch and Savvy.

3. RUPA section 308 parallels UPA section 16, except that it calls persons liable under that section "purported partners," rather than "partners by estoppel"(see Professor Painter's analysis referred to in *Volkman*). The only other changes to UPA section 16 are for the purpose of clarification.

Chapter 12

Limited Partnerships

A. Introductory Note

The Revised Uniform Limited Partnership Act (RULPA) defines a limited partnership as "a partnership formed by two or more persons . . . , having one or more general partners and one or more limited partners." RULPA § 101(7). Subject to certain limitations, a "general partner" in a limited partnership "has the rights and powers and is subject to the restrictions and liabilities of a partner in a partnership without limited partners." RULPA § 404. Limited partners, on the other hand, have only limited rights and obligations. Limited partners generally are not liable for partnership obligations. RULPA § 303. Limited partners have no general right to participate in the management of the business, but only such voting rights as given under the limited partnership agreement. RULPA § 302. In fact, as discussed later in this chapter, limited partners who participate in the "control" of the limited partnership's business become liable as general partners for obligations of the limited partnership. RULPA § 303.

As discussed in the following extract from *Klein v. Weiss*, 284 Md. 36, 395 A.2d 126 (1978), the limited partnership form of business association began in the late 1700s and early 1800s:

> Limited partnerships were unknown at common law; they are exclusively a creature of statute, their main purpose being to permit a form of business enterprise, other than a corporation, in which persons could invest money without becoming liable as general partners for all debts of the partnership. "The general purpose of [limited partnership] acts was not to assist creditors, but was to enable persons to invest their money in partnerships and share in the profits without being liable for more than the amount of money they had contributed. The reason for this was to encourage investing." *Gilman Paint & Varnish Co. v. Legum*, 197 Md. 665, 670, 80 A.2d 906, 908 (1951).
>
> The first limited partnership statute in the United States was enacted by New York in 1822; Maryland adopted a similar statute [in] 1836. These early statutes required the recording of a partnership certificate giving notice to the public of the exact terms of the partnership, including the amount of the capital contributions of the limited partners, so that the public could deal with the partnership "advisedly." *Lineweaver v. Slagle*, 64 Md. 465, 2 A. 693 (1886). The fundamental difference between the liability of general and limited partners under these statutes was "that the former are responsible *in solido* for the debts and obligations of the firm, as in the case of ordinary partnerships, without regard to the amounts contributed by them to the social capital; whilst the latter is not personally liable if the statute has been complied with, because his cash contribution is substituted for a personal liability." *Safe Deposit Co. v. Cahn*,

102 Md. 530, 546, 62 A. 819 (1906). Strict compliance with all statutory provisions was deemed essential to create a limited partnership under these early statutes, since they were in derogation of the common law. As a consequence, even minor or trivial infractions of the statute were held by some courts to subject the limited partners to unlimited liability as general partners. Because the strict construction of these statutes inhibited the effective accomplishment of the purpose for which they were intended, the National Conference of Commissioners on Uniform State Laws proposed the adoption in 1916 of a Uniform Limited Partnership Act [(ULPA)]. Maryland enacted the [ULPA in] 1918, and the statute with minor modifications is now in effect in every state in the country except Louisiana. The Act's provisions are intended to govern the determination of essentially all questions arising out of the formation and operation of limited partnerships. The rule that statutes in derogation of the common law are to be strictly construed is expressly made inapplicable to the [ULPA].

Decisions interpreting the [ULPA] recognize that a limited partnership consists of general partners who conduct the business and who have unlimited liability to creditors for its obligations, and of limited partners who have no right to participate in the management of the business, and whose liability is limited to the amount of their capital contribution. As the Official Comment to section 1 of the [ULPA] makes clear, a limited partner, though so called by custom, is not "in any sense" either a partner or a principal in the business or transactions of the partnership; his liability, except for known false statements in the certificate of partnership, is to the partnership, and not to its creditors. Succinctly put, a limited partnership interest in a business is in the nature of an investment. Section 17(a) of the [ULPA] delineates the extent of the limited partner's investment in the business; it makes him liable to the partnership:

> (1) For the difference between his contribution as actually made and that stated in the certificate as having been made; and
>
> (2) For any unpaid contribution which he agreed in the certificate to make in the future at the time and on the conditions stated in the certificate.

The creation of a limited partnership is not a mere private, informal, voluntary agreement as in the case of a general partnership, but is a public and formal proceeding which must follow the statutory requirements of the [ULPA]. [Section 2(2) of the ULPA] prescribes that a limited partnership is formed "if there has been substantial compliance in good faith" with the requirements contained in section 2(1). That subsection mandates that a certificate of a partnership be signed by the parties, acknowledged, and recorded with the clerk of the court. It requires that the certificate set forth designated partnership details, including the name of the partnership, the character and location of the business, the identity of the general and limited partners, the term of the partnership, the cash contributions made by the limited partners, and such additional contributions, if any, which the limited partners have agreed to make in the future. The certificate is a statutory prerequisite to creation of a limited partnership and until it is filed, the partnership is not formed as a limited partnership. The principal function of the certificate is to give third persons notice of the essential features of the limited partnership. Of course, whether a limited partnership has been formed is of particular importance in determining whether a person has achieved the status of a limited partner with the attendant limitation of his liability to third persons dealing with the partnership.

The ULPA, first promulgated in 1916, was eventually adopted by virtually all of the fifty states. The ULPA has now largely been supplanted by the RULPA. The RULPA, adopted by the National Conference of Commissioners on Uniform State Laws in 1976 and substantially amended in 1985, has now been adopted in forty-six states.

For further information regarding the development of limited partnership law generally, and especially the 1985 RULPA, *see* Closen, *Limited Partnership Reform: A Commentary on the Proposed Illinois Statute and the 1976 and 1985 Versions of the Uniform Limited Partnership Act,* 6 N. ILL. L. REV. 205 (1986).

B. Defective Limited Partnerships

Dwinell's Central Neon v. Cosmopolitan Chinook Hotel

21 Wash. App. 929, 587 P.2d 191 (1978)

McINTURFF, Judge.

Cosmopolitan Chinook Hotel (Cosmopolitan) appeals from a summary judgment, holding it liable as a general partnership and not as a limited partnership in connection with an action brought by Dwinell's Central Neon (Dwinell's) for breach of contract.

On October 25, 1972, Cosmopolitan and Dwinell's entered into three separate agreements for the lease-sale of neon signs. Dwinell's was represented by one of its salesmen and Cosmopolitan was represented by two of its partners. The contracts contained an acceleration clause in the event of Cosmopolitan's default and a provision for a reduction in the monthly payment should Dwinell's fail to properly maintain the signs.

In October, 1976, Cosmopolitan was behind on its payments and Dwinell's brought suit to accelerate the balance due under the contract. The complaint averred that Cosmopolitan was a general partnership due to its failure to comply with the statutory filing requirements of the [ULPA]. Cosmopolitan, on the other hand, claimed limited partnership status and stated that their status was known by Dwinell's at the time of contracting and was a matter of common knowledge in the community.

We are asked to consider whether summary judgment was proper in light of the following alleged factual issues left unresolved:

(1) Whether Dwinell's had actual knowledge of Cosmopolitan's limited partnership status at the time of contracting;

(2) Whether the court erred in concluding that Cosmopolitan was a general partnership;

At the time Dwinell's and Cosmopolitan entered into the lease-sale agreements, Cosmopolitan had taken no steps to comply with the filing requirements of [ULPA section 2]. It was not until February 1973, several months following execution of the contract with Dwinell's, that the certificate of limited partnership was filed. Cosmopolitan argues, however, that it was widely known in Yakima that a limited partnership had purchased the Chinook Hotel. Further, Cosmopolitan states that this fact was communicated to Dwinell's via its salesman. This information was allegedly communicated in the following manner—the word "partnership" was circled as identifying the "user" under the contract and the contract was signed, "Evan Bargman, V.P., R. Powers, President." According to Cosmopolitan, circling the word "partnership" best indicated its status as a limited partnership and the signatures clearly indicated that Bargman and Powers were not signing as general partners but as corporate officers of the general partnership.

The bare allegation in Cosmopolitan's affidavit "it was widely known and publicized in Yakima that it (the hotel) had been purchased by a limited partnership" is insufficient to raise a genuine issue of fact. It must furnish the factual evidence upon which it relies. Here, there is no factual evidence to support the allegation.

Secondly, a third party's knowledge regarding the status of a limited partnership is irrelevant when at the time of contracting, the partners have made no attempt to comply with the statutory information and filing requirements of the [ULPA].

Limited partnerships were unknown at common law and are purely creatures of statute. Parties seeking the protection of limited liability within the context of a partnership must follow the statutory requirements. To form a limited partnership, a certificate of limited partnership must be drafted and filed pursuant to [ULPA section 2]. While our courts no longer require literal compliance with the statute at one's peril, the statute does contemplate at least "substantial compliance with the requirements." [ULPA § 2(2)]. Here, there was no compliance with the statute at the time of contracting and the certificate of limited partnership was not filed until several months later. The object of statutory regulation of limited partnerships is to insure that limited partners do not find themselves exposed to the unlimited liability of a general partner.

The statute specifies the acts which must be performed by persons desiring to become limited partners. Cosmopolitan had not complied with any requirements of the statute at the time it entered into the contract with Dwinell's. Obviously, the purpose of the filing requirement was thwarted, that is, to acquaint third persons dealing with the partnership of the details of the partnership arrangement. A creditor has a right to rely upon there being substantial compliance with [ULPA section 2] before the protection of its provisions are afforded to any member of a partnership. Here there was no compliance.

Cosmopolitan, relying on the case of *Stowe v. Merrilees*, 6 Cal. App. 2d 217, 44 P.2d 368 (1935), contends that because [ULPA section 2] is silent as to when the certificate must be filed, a reasonable time is implied. Cosmopolitan submits that it substantially complied with the requirements of the statute by filing a certificate of limited partnership some 90 days *after* the contract went into effect. Reliance on *Stowe v. Merrilees* is misplaced. There, the partners executed a partnership agreement but failed to file the certificate until 49 days later. The court held that the firm became a limited partnership as to third parties who extended credit *subsequent* to the act of filing. Cosmopolitan wants the effect of filing the certificate of limited partnership to relate back to a contract previously entered into. To adopt this reasoning would render the statutory requirement of [ULPA section 2] meaningless and business relationships would be rendered unstable and unpredictable.

Thus, since there was no compliance with the [ULPA], the court was correct in holding as a matter of law that Cosmopolitan was liable as a general partnership on the contract with Dwinell's.

The judgment of the superior court is affirmed.

Voudouris v. Walter E. Heller & Co.

560 S.W.2d 202 (Tex. Civ. App. 1977)

COLEMAN, Chief Justice.

Walter E. Heller & Company brought suit against Nick Wayne Voudouris and Johnny Voudouris d/b/a Carpet Gallery of Austin, Ltd. A judgment was entered against Nick Wayne Voudouris, who subsequently went through bankruptcy. The case was severed, and after a trial before the court, judgment was entered against Johnny Voudouris. This appeal resulted.

Johnny Voudouris denied that he had ever been a general partner in the business of Carpet Gallery of Austin, and alleged that he had not taken part in the control of the business; that he had never accepted nor received any profits, other compensation, or income from Carpet Gallery of Austin; that Carpet Gallery of Austin, Ltd. was a limited partnership at all times; that Nick Wayne Voudouris was the general partner and Johnny Voudouris was a limited partner in the limited partnership, which was formed on or about October 30, 1973 and was ended on or about April, 1974.

After the plaintiff had introduced documentary evidence to prove up the account owed to it by Carpet Gallery of Austin, he called the defendant Johnny Voudouris as a witness. All of the testimony relating to the issue of partnership, with exceptions to be noted, was given by this witness.

Johnny Voudouris testified that in 1974 he was a county commissioner in Travis County and owned an interest in two janitorial services. He testified that he was engaged as a limited partner in the business known as Carpet Gallery of Austin and that he knew nothing of the carpet business in general and very little about this particular business. He thought that Nick sold and installed carpet in homes and apartment houses. He wasn't sure whether it was largely a subcontracting business. He did not know how many employees worked at the premises. He thought the business was located at 1924 South First Street. No inventory of carpet was maintained at that office and he didn't know whether an inventory was maintained at any other location. A written partnership agreement was prepared by attorneys selected by Nick Voudouris. Johnny contributed capital to the partnership by co-signing a promissory note with Nick. Johnny had to pay off the loan to the bank. He did not participate in the day by day operation of the business and did not have access to the books and records of this business. When he found out that Nick was not paying his bills, he immediately told him that he did not want to be involved in something that wasn't being taken care of and that he didn't [want] to be involved with him at all under any conditions. He then secured a list of creditors from Nick and wrote letters to each creditor informing them that he had sold his interest to Nick Voudouris and was no longer liable on any past or future indebtedness. A copy of this letter was introduced into evidence by the plaintiff and bears the date May 6, 1974. Johnny's secretary informed him that people had been calling. Johnny then began investigating and discovered that Nick had used a copy of his financial statement in establishing credit with the plaintiff and others. Johnny testified that he had no letterheads and that the letters were typed on plain paper and his secretary had apparently secured envelopes bearing the logo of Carpet Gallery of Austin from Nick and mailed the letters to the creditors in them. He testified that he did not file the limited partnership agreement with the Secretary of State and did not pay any filing fees. He left all of that to Nick and he assumed Nick had filed it. He did not check to see if in fact it had been filed with the Secretary of State.

In answers to questions from his own counsel Johnny Voudouris testified that Nick Voudouris came to him for assistance in getting the carpet business started. Nick told him that he was unable to borrow money from the bank unless Johnny would co-sign a note for him. He did co-sign the note and required Nick to draw the papers up because he did not want to be involved and wanted no responsibility for the business. He testified that he was strictly an investor. He had never been involved in any other transaction with Nick. He did not give his financial statement to Nick or make it available to him and had no idea how he got it. He testified that after he learned that Nick had not been paying his bills he demanded a release of liability and that Nick signed one in return for his interest in the business. The written indemnification agreement was introduced into evidence then. He did not take an active role in the operation of Carpet Gallery at any time and never intended to take an active role. When he found out in May of 1974 that Nick was representing that he, Johnny, was interested in the business he renounced the partnership within a week and entered into the indemnity agreement with Nick.

The indemnification agreement bears the date May 6, 1974 and recites the formation of a limited partnership agreement and the dissolution of said agreement.

[ULPA section 1] provides: "A limited partnership is a partnership formed by two or more persons under the provisions of this Act and having as members one or more general partners and one or more limited partners. The limited partner as such shall not be bound by the obligations of the partnership." [ULPA section 2] requires that the persons desiring to form a limited partnership sign and swear to a certificate stating certain specified information and file for record the certificate in the office of the Secretary of State.

[ULPA section 7] provides: "A limited partner shall not become liable as a general partner unless, in addition to the exercise of his rights and powers as a limited partner, he takes part in the control of the business."

[ULPA section 11] provides: "A person who has contributed to the capital of a business conducted by a person or partnership erroneously believing that he has become a limited partner in a limited partnership is not, by reason of his exercise of the right of a limited partner, a general partner with the person or in the partnership carrying on the business, or bound by the obligations of such person or partnership; provided that on ascertaining the mistake he promptly renounces his interest in the profits of the business, or other compensation by way of income."

[ULPA section 28] provides: "(1) The rule that statutes in derogation of the common law are to be strictly construed shall have no application to this Act. (2) This Act shall be so interpreted and construed as to effect its general purpose to make uniform the law of those states which enact it."

The rules for determining the existence of a partnership are set out in [UPA section 7]: "(1) Except as provided by Section 16 persons who are not partners as to each other are not partners as to third persons." (2)...(3) The sharing of gross returns does not of itself establish a partnership, whether or not the persons sharing them have a joint or common right or interest in any property from which the returns are derived. (4) The receipt by a person of a share of the profits of a business is prima facie evidence that he is a partner in the business."

[Prof.] Alan R. Bromberg states that paragraph (1) is highly important because of the frequent attempts of third persons to charge one person with obligations incurred by another on the theory that they are partners. Some Texas cases are more willing to find a partnership as to third persons than among the alleged partners. However the better view has considered only arrangements between the partners unless some holding out creates an estoppel. Mr. Bromberg concludes that this view is the rule promulgated by paragraph (1), for [UPA section 16] deals with estoppel.

There is no evidence in this record from which an inference could be drawn that Johnny Voudouris and Nick Voudouris were general partners as to each other. Walter E. Heller & Company stipulated that Johnny Voudouris made no representations which induced them to extend credit and that there was no basis upon which that company could raise an estoppel. There is no evidence that the business made a profit or that Johnny Voudouris received any share of the profits of the business. The burden was upon the plaintiff to establish a partnership between Johnny Voudouris and Nick Voudouris. There is no evidence that Johnny Voudouris had the right to operate the business as a co-owner. There is no evidence that he had a right to direct the operation of the business. There is no evidence that he had a right to contract on behalf of the business.

The limited partnership agreement evidences the fact that Johnny Voudouris agreed to become a limited partner and contributed $9,500.00 to the capital of the business. It further recites that Nick Voudouris is a general partner. While these recitations are not established to the extent that they cannot be contradicted by other evidence, there is no evidence to contradict these recitations. While the limited partnership agreement never became effective according to its terms because it was never filed with the Secretary of State, it does illuminate the intent of the parties. Whether a particular association is in fact a partnership depends largely on the intention or understanding of the parties involved. They must ordinarily agree and intend to become partners.

An indication of the interpretation to be given [ULPA section 11] is found in *United States v. Coson*, 286 F. 2d 453 (9th Cir. 1961). The court quoted from *Giles v. Vette*, 263 U.S. 553, 44 S. Ct. 157, 161, 68 L. Ed. 441, where the Supreme Court said:

> Section 11 is broad and highly remedial. The existence of a partnership limited or general is not essential in order that it shall apply. The language is comprehensive, and covers all cases where one has contributed to the capital of a business conducted by a partnership or person erroneously believing that he is a limited partner. It ought to be construed liberally, and with appropriate regard for the legislative purpose to relieve from the strictness of the earliest statutes and decisions.

In a footnote the court said:

> Of course an intent to become a general partner may be inferred from conduct. In this case no such conduct was shown. Coson had nothing to do with

management of Moulin Rouge, or with its organization. The only conduct shown on his part was consistent solely with his belief that he was dealing with a limited partnership. The ancient rule that failure to comply with statutory provisions required to form a limited partnership renders the association a general partnership vanished with the enactment of [the ULPA]. As stated in the Commissioners' note on the act:

> Third: The limited partner not being in any sense a principal in the business, failure to comply with the requirements of the act in respect to the certificate, while it may result in the nonformation of an association, does not make him a partner or liable as such. The exact nature of his liability in such cases is set forth in Section 11.

The 9th Circuit went on to hold that it was not important whether the renunciation operated to relieve Coson from liability ab initio or whether it operated to compel a finding that Coson was not a general partner at any time, first because he never had the necessary intent to join a partnership in that capacity, and second because his renunciation under Section 11 was fully effective.

Here we find that the limited partnership failed to become effective because it was not filed with the Secretary of State. There is testimony from the defendant that immediately upon learning that the partnership agreement had not been filed he renounced the partnership.

The failure to file the limited partnership agreement with the Secretary of State did not result in the formation of a general partnership. It was stipulated that there was no basis for a finding of partnership by estoppel. The remaining circumstances are legally insufficient as a basis for a finding that the formation of a general partnership between Johnny and Nick Voudouris was intended by the partners.

The judgment of the trial court is reversed and judgment is here rendered that Walter E. Heller & Company take nothing.

Notes

1. Compare ULPA section 11 and RULPA section 304.

2. Suppose Connie Capital invested $2,000 in a business, believing in good faith that she had become a limited partner, although, in fact, the general partner never filed any certificate of limited partnership. Connie first learned that she was not a limited partner when a creditor of the business approached her to pay off a debt of the business. At that time, Connie already had received distributions of profits from the business. May Connie keep the profits already paid, or must she repay them? *See* RULPA § 304(a)(2). Would the same result follow under the ULPA? *See Gilman Paint & Varnish Co. v. Legum*, 80 A.2d 906 (Md. 1951) (investor need not return profits already received).

3. Suppose that, instead of renouncing a share of the profits, Connie instead procured a filing of a certificate of limited partnership. What result then as to liabilities arising before filing? After filing? *See* RULPA § 304(a)(1). What result would follow under ULPA section 11?

4. The 1976 version of RULPA section 304(b) limited RULPA section 304(a) by allowing a third party who had transacted business with the "limited partnership" prior to the curative act (filing or withdrawal) to hold persons who had thought they

were limited partners liable where the third party believed in good faith that the persons were general partners. Is this consistent with UPA section 16, which only holds non-partners liable in estoppel based on their own conduct or consent? The 1985 version of RULPA requires not only that the third party have believed that the limited partner was a general partner, but *also* requires that the third party's belief be based on the limited partner's own conduct.

5. For additional discussion, *see* Closen, *Limited Partnership Reform: A Commentary on the Proposed Illinois Statute and the 1976 and 1985 Versions of the Uniform Limited Partnership Act,* 6 N. ILL. L. REV. 205, 255-58 (1986).

C. Participation in Control

Gast v. Petsinger

228 Pa. Super. 394, 323 A.2d 371 (1974)

HOFFMAN, Judge:

This appeal is from a summary judgment involving a contract dispute. Appellant charges in his Complaint that he was employed by LNG Services as a project engineer in 1968. For over a year, he was paid his agreed salary of $15,000.00 per year. From October of 1969 until March of 1971, when he severed his employment from the business, he continued in his capacity without pay. Upon tendering notice of termination of employment, appellant submitted a claim for back pay and expenses. This amount was never paid and a suit in assumpsit was thereupon instituted. The Complaint states that the business known as LNG Services is formally a limited partnership. The only named general partner is the defendant, Robert E. Petsinger. Nevertheless, appellant claims that the other named individual defendants, while ostensibly limited partners, were, by virtue of their participation in the enterprise, acting as general partners, and should therefore be liable for the monies due him.

[T]he Court entered an Order granting defendants' Motion of Summary Judgment. The plaintiff-appellant has appealed to this Court asserting that the [record] establish[es] certain involvement in the partnership by the named defendants that presents a factual dispute on the question of control which should be submitted to a jury.

We have examined the record in this case and find the following to be degree and kind of participation of the Limited Partners in LNG Services:

1. All Limited Partners have the following rights and powers as described in the Limited Partnership Agreement:

(a) the right to receive distributions from time-to-time and upon dissolution;

(b) the right to prevent the transfer of assets and other acts 'outside the ordinary business of the partnership' unless an aggregate of 50% in interest give written consent to the transfers of acts;

(c) the right to examine the books and records of the partnership at the principal office of the partnership;

(d) the right to attend meetings 'for the purpose of receiving the report of the General Partner and for taking any action referred to' in clause (b), *supra*;

(e) the right to transfer, sell or assign their interests to third parties;

(f) and, upon the death of a Limited Partner, to have his or her share of the profits and distributions inure to his or her Estate.

2. According to the Limited Partnership Agreement, 'the management and control of the Partnership's day-to-day operation and maintenance of the property of the Partnership shall rest exclusively with the General Partner.' Consistent with statutes regulating limited partnerships, the Agreement places the 'control' of the business in the hands of the General Partner. The Limited Partners, by virtue of their capital contributions, have the powers mentioned above, and prohibited from taking any 'part in the conduct or control of the Partnership and its business and shall have no right or authority to act for, or bind, the Partnership.'

3. The organization of LNG Services is in conformance with the [ULPA]. The certificate is in good order, and the Agreement delineates the powers, rights and liabilities of the General and Limited Partners in express terms. None of the powers mentioned therein exceed the degree of 'control' which converts the status of a limited partner to that of general partner. In two sections of the ULPA, the statute clearly limits the liability of the limited partner: "A limited partner shall not become liable as a general partner unless, in addition to the exercise of his rights and powers as a limited partner, he takes part in the control of the business." [ULPA § 7.]

In [*Freedman v. Philadelphia Tax Review Board*, 212 Pa. Super. 442, 446, 243 A.2d 130, 133 (1968)], we defined the limited partnership as

> an entity in which one or more persons, with unlimited liability, manage the partnership, while one or more other persons only contribute capital; these latter partners have no right to participate in the management and operation of the business and assume no liability beyond the capital contributed.

We concluded that: "By adhering to this arrangement, the limited partner is exempted from general liability and places his capital alone at the peril of the business."

Each of the limited partners in the instant case contributed capital to the partnership and enjoyed certain powers and rights which have been recognized as consistent with the concept of a 'limited partner.' Each received reports and materials periodically concerning the Partnership sent by the General Partner. The record discloses that [certain] limited partners also on occasion attended meetings of the partnership called by the General Partner between March and July 1969 for the purpose of reporting on the business of the partnership and amending the Agreement. In addition, [certain limited] partners attended personal meetings between the General Partner and certain employees for the purpose of raising additional capital. [Other limited] partners did no more than receive the aforementioned reports of the partnership.

Only Dr. Garwin and Jerome Apt, Jr., appear to have acted in capacities which require some discussion and evaluation. In addition to receiving reports and attending meetings wherein status reports and additional capital investments were discussed, Dr. Garwin was employed by the Partnership as an independent engineering consultant with respect to certain projects undertaken by LNG Services for which service he was retained by the General Partner and in which, he and the General Partner assert, he remained subject to the supervision and control of Petsinger, the General Partner. Apt was also engaged from time to time as an independent consultant on certain projects. These individuals were described as 'Project Managers' on several booklets which were attached to appellant's deposition as exhibits.

Accepting all the facts as asserted by the plaintiff as true, we do not believe that, at least with respect to several of the appellees, this case so clearly was devoid of a single factual issue as to remove the matter from the deliberation of a jury.

The key issue before the lower court was whether the appellant had presented an arguable case demonstrating that some or all of the appellees had 'take(n) part in the control of the business.' The question of 'control' has not been squarely met in Pennsylvania. We are, however, guided by decisions in a number of jurisdictions following the ULPA which have construed the term in various factual contexts. One excellent Harvard Law Review article examining this problem identifies the problem and the important factors to consider. "Investing Partners want to limit their liability in connection with the enterprise. They will not participate in managing the partnership's ordinary investment activities (h)owever, as a practical matter, it is unlikely that major commitments of capital would be made without informing and perhaps consulting with Investing Partners." Feld, *The 'Control' Test for Limited Partnerships*, 82 Harv. L. Rev. 1471, 1474.

State and federal courts have taken a similar view. The courts have held, without satisfactorily describing the standards by which to judge a limited partner's activities, that the following did not constitute taking part in the 'control' of the business: acting as a foreman in the employ of the partnership, with the power to purchase parts as necessary without consulting the general partner, but without the power to extend credit without prior approval from the general partner or deal with the partnership account, acting as a member of the board of directors of the partnership (although the Court noted that he never did actually serve as such), acting as sales manager in a new car sales department of the partnership without power to hire or fire, and, with power to order cars only with the general partner's approval, and, participating in the choice of key employees and giving a certain degree of 'advice.'

An analysis of the cases reveals that they were decided on their own facts and are of little use in forming rules or standards. In each case, it was not the position of the limited partner that was stated as permissible, but the actual role and degree of participation that each had in relation to the general partner. A reading of those cases reinforces the belief of this Court that the determination must be made on an *ad hoc* basis, and while employment may not be conflicting with the status of a limited partner, the 'control' that partner has in the day-to-day functions and operations of the business is the key question. Does the limited partner have decision-making authority that may not be checked or nullified by the general partner? As Alan Feld notes in his article:

> [While] some cases would permit the limited partner to 'advise' the general partners, it is not at all clear that Investing Partners may do so without fear of liability in view of the weight their advice is likely to carry, both because of the size of their investment and because they are 'carrying' Managing Partners' interests. The determination of control is a factual one and this relationship may, as a practical matter, give any 'advice' the color of a command in the partnership.

Here, the appellant testified that partners Apt and Garwin acted in the partnership as 'Project Managers.' He stated in his deposition that the appearance of their names on brochures and reports, the obvious weight their 'advice' carried in their recommendations and report on key projects, and their managerial responsibilities, all contributed to a belief that they exercised 'control.' The defendant Petsinger, the General Partner, confirms the fact that these two individuals acted as independent 'consultants' on various 'projects.' He denies their authority or right to control the business decisions. His statement as defendant is conclusionary, and since we are reviewing this appeal on a summary judgment, the inference most favorable to the plaintiff must be made.

It may be true that once all the facts are in the appellees, Apt and Garwin, will have been found not to have exercised the degree of 'control' necessary to impose general liability upon them. We agree that the nature of the business of LNG Services, described as having as its purposes 'the management of the development, engineering, and technical advice relating to the development or uses for liquefied natural gas, etc.,' required the utilization of expert opinion of technical minds. It is not apparent from the face of the record that the technical skills and training of Apt and Garwin did not by virtue of their retention as 'Project Managers' place them in a position where their 'advice' did influence and, perhaps, control the decisions of the General Partner, whose particular expertise is unknown.

With respect to the [other limited partners], we affirm the order of the court below granting defendants' motion for summary judgment. None of [those limited] partners is shown to have engaged in any activity or participated beyond those lawfully and expressly stated in the Limited Partnership Agreement. With respect to the appellees, Jerome Apt, Jr., and Dr. Leo Garwin, we reverse the order and judgment of the court below, and remand the case for further proceedings consistent with this opinion.

Frigidaire Sales Corp. v. Union Properties, Inc.

14 Wash. App. 634, 544 P.2d 781 (1976),
aff'd 88 Wash. 2d 400, 562 P.2d 244 (1977)

CALLOW, Judge.

The plaintiff, Frigidaire Sales Corporation, appeals from a superior court judgment dismissing its claim against defendants Leonard Mannon and Raleigh Baxter. The sole issue presented on appeal is whether individuals who are limited partners become liable as general partners when they also serve as active officers or directors, or are shareholders of a corporation which is the managing general partner of the limited partnership.

The parties agreed on the facts. On January 15, 1969, Frigidaire Sales Corporation entered into a contract with Commercial Investors, a limited partnership, for the sale of appliances to Commercial. The contract was signed on behalf of Commercial Investors by defendants Mannon and Baxter in their respective capacities as president and secretary-treasurer of Union Properties, Inc., the corporate general partner of Commercial Investors. Mannon and Baxter were also directors of Union Properties, Inc., and each owned 50 percent of the outstanding shares of Union Properties, Inc. In their capacities as directors and officers of Union Properties, Inc., the defendants exercised the day-to-day management and control of Union Properties, Inc. Both defendants also held one limited partnership unit out of a total of 52 outstanding partnership investment units in Commercial Investors.

Frigidaire Sales Corporation, as the creditor, instituted this action against the general partner Union Properties, Inc. and the defendants Mannon and Baxter individually when Commercial Investors, as the debtor and as the purchaser of the appliances, failed to pay the November 1970 installment and all subsequent installments due on the contract. The trial court entered judgment for the plaintiff against Union Properties, Inc., but dismissed the plaintiff's claim against Mannon and Baxter. The plaintiff appeals the dismissal of the individual defendants.

Is the Dominant Consideration Creditor Reliance or Prohibited Control?

The plaintiff contends that the defendants, as limited partners, controlled the business because they were (1) sole shareholders of Union Properties, Inc., the general partner; (2) on the board of directors of Union Properties, Inc.; (3) president and secretary of Union Properties, Inc.; and (4) exercised the day-to-day management of Union Properties, Inc. The defendants contend, on the other hand, that the limited partnership was controlled by its general partner Union Properties, Inc., a distinct and separate legal entity, and not by the defendants in their individual capacities.

The precise issue has not been previously raised in Washington, and the term "control" as used in [ULPA section 7] has not been defined with the present problem in mind.

The issue recently received attention in Texas. In *Delaney v. Fidelity Lease, Ltd.*, 526 S.W.2d 543 (Tex. 1975), the limited partners controlled the business of the limited partnership as officers, directors and stockholders of the corporate general partner. The Texas Supreme Court held at 545:

> [T]hat the personal liability, which attaches to a limited partner when "he takes part in the control and management of the business," cannot be evaded merely by acting through a corporation.

The opinion overrules the decision of the Texas Court of Civil Appeals, in which it had been stated:

> The logical reason to hold a limited partner to general liability under the control prohibition of the Statute is to prevent third parties from mistakenly assuming that the limited partner is a general partner and to rely on his general liability. However, it is hard to believe that a creditor would be deceived where he knowingly deals with a general partner which is a corporation. That in itself is a creature specifically devised to limit liability. The fact that certain limited partners are stockholders, directors or officers of the corporation is beside the point where the creditor is not deceived.

Delaney v. Fidelity Lease, Ltd., 517 S.W.2d 420, 425 (Tex. Civ. App. 1974).

The Supreme Court opinion in *Delaney* was concerned that the statutory requirements of at least one general partner with general liability in a limited partnership could be circumvented by limited partners operating the partnership through the corporation with minimum capitalization and, therefore, with limited liability. The fear is, however, not peculiar to a limited partnership with a corporate general partner. An individual may form a corporation with limited capitalization and thereby attempt to avoid personal liability. When one acts in such fashion, however, the inadequate capitalization is a factor in determining whether to disregard the corporate entity. If a corporate general partner in a limited partnership is organized without sufficient capitalization so that it was foreseeable that it would not have sufficient assets to meet its obligations, the corporate entity could be disregarded to avoid injustice. We find no substantive difference between the creditor who does business with a corporation that is the general partner in a limited partnership and a creditor who simply does business with a corporation. In the absence of fraud or other inequitable conduct, the corporate entity should be respected.

We note that the decision of the Supreme Court of Texas in *Delaney* relies upon the reasoning of the dissent filed in the Texas Court of Civil Appeals. We believe that the dissent, however, is based in part upon the incorrect premise that a corporation may not be a general partner under the Uniform Limited Partnership Act. We have shown that this is not so under the Washington Act. Moreover, the dissent based its reasoning upon the assumption that, because the limited partners acted as officers of the corporate general partner, they "were obligated to their other partners to so operate the corporation as to benefit the partnership." We find no inherent wrong in this. Persons in the position of the individual defendants in this case would be bound to act in the best interests of both the corporate general partner and the limited partners under the guidelines of [ULPA section 12]. The dual capacities are not inimical as asserted.

Apparently prior to the filing of the Texas Supreme Court decision in *Delaney*, a law review article discussing the Texas Court of Civil Appeals decision in *Delaney v. Fidelity Lease, Ltd.*, 517 S.W.2d 420 (Tex. Civ. App. 1974), appeared in 6 Texas Tech. L. Rev. 1171 (1974). Therein the author observed:

> In *Delaney* the court was confronted squarely with the choice of adopting a creditor reliance test or imposing personal liability because of the statutory control prohibition, even though the plaintiff originally did not require the defendant's personal guaranty in the execution of the lease. By adopting the creditor reliance test the court has expanded the permissible forms of business organizations. Texas businessmen now can combine the advantages of both the partnership and the corporation. The desirability of the court's decision is demonstrated by the fact that under such an arrangement the limited partners may enjoy the conduit theory of income taxation as well as complete protection from personal liability. The additional benefit flowing from the *Delaney* decision is that the businessman now can take advantage of these previously existing benefits without forfeiting managerial control of the organization.

Moreover, a literal reading of [ULPA section 7] that disregards the existence of the corporate entity as a general partner is not justified. The consideration of the issue must inquire not only whether a limited partner has participated in a forbidden control, but also whether the corporate entity should be regarded or disregarded. In Horowitz, *Disregarding the Entity of Private Corporations,* 15 Wash. L. Rev. 1, 11 (1940), certain principles are suggested for testing whether corporate entities should be acknowledged or disregarded. The principles, pertinent to our inquiry, were stated to be:

> (a) If there is an overt intention to regard or disregard the corporate entity, effect will be given thereto unless so to do will violate a duty owing.

(b) The overt intention is that of the corporation whose entity is sought to be disregarded or of the person or persons owning its stock and sought to be visited with the consequence of regard or disregard of the corporate entity.

(c) The duty owing must be owing to the person seeking to invoke the doctrine, and such duty may arise from common law and equity, contract or statute.

Here, there was an overt intention to regard the corporate entity and no showing of the violation of any duty owing to the creditor. The creditor dealt with the corporate general partner in full awareness of the corporate status of the general partner. There is no showing of any fraud, wrong or injustice perpetrated upon the creditor, merely that [ULPA section 7] provides that a limited partner becomes liable as a general partner if he takes part in the control of the business. When these are the circumstances, we hold that the corporate entity should be upheld rather than the statute applied blindly with no inquiry as to the purpose it seeks to achieve. As observed in the comment to section 1 of the ULPA :

> No public policy requires a person who contributes to the capital of business, acquires an interest in the profits, and some degree of control over the conduct of the business, to become bound for the obligations of the business; provided creditors have no reason to believe at the times their credits were extended that such person was so bound.

A limited partner is made liable as a general partner when he participates in the "control" of the business in order to protect third parties from dealing with the partnership under the mistaken assumption that the limited partner is a general partner with general liability. If a limited partnership certificate pursuant to [ULPA section 2(1)] is properly prepared and filed and the limited partner does not participate in the control of the business, it is unlikely that third parties will be misled as to the limited liability of the limited partners. The underlying purpose of the control prohibition of [ULPA section 7] is not furthered, however, by prohibiting limited partners from forming a corporation to act as the sole general partner in a limited partnership. A third party dealing with a corporation must reasonably rely on the solvency of the corporate entity. It makes little difference if the corporation is or is not the general partner in a limited partnership. In either instance, the third party cannot justifiably rely on the solvency of the individuals who own the corporation.

We hold that limited partners are not liable as general partners simply because they are active officers or directors, or are stockholders of a corporate general partner in a limited partnership.

Affirmed.

Note

Before the adoption of the ULPA, a limited partner could be held liable for partnership obligations if the limited partner participated in the *conduct* of partnership business. ULPA section 7 was intended to liberalize the law: a limited partner would not become liable as a general partner unless the limited partner participated in the *control* of the business (as opposed to merely participating generally).

Frigidaire Sales Corp. v. Union Properties, Inc. and *Delaney v. Fidelity Lease, Ltd.* (discussed in *Frigidaire Sales Corp.*) stand on opposite sides of a *second*, modern, development with respect to limited partner participation. *Frigidaire Sales Corp.*, and similar cases, impose an additional *creditor reliance* test to limited partner liability: it is not enough that the limited partner have participated in control, that participation must also have *misled* creditors as to the limited partner's status. The *Delaney* case quite rightly points out that ULPA section 7 says nothing about reliance (why not?). However, *Delaney* is on the wrong side of historical forces: RULPA section 303 adopted *Frigidaire Sales Corp.*'s requirement of creditor reliance.

> [The creditor reliance test] was adopted partly because of the difficulty of determining when the "control" line has been overstepped, but also (and more importantly) because of a determination that it is not sound public policy to hold a limited partner who is not also a general partner liable for the obligations of the partnership except to persons who have done business with the limited partnership reasonably believing, based on the limited partner's conduct, that he is a general partner.

RULPA § 303, Official Comment.

RULPA section 303(b) also added a non-exclusive "laundry list" of activities that are not participation in control. The list of permitted limited partner activities is wide ranging, running from acting as a shareholder, director, or officer of a corporate general partner (thus adopting the *Frigidaire Sales Corp.* holding) to consulting with and advising a general partner, to voting on any matter with respect to which a limited partner vote is required by the RULPA *or by the limited partnership agreement.*

> Paragraph (b) is intended to provide a "safe harbor" by enumerating certain activities which a limited partner may carry on for the partnership without being deemed to have taken part in control of the business. This "safe harbor" list has been expanded beyond that set out in the 1976 Act to reflect case law and statutory developments and more clearly to assure that limited partners are not subjected to general liability where such liability is inappropriate.

RULPA § 303, Official Comment.

For additional discussion, *see* Closen, *Limited Partnership Reform: A Commentary on the Proposed Illinois Statute and the 1976 and 1985 Versions of the Uniform Limited Partnership Act*, 6 N. Ill. L. Rev. 205, 250-55 (1986).

Chapter 13

Partnership Liabilities

A. Preliminary Note on Entity v. Aggregate

A recurring dispute in partnership law is the "nature" of a partnership. At common law, a partnership was generally viewed as a *relationship* among the partners. That is, "the partnership" was considered to be the *aggregate* of its partners. Unlike a corporation, "the partnership" was not an *entity*, a legal person separate from the partners.

The competing concepts of the nature of a partnership have had a significant impact on the development of partnership law. Courts often have looked to the nature of a partnership in determining the substantive rights and obligations arising out of partnerships. For example, the early common law, with its aggregate concept of partnerships, tried to describe partnership rights and obligations *solely* in terms of existing concepts of ownership and liability. Unfortunately, many of those concepts were not suitable in a partnership context. As a result, the early common law put too much emphasis on the *individual* rights and obligations of the partners and too little emphasis on the *collective* rights and obligations of all the partners. Similarly, treating a partnership solely as an entity puts too much emphasis on the (collective) rights and obligations of the partnership "person," and too little emphasis on the individual rights and obligations of each partner.

Partnerships are part aggregate *and* part entity. In some contexts, it is better to treat the partners *separately*—as if the partnership were an aggregate—while in other contexts it is better to treat the partners *collectively*—as if the partnership were an entity. The problem with a purely *conceptual* approach to partnership law is that it determines partnership rights and obligations *exclusively* on the basis of the perceived "true" nature of a partnership. As a result, conceptualism leaves partnership law too little flexibility.

Instead, partnership law requires a *functional* approach that recognizes the *unique* nature of partnerships. The UPA arguably reflects just such an approach. Instead of adopting the legal person concept, it retained the aggregate concept without being limited by it. Instead, it adopted a functional approach that allows either the individual or the collective rights of partners to be emphasized according to the particular factual and policy context. Nevertheless, many commentators have argued that the only way to account for the UPA's treatment of partnership rights and obligations is by an implied adoption of the entity concept of a partnership. For additional discussion, *see* Rosin, *The Entity-Aggregate Dispute: Conceptualism and Functionalism in Partnership Law,* 42 Ark. L. Rev. 395 (1989).

RUPA section 201 specifies that a partnership is "*an entity resulting from the* association of two or more persons to carry on as co-owners a business for profit" (emphasis added). Nevertheless, as the Prefatory Note to the RUPA makes clear, the

"RUPA does not require relentless application of the entity approach. The aggregate approach is retained for some purposes."

In reading partnership materials, the student should begin by looking at any applicable UPA (or RUPA) provisions. The student should then look at the particular *context* in which the courts are required to determine partnership-related rights and obligations. The student should then ask whether, in view of the provisions of the UPA and the context, it is more appropriate to treat the partners separately (as an aggregate) or collectively (as an entity). The student should also observe whether a court takes a functional or a conceptual approach.

B. The Nature of a Partner's Liability for Partnership Obligations

Swiezynski v. Civiello

489 A.2d 634 (N.H. 1985)

BATCHELDER, Justice.

The issue before us is whether a partnership employee who has received workers' compensation benefits for an injury received in the course of employment may maintain a negligence action against an individual partner who owns the work premises for this same injury. The resolution of this issue turns on whether an individual partner is an employer under the Workers' Compensation Law, and thereby is entitled to immunity from certain employee suits.

The plaintiff, Margaret Swiezynski, was employed as a grocery clerk at the Garden Street Superette in Milford. The grocery store was operated by the defendants, Rocco V. Civiello and William B. Crawford, as a partnership. The premises were owned by the defendants individually as tenants in common. On March 16, 1981, the plaintiff was injured when she fell in the store. The plaintiff subsequently received workers' compensation benefits for her injuries. She thereafter filed the instant action against the defendants, alleging that her injury resulted from a breach of a duty of care owed to her by each of the defendants as the landowners.

Without consulting the partnership agreement between the defendants, the Superior Court dismissed the plaintiff's suit, holding that the individual defendants are immune from the plaintiff's suit because they are employers within the meaning of the statute.

In *Holzworth v. Fuller*, 122 N.H. 643, 645, 448 A.2d 394, 395 (1982), we held that an employer's provision of workers' compensation insurance insulated the employer-landowner from a suit which alleged that the employee's injury had resulted from the employer's breach of his duty of care arising from his ownership of the premises. Whether the plaintiff may maintain her claims depends on whether the defendants are employers under the statute and thereby enjoy protection under *Holzworth*.

Under the Workers' Compensation Law, "employer" is defined as "a person, *partnership*, association, corporation, or legal representative of a person, *partnership*, association or corporation, who employs one or more persons." (emphasis added). We find that, for purposes relevant here, a partnership has no legal identity distinguishable from its partners who have retained their statutory rights of management and hence that such partners qualify as employers under the statute. Our holding is necessitated by the Workers' Compensation Law's conception of what constitutes an employment relationship and by the statute's underlying policy. Our conclusion that a partnership does not, in this context, constitute a legal entity distinguishable from its partners is consistent with New Hampshire partnership law, case law under the Workers' Compensation Law, and the decisions of the vast majority of the jurisdictions that have considered this question.

The Workers' Compensation Law refers to a private employment relationship as "any contract of hire, express or implied, oral or written." RSA 281:2, III (Supp. 1983). Such a contract confers on the employer a right to the labor of the employee and on the employee a corresponding right to compensation.

The dispositive characteristic of the employer's status is his right to control the employee's work performance. Under the Workers' Compensation Law, the distinguishing features of an employment relationship, therefore, are the employer's right to the employee's labor and his right to control the employee's performance and the employee's corresponding right to compensation.

Under New Hampshire law, these features are present in the relationship between a partner and a partnership employee. Unless the partnership agreement provides otherwise, partners by law have "equal rights in the management and conduct of the partnership business." [UPA § 18(e)]. Consequently, each partner has an equal right to control the work performance of a partnership employee. Partners are personally liable for partnership obligations, [UPA § 15], including an employee's claim for compensation.

As the Supreme Court of New Jersey stated in a similar case, "we cannot conceive of any incident of the employer-employee relationship which is here lacking." [*Mazzuchelli v. Silberberg*, 29 N.J. 15, 22, 148 A.2d 7, 11 (1959)]. Professor Larson is in accord:

> [I]n any ordinary partnership each partner has by law an equal share in management, and is therefore in actual possession of the powers of the employer. *Unless he has contracted away these powers*, which he can theoretically do, he is as much the employer as anyone can be, not as a matter of conceptual reasoning but as a matter of actual functions and rights.

1C A. Larson, [The Law of Workmen's Compensation § 54.32, at 9-202-9-203 (1982)] (emphasis added). Accordingly, we hold that a partner retaining his right of management is in an employment relationship with a partnership employee and, thus, constitutes an employer under the Workers' Compensation Law.

The Workers' Compensation Law balances the interests of the employee against those of the employers. The employee receives a right to receive insurance benefits for work-related injuries in exchange for his forfeiture of his corresponding rights of action against the employer; the employer receives statutory immunity from employee suits in exchange for his provision of insurance benefits. Under New Hampshire law, partners are personally liable for all debts of the partnership, [UPA § 15], including the liability for workers' compensation insurance.

To construe "employer" not to include individual partners would require partners to endure the liability for compensation insurance without the enjoyment of the corresponding benefit of immunity from employee suits. This construction would frustrate the policy underlying the Workers' Compensation Law. Where reasonably possible, a statute should be construed to effectuate its underlying policy. Construing the term "employer" to include individual partners, therefore, is preferable because it gives force to a policy central to the act.

The Uniform Partnership Act ("UPA"), which states the law governing partnerships in this State, is instructive on the issue before us. The UPA commingles the entity theory, which regards a partnership as an independent legal entity, with the aggregation theory, which holds that a partnership has no such independent status. The plaintiff asks us to extrapolate from the UPA's partial adoption of the entity theory the conclusion that a partnership is a distinct legal entity for the purposes relevant here. We are mindful, however, that "[u]ltimately it is not too important whether a specific result directed by the uniform law is dressed in garb of the entity concept, provided the fictional personification is confined to the specific result and is not used as a premise for syllogistic thrusts elsewhere." *Mazzuchelli v. Silberberg*, 29 N.J. at 21, 148 A.2d at 11.

A partnership is not considered an entity separate from its members, except in limited circumstances. The entity theory governs only in matters of procedure, *see, e.g.*, [UPA §§ 11, 12, 27, 28, 30], and in the holding and conveyancing of property, *see, e.g.*, [UPA §§ 10, 24-26], including the marshalling of assets, *see* [UPA § 40(h), (i)].

The aggregation theory controls in matters relating to the substantive liabilities and duties of the partners. Our statute defines a partnership as "an *association* of two or more persons to carry on as *co-owners* a business for profit." [UPA § 6] (emphasis added). "To state that partners are co-owners of a business is to state that they each have the power of *ultimate* control." [UPA § 6, comment (1)] (emphasis added). Partners accordingly "have equal rights in the management and conduct of the partnership business," [UPA § 18(e)], and are personally liable for partnership obligations, [UPA § 15]. In short, "[t]he Uniform Partnership Act does not make a legal partnership an independent juristic entity, and whatever recognition is given therein to the entity theory is solely for procedural or conveyancing purposes." *Carlson v. Carlson*, [346 N.W.2d 525, 527 (Iowa 1984)].

A number of jurisdictions have considered the precise issue before us; namely, whether a partner is an employer under a workers' compensation statute and thereby is entitled to immunity from employee suits. The vast majority of these jurisdictions has held that a partner is an employer.

A number of cases expressly considered the UPA. With but one exception, these cases held that under the act a partnership is not a legal entity distinct from its partners. Because we construe the UPA as enacted in New Hampshire "to make uniform the law of those states which [have] enact[ed] it," [UPA § 4(4)], we treat this majority rule as persuasive.

Where reasonably possible, statutes should be construed as consistent with each other. Construing the term "employer" in the Workers' Compensation Law not to include individual partners would frustrate a policy of the UPA and therefore should be avoided. The UPA expressly recognizes that title to real property owned by the partnership may be held in the names of all the partners. *See* [UPA § 10(4), (5)]. The plaintiff claims that she may maintain her negligence action against the defendants because they held title to the supermarket in their names as tenants in common and not in the name of the partnership. If we accept this argument, the defendants will be penalized for holding their property in a form expressly condoned by the UPA and members of other business partnerships will be discouraged from adopting this statutorily sanctioned form of partnership. This final circumstance further recommends our holding.

We remand for a determination as to whether the partnership agreement provided that the defendants did not retain their legal rights of management. Unless it so provided, the defendants are employers under the Workers' Compensation Law.

Order vacated, remanded.

Note

Would the adoption by New Hampshire of the RUPA, including RUPA section 201(a) defining a partnership as an entity, change the result in *Swiezynski v. Civiello*?

Head v. Henry Tyler Construction Corp.

539 So. 2d 196 (Ala. 1988)

BEATTY, Justice.

This is an appeal by Beverly P. Head, Jr., and James R. Forman, Jr., from a summary judgment rendered against them in favor of Henry Tyler Construction Corporation ("HTCC") in Jefferson Circuit Court.

On May 30, 1985, HTCC entered into a construction contract with Costa and Head (Atrium), LTD. ("Atrium"), an Alabama limited partnership. The contract provided that HTCC would be compensated on a time and material basis. During the course of construction, HTCC submitted applications for payments, which were paid by Atrium. However, on the final request for payment, Atrium paid HTCC the sum of $37,448.23, leaving a balance owed of $39,639.98.

Approximately four months later, HTCC brought suit for the balance due under the construction contract and for the enforcement of a materialman's or mechanic's lien. The complaint, as amended, listed as defendants: Atrium; Costa and Head (Birmingham One), Ltd. ("Birmingham One"), a limited partnership; Costa and Head Land Company ("Land Company"), an Alabama general partnership; and Pedro C. Costa; Nelson H. Head; Beverly P. Head, Jr.; James R. Forman, Jr.; and Thomas L. Howard as individuals. The complaint alleged that Birmingham One was the sole general partner of Atrium and that Birmingham One had, as its sole general partner, Land Company. The basis of HTCC's complaint against the individual defendants was that they, as general partners of Land Company, were in turn jointly and severally liable for the debts of Birmingham One and Atrium.

After various pleadings and motions of the parties, it was learned that Atrium, Birmingham One, and Land Company had filed for bankruptcy under 11 U.S.C. §§ 110-1 et seq. Thereafter, the trial court heard oral argument and reviewed various documents offered in connection with a motion for summary judgment filed by HTCC against Beverly Head and James Forman requesting that judgment be entered against them for the amount of the indebtedness set forth in the complaint. In an opinion with detailed findings of fact and conclusions of law based on the evidence presented, the trial court granted summary judgment in favor of HTCC. The judgment was in the amount of $44,896.78 and was made final.

The balance of indebtedness owed by Atrium to HTCC is not in dispute. Also, it is undisputed that Atrium's general partner is Birmingham One, and that Birmingham One's general partner is Land Company. Under [ULPA section 9(1)], the general partner of a limited partnership is subject to the same liabilities as the partner of a general partnership. A partner of a general partnership is jointly and severally liable for all debts and obligations of the partnership. [UPA § 15].* Thus, Birmingham One, as the general partner of Atrium, is jointly and severally liable for the debt owed by Atrium. Also, because Birmingham One is itself a limited partnership, Land Company, as the general partner of Birmingham One, is jointly and severally liable for the obligations of Birmingham One. Furthermore, the partners of Land Company—Pedro Costa, Beverly Head, Jr., James Forman, Jr., and Thomas Howard—are likewise jointly and severally liable for the debts and obligations of Land Company pursuant to [UPA section 15]. Indeed, Head and Forman concede in their brief that they are liable for the debt in question. However, they assert that under Alabama law a condition precedent exists to holding them liable. They maintain that a partnership creditor must first exhaust efforts to obtain payment from the partnership or prove that the partnership has no assets before proceeding directly against the individual partners and their assets. Therefore, the sole issue to be decided in this case is whether the trial court was correct in its determination that no such condition precedent exists under Alabama law.

The general common law rule is that partnership contracts create only a joint liability among the partners. The partners are not individually liable for partnership contracts, unless assets of the partnership are inadequate to pay the partnership debts or there is no effective remedy without resort to the property of individual partners. The Uniform Partnership Act, § 15(b), provides that partners are jointly liable for all debts and obligations of a partnership, except those arising from a tort or breach of trust. This is a codification of the common law rule.

By statute, however, Alabama long ago abandoned this common law rule of imposing only joint liability on partners for partnership debts and obligations. In *Dollins & Adams v. Pollock & Co.*, 89 Ala. 351, 7 So. 904 (1890), this Court recognized that the Alabama Code of 1886 provided for *joint and several liability* on the partners for partnership obligations and permitted a creditor to sue them jointly or severally at his option. Likewise in *First National Bank v. Capps*, 208 Ala. 207, 94 So. 109 (1922), the Court conceded that, in the absence of a statutory provision to the contrary, partnership contracts are joint and not several and that under the common law, liability of partners was so treated. The Court then cited the Code of 1907, which authorized a creditor of the partnership to sue one partner for the obligation of all. This statute, the Court stated, "gave the creditor of a partnership the right to sue any member of the firm, and by such suit to change the nature of the partnership obligation from joint to joint and several."

Consequently, when the Uniform Partnership Act was being proposed for adoption in Alabama, § 15(b), providing for only joint liability, was the subject of debate.

* [Note by editors.] As discussed by the court below, Alabama's version of the UPA varies from UPA section 15 in making partners jointly and severally liable for *all* partnership obligations.

In 1962, a subcommittee of the Alabama State Bar's Committee on Jurisprudence and Law Reform suggested that the section be changed to conform to existing Alabama law. The report of the subcommittee's findings state:

> Our committee has recommended only two changes in the terminology of the Uniform Partnership Act as originally drawn by the Commissioners. Section 15 provides that partners were jointly and severally liable for breaches of trust and wrongful acts and omissions causing loss or injury but that they are jointly liable only for all other debts and obligations of the partnership. This appears to be a statement of the common law rule as understood in most jurisdictions. However, Section 141, Title 7, *Code of Alabama*, expressly authorizes actions against one or more of the partners for the 'obligations' of the partnership, thus, in effect, converting the liability at the election of the party bringing the action to joint and several liability for all practical purposes except set-off and recoupment. In view of this situation, the subcommittee, with one member dissenting, felt that it would be more in keeping with the existing Alabama law and procedure to amend Section 15 by providing simply that all partners shall be liable jointly and severally for all debts and obligations of the partnership.

Woolf, *New Partnership Act Proposed by Committee on Jurisprudence and Law Reform*, 24 Ala. Law. 115, 116 (1963).

The Alabama legislature eventually enacted the Alabama Partnership Act, patterned after the Uniform Partnership Act, but adopted the suggested change to § 15(b). The provision of the Act dealing with partner liability unequivocally states that partners are "jointly and severally" liable for all debts and obligations of the partnership. Appellant still contends, however, that a creditor must first exhaust any remedies against the partnership before initiating an action against individual partners. This argument is without merit because it does not recognize the legal impact, through the years, of Alabama's statutes making partners severally liable on partnership contracts in addition to the already existing common law joint liability.

The major impact of making partners not merely jointly liable but also severally liable is that if a creditor chooses to bring an action against one of the partners, that partner is liable for all of the partnership debts, regardless of whether the creditor first attempted to recover the debt from the partnership or prove that the partnership had no assets. Several liability is "[l]iability *separate and distinct from liability of another* to the extent that an independent action may be brought without joinder of others." *Black's Law Dictionary* (5th ed. 1979) at 1232. (Emphasis added.) The individual liability associated with partners that are jointly liable is not separate and distinct from the liability of all the partners jointly. Rather, the individual liability arises only after it has been shown that the partnership assets are inadequate. No direct cause of action may be maintained against the individual partners until the above condition is met. Several liability, on the other hand, imposes no such conditions precedent before one can be held individually liable. As stated in 59A Am. Jr. 2d *Partnerships*, § 709 at 590 (1987):

> Where partners are considered jointly and severally liable on partnership obligations, establishing personal unlimited liability of partners as individuals, each individual partner thus pursued must be made a party to the action without the necessity of joining all partners in the suit as indispensable parties, nor must

the plaintiff bring a prior action against the partnership. A direct right of action exists against the partner.

Alabama has long recognized the legal effect of joint and several liability of partners for partnership debts:

> As a general rule, each individual partner is liable to creditors of the firm for the whole amount of every debt due therefrom. *Nor is a creditor of the firm, except, perhaps, as to individual creditors of a member thereof, required to resort to the firm assets before looking to the individual property of the respective members of the said firm for the satisfaction of this debt.*

Cleckler v. First National Bank of Anniston, 204 Ala. 268, 269, 85 So. 484, 484 (1920). (Emphasis added.) Likewise, other jurisdictions that have adopted joint and several liability provisions in their partnership acts hold that creditors of the partnership do not have to pursue partnership assets before looking to any of the individual partners for payment of the entire debt.

Therefore, we affirm the trial court's grant of summary judgment. This does not place an undue burden on partners, as the Alabama Partnership Act allows every partner indemnification from the partnership for personal liabilities incurred, absent any modification agreed upon by the partners themselves. [UPA § 18(b)].

AFFIRMED.

Note

The RUPA makes two changes in the liability of partners. First, partners would be jointly and severally liable for *all* partnership debts and obligations. RUPA § 306. Second, notwithstanding the joint and several nature of the partners' liability, judgment creditors would generally be required to exhaust partnership assets before proceeding against the individual assets of partners. RUPA § 307(c).

C. Suits Against Partnerships and Partners

Mansour v. Massey

336 S.E.2d 15 (S.C. 1985)

NESS, Chief Justice.

Respondent Mansour brought suit against four defendants to recover a debt for liquor sold. Three of the defendants were never served. The trial judge granted an involuntary nonsuit without prejudice as to the three defendants not served, and entered judgment against appellant Leake.

The complaint seeks recovery against four defendants, purportedly on the basis of a joint and several debt. Mansour's testimony was ambiguous as to whether he sought recovery against the defendants individually or on the basis of partnership liability. Leake asserted the debt was a corporate debt. The trial judge found the capacity of the parties was unclear, but he granted judgment in full against Leake based on his personal liability for partnership debts.

Individual partners are jointly liable for partnership debts. [UPA § 15(b)]. All partners must be joined in an action for a partnership debt.

The trial judge erred in entering judgment against Leake in the absence of the other persons. The judgment below is reversed.

Allgeier, Martin & Associates v. Ashmore

508 S.W.2d 524 (Mo. App. 1974)

PER CURIAM:

The sole named plaintiff in this cause is "Allgeier, Martin and Associates." Plaintiff's petition commences: "Comes now the Plaintiff and for its cause of action states: 1. That Plaintiff is a partnership." The balance of this pleading, in two alternative counts, prayed for a money judgment against one corporation and three individuals (Tom, Philip and Michael Ashmore) for the reasonable value of "work, labor and services" rendered by plaintiff at the request of defendants. Sheriffs' returns to issued summons and alias summons attest that service was effected on the corporation and upon Tom and Philip Ashmore; a non est return was filed to the summons issued for Michael Ashmore. Under date of December 3, 1970, the Circuit Court of Jasper County entered a default judgment against the corporation and Tom Ashmore. The judgment correctly stated that Michael Ashmore had not been served with process; it erroneously declared that Philip had not been served and ordered "that this case remain on the active docket pending the service of process on these two defendants." On February 3, 1972, Tom Ashmore filed "Motion to Set Aside Default Judgment" which was sustained on February 5, 1973. Thereafter, on February 13, 1973, "Allgeier, Martin and Associates, the above named plaintiff," filed a notice of appeal "from the order and Judgment entered in this action on the 5th day of February 1973, setting aside the default judgment."

Whether the court nisi erred vel non in setting aside the default judgment as asserted in the points raised by appellant need not be discussed or decided, for albeit no one except us has raised the subject, the partnership cannot recover in any event and all involved should be spared the effort and cost of prolonging litigation that cannot legally survive.

Missouri follows the common law or aggregate theory of partnership rather than the entity theory. The Uniform Partnership Law did not transform a partnership into a separate or juristic entity and, generally, all partners are necessary parties-plaintiff in actions to enforce an obligation due the partnership. Absent statutory authority, a partnership cannot sue in the firm name and a judgment rendered for a partnership so suing will be reversed on appeal on the principle that a partnership has no legal existence apart from its members, but is a mere ideal entity.

To augment the confusion, in its order of February 5, 1973, the trial court not only set aside the default judgment but also granted defendants leave to file an answer and counterclaim or cross bill. Just as plaintiff may not maintain this suit in the partnership name, so too "in a suit [or counterclaim] against a partnership in its firm name only, there is no legal entity before the court against which lawful judgment may be rendered, [which] constitutes a fatal defect not waived by failure to object, and a judgment against the partnership in its firm name alone is void." *Davison v. Farr*, [273 S.W.2d 500, 503 (Mo. App. 1954)].

The situation presented is one in which plaintiff, by default or otherwise, cannot secure a valid judgment against the defendants or any of them, and where the defendants, singularly or collectively, cannot obtain a valid judgment against the plaintiff via a counterclaim or otherwise. In fine, the parties are but caponized litigants whose crowings will gain them neither success nor posterity. We have no choice but to direct the judgment which the trial court should have entered, and that is to dismiss the cause in its entirety. Therefore, the order and judgment appealed from is reversed and the cause is remanded with directions to enter a judgment dismissing the cause.

Notes

1. The common law rule that partnerships, because they are not legal persons, have no capacity to sue and be sued in partnership name has been modified in many jurisdictions by so-called "common name" or "joint debtor" statutes authorizing suits *against the partners* in the partnership name.

2. RUPA section 307(a) permits a partnership "to sue and be sued" in the partnership name.

3. What is the effect of a judgment rendered in a suit in partnership name?

Foster Lumber Co., Inc. v. Glad

303 N.W.2d 815 (S.D. 1981)

WOLLMAN, Chief Justice.

The trial court entered a default judgment against Malcolm W. Glad (appellant) and Kenneth H. Olson (Olson). Appellant appeals from the order of the trial court denying his motion for relief from judgment.

Appellee, Foster Lumber Company, Inc., brought an action against the partnership of appellant and Olson, who were doing business as Exterior Designers. Although Olson was served with a copy of the summons and complaint, appellant was never served. A default judgment was entered against Olson and appellant individually. Appellant filed a motion for relief from judgment on the basis that the trial court was without jurisdiction to enter judgment against him individually because he had not been served with process. The trial court denied the motion.

[The] issue on appeal is whether, in an action against a partnership, a valid judgment can be rendered against an individual partner without service of process on that partner.

SDCL 15-6-17(b) provides as follows:

> When two or more persons associated in any business, transact such business under a common name, whether it comprises the names of such persons or not, the associate may sue or be sued by such common name, the summons in such cases being served on one or more of the associates. *The judgment in the action shall bind the joint property of all the associates, and the individual property of the party or parties served with process, in the same manner as if all had been named defendants and had been sued upon their joint liability.* (Emphasis added.)

SDCL 15-8-2 reads as follows:

> If an action be against defendants jointly indebted upon contract, the plaintiff may proceed against the defendant served unless the court otherwise direct; and if he recover judgment, *it may be entered against all the defendants thus jointly*

> *indebted so far only as that it may be enforced against the joint property of all, and the separate property of the defendants served* and if they are subject to arrest, against the persons of the defendants served. (Emphasis added.)

The language of the foregoing rule and statute indicates that a judgment can bind the individual property of only those parties served with process. Additionally, due process requires personal service on a partner to bind his individual assets.

Accordingly, we hold that in an action against a partnership, a judgment cannot be rendered against an individual partner unless that partner has been served with process.

Since appellant was not served with process, the default judgment insofar as it relates to appellant individually is invalid. The order of the trial court denying appellant's motion for relief from judgment is reversed, and the case is remanded to the trial court for further proceedings consistent with this opinion.

Jefferson State Bank v. Welch

229 Or. 335, 702 P.2d 414 (1985)

JONES, Justice.

The defendants appeal from the decision of the Court of Appeals which held that the trial court erred in allowing the defendants' motion for summary judgment.

Plaintiff, Jefferson State Bank (the Bank), brought an action against the defendants, Welch, Sr., Welch, Jr., and Juhl, doing business as W.R. Welch Construction, a partnership. This action was filed after defendants defaulted, for a second time, on a $50,000 secured note which had become due. The Bank brought the action against the three defendants on a theory of joint liability. Welch, Jr., failed to respond to the complaint and summons, and on October 18, 1982, the Bank was granted what the circuit court labeled a "default judgment" against Welch, Jr., for the total amount of money due plus interest and costs. The Bank proceeded to execute upon this default judgment. Shortly following this execution by the Bank, defendant Welch, Jr., filed for bankruptcy. The Bank continued to execute upon the default judgment and received an undisclosed sum in the bankruptcy settlement.

Defendants Welch, Sr., and Juhl filed a motion for summary judgment claiming that because the Bank had executed on the default judgment against defendant Welch, Jr., the joint obligation was merged into the default judgment. Defendants Welch, Sr., and Juhl assert that the Bank was thereby prevented from proceeding further with the action against them. The trial court granted defendants' motion for summary judgment. The Court of Appeals reversed on the ground that the so-called "default judgment" was not a final judgment.

Defendants urge that the so-called "all-or-none" rule is substantive law which should control the disposition of this case. The all-or-none rule provides that a creditor, after obtaining judgment against any one of several joint debtors, cannot subsequently obtain a judgment on the same obligation against the other joint debtors. Defendants also urge that the "merger rule" is an extension of the all-or-none rule, and is also substantive law. The merger rule provides that where a partnership obligation is joint, as opposed to joint and several, a judgment rendered on the obligation against fewer than all of the partners serves to merge the entire obligation of the partnership into the judgment.

Welch, Sr., and Juhl argue that the obligation of the partnership was merged into the default judgment which the Bank obtained and executed upon against defendant Welch, Jr.

The Bank contends that it never received a final judgment against defendant Welch, Jr., and that, therefore, there is no basis for the application of either the all-or-none rule or the merger rule.

In the case at bar, had the trial court made certain determinations, the default judgment would have become a final judgment. As such, the defendants' argument pertaining to the all-or-none rule and the merger rule would have to be addressed. However, we do not reach this issue because there was no final judgment regarding defendant Welch, Jr. The execution on the intermediate "default judgment" did not bar further proceedings against defendants Welch, Sr., and Juhl. The summary judgment should not have been granted.

The Court of Appeals is affirmed.

Notes

1. The "all-or-none" and "merger" doctrines mentioned in *Jefferson State Bank v. Welch* do not apply where liability is joint *and several.* In some jurisdictions, these doctrines have been eliminated by statute. *E.g.*, MODEL JOINT OBLIGATIONS ACT § 2 (1925).

2. Although a judgment against some, but not all, joint and several debtors does not relieve the remaining debtors of liability, recall that under the general rule (*Foster Lumber Co., Inc. v. Glad*), the judgment may not be enforced against the individual assets of unserved partners. The judgment creditor must bring a *new* suit against such partners.

Moreover, the prior judgment may not even have any *collateral estoppel* effect, so the creditor will have to *relitigate* the *partnership's* obligation! *See, e.g., Wendland v. Commissioner*, 739 F.2d 580 (11th Cir. 1984).

Note that the modern trend is toward greater scope of collateral estoppel. For example, some courts hold that persons may be bound by judgments in suits to which they were not parties where they were "virtually represented" by parties to the suit. *See, e.g., United States v. Geophysical Corp.*, 732 F.2d 693 (9th Cir. 1984).

Unfortunately, because of (i) UPA section 15(b) making partners only jointly liable for partnership contracts, and (ii) the merger doctrine mentioned in *Jefferson State Bank v. Welch*, there are few cases discussing the effect of a judgment against the partnership in a suit against unserved partners. As a result, courts—and the lawyers that argue before them—may not be well equipped to recognize—much less grapple with—the problems involved. *See, e.g., Storch Engineers v. D & K Developers*, 593 A.2d 245 (N.H. 1991).

Chapter 14

Management and Conduct of Partnership Business

A. Dealings with Third Parties

Burns v. Gonzalez

439 S.W.2d 128 (Tex. Civ. App. 1969)

CADENA, Justice.

Plaintiff, William G. Burns, sued Arturo C. Gonzalez and Ramon D. Bosquez, individually and as sole partners in Inter-American Advertising Agency (herein called "the partnership"), to recover on a $40,000.00 promissory note executed by Bosquez in his own name and in the name of the partnership. After an interlocutory default judgment had been entered in favor of plaintiff against Bosquez, the trial court, sitting without a jury, entered the judgment appealed from, denying Burns any recovery against Gonzalez.

The sole business of the partnership was the sale, on a commission basis, of broadcast time on XERF, a radio station located in Ciudad Acuna, Mexico, and owned and operated by a Mexican corporation, Compania Radiodifusora de Coahuila, S.A. (herein called "Radiodifusora"). Bosquez and Gonzalez each owned 50% of the Radiodifusora stock, with Bosquez acting as president of the corporation.

The events culminating in this litigation began in 1957 when a written contract was entered into between Radiodifusora and the partnership, on the one hand, and Roloff Evangelistic Enterprises, Inc., and Burns, on the other. Under this contract Radiodifusora and the partnership, in consideration of the payment of $100,000.00 by Roloff and Burns, agreed to make available to them two 15-minute segments of broadcast time daily over XERF so long as the franchise of the radio station remained in force, beginning July 1, 1957. In accordance with the terms of the contract, Roloff and Burns paid the $100,000.00 in four equal installments on July 1, 1957, November 1, 1957, March 1, 1958, and July 1, 1958, with Burns retaining 15% of such payments as his commission, as he had a right to do under the terms of the contract.

Subsequently, Roloff assigned all of its rights under this contract to Burns, effective June 16, 1962. Both Radiodifusora and the partnership approved such assignment.

Because of labor disputes and other circumstances, the radio station was shut down at various times. With some exceptions, the broadcast periods described in the 1957 contract were not made available to Burns or to persons to whom he sold such broadcast periods, after June 16, 1962.

On November 28, 1962, Bosquez, purporting to act on his own behalf and on behalf of the partnership, executed the note in question, payable to Burns on November

28, 1964. According to a separate instrument signed by Bosquez on the same date, the radio station was in receivership and it was unlikely that the broadcast periods to which Burns was entitled under the 1957 contract would be made available to him for the two-year period ending November 28, 1964, the date on which the note was payable. This instrument recited that since Burns would derive an income of $20,000.00 a year from sale of such broadcast periods, the note in the amount of $40,000.00 had been executed and delivered to Burns to compensate him for the income which he would have derived during the two-year period ending November 28, 1964. Bosquez testified, and Burns does not deny, that "one of the reasons" why he executed the note was the promise by Burns not to sue Radiodifusora.

The next relevant instrument is dated May 24, 1963. It is a contract between Burns and Bosquez, who purported to act on behalf of Radiodifusora and the partnership. The preamble to this agreement refers to the 1957 contract, the assignment of Roloff's rights thereunder to Burns, the approval of such assignment by Radiodifusora and the partnership, and the breach of such contract. No mention is made of the 1962 note. After this reference to the prior course of dealings between the parties, the agreement recognizes the rights of Burns under the 1957 contract, and Radiodifusora agrees to make the broadcast periods described in that contract available to Burns beginning September 1, 1963. As consideration for this promise by Radiodifusora, Burns agreed to pay Radiodifusora one-half of the amounts realized by him from sale of such time, and agreed not to file suit against Radiodifusora. The contract concludes with the recital that all understandings between the parties had been reduced to writing and were embodied therein.

Although Gonzalez denied under oath the authority of Bosquez to execute the 1962 note, the trial court held that the note was an obligation of the partnership. The judgment in favor of Gonzalez was based on the theory that he had been relieved of liability on the note as a result of the 1963 agreement.

Under Sec. 9(1), UPA, "Every partner is an agent of the partnership for the purpose of its business, and the act of every partner, including the execution in the partnership name of any instrument, *for apparently carrying on in the usual way the business of the partnership* of which he is a member, binds the partnership, unless the partner so acting has in fact no authority to act for the partnership in the particular matter, and the person with whom he is dealing has knowledge of the fact that he has no such authority." (Emphasis added.) In this case, in fact, Bosquez had no authority to bind the partnership by executing a negotiable instrument. But, since this express limitation on the authority of Bosquez to bind the partnership by executing a negotiable instrument was unknown to Burns, then, under the language of Sec. 9(1), his act in executing the note would bind the partnership if such act can be classified as an act "for apparently carrying on in the usual way the business of the partnership."

As we interpret Sec. 9(1), the act of a partner binds the firm, absent an express limitation of authority known to the party dealing with such partner, if such act is for the purpose of "apparently carrying on" the business of the partnership in the way in which other firms engaged in the same business in the locality usually transact business, or in the way in which the particular partnership usually transacts its business. In this case, there is no evidence relating to the manner in which firms engaged in the sale of advertising time on radio stations usually transact business. Specifically, there is no evidence as to whether or not the borrowing of money, or the execution of negotiable instruments, was incidental to the transaction of business, "in the usual way," by other advertising agencies or by this partnership, Inter-American Advertising Agency. It becomes important, therefore, to determine the location of the burden of proof concerning the "usual way" of transacting business by advertising agencies.

Sec. 9(1) states that the act of a partner "for apparently carrying on in the usual way the business of the partnership" binds the firm. This language does not place the burden of proof on the nonparticipating partner to establish the nonexistence of the facts which operate to impose liability on the firm. If the Legislature had intended to place the burden of proof on the non-participating partner, it could have done so easily. The statute could have been drafted to declare that the act of a partner binds the firm "unless it is shown that such act was not for apparently carrying on in the usual way the business of the partnership." Actually, the liability-imposing language of Sec. 9(1) indicates that the burden of proof is on the person seeking to hold the non-participating partner accountable. It is not couched in terms appropriate for the establishment of a presumption, "administrative" or otherwise. The language relating to carrying on in the usual way the business of the partnership is no more than a statement of the rule concerning vicarious liability based on "apparent" authority.

We conclude that, under a reasonable interpretation of the language of Sec. 9(1), the burden of proving the "usual way" in which advertising agencies transact business was upon Burns.

Our conclusion is supported by the fact that the liability of partners with respect to third persons is largely determined by reference to the principles of law of agency. UPA, Sec. 4(3). One who asserts that the particular act of an agent is within the scope of the agent's authority has the burden of proving the extent of such authority. We recognize, of course, that there are aspects in which the partner-agent differs from the "ordinary" agent. But we know of no distinction which compels application of different rules concerning the burden of proof in connection with establishment of the extent of the agent's power. The principle for imposing liability on the non-acting party, be he partner or ordinary principal, is that he has "held out" the actor as being empowered to perform acts of the nature of the act in question. If A seeks to impose liability on B for the act of C on the theory that B held C out as having power to do such act, clearly the burden of establishing the facts which constitute such holding out is on A.

In the case of an ordinary agent, "holding out" is established by showing that the principal placed the agent in a position which ordinarily carries with it generally recognized powers. The agent will then have, as far as third parties are concerned, the power to do the things ordinarily done by one occupying such a position, unless the third party has knowledge of limitations on the powers of the agents. In *Collins v. Cooper*, 65 Tex. 460, 464 (1886), the Supreme Court said that in determining the extent of an agent's power, it "becomes necessary, to consider the character of the business, the manner in which it is usual to carry on such a business, and where the agency has continued for a long time, the manner in which the particular business was carried." This is the same principle which is made applicable to problems concerning the power of partners by Sec. 9(1).

There are many statements to the effect that members of a "trading" partnership have implied authority to bind the partnership by issuing commercial paper, while members of a "non-trading" partnership have no such implied authority. But we do not base our holding on the ground that the partnership here was the non-trading type. It is apparent that the attempted distinction between the two types of partnership is nothing more than a shorthand rendition of the notion that B is liable for the act of C if B has "held out" to other persons that C is empowered to perform acts of that particular nature. The nature of the distinction is revealed by the language of Chief Justice Stayton in *Randall v. Meredith*, 76 Tex. 669, 13 S.W. 576, 582-583 (1890):

> If the partnership contemplates the periodical or continuous or frequent purchasing, not as incidental to an occupation, but for the purpose of selling again the thing purchased, either in its original or manufactured state, it is a trading partnership; otherwise, it is not. There is no doubt that all partnerships which fall within this definition are trading partnerships, and it may be that it is broad enough to cover all that should be so classed. If these were not embraced within this definition, in which each partner is clothed with power to borrow money, they may be recognized by the character of the business pursued, which makes frequent resort to borrowing a necessity, not existing by reason of embarrassments, or on account of some fortuitous event, but for the advantageous prosecution of even a prosperous business.
>
> An act may be necessary for the carrying on of the business of a partnership, but when done by one partner the firm cannot be bound by it, unless he has express or implied power to do the act. Whether he has the implied power depends on whether the act be "necessary to carry on the business in the ordinary way. A partner's power is to do only what is usual, and not what is unusual because necessary."
>
> Whether the work was done in the usual course of business, or was necessary, was not the inquiry to which the mind of the jury should have been directed. The work may have been done in the usual course of business, or necessary, but this would not confer on the partner power to borrow money to pay for it, unless the exercise of that power was usual in the ordinary conduct of such a business.

It appears that the tests announced in *Randall* for determining whether a partnership is to be classed as trading or non-trading is exactly the same test for imposition of liability embodied in Sec. 9(1). This explains the fact that the UPA makes no mention of the distinction between trading and non-trading firms.

We are aware of the language in *Crozier, Rhea & Co. v. Kirker*, 4 Tex. 252, 258-259 (1849), to the effect that every partner has implied power to bind his co-partners by executing notes for commercial purposes consistent with the object of the partnership. Similar language is found in *Brewer v. Big Lake State Bank*, 378 S.W. 2d. 948, 951 (Tex. Civ. App.—El Paso 1964), and *Ft. Dearborn Nat. Bank v. Berrott*, 23 Tex. Civ. App. 662, 57 S.W. 340, 341 (San Antonio, 1900). But in each of these cases the partnership business contemplated "the periodical or continuous or frequent purchasing, not as incidental to an occupation, but for the purpose of selling again the thing purchased." Where the partnership business is of that nature, it is usual and customary to purchase on credit and to execute paper evidencing the existence of the partnership debt. That is, to use the language of Sec. 9(1), in such partnership, "carrying on in the usual way the business of the partnership" involves borrowing and the issuance of commercial paper. Or, to use the language of *Randall*, the nature of such a partnership "makes frequent resort to borrowing a necessity, not existing by reason of embarrassments, or on account of some fortuitous event, but for the advantageous prosecution of even a prosperous business." The statements in *Crozier*, *Brewer* and *Berrott* relating to implied authority of a partner to issue negotiable paper must be construed as being applicable to the types of partnerships there involved. If not so limited, then the assertions that every partner has implied authority to bind the firm by executing negotiable instruments must be disregarded as incorrect, irreconcilable with the analysis of the problem in *Randall*, and inconsistent with the plain language of Sec. 9(1). The power of a partner to issue commercial paper arises not from the existence of the partnership, but from the nature of the partnership business and the manner in which such business is usually conducted. This is the plain meaning of Sec. 9(1).

The only thing we know of the nature of the partnership here is that it was restricted to sale of broadcast time over XERF on a commission basis. There is nothing to show that the transaction of such business required "periodical or continuous or frequent purchasing" or made "frequent resort to borrowing a necessity, not existing by reason of embarrassments, or on account of some fortuitous event, but for the advantageous prosecution of even a prosperous business." The assets of the partnership consisted of a few desks, chairs, typewriters and office supplies.

We disagree with the contention put forward by Burns to the effect that Bosquez was the managing partner. At best, the record reflects that both Bosquez and Gonzalez were active in the management of the business. As a matter of fact, with the exception of the transactions involving the 1962 note and the 1963 agreement, the record discloses that all instruments significantly affecting the relations between the partners and Burns were signed by both Bosquez and Gonzalez.

Since the evidence does not disclose that Bosquez, in executing the 1962 note, was performing an act "for apparently carrying on in the usual way the business of the partnership," there is no basis for holding that the note sued on was a partnership obligation.

Since Burns filed no pleadings alleging that Gonzalez had ratified the act of Bosquez, or that Gonzalez had been guilty of any acts giving rise to an estoppel, it is not possible to hold Gonzalez liable on any theory of ratification or estoppel.

The judgment of the trial court is affirmed.

Notes

1. Under RUPA section 301(1) the unauthorized act of a partner binds the partnership to third parties without *knowledge* of the partner's lack of authority if the act is for "apparently carrying on in the usual way" *either* the partnership business (as actually conducted by the partnership) *or* business of the kind carried on by the partnership.

2. Does a partner's unauthorized act within the scope of UPS section 9(1)/RUPA section 301(1) bind the partnership if the third person with whom the partner deals does not know that the partner is a partner?

3. Is a partner's power to bind the partnership under UPA section 9(1) and RUPA section 301(1) authority, apparent authority, estoppel or inherent agency power?

Kelsey-Seybold Clinic v. Maclay

466 S.W.2d 716 (Tex. 1971)

WALKER, Justice.

This is a suit for alienation of affections in which the trial court rendered summary judgment for one of the defendants, Kelsey-Seybold Clinic, a medical partnership.

The suit was brought by John Dale Maclay against Dr. Earl J. Brewer, Jr., M.D. and the Clinic. After sustaining the Clinic's motion for summary judgment, the trial court ordered that this part of the case be severed from the suit against Dr. Brewer. Plaintiff appealed to the Court of Civil Appeals, which reversed the trial court's judgment in favor of the Clinic and remanded the cause for trial.

Plaintiff alleged that Dr. Brewer and the Clinic had treated him, his wife and their children for several years; that Dr. Brewer, who is a pediatrician and one of the partners in the Clinic, was the doctor to whom his wife had taken their children; that beginning in late 1966, Dr. Brewer conceived and entered into a scheme to alienate the affections of plaintiff's wife, Mrs. Maria Maclay; that he showered his attentions and gifts upon her until April or May, 1967, when her affections were alienated as a direct result of his actions, causing her to separate from plaintiff on or about July 25, 1967.

Plaintiff further alleged that Dr. Brewer's actions designed to alienate Mrs. Maclay's affections occurred while he was acting as a medical doctor for plaintiff's family and in the course and scope of his employment as a partner in the Clinic; that various acts of undue familiarity occurred both on and off the premises of the Clinic; that prior to April, 1967, the Clinic, through Dr. Mavis Kelsey, one of the senior partners, had knowledge of Dr. Brewer's actions; that at the time this knowledge was acquired, the Clinic was providing medical treatment for plaintiff and his entire family; and that "the partnership approved of, consented to, and ratified and condoned such conduct of its partner, Brewer, and refused to come to the aid of your plaintiff or in any way attempt to halt or disapprove the actions of Brewer."

Dr. Kelsey stated that he had treated plaintiff ten or fifteen years before and that other doctors in the Clinic had treated plaintiff, his wife and children since then. At some time in the Spring of 1967, plaintiff complained to Dr. Kelsey that Dr. Brewer was having an affair with Mrs. Maclay. According to Dr. Kelsey's recollection of this conversation, plaintiff stated that he and his wife had separated. At about the same time Dr. Kelsey received a telephone call from Mrs. Maclay's uncle, who inquired what Dr. Kelsey 'knew about this affair.' Two or three weeks later plaintiff telephoned Dr. Kelsey a second time.

It was Dr. Kelsey's impression that the purpose of plaintiff's two telephone calls was to seek sympathy. Plaintiff did not ask him to do anything, and he had done nothing. He did not talk with Dr. Brewer about the matter until after this suit was filed. The witness did not believe that anything improper had occurred at the Clinic. If anyone had known of conduct such as that alleged by plaintiff, the partners 'wouldn't put up with that.' Dr. Kelsey also stated that the Clinic had not adopted a policy of intentionally alienating Mrs. Maclay's affections. A nurse is always present when a female patient is examined or treated by a doctor in the Clinic, but Dr. Kelsey felt that it would be impossible to keep up with the private lives, outside the Clinic, of over fifty doctors.

Plaintiff stated that in his telephone conversation with Dr. Kelsey, he inquired whether the latter was aware that Dr. Brewer had a romantic interest or involvement with his wife. Dr. Kelsey replied that he was aware of the matter and had talked with Mrs. Maclay's uncle about it. The Clinic filed an affidavit by all members of its executive committee, except Dr. Brewer, stating that the committee is charged with responsibility for setting policy for the partnership, that the business of the partnership is that of operating a medical clinic, that Dr. Brewer was not authorized by the partnership at any time to do any act which might result in the alienation of Mrs. Maclay's affections from her husband, and that the partnership had done no act with the purpose, intent or design to alienate her affections.

The bases of liability alleged in the petition are: (1) that Dr. Brewer's wrongful conduct was in the course and scope of the partnership business and was approved, consented to, ratified and condoned by the Clinic; and (2) that the Clinic, after notice of the alleged relationship between Dr. Brewer and Mrs. Maclay, failed to take any action. Plaintiff is thus relying upon the vicarious or partnership liability of the Clinic for the acts of one of the partners and also its liability for breach of a duty owing by the Clinic when it learned of Dr. Brewer's relationship with Mrs. Maclay.

On the question of vicarious liability, [w]e are unwilling to believe that plaintiff seriously expects to prove in a conventional trial that the acts alleged to have been committed by Dr. Brewer were in the course and scope of the partnership business or were either authorized or ratified by the Clinic. Rather than concern ourselves about possible deficiencies in the affidavit filed by the Clinic, we assume for the purpose of this opinion that Dr. Brewer was not acting in the ordinary course of the Clinic's business and that his conduct was neither authorized nor ratified by the partnership. This will enable us to reach questions that may well arise at the trial of the case.

The Court of Civil Appeals reasoned that the summary judgment was improper because the Clinic had not conclusively negated consent on its part to the alleged wrongful conduct of Dr. Brewer. In reaching this conclusion, it relied on our opinion in *K & G Oil Tool & Service Co. v. G & G Fishing Tool Service*, 158 Tex. 594, 314 S.W.2d 782, where it was stated that:

> A non-participating partner is ordinarily not personally liable for the wrongful, tortious or criminal acts of the acting partner unless such acts are within the scope of the partnership's business or were consented to, authorized, ratified or adopted by the non-participating partner.

There was no question of consent in *K & G*, and it was held that the non-participating partner was not liable. Similar statements have been made by other courts in connection with similar holdings. Two courts apparently entertain the view that mere tacit consent is enough to make the non-participating partner liable for the willful tort of the acting partner outside the scope of the partnership business. Their conclusion in this respect appears to be due, at least in part, to an erroneous interpretation of the opinion in *Williams v. F. & W. Grand Five, Ten and Twenty-five Cent Stores*, 273 Pa. 131, 116 A. 652. The plaintiff there was accused of stealing a tooth brush. While being interrogated in defendant's store, she was assaulted by the operative of a private detective agency employed by defendant to guard the store. The trial court rendered judgment on the verdict in favor of the plaintiff, and it was contended on appeal that defendant could not be responsible for an assault committed by the employee of an independent detective agency. The appellate court pointed out that the jury had been instructed to find for the plaintiff if they believed that the manager of the store was present and participated in the acts or permitted the operative to insult and assault the plaintiff when he could and should have protected her. It then observed that the defendant was held responsible not for the acts of the operative but for those of its own manager.

Where a partner proposes to do, in the name or for the benefit of the partnership, some act that is not in the ordinary course of the business, consent by the other partners may constitute his authority to do the act for the partnership. We also recognize that even a willful or malicious act outside the ordinary scope of the partnership business may be so related to the business that tacit consent of the other partners could fairly be regarded as a grant of authority. In this instance, however, Dr. Brewer was acting solely for his own personal gratification. His conduct could not benefit the Clinic in any way, and no one would have supposed that he was acting for the partnership. It is our opinion that in these circumstances the 'consent' that might be inferred from the silence or inaction of the Clinic after learning of his conduct does not render the Clinic vicariously liable for the damages claimed by plaintiff.

On the basis of the present record and the facts we are assuming in this case, the liability of the Clinic must rest, if at all, upon some theory akin to that recognized by the court in *Williams*. The Clinic was under a duty, of course, to exercise ordinary care to protect its patients from harm resulting from tortious conduct of persons upon the premises. A negligent breach of that duty could subject the Clinic to liability without regard to whether the tortious conduct immediately causing the harm was that of an agent or servant or was in the ordinary scope of the partnership business.

We are also of the opinion that the Clinic owed a duty to the families of its patients to exercise ordinary care to prevent a tortious interference with family relations. This duty relates only to conduct of a partner or employee on the premises of the Clinic or while purportedly acting as a representative of the Clinic elsewhere. Failure to exercise ordinary care in discharging that duty would subject the Clinic to liability for damages proximately caused by its negligence.

The rather meager information in the present record does not necessarily indicate that the Clinic was under a duty to act or that it could have done anything to prevent the damage when Dr. Kelsey first learned of the situation. On the other hand, it does not affirmatively and clearly appear that the Clinic could or should have done nothing. In our opinion the Clinic has failed to discharge the heavy, and in a case of this character virtually impossible, burden of establishing as a matter of law at the summary judgment stage that it is not liable under any theory fairly presented by the allegations of the petition.

The judgment of the Court of Civil Appeals is affirmed.

Notes

1. UPA section 13 provides that a partnership is liable for a partner's wrongful act or omission if the partner acted "in the ordinary course of business of the partnership or with the authority of his co-partners." Instead of applying UPA section 13, the court in *Kelsey-Seybold Clinic v. Maclay* applied common law respondeat superior. Does it make sense to apply the "scope of employment" test to the conduct of a partner?

2. UPA section 14 also holds the partnership responsible for a partner's misapplication of property, where the property *either* was received by the partnership in the course of its business, UPA § 14(b), *or* was received by the partner within the scope of his apparent authority, UPA § 14(a). What agency principles is UPA Section 14 equivalent to?

3. RUPA section 305(a) *combines* UPA sections 13 and 14(a):

> A partnership is liable for loss or injury caused to a person or for a penalty incurred as a result of actionable conduct by an act or omission of a partner acting in the ordinary course of business of the partnership or with the actual or apparent authority of the partnership.

How does RUPA section 305(a) change the scope of either UPA section 13 or UPA Section 14(a)?

RUPA section 305(b) is the RUPA equivalent of UPA section 14(b).

B. Rights of Partners Among Themselves

1. Authority of a Partner—Generally

National Biscuit Co., Inc. v. Stroud

259 N.C. 467, 106 S.E.2d 692 (1959)

The case was heard in the Superior Court upon the following agreed statement of facts:

On 13 September 1956 the National Biscuit Company had a Justice of the Peace to issue summons against C. N. Stroud and Earl Freeman, a partnership trading as Stroud's Food Center, for the nonpayment of $171.04 for goods sold and delivered. After a hearing the Justice of the Peace rendered judgment for plaintiff against both defendants for $171.04 with interest and costs. Stroud appealed to the Superior Court: Freeman did not.

In March 1953 C. N. Stroud and Earl Freeman entered into a general partnership to sell groceries under the name of Stroud's Food Center. Thereafter plaintiff sold bread regularly to the partnership. Several months prior to February 1956 the defendant Stroud advised an agent of plaintiff that he personally would not be responsible for any additional bread sold by plaintiff to Stroud's Food Center. From 6 February 1956 to 25 February 1956 plaintiff through this same agent, at the request of the defendant Freeman, sold and delivered bread in the amount of $171.04 to Stroud's Food Center. Stroud and Freeman by agreement dissolved the partnership at the close of business on 25 February 1956, and notice of such dissolution was published in a newspaper in Carteret County 6-27 March 1956.

The relevant parts of the dissolution agreement are these: All partnership assets, except an automobile truck, an electric adding machine, a rotisserie, which were assigned to defendant Freeman, and except funds necessary to pay the employees for their work the week before the dissolution and necessary to pay for certain supplies purchased the week of dissolution, were assigned to Stroud. Freeman assumed the outstanding liens against the truck. Paragraph five of the dissolution agreement is as follows: "From and after the aforesaid February 25, 1956, Stroud will be responsible for the liquidation of the partnership assets and the discharge of partnership liabilities without demand upon Freeman for any contribution in the discharge of said obligations." The dissolution agreement was made in reliance on Freeman's representations that the indebtedness of the partnership was about $7,800 and its accounts receivable were about $8,000. The accounts receivable at the close of business actually amounted to $4,897.41.

Stroud has paid all of the partnership obligations amounting to $12,014.45, except the amount of $171.04 claimed by plaintiff. To pay such obligations Stroud exhausted all the partnership assets he could reduce to money amounting to $4,307.08, of which $2,028 was derived from accounts receivable and $2,278.44 from a sale of merchandise and fixtures and used over $7,700 of his personal money. Stroud has left of the partnership assets only uncollected accounts in the sum of $2,868.77, practically all of which are considered uncollectible.

Stroud has not attempted to rescind the dissolution agreement, and has tendered plaintiff, and still tenders it, one-half of the $171.04 claimed by it.

From a judgment that plaintiff recover from the defendants $171.04 with interest and costs, Stroud appeals to the Supreme Court.

PARKER, Justice.

C. N. Stroud and Earl Freeman entered into a general partnership to sell groceries under the firm name of Stroud's Food Center. There is nothing in the agreed statement of facts to indicate or suggest that Freeman's power and authority as a general partner were in any way restricted or limited by the articles of partnership in respect to the ordinary and legitimate business of the partnership. Certainly, the purchase and sale of bread were ordinary and legitimate business of Stroud's Food Center during its continuance as a going concern.

Several months prior to February 1956 Stroud advised plaintiff that he personally would not be responsible for any additional bread sold by plaintiff to Stroud's Food Center. After such notice to plaintiff, it from 6 February 1956 to 25 February 1956, at the request of Freeman, sold and delivered bread in the amount of $171.04 to Stroud's Food Center.

In *Johnson v. Bernheim*, 76 N.C. 139, this Court said: "A and B are general partners to do some given business; the partnership is, by operation of law, a power to each to bind the partnership in any manner legitimate to the business. If one partner go to a third person to buy an article on time for the partnership, the other partner cannot prevent it by writing to the third person not to sell to him on time; or, if one party attempt to buy for cash, the other has no right to require that it shall be on time. And what is true in regard to buying is true in regard to selling. What either partner does with a third person is binding on the partnership. It is otherwise where the partnership is not general, but is upon special terms, as that purchases and sales must be with and for cash. There the power for each is special, in regard to all dealings with third persons at least who have notice of the terms." There is contrary authority. 68 C.J.S. Partnership § 143, pp. 578-579. However, this text of C.J.S. does not mention the effect of the provisions of the [UPA].

[UPA section 9] is entitled "Partner Agent of Partnership as to Partnership Business," and subsection (1) reads: "Every partner is an agent of the partnership for the purpose of its business, and the act of every partner, including the execution in the partnership name of any instrument, for apparently carrying on in the usual way the business of the partnership of which he is a member binds the partnership, unless the partner so acting has in fact no authority to act for the partnership in the particular matter, and the person with whom he is dealing has knowledge of the fact that he has no such authority." [UPA section 9(4)] states: "No act of a partner in contravention of a restriction on authority shall bind the partnership to persons having knowledge of the restriction."

[UPA section 15] provides that "all partners are jointly and severally liable for the acts and obligations of the partnership."

[UPA section 18] is captioned "Rules Determining Rights and Duties of Partners." Subsection (e) thereof reads: "All partners have equal rights in the management and conduct of the partnership business." Subsection (h) hereof is as follows: "Any difference arising as to ordinary matters connected with the partnership business may be decided by a majority of the partners; but no act in contravention of any agreement between the partners may be done rightfully without the consent of all the partners."

Freeman as a general partner with Stroud, with no restrictions on his authority to act within the scope of the partnership so far as the agreed statement of facts shows, had under the Uniform Partnership Act "equal rights in the management and conduct of the partnership business." Under [UPA section 18(h)] Stroud, his co-partner, could not restrict the power and authority of Freeman to buy bread for the partnership as a going concern, for such a purchase was an "ordinary matter connected with the partnership business," for the purpose of its business and within its scope, because in the very nature of things Stroud was not, and could not be, a majority of the partners. Therefore, Freeman's purchases of bread from plaintiff for Stroud's Food Center as a going concern bound the partnership and his co-partner Stroud. The quoted provisions of our Uniform Partnership Act, in respect to the particular facts here, are in accord with the principle of law stated in *Johnson v. Bernheim, supra.*

In Crane on Partnership, 2d Ed., p. 277, it is said:

> In cases of an even division of the partners as to whether or not an act within the scope of the business should be done, or which disagreement a third person has knowledge, it seems that logically no restriction can be placed upon the power to act. The partnership being a going concern, activities within the scope of the business should not be limited, save by the expressed will of the majority deciding a disputed question; half of the members are not a majority.

At the close of business on 25 February 1956 Stroud and Freeman by agreement dissolved the partnership. By their dissolution agreement all of the partnership assets, including cash on hand, bank deposits and all accounts receivable, with a few exceptions, were assigned to Stroud, who bound himself by such written dissolution agreement to liquidate the firm's assets and discharge its liabilities. It would seem a fair inference from the agreed statement of facts that the partnership got the benefit of the bread sold and delivered by plaintiff to Stroud's Food Center, at Freeman's request, from 6 February 1956 to 25 February 1956. But whether it did not, Freeman's acts, as stated above, bound the partnership and Stroud.

Affirmed.

Covalt v. High

100 N.M. 700, 675 P.2d 999 (App. 1983)

DONNELLY, Judge.

Can a partner recover damages against his co-partner for the co-partner's failure or refusal to negotiate and obtain an increase in the amount of rental of partnership property?

The plaintiff, Louis E. Covalt, filed suit against defendant, William L. High, seeking (1) the sale of real property in lieu of partition, (2) an accounting as to former partnership property, and (3) seeking both actual and punitive damages. Covalt alleged High had breached his fiduciary duty as a partner resulting in a loss of increased rentals. Covalt also filed a separate action against Concrete Systems, Inc. (CSI), Mildred L. High and Mark High (wife and son of William High), as corporate shareholders, seeking dissolution of the corporation, damages for alleged misuse of corporate funds, and seeking a dissolution and accounting of partnership assets. By order of the district court the two cases were consolidated for trial.

The answers of defendants denied any wrongdoing and contained a counterclaim asserting, *inter alia*, that Covalt as former employee of CSI had wrongfully converted corporate assets and wrongfully interfered with contractual relations between the corporation and others.

The trial court ordered that Covalt's claim for loss of rental income, allegedly owed by defendant to the former partnership, be bifurcated from the remaining issues and tried separately to the court. Following trial thereon, Covalt was awarded judgment against William L. High, individually, in the sum of $9,500, plus prejudgment interest in the sum of $2,269.

High appeals the partial judgment entered solely against him. The single issue presented on appeal is whether the trial court erred by ruling that High breached a fiduciary duty of fairness to his former partner Covalt by failing to negotiate and obtain an increase in the amount of rental for the partnership realty.

Covalt and High were corporate officers and shareholders in CSI. Covalt owned 25% of the stock and High owned the remaining 75% of the stock. Both men received remuneration from the corporation in the form of salaries and bonuses. In late 1971, after both High and Covalt had become corporate officers, they orally agreed to the formation of a partnership. The partnership bought real estate and constructed an office and warehouse building on the land. In February, 1973, CSI leased the building from the partnership for a five-year term. Following the expiration of the initial term of the lease, CSI remained a tenant of the building; the corporation and the partnership orally agreed to certain rental increases. The corporation made substantial improvements to the leasehold. Under the original lease any improvements to the premises were to accrue to the partnership upon termination of the lease.

In December, 1978, Covalt resigned his corporate position and was employed by a competitor of CSI. Covalt, however, remained a partner with High in the ownership of the land and the building rented to CSI. On January 9, 1979, Covalt wrote to High demanding that the monthly rent for the partnership real estate leased to CSI be increased from $1,850 to $2,850 per month. Upon receipt of the letter, High informed Covalt he would determine if the rent could be increased. Thereafter, however, High did not agree to the increased rent and took no action to renegotiate the amount of the monthly rent payable.

At the trial, High testified that he felt CSI could not afford a higher rent and that the corporation had a poor financial status. The trial court, however, adopted findings that CSI could afford the requested rental increase and that High's failure to assent to his partner's demand was a breach of his fiduciary duty. The trial court also found that at the time of Covalt's demand, a reasonable monthly rental would have been $2,850 per month or more.

The trial court adopted findings of fact, that:

> 18. At all material times, William High was the managing partner of the partnership and had a duty of utmost fairness to his partner, Mr. Covalt, which required him to obtain a reasonable rental on the property.
>
> 55. William High refused to see that the rental on the Richmond property was raised to $2,850 a month, and said refusal was a breach of his fiduciary duty of utmost fairness to his partner, Louis Covalt.

The court also found that the partnership between High and Covalt was dissolved by written agreement dated August 27, 1980. Under the terms of the dissolution, High paid Covalt $170,000, in cash, plus installment payments for his one-half interest as a partner, and for other property in which the two parties held joint interests.

The court further found that the rental rate in effect when the written lease expired on January 31, 1978, was $1,850 per month, no other written lease was ever executed by the partnership and CSI, and that the partners never had any specific agreement as to how the partnership would set the rent to be charged CSI. As between the partners, that calculation was left up to High. The court adopted a finding that High, as Covalt's partner, did not agree with Covalt's demand to raise the monthly rental payable by CSI.

The trial court also found:

> 34. On January 9, 1979, when Covalt made his demand on [CSI] for a rental increase, High, as President of [CSI] owed a duty to the Corporation and all shareholders, including Covalt, to exercise his best judgment to operate the Corporation as profitably as possible.
>
> 35. That High, in failing or refusing to accede to the demand by Covalt to raise the rent, was fulfilling this duty owed to the Corporation and its shareholders, including Covalt.

Based on the foregoing findings, the trial court concluded that High breached his fiduciary duty to Covalt, resulting in damage to Covalt in the sum of $9,500 as lost rentals, plus prejudgment interest through April 30, 1982, in the amount of $2,269.66.

Fiduciary Duty as a Partner

Did High breach a fiduciary partnership duty to Covalt warranting an award of damages?

The status resulting from the formation of a partnership creates a fiduciary relationship between partners. The status of partnership requires of each member an obligation of good faith and fairness in their dealings with one another, and a duty to act in furtherance of the common benefit of all partners in transactions conducted within the ambit of partnership affairs.

The problems which have arisen between the parties herein emphasize the importance of formulating written partnership agreements detailing the rights and obligations of the partners. Here, at the time of Covalt's demand for an increase in rents, both he and High simultaneously occupied the positions of corporate shareholders in CSI and as partners engaged in the ownership and rental of real property to the same corporation. Prior to Covalt's resignation as a corporate officer, he also served as vice president of CSI. The trial court found that High occupied the position of managing partner of the partnership.

Except where the partners expressly agree to the contrary, it is a fundamental principle of the law of partnership that all partners have equal rights in the management and conduct of the business of the partnership. [UPA § 18(e).] As specified in the Uniform Partnership Act..., where there is a difference of opinion between the partners as to the management or conduct of the partnership business, the decision of the majority must govern. [UPA § 18(h).]

Under [UPA section 18(e)], Covalt was legally invested with an equal voice in the management of the partnership affairs. Assuming, but not deciding, that High's status as a managing partner is not to be considered, neither partner had the right to impose his will or decision concerning the operation of the partnership business upon the other. The fact that a proposal may in fact benefit the partnership does not mandate acceptance by all the partners. As specified in [UPA section 18(h)], "any difference arising as to ordinary matters connected with the partnership business may be decided by a majority of the partners; but no act in contravention of any agreement between the partners may be done rightfully without the consent of all the partners."

As stated in *Lindley on the Law of Partnership*, at 354 (E. Scamell 12th ed. 1962) (hereinafter referred to as *Lindley*), as to differences arising in the ordinary scope of the partnership business:

> [I]f the partners are equally divided, those who forbid a change must have their way. [O]ne partner cannot either engage a new or dismiss an old servant against the will of his co-partner; nor, if the lease of the partnership place of business expires, insist on renewing the lease and continuing the business at the old place.

In *Summers v. Dooley*, 94 Idaho 87, 481 P.2d 318 (1971), the Supreme Court of Idaho was confronted with a similar problem arising out of a partnership of two individuals. There, the partners were engaged in a trash collection business and each contributed to the necessary labor. Over the objection of one partner, the other hired an additional employee. The disagreement over the hiring and compensation of the new employee resulted in a suit between the partners. The one partner sought to compel his co-partner to contribute to the expenses for hiring the additional man. The court held that, based upon the Idaho statute, mirroring the Uniform Partnership Act and identical to that adopted by New Mexico, the statutory language that any differences between partners as to the ordinary course of partnership business "may be decided by a majority of the partners" is mandatory rather than permissive in nature.

In keeping with *Lindley* and *Summers*, as between the partners themselves, in the absence of an agreement of a majority of the partners—an act involving the partnership business may not be compelled by the co-partner. If the parties are evenly divided as to a business decision affecting the partnership, and in the absences of a written provision in the partnership agreement providing for such contingency, then, as between the partners, the power to exercise discretion on behalf of the partners is suspended so long as the division continues. The rule is different, however, as to transactions between partners and third parties. *See Dotson v. Grice*, 98 N.M. 207, 647 P.2d 409 (1982) (holding that in dealing with third parties a partner has the authority to act on behalf of the partnership in the usual way, even without the consent of the other partner).

Similarly, it is observed in 1 J. Barrett & E. Seago, *Partners and Partnerships Law and Taxation*, at 484 (1956):

> Where the partnership consists of only two partners there is ordinarily no question of one partner controlling the other and there is no majority. The rights of each of the two partners are equal. If the partners are unable to agree and if the partnership agreement does not provide an acceptable means for settlement of this disagreement, the only course of action is to dissolve the partnership.

At the time of the formation of the partnership, both Covalt and High were officers and shareholders of CSI. Each was aware of the potential for conflict between their duties as corporate officers to further the business of the corporation, and that of their role as partners in leasing realty to the corporation for the benefit of the partnership business. In the posture of being both a landlord and representatives of the tenant they had conflicting loyalties and fiduciary duties. After Covalt's resignation as an officer of the corporation he continued to remain a shareholder of the corporation. Each party's conflict of interest was known to the other and was acquiesced in when the partnership was formed.

Under the facts herein, in the absence of a mutual agreement between the partners to increase the rent of the partnership realty, we hold that one partner may not recover damages for the failure of the co-partner to acquiesce in a demand by the plaintiff that High negotiate and execute an increase in the monthly rentals of partnership property with CSI. Thus, there was no breach of a fiduciary duty. In the absence of a mutual agreement, or a written instrument detailing the rights of the parties, the remedy for such an impasse is a dissolution of the partnership.

[T]he judgment awarding damages is reversed.

Notes

1. What is the difference between *National Biscuit Co., Inc. v. Stroud* and *Covalt v. High*, on the one hand, and *Burns v. Gonzalez*, on the other?

2. Under the opinions in *National Biscuit Co., Inc. v. Stroud* and *Covalt v. High*, when does a partner act *rightfully* (as against the other partners) in the partnership business? What is the *source* of a partner's *right* to act in the partnership business? Is it possible to reconcile the *results* of *National Biscuit Co., Inc. v. Stroud* and *Covalt v. High*?

3. The provisions of UPA section 18(h) may be varied by agreement among the partners. For example, partners often agree to vote according to their *interests*, rather than *per capita*. Any agreement intended to apply to matters that would require partner *unanimity* under the UPA should do so expressly and unambiguously. Several

cases have *limited* the provisions of partnership voting agreements to votingd agreements to voting on *ordinary* matters, reasoning that voting rights as to "extraordinary" are so "fundamental and vital" that any ambiguity as to the application of the agreement should be resolved *against* surrender of such rights. *E.g.*, *Wilzig v. Sisselman*, 182 N.J. Super. 519, 535, 442 A.2d 1021, 1030 (1982). *See generally*, A. BROMBERG & L. RIBSTEIN, BROMBERG & RIBSTEIN ON PARTNERSHIP 6:40–41, 6:436–49 (1988).

4. RUPA sections 401(f) and 401(j) are the RUPA equivalents of UPA sections 18(e) and 18(h).

5. What does UPA section 18(e) (equal rights to participate in management) have to do with whether the defendant in *Covalt v. High* violated defendant's duty of loyalty?

2. Additional Limitations on the Authority of a Partner

Vinson v. Marton & Associates

159 Ariz. 1, 764 P.2d 736 (App. 1988)

KLEINSCHMIDT, Judge.

This is an appeal from summary judgment in favor of defendants in a lawsuit for specific performance of a real estate contract. We must determine whether the unanimous consent of the partners was required to convey the partnership's sole asset.

Marton & Associates was a partnership formed in 1960 for the purpose of buying, selling and exchanging real property. The partnership's sole asset was a 238 acre parcel of land near Buckeye, Arizona. The original partners were Larry Marton, Larry Melcher, Dr. A.J. Silva, Richard Stephenson, Dr. Franklin Laneback, Robert Creighton, Charles Johnston and Powell Gillenwater. After Dr. Silva's death, his interest in the property passed by inheritance to Mary Silva, John Silva and the Celeste Silva-Brock Trust; after Dr. Laneback's death, his interest passed to his widow Phyllis Laneback; and after Powell Gillenwater's death, his interest passed to Danielle Gillenwater-Civer. Robert Creighton's interest was transferred to the Robert and Catherine Creighton Trust. The record does not disclose what happened to the interests of Richard Stephenson and Charles Johnston.

In November 1985, John Vinson entered into a contract to purchase the parcel of land owned by Marton & Associates. The purchase agreement was signed by Larry Melcher and John Silva for the sellers. Vinson alleged that Melcher, Silva and their realtor, C.B. Stauffer, represented that they were authorized to sign on behalf of the partnership. At the time Melcher signed the contract he held powers of attorney executed in 1979 from Larry Marton, the Creighton Trust and Phyllis Laneback. Stauffer informed Vinson that the land had been listed for sale by the partnership for several years.

Escrow instructions were issued on December 2, 1985, and were signed by Larry Marton, Larry Melcher, Mary Silva, Celeste Silva-Brock, John Silva, Phyllis Laneback, Robert Creighton and Catherine Creighton. Danielle Gillenwater-Civer was the only person with an interest in the property who did not sign the escrow instructions. After the escrow instructions were signed, Stauffer presented the partnership with another offer to purchase the property at a higher price. Subsequently, the partnership and the individual partners refused to convey the property to Vinson.

Vinson filed suit alleging two counts for breach of contract against the partnership and the individual partners and seeking specific performance of the contract. Alternatively, Vinson sought damages in a third count against John Silva and Larry Melcher for damages resulting from their having entered into a contract without authority to do so. In count four, the plaintiffs sought damages against Melcher, Silva, Stauffer, and P.R. Powell and Associates, Stauffer's employer, for false representation.

All parties filed motions and cross motions for summary judgment, and the trial court granted judgment in favor of defendants on the first two counts of the complaint.

After the appeal relating to counts one and two of the complaint was filed, Vinson, Melcher, Powell and Stauffer entered into a settlement agreement respecting counts three and four. The settlement agreement specifically permitted Vinson to proceed with his appeal on counts one and two. Vinson agreed to release Melcher, Stauffer and Powell from any liabilities arising from the sale of the property at issue and not to sue Melcher individually or as a partner in Marton & Associates under counts one and two of the complaint. It permits Vinson to do whatever is necessary to preserve his rights to proceed against the other defendants under counts one and two of the complaint. Silva and his wife refused to enter into the settlement agreement.

The Sale Was Controlled by the Partnership Agreement

The trial court's minute entry granting summary judgment provides in part:

> The plaintiffs entered into a contract for the sale of the sole partnership asset with some but not all of the partners. The plaintiffs contend that Article VII of the Partnership Agreement allows a majority of the partners to conduct all business of the partnership. *Because a number of original partners are now deceased, this provision is not controlling upon the successor partners.* (All apparently agree that a partnership of some sort does exist.)
>
> With no controlling language in the agreement, the provision of [UPA section 9] controls. In a recent decision the Court of Appeals has held that the concurrence of all of the partners is necessary to conclude a sale such as the one proposed in this case. (Emphasis added.)

In referring to [UPA section 9] as controlling, the trial court was apparently relying on subsection [(3)(c)], which requires unanimous consent of the partners to do any act that would make it impossible to carry on the ordinary business of the partnership. We disagree with the trial court's conclusion that the death of some of the partners rendered the partnership agreement inapplicable to this transaction. Article IX of the agreement provides:

> It is further agreed that *the death or insanity of one or more of the partners of this partnership shall not dissolve the partnership*, but the same shall be continued by the remaining partners, and in the event of the death of any partner his personal representative shall immediately offer the partnership interest of the deceased partner for sale, first to the partnership and upon its refusal, then to as many of the partners individually as wish to participate, at its actual value to be determined by three arbitrators. (Emphasis added.)

Accordingly, the partnership agreement pursuant to its own terms continued in force after the death of any partner.

[UPA section 18] provides in part that "[t]he rights and duties of the partners in relation to the partnership shall be determined, *subject to any agreement between them*, by the following rules." (Emphasis added.) Other jurisdictions that, like Arizona, have adopted the Uniform Partnership Act recognize that partners may agree to terms different from the Uniform Partnership Act and be bound by those terms.

The rule that a partnership agreement controls over the Uniform Partnership Act has been acknowledged specifically with respect to death provisions in such an agreement. Accordingly, we find that the partnership agreement remained effective and there was no dissolution of Marton & Associates because of the death of some of the original partners.

Unanimous Consent of All Partners Was Not Required for the Sale of the Property at Issue

Article VII of the partnership agreement provides in part:

> *All business* of this partnership shall be carried on by, and only by, the majority vote of the partners, however, it is agreed that this partnership shall never allow the annual payments on its investment to exceed $500 per unit without the unanimous written consent of the partners. (Emphasis added.)

Marton & Associates argues that Article VII does not govern the sale of the sole partnership asset because it is not a sale in the ordinary course of business. Rather, it argues that the sale is controlled by the provisions of [UPA section 9], which requires a unanimous vote of the partners.

Vinson contends that [UPA section 9] is inapplicable because the partnership agreement expressly permits an act with less than a unanimous vote. He argues that "all business" includes a sale of the partnership's sole asset. He also argues that, even assuming arguendo that "all business" means the "ordinary business" of the partnership, this sale was in the ordinary course of business under [UPA section 9].

[UPA section 9(1)] provides:

> Every partner is an agent of the partnership for the purpose of its business, and the act of every partner, including the execution in the partnership name of any instrument, for apparently *carrying on in the usual way the business of the partnership* of which he is a member binds the partnership, unless the partner so acting has in fact no authority to act for the partnership in the particular matter, and the person with whom he is dealing has knowledge of the fact that he has no authority [(emphasis added)].

[UPA section 9(3)] provides that the authorization of all partners is required to do certain acts, including:

> [(b)] Dispose of the good-will of the business.
>
> [(c)] Do any other act which would make it impossible to carry on the ordinary business of a partnership.

Marton & Associates cites cases standing for the general proposition that unanimous consent of all partners must be obtained in order to sell the capital assets of the partnership.

However, numerous cases interpreting § 9 of the Uniform Partnership Act hold that where the business of the partnership is to sell real estate, the sale of real estate, including real estate that is the sole asset, is a sale in the usual course of business.

Marton & Associates cites *Jolly v. Kent Realty, Inc.*, 151 Ariz. 506, 729 P.2d 310 (App. 1986), for the proposition that the sale of a sole partnership assert requires unanimous approval of all partners under [UPA section 9]. This misstates the holding of that case. In *Jolly* this court found that the sale of the partnership's capital asset was not "carrying on in the usual way of business" under [UPA section 9(1)]. In concluding that one partner could not bind the partnership to the sale of an apartment complex, the court found no evidence to establish that the partnership's "usual business" was the "selling or exchanging of apartment investments." It treated the partnership as one whose "usual business" was *operating* the apartment complex. Thus the court held that one partner could not bind the partnership to a sale of the complex because the agreement provided that 51% of the partners approve "decisions affecting the future worth of the investment."

In contrast to *Jolly* the record in this case reflects that the partnership was established to buy and sell property. It held the undeveloped land as an investment to sell for profit. This was its only business—its "stock in trade."

[*Kristerin Dev. Co. v. Granson Inv.*, 394 N.W.2d 325 (Iowa 1986)] involved circumstances very similar to the instant case. In 1976, the partnership bought an apartment building. In 1980, the building was listed for sale with a realtor. Two of the three partners executed the purchase contract and assured the buyer that two signatures were sufficient to bind the partnership. The partnership ultimately refused to go through with the sale, and the buyer sued for breach of contract. The trial court directed a verdict in favor of the partnership on grounds that the partnership could only be bound by a contract signed by all partners. In reversing the trial court the Iowa Supreme Court stated:

> [A] contract executed by one partner alone to sell partnership real estate is binding on the other partners provided the partnership is in the business of buying or selling real estate.

The Iowa Supreme Court considered [UPA section 9(1)] and found that the "apparent scope of the partnership business depends primarily on the conduct of the partnership and its partners and what they cause third persons to believe about [their] authority." Further, the court rejected the partnership's contention that the fact that the partnership owned only one asset took the sale out of the "usual course of business."

Vinson argues that, since Marton & Associates was in the business of investing in land, the fact that it sold its sole asset did not prevent it from continuing business. It could have chosen to reinvest in other property. A partnership in the business of buying and selling property does not necessarily cease to do business if it sells all its real property. Thus, he argues that [UPA section 9(3)] is not applicable to this transaction. We agree.

In addition, we find that the partnership agreement itself authorizes "all business" to be transacted by a majority vote with one stated exception—the authorization of investment expenditures to exceed $500 per unit. The expression in a contract of one or more things in a class implies the exclusion of all other things. Thus, by identifying expenditures as requiring unanimous approval, the contract impliedly excludes other decisions. We find that under the partnership agreement and [UPA section 9], a majority of the partners of Marton & Associates had authority to sell the real property at issue.

Summary judgment in favor of defendants is reversed, and this matter is remanded to the trial court for proceedings in accordance with this opinion.

Wasserman v. Wasserman

7 Mass. App. 167, 386 N.E.2d 783 (1979)

GRANT, Justice.

This is an action brought in the Superior Court by Peter Wasserman (Peter) against Max Wasserman (Max) and Jeanne L. Wasserman (Jeanne) by which Peter seeks to establish his position as the sole general partner of a limited partnership known as Sherman Associates, an order that Max and Jeanne turn over to him the books and records of the partnership, an injunction against their interfering with his management of the affairs of the partnership, and an accounting with respect to certain fees which the partnership has paid Jeanne for her services in managing the real estate owned by the partnership. The action was heard and determined on cross motions for summary judgment. Peter's motion was denied, the defendants' motion was allowed, and Peter has appealed from the ensuing final judgment of dismissal.

On January 4, 1971, Max and Jeanne entered into a written agreement of limited partnership for the purpose of acquiring, constructing and operating a project of low and moderate income housing in Cambridge. By the terms of that agreement Max was constituted the sole general partner of the partnership, and Max and Jeanne became the only Class B limited partners. The agreement expressly provided, among other things, that it had been made and entered into pursuant to the provisions of the [ULPA] and that the general partner (Max) should have "no authority to admit a person as a general partner." [ULPA § 9(f).] The certificate required by [the ULPA] was executed by Max and Jeanne in the capacities already indicated, was sworn to by them, and was filed on February 9, 1971.

On or about July 15, 1971, Max and Jeanne entered into an agreement in writing which superseded and recast the provisions of the agreement of the previous January. Max continued as the sole general partner, and Max and Jeanne continued as the only Class B limited partners. Section 10.2 of the amended agreement reads in material part as follows:

> At any time the then General Partners or Partner by unanimous consent or in the event there shall be no General Partners, Wasserman Development Corporation, may designate any one or more of the following individuals to become a General Partner without approval of any Limited Partner: (1) Any officer or director of Wasserman Development Corporation or Jacet Construction Corporation. (2) Any fiduciary under the will or a trust instrument of Max Wasserman. (3) Any other Person whose designation shall receive the consent of the Limited Partners.[6] This agreement shall constitute the written consent of every Limited Partner to admit as a General Partner any Person designated in the manner above provided.

6. The words "Consent of the Limited Partners" are defined in the amended agreement as "the written consent or approval of Class A Limited Partners whose aggregate Capital Contributions represent at least sixty percent (60%) of the Class A Class Contribution."

The agreement was signed by Max in his capacities as the general partner and a Class B limited partner and by Jeanne in her capacity as a Class B limited partner. Acting in those same capacities, Max and Jeanne executed, swore to, and, on October 14, 1971, filed an amendment of the certificate of limited partnership.

Following the execution of the foregoing amendment of the partnership agreement, fourteen persons were admitted as Class A limited partners of Sherman Associates. Each of the fourteen signed a counterpart of the amended agreement. On March 3, 1972, there was filed with the Secretary of the Commonwealth a second amendment of the certificate of limited partnership which reflected the admission of the Class A limited partners and which was signed and sworn to by Max as the general partner and as a Class B limited partner and by Max as "attorney in fact" for Jeanne and all the Class A limited partners.

At some point (the actual sequence of events is not clear from the record) Max, as the general partner, entered into an agreement with Jeanne, as the principal of a concern known as Sandell Management Company, under which the partnership agreed to pay Jeanne six percent of the gross collections from the operation of the project for her services in managing the project. The agreement with Jeanne was to last through May 31, 1977, and has yielded her a gross of approximately $42,000 annually.

On January 21, 1975, Max, utilizing the letterhead of Wasserman Development Corporation, wrote each of the limited partners, advising them that the project had been fully rented and was showing a positive cash flow, that he desired to retire, and that he intended to name Peter as the general partner of Sherman Associates pursuant to the provisions of the above quoted [section] 10.2 of the amended partnership agreement. On February 3, 1975, Max, purporting to act under [section] 10.2, executed a formal written designation of "Peter W. Wasserman, Vice President of Wasserman Development Corporation to be a new general partner of the Partnership," subject to the performance of certain conditions which were later fulfilled.[11] On March 1, 1975, Max executed a written assignment to Peter of Max's entire interest as general partner of the partnership. On March 10, 1975, Peter executed a written acceptance of his designation as general partner, in which he agreed to be bound by the terms and provisions of the amended partnership agreement.

On March 18, 1975, there was filed a third amendment of the certificate of limited partnership which recited on its face that it was being filed "(i)n order to reflect the admission of Peter Wasserman as an additional general partner and the subsequent retirement of Max Wasserman as general partner." This amendment was signed and sworn to by Max as "former General Partner and Class B Limited Partner," by Peter as "General Partner," and by Peter as "attorney-in-fact" for Jeanne and all the Class A limited partners.

Between March 1, 1975, and May 31, 1977, Peter performed various functions which would normally be expected of the general partner, such as the execution and filing of the partnership's Federal income tax returns for the years 1975 and 1976 and the execution and delivery of various financial reports required by the United States Department of Housing and Urban Development. On the latter date Peter notified Jeanne that the partnership would not renew the aforementioned management agreement which Max had entered into with her and which was due to expire on

---

11. It is agreed that Peter was an officer of Wasserman Development Corporation on February 3, 1975.

May 31, 1977. Max and Jeanne immediately took the position that Max was still the sole general partner of Sherman Associates, and on May 19, 1977, Max purported to extend the life of the agreement with Jeanne until May 31, 1979. Those actions, and Max's refusal to deliver the partnership books and records to Peter, led to the commencement of the present action.

The principal controversy between the partners is as to the effect which should be given to the provisions of [ULPA sectioch reads:

> A general partner shall have all the rights and powers and be subject to all the restrictions and liabilities of a partner in a partnership without limited partners, except that without the written consent or ratification of the specific act by all the limited partners, a general partner or all of the general partners have no authority to (A)DMIT A PERSON AS A GENERAL PARTNER.

Peter contends (1) that Max and Jeanne gave the only consent required by [ULPA § 9(1)(e)] when, as limited partners, they signed the amended partnership agreement of July 15, 1971, and (2) that, in any event, they have, by their subsequent actions, consented to or ratified Max's actions in substituting Peter as the sole general partner. Max and Jeanne dispute both propositions and rely on affidavits submitted by Jeanne and by two of the Class A limited partners to the effect that none of them has, as matter of fact, consented to or ratified any such substitution.

It is clear to us, as matter of construction, that the purpose and intent of § 10.2 of the amended agreement of partnership were to express and supply in advance, and without prior consultation with them, whatever consent might be required of the other limited partners to Max's designation as a general partner of "(1) Any officer or director of Wasserman Development Corporation or Jacet Construction Corporation (or) (2) Any fiduciary under the will or a trust instrument of Max Wasserman" and that Max was to be required to consult and obtain the consent of the other limited partners only in the event he should wish to designate "(3) Any person" not embraced within (1) or (2). Given (a) the fact that (1) was preceded by the words "without approval of any Limited Partner" and (b) the concluding sentence ("This agreement shall constitute the written consent of every Limited Partner to admit as a General Partner any Person designated in the manner above provided"), we see no other sensible construction of § 10.2.

The question remains whether an agreement such as the foregoing can constitute the "written consent" contemplated by [ULPA section 9(1)]. The question was left unanswered in *Lehrberg v. Felopulos*, 356 Mass. 148, 155, 248 N.E.2d 648 (1969). However, the cases from other jurisdictions which have considered the question have either held or assumed that the required consent can be found in the express provisions of a partnership agreement. The rationale appears to have been that in the absence of an express prohibition, the Act leaves the members of a limited partnership free to determine their rights with respect to each other by any contractual agreement which does not contravene public policy or run afoul of the common law.

Jeanne points to [RULPA section 401], and particularly to the Commissioners' Comment thereon. [RULPA section 401 reads] as follows: "After the filing of a limited partnership's original certificate of limited partnership, additional general partners may be admitted only with the specific written consent of each partner." The comment reads: "Section 401 is derived from Section 9(1)(e) of the prior law and carries over the unwaivable requirement that all limited partners must consent to the admission of an additional general partner and that such consent must specifically identify the general partner involved." We see nothing in the proposed new section, or in the comment, which precludes a conclusion that the written consent contemplated by § 9(1)(e) can be found in the provisions of a partnership agreement. The purpose of that section, as well as of the proposed new section, is to give each limited partner, who has no voice in the operation of the partnership business, the opportunity to prevent his investment from falling into the hands of an unknown or unwanted general partner. We think that purpose was served by the express provisions of § 10.2(1) of the amended partnership agreement in the present case. Nor do we perceive any difficulty with the Commissioners' concern for specificity; Jeanne, who is Max's wife and Peter's mother, is hardly in a position to say she did not know who controlled Wasserman Development Corporation or that Peter was a stranger to her or the corporation.

We hold that Jeanne gave her consent to the designation of Peter as a general partner when she signed the amended partnership agreement of July 15, 1971. Accordingly, it becomes unnecessary to consider whether Jeanne may also have consented to or ratified that designation in 1975 or at any subsequent time.

The order allowing the defendants' motion for summary judgment and the judgment are reversed.

Note

Section 401 of the 1985 version of RULPA follows *Wasserman v. Wasserman* and expressly allows the limited partners to agree *in advance* to the admission of a new general partner.

3. Partner's Fiduciary Duties

Starr v. International Realty, Ltd.

271 Or. 396, 533 P.2d 165 (1975)

TONGUE, Justice.

This is a suit by the partners in a real estate venture to require the Realtor and promoter of the venture, who was also a partner, to account to the partnership for the commission received by him as the Realtor without consent of the remaining partners and to hold in trust for the partnership the vendor's interest in the real estate purchased, which he also acquired without their consent. Defendants appeal from an adverse decree and plaintiffs cross-appeal from other portions of that decree.

The case involves a group of prominent Portland doctors and others in high income tax "brackets" and in need of "tax shelters." They were persuaded by one Stanley G. Harris, a Portland "expert" in real property investments, that by investing $285,000 and joining with him in a partnership for the purchase of an apartment house then under construction, the entire down payment of $265,000 could be treated for federal income tax purposes as "prepaid interest," thereby saving large amounts otherwise payable in income taxes.

It would serve no useful purpose to summarize the entire transaction for the purchase of this property for the sum of $2,010,000 in all of its details, as "put together" by Harris. Suffice to say that we have reviewed the lengthy transcript of the testimony of some 21 witnesses, together with 94 exhibits, and agree with the trial court in its findings that Harris did not reveal to his partners that the property could have been purchased for $907,500 "net" to the seller (including $207,500 to the seller to "cash [him] out of the transaction" and the assumption of a $700,000 mortgage), and that a commission of $100,000, together with an escrow fee of $2,500, was to be paid to International Realty Ltd., of which Harris was president, or that Harris had made an agreement with the seller of the property under which International or Harris would acquire the vendor's interest to the contract under which the property was being purchased by the partnership.

1. *Defendants' failure to disclose the receipt of the broker's commission.*

In *Liggett v. Lester*, 237 Or. 52, 58, 390 P.2d 351 (1964), although under different facts, we stated that:

> The rule which requires an accounting for secret profits applies to commissions and discounts *secretly obtained* by a partner on purchases made by him for the firm. It was Lester's duty to obtain petroleum products for the partnership at the best price possible.
>
> The case at bar involves purchases for the partnership resulting in *secret commissions* or discounts. Where a secret discount is withheld by one partner on purchases which he has made on behalf of the partnership, the entire amount of the discount must be accounted for. (Emphasis added.)

To the same effect, see Crane and Bromberg on Partnership 389-90, § 68 (1968). The question to be decided in this case, however, is whether the $100,000 commission paid to International of which Harris was the president, was a "secret" commission.

Defendants contend that the broker's commission paid to International was not "secret" or "concealed"; that "explicit consent" is not required; and that "sufficient disclosure" was made "through documents, through the plaintiffs' general knowledge of the general manner in which real estate transactions are conducted, and through specific conversations." Defendants "do not contend that plaintiffs explicitly and expressly consented to the commission."

It appears from the testimony that most of the plaintiffs knew or should have known that Harris and International were in the real estate business and that a Realtor's commission in some amount would normally be paid to some Realtor on this transaction. Apparently, because their interest in the income tax advantages of the transaction was so dominant and overriding, the doctors did not inquire whether such a commission would be paid to Harris or to International, or in what amount, and Harris did not tell them. It is contended by the doctors, however, that in this case they are entitled to the benefit of the equivalent of a role more familiar to them in the practice of medicine—that of "informed consent."

In *Liggett v. Lester*, *supra*, we also said:

> Although Liggett was aware of Lester's bulkplant operation, it is clear that Lester failed to disclose the additional discounts he was receiving on the sales to the partnership. Lester not only failed to offer his partner an opportunity to share in the discount, but he tried to keep Liggett from learning of it. Liggett discovered this state of affairs by chance. Lester cannot rely upon the foregoing right to engage in other business since Liggett's consent was not truly obtained.

It is contended by defendants that *Liggett* is not controlling because the defendant in that case "actively attempted to keep his partner from learning of the discount." In our view, however, the rule as stated by this court in *Liggett* is not limited to cases involving "active attempts" to conceal.

[UPA section 21(1)] provides:

> Every partner must account to the partnership for *any benefit*, and hold as trustee for it any profits derived by him *without the consent* of the other partners from any transaction connected with the formation, conduct, or liquidation of the partnership or from any use by him of its property. (Emphasis added.)

In *Fouchek et al. v. Janicek*, 190 Or. 251, 262, 225 P.2d 7 83 (1950), we said that this section from the [UPA] states "the essence of the fiduciary [duty] of a partner," as stated by Justice Cardozo in *Meinhard v. Salmon*, 249 N.Y. 458, 463, 164 N.E. 545 (1929), as follows:

> Joint adventurers, [and] copartners, owe to one another, while the enterprise continues, the duty of the finest loyalty. Many forms of conduct permissible in a workaday world for those acting at arm's length are forbidden to those bound by fiduciary ties. A trustee is held to something stricter than morals of the market place. Not honesty alone, but the punctilio of an honor the most sensitive, is then the standard of behavior. As to this there has developed a tradition that is unbending and inveterate. Uncompromising rigidity has been the attitude of courts of equity when petitioned to undermine the rule of undivided loyalty by the 'disintegrating erosion' of particular exceptions. Only thus has the level of conduct for fiduciaries been kept at a level higher than that trodden by the crowd. It will not consciously be lowered by any judgment of this court.

Real estate brokers are subject to potential conflicting interest in many transactions. Even when a real estate broker does not become a partner in a venture involving the purchase of property this court has held that he owes a fiduciary duty to protect his client's interests and also "to make a full, fair and understandable explanation to his client before having him sign any contract."

When, as in this case, a real estate broker undertakes to join as a member of partnership or joint venture in the purchase of real property on which he holds a listing, he is also subject to the fiduciary duties of undivided loyalty and complete disclosure owed by one partner to another. Indeed, one of the fundamental duties of any partner who deals on his own account in matters within the scope of his fiduciary relationship is the affirmative duty to make a full disclosure to his partners not only of the fact that he is dealing on his own account, but all of the facts which are material to the transaction. As held in *Duniway v. Barton*, 193 Or. 69, 78, 237 P.2d 930 (1951), although not involving a partnership, a fiduciary has a duty "not only not to misrepresent," but to "disclose fully all the material facts within his knowledge."

It follows that the "consent of the other partners" required by [UPA section 21(1)] before any partner may retain "any benefit" from "any transaction connected with the formation [or] conduct" of a partnership must necessarily be an "informed consent" with knowledge of the facts necessary to the giving of an intelligent consent.

In this case, Harris did not inform plaintiffs or disclose to them the fact that this property could have been purchased for $907,500 "net" to the seller or that upon its purchase for $1,010,000 Harris or International (of which Harris was the president) would be paid a commission in the amount of $100,000. In the absence of such a disclosure there could be no effective "consent" by plaintiffs to the payment or retention by Harris of any such "benefit" from that transaction, for the purposes of [UPA section 21(1)].

For these reasons we must reject defendants' contention that the broker's commission paid to International was "neither secret nor concealed." For the same reasons, the trial court did not err in requiring defendants to account to the partnership for that commission.

2. *Defendants' failure to disclose the agreement to receive an assignment of the vendor's interest in the sales contract.*

Defendants make no contention that they originally informed plaintiffs of the agreement by which the vendor's interest in the contract under which this property was being purchased by the partnership would be assigned to International. Defendants contend, however, that in 1970 Harris "spoke with each of the partners except [one] about possible acquisition of the vendor's interest" and that "none of the partners expressed any desire to purchase the interest, even though Harris apparently offered it at a substantial discount." Defendants also cite cases from other states in support of the contention that "a partner may purchase the fee to the property which the partnership has leased, provided he practices no deception or fraud upon his co-partners."

Again, we consider the better rule, and the established rule in Oregon to be that the absence of "deception or fraud" is not sufficient to justify a partner in acquiring such an interest in property being purchased under contract by the partnership. On the contrary, we hold that the acquisition by International (and subsequently by Harris and his wife) of the vendor's interest in the property being purchased under contract by the partnership of which Harris was a member was a "benefit" that was connected with the formation [and] conduct" of the partnership and was subject to [UPA Section 21], so as to require "consent" by the other parties and so as also to be subject to the duty of full disclosure to the same extent as the receipt of the commission on the sale, as previously discussed.

The same result also follows under established rules of agency. Thus, as stated in Restatement 2d of Agency 208-09, § 390, comment *a*:

> One employed as agent violates no duty to the principal by action for his own benefit *if he makes a full disclosure of the facts* to an acquiescent principal and takes no unfair advantage of him. Before dealing with the principal on his own account, however, *an agent has a duty, not only to make no misstatements of fact, but also to disclose to the principal all relevant facts fully and completely.* A fact is relevant if it is one which the agent should realize would be likely to affect the judgment of the principal in giving his consent to the agent to enter into the particular transaction on the specified terms. Hence, the disclosure must include not only the fact that the agent is acting on his own account, but also all other facts which he should realize have or are likely to have a bearing upon the desirability of the transaction from the viewpoint of the principal. (Emphasis added.)

It follows that the trial court did not err in holding that Harris holds the vendor's interest in this contract in trust for the benefit of the partnership.

4. *Plaintiffs are entitled to the full amount of the sums misappropriated without deduction of amounts paid to employees.*

Plaintiffs' remaining contention on cross-appeal is that the trial court erred in allowing defendants a set-off of some $34,656.10, representing that portion of the $82,500 found to have been misappropriated by the defendants which was paid to salesmen who secured the original listing and who secured the various "clients" who became partners in the venture. Plaintiffs again cite *Liggett v. Lester*, in which we distinguished cases involving "dealings with third parties" and held, under the facts of that case, that a partner who had withheld a "secret discount" must account for that "entire amount."

To the same effect, the following rule is stated in 1 Rowley on Partnership 532, § 21.1 (2d ed. 1960):

> The partner receiving secret commissions on the partnership transactions must account for the whole amount of the commissions so received even though he may have been assisted in the deal by a third person, to whom he paid a part of such commissions.

Defendants contend, on the contrary, that "[t]he power of a court of equity to fashion justice should not be limited" and that "[r]emedies should be shaped to meet the needs of justice required by the facts of each case."

After a review of this record, however, we believe that the facts of this case are sufficiently aggravated that the defendants should be held liable to account for payment to the partnership of the full amount misappropriated by defendants, without deductions or set-off of payments made to employees.

The fact that in this case the commission received by International and by Harris was shared with salesmen employed by them does not, in our opinion, require a different result under the facts of this case.

Except as modified by the disallowance of the set-offs claimed by defendants, the decree of the trial court is affirmed and the case is remanded for the purpose of computing the amount to be awarded by the final judgment.

Notes

1. A partner's duty of loyalty extends beyond transactions between the partnership and the partner. It also extends to transactions *between partners*. Consider, for example, *Johnson v. Buck*, 540 S.W.2d 393 (Tex. Civ. App. 1976).

Johnson and Buck were partners in a real estate development partnership, with Johnson as managing partner. Johnson convinced Buck that they were in danger of losing their entire investment. Johnson misrepresented the financial condition of the partnership and their bank's willingness to renew partnership loans that were coming due. Buck then sold his interest in the partnership to Johnson for substantially less than its true value. In fact, the business was not only currently making money, Johnson anticipated it would continue to do so. Not only had the bank not cut off the partnership's credit, it had loaned money to Johnson so he could buy out Buck.

The court placed on Johnson the burden of proving that his dealings with Buck were fair, and had little difficulty in finding that Johnson had violated his duty of loyalty. Not only had he failed to make full disclosure of all material facts, he had actively misrepresented the facts. The court found that Buck was entirely justified in relying solely on his partner without any independent verification, especially when the partner relied on was the managing partner.

2. A partner's duty of loyalty also applies to a partner's management of partnership business, even when the partner is not engaging in a transaction with the partnership or another partner. Consider, for example, *Labowitz v. Dolan*, 189 Ill. App. 3d 403, 545 N.E.2d 304 (1989). The limited partners of a partnership alleged that its general partner, Dolan, had tried to "freeze" the limited partners out of a limited partnership by refusing to distribute *any* cash to the partners. (For federal tax purposes, a partnership is not taxed on its income. Instead, the partners are directly taxed on the share of partnership income. If the general partner fails to distribute any cash to the partners, they suffer twice: not only are they not *benefiting* from the partnership's income, they suffer a *detriment*, because they must come out of pocket to pay taxes on their share of partnership income.)

The trial court *dismissed* the limited partner's *complaint with prejudice*, reasoning that the partnership agreement vested him with *sole discretion* in managing the partnership's affairs, including determining when and whether to distribute cash. The appellate court *reversed*, holding that Dolan's discretion was limited by his duty to act in good faith, with honesty and fairness (to the limited partners) in managing the partnership's business.

3. RUPA section 404 imposes on partners two basic fiduciary duties: the duty of loyalty, and the duty of care.

Note on Necessity for Accounting

A traditional principle of partnership law is that one partner may not sue the partnership or another partner on a matter arising out of partnership affairs until the partnership has been dissolved, its affairs wound up, and there has been an *accounting* of such affairs. This principle has several theoretical bases. First, to the extent a partnership is an aggregate, a partner's suit against the partnership is really a suit against the suing partner. Second, partnerships result in an interconnected web of financial relationships. Even though the "partnership" may be liable to a partner, that partner is responsible for a proportionate part of all partnership losses. UPA § 18(a). Moreover, the other partners may also have claims arising out of partnership affairs. The only way to tell if any particular partner is due anything is to close the partnership down and resolve *all* its affairs.

This rule is subject to numerous exceptions. Professors Bromberg and Ribstein list ten different contexts in which courts have allowed a suit between partners without a prior accounting. 2 A. BROMBERG & L. RIBSTEIN, BROMBERG & RIBSTEIN ON PARTNERSHIP 6:102-10 (1989). The primary exception is a suit arising out of a transaction sufficiently isolated from other partnership affairs that it can be resolved without a review of all partnership affairs. *Id.* at 6:107-08. In that connection, note that a minority of courts do not require a prior accounting in a suit between persons who are only joint venturers. *Compare Kaufmann v. Nolan*, 81 Or. App. 237, 724 P.2d 912, 913 (1986) (recognizing, but not applying, rule that accounting is not always required in a joint venture) *with Kartalis v. Commander Warehouse Joint Venture*, 773 S.W.2d 393 (Tex. App. 1989) (requiring prior accounting).

The rule that a partner may not sue another partner on a matter arising out of partnership affairs until there has been dissolution and an accounting has come under increasing criticism. At least one state's supreme court has already abolished it. *Sertich v. Moorman*, 783 P.2d 1199 (Ariz. 1989). RUPA section 406 specifically permits both partnership and partner suits. The Comment makes clear the intent to abolish the rule requiring a prior accounting.

Chapter 15

Partnerships and Property

A. What Property Is Partnership Property?

Eckert v. Eckert

425 N.W.2d 914 (N.D. 1988)

GIERKE, Justice.

Gaila Eckert, as personal representative of the estate of Donovan Eckert, appeals from a district court judgment dismissing her action against Ben Eckert.

Ben Eckert was Donovan Eckert's uncle. In 1959 the two formed a partnership and engaged in farming and ranching as the "E-7 Ranch." No formal partnership agreement was ever executed. Donovan died in 1982, and Gaila commenced this action seeking dissolution and liquidation of the partnership.

The parties have reached an agreement for division of all partnership property except for cooperative patronage credits with the Minot Farmers Union Elevator, Minot Farmers Union Oil, and Harvest States Cooperative. Gaila asserts that these patronage credits are partnership property which should be equally split. Ben asserts that these credits were titled in his name individually and are not partnership property.

As explained in this record, a portion of the cooperatives' profits each year are allocated to each member-patron and the cooperative is required to pay out at least twenty percent of this amount in cash to the member-patron. The remaining eighty percent is retained by the cooperative but shows on its books as a patronage credit to the member-patron. Although this portion is not distributed to the member-patron at the time it is earned, it must be reported as income by the member-patron. These unpaid distributions typically are retained by the cooperative until the member-patron reaches a certain age or the cooperative's board of directors votes to "retire" the credits for a specified past year.

In this case, patronage credits were earned on business generated by the partnership. The twenty percent annual cash distributions were paid to Ben Eckert, who placed them in the partnership account and included them as income to the partnership on the partnership tax return. The partnership return then allocated one-half of this income to Ben and one-half to Donovan. The eighty percent patronage credits were also included as partnership income each year, and again one-half of this income was allocated to each partner.

Upon reaching age 65 in 1978, Ben began receiving distributions of the retained patronage credits from Farmers Union Oil. Between 1978 and 1983, Ben received $28,612.28 in retirement of those credits. Ben has retained all of these funds. None of the retained patronage credits earned on partnership business with Farmers Union Elevator and Harvest States had been distributed at the time of trial.

The trial court placed upon Gaila the burden of proving that the patronage credits earned through partnership business were partnership property. The trial court concluded that Gaila had failed to meet her burden of proof and dismissed her action. Gaila asserts on appeal that the trial court erred in failing to apply a statutory presumption which would shift the burden of proof to Ben. We agree.

The trial court relied heavily upon the fact that the patronage credits were held in Ben's name, but that fact is not conclusive of the issue of ownership. Property which is titled in the name of an individual partner may nevertheless be partnership property. The determination whether property held in the name of an individual partner belongs to the partnership is a question of fact. The relevant inquiry is whether the partners intended that the property in question be partnership property or individual property.

[UPA section 8] provides in pertinent part:

> Partnership Property.—
>
> (1) All property originally brought into the partnership stock or subsequently acquired by purchase or otherwise, on account of the partnership, is partnership property.
>
> (2) Unless the contrary intention appears, property acquired with partnership funds is partnership property.

[UPA Section 4(4)] provides that any provision in the [UPA] "must be so construed as to effectuate its general purpose to make uniform the law of those states which enact it." Thus, we look to decisions of other states which have adopted the Uniform Partnership Act for guidance in construing our provisions.

The above-quoted provisions of the Uniform Act have consistently been construed to create a presumption that property acquired with partnership funds is partnership property. For example, the Court of Civil Appeals of Texas stated in *Conrad v. Judson*, [465 S.W.2d 819, 828 (Tex. Civ. App. 1971)]:

> We think there is a presumption, under the above authorities, and particularly the Texas Uniform Partnership Act, that property purchased with partnership funds is intended to be partnership property; and if one would contend otherwise the burden would be on him or her to offer proof of a different intention and to obtain an affirmative jury finding thereon.

Cases from other jurisdictions which have adopted the Uniform Partnership Act are in accord. The presumption extends beyond purchases with partnership funds to any acquisition of property derived from partnership labor, materials, or other assets.

In this state, a presumption shifts the burden of proof to the party against whom it is directed. A review of the record in this case establishes that the presumption should have been applied and the burden of proof shifted to Ben. Ben does not dispute that the vast majority of the patronage credits were derived from partnership business with the cooperatives.[1] Inasmuch as these credits were property acquired or derived through partnership funds, assets, labor, or materials, they are presumed to be part-

1. Ben does assert that some amount of the patronage credits is attributable to business conducted with the cooperatives in his individual capacity. Because it concluded that none of the patronage credits were partnership property, the trial court did not reach this issue. Ben will have the opportunity on remand to again present this issue.

nership property pursuant to [UPA section 8]. The burden then shifts to Ben to establish that there was an intention between the partners that the patronage credits earned through partnership business were to be Ben's individual property.

The judgment of the district court is reversed and the matter is remanded for a new trial in accordance with this opinion.

Notes

1. Banker owns a building on the courthouse square in downtown Podunk. Banker and Merchant decide to open a hardware business as equal partners. Banker and Merchant agree to use Banker's building as their store. Is the building partnership property?

2. RUPA sections 203, 204 and 302 are the RUPA provisions equivalent to UPA sections 8 and 10.

B. Title to Partnership Property

At common law, deeds in the *partnership name* were generally held ineffective to convey legal (as opposed to equitable) title to real property. First, because a partnership was not a legal person, it was incapable of holding title to realty. Second, the partnership name did not describe the *partners* using that name with sufficient certainty to vest legal title in them. *See* Rosin, *The Entity-Aggregate Dispute: Conceptualism and Functionalism in Partnership Law*, 42 ARK. L. REV. 395, 408-15 (1989).

UPA section 8(3) changes the common law rule, and makes conveyances in the partnership name *effective* to pass legal title. Under a conveyance in the partnership name, who holds legal title to partnership property?

Putnam v. Shoaf

620 S.W.2d 510 (Tenn. App. 1981)

NEARN, Judge.

This dispute is over the sale of a partnership interest in the Frog Jump Gin Company.

The Frog Jump Gin had operated for a number of years showing losses in some years and profits in others. In the time immediately preceding February, 1976, it appears that the gin operated at a loss. Orginally, the gin was operated as an equal partnership between E. C. Charlton, Louise H. Charlton, Lyle Putnam and Carolyn Putnam. In 1974 Mr. Putnam died and Mrs. Putnam, by agreement, succeeded to her husband's interest. The gin operated under that control and management until February 19, 1976, when Mrs. Putnam desired to sever her relationship with the other partners in Frog Jump Gin. At that time the gin was heavily indebted to the Bank of Trenton and Trust Company, and Mrs. Putnam desired to be relieved of this liability. John A. and Maurine H. Shoaf displayed an interest in obtaining Mrs. Putnam's one-half interest in the partnership. An examination by the Shoafs of the financial records of the gin, evidenced by a statement from the gin bookkeeper, indicated a negative financial position of approximately $90,000.00. The Shoafs agreed to take over Mrs. Putnam's position in the partnership if Mrs. Putnam and the Charltons would each pay $21,000.00 into the partnership account. The Shoafs agreed to assume personal liability for all partnership debts, including Putnam's share of any partnership debts made prior to their coming into the partnership, although the Uniform Partnership Act would only make him [sic] personally liable for debts made after his [sic] entry into the partnership unless he agreed to more. *See* [UPA § 17]. Both the Charltons and Mrs. Putnam paid their respective amounts into the partnership account, and Shoaf [sic] assumed all partnership obligations as aforesaid.

At the time of this agreement the known assets of the Frog Jump Gin consisted primarily of the gin, its equipment, and the land upon which they were located. All gin assets, including the land, were held in the name of the partnership. Mrs. Putnam conveyed her interest in the partnership to the Shoafs by means of a quit claim deed. Upon Shoafs' assumption of the position of a partner, the services of the old bookkeeper were terminated and a new bookkeeper was hired.

In April, 1977, with the assistance of the new bookkeeper, it was learned that the old bookkeeper had engaged in a scheme of systematic embezzlement from the Frog Jump Gin Company from the time of Mr. Putnam's death until the bookkeeper's services were terminated. This disclosure led to suits being filed by the gin against the bookkeeper and the banks that had honored checks forged by the bookkeeper. There is no need to go into the details of all that litigation. Suffice it to say that Mrs. Putnam was allowed to intervene claiming an interest in any fund paid by the banks and the upshot of it all was a judgment paid into Court by the banks in excess of $68,000.00. One-half of that sum, by agreement, has been paid to the Charltons as owners of a one-half interest in the gin, and the other half is the subject of this dispute between the Shoafs and Mrs. Putnam's estate. She has died pending this litigation and the case revived.

Mrs. Putnam had died before the hearing of the case, thus the only proof before the Trial Judge on the issue at hand was the pleadings, the documents signed by the parties of interest and the deposition of Mr. Shoaf. The Trial Judge dismissed the claim of Putnam and held that Mrs. Putnam had no interest in the fund. The Putnam estate has appealed, citing numerous alleged "issues."

The basis of the Trial Judge's decision was that Mrs. Putnam intended to convey all of her interest in the partnership to Shoaf and, therefore, the Court could not reform the sale and hold that the unknown right of action against the banks for payment of forged checks was not conveyed by Mrs. Putnam in the conveyance to the Shoafs.

The conveyance between Mrs. Putnam and the Shoafs is evidenced by what is styled a "Quitclaim Deed" executed by Mrs. Putnam on February 19, 1976, which is as follows:

> FOR AND IN CONSIDERATION of the sum of One Dollar ($1.00), cash in hand paid, the receipt of which is hereby acknowledged, and the assumption by Grantees of all Grantor's obligations arising or by virtue of her partnership interest in the Frog Jump Gin Company, including three notes to Bank of Trenton and Trust Company, I, CAROLYN B. PUTNAM, a widow, have this day bargained and sold and by these presents do hereby sell, transfer, convey and forever quit-claim unto JOHN A. SHOAF and wife, MAURINE H. SHOAF, their heirs and

assigns, all the right, title and interest (it being a one-half (½) undivided interest) I have in and to the following described real and personal property located in the 25th Civil District of Gibson County, Tennessee, and described as follows; to-wit:

(The legal description of the real property follows.)

PERSONAL PROPERTY:

All of the personal property and machinery in said Frog Jump Gin Company's buildings and on said properties described and used in the operation of its cotton gin plant on the above described parcel of land, including two Moss Gordin 75 saw gin stands; one Overhead incline cleaner; stick and green leaf machine; two Moss Gordin lint cleaners; two Mitchell Feeders; two Mitchell burners; one Hardwick Etter all steel press; condensers; fans; motors; pulleys; shafting; all piping; belting and machinery and appliances and other personal property, including all cotton trailers, on said parcel of land and used in connection with the operation of said cotton gin, accounts receivable, inventory and all other assets of Frog Jump Gin Company.

TO HAVE AND TO HOLD the said real and personal property with the appurtenances, estate, title and interest thereto belonging unto the said John A. Shoaf and wife, Maurine H. Shoaf, their heirs and assigns, forever.

Witness my signature this the 19th day of February, 1976.

On the same day Mrs. Putnam and the Charltons executed the following agreement:

This Agreement made and entered into on this the 19th day of February, 1976, by and between E. C. Charlton and wife, Louise H. Charlton, party of one part, and Carolyn B. Putnam, party of the other part, all of Trenton, Gibson County, Tennessee;

WITNESSETH: THAT WHEREAS, the parties have heretofore been conducting a business, as partners, under the firm name and style of Frog Jump Gin Company; and

WHEREAS, Carolyn B. Putnam has agreed to pay into the partnership the sum of Twenty-one Thousand Dollars ($21,000.00), the receipt of which is hereby acknowledged, and has sold and conveyed her interest in the partnership to John A. Shoaf and wife, Maurine H. Shoaf.

NOW, THEREFORE, it is mutually agreed that the partnership be and hereby is dissolved. It is further mutually agreed that the parties do hereby release and forever discharge each other from any and all claims and demands on account of, connected with, or growing out of the said partnership, or the division of the assets thereof; and it is expressly understood and agreed that Carolyn B. Putnam is completely released and discharged from any and all liability, debts, or causes of action of the Frog Jump Gin Company, presently existing, contingent, or otherwise, including notes owed to Bank of Trenton and Trust Company, and that E. C. Charlton and wife, Louise H. Charlton, assume all liability and indebtedness of the said partnership and covenant to indemnify and save harmless the said Carolyn B. Putnam in the premises.

In Witness Whereof, the parties have hereunto set their signatures, this day and date first above written.

At approximately the same time, Mrs. Putnam obtained from the Bank of Trenton a complete release from all personal liability for note indebtednesses to the Bank in the face amount of $105,000.00 in consideration of the Shoafs' assumption of all obligations of the Frog Jump Gin.

Counsel for Putnam argues that the proof shows there was no meeting of the minds to convey the unknown asset of the claim against the bank, first because its existence was admittedly unknown by both parties and second, the quit claim deed makes no mention of cash or money in the bank and the items that are there mentioned are in fact physical assets, readily ascertainable items that could be identified for the purpose of securing loans and paying debts. Further, counsel argues that the words "all other property" used in the quit claim deed must be construed in accordance with the true intent of the parties.

First, we must discover the nature of the ownership interest of Mrs. Putnam in that which she conveyed. Under the Uniform Partnership Act, her partnership property rights consisted of her (1) rights in specific partnership property, (2) interest in the partnership and (3) right to participate in management. [UPA § 24]. The right in "specific partnership property" is the partnership tenancy possessory right of equal use or possession by partners for partnership purposes. This possessory *right* is incident to the partnership and the possessory right does not exist absent the partnership. The possessory right is not the partner's "*interest*" in the assets of the partnership. [UPA § 25]. The real interest of a partner, as opposed to that incidental possessory right before discussed, is the partner's interest in the partnership which is defined as "his share of the profits and surplus and the same is personal property." [UPA § 26]. Therefore, a co-partner owns no personal specific *interest* in any specific property or asset of the partnership. The *partnership* owns the property or the asset. [UPA § 8]. The partner's interest is an undivided interest, as a co-tenant in all partnership property. [UPA § 25]. That interest is the partner's pro rata share of the net value or deficit of the partnership. [UPA § 26]. For this reason a conveyance of partnership property held in the name of the partnership is made in the name of the partnership and not as a conveyance of the individual interest of the partners. *See* [UPA § 8].

This being true, all Mrs. Putnam had to convey was her interest in the partnership. Accordingly, she had no specific interest in the admittedly unknown choses in action to separately convey or retain. Therefore, the determinative question is: Did Mrs. Putnam intend to convey her interest in the partnership to the Shoafs? There can be no doubt that such was the intent of Mrs. Putnam, as she had no other interest to convey. To give any other intent to the actions of Mrs. Putnam would require a fraudulent intent on her part, which intent certainly did not exist. Therefore, the intent of Mrs. Putnam was to convey the interest she owned which was "her share of the profits and surplus." [UPA § 26].

Since neither the Shoafs nor Mrs. Putnam knew of the embezzlement by accountant Bennie Johnston, there can be no doubt that neither the Shoafs nor Mrs. Putnam knew of the valuable asset that the partnership possessed in its claim against the banks. However, it was the partnership's asset and not her personal asset. Just as she could not have retained it, had she known of it, and at the same time conveyed her partnership interest, we cannot now say she conveyed her partnership interest in 1976, but is still entitled to a share in it. This situation is no different from a hypothetical oil discovery on the partnership real property after transfer of a partnership interest with neither party believing oil to be present at the time of the conveyance. The interest in the real property always was and remained in the partnership. Of course, the transferor would not have transferred his partnership *interest* had he known of the existence of oil on partnership property; but, mutual ignorance of the existence of the oil would not, in our opinion, warrant a "reformation" of the contract for sale of the partnership interest, or warrant a decree in favor of the transferor for a share of the value of the oil.

It is inescapable to us that the interest in the choses in action remained in the partnership at all times regardless of the composition of the partners; and, it is equally inescapable that Mrs. Putnam intended to convey her partnership interest.

This is not a case of mutual mistake but one of mutual ignorance. They are not necessarily the same thing. Those cases cited by appellant as authority for a reversal of the Chancellor... are not applicable to the facts of this case. The results in those cases are primarily based on the finding that the transferor could not have intended to convey that which the transferee received for less than valuable consideration. In this case Mrs. Putnam had to intend to convey her interest in the partnership. Hindsight now shows that it had more value than either party thought. But, hindsight is not a basis for a money judgment, a revision or a reformation. We wonder what would be the position of Mrs. Putnam, or the estate, had the Frog Jump Gin failed, leaving a sizeable deficit, even after the influx of the bank's refund. Would she accept a partner's share of the Frog Jump Gin's liabilities for a share of the bank's refund? The question answers itself and we pose it only to show that she did not have a specific interest in any specific assets of the Frog Jump Gin, either to retain or convey. All she had was a partner's interest in a "share of the profits" (and losses) which she certainly intended to convey.

In looking at the pleadings we note that in Mrs. Putnam's complaint it states that she "sold her undivided one-half interest to John Shoaf and wife, Maurine H. Shoaf."

We also note that in the agreement made with the Charltons, on the same day, she stated that she had "sold and *conveyed her interest in the partnership* to John Shoaf and wife, Maurine H. Shoaf."

We hold that the evidence does not preponderate against the Trial Judge's finding regarding interest.

The result is the judgment below is affirmed with costs of appeal adjudged against the Putnam estate.

Notes

1. UPA section 25(1) specifies that the *partners* are co-owners of "specific partnership property," holding in a *tenancy in partnership*. But note that the rights of partners in specific partnership property are very narrow. A partner has the right to *possess* partnership property for partnership purposes *only*. UPA § 25(2)(a). Moreover, a partner's rights as a tenant-in-partnership cannot *separately* be conveyed or attached for individual (non-partnership purposes). The only property right of a partner that can be *individually* conveyed is the *interest in the partnership*—the partner's share of profits and surplus. As *Putnam v. Shoaf* indicates, the interest in the partnership is an undivided interest in *all* of the partnership property, *taken as a whole*, and *not* in any *individual* part:

> A partner has a beneficial interest in partnership property considered as a whole. As profits accrue, he has a right to be paid his proportion, and on winding up of the business, after obligations due third persons have been met, he has a right to be paid in cash his share of what remains of the partnership property. *These rights considered as a whole are his interest in the partnership*; and this beneficial interest he may assign in whole or in fractional part, as is indicated in section 27.

UPA § 25 Official Comment (emphasis added).

2. On the whole, courts and commentators have not been receptive to the intent of the UPA to create a new estate in land—the tenancy in partnership. *See* Rosin, *The Entity-Aggregate Dispute: Conceptualism and Functionalism in Partnership Law*, 42 ARK. L. REV. 395 (1989). Many courts and commentators argue (as did *Putnam v. Shoaf* in dicta) that under the UPA the *partnership* itself as a separate entity owns partnership property. They reason that UPA section 25(2) so limits partners' "rights" as to leave them no real "ownership" in the traditional sense. Instead, all the partner owns is an interest in the partnership itself.

For most purposes, it is *irrelevant* who "owns" partnership property. The real issue is the *functional* rights of partners and others in partnership property. By its nature (and under the UPA), partnership property is to be used only for partnership purposes; individual partners, and persons claiming under them, may not use, convey, or attach partnership property for a non-partnership purpose. That is true regardless of how the nature of the ownership is *conceptualized.*

3. Under the RUPA, title to partnership property vests in the partnership itself (sections 203 & 204). The substance of UPA section 25(2) remains unchanged—the partners have no *transferable* interest in partnership property (section 501). Instead, a partner has only an interest in the partnership—which the RUPA renames a "transferable interest in the partnership," but otherwise does not change. RUPA § 502.

C. Interest in the Partnership

Beach v. Anderson

417 N.W.2d 709 (Minn. App. 1988)

PARKER, Judge.

Larry Anderson and Vernon Beach resolved their partnership dissolution lawsuit by stipulating before a court reporter. Subsequently, Anderson refused to honor the stipulation. Beach brought a motion to compel settlement, and Anderson brought a motion to return the parties to *status quo ante.* The trial court granted the motion to compel settlement.

In the spring of 1984, Beach and Anderson entered into an oral partnership agreement to own and operate an amusement center in Brainerd, Minnesota, called Vacationland Park. Together they purchased real estate for the venture and constructed a go-cart track. Shortly after opening in August 1984, the parties disagreed on the management of the center. As a result of the disputes, during 1985 and 1986 they agreed to alternate management of the park. Each would operate the park for two days, pay the expenses incurred for the time he was in control and retain the income during his operation.

After substantial negotiations, the parties failed to agree upon the terms of a written partnership agreement, and Beach filed suit for dissolution of the oral partnership. A trial date certain was set, and on February 19, 1987, the parties met for scheduled depositions with their wives and attorneys present. Over a period of several hours, the attorneys negotiated a settlement which was stipulated before the court reporter.

In pertinent part the agreement held:

> (1) Beach would pay Anderson $85,000 for his interest in the partnership and personal property.

Beach moved for an order giving him sole possession of Vacationland Park until the court ruled on his initial motion compelling settlement. Anderson then brought a counter-motion seeking a return to *status quo ante.*

At the motion hearing the trial court refused to return to *status quo ante*, but required Beach to provide a weekly listing of income and expenses. At a subsequent proceeding, the trial court granted Beach's motion to compel settlement against both Larry and Kim Anderson. Anderson appeals.

The transcript reveals that the stipulation is for the sale of an "interest in the partnership which is the subject of this litigation." The partnership assets included equipment, go-carts and real estate.

Anderson argues that the statute of frauds applies because the stipulation involved the transfer of real estate, but the stipulation clearly transfers the "partnership interest":

> Plaintiff Vernon Beach will pay to defendant Larry Anderson, the sum of $85,000 for his *interest in the partnership* which is the subject of this litigation, and that partnership having been previously operated under the name of Vacationland Park. Of that amount, $5,000 earnest money will be paid today in the form of a check payable to the trust account of Caldis & Caldis, Attorneys at Law, to be held by that firm pending the closing of this transaction. The balance of $80,000 will be paid on March 31, 1987. At that time Andersons will deliver to Beaches a quit claim deed and an assignment of contract for deed for the real property involved in the matter, *and other such documentation as may be necessary to transfer the partnership interest which is being conveyed to Beach.* (Emphasis added).

As a contract for the sale of a partnership interest, [UPA section 26] applies:

> A partner's interest in the partnership is that partner's share of the profits and surplus, and the same is *personal property.* (Emphasis added.)

From this language it is evident that the conveyance of deeds and "other such documentation" connected to real estate transfer is merely ancillary to the partnership transfer. This is not a stipulation for the sale of land within the statute of frauds, as Anderson would characterize it.

Real estate owned by a partnership is considered personalty. Under [UPA section 26], once a partnership acquires realty with partnership funds and for partnership purposes, it then becomes personalty for all purposes.

In *Arnold v. Wainwright*, 6 Minn. 358 (Gil. 241) (1861), the issue was the disposition of jointly owned real estate. Because the partnership was an oral one, appellant contended the conveyance of real estate must conform with the statute of frauds. The court first determined that a valid partnership existed and then offered this analysis of the real estate involved:

> In regard to all lands which are ascertained to be partnership property, the rule in equity is, that they shall be treated as mere personalty, and be governed by the rules and general doctrines applicable to that species of property.

Addressing the conveyance of such real estate, the court said:

> [W]hen it is part of the partnership effects, it is to be treated in equity, to all intents and purposes, as a part of the partnership funds; and whatsoever may be the form of the conveyance, it will be held subject to all the equitable rights and liens of the partners which would apply to it, if it were personal estate.

Under this analysis the statute of frauds does not apply, because the real estate in issue is personalty "to all intents and purposes."

Anderson also raises the issue of whether his wife can be required to join him in signing a quit-claim deed. [UPA section 25(2)(e)] states:

> A partner's right in specific partnership property is not subject to dower, curtesy, the statutory interest of a surviving spouse, or allowances to a surviving spouse, heirs or next of kin.

Therefore, it does not appear that Kim Anderson has any individual interest in the property, because she is not personally interested in the partnership. We remand to the trial court for consideration of an appropriate order effectuating the transfer pursuant to the agreement.

Affirmed and remanded.

Note

Beach v. Anderson and UPA section 26 restate the doctrine of so-called "out-and-out conversion" of partnership real property in personal property. A more accurate way of understanding this principle is that a partner has no separate, transferable right in any specific partnership property. UPA § 25(2). Instead, a partner only has the (transferable) interest in the partnership, which is only the *surplus* of partnership property after it is no longer required for partnership purposes. UPA § 26. Because each partner has the right to have the partnership assets sold and his/her share in *cash*, UPA § 38(1), the interest in the partnership can only be personal property (as stated in UPA section 26 and RUPA section 502(a)).

Centurion Corp. v. Crocker National Bank

208 Cal. App. 3d 1, 255 Cal. Rptr. 794 (1989)

KLINE, Presiding Justice.

Jon Perroton (Perroton) appeals the denial of his motion for an order voiding an order granting Crocker National Bank's motion for sale of Perroton's interest in limited partnership known as Turn-Key Storage. He contends: (1) the trial court erred in ordering the sale of his partnership interest at an execution sale where the partnership was not the judgment debtor and (2) the order directing sale was precluded by the [ULPA] and by the partnership agreement itself.

[R]espondent Crocker National Bank (Crocker) obtained a judgment against Perroton for $1,431,688.29. Thereafter, on February 6, 1985, the bank obtained an order pursuant to [ULPA section 22] charging Perroton's interest in the limited partnership known as California Self Storage with payment of the unsatisfied judgment plus interest. The charging order was subsequently corrected to change the name of the partnership to Turn-Key Storage doing business as California Self-Storage.

As of November 1985, Crocker had received no monies as a result of the charging order against Turn-Key Storage. Therefore, Crocker moved for an order of sale of Perroton's interest in Turn-Key Storage. Notice was served on Perroton, the only limited partner, in care of the Federal Metropolitan Correctional Center in Tucson, Arizona, where he was a prisoner. Notice was also served on counsel for Perroton's mother, Bette Perroton, the only general partner of Turn-Key Storage.

No opposition was filed to the motion for sale. Bette Perroton filed a statement of "conditional non-opposition" to the sale.[1]

After hearing, the limited partnership interest in Turn-Key Storage was ordered sold. Perroton, Bette Perroton as general partner, and counsel for the general partner received notice of the order for sale of Perroton's interest in the limited partnership on January 27, 1986.

Approximately 15 months later, Perroton moved to void the order of sale. This motion was filed after Perroton had filed for bankruptcy and after Crocker had obtained relief from the automatic stay in the bankruptcy to allow it to sell the limited partnership interest of Perroton in Turn-Key Storage.

Perroton's motion to void the order of sale was denied; Perroton filed a notice of appeal.

The Court Did Not Abuse Its Discretion in Denying Perroton's Motion To Void the Prior Order of Sale

"A motion for relief [from a trial court order] is addressed to the sound discretion of the trial court and an appellate court will not interfere unless there is a clear showing of an abuse. [T]he moving party has the burden of showing good cause." (*Davis v. Thayer* (1980), 113 Cal. App. 3d 892, 904, 170 Cal. Rptr. 328.) If the [ULPA] absolutely bars the sale of a partnership interest in satisfaction of a debt of an individual partner, abuse of discretion would be established. However, under the facts presented, we conclude that the order of sale was not void. Hence, the court did not abuse its discretion in denying Perroton's motion.

"A creditor with a judgment against a partner but not against the partnership ordinarily cannot execute directly on partnership assets or on the partner's interest in the partnership." (*Advising California Partnerships* (Cont. Ed. Bar 1988), § 6.88, p. 428; see also [UPA § 25(2)(c)].)[3] The reasons for the rule were discussed at some

1. According to this declaration: "4. The Partnership does not object to the sale of Jon Perroton's partnership interest at Sheriff's Sale as sought by Crocker Bank provided that the rights of the purchaser at such sale are limited as set forth in the Stipulation and Order and amendment to Certificate of Limited Partnership as described above; to wit, the successor [sic] would have the rights to profits and losses but would not become a substituted limited partner in the Partnership."

3. Code of Civil Procedure, section 699.720, lists among the types of property not subject to levy under a writ of execution, "(2) The interest of a partner in a partnership where the

length in *Taylor v. S & M Lamp Co.*, 190 Cal. App. 2d 700, 707-709, 12 Cal. Rptr. 323:

> Prior to California's adoption of the Uniform Partnership Act a judgment creditor of a partner whose personal debt, as distinguished from partnership debt, gave rise to the judgment, could cause a sale at execution of partnership assets, including specific items of partnership property, to satisfy his judgment.
>
> Lord Justice Lindley gave the following reason for the English rule forbidding execution sale of a partner's interest in the partnership to satisfy his nonpartnership debt:
>
> > When a creditor obtained a judgment against one partner and he wanted to obtain the benefit of that judgment against the share of that partner in the firm, the first thing was to issue a *fi.fa.*,[4] and the sheriff went down to the partnership place of business, seized everything, stopped the business, drove the solvent partners wild, and caused the execution creditor to bring an action in Chancery in order to get an injunction to take an account and pay over that which was due the execution debtor. A more clumsy method of proceeding could hardly have grown up.
>
> It was to prevent such "hold up" of the partnership business and the consequent injustice done the other partners resulting from execution against partnership property that the quoted code sections and their counterparts in the Uniform Partnership Act and the English Partnership Act of 1890 were adopted. As we view those code sections they are not intended to protect a debtor partner against claims of his judgment creditors where no legitimate interest of the partnership, or of the remaining or former partners, is to be served.

Therefore, a judgment creditor must seek a charging order to reach the debtor partner's interest in the partnership. (See [UPA § 28].) Through a charging order, the court may charge the debtor's interest in the partnership with payment of the unsatisfied judgment, plus interest. The court may also appoint a receiver of subsequent profits or other money due to the debtor partner. ([UPA § 28(1); ULPA § 22].)

Perroton concedes the validity of the charging order obtained by Crocker. He contends, however, that under the foregoing statutory scheme, the court may not order sale of his partnership interest at execution sale. We conclude that the authorities support the order for sale of a judgment debtor partner's partnership interest as distinct from the property of the limited partnership, where the creditor has shown that it was unable to obtain satisfaction of the debt under the charging order, and where the remaining partner, here the general partner Bette Perroton, has consented to the sale.

It is clear that

---

partnership is not a judgment debtor." [UPA § 25(2)(c)] provides in relevant part: "A partner's right in specific partnership property is not subject to enforcement of a money judgment, except on a claim against the partnership."

4. The abbreviation for "*Fieri facias*," literally "that you cause to be made," the term used to describe a writ of execution commanding the sheriff to levy and take the amount of a judgment from the goods and chattels of the judgment debtor. (Black's Law Dictionary (4th ed. 1968 rev.) p. 754.)

> the limited partner is given no property interest in the specific partnership assets as such. Rather, he is entitled, among other things, "to receive a share of the profits or other compensation by way of income, and to the return of his contribution." ([ULPA § 19(3)].) [T]he limited partner has no interest in the partnership property by virtue of his status as a limited partner. Thus, such assets are not available to satisfy a judgment against the limited partner in his individual capacity. [T]he very nature of the limited partner's relationship with the business organization indicates that he has no property interest in the specific partnership assets which would render them available to his personal creditors. (*Evans v. Galardi*, 128 Cal. Rptr. 25, 546 P.2d 313.)

The question remains whether, nevertheless, the court may order sale of the debtor's partnership interest itself as distinct from the partnership assets in the circumstances presented here. We think the answer is yes.

[UPA section 28] itself, which sets forth the creditor's charging order remedy, refers to the possible court ordered sale of a partnership interest which is subject to a charging order. Subsection (2) provides:

> The interest charged may be redeemed at any time before foreclosure, *or in case of a sale being directed by the court* may be purchased without thereby causing dissolution: (a) With separate property, by any one or more of the partners, or (b) With partnership property, by any one or more of the partners with the consent of all the partners whose interests are not so charged or sold. (Emphasis added.)

Referring to this provision, an authoritative treatise on California partnerships states as follows:

> The judgment creditor does not own the partnership interest by virtue of the charging order but may become the owner by foreclosing the interest. Any of the other partners may, however, redeem the interest before foreclosure *or court-ordered sale*, using their individual property or partnership property if all the partners other than the debtor consent. (*Advising California Partnerships*, at p. 129, emphasis added.)

Cases requiring creditors to obtain charging orders also indicate that sale of the partnership interest is permissible where the creditor has first obtained a charging order and has demonstrated the monies collected under the charging order are insufficient to satisfy the judgment.

In *Evans v. Galardi*, the court refused to allow a levy on partnership assets to satisfy a partner's debt. The court required the creditor to use the charging order instead. However, in so holding, the court stated: "Where, as in the instant case, the partnership is a viable business organization and plaintiff does not show that he will be unable to secure satisfaction of his judgment by use of a charging order or by levy of execution against the debtors' other personally owned property, there is no reason to permit deviation from the prescribed statutory process." The clear implication is that such levy and sale may, in certain circumstances, be permitted even in the absence of fraud.

In *Taylor v. S & M Lamp Co.*, 190 Cal. App. 2d 700, 12 Cal. Rptr. 323, the creditor obtained a charging order and thereafter, without obtaining any court order supplementing the charging order, obtained a writ of execution on his judgment against two partners and caused the sheriff to levy on all the beneficial interests of the two partners in the partnership. The trial court memorandum of opinion read: "The charging order . . . impressed a lien on the interests of Ben and Eugene Stephens in the partnership, but the proceeding thereafter followed by plaintiff did not conform to the law. Another order could have been obtained directing the sale of said interests." The Court of Appeal termed the trial court memo "a correct statement of the law as applied to the ordinary case," where the partnership continues and where no fraudulent transfer is made.

Thus, both the [UPA] and the cases seem to contemplate that a court may authorize sale of the debtor partner's partnership interest even in the absence of fraud, where the conditions are met: first, the creditor has previously obtained a charging order, second, the judgment nevertheless remains unsatisfied; *and third, all partners other than the debtor have consented to the sale of the interest.*

The concerns which form the basis for the exemption of partnership interests and property are satisfied by this procedure. Allowing sale in such instance is consistent with the purpose of these code sections to avoid disruption to the partnership business and with the observation of *Taylor* that the sections "are not intended to protect a debtor partner against claims of his judgment creditors where no legitimate interest of the partnership, or of the remaining or former partners is to be served."

Because the Sale Is of the Limited Partner's Interest in the Partnership and the Remaining Partner Has Consented, the Order of Sale Does Not Violate the Partnership Agreement

Perroton contends that the order of sale was void as it was inconsistent with the terms of the Limited Partnership Agreement. Perroton points out that he is strictly a limited partner, his interest in the partnership is limited by the Agreement to fifty percent of the capital and profits; and he has no cognizable or legal "interest" whatsoever in either the real or personal property of the partnership. Further, he argues that as a limited partner, he has no right to be active in the affairs of the partnership, and he may not sell, assign or encumber his interest in the partnership.

"The judgment creditor does not acquire any greater rights than the debtor is entitled to for his own benefit." (UPA, Official Comment to section 28.) Just as a charging order cannot grant the creditor a greater interest in the partnership than that of the debtor partner at the time of the order, a supplementary order for sale does not allow the purchaser to acquire more rights in the partnership than the debtor partner possessed.

Nevertheless, as the Nevada Supreme Court pointed out in rejecting a debtor partner's claim that assignment of his partnership interest was inconsistent with the terms of the partnership agreement: "[T]he partnership agreements could not divest the district court of its powers provided by statute to charge and sell an interest of a partner in a partnership." (*Tupper v. Kroc* (1972), 88 Nev. 146, 494 P2d 1275, 1250.)

Crocker concedes that the

> sale of Perroton's interest in Turn-Key Storage ordered by the Superior Court is *not* an order for the sale of any real or personal property owned by Turn-Key Storage. To the contrary, it is simply a sale of whatever interest, legal, equitable, or otherwise, which Perroton holds in Turn-Key Storage by virtue of his being

a limited partner. The eventual purchaser will acquire no greater rights than Perroton would have if he had remained a limited partner.

Further, both the Limited Partnership Agreement and the consent to the sale by Bette Perroton make clear that a purchaser of Perroton's limited partnership interest would have rights to profits and losses, but would not become a substituted limited partner in the Partnership, absent consent by the general partner.

As we see no statutory prohibition on the sale in these circumstances and sale does not violate the terms of the limited partnership agreement, the court did not abuse its discretion in denying Perroton's 473 motion.

THE JUDGMENT IS AFFIRMED.

Notes

1. In *Centurion Corp.*, the court indicates that a foreclosure on a debtor partner's interest in the partnership requires the "consent" of the other partners. This is not strictly true. As indicated in *Tupper v. Kroc* (discussed in *Centurion Corp.*), the partnership agreement cannot override the creditor's rights under UPA section 28 (RUPA section 504). However, UPA section 28(2) gives the other partners the right to *redeem* the affected interest in the partnership at any time before "foreclosure" of the charging order. UPA § 28(2).

2. UPA section 27 specifies the rights of an assignee of a partner's interest in the partnership. Of the three partner "property rights" listed in UPA section 24, an assignee, *as such*, only gets the assigned portion of the *interest in the partnership*—profits during the continuance of the partnership (UPA § 27(1)), and the "interest"—the surplus—*after* dissolution (UPA § 27(2)). Note that under the UPA, an assignee is not entitled to an accounting, or even to books and records, until *after* dissolution.

3. As indicated in *Centurion Corp.*, a limited partner has no rights in specific partnership property and no right to participate in management. That is, a limited partner has *only* an interest in the partnership. *See* ULPA §§ 10, 19; RULPA § 702.

4. The assignee of an interest in the partnership does *not* become a *partner* or a limited partner absent the consent of *all* (general) partners. *See* UPA § 18(g), RULPA §§ 301, 702.

5. There is some confusion as to whether all of a partner's financial claims arising out of the partnership are included in the interest in the partnership. This question will be considered in chapter 17, "Dissolution: Accounting," when we consider the cases *Hamilton Airport Advertising, Inc. v. Hamilton.*

Chapter 16

Dissolution: Causes of Dissolution; Liquidation v. Continuation

A. Causes of Dissolution

Canter's Pharmacy, Inc. v. Elizabeth Associates

578 A.2d 1326 (Pa. Super. 1990)

CIRILLO, President Judge:

Westbrook Pharmacy and Surgical Supply ("Westbrook") appeals from an order entered on June 2, 1989, in the Allegheny County Court of Common Pleas granting Elizabeth Associates' motion to stay the proceedings pending arbitration.

On January 7, 1987, Schneider Health Services, Inc. ("SHS"), Orrie M. Rockwell, Jr., and Westbrook entered into a partnership agreement for the purpose of operating a personal care facility in Elizabeth, Pennsylvania. The partnership was conducted under the name of Elizabeth Associates ("Elizabeth"). The partnership agreement contained an arbitration provision:

> *Arbitration.* If for any reason the Partners cannot agree in a matter or matters of Partnership affairs, the dispute shall be decided by a majority decision of three (3) arbitrators, by which the Partners agree to abide. Each Partner shall have the right to appoint one arbitrator. The decision of the arbitrators shall be final, and the cost of the same shall be borne equally by the Partners.

After the partnership commenced operations, it began to suffer financial losses which required, pursuant to the agreement, additional capital contributions by the partners. Disputes arose concerning the extent of the losses and the management of the partnership. In sum, Westbrook refused to contribute any additional operating capital.

On January 24, 1989, Elizabeth instituted a civil action in the Allegheny County Court of Common Pleas against Westbrook to recover capital contributions allegedly owed by Westbrook to the partnership. On March 7, 1989, Westbrook responded by answering Elizabeth's complaint and filing a counterclaim against Elizabeth seeking equitable relief in the form of a partnership accounting and a dissolution of the partnership. Subsequently, on March 8, 1989, Westbrook commenced a separate equity action alleging various breaches of the partnership agreement. Elizabeth did not respond to this separate equity action.

On March 28, 1989, the trial court granted Westbrook's petition to consolidate the civil action commenced by Elizabeth with the equity actions instituted by Westbrook. On May 10, 1989, Elizabeth filed a motion to stay the consolidated proceedings pending arbitration pursuant to the arbitration provision in the partnership agreement. On June 2, 1989 the trial court entered an order staying the proceedings pending arbitration, and this timely appeal followed. Westbrook presents one issue for our consideration:

> When a contract contains a provision that all disputes arising under the contract will be decided by Arbitration, can the parties, by their conduct, waive or revoke the Arbitration provision and resort to suit under the jurisdiction of the Court of Common Pleas?

It is well settled that when one party to an agreement seeks to prevent the other from proceeding to arbitration, our inquiry is limited to determining whether an agreement to arbitrate was entered into and whether the dispute involved is within the scope of the arbitration provision.

Westbrook maintains that since its separate equity action seeking dissolution of the partnership cannot be heard in arbitration that these consolidated actions are not subject to arbitration.

It is clear that in certain circumstances a partnership may be dissolvable by the express will of any partner at any time. As the following discussion will illustrate, Westbrook's filing of an equity action seeking a dissolution effectively expressed its desire to dissolve the partnership at-will.

> Dissolution of a partnership is caused under [UPA section 31(1)(ii)] "by the express will of any partner." The expression of that will need not be supported by any justification. *If no "definite term or particular undertaking [is] specified in the partnership agreement," such an at-will dissolution does not violate the agreement between the partners; indeed, an expression of a will to dissolve is effective as a dissolution even if in contravention of the agreement.* We have recognized the generality of a dissolution at will. If the dissolution results in breach of contract, the aggrieved partners may recover damages for the breach and, if they meet certain conditions, may continue the firm business for the duration of the agreed term or until the particular undertaking is completed.

Girard Bank v. Haley, 460 Pa. 237, 243, 332 A.2d 443, 446-47 (1975) (emphasis added). The concept is simple: one cannot be coerced to remain in a partnership against his or her wishes.

Also, it is significant that the dissolution of a partnership does not mean that the partnership ceases doing business; rather dissolution "is the change in the relation of the partners caused by *any partner* ceasing to be associated in the carrying on, as distinguished from the winding up, of the business." [UPA § 29](emphasis added). Here, although the partners drafted a provision concerning the termination of the partnership, the agreement is silent as to dissolution.

The termination of a partnership is markedly different from the dissolution of a partnership. When a partnership has terminated it ceases doing business; when a partner effects a dissolution it simply means that partner is no longer associated with the business of the partnership.[4] Consequently, since the instant agreement does not

---

4. The authors of the Uniform Partnership Act suggest the following delineation in distinguishing among various terms which apply to that process which leads to the final settlement of all partnership affairs: "Dissolution" designates that point in time when the partners cease

concern the dissolution of the partnership, the relevant provisions of the [UPA] will control.

We must now determine if this partnership was for a definite term or for a particular undertaking. Once again, if the partnership was for an indefinite term or not for a particular undertaking, Westbrook was free to dissolve the partnership at-will without violating the agreement. [UPA § 31(1)(b)]. A review of the partnership agreement reveals that the partnership is not for a fixed term, and its purpose is set forth as follows:

> The purpose of the Partnership shall be renovation, equipping and operation of a large personal care facility to be known as Old Elizabeth Manor and to be located at 310 Third Street, Elizabeth, Pennsylvania and to do and perform any and all other acts as shall be necessary or incidental thereto.

In *Haley*, the partnership's purpose was to maintain and lease buildings on a tract of real property. The supreme court found that this undertaking was general and could not be said to set forth a "particular undertaking" within the meaning of the Act.

> A "particular undertaking" under the statute must be capable of accomplishment at some time, although the exact time may be unknown and unascertainable at the date of the agreement. Leasing property, like many other trades or businesses, involved entering into a business relationship which may continue indefinitely; there is nothing "particular" about it.

The purpose of the instant partnership was to renovate, equip and operate a personal care facility. Operating a personal care facility, like leasing property, may continue indefinitely; there is nothing particular about it. Accordingly, Westbrook's decision to dissolve was not in violation of the agreement.

Having concluded that Westbrook did not violate the agreement when it effected a dissolution of the partnership, we further find that these parties should not be forced into arbitration. Since an expression of a will to dissolve is effective as a dissolution, Westbrook's equity action seeking dissolution effectively caused a dissolution of the partnership. Arbitration, by its very nature, presupposes the existence of a dispute and an ability to decide in favor of one party and against another. Clearly, when a party has an unqualified right to dissolve a partnership at-will there is nothing to arbitrate. Indeed, arbitration, in this case, would be futile. Therefore, since Westbrook's decision to dissolve at-will is not subject to arbitration, the trial court erred in staying these proceedings pending arbitration.

Order reversed.

Notes

1. Why should a partner have the power to dissolve a partnership agreement in breach of an agreement to remain a partner for a definite term or particular undertaking?

2. A partnership in which there is no agreed definite term or particular undertaking is often called an "at will" partnership. Given that a partner may dissolve a

---

to carry on the business together; "termination" is the point in time when all the partnership affairs are wound up; and "winding up" or "liquidation" is the process of settling partnership affairs after dissolution. This is judicially recognized as the correct sequence of events. [UPA § 30.]

difinite term/particular undertaking partnership "at will," UPA § 31(2), aren't *all* partnerships in some sense "at will"?

3. Under the RUPA, partners retain the power to *withdraw* ("dissociate") from a partnership at will, RUPA § 601(1), even where that withdrawal violates the partnership agreement (as in a partnership for a definite term or particular undertaking), RUPA § 602.

Gates Rubber Co. v. Williford

530 S.W.2d 11 (Mo. 1975)

ROBERT R. WELBORN, Special Judge.

On November 7, 1969, The Gates Rubber Company, a corporation, obtained a judgment in the Jackson County Circuit Court against Samuel H. Deese for $3,987.31. Pursuant to the application of Gates, the circuit court issued an order charging the interest of Deese, if any, in a partnership consisting of Deese, Price Williford, Duren Sleyster and Mark Deese, with the payment of the judgment. A special execution issued, pursuant to which Samuel Deese's interest in the partnership was sold at public sale to Gates for $500.00. Gates thereafter brought this action against Williford, Williford's wife, Sleyster, Sleyster's wife and Mark Deese. By Count I of the action, Gates sought a dissolution of the partnership profits, losses and affairs and for a proper distribution of the net assets of the partnership. Count II sought to quiet title in the partnership, title to which was held by Williford and Sleyster. By their answer, defendants alleged that Williford, prior to the sheriff's sale, had acquired the interest of Deese in the partnership and that "there is no interest with which the petition herein is applicable." At a trial of the cause, the court sustained defendants' motion to dismiss plaintiff's cause of action at the close of plaintiff's case. This appeal followed.

In February, 1963, Samuel H. Deese, Mark E. Deese, Price B. Williford and Duren N. Sleyster entered into an oral partnership to engage in the business of manufacturing and selling furniture. The partnership name was "Diversified Activities." The business operated under the name "Bishop Furniture Company," at a building at 1341 Knox, North Kansas City, Missouri. The partnership arrangement was for a 25% interest in each partner.

The real estate described in Count II of plaintiff's petition was the property at 1341 Knox. It was conveyed by the Small Business Administration to Williford and Sleyster on or about December 27, 1963. Williford advanced a portion of the money for the down payment of the purchase price, but was reimbursed by the partnership. The partnership provided the balance of the down payment. The balance of the purchase price was borrowed from the Raytown Bank and Williford and Sleyster and their wives executed a deed of trust on the property to secure the indebtedness. Payments on the note through March 11, 1969 were made by the partnership. The land and building were shown as an asset on the books of the partnership until at least February 28, 1969. In answer to interrogatories, in connection with this case, Williford and Sleyster asserted ownership of a 25% interest in the property.

The partnership operated at a profit in 1967 of $36,800.01, shared equally among the four partners according to the partnership's federal income tax return. The next two years were less successful, with a loss of $78,532.06 for the year ending in

December 31, 1968, and a loss of $79,588.72 for the following year, again equally apportioned among the four partners. Sometime during 1969, the inventory of the Bishop Furniture Company was sold. The record is silent as to subsequent activity of the partnership.

On November 7, 1969, appellant, The Gates Rubber Company, obtained a judgment in Jackson County Circuit Court against Samuel H. Deese for $3,987.31.

On January 16, 1970, appellant, pursuant to [UPA section 28], filed an application for an order charging the interest of Samuel H. Deese in the partnership with the payment of the judgment debt. An order was issued directed to Deese, Williford, Sleyster and Mark Deese, calling upon them to answer Gate's application and show cause why an order should not be issued charging the interest of Deese.

A hearing was held on February 6, 1970, at which the four partners were represented by attorneys. The court found the existence of the unpaid judgment debt and further found "that the said Samuel H. Deese is a partner in the firm of Diversified Activities, d/b/a Bishop Furniture Company, a partnership consisting of Samuel H. Deese, Price Williford, Duren Sleyster, and Mark Deese, with place of business at 1341 Knox in North Kansas City, Missouri."

The order continued:

> IT IS THEREFORE ORDERED that the interest of said partnership of Samuel H. Deese, Price Williford, Duren Sleyster and Mark Deese, known as Diversified Activities, and doing business under the name of Bishop Furniture Company, is hereby charged with the payment of said sum of $3,987.31, the unsatisfied amount of said judgment debt, together with the interest thereon and with the costs of collection of said unsatisfied judgment debt and interest thereon[.]

A special execution was issued, ordering the sale of Deese's interest in the partnership to satisfy the judgment. On April 20, 1971, the sheriff, at public venue, sold the interest of Deese to appellant for $500.00. A Sheriff's Bill of Sale issued and the court confirmed the sale on May 19, 1971.

The petition in this case was filed May 26, 1971. It alleged the existence of the partnership and generally the matters above recited. It further alleged that since on or before April 9, 1970, the partnership had not engaged in the business of manufacturing and selling furniture, but that no steps had been taken to liquidate the partnership. It alleged the ownership by the partnership of the building at 1341 Knox and that Williford and Sleyster were receiving rent and profits therefrom without accounting therefor to plaintiff. Count II related to the ownership of the real property. By their answer, defendants alleged that plaintiff had no interest in the partnership because Williford had purchased the interest of Samuel Deese on February 28, 1969.

At the trial of the case, plaintiff introduced documentary evidence which included income tax returns of the partnership, the Willifords and the Sleysters, the record of the charging procedure in the circuit court and profit and loss records of the partnership for the years 1968 and 1969. The accountant who prepared the profit and loss statement also testified on behalf of plaintiff. Plaintiff's attempt to show by that witness statements by Williford to him in February, 1969, as to the partnership's members, was precluded by an objection of defendants, sustained by the trial court, based upon the failure of plaintiff, in response to interrogatories, to indicate that the witness would be relied upon as a source of evidence of matters alleged in plaintiff's petition.

At the conclusion of plaintiff's case, defendants' motion to dismiss was sustained, the trial court in its order reciting that plaintiff had failed to introduce evidence that its predecessor, Samuel Deese, had an interest in the partnership and that plaintiff had failed to prove that it had an interest in the partnership. After its motion for new trial had been overruled, this appeal followed.

Appellant here contends that the evidence below was sufficient to show that Deese had an interest in the partnership which it acquired by virtue of the sheriff's sale, following the charging order. Appellant points to all of the evidence which it adduced in support of its position, but its primary reliance was upon the finding of the court in the charging order of the existence of the partnership and of Deese's interest in the partnership. Respondents contend that the charging order[, because it] is directed at Deese's interest, "if any," in the partnership[,] negates any finding in the order of the existence of such a partnership and Deese's interest in it.

The application for the charging order alleged the existence of the partnership and Deese's interest therein. The order directed to the respondents directed them to appear and show cause why the interest of Deese in the partnership should not be charged with the payment of appellant's judgment. By their attorneys, respondents did appear at the show cause hearing. The respondents filed no formal response to the application for the charging order but they must be held responsible for knowing the possible adverse effect upon their partnership interest which a charging order would produce. Insofar as they were concerned, the proceeding was an adversary one and they took no steps to appeal the order, adverse to their interests. Respondents are now estopped to question the affirmative finding of the court that said Samuel H. Deese is a partner in the firm of Diversified Activities.

The fact that the order charged Deese's interest, "if any," does not negate the affirmative finding of the court of the existence of the partnership and of Deese's interest. The "if any" condition was nothing more than a recognition of the nature of Deese's interest. Under [UPA section 26], "A partner's interest in the partnership is his share of the profits and surplus, and the same is personal property." Thus Deese would have had an interest subject to being charged only if the partnership had profits and surplus, unknown factors at that time and a matter certainly of possible doubt in view of the then dormant status of the firm's business activity.

Respondents' attempt to justify the trial court's ruling on the grounds that appellant made an election of remedies which destroyed any right it obtained under the charging order is without merit. The sale of the partner's interest subject to the charging order is authorized by [UPA section 28]. The purchaser of the interest at such sale has the right to apply thereafter for the dissolution of a partnership at will, such as this was. [UPA § 32(2)(b)]. Thus, the action here taken was entirely consistent with the charging order and no question of election of remedies is involved.

This being an equity case, this court on appeal reviews the evidence and arrives at its own conclusions of fact and law. There is no question of resolving conflicting testimony in this case and therefore no deference is to be accorded the trial court's findings. Furthermore, defendants having rested their case on a motion to dismiss at the close of plaintiff's case, they are considered to have submitted the case for final determination on plaintiff's evidence.

In this situation, as above indicated, plaintiff's evidence did show that it was entitled to the relief sought in Count I of its petition. As for Count II, plaintiffs' evidence showed that, although the property there described was acquired in the name of Sleyster and Williford, the evidence further showed that they were reimbursed by the partnership for funds they advanced for the purchase; that payments on the loan made to provide a portion of the purchase price were made from partnership funds through early 1969; that the partnership paid the taxes on the property through 1967 and established a tax reserve with a bank for payment of the 1968 taxes; that the partnership paid the insurance premiums on the property through 1968; that the property was carried as an asset on the books of the partnership and was depreciated on the partnership income tax returns. Finally, in response to interrogatories, respondents each claim a 25% interest in the property and named Deeses as owners of the other interests in the property.

Plaintiff's evidence, therefore, did establish that the real estate in question was partnership property. The trial court should have so decreed in response to Count II of plaintiff's petition.

Judgment reversed and cause remanded with direction to enter new decree, granting plaintiff relief sought in both counts of its petition.

Notes

1. Under UPA section 32(2), the *purchaser* of an interest in the partnership, whether by way of voluntary assignment or on foreclosure of a charging order, is entitled to petition a court to dissolve an "at will" partnership (either originally without, or after expiration of, a definite term or particular undertaking). Presumably, this right is not available to one acquiring an interest in the partnership other than through purchase, such as by gift or inheritance. *But see In re Bell & Beckwith*, 64 B.R. 620 (Bankr. N.D. Ohio 1986) (bankruptcy trustee for the liquidation of the estate of a partner allowed to petition for dissolution of the partnership). How might a partnership agreement be drafted to deal with this possibility?

2. RUPA section 801(6) is the RUPA provision, equivalent to UPA section 32(2), that permits *transferees* of transferable interests in a partnership to have a court *wind up* the partnership business.

Note on Causes of Dissolution

1. *Voluntary Dissolution.*

As discussed in *Canter's Pharmacy, Inc. v. Elizabeth Associates*, each partner has the inherent *power* to dissolve a partnership at any time. If the partners agreed to be partners for a definite term or during a particular undertaking, the exercise of the power to dissolve violates that agreement. UPA § 31(2). If the partners did not agree to a definite term or a particular undertaking, or if the agreed term has expired (or the agreed undertaking has been completed), then the partnership is said to be a partnership "at will." That is, each partner may exercise the power to dissolve as a matter of right, *without violating the partnership agreement.* UPA §§ 31(1)(a), (b).

In a partnership at will, can partners exercise the power to dissolve in "bad faith"? Suppose that a dissolving partner dissolved with the intent of "freezing" the other partner(s) out of the partnership business and arrogating it to himself or herself. Has the partner acted wrongfully? If so, what is the appropriate remedy? Several cases have confronted similar facts. Although the courts have allowed the dissolution to stand, they have held the dissolving partner liable in damages for "wrongful" dissolution. *See, e.g., Arford v. Blalock*, 199 Ga. App. 434, 405 S.E.2d 698 (1991); *Page v. Page*, 55 Cal. 2d 192, 10 Cal. Rptr. 634, 359 p.2d 41 (1961). When you read *Monteleone v. Monteleone* (later in this chapter), consider whether the innocent partner should also be allowed to continue the partnership business without liquidation.

Note that if a partner assigns in whole or in part the partner's interest in the partnership, the *remaining* partners, by unanimous agreement, may *rightfully* dissolve notwithstanding any agreed term or undertaking. UPA § 31(1)(c).

2. *Dissolution as a Matter of Law.*

A partnership also *automatically* dissolves on the happening of any of the following events:

(i) the partnership business becomes unlawful (or may not lawfully be carried on in a partnership), UPA § 31(3);

(ii) the death of any partner, UPA § 31(4) (Texas: unless the partnership agreement provides otherwise);

(iii) the bankruptcy of any partner or of the partnership, UPA § 31(5); or

(iv) a court decree under UPA section 32, UPA § 31(6).

Although neither ULPA nor RULPA expressly say so, the death, bankruptcy, insanity, expulsion, or withdrawal of a *limited partner* does not dissolve a limited partnership. Why not?

3. *Partner's Right to Petition for Court Dissolution.*

UPA section 32(1) gives any *partner* the right, under certain circumstances, to petition a court to dissolve a partnership. These circumstances include:

(i) the physical or mental incapacity of a partner, UPA §§ 32(1)(a), (b);

(ii) wrongful conduct on the part of a partner (including conduct that makes it "not reasonably practicable" to carry on the partnership business with that partner), UPA §§ 32(1)(c), (d);

(iii) the partnership business can only be carried on at a loss, UPA § 32(1)(e); and

(iv) whenever other circumstances make it equitable to do so, UPA § 32(1)(f).

Dissolution on account of a partner's wrongful conduct will be discussed in *Lonning v. Kurtz*, below, and the notes following.

4. *Retirements and Withdrawals.*

Suppose that a partner decides to "retire." The partner assigns his or her interest in the partnership to the other partners, who continue doing business. What is the effect of the retirement on the partnership?

UPA section 27 provides that the assignment of a partner's interest in the partnership does not of itself dissolve the partnership.

On the other hand, UPA section 29 defines dissolution as a change in relationship *caused* by any partner *ceasing to be associated* in the carrying on of partnership business. Certainly, the retiring partner is no longer associated in carrying on partnership business.

At pre-UPA common law, any *change in the composition* of the partners constituting the partnership dissolved the partnership. Where the remaining partners continued doing business, technically they did so in a *new* partnership.

Post-UPA cases reach the same result, either *via* UPA section 29 or by finding an implied expression of will to cease being a partner (dissolve). *See, e.g., Thomas v. American Nat'l Bank*, 704 S.W.2d 321 (Tex. 1986).

As to limited partnerships, recall that under ULPA section 20 and RULPA section 801(3), the retirement (or other withdrawal) of a general partner will dissolve the limited partnership unless the business is rightfully continued by the remaining general partners.

5. *Changes in Partner Composition* ***without*** *Dissolution.*

The concept that any change in the composition of the partners constituting a partnership dissolves that partnership is far reaching. For example, remaining partners continuing business after a retirement, do so as a *new* partnership.

The idea that a *new* partnership arises after a change in partner composition results from an analytic mishmash of the entity and aggregate concepts. If a partnership is viewed purely as an aggregate, a *relationship* among the partners, the loss or addition of a partner changes the relationship with the retiring or admitted person, but does not change the relationship among the *other* partners. Similarly, if a partnership is viewed as an entity fully independent of its partners, changes in partners are irrelevant so long as the entity continues. Only if a partnership is a quasi-entity dependent on a *unique* relationship among *particular* persons should a change in partner composition of a continuing business result in *complete* dissolution.

Under the *Texas* UPA, the partnership agreement may provide that the *death* of a partner will not dissolve the partnership. TEX. REV. CIV. STAT. ANN. art. 6132b § 31(4) (Vernon 1970). Similarly, RULPA provides that on the "withdrawal" of a partner [which would include the partner's death, RULPA § 402(6)], the limited partnership agreement may provide that the limited partnership is not dissolved. RULPA § 801(4). Substantially the same rule applies in ULPA section 20.

6. *RUPA: Partner Dissociation, Winding Up and Dissolution.*

The RUPA fundamentally alters the UPA concept of dissolution. First, the RUPA separates the concepts of partner dissociation from the partnership, section 601, and winding up of the partnership business, section 801. Second, partnerships will *not* dissolve merely because a person ceases to be a partner. Instead, dissolution will occur *only* when the partnership begins winding up. RUPA § 801. If there is no winding up and the remaining partners instead continue doing business, the partnership will *not* dissolve—the partnership entity will continue.

The events that will cause a partner to dissociate from the partnership are set forth in RUPA section 601. RUPA section 601 largely reorganizes (and elaborates on) UPA sections 31(1), 31(2), 31(4), 31(5), and 32(1)(a)-(d). For example, the events that will cause a partner to dissociate from the partnership include:

(1) the partner's express will, RUPA § 601(1);

(2) a partner's bankruptcy, RUPA § 601(6) or death, incompetency or judicially determined incapacity, RUPA § 601(7); and

(3) expulsion of the partner, either under the partnership agreement, RUPA § 601(3), by a court, RUPA § 601(5), or by vote of the other partners, RUPA § 601(4).

The events that cause a winding up of the partnership business are set forth in RUPA section 801. Most of these events will be discussed in the next section of this chapter.

B. Liquidation v. Continuation

1. Liquidation by Sale

Dreifuerst v. Dreifuerst

90 Wis. 2d 566, 280 N.W.2d 335 (1979)

BROWN, Presiding Judge.

The plaintiffs and the defendant, all brothers, formed a partnership. The partnership operated two feed mills, one located at St. Cloud, Wisconsin and one located at Elkhart Lake, Wisconsin. There were no written Articles of Partnership governing this partnership.

On October 4, 1975, the plaintiffs served the defendant with a notice of dissolution and wind-up of the partnership. The action for dissolution and wind-up was commenced on January 27, 1976. The dissolution complaint alleged that the plaintiffs elected to dissolve the partnership. There was no allegation of fault, expulsion or contravention of an alleged agreement as grounds for dissolution. The parties were unable, however, to agree to a winding-up of the partnership.

Hearings on the dissolution were held on October 18, 1976 and March 4, 1977. Testimony was presented regarding the value of the partnership assets and each partner's equity. At the March 4, 1977 hearing, the defendant requested that the partnership be sold pursuant to sec. 178.33(1), Stats., and that the court allow a sale, at which time the partners would bid on the entire property. By such sale, the plaintiffs could continue to run the business under a new partnership, and the defendant's partnership equity could be satisfied in cash.

On February 20, 1978, the trial court, by written decision, denied the defendant's request for a sale and instead divided the partnership assets in-kind according to the valuation presented by the plaintiffs. The plaintiffs were given the physical assets from the Elkhard Lake mill, and the defendant was given the physical assets from the St. Cloud mill. The defendant appeals this order and judgment dividing the assets in-kind.

Under [UPA section 29], a partnership is dissolved when any partner ceases to be associated in the carrying on of the business. The partnership is not terminated, but continues, until the winding-up of partnership is complete. [UPA section 30]. The action stated by the plaintiffs, in this case, was an action for dissolution and wind-up. The plaintiffs were not continuing the partnership and, therefore, [UPA sections 41 and 42] do not apply. The sole question in this case is whether, in the absence of a written agreement to the contrary, a partner, upon dissolution and wind-up of the partnership, can force a sale of the partnership assets.

At the outset, we note, and the parties agree, that the appellant was not in contravention of the partnership agreement since there was no partnership agreement. The partnership was a partnership at will. They also agree there was no written agreement governing distribution of partnership assets upon dissolution and wind-up. The dispute, in this case, is over the authority of the trial court to order in-kind distribution in the absence of any agreement of the partners.

[UPA section 38(1)] provides:

> When dissolution is caused in any way, except in contravention of the partnership agreement, each partner, as against his copartners and all persons claiming through them in respect to their interests in the partnership, *unless otherwise agreed*, may have the partnership property applied to discharge its liabilities, and the surplus applied to pay *in cash* the net amount owing to the respective partners. [Emphasis supplied.]

The appellant contends this statute grants him the right to force a sale of the partnership assets in order to obtain his fair share of the partnership assets in cash upon dissolution. He claims that in the absence of an agreement of the partners to in-kind distribution, the trial court had no authority to distribute the assets in-kind. He is entitled to an in-cash settlement after judicial sale.

The respondents contend the statute does not entitle the appellant to force a sale and grants the trial court the power to distribute the assets in-kind if in-kind distribution is equitably possible and doesn't jeopardize the rights of creditors.

We do not believe that the statute can be read in any way to permit in-kind distribution unless the partners agree to in-kind distribution or unless there is a partnership agreement calling for in-kind distribution at the time of dissolution and wind-up.

A partnership at will is a partnership which has no definite term or particular undertaking and can rightfully be dissolved by the express will of any partner. [UPA section 31(1)(b)]. In the present case, the respondents wanted to dissolve the partnership. This being a partnership at will, they could rightfully dissolve this partnership with or without the consent of the appellant. In addition, the respondents have never claimed the appellant was in violation of any partnership agreement. Therefore, neither the appellant nor the respondents have wrongfully dissolved the partnership.

Unless otherwise agreed, partners who have not wrongfully dissolved a partnership have a right to wind up the partnership. [UPA section 37]. Winding-up is the process of settling partnership affairs after dissolution. Winding-up is often called liquidation and involves reducing the assets to cash to pay creditors and distribute to partners the value of their respective interests. Thus, lawful dissolution (or dissolution which is caused in any way except in contravention of the partnership agreement) gives each partner the right to have the business liquidated and his share of the surplus paid *in cash*. In-kind distribution is permissible only in very limited circumstances. If the partnership agreement permits in-kind distribution upon dissolution or wind-up or if, at any time prior to wind-up, all partners agree to in-kind distribution, the court may order in-kind distribution. While at least one court has permitted in-kind distribution, absent an agreement by all partners, *Rinke v. Rinke*, 330 Mich. 615, 48 N.W.2d 201 (1951), the court's holding in that case was limited. In *Rinke*, the court stated:

> The decree of the trial court provided for dividing the assets of the partnerships rather than for the sale thereof and the distribution of cash proceeds. Appellants insist that such method of procedure is erroneous and not contemplated by the Uniform Partnership Act. Attention is directed to Section 38. Construing together pertinent provisions of the statute leads to the conclusion that it was not the intention of the legislature in the enactment of the Uniform Partnership Act to impose a mandatory requirement that, under all circumstances, the assets of a dissolved partnership shall be sold and the money received therefor divided among those entitled to it, particularly so, as in the case at bar, where there are no debts to be paid from the proceeds. *The situation disclosed by the record in the present case is somewhat unusual in that no one other than the former partners is interested in the assets of the businesses. In view of this situation and of the nature of the assets*, we think that the trial court was correct in apportioning them to the parties. There is no showing that appellants have been prejudiced thereby. [(Emphasis supplied.)]

The Michigan court's holding was limited to situations where: (1) there were no creditors to be paid from the proceeds, (2) ordering a sale would be senseless since no one other than the partners would be interested in the assets of the business, and (3) an in-kind distribution was fair to all partners.

That is not the case here. There was no showing that there were no creditors who would be paid from the proceeds, nor was there a showing that no one other than the partners would be interested in the assets. These factors are important if an in-kind distribution is to be allowed. [UPA section 38 is] intended to protect creditors as well as partners. In-kind distributions may affect a creditor's right to collect the debt owed since the assets of the partnership, as a whole, may be worth more than the assets once divided up. Thus, the creditor's ability to collect from the individual partners may be jeopardized. Secondly, if others are interested in the assets, a sale provides a more accurate means of establishing the market value of the assets and, thus, better assuring each partner his share in the value of the assets. Where only the partners are interested in the assets, a fair value can be determined without the necessity of a sale. The sale would be merely the partners bidding with each other without any competition. This process could be accomplished through negotiations or at trial with the court as a final arbitrator of the value of the assets. With these policy considerations in mind, we think the Michigan court's holding in *Rinke* was limited to the facts of that case. Those facts not being present in this case, we do not feel an in-kind distribution in this case was proper.

However, even assuming the respondents in this case can show that there are no creditors to be paid, no one other than the partners are interested in the assets, and in-kind distribution would be fair to all partners, we cannot read [UPA section 38] as permitting an in-kind distribution under any circumstances, unless all partners agree. [UPA section 38 is] quite clear that if a partner may force liquidation, he is entitled to his share of the partnership assets, after creditors are paid *in cash*. To the extent that *Rinke v. Rinke* creates an exception to cash distribution, we decline to adopt that exception. We, therefore, must hold the trial court erred in ordering an in-kind distribution of the assets of the partnership.

The last question that arises is whether the appellant can force an actual sale of the assets or whether the trial court can determine the fair market value of the assets and order the respondents to pay the appellant in cash an amount equal to his share in the assets.

As discussed above, a sale is the best means of determining the true fair market value of the assets. Generally, liquidation envisions some form of sale. Since the statutes provide that, unless otherwise agreed, any partner who has not wrongfully dissolved the partnership has the right to wind up the partnership and force liquidation, he likewise has a right to force a sale, unless otherwise agreed. While judicial sales in some instances may cause economic hardships, these hardships can be avoided by the use of partnership agreements.

Judgment reversed and cause remanded for further proceedings not inconsistent with this opinion.

Notes

1. There are two chief reasons why UPA section 38(1) gives each partner the right to require liquidation by sale. The first is that mentioned in *Dreifuerst v. Dreifuerst*: a sale is the best way to determine the true market value of partnership assets.

The second reason is at least as important. Notwithstanding the dissolution of the partnership, partners remain liable for all partnership obligations. UPA § 36(1). In a liquidation by sale, the process of winding up partnership affairs discharges partnership obligations in three important ways. First, the partnership will complete "unfinished business"—transactions begun, but not completed, before dissolution. Second, the proceeds of the sale of partnership property will be applied to pay partnership liabilities. Third, if such proceeds are inadequate to cover partnership liabilities, the partners must contribute their shares of this "loss." UPA §§ 18(a), 40(a), 40(d). See the chapter entitled "Dissolution: Accounting."

2. RUPA sections, 802 and 808(a) continue the rule that a partner in a partnership at will is entitled to liquidation by sale.

2. Continuation of the Partnership Business Without Liquidation

Liquidation by sale is not the inevitable result of dissolution of the partnership. First, UPA section 38(1) applies only if the partners have not agreed otherwise. Second, the UPA limits a partner's liquidation right in certain circumstances, and permits the other partners to continue the business of the partnership.

Given *each* partner's general UPA section 38(1) right to liquidation by sale, continuation of the partnership business without liquidation generally requires the consent of *all* the partners, or a right to do so under the UPA or the partnership agreement.

Lonning v. Kurtz

291 N.W.2d 438 (N.D. 1980)

VANDE WALLE, Justice.

Gordon E. Lonning appeals from a judgment entered on May 17, 1979, by the Burleigh County district court, holding that Lonning's interest in a partnership with Philip J. Kurtz, Adrian J. Fischer, and Richard A. Fischer was dissolved no later than

August 5, 1977, and that Lonning was entitled to the value of his partnership interest as of that date.

The record shows that Kurtz was the owner of certain real property in Burleigh County upon which he was attempting to develop a mobile home park. Kurtz began developing the project but encountered financial difficulties. He approached Adrian Fischer for possible financial backing and through him became acquainted with Richard Fischer and the plaintiff, Gordon Lonning. These parties entered into a partnership agreement to develop the property. On June 30, 1977, the parties reduced their agreement to written form.

In conjunction with the partnership agreement, a contract for deed was entered into whereby Kurtz agreed to sell to each of the other partners an undivided 20 percent interest for a $52,000 payment in the property intended for development. After receiving the specified down-payment of $10,400 plus a mortgage on the balance due from each other partner, Kurtz was to convey a partial interest in the property to the other partners who would in turn convey their interests to the partnership in order to become general partners. Because of financial difficulties, the other partners were unable to pay the total down-payment required, so Kurtz agreed to forego his right to demand immediately the full down-payment. However, no deed for the property was ever delivered under this contract.

Dissension developed among the partners. On August 5, 1977, Lonning wrote to the remaining partners stating they had indicated to him that they no longer wanted him in the business. He went on to say he wished to remain in the partnership but offered to accept a certain sum, plus certain equipment and materials in settlement of his interest, "instead of invoking Article XI" of the partnership agreement, which provided for the settlement of partnership interests in the event a partner left the partnership for whatever reasons. If the offer was unacceptable, Lonning stated, the letter was to be considered notice to sell his interest in the partnership and that the other partners should prepare to call appraisers pursuant to Article XI. The partners met to discuss the matter but were unable to reach agreement. Thereafter, Lonning did not associate himself with the partnership, and the remaining partners arranged financing and continued to develop the property as a partnership without the involvement of Lonning.

In February of 1978, Lonning sued for an accounting and appraisal of the partnership assets along with an interest in the assets commensurate with his investment. The district court found that the partnership had been dissolved not later than August 5, 1977, by Lonning's withdrawal or expulsion or his letter of August 5, 1977, and that, pursuant to Article XI of the partnership agreement, Lonning was entitled to an accounting. It ordered that Lonning was entitled to the value of his interest in the partnership property, which the court found to be one percent.[1]

Lonning now appeals from this judgment. On appeal Lonning contends that the partnership he entered with Kurtz and the Fischers has not been dissolved, either by agreement or by operation of law. While it is true that a partnership may be dissolved

---

1. This computation was based upon a finding that Lonning had paid a total of $2,600 into the partnership, which amounted to five percent of the $52,000 required to be paid in order to entitle Lonning to a 20 percent interest in the partnership. This is one percent of the total partnership property.

by an agreement of the partners [UPA § 31(1)(c)], or by court order [UPA § 32], these are not the only ways to dissolve a partnership.

"Dissolution," as the term is used in the Uniform Partnership Act, "is the change in the relation of the partners caused by any partner ceasing to be associated in the carrying on as distinguished from the winding up of the business." [UPA § 29]. It designates the point in time when the partners cease to carry on the business *together*. So defined, "dissolution" is a technical legal concept, unlike the usage found in other areas of the law such as corporations. "Dissolution," under the Uniform Partnership Act, is not synonymous with "winding up" and "termination," which are additional steps in completing the affairs and ending a partnership.

[UPA section 31] states in part that dissolution is caused without violation of a partnership agreement:

> d. By the expulsion of any partner from the business bona fide in accordance with such a power conferred by the agreement between the partners.

The agreement entered by the parties here on June 30, 1977, contained such a provision for expulsion. Article XII of the agreement states:

> The partnership may expel any partner by a vote of the remaining partners holding eighty percent (80%) of the partnership interest for any reason that the remaining partners may deem appropriate. Any partner who shall be expelled from the partnership shall be entitled to the same rights, obligations and interests provided in Article XI for departing partner.

Furthermore, [UPA section 38(1)] provides:

> 1. When dissolution is caused in any way, except in contravention of the partnership agreement, each partner, as against his copartners and all persons claiming through them in respect of their interests in the partnership, *unless otherwise agreed*, may have the partnership property applied to discharge its liabilities, and the surplus applied to pay in cash the net amount owing to the respective partners. But if dissolution is caused by [the] expulsion of a partner, bona fide under the partnership agreement and if the expelled partner is discharged from all partnership liabilities, either by payment or agreement under [UPA section 36(2)], he shall receive in cash only the net amount due him from the partnership." [(Emphasis added.)]

In Crane & Bromberg, *Law of Partnership*, § 74(d) (1968), the authors, in discussing partnership agreement provisions for expulsion, state:

> The partnership agreement may provide for expulsion of a partner, either automatically or by vote of a designated portion of the remaining partners. The expulsion may be conditioned on specific causes, which must be shown to exist in fact to justify the exercise of the power. Or it may be authorized when the other partners deem it desirable in the interests of the partnership, or entirely without cause.
>
> Expulsion provisions are rare because of each partner's fear that the others may gang up on him. However, if properly limited, they are useful, especially for professional firms which might be disqualified by the actions of a member. Whatever their merit, expulsion provisions carry the significant consequence that

> the expelled partner is entitled only to a cash settlement, without liquidation of the business.

We believe the evidence was sufficient for the district court to determine that Lonning has been expelled pursuant to the partnership agreement.

In addition, the district court found:

> If he withdrew, as he also had the right to do under the partnership agreement, the withdrawal would likewise cause a dissolution of his interest.

Even if the partnership agreement had not provided for dissolution upon expulsion or voluntary withdrawal, any partner could have dissolved the partnership at any time.

Even if, as Lonning argues, there was no agreement or court order for dissolution, we believe that the record clearly shows that after August 5, 1977, Lonning was no longer "associated in the carrying on . . . of the business." Under these circumstances we find no error in the district court's determination that Lonning's partnership with the others had been dissolved.

After dissolution, a partnership continues until the winding up or liquidation of partnership affairs is completed. Then the partnership terminates. [UPA § 30]. Although dissolution may be followed by liquidation, this need not occur if the partnership agreement provides for continuation of the partnership business after dissolution and the departing partner is paid for his partnership contribution and share of accumulated profits.

The partnership agreement entered by Lonning and the others contained the following provisions:

> ARTICLE X
>
> The death, retirement, expulsion or absence of any partner will not dissolve the partnership as to the other partners unless agreed by all partners.
>
> ARTICLE XI
>
> In the event any partner leaves the partnership by reason of death, disability, expulsion, retirement, or for any other reason, the departing partner or successor in interest, must first offer and sell to the remaining partners its partnership interest. Said option to purchase by the remaining partners shall extend for a period of ninety (90) days after written notice to the remaining partners. Said departing partner must make his share available pro-rata to the remaining partners. For purposes of any purchase under the terms of this Article, if the partners cannot agree on a price, the selling price of said departing partner's interest in the partnership's real property shall be determined by competent real estate appraisers. The parties to this agreement must elect two appraisers and the two selected appraisers shall select a third appraiser. The three appraisers must agree to a market value of said property for the purpose of distribution to the departing partner. If the three appraisers cannot agree, new appraisers shall be selected, again pursuant to this Article. The decision of the three appraisers shall become binding on all partners.

In addition, the record reveals that Lonning had been discharged from his partnership liabilities by agreement as provided under [UPA section 36(2)].

Lonning, along with the others, had signed an unsecured note with the State Bank of Burleigh County for a $10,000 loan made to the partnership as preliminary financing to start the project. He also, with the others, signed a personal guaranty on credit to be extended to the partnership. But Mr. Ronald Lamphear, who handled the loan file for the bank, stated that Mr. Lonning was not liable on the note nor under the guaranty. The note, which Lonning had signed along with the others, had been paid off with moneys from a $300,000 loan made to Kurtz and the Fischers. Lonning had signed neither the note nor the mortgage on the $300,000 loan. The bank still has the personal guaranties signed by Lonning and the others for any credit extended to the partnership, but the $300,000 loan was made to the remaining partners individually, and the bank has not made any loans in the name of the partnership. Mr. Lamphear indicated the bank would be willing to tear up the guaranty signed by Lonning if the other remaining partners signed a new one.

Prior to the finalization of the $300,000 loan, Kurtz indicated to Lamphear that Lonning was no longer a partner and that responsibility for the loan rests with the remaining partners. Sometime after the $300,000 loan was made, Lonning himself contacted the bank and was informed by Lamphear that he was not liable for either the $10,000 loan or the $300,000 loan. We believe the trial court could infer from these facts that Lonning had been released from any partnership liability existing at the time his partnership with the others was dissolved.

We affirm the judgment of the district court with costs, and order that Lonning be paid for his partnership interest as of August 5, 1977, in accordance with the provisions of Article XI of the partnership agreement.

Levy v. Nassau Queens Medical Group

102 A.D.2d 845, 476 N.Y.S.2d 613 (1984)

MEMORANDUM BY THE COURT.

In an action to recover damages for breach of contract and prima facie tort, plaintiffs appeal from an order of the Supreme Court, Queens County, dated February 15, 1984, which granted defendant's motion to dismiss the complaint for failure to state a cause of action.

Plaintiff's decedent, Dr. Sidney Levy, was a physician engaged in the practice of medicine as a partner in the defendant Nassau Queens Medical Group. By a majority vote of the partnership executive committee, Levy was expelled from the partnership on the ground that he was more than 70 years of age. Under the partnership agreement, a partner could be terminated by a majority vote if he has reached the age of 70. In this action to recover damages for breach of the agreement and for prima facie tort, plaintiffs alleged that the termination was made in bad faith because other persons over the age of 70 were not expelled from the partnership and the real reason for the termination was Levy's criticisms of partnership decisions. Special Term granted defendant's motion to dismiss the complaint for failure to state a cause of action.

The purpose of the termination clause was to provide a simple, practical and speedy method of separating a partner from the partnership, and in the absence of undue penalty or unjust forfeiture, the court may not frustrate this purpose. While bad faith may be actionable, there must be some showing that the partnership acted out of a desire to gain a business or property advantage for the remaining partners.

Policy disagreements do not constitute bad faith since "at the heart of the partnership concept is the principle that partners may choose with whom they wish to be associated."

Accordingly, there should be an affirmance.

Notes

1. Under UPA section 38(1), a person expelled as partner under a right given in the partnership agreement does not have an absolute right to require liquidation by sale, *even in a partnership at will*. So long as the expelled partner is *discharged* from partnership liabilities, the expelled partner has only the right to be paid the value of his or her interest in the partnership (the "net amount due him"). After an expulsion, each of the *other* partners has the right to liquidation by sale unless the partnership agreement provides otherwise.

2. The RUPA continues the right of partners to expel a partner pursuant to a right given in the partnership agreement. RUPA § 601(2).

In a partnership for a *definite term or specific undertaking*, RUPA section 801(2) gives only the *other* partners the right to a winding up. Similarly, *in a partnership at will*, the expelled partner no longer has the RUPA section 801(1) right to cause a winding up; the *other* partners, of course, retain that right. In either case, if the other partners all wish to continue business, they may do so by purchasing the interest of the expelled partner. RUPA § 701(a). Note that the RUPA only requires that the expelled partner be *indemnified* against (rather than released from) existing liabilities. RUPA § 701(d).

Monteleone v. Monteleone

147 Ill. App. 3d 265, 497 N.E.2d 1221 (1986)

Justice McMORROW:

Nick Monteleone and Lorenzo Monteleone (Nick and Lorenzo) appeal from the order of the judicial sale of the Monte Auto Body Shop, of which Nick and Lorenzo are partners in conjunction with Jerry Monteleone (Jerry). The primary question presented for our review is whether the trial court erred in ordering a judicial sale of the partnership assets prior to adjudicating whether Nick and Lorenzo have a right to retain the partnership business and reimburse Jerry for the value of his interest in the partnership, on the ground that Jerry wrongfully terminated the partnership.

Jerry instituted proceedings to dissolve his partnership with Nick and Lorenzo in the Monte Auto Body Shop on January 5, 1984. Thereafter Nick and Lorenzo filed an answer to Jerry's complaint and presented a counter-claim requesting dissolution of the partnership and recognition of their right to continue the business and to reimburse Jerry for his interest in the partnership, less damages for his wrongful termination of the partnership.

It is undisputed between the parties that Jerry, Nick, and Lorenzo formed an oral partnership in April 1979 to own and operate an automobile body repair business named Monte Auto Body Shop in Melrose Park, Illinois. Jerry, Nick, and Lorenzo dispute who among them caused the dissolution of partnership.

Jerry stated in his complaint that Nick and Lorenzo "wrongfully executed [Jerry] from the partnership premises" on or about October 31, 1983, thereby effecting a dissolution of the partnership. He alleged that Nick and Lorenzo subsequently failed to conclude partnership business, but instead continued to operate the auto body shop partnership without complying with the requirements of section 38(2)(b) of the Uniform Partnership Act. Jerry's pleading requested dissolution of the partnership. This behavior included, in essence, misappropriation of partnership funds, failure to contribute to the operation of the business, a wrongful demand that Jerry's son be made a partner in the business and that a certain employee be immediately discharged, and refusal to return partnership books and records. They stated that after the partnership "was dissolved in October of 1983 [by Jerry's wrongful termination]," Nick and Lorenzo, "being a surviving majority, formed a new partnership." Apparently this enterprise operates under the name Monte Auto Body Shop in the same location as the presently disputed partnership and continues ownership and operation of that partnership in auto body repair work. Based upon these allegations, Nick and Lorenzo requested that the court declare the partnership dissolved by virtue of Jerry's wrongful conduct in October 1983, the value of partnership assets to be determined as of October 1983, Nick and Lorenzo be permitted to purchase Jerry's interest, Nick and Lorenzo "be decreed to be the surviving partners and to continue the partnership business," an accounting to be performed, and Jerry "be assessed all damages and costs incurred by the partnership and/or [Nick and Lorenzo]" because of Jerry's wrongful termination of the partnership.

Although hearings on the parties' allegations had commenced, the trial court never made a final adjudication of the merits of their claims. Thereafter Jerry filed a motion requesting that the court order a judicial sale of partnership assets prior to the court's decision on the issues of the parties' interests in the business, the dissolution of the partnership and its wrongful termination, and the parties' rights upon dissolution. Following a briefing and oral argument, the trial court granted the motion in a written order for the judicial sale of partnership assets. The court's order found that the partnership was dissolved over two years ago. Based upon "the obvious dispute concerning the value of assets," the court ordered a judicial sale of "all of the partnership assets" with directions that, following the sale, "the sheriff shall * * * hold the proceeds subject to confirmation and appropriate proceeds order by this court based upon reasonable value and other equitable and legal considerations * * * ." The court found no just reason to delay enforcement of or appeal from its order of judicial sale. The timely expedited appeal of Nick and Lorenzo followed.

As previously noted, the primary question presented for our review is whether the court could properly order a judicial sale of the "partnership assets" of Monte Auto Body Shop prior to a determination of the claim of Nick and Lorenzo that they could continue operation of the partnership business because of Jerry's wrongful termination of the partnership.

Under section 38(2)(b) of the Uniform Partnership Act, innocent partners have the right to continue partnership business where another partner has wrongfully terminated the partnership. Nick and Lorenzo thus may have the right to continue ownership and operation of the Monte Auto Body Shop partnership, if they are able to establish at a subsequent proceeding that Jerry's conduct constituted a wrongful termination of the partnership.

The rights of partners upon a partner's wrongful termination of the partnership are governed by section 38(2) of the Uniform Partnership Act. This section provides in relevant part:

(2) When dissolution is caused in contravention of the partnership agreement the rights of the partners shall be as follows:

(a) Each partner who has not caused dissolution wrongfully shall have,

II. The right, as against each partner who has caused the dissolution wrongfully, to damage for breach of the agreement.

(b) The partners who have not caused the dissolution wrongfully, if they all desire to continue the business in the same name, either by themselves or jointly with others, may do so, during the agreed term for the partnership and for that purpose may possess the partnership property, provided they secure the payment by bond approved by the court, or pay to any partner who has caused the dissolution wrongfully, the value of his interest in the partnership at the dissolution, less any damages recoverable under clause (2a II) of this section, and in like manner indemnify him against all present or future partnership liabilities.

(c) A partner who has caused the dissolution wrongfully shall have:

II. If the business is continued under paragraph (2b) of this section the right as against his co-partners and all claiming through them in respect of their interests in the partnership, to have the value of his interest in the partnership, less any damages caused to his co-partners by the dissolution, ascertained and paid to him in cash, or the payment secured by bond approved by the court and to be released from all existing liabilities of the partnership; but in ascertaining the value of the partner's interest the value of the good will of the business shall not be considered.

A partner's conduct is considered "wrongful" when it is taken in derogation of the duties imposed either explicitly by the partnership agreement or implicitly by virtue of the nature of the partnership itself. The Uniform Partnership Act empowers a court to order partnership dissolution whenever, for example, a "partner has been guilty of such conduct as tends to affect prejudicially the carrying on of the business, [or whenever a] partner willfully or persistently commits a breach of the partnership or agreement, or otherwise so conducts himself in matters relating to the partnership business that it is not reasonably practicable to carry on the business in partnership with him." [UPA § 32(1)(c), (1)(d)].

Nick and Lorenzo alleged in their counter-claim that the oral partnership between Nick, Lorenzo, and Jerry specified that "each partner would contribute equally to the capital and equally share all profits and losses and further, that each partner would contribute an equal amount of labor to the operation of the partnership, and each partner would receive weekly compensation for his labor." Their pleading then alleged in substance that Jerry had violated this agreement in several specified respects. They claimed before the trial court and in this appeal that these allegations also constituted a breach of Jerry's fiduciary duties to the partnership.

Jerry concedes in this appeal that for the purposes of analysis, "we must assume that [Jerry] took draws in excess of his percentage of ownership and committed the conduct alleged in the counter-claim." In our opinion these allegations in the counter-claim of Nick and Lorenzo were sufficient to state a claim that Jerry's behavior was in contravention of the partnership agreement or a breach of Jerry's fiduciary duties, and would amount to "wrongful termination" of the partnership. Such alleged wrongful termination of the partnership is sufficient to order dissolution of the partnership and to recognize the right of Nick and Lorenzo to continue operation of the business rather than be subjected to the possibility of a contrived judicial sale from which they would receive a monetary payment for their respective interests in the partnership. (See [UPA § 38(2)].) As a result, the court's order of judicial sale of the partnership before a finding of whether Jerry wrongfully terminated his participation in the partnership was premature, and amounted to reversible error.

Jerry argues that his conduct, even if it amounts to wrongful termination, would not justify the continuation of the partnership business by Nick and Lorenzo, because the oral partnership agreement between them was not for a fixed term and was therefore a partnership at will. *See* [UPA § 31].

We find this argument unpersuasive. Section 38 of the Uniform Partnership Act does not explicitly limit the rights of innocent partners conferred in the provision to those partners who have agreed to a partnership for a fixed term. Furthermore, the fact that subsection (2) permits the innocent partners to "continue the business in the same name during the agreed term for the partnership" is not reasonably interpreted, in our view, as a limitation upon the application of section 38 solely to fixed-term partnerships. Instead it recognizes that the term originally agreed upon by the partners (here, at will) shall remain in effect during the innocent partners' continuation of the partnership business.

In our view section 38 does not contemplate that Nick and Lorenzo should be precluded from continuing the partnership business under these circumstances merely because their oral agreement set no fixed date for the termination of the partnership.

Parenthetically we also find without merit Jerry's contention that, in the interest of judicial economy, a judicial sale is preferable to a hearing wherein the parties present evidence of the appraised value of partnership assets. Section 38(2) accords to innocent partners the right to continue the partnership enterprise, rather than to share in the proceeds of sale or liquidation of the partnership estate.

REVERSED AND REMANDED.

Note on Section 38(1½): Application of UPA Section 38(2) to Partnerships at Will

The *Monteleone* court held that UPA section 38(2)(b) permits "partners who have not caused dissolution wrongfully" to continue the business of an *at will* partnership in the case of misconduct by another partner. Does that make sense? If a partnership is "at will," the partners have not agreed to be partners for any definite term or particular undertaking. That is, the partners have no legally enforceable expectation as to how long they will be partners. Any partner can rightfully dissolve the partnership "at will," UPA § 31(1)(b), and insist on liquidation by sale, UPA § 38(1). If that is the case, how can the partners "bootstrap" themselves to a right to continue without liquidation and *without the consent of **all** the partners*?

Moreover, despite *Monteleone*, UPA section 38(2) does not *clearly* permit continuation except in the case of an *early* dissolution of a partnership for a definite term or particular undertaking. The introductory clause to section 38(2) makes that section applicable only where the dissolution is caused *in contravention of the partnership agreement*.

UPA section 31(2) provides that dissolution is caused "in contravention of the partnership agreement" when a partner exercises the *power* to dissolve without having the *right* to do so under section 31(1). Similarly, section 31(1)(c) provides that dissolution at the express will of any partner occurs "*without violation of the agreement between the partners*" where there is no definite term or particular undertaking.

UPA section 38(2)(b) allows the other partners to continue only for the remainder of "the agreed term of the partnership." Thus, (notwithstanding *Monteleone*) section 38(2) does *not* apply to *any* dissolutions other than an early voluntary termination of a partnership for a definite term or specific undertaking.

Nevertheless, *Monteleone* is not an isolated case. Courts often do allow continuation in circumstances involving partner misconduct, applying what might be called "*section 38(1½)*." That is, they purport to apply UPA section 38(2) to UPA section 32(1) court dissolutions on account of partner misconduct.

The RUPA limits the statutory right to continue without winding up. Under RUPA section 701, if no event causes winding up under RUPA section 802 after a partner dissociation, the partnership must purchase, and the dissociating partner must sell, the interest in the partnership of the dissociating partner.

As to *partnerships at will*, although expulsion of a partner for misconduct is *not* a wrongful dissociation giving rise to damages, RUPA § 602, the expelled (dissociated) partner has no right to cause winding up. Only the other (innocent) partners have the right to cause winding up. RUPA § 801(1).

As to partnerships for a *term or undertaking*, *only* the other (innocent) partners have the right to winding up after a partner dissociates early. That is true regardless of whether the dissociation occurs as a result of express will, RUPA § 801(2), wrongful conduct or expulsion, RUPA § 801(2), or death, RUPA § 801(3). Note that the RUPA *expands* the definition of expulsion to include not only expulsions in accordance with the partnership agreement, RUPA § 601(2), but also expulsions by a *court* on account of partner misconduct, RUPA § 601(3)).

Note on Section 32(1): Dissolutions by a Court on Account of Partner Misconduct

1. Dissolution of a partnership under UPA section 32(1)(c) or (d) is an equitable remedy that speaks to the discretion of the trial court:

> [A]n action of a partner which is merely trifling in nature or a temporary grievance without permanent damage does not form adequate grounds for dissolution. Rather the conduct must be legally substantial and evidence either gross misconduct or want of good faith or cause serious and permanent injury to the partnership.

Wood v. Holiday Mobile Home Resorts, Inc., 128 Ariz. 274, 625 P.2d 337, 343 (App. 1980) (action of general partner in mortgaging partnership property without authority and in taking unauthorized management fees justified court dissolution of limited partnership).

2. In *Monteleone*, the partners engaged in "self-help" and "expelled" another partner without having a right to do so under the partnership agreement, *and* without the benefit of court review of the facts. First, their own actions were the formal *cause* of dissolution, regardless of their motivation. Second, as a policy matter the law should require partners who have not bargained for a right to expel to go before a court to prove the justness of their "cause."

3. Under RUPA section 601(5), a partner may petition a court to "expel" (dissociate) a partner on account of the partner's "wrongful" conduct.

Note on Continuations under UPA Section 38(2)

1. A UPA section 38(2) continuation differs from a UPA section 38(1) expulsion in two respects. First, a partner wrongfully causing dissolution is liable in damages. UPA § 38(2)(a)(II). Second, in determining the value of the outgoing partner's interest in the partnership, a partner wrongfully causing dissolution is not entitled to a share of the *goodwill*. UPA § 38(2)(b)(II). Where a court allows an equitable continuation as in *Nicholes v. Hunt* (following), what are the rights of a non-continuing partner?

2. Unless the partnership agreement provides otherwise, the consent of *all* of the innocent partners is required before the business can be continued under UPA section 38(2). That is, each of the innocent partners has the right to liquidation by sale. UPA § 38(2)(a)(I).

3. The innocent partners are entitled to damages from the partner wrongfully causing dissolution. If the innocent partners elect to continue the partnership business, the partner wrongfully causing dissolution is only entitled to be paid the value of the partner's interest in the partnership, but without including any value for goodwill of the partnership business, and less any damages. UPA § 38(2)(c). In addition, the partner wrongfully causing dissolution must be *released* from existing liabilities of the partnership. Under the *Texas* version of the UPA, as under RUPA section 701(d), the innocent partners may instead *indemnify* the partner wrongfully causing dissolution against existing liabilities. TEX. REV. CIV. STAT. ANN. art. 6132b § 38(2)(b), (c) (Vernon 1970).

Nicholes v. Hunt

273 Or. 255, 541 P.2d 820 (1975)

BRYSON, Justice.

Plaintiff seeks a decree for the dissolution of a partnership pursuant to [UPA section 32(1)(c) & (d)]. Plaintiff alleged that defendant wrongfully excluded plaintiff from the partnership; that there be an accounting and prayed for a dissolution of the partnership and determination of each party's interest. Defendant filed an amended answer denying plaintiff's allegations and affirmatively alleged that plaintiff breached the partnership agreement and that defendant be allowed to continue the business pursuant to an "implied term" in the partnership agreement.

The trial court found that the parties had formed a partnership at will and that defendant, in good faith, had dissolved the partnership on May 27, 1973; that the partnership could be "terminated at will" and entered a decree ordering the dissolution of the partnership and the distribution of the partnership assets. Plaintiff appeals and defendant cross appeals.

Prior to 1972 defendant, as sole proprietor, was engaged in the manufacture and sale of lead shot for shotgun shells under the name West Coast Shot Manufacturing Company. Defendant had developed a "miner" and special equipment to recover used shot from trap shooting fields which was then melted down to produce new shot for sale on the market.

In the spring of 1972 plaintiff met defendant in Medford, Oregon, and the parties orally agreed to form an equal partnership for the mining, manufacture, and sale of shot. Plaintiff was to purchase one-half of defendant's existing business for $50,000. It was also agreed that plaintiff would make an initial payment of $10,000 and transfer one-half interest in his airplane to the partnership. The balance of $35,000 was to be reduced by annual payments of $5,000 together with interest at 7 percent. Defendant, being experienced, was to devote his best effort to the business. No written partnership agreement was executed. However, the evidence and tax returns show that they operated as an equal partnership beginning May 29, 1972.

The record shows the original equipment was improved and upgraded and the new venture was a financial success but subject to considerable dissension between the partners. However, by December of 1972 the parties had "pretty well patched everything up, everything was happy." On May 28, 1973, approximately six months later, defendant informed plaintiff by phone that their business relationship was at an end.[5] Following the telephone notice of dissolution, defendant sent plaintiff a letter which stated in part as follows:

> May 31, 1973
>
> Please accept this letter as notice of termination of our business relationship. This notice is meant to be effective whether our business relationship is characterized as an agreement to form a partnership, or a partnership. In either event, I will continue to operate West Coast Shot Company henceforth.
>
> You are specifically not authorized henceforth to act on behalf of West Coast Shot Company or myself as employee, agent, or partner. This termination is to be effective upon today's date, May 31, 1973.
>
> [T]he $35,000.00 balance was to be paid at $5,000 per annum with seven percent (7%) interest upon the unpaid balance. The first $5,000.00 payment, plus interest, was due May 1, 1973, and you have failed to make that payment.

On June 4, 1973, plaintiff's attorney wrote to defendant stating:

> Our client feels you have wrongfully dissolved the partnership.
>
> Pursuant to [UPA section 38(2)(b)], our client hereby elects to continue the business of the partnership under the same name by himself and hereby demands that you immediately give him possession of all of the partnership property for that purpose. In addition, he demands that you submit an accounting of all the partnership affairs to date.

After May 27, 1973, the defendant continued to operate the business but maintained a record of all transactions, assets and profits.

Each party contends that he is entitled to buy the 50 percent share of the other partner and continue the business as a sole proprietor.

The evidence shows that defendant elected to and did exercise his right to dissolve the partnership pursuant to [UPA section 31(1)(b)] and fully notified the plaintiff of this election on the morning of May 28, 1973. This was confirmed in the letter

5. At trial, defendant testified that he terminated the partnership because plaintiff failed to carry out instructions, did not devote his full time to the business, and did not meet his annual payment of $5,000 for 1973. "Most of it was based on a year of bickering and arguing * * * ."

previously quoted dated May 31, 1973. Prior to adoption of the Uniform Partnership Act, in *McKinnis v. Dodge*, 103 Or. 9, 13, 203 P. 876, 878 (1922), this court held:

> A partnership is dissolved by notice of one partner to his associates of his election to terminate the partnership. No particular form of notice is required.

Nevertheless, plaintiff contends that the dissolution was in contravention of the partnership agreement and relies on *Page v. Page*, 10 Cal. Rptr. 634, 646, 359 P.2d 41, 44 (1961), to support his contention that defendant, as a fiduciary, was obligated to exercise his power to dissolve the partnership in good faith.[6]

Plaintiff directs us to evidence produced at trial of an "unfair design" on defendant's part to "freeze out" plaintiff from a profitable enterprise. Defendant directs us to evidence of his good faith dissolution and the refusal of plaintiff to devote his full time to the business and failure to follow defendant's "major decisions." Assuming that there was such a duty of good faith in this case, the evidence proves that defendant acted in good faith and did not act in contravention of the oral partnership at will. In *Timmermann v. Timmermann*, 538 P.2d 1254, 1259 (1975), we held:

> A partnership at will may be dissolved without violation of the agreement between the partners by the express will of any partner when no definite term or particular undertaking is specified [UPA § 31(1)(b)].

The trial court did not err in this respect, and we find under the facts of this case that defendant dissolved the partnership in good faith as of May 27, 1973.

Plaintiff also contends that he is entitled to purchase defendant's interest in the partnership and continue the same or that the dissolution requires a liquidation and sale of assets before distribution. There is no express provision in [the] Uniform Partnership Act which establishes liquidation by sale as the exclusive mode of distributing partnership assets after dissolution. Although the basic rule is that any partner has the right to force liquidation by sale, the rule has been subject to criticism under facts similar to those in this suit.

> While situational variants make it dangerous to generalize, the liquidation right will be injurious to the business in many, perhaps in most, cases. One authority has described it as "ruinous." Whether it really is depends on the relative value of the business sold and the business retained. Such values are partly subjective and partly influenced by specific facts. But, it is rare that a small business, which is the kind most partnerships are, can be sold for as much as the owners think it is worth to themselves. This is true if it is disposed of intact as a going concern, and even more so if it is sold piecemeal. In short, the likelihood of loss of value is great enough to require every partnership to look to the ways of denying or restricting the liquidation right.
>
> The partners are frequently the best prospects for purchase. They have knowledge of the business, experience in its operations, and, perhaps, confidence in its future. They have an exisiting financial and psychological stake in it, and

6. "A partner at will is not bound to remain in a partnership, regardless of whether the business is profitable or unprofitable. A partner may not, however, by use of adverse pressure "freeze out" a co-partner and appropriate the business to his own use. A partner may not dissolve a partnership to gain the benefits of the business for himself, unless he fully compensates his co-partner for his share of the prospective business opportunity."

> the corollary opportunity to acquire the remaining interest for smaller outlay than a third party would need in order to buy the whole thing. The substantial problems of selling a business to a stranger for a good price may be avoided by a sale to an existing partner if such can be done on price and terms fair to the outgoing interest. Bromberg, *Partnership Dissolution—Causes, Consequences, and Cures*, 43 Tex. L. Rev. 647-48, 649 (1965).

Courts, both prior and subsequent to adopting the UPA, have, under certain circumstances, relied upon their equitable powers to distribute partnership assets without resort to a sale.

In *Rinke v. Rinke*, 330 Mich. 615, 48 N.W. 2d 201, 207 (1951), a suit for dissolution of a partnership, the Michigan Supreme Court refused to order a liquidation sale to a third party and interpreted the Uniform Partnership Act by stating

> [T]he decree of the trial court provided for dividing the assets of the partnership rather than for the sale thereof and the distribution of cash proceeds. Appellants insist that such method of procedure is erroneous and not contemplated by the Uniform Partnership Act. Construing together pertinent provisions of the statute leads to the conclusion that it was not the intention of the legislature in the enactment of the Uniform Partnership Act to impose a mandatory requirement that, under all circumstances, the assets of a dissolved partnership shall be sold and the money received therefor divided among those entitled to it, particularly so, as in the case at bar, where there are no debts to be paid from the proceeds. The situation disclosed by the record in the present case is somewhat unusual in that no one other than the former partners is interested in the assets of the businesses. In view of this situation and of the nature of the assets, we think that the trial court was correct in apportioning them to the parties.

The position taken by the Michigan Supreme Court is not an isolated one.

> [I]n some circumstances and in jurisdictions where the Uniform Partnership Act is in effect, surplus assets have been apportioned among the partners, and apart from the act distribution of the surplus partnership stock in kind has sometimes been made by the court in cases where there were no firm debts and a division in kind could be fairly and equitably made. 1 Rowley on Partnership, § 38.0, at 737.

In *Greg v. Bernards*, 250 Or. 458, 443 P.2d 166 (1968), a suit for dissolution of a partnership, plaintiff appealed from a decree which dissolved the partnership and vested in defendants the title to the partnership assets upon payment by them to plaintiff for the value of his partnership assets and also his share of the profit. Without expressing our reasoning, we held that the trial court reached the correct conclusion and affirmed.

In the case at bar, payment of creditors is not a problem. The partnership debts had been paid by the defendant, the managing partner who started the business. A large portion of the assets have been reduced to cash and bank time certificates of deposit. The audit on which the trial court based its distribution of assets included a substantial sum for "good will." Although plaintiff contributed to the success of the shot manufacturing business there is evidence that plaintiff was not always attentive to the business or to the decisions and recommendations of defendant, the managing partner.

We conclude, as defendant contends and as the trial court found, that the equities lie with the defendant in this case. Further, since there was no evidence regarding the value which the partnership assets might command on the market, it is difficult for us to determine whether a sale would be beneficial or prejudicial to the respective parties. As earlier described, this is a unique, or unusual, business which requires particular knowledge of the remanufacturing process and ability to repair and operate the necessary machinery. Plaintiff argues that he is entitled to purchase the 50 percent share of the defendant but his is no answer to the problem that confronted the trial court. The defendant conceived and designed the machinery and the method of operation, which was successfully operated for a number of years before formation of the partnership at will. Plaintiff is not precluded from engaging in a like or similar business.

The judgment of the trial court is affirmed as modified and remanded for a determination of the plaintiff's share of the profits from the date of the dissolution to the date of the accounting and to determine reasonable compensation for defendant in winding up the partnership affairs.

Notes

1. Note that the *Nicholes* court did *not* allow the inventor to continue the partnership business pursuant to UPA section 38(2). In fact, the court held that dissolution was not caused in bad faith or in contravention of the agreement. On the other hand, the court did not require liquidation by sale. Why not? What did the court do instead? What difference would it have made if the court had allowed the inventor to proceed under UPA section 38(2)?

2. Is it clear to you that the court's ruling was fair and equitable?

3. The inventor here was fortunate in that the court gave him "custody" of the partnership business. If you had represented the inventor during the formation of the partnership, what contractual safeguards could you have used to protect the inventor's rights?

Chapter 17

Dissolution: Accounting

A. General Rule

Parker v. Northern Mixing Co.

756 P.2d 881 (Alaska 1988)

RABINOWITZ, Chief Justice.

A partnership dissolved, and the partners sued each other over the proper distribution of assets and losses. This appeal raises legal issues regarding awards of prejudgment interest and the sharing of partnership losses. The parties also challenge factual findings of the superior court concerning specific aspects of the partnership agreement, various elements of damages, and disputes over items allowed and disallowed in the final accounting.

Early in 1984, long-time acquaintances Douglas Guthrie ("Douglas") and Daniel Mark Parker, III ("Ike") discussed the possibility of operating an asphalt plant in the central Kenai Peninsula area. Ike had considerable experience in the asphalt paving business and, in 1983, he established his present business, Parker Paving Corporation ("PPC"). Douglas is employed as a salesman by Guthrie Machinery Company ("GMC"), a corporation owned by his father, C.J. Guthrie ("C.J."), which sells new and used asphalt plants and accessories.

In June 1984, Douglas, Ike, and C.J. orally agreed to purchase an asphalt plant located in Kamloops, British Columbia. After transporting the plant to Soldotna, they would commence operations to supply asphalt to PPC. The terms of this agreement are disputed. Douglas and C.J. ("the Guthries") claim that C.J. individually or through GMC would supply start-up capital for the asphalt venture (known as Northern Mixing Company or "NMC"), and that C.J.'s advance would be replaced by permanent financing provided by an institutional lender. The Guthries also claim that, pursuant to the agreement: Douglas and Ike would be equally responsible for repayments of the permanent financing and would each provide financial statements, security for his share of the financing, and a statement of work in progress; Douglas and Ike would manage NMC and each own 40% of the corporate stock; and Douglas would be paid $2,500 per month for managing the operation of the asphalt plant. Finally, they claim that C.J. was to own the remaining 20% of the corporate stock in return for securing the financing, and that Ike agreed to make available his and PPC's financial statements and to furnish real property in Oregon as security.

Ike agrees that C.J. was to secure financing for NMC and that NMC was intended to be a corporation. Ike further agrees that he and Douglas were to be responsible for the business, but he disputes any agreement that he was to provide security or any financial statements in connection with long-term financing of NMC or that

Douglas was to receive any additional compensation for his participation in managing the business.

The superior court found that all the parties expected C.J. to be able to secure long-term financing to replace his initial investment. It found further that Ike would provide financial information to aid the financing, but that Ike's obligation to provide security arose only when a likely source of financing had been identified. The superior court also found that, although the reasonable value of Douglas's services for the period during which he worked was $2,500 per month, "there was no meeting of the minds among the principals of NMC" to pay him a salary in that or any other amount.

The asphalt plant operated for only about two months, in 1984. When the parties decided to discontinue the business relationship in the winter of 1984-85, they were not able to reach an agreement concerning the allocation of NMC's assets, profits, and liabilities.

The Guthries filed a complaint against Ike in superior court seeking possession of the asphalt plant, damages for diminution in the plant's value equal to its reasonable rental value while in Ike's possession, and an accounting of all income and disbursements of NMC. C.J. (through GMC) claimed expenses of $93,477.16 incident to the original financing of NMC, of which $84,829.09 is acknowledged by Ike as properly chargeable to NMC. Included in the $6,022.84 of disputed charges[2] are a fine and attorney's fees incurred as a result of operating the asphalt production plant without a required environmental permit, and certain credit card charges. C.J. also claimed $19,863.68 in interest on his advances, all of which Ike disputes. Ike (through PPC) in turn claimed expenses incident to operation of NMC of $151,291.66, of which $95,413.39 is acknowledged by the Guthries as chargeable to NMC. Included in the $55,878.27 of disputed charges are trucking and equipment rental charges, land rent, approximately $22,000 for rock, certain payroll charges, and the cost of repair work—application of a "slurry coat" to a finished project—necessitated by the plant's production of some faulty batches of asphalt. PPC also owes NMC $92,320.00 for asphalt produced and sold to PPC in 1984.

The superior court found that the fine, attorney's fees, and the cost of the repair work were properly charged against the business. Pursuant to its finding that NMC, although intended ultimately to be a corporation, was a *de facto* partnership of Ike and Douglas, the superior court applied Alaska's Uniform Partnership Act to settle their rights and liabilities.[3] The superior court found that the partnership was dissolved during the winter of 1984-85 due to the parties' inability to reach an agreement for the operation of the asphalt plant in 1985. According to the superior court, neither party was at fault in causing the dissolution of the partnership since either could terminate it at will under [UPA section 31(1)(b)].

The court determined that C.J. was at all material times a creditor of NMC based on his furnishing the start-up capital for the company, that he never became a shareholder because NMC never issued any stock or operated as a going business, and that although he was to share in NMC's gross returns, he was not for that reason

2. This figure, stated by the superior court, appears incorrect since $93,477.16 − $84,829.09 = $8,648.07.

3. The specific provision applied by the superior court was [UPA section 40].

alone a partner.[5] The superior court further found that there was no agreement by the partnership or its individual partners to pay C.J. any interest.

The superior court determined that the partnership's sole assets were the plant itself and related equipment, and the accounts receivable from PPC. Based on C.J.'s testimony, the court's valuation of the plant was $76,887.73, and the PPC receivable was $92,320.00. NMC's total asset value, including prejudgment interest of $13,625.28, was thus $182,833.01.[7] The amount owed C.J., NMC's sole creditor, was established as $88,956.40. As indicated previously, the court found that there were no agreements between Ike and Douglas concerning compensation for each other's services and concluded that, because NMC produced no profits for distribution, the only sums due the partners were for their contributions. Douglas contributed services valued at $7,500 and Ike contributed services, equipment and expenditures of $134,477.62.

The superior court's accounting for the partnership under [UPA section 40] was thus as follows:

ASSETS OF NMC	
Plant	$ 76,887.73
PPC Receivable	$ 92,320.00
Prejudgment Interest	$ 13,625.28
TOTAL	$182,833.01
AMOUNT DUE CREDITOR	
C.J. Guthrie d/b/a GMC	$ 88,956.40
BALANCE AVAILABLE FOR PARTNER'S CONTRIBUTIONS	$ 93,876.61
PRO-RATA DISTRIBUTION TO PARTNERS (56.52% of Contribution)	
Douglas Guthrie	$ 4,960.00
Ike Parker	$ 88,916.61

Accordingly, the net liability/recovery of the parties was calculated as:

Ike Parker d/b/a/ PPC	
Prejudgment Interest	($ 13,625.28)
Account Payable NMC	($ 92,320.00)
Return of Contribution	$ 88,916.61
Balance—Contribution	($ 17,028.67)
Douglas Guthrie	
Return of Contribution	$ 4,960.00
C.J. Guthrie	
Value of Plant	$ 76,887.73
Balance Due—Cash	$ 12,068.67

Finally, the superior court rejected all claims of the parties against each other, except those included in the accounting. The court concluded in particular that neither party's

5. The court cited [UPA section 7(3)] in support of this conclusion.

7. Upon motion for reconsideration, the superior court amended its original Findings of Fact, Conclusions of Law and Order to include prejudgment interest.

actions support a claim for breach of any joint venture or partnership agreement since the partnership was at will and no specific agreement existed; that GMC was not a seller of goods to NMC or to either of its partners; and that the Guthries have no claim for punitive damages because Ike's conduct was not willful or malicious. Therefore, the superior court ordered:

1. Judgment for NMC against Ike in the amount of $17,028.67;

2. Judgment for Douglas against NMC in the amount of $4,960.00

3. Transfer by NMC, Douglas, and Ike to C.J. of all rights, title and interest in the plant in satisfaction of all of C.J.'s claims (except as otherwise provided in the court's order);

4. Judgment for C.J. against NMC of $12,068.67.

The superior court also ordered each party to bear its own costs and attorney's fees based on its view that neither party "prevailed" as that term is used in Civil Rules 79 and 82.

This appeal and cross-appeal followed.

Partners are entitled to repayment of their contributions only *after* other liabilities of the partnership (i.e., those owing to creditors other than partners and to partners other than for capital and profits) are satisfied. *See* [UPA § 40(b)II].

Ike contends that it necessarily follows from the "undisputed evidence" that the parties agreed to share partnership profits equally that they also agreed to share losses equally. Accordingly, he argues, the superior court erred in allocating NMC's liabilities between the parties based on the amounts of their respective capital contributions. We reverse the superior court's determination of the repayment of capital contributions.

The capital account of a partnership is, by definition, the difference between its assets and liabilities. The partnership had total assets of $182,833.01. From this amount $88,956.40 was due to its sole creditor, C.J. Guthrie.* The partnership's remaining assets thus totaled $93,876.61. Each partner made the following contributions to capital:

Parker	—	$134,477.62
Guthrie	—	$ 7,500.00[14]
Total Capital		$141,977.62

Since only $93,876.61 in partnership assets remained after paying C.J., the partnership suffered a loss of $48,101.01.

Since there was no agreement to the contrary, [UPA section 18(a)] determines the division of this loss between the parties: "each partner shall contribute towards the losses, whether of capital or otherwise according to the partner's share in the profits." Since the partners agreed to share profits equally, the loss sustained by the

* [Note by editors.] Earlier in its opinion, the court had affirmed the trial court's finding that C.J. Guthrie was not a partner.

14. This amount is disputed and in accordance with this opinion is remanded for further findings.

partnership capital account should be shared equally. Thus:

$48,101.01 ÷ 2 = $24,050.50.

Guthrie's capital account:

$ 7,500.00	Capital contribution
($24,050.50)	½ of loss
($16,550.50)	

Parker's capital account:

$134,477.62	Capital contribution
($ 24,050.50)	½ of loss
$110,427.12	

Guthrie must therefore pay $16,550.50 to the partnership. When he makes that payment his capital account will be zero, the net assets of the partnership will be $110,427.12, and Parker's capital account will remain at $110,427.12.[17]

In view of the foregoing we reverse the superior court's pro rata repayment of capital contributions.

Notes

1. Guthrie was required to contribute $16,550.50 to equalize losses, including capital losses. After Guthrie makes that contribution, and Parker is paid $110,427.12, how much will each partner have lost?

2. Suppose that partnership assets were only $30,934.02 (*before* paying C.J.).

a. What would be the result under the accounting rules of UPA section 40?

b. Suppose that Guthrie is bankrupt, with individual assets of $100,000.00 and claims by individual (separate) creditors of $100,000.00. How would that affect your answer? Note that the portion of UPA section 40(h) giving individual creditors priority on individual property has been pre-empted by U.S. Bankruptcy Code Section 723(c). Under that provision, unsatisfied partnership creditors have *equal* priority with a partner's individual general creditors (as against individual property). Note that Draft RUPA section 808 *deletes* UPA section 40(h)-(i).

3. Suppose instead that *after* paying off C.J., the remaining partnership assets amounted to $241,977.62. What would each of Parker and Guthrie have been entitled to under UPA sections 18(a) and 40?

4. RUPA section 401(a)-(b) and 808 set forth the RUPA provisions, equivalent to UPA sections 18(a) and 40, regarding the settlement of partnership accounts on dissolution.

17. In other words Guthrie must pay $16,550.50 to NMC, rather than receive back $4,960.00.

B. Service Partners and Liquidation Accounting

Becker v. Killarney

177 Ill. App. 3d 793, 532 N.E.2d 931 (1988)

Justice SCOTT:

It is rare that parties come together, form a partnership, and plan to lose money in their endeavors. Nevertheless, the old saw teaches that the "best laid plans of mice and men" will occasionally go awry. This is the legal culmination of just such an ill-fated endeavor.

Prior to June 1975, First Federal Savings and Loan Association of Peoria advanced money for the expansion of the Voyager Inn, an existing hotel in downtown Peoria. Before the expansion was complete, First Federal had taken possession of the property as mortgagee. Thereupon, First Federal entered into negotiations with G. Raymond Becker, one of the plaintiffs, to strike a deal under which Becker would take over the parcel and complete the hotel addition. In furtherance of that deal, Becker formed the partnership which was to become the subject of the instant dispute.

Becker assembled a partnership team that included parties with various skills and services that could be valuable to the enterprise. He himself was a developer and president of a construction company, Gordon E. Burns was an architect, John P. Dailey was a financier, John C. Parkhurst was an attorney, and Rosel was the prospective hotel manager. These original five partners entered into a formal written agreement on June 20, 1975. None of the original five partners funded the partnership with any cash capital, but each agreed to contribute his services; the evidence adduced in the trial court establishes that the five partners did so throughout the partnership's operation of the hotel.

With the exception of Rosel, and his successor White, who also managed the hotel, the original partners were not compensated for their services. Salaries were prohibited by the partnership agreement. The cash contributions necessary to get the partnership off the ground came from Thomas Killarney and Bernard Feely. Within months following the original formation of the partnership, Killarney had contributed \$160,000 for an 8% interest and Feely had contributed \$100,000 for a 5% interest. Both Killarney and Feely had been previous business associates of Becker, and both signed identical amendments to the partnership agreement setting forth the rights and obligations of the new partners.

The project proceeded, aided by a \$10,500,000 non-recourse first mortgage loan from First Federal and credit extended by the contractor, Becker Bros., Inc., Becker's construction company. The capital contribution of Killarney and Feely provided working capital for the partnership. It appears, however, that the hotel, once constructed and open, was something less than a commercial success. After the hotel had been open for some time, it became necessary to negotiate an additional \$500,000 loan from First Federal to be used as working capital. Indeed, the hotel consistently lost money, not just tax shelter losses but real cash losses, and the losses increased as time passed. In August of 1979, the partners were assessed \$100,000 according to their respective interests, in order to raise money to pay the bills. Again in April of 1980, a second assessment of $100,000 was necessary, and all the partners paid their percentage shares.

As the losses mounted, in September 1984 the hotel property was transferred back to First Federal. Unlike the original mortgage loan, not all obligations of the partnership feature non-recourse agreements to protect the partners. A dispute arose as to the obligations of the various partners to pay for these partnership debts and the subject lawsuit resulted. In the circuit court of Peoria County, four of the original partners, Becker, Burns, Dailey and Parkhurst, complained for a money judgment against the two defendant partners, Killarney and Feely, for their shares of the partnership debts. The defendant partners counterclaimed, alleging that the plaintiffs owed money to the partnership. After a trial extending for a period of weeks, the Peoria court entered judgment against the plaintiffs and for the defendants. The plaintiffs appeal that judgment.

The circuit court concluded the law required that the partnership capital accounts of Killarney and Feely should reflect their cash contributions and be applied to their share of the net loss; that is, the net losses of the partnership should be calculated according to each partner's percentage commencing with the first dollar of loss, and not simply those losses which exceeded the original capital contributions of Killarney and Feely. The plaintiffs, those partners who contributed services rather than cash to the partnership, believe the circuit court erred in permitting the "cash partners" to apply their original investment totaling $260,000 against their share of the losses.

In Illinois, the relations among partners are governed by the Uniform Partnership Act. [UPA section 40] provides for the settling of accounts between the parties. The circuit court, relying on the statute, concluded that the $260,000 capital contribution of the "cash partners," Killarney and Feely, was a liability of the partnership and therefore subject to contributions from all the partners for payment.

The plaintiffs urge that such an unbending application of the statute yields an unfair and inequitable result. Killarney and Feely, the cash partners, receive a preference in the payment of their contribution to the partnership because that contribution was made in cash, but Becker, Dailey, Burns and Parkhurst receive no payment for their contribution because it was made in the form of services. One might reasonably assume that the partners themselves determined the services, skill and know-how of the plaintiffs to be of proportionate value of the partnership as the partners' shares of the profits; there was no preference in sharing profits (or losses) for those who contributed cash as opposed to services.

The "service partners" urge that equity and fairness demand that their contribution of services, skill, know-how or sweat-equity, however it be labeled, must be accounted for in the same manner as the cash contribution of the "cash partners." The plaintiffs cite no provision of the Uniform Partnership Act in support of their position, but argue instead that where the Act is silent, the general principles of law and equity apply ([UPA § 5]), and equity would militate against this unjust enrichment of the defendants. The plaintiffs rely on the California court's decision in *Kovacik v. Reed* (1957), 49 Cal. 2d 166, 315 P.2d 314, as the correct rule of law in cases such as this.

The *Kovacik* court, while recognizing the general rule with respect to loss sharing among partners, also notes:

> it appears that in the cases in which the above stated general rule has been applied, each of the parties had contributed capital consisting of either money or land or other tangible property, or else was to receive compensation for services rendered to the common undertaking which was to be paid before computation of the profits or losses. Where, however, as in the present case, one partner or joint adventurer contributes the money capital as against the other's skill and labor, all the cases cited, and which our research has discovered, hold that neither party is liable to the other for contribution for any loss sustained. Thus, upon loss of the money the party who contributed it is not entitled to recover any part of it from the party who contributed only services. (I)n such a situation, the parties have, by their agreement to share equally in profits, agreed that the value of their contributions—the money on the one hand and the labor on the other—were likewise equal; it would follow that upon the loss, as here, of both money and labor, the parties have shared equally in the losses.

We find the rationale set forth in *Kovacik* to be persuasive, inconsistent with no express provision of the Uniform Act, and consistent with long-held equitable principles which form the foundation of our jurisprudence.

The defendant would have us conclude that *Kovacik* is inconsistent with [UPA section 40]. We disagree. While the liabilities of the partnership may well include payments "owing to partners in respect of capital," we do not agree that such capital cannot be intangibles such as special skills or know-how as well as tangibles such as cash. In fact, it is more likely that the parties "by their agreement to share equally in profits, agreed that the value of their contributions—the money on the one hand and the labor on the other—were likewise equal." *Kovacik*, 315 P.2d at 316.

Likewise, we find no inconsistency between the *Kovacik* rule and the express provisions of the partnership agreement itself. Defendants' expert finds such an inconsistency in a provision in the two agreement amendments which reads as follows:

> Additional cash contributions of capital may be made by any or all of the partners from time to time and any such cash contributions shall be returned to such partners before any distribution of assets is made upon the sale of assets or dissolution of the partnership.

The experts who testified were not unanimous as to the meaning and application of the quoted provision. It is ambiguous, but in its ambiguity, it is not inconsistent with the unique rule of *Kovacik*.

For the reasons stated, we agree that in cases such as this, the *Kovacik* rule should apply. Equity requires that the value of services be recognized and capitalized, so as to prevent unjust enrichment. Absent an agreement to the contrary, and we find no such agreement under the instant facts, *Kovacik* should apply. We direct the circuit court to apply the principles therein and enter judgment accordingly.

REVERSED AND REMANDED.

Parker v. Northern Mixing Co.

756 P.2d 881 (Alaska 1988)

[Re-read the *facts* set out earlier in this chapter.]

Ike contends that the superior court erred in crediting Douglas for a partnership contribution of $7,500 in services. He argues that such credit is contrary to the court's express finding that, although Douglas worked full time running the asphalt plant for approximately three months in 1984 and the reasonable value of his services was $2,500 per month, "there was no meeting of the minds among the principals of NMC that he be paid a salary in that or any other amount."

In *Schymanski v. Conventz*, 674 P.2d 281, 284-85 (Alaska 1983), this court distinguished between non-cash capital contributions to a partnership and remuneration for ordinary services:

> The general rule is that, in the absence of an agreement to such effect, a partner contributing only personal services is ordinarily *not* entitled to any share of partnership capital pursuant to dissolution. Personal services may, however, qualify as capital contributions to a partnership where an express or implied agreement to such effect exists.
>
> To be distinguished from non-cash capital contributions to a partnership is compensation or remuneration for a partner's services performed in the course of day-to-day affairs of the partnership. In the absence of an agreement to provide for such compensation, remuneration for a partner's services performed in the course of partnership affairs is prohibited by statute.[12]

In light of *Schymanski*, it seems clear that the superior court meant, by its finding that no meeting of the minds occurred regarding payment of any *salary* to Douglas, that the parties entered no agreement that would lift the [UPA section 18(f)] proscription against compensation for acting in the partnership business. That does not, however, necessarily answer the question of whether the court found an express or implied agreement that Douglas's services would qualify as capital contributions to the partnership. Douglas argues that the superior court could reasonably have found such an implied agreement since he was to operate the plant full time, whereas Ike had other employment and income.

The superior court made no specific findings as to the existence of an agreement to treat Douglas's services as capital contributions. The court did, however, find that

> [t]here were no agreements between the partners for compensation for either's services. There are no profits to be distributed. Consequently the only sums due the partners are with respect to their contributions.

The superior court then proceeded to find that Douglas "contributed services to the joint venture in the amount of $7,500," and that Ike "contributed services, equipment and expenditures" totalling $134,477.62. From these findings collectively, it could be inferred that the superior court found an implied agreement between Douglas and Ike that their services would constitute capital contributions to NMC.

Given the foregoing, however, we conclude that the question of the existence or non-existence of such an agreement should be remanded to the superior court for explicit findings of fact as to whether it was agreed that Douglas's services would constitute capital contributions.

---

12. [UPA section 18(f)] provides, with an exception not here relevant, that subject to any agreement between the partners, no partner is entitled to remuneration for acting in the partnership business.

Notes

1. UPA section 18(f) says that a partner may not receive remuneration for acting in the partnership business. In *Parker v. Northern Mixing Co.*, did the trial court indirectly compensate Guthrie (the service partner) for services? What different effect does giving Guthrie a $7,500 implied capital contribution (rather than a $2,500 a month salary) have on Parker (the capital partner)?

Suppose the *Parker* partnership had lasted 12—or even 24 or 36—months before dissolving. What would Guthrie's implied capital contribution be by then?

2. Just as a partner is not entitled to remuneration for acting in the partnership business, a partner contributing capital is not entitled to *interest* on that capital until after the date the capital was to be repaid (generally, after dissolution). The theory in both cases is that partners are compensated for contributing their capital and services by their share of the profits.

3. *Becker v. Killarney* reasons that because the capital and service partners agreed to share profits equally, the partners must have viewed their "contributions" to the partnership as being equal. Yet partners can "contribute" in more than one way. First, they can contribute to the partnership's *profit-producing potential*. Second, they can contribute *directly* to the partnership's *wealth*. Note that a contribution to profit-producing potential *indirectly* results in an increase in the partnership's wealth, but only to the extent that potential is *realized* as actual profits.

In the case of a capital/service partnership, one partner "contributes" only property, and the other only services. What, if anything, does the fact that the partners share profits equally imply about the partner's relative contributions to the partnership's profit-producing potential? Their relative contributions to the partnership's wealth? Consider the following problems:

Problem 1. Suppose that Capital and Labor have formed a partnership to run a convenience store. Capital owns a suitably located building, and has agreed to let the partnership use the building rent-free. In order to buy the inventory, the partnership borrowed $20,000 from Bank. Labor has agreed to devote full-time and best efforts to the partnership business. Capital, a doctor, will not work in the partnership business. Capital and Labor have agreed to share profits equally. There is no agreement to pay Labor a salary.

Six months later, the store has not been successful, so Capital and Labor decide to liquidate the partnership. The partnership's sole property consists of inventory worth $10,000. The partnership's sole creditor is Bank, which is still owed $20,000. That is, the partnership has *lost* $10,000.

What did each partner contribute to the partnership's profit-producing potential? To its wealth? How should the operating losses be divided?

Problem 2. Suppose that instead of borrowing the start-up funds from Bank as in Problem 1, *Capital* had advanced (lent) the partnership $20,000. What were the parties relative contributions to the partnership's profit-producing potential and its wealth? How should the operating losses be divided now?

Problem 3. Suppose Capital had instead made a $20,000 cash capital contribution to the partnership. What were the parties relative contributions to the partnership's profit-producing potential and its wealth? How should the operating losses be divided now?

4. The RUPA is more clear concerning the nature of the "contributions" that rise to rights to distributions. RUPA section 401(a) provides:

> (a) A partnership shall establish an account for each partner which must be credited with an amount equal to the cash plus the value of any other property, net of the amount of any liabilities, the partner contributes to the partnership and the partner's share of the partnership profits. Each partner's account must be charged with an amount equal to the cash plus the value of any other property, net of the amount of any liabilities, distributed by the partnership to the partner and the partner's share of the partnership losses.

How do this change bear on the service partner question?

5. How could a service partner and a capital partner protect their interests when forming a partnership?

C. Scope of the Interest in the Partnership

Hamilton Airport Advertising, Inc. v. Hamilton

462 N.E.2d 228 (Ind. App. 1984)

MILLER, Judge.

The multiple corporate, partnership and individual defendants-appellants herein seek the reversal of the trial court judgment awarding Renetta Hamilton $65,977.25 due her as administratrix and sole heir of William S. Hamilton, deceased brother and business associate of the appellants. Their chief contention is that Renetta has failed to prove she is entitled to monies allegedly due her from two corporations and a partnership as occasioned by William's death and applicable buy-sell agreements regarding his business interests.

The following issues are dispositive of this case:

> Did Renetta have a valid and binding agreement, executed after William's death, settling disputed amounts due to her for William's business interests?
>
> Did the court err in determining Renetta was entitled to undrawn accumulated earnings left in William's account in the partnership?

The following stipulated facts adequately serve as a skeletal foundation for this relatively complex state of affairs:

> 1. Renzie M. Hamilton began a display manufacturing business in the late 1940's in which his brother, Kenneth H. Hamilton, subsequently joined him as a partner and, afterwards, a third brother, William S. Hamilton, joined in the business as a partner. A partnership was entered into in January, 1955 [called Hamilton Display Manufacturing Company].
>
> 2. Hamilton Airport Advertising, Inc. [Airport Advertising] and Hamilton Building Corporation [Building Corp.] were later formed by the three brothers for the purpose of holding title to various buildings and real estate.

3. On January 11, 1962, the three brothers entered into buy-sell agreements relative to each of the corporations, and new Articles of Partnership for Hamilton Display Manufacturing Company [Display Mfg.].

4. At all times pertinent here, Renzie, Kenneth and William Hamilton were the sole officers, shareholders and directors of each of the corporations and equal partners in the partnership.

5. William Hamilton died on November 24, 1969.

6. In December, 1969, proceeds from a policy of life insurance carried by the partnership on the life of William was paid in the total amount of $57,713.76, which funds were deposited by Renzie and Kenneth in the partnership business.

7. At all times pertinent here, Renetta E. Hamilton was the wife, sole heir and beneficiary, and administratrix of the estate of William S. Hamilton.

8. Renetta Hamilton disputed the figure suggested by Mr. Suttles [of $95,238 as the amount due to William's estate under the pertinent buy-sell agreements].

11. On June 5, 1970, Renzie Hamilton and Renetta Hamilton met and a document, stipulated Exhibit 4, was prepared and signed by each of them[, which] reads as follows:

TO WHOM IT MAY CONCERN:
RE: ESTATE OF WILLIAM S. HAMILTON, DECEASED

Based upon projected estimates relevant to "Buy-Sell" Agreement with the Estate of William S. Hamilton, the approximate value of the Deceased's interest in the Hamilton Display Manufacturing Co. is determined to be [$63,800.00].*

/s/ *Renzie M. Hamilton*
Renzie M. Hamilton
President, Hamilton Display Mfg. Co.

/s/ *Renetta E. Hamilton*
Renetta E. Hamilton
Admx. of the Estate of William S. Hamilton Deceased

Subsequently, payments were made to William S. Hamilton Estate.

12. The last payment was made December, 1974 and brought the total of payments to her [to $46,100].

Renetta brought her suit against William's brothers, Renzie and Kenneth, and the three companies, Display Mfg. (partnership), Airport Advertising and Building Corp. in March 1976. She sought recovery for an accounting and money judgment based on the business affairs of the three companies. The appellants answered, moved to dismiss [for failure to state a claim] and counterclaimed for overpayment to William's estate. The trial court sustained the motion to dismiss as to Renetta's claim for an accounting.

The cause went to trial by the court in July, 1981, with the parties presenting evidence not only of the document signed by Renetta and Renzie and its surrounding

* [Note by editors.] The parties estimated the amount due for *all three* companies as $125,000.00. Based on the Court's allocation of payments made, $63,800 was the portion of the estimate allocated to the partnership, Display Mfg.

circumstances, but also, and without objection, evidence of the buy-sell agreements and alleged sums due and owing from the appellants to William and vice versa. There was no significant dispute regarding the monies due William for his stock in the two corporations. The petulant battle here centers on the meaning and interpretation of language in the partnership buy-sell agreement, which purported to delineate the partner's rights and liabilities upon the death of one. We quote these pertinent provisions.

Hamilton Display Manufacturing Company
Article V

Death, Bankruptcy, etc.

(6) If an[d] in the event that either [sic] of the partners, during the term of this partnership, shall die, or shall be adjudged bankrupt, insolvent, or incompetent, or shall take proceedings for liquidation by arrangement with his creditors, or shall assign or attempt to assign his interest in the partnership in violation of these Articles, then this partnership shall terminate at once, without notice, as to him, and he, or his personal representatives, fiduciaries, or assigns, as the case may be, shall have no interest in common with the other partners in the property of the partnership, but shall be considered in equity as vendor to the surviving or other partners, of his entire share and interest in the partnership, as and from the day of his said death, adjudication, taking proceedings or assigning, as aforesaid, at a price determined and payable upon terms and conditions as stated in paragraph (7) of this Article V. And the surviving or other partners in any such case shall be considered as having bought the interest of said partner to whom such event shall have happened, and they promise to carry out such purchase and pay said purchase price therefor as herein provided.

Price.

(7) The price to be paid to such partner as shall retire, as provided herein, or to the estate of a deceased partner, shall be the sum of Twenty-Five Thousand Dollars ($25,000.00), to be paid, in the event of death... In addition to the above, such partner as shall retire, as provided herein, or to the estate of a deceased partner, shall be paid a sum equal to the amount that would have been distributable to said retired or deceased partners out of net profits during the ensuing twelve (12) months of said partnership. This amount shall be paid in twelve (12) equal monthly installments, beginning one year and one month from the established date of death or retirement of such partner.

Significantly, Renetta presented evidence that at William's death, he had $60,268 in what was alternatively denominated by the parties as a "drawing account" or "capital account" in the partnership. At the same time, Renzie had $11,829 in his account and Kenneth, $51,027 in his. The federal partnership tax returns, along with other testimony, clearly indicated that the annual income from the partnership was divided evenly among the three partners and the equal shares credited to each partner's account. From their respective accounts, each partner was entitled to a weekly draw of $125. However, through the years, each partner had made additional draws, Renzie, of course, drawing out the largest amount by the time William died, as evidenced by the smaller amount remaining in his account. The reason for leaving such funds in the accounts was to accommodate cash flow problems in the business, and withdrawal of one's entire account would have hurt the company.

The following portions of the partnership agreement are the only memorialized references to these accounts:

Article II

Capital and Partners' Interest

Capital

(1) Capital, now held and employed by the partnership, is apportioned as reflected on the partnership books of account.

Profits and Losses

(2) The net profits or losses of the partnership, after the payment of the weekly drawing accounts as provided for in paragraph 6 [sic], Article II hereof, shall be divided equally among the partners.

Loans

(3) If any one of the partners, with the consent of the others, shall loan or advance funds to or for the partnership, such funds shall not be considered capital but shall be a loan or loans, evidenced by the promissory note or notes of the partnership.

No Salary or Interest

(4) None of the partners shall receive any salary for services rendered to the partnership or be paid any interest upon his original or any subsequent contribution to the partnership capital except as provided in paragraphs (3) and (5) of Article II hereof.

Drawing Accounts, etc.

(5) The partners shall have weekly drawing accounts to be charged against the earnings of the partnership in the following amounts:

To Renzie M. Hamilton, Kenneth H. Hamilton and William S. Hamilton, the sum of One Hundred and Twenty-five Dollars ($125.00) each week.

Other distributions of earnings shall be made on the basis of one-third (⅓) of such total amount as shall be distributed to each partner at such time and in such amounts as the partners shall agree upon, including withdrawals found to be necessary for the payment of U.S. income taxes.

Both sides sponsored expert testimony from accountants, who tendered documentary fiscal summaries of monies due to or from William's estate. Renetta's accountant witness Richard Bell testified to the import of the immediately foregoing sections of the partnership agreement. He opined that because the partners had not withdrawn funds in equal measure from their drawing accounts, William must be credited as having *loaned* the partnership the difference. Thus his estate would be entitled to $48,438.78 from his drawing account as the difference between his total account set at $60,268.07 and Renzie's, as the smallest, at $11,829.29. Bell added this sum to the purchase price actually set out in the buy-sell agreement. He indicated the following sums were due William's estate as based on his valuations and the terms of the agreements.

	Payments Made	Payments Due	Net Amounts Due
<u>DISPLAY MFG.</u>			
(Partnership)	$46,100.00	$83,092.78	$36,992.78

[Appellants] also took issue with the alleged status of the partnership accounts as loans because there were no promissory notes as required by the partnership agreement.

The appellants' accountant witness Leroy Prall, on the other hand, presented his own interpretation of the drawing (or capital) accounts in the partnership:

> It's any capital contributions at the outset plus additionally during the existence of the partnership, plus any share of the profits less any withdrawals.

He then determined William's partnership share by equalizing the accounts as current at his death ($11,829 + $51,027 + $60,268 = $123,124) for an average of $41,041. This average was taken from the actual sum in William's account, giving his account a credit of $19,227. However, this expert did not consider William's account when he computed the amount due under the buy-sell agreement because said agreement made no mention of the capital amount. Thus, the appellants' calculations indicate the business overpaid William's estate.[4]

	Payments Made	Payments Due	Difference (Over) Under
DISPLAY MFG.			
Assumption 1	$46,100	$34,303	$(11,797)
Assumption 2	46,100	27,405	(18,695)

In accordance with the parties' requests for findings of facts, the trial court obliged with a lengthy discourse, incorporating the above-quoted stipulations of the parties. In addition, the court interpreted the partnership provisions regarding the capital (or drawing) accounts and the alleged $125,000 settlement agreement signed by Renetta and Renzie. The trial court then propounded the following conclusions and judgment, apparently accepting Renetta's figures.

> CONCLUSIONS OF LAW
>
> Based upon the foregoing Findings of Fact, the Court makes the following conclusions:
>
> 1. The law is with [Renetta] and against the Defendants.
>
> [2]. The Defendant, Hamilton Display Manufacturing Company, was indebted to William S. Hamilton on the date of his death in the amount of $48,438.78 for monies loaned to such partnership as a result of unequal distributions of partnership profits among the three partners and [Renetta] is entitled to collect such indebtedness from such partnership in addition to the additional monies owing from each of the Defendants pursuant to the Stock Purchase Agreement and the Buy-Sell [sic] Provisions of the partnership agreement.
>
> JUDGMENT
>
> The Court on the basis of the foregoing Findings of Fact, Conclusions of Law now therefore enters Judgment in this cause as follows:
>
> The Court finds, adjudges and decrees that [Renetta] shall recover the sum of $36,992.78 plus prejudgment interest from the Defendants Hamilton Display Manufacturing Company, Renzie Hamilton and Kenneth Hamilton.

4. The [following table sets forth] two sets of calculations by Prall for valuation of Display Mfg. [The reasoning for this] is not pertinent to our decision. In actuality, it reflects the difference with and without the inclusion of Airport Advertising income as interpreted from the buy-sell agreements.

Decision

"Settlement Agreement"

We are first compelled to dispose of all issues concerning the document signed by Renetta and Renzie, which stated William's interest in the three business associations was $125,000. The trial court made findings of fact, which in effect construed the document to be a valid and binding settlement agreement of a dispute between Renetta and the appellants concerning money due to William's estate. However, closer scrutiny of the actual conclusions of law and judgment reveal the court did not necessarily base its ultimate decision on this document as the basis of recovery. Instead, the trial court admitted evidence and testimony, without a relevant objection, regarding the buy-sell agreements and the *actual* valuation of assets and accounts involved in each enterprise such that Renetta's dismissed complaint for an accounting was actually litigated by consent of the parties. It was, thus, that the total amount of money (without interest) exceeded the sum stated in the alleged settlement agreement. And where the parties have tried an issue by consent, despite the stance of the formal complaint, we will uphold a judgment based thereon. (Indeed, the appellants have no cause for quarrel when one of their counterclaims alleged overpayment and an accounting would have been a necessity to such recovery to determine those damages.) We, of course, note the fact that trial court's written judgment makes direct reference to Renetta's complaint on the settlement agreement when it declared she was recovering pursuant to Count I. However, because we find the basic legal reasoning in the judgment to be correct, we feel justified in ignoring minor technical discrepancies in an otherwise valid judgment. Therefore, after due consideration, we need not further address any other issues raised by the appellants regarding this document.

At this point, the construction of the partnership agreement's buy-sell arrangements becomes crucial. Article V, paragraph 6 states that when any partner dies, the partnership shall terminate as to him, and he will be considered the vendor to the others

> of his entire share and interest in the partnership at a price determined and payable upon terms and conditions as stated in paragraph (7) of this Article V.

The parties generally have no quarrel with the price affixed in the said paragraph 7—$25,000 plus ⅓ net profits of the next year's business. The problem is whether this price is for the purchase of all claims to and interests in the partnership, including William's partnership account. We do not believe it is.

The terms used in the pertinent provision envision the purchase of William's "entire share and interest in the partnership." There is no mention of a payment for William's contribution to capital, and our statutes clearly eliminate the possibility that capital is within the definition of partnership interest.

The Uniform Partnership Act delineates three types of rights in a partnership, two of which are: 1) rights in specific partnership property [UPA § 25] and 2) interest in the partnership as one's share of the profits and surplus [UPA § 26]. The latter we believe to be the contemplated item of purchase in the buy-sell agreement. And there is a distinction between the partnership interest and capital. *See, e.g.*, [UPA § 18] (the two are referred to as separate interests). A partnership interest is a salable capital asset of the individual partner. Capital, on the other hand is a liability, a debt of the partnership to a partner. [UPA § 40].

> It is clear that when these profits were calculated and divided according to the terms of the agreement, and the share of each partner was put to his credit, then, as between the partners, these profits *ceased to be assets of the firm, and became debts due from the firm to each member of the firm.*

Molineaux v. Reynolds, 35 A. at 538. A more recent Illinois case declares:

> Due to the nature of a partnership, a partner not only has rights in partnership assets and profits but also has the right to be repaid the amount of his contributions to the capital of the partnership.

In re Marriage of Wilson, (1982) 110 Ill. App. 3d 809, 814, 66 Ill. Dec. 508, 511-512, 443 N.E.2d 31, 34-35. And from a purely practical standpoint, a partner could be repaid his capital contribution in full, but his partnership interest would remain.

It is undeniable the two are intertwined in the valuation of a partnership in a buy-sell agreement because such arrangement is a dissolution. The worth of one's rights to profits and surplus, the partnership interest, *has* been equated with one's capital contributions and/or capital account for purposes of valuation and sale. *See, e.g., Smith v. Commissioner*, (7th Cir. 1964) 331 F.2d 298. However, in *Smith*, the value of the capital account was specifically agreed upon as the value of the partnership interest. Indeed, partners may perhaps agree that the actual generation of profits is caused by specific capital contributions, and thus the measure of the partnership interest is the valuation of such capital. However, such agreement is not present in the case before us. Also, we are led by another of our statutes which states that the sale of a partner's interest in the partnership entitles the buyer only to the profits. [UPA § 27]. There is no mention of payment of the capital debt owed the selling partner in *addition* to such profits. Thus, we find guidance in decisions of sister states wherein one's capital account is an asset separate and distinct from the partnership interest in valuation for dissolution:

> First, the difference between the fair market value of the partnership's assets, both real and personal, and in its liabilities is determined. Next, the partner's capital accounts, which are debts of the partnership, are subtracted from that figure. Out of the remainder, the partner's percentage interest is determined. *The partner's capital account in full is an additional, separate asset to be included in the division of property.*

Johnson v. Johnson, (1979) Minn. 277 N.W.2d 208, 213. The rationality of this decision to so differentiate is seen most clearly in terms of a practical situation. If we were to limit the value of a partner's interest in the partnership to the contribution of capital, what happens to the value as the partnership repays the capital? The book value of the assets logically increases while the debt of capital is diminishing. However, the partnership interest remains, according to statute as does the right to partnership property. It, therefore, makes more sense to base the value of the partnership interest on the debt-free partnership assets apart from the capital liability. Thus, we agree with a federal court in declaring the partnership's buy-sell agreement meant "the *interest* of the deceased [William] in the partnership was purchased, i.e., his right to his share of the *surplus* of assets over liabilities." *Anderson v. United States*, (S.D. Cal. 1954) 131 F. Supp. 501. The capital was not included.

Of course, the internal operation of a partnership and the duties and obligations imposed upon the partners as to each other, set out in our statutes, can be altered by agreement of said partners, but there is no such modification here. In this case, the brothers Hamilton merely agreed to the purchase price of a dead partner's interest. This arrangement did not absolve them of the partnership's liability to repay the undrawn capital contributions. Therefore, under the evidence the court would have been justified in awarding up to $60,268 as the amount representing the capital account, in addition to the agreed price.

The parties here do not dispute that the appellants have paid Renetta $46,100, to date, for William's partnership holdings. It is clear that $25,000 of that represents the $25,000 agreed purchase price for his partnership interest. There was evidently some difference in opinion as to the amount of net profits from the partnership that was due the estate for the twelve months following William's death. However, the trial court settled upon a figure of $9,654 which appellants have not attacked on appeal. Therefore, the buy-sell agreement was interpreted as requiring $34,654 be paid to Renetta under the specific terms of the agreement. The trial court calculated that William's capital account was worth $48,438.78, a figure that is well within the evidence here. Adding the two sums, $34,654 and $48,438.78, the trial court reached a total of $83,092.78. Subtracting the $46,100 already paid, the trial court awarded Renetta $36,992.78 as the amount still owing. Again, this was within the evidence; there was no error.

[W]e affirm in part and reverse in part.

Notes

1. Consider the following extract from the Official Comment to UPA section 25(2)(b):

> A partner has a beneficial interest in partnership property considered as a whole. As profits accrue, he has a right to be paid his proportion, and on the winding up of the business, after the obligations due *third persons* have been met, he has a right to be paid in cash his share of what remains of the partnership property. These rights considered as a whole are his interest in the partnership; and this beneficial interest he may assign in whole or in fractional part, as is indicated in section 27 (emphasis added).

According to the principles studied in *Parker v. Northern Mixing Co.*, how is a partner's distributive share of partnership property determined? Is *Hamilton Airport Advertising, Inc. v. Hamilton* consistent with those principles?

In *Rasmussen v. Thomas*, 98 Nev. 216, 644 P.2d 1030 (1982), the Nevada Supreme Court reversed a trial court order returning to a partner of a dissolved partnership the partner's capital contribution:

> Upon dissolution, the respondents in this case were entitled to the value of their respective shares in the partnership business, not to a return of capital invested. *See* [UPA § 38(1)]. Without an accounting of the partnership affairs, ascertaining what surplus, if any, remained after discharging liabilities and collecting assets, an accurate money judgment award, returning to respondents Clarence and Richard Thomas their interest in the partnership, could not be rendered.

Recall that at common law, partners could not sue each other on matters arising out of partnership affairs. As discussed in chapter 14, one of the chief reasons for requiring a prior accounting is that partners must bear their proportionate shares of profits *or losses*. Thus, partners are not unqualifiedly entitled to a return of contributions. For example, in *Parker v. Northern Mixing Co.*, although Parker had made $134,477.62 in contributions, he was only entitled to receive $110,427.12 after taking into account his share of the losses.

2. If UPA section 18(a) does *not* make a partner's right to return of capital an asset separate from the interest in the partnership, what is its purpose?

3. RUPA section 502(a) defines a partner's "transferable interest in the partnership" as the partner's right to distributions. Under RUPA sections 808 and 401, a partner's right to distributions on dissolution are determined according to the partner's "account." Sections 401(a), 401(b) and 808(b) make it clear that "contributions," "profits," and "losses" are *not* separate assets, but rather only *items* to be credited or charged to the partner's account.

4. Additional discussion of this question may be found in Rosin, *The Entity-Aggregate Dispute: Conceptualism and Functionalism in Partnership Law*, 42 ARK. L. REV. 395, 443-65 (1989).

Chapter 18

Dissolution: Rights of Dissociating Partners; Fiduciary Duties; Rights of Third Parties

A. Rights of Dissociating Partners When Business Continued Without Settlement of Accounts

UPA section 42 addresses the rights of a retiring (dissociating) partner (or the partner's estate) when the remaining partners continue the partnership business, but have not yet "settled" with the dissociating partner/estate. First, the withdrawing partner/estate is entitled to have the value of the dissociating partner's interest in the partnership ascertained (determined). Second, the dissociating partner/estate is then entitled to payment *as an ordinary creditor* (but junior to partnership creditors as of the date of the dissociation) of an amount equal to the value of the interest in the partnership as so determined. Last, the dissociating partner/estate is entitled to compensation for delay. The dissociating partner/estate can choose the form of that compensation—either (money) interest or the "profits attributable to the use of his right in the property of the dissolved partnership."

Rosen Trust v. Rosen

53 A.D.2d 342, 386 N.Y.S. 491 (1976)

MOULE, Justice.

The issues presented on this appeal involve the validity of an interlocutory judgment and certain subsequent intermediate orders made in connection with the dissolution of a partnership as well as the propriety of the final judgment determining plaintiff's share of the assets and profits of the business.

On October 1, 1958 plaintiff's decedent, Harold J. Rosen, and defendants, Herbert S. and Maurice L. Rosen, three brothers, formed a partnership with offices in Syracuse for the purpose of engaging "in the business of purchasing, selling, leasing and managing real estate and constructing buildings thereon." While all three partners initially made contributions to capital, they contemplated that Harold and Herbert, who were both highly paid executives with the Helene Curtis Cosmetic Co., Inc., would contribute the necessary money to operate the business and that Maurice, a licensed real estate broker, would be responsible for managing the partnership.

To reflect this arrangement, the partnership agreement provided that net profits or net losses would be divided equally even though one partner's capital or income account might be considerably greater than another's and that no partner would receive any salary for services rendered to the partnership. It further provided that, upon the death of a partner, the partnership would not terminate but rather would continue under the management of the surviving brothers. The deceased partner's legal representative could participate in the profits and losses of the business or, at his option and with notice to the surviving partners, he could elect to withdraw. If such election was made, the surviving partners were required either to purchase the deceased partner's interest or else to terminate the business with reasonable promptness. In any event, however, the agreement provided that no compensation would be paid to the surviving partners for their services in liquidation of the partnership.

Thereafter, on August 24, 1964, Harold J. Rosen died and, pursuant to the terms of the partnership agreement, his estate notified defendants on November 8, 1964 that it intended to withdraw from the partnership as of December 31 of that year. Herbert and Maurice did not purchase the estate's share of the business and, in accordance with Article 11 of the partnership agreement, they were under a duty to liquidate the business promptly and to distribute the assets.

On October 9, 1967, plaintiff commenced an action [seeking] a judicial dissolution of the partnership, an accounting, the appointment of a receiver, liquidation and distribution of the partnership assets.

Thereafter, in an interlocutory judgment entered on October 8, 1970, the court made the following determinations:

> That the partnership was legally dissolved as of December 31, 1964;
>
> That defendants were required to submit an accounting within 60 days of the entry of the judgment to establish plaintiff's share in the assets as of December 31, 1964 as well as its share in post-dissolution profits up to the entry of the judgment;
>
> That, upon submission of the accounting, plaintiff could elect to receive [its share] in the partnership assets valued as of December 31, 1964 either with interest on that amount up to the date of the entry of judgment or with one-third of the post-dissolution profits up to the same date.

In an order entered on December 28, 1972 the court directed that the matter be submitted to a referee who would determine the value of the estate's interest in the partnership assets as of December 31, 1964, as well as the estate's share in the post-dissolution profits from December 31, 1964 to December 31, 1971.

Hearings before the referee were conducted in March and April, 1973. Thereafter, on August 13, 1973 the referee rendered his final report in which he valued the estate's share in the partnership assets at $265,079.74 as of December 31, 1964. He also determined that the estate's share in the post-dissolution profits was $233,866.75.

In an order entered on May 13, 1975, the court accepted without modification the referee's valuation as to the plaintiff's share in the post-dissolution profits.

The final order and judgment, which was entered on May 19, 1975 and which merely elaborated upon the order of May 13, 1975, reflected plaintiff's election to receive one-third of the post-dissolution profits between December 31, 1964 and December 31, 1971. It is from this judgment as well as from the interlocutory judgment and the orders of December 28, 1972 and May 13, 1975 that plaintiff and defendants appeal.

The question presented on this appeal concerns whether the plaintiff's share of post-dissolution profits should be the same as decedent's equitable percentage share of the partnership's total assets as of December 31, 1964 which was 38 percent. This distribution was rejected by the court in its interlocutory judgment of October 8, 1970 and plaintiff was limited to a 33⅓ percent share of the post-dissolution profits.

[UPA section 42] provides in part as follows:

> When any partner retires or dies, and the business is continued under any of the conditions set forth in section seventy-two, subdivisions one, two, three, five and six, or section sixty-nine, paragraph (b) of subdivision two, without any settlement of accounts as between him or his estate and the person or partnership continuing the business, unless otherwise agreed, he or his legal representative as against such persons or partnership may have the value of his interest at the date of dissolution ascertained, and shall receive as an ordinary creditor an amount equal to the value of his interest in the dissolved partnership with interest, or, at his option or at the option of his legal representative, in lieu of interest, *the profits attributable to the use of his right in the property of the dissolved partnership*. (Emphasis supplied).

In rejecting the 38 percent ratio the court stated that this statutory provision was superseded by Article 4 of the partnership agreement, which provided that net profits or losses be divided equally, and by Article 5, which provided that "[n]o additional share of profits shall inure to any partner by reason of his capital or income account being proportionately in excess of the capital or income accounts of the others." However, it is clear from a reading of the entire agreement that these provisions do not specifically apply to post-dissolution distribution. In the absence of such specific application, the predissolution percentage shares do not serve to supersede the statutory share of [UPA section 42]. Thus we hold that the court erred in limiting plaintiff's share in the post-dissolution profits to 33⅓ percent.

In implementing the provisions of [UPA section 42], it is necessary to ascertain the ratio of the decedent's share in the assets of the partnership to the total assets. In the instant case, the total net worth of the partnership, as of December 31, 1964, was $629,631.85. [T]he plaintiff's total value in the assets of the partnership amount[ed] to $241,890.69.* When this figure is proportionately compared to the total net worth of the partnership ($629,631.85), we arrive at a ratio of 38 percent which reflects plaintiff's percentage share in the post-dissolution profits for the period 1965-1971.

The post-dissolution profits of the partnership from January 1, 1965 through December 31, 1971, as found by the referee, totaled $701,600.24. [After certain adjustments], we arrive at a net post-dissolution profit of $510,375.24. Applying a rate of 38 percent to this sum we find plaintiff's proportionate share to be $193,942.59.

Therefore the order of May 13, 1975 and judgment of May 19, 1975 should be further modified to provide that judgment be entered in favor of plaintiff in the amount of $241,890.69 for assets plus $193,942.59 for profits. Except as herein modified the

---

* [Note by the editors.] In a portion of the opinion not appearing in this book, the Court adjusted the referee's accounting.

aforesaid order of May 13, 1975 and the judgment of May 19, 1975 are otherwise affirmed.

Notes

1. UPA section 42 does *not* give the remaining partners the *right* to continue under circumstances where that right is not available under the agreement or under UPA section 38. Instead, it only addresses the rights of the dissociating partner/estate where business is *rightfully* continued.

2. Suppose that Alice, Bruce, and Carol are partners. Carol dies, and Alice and Bruce continue the partnership business under a right given in the partnership agreement. Carol's estate elects under UPA section 42 to take a share of the profits as compensation for delay in paying the estate the value of Carol's interest in the partnership. Is Carol's estate liable for an entirely new partnership obligation arising after Alice and Bruce continued the business? Why or why not?

3. Note that under RUPA section 701(b), a dissociating partner (or estate) will not be able to elect a share of post-dissolution profits, but will *only* be entitled to (money) interest as compensation for delay.

Note on *Timmermann v. Timmermann*

One issue that arises frequently under UPA section 42 is whether, in calculating the profits the departing partner is entitled to share, the continuing partners are entitled to a *compensation for their services.*

UPA section 18(f) provides that in the absence of an agreement otherwise, partners are not entitled to remuneration for services in the partnership business (they are compensated by a share of the profits). The only exception is a *surviving* partner who winds up partnership affairs after the death of a partner. Nevertheless, as indicated by the following extract from *Timmermann v. Timmermann*, 272 Or. 613, 538 P.2d 1254, 1262-63 (1975), the majority rule is that an allowance for services is proper under UPA section 42:

> Plaintiff's contention, that the accounting should have made no allowance to Stanley and Ernest for their labor and management after dissolution, is incorrect. Although this question has never before directly arisen in Oregon, we feel that one who continues the partnership business after dissolution and contributes substantial labor and management services thereto is entitled to compensation for that share of the profits which are attributable to such services. Such a rule is comparable with [UPA section 42], which allows a retiring partner only those "profits attributable to the use of his right in the property." Thus, he should have no interest in profits attributable to the labor and management services of the continuing partners.
>
> The above rule is in accord with the better reasoned decision from other jurisdictions. As stated in *Essay v. Essay*, 175 Neb. 730, 123 N.W.2d 648, 649 (1963):
>
> Where the profits earned after dissolution and before a final accounting are attributable in part to the personal skill or services of a partner, it is a factor to be considered in the apportioning of the shares of the partners.
>
> 1 Rowley on Partnership 814, 815, § 42.3 (2d 1960) states:

> The best considered authorities hold that the former partner or his estate is entitled to the profits which were earned by his share of the assets, or according to his share of the capital, after deducting such share as is attributable to the skill and services of those who have continued to carry on the business.
>
> If the business is continued by consent of those who are entitled to an account and they elect to take profits, the partner who so continues the business is usually held to be entitled to compensation.

But see Wikstrom v. Davis, 211 Or. 254, 281, 315 P.2d 597 (1957) [(in calculating UPA section 42 profits, partners *wrongfully* continuing business are not entitled to compensation for services)].

In *Vangel v. Vangel*, 291 P.2d at 28, the California Supreme Court discussed the related question of allowing compensation for a withdrawing partner who continued to render valuable services in the operation of a citrus farm. The court said:

> As a practical matter, his share of the profits usually is computed on the basis of the ratio that his share of the partnership assets bears to the whole of them. However, that division may not be equitable when the contribution to profits from capital is relatively minor in comparison to the contribution from the skills or services of one conducting the business. In such a case, the managing partner may be entitled to a greater share of the profits. Although such a method of dividing profits is usually spoken of in terms of providing extra compensation for the managing ex-partner, in reality it merely reflects the statutory requirement that the retired or deceased partner be allowed the profits *attributable* to his right in the assets used in the business. (Emphasis in original.)

In summary, we find that a trial court, in determining profits attributable to the use of a withdrawing partner's right in the property of the dissolved partnership, is entitled to make an equitable allowance for the services of the continuing partners.

An accounting to determine the profits attributable to the use of Lynne's rights in the property of the partnership should allocate to plaintiff his proportional share of the total profits of the partnership less compensation to the continuing partners for their services to the partnership after dissolution. Thus, it will be necessary for the trial court to hold a hearing and determine the value of each continuing partner's service to the partnership.

> The court below must determine what is the fair value of such services by a consideration of the nature of the work, the time spent, and the skill used. *Bracht v. Connell*, 170 A. at 300.

The trial court should allow a sum for each continuing partner from the date of dissolution to the date of the accounting to be subtracted from the total profits of the partnership. Plaintiff should then be allocated his proportional share (33.78%) of the remaining profits. By the use of such method, defendants will be compensated for their services to the partnership and plaintiff will receive the profits attributable to the use of his right in the property of the partnership.

B. Fiduciary Duties During Liquidation

Fulton v. Baxter

596 P.2d 540 (Okla. 1979)

SIMMS, Justice:

Plaintiff-Appellee commenced an action seeking an accounting and damages. Plaintiff alleged that Defendant-Appellant had destroyed a partnership and converted certain partnership assets. Verdict was returned in plaintiff's favor and judgment was accordingly entered on the verdict. Defendant appeals. The Court of Appeals, Division I, reversed and remanded for further accounting.

The operative facts, as disclosed from the record, are that plaintiff and defendant formed a partnership in April, 1970, to sell life, health, and disability insurance. The partnership, known as Fulton-Baxter & Associates, acquired non-exclusive general agency contracts with various insurance companies. In addition to sales made by the partners, policies were sold through the partnership by a number of appointed agents. When these agents sold policies written by insurance companies with which Fulton-Baxter had an agency contract, the partnership was paid an override commission. After 1970, these agents accounted for the bulk of gross sales processed through the partnership.

On or about September 25, 1975, the defendant informed plaintiff of his desire to terminate the partnership and divide the assets. The plaintiff agreed to the dissolution and suggested that each partner place a value on the partnership assets with one partner to have the option of buying or selling at the stated value. Defendant agreed.

Pursuant to the agreement, both partners prepared separate valuations of the assets. Plaintiff placed a value of $6,000 on partnership "goodwill." Defendant listed "goodwill" as an asset having no value. Plaintiff placed a value on the group contracts and override commissions totalling $40,000. Defendant listed these contracts as assets with no value to the partnership. The parties were unable to reach a settlement of their differences.

Thereafter, defendant entered into new general agency contracts with the insurance companies serviced by the partnership. These new contracts were in the name of L. W. Baxter & Associates.

Contracts with Fulton-Baxter, the partnership, were subsequently cancelled, but not before some policies were processed under the L. W. Baxter contract. Defendant had the Yellow Page listing changed from Fulton-Baxter to L. W. Baxter & Associates. Defendant also had the telephone company change its records to show that the telephone number used by the partnership was now to be used by L. W. Baxter & Associates. Defendant instructed the post office not to release partnership mail when the plaintiff requested it. Defendant continued to occupy the partnership offices and when the lease expired, defendant renewed it in the name of L. W. Baxter. In short, all the assets evaluated by the defendant to be worthless, ultimately came to be the assets of defendant's new insurance agency.

In order to determine whether the jury correctly concluded that defendant appropriated partnership property, this Court must resolve three questions: (1) What was the extent of defendant's duty relative to partnership property? (2) Did the defendant breach that duty? (3) Did the evidence support the amount of damages awarded?

The duty concerning profits derived from a partnership is found at [UPA section 21(1)], which provides:

> Every partner must account to the partnership for any benefit, and hold as trustee for it any profits derived by him without the consent of the other partners from any transaction connected with the formation, conduct, or liquidation of the partnership or from any use by him of its property.

[UPA section 21(1)] is unambiguous and imposes an absolute duty. This duty remains undiminished by the fact that a partnership has been dissolved. [UPA section 30] provides that on dissolution of a partnership, the partnership is not terminated, "but continues until the winding up of partnership affairs is completed."

This Court has consistently held that good faith is most especially required where one partner is trying to oust another partner. [T]hroughout the period in question, the defendant was bound to exercise good faith relative to partnership transactions and property.

Evidence in this case shows that defendant purposely brought about the termination of the partnership lease and renewed it in the name of L. W. Baxter. Conduct of this category is not to be permitted in the context of the partnership affiliation. In *Waller v. Henderson*, [135 Okla. 231, 275 P.2d 323 (1929)], we adopted the rule that a partner may not obtain a renewal of a partnership lease for his own purpose to commence after the expiration of the original lease, or after the termination of the partnership without disclosing those facts to his co-partners. The rule is succinctly stated at 60 Am. Jur. 2d *Partnership*, § 127, at 53:

> Even after dissolution of the partnership, the equitable expectancy of renewal (of the lease) remains a partnership asset for the purposes of liquidation, to be taken into account and disposed of for the common benefit of the partners, and hence, a renewal after dissolution of the firm, taken by less than all the partners, inures to the benefit of the firm.

We therefore have no difficulty in finding that defendant breached his fiduciary duty and wrongfully appropriated the partnership lease to his own benefit, notwithstanding his insistence that the offices occupied by the partnership were of no value to the partnership.

We are unpersuaded by defendant's argument that the business relationships, overrides, and agency contracts could not be wrongfully appropriated since they were contingent or cancellable at will. We agree with the statement found in *Rowley on Partnerships*, § 21.1, at 544 (1960), which reads:

> The same rule which governs the securing of leases applies to other benefits, and if a member of an insurance partnership secures a renewal of agencies in himself and for his own benefit, it is held that he takes them for the use of the firm, and this even though the other partners contemplated going out of business.

In the instant case, the defendant not only renewed the agencies in himself, he processed policies through his own agencies before the partnership contracts were cancelled.[1]

The record reveals sufficient evidence from which the jury could conclude that defendant wrongfully appropriated valuable partnership assets and converted them to his own use. There was sufficient evidence regarding partnership income for the years preceding dissolution, and testimony regarding income generated by at least one agency contract following dissolution. There was also presented testimony concerning the proceeds realized from a project conceived in the course of the partnership and consummated following dissolution. We find the amount of the verdict supported by competent evidence.

The opinion of the Court of Appeals is therefore vacated, and the judgment of the trial court is Affirmed.

Notes

1. "Goodwill" has been defined as the reasonable expectation of continued patronage of a business by its clientele. That is, goodwill is the business's expected future income. Goodwill is based largely on the *reputation* of the business, and depends on several factors, including continuity of location, continuity of name, customer lists, contracts with employees, customers and suppliers, and the like.

2. Conflicts between partners regarding the valuation of a partnership's goodwill often arise after the dissolution of a partnership, particularly where some of the partners wish to continue the partnership's business. Often, as in *Fulton v. Baxter*, the continuing partners wish to minimize the valuation of goodwill. They do so not because they think goodwill is not valuable (or else why do they wish to *continue doing business*?) but because they do not want to *pay* the departing partner for his or her *share* of goodwill. Such conflicts can be avoided at the planning stage by having the partners agree *in advance* as to the method of valuing goodwill.

3. Professional partnerships—lawyers, doctors—pose special problems in considering the question of goodwill. Until somewhat recently, the common law rule was that partnerships in businesses involving personal skills had no goodwill as a partnership. Because the reputation of the business could not be separated from the *individual* skills and reputations of each partner, not only was there no *partnership* asset of goodwill, even the individual goodwill was inherently unsalable.

Most modern courts have rejected this reasoning, and recognize that professional partnerships may have goodwill. As the following case indicates, professional partnerships still raise thorny questions.

Rosenfeld, Meyer & Susman v. Cohen

145 Cal. App. 3d 853, 194 Cal. Rptr. 180 (1983)

NEBRON, Associate Justice.

This is an appeal from a judgment on the pleadings, a partial summary judgment.

The issue which underpins all causes of action here involved may be generally stated as follows: Given the facts of this case, does a former partner of a partnership

---

1. Partners, ordinarily, are under a duty not to compete with the partnership but a discussion of this topic is not essential for resolution of the issues raised in this case.

at will owe any fiduciary duty to former partners after dissolving the partnership and subsequently agreeing with former clients of the dissolved partnership to accept and carry on business which was originally a portion of the assets of the dissolved partnership?

Appellant Rosenfeld, Meyer and Susman (hereinafter called RM & S) consists of the 17 former partners of a dissolved at-will law partnership suing in the name of the dissolved RM & S partnership as both winding up partners and in their individual capacities. Respondents Peter R. Cohen and Deborah D. Riordan, as administratrix of the estate of Edward J. Riordan, deceased (hereinafter called C & R), are the two former partners who dissolved that at-will partnership. International Rectifier Corporation (hereinafter called Rectifier) is a former client of the dissolved RM & S partnership.

In late 1968, Rectifier sought attorneys to bring a major patent antitrust action on a contingent fee basis. After considering the proposals of several law firms, Rectifier entered in a written agreement with RM & S in March 1969, employing RM & S to represent Rectifier in that litigation. The agreement provided that RM & S would be paid limited fees of $30 per hour up to a maximum of 1,000 hours per year for five years against one-third of any recovery and that Rectifier would bear all costs and expenses.

Most of the attorney services rendered by RM & S were performed by C & R, the two senior litigators at RM & S, both experienced in antitrust litigation. From March 1969 through April 30, 1974, RM & S attorneys spent in excess of 19,000 hours on the case. Moreover, RM & S also supervised almost 60,000 hours of paralegal and document clerk services. Other than C & R, no partner had anything but a passing acquaintance with the Rectifier case. The Rectifier account substantially increased RM & S's expenses. RM & S was required to rent additional office space, hire additional support personnel for the Rectifier action and employ additional attorneys to handle matters which otherwise would have been attended to by C & R.

[E]ach partner's profit percentage was fixed by a committee and approved by the partnership. Profits were determined only after fees were received by RM & S and then divided among the partners pursuant to their current partnership percentage, regardless of a partner's work on any particular matter. Throughout the five years that C & R handled the Rectifier action, they received approximately $800,000 from RM & S, despite the fact that they produced virtually no income for the firm during this period. The other partners of RM & S expected to share in the fee from the Rectifier action should it eventually materialize.

By late 1973, C & R believed the trial of the Rectifier action would commence in the fall of 1974 and that the case would settle for between $20 million and $50 million, or, if tried, that the judgment would be approximately $100 million before trebling. Sometime in December 1973, or January 1974, C & R demanded that they be allocated double their partnership percentage of the fee to be paid by Rectifier in connection with the Rectifier action. C & R threatened that if RM & S did not agree to change the partnership allocation, they would withdraw from RM & S. Thereafter, RM & S partners negotiated with C & R to avoid their withdrawal or to make arrangements for C & R to complete the Rectifier action should they withdraw from the firm. As these negotiations progressed, C & R made new demands and stated to two of the partners of RM & S that they would never settle the dispute which they had created. As late as March 26th, or 27th, Riordan told a third partner that C &

R no longer needed RM & S. Riordan stated his belief that if C & R withdrew from the firm Rectifier would hire C & R to complete the case,[2] and would provide the necessary financing.

On March 28, 1974, RM & S partners and C & R met with Rectifier's president (Lidow) and vice-president/general counsel (Koris). RM & S described the problem at the firm and explained that the firm was willing to make concessions to C & R, but that C & R would not agree. RM & S also assured Rectifier that if C & R withdrew, RM & S would do whatever was necessary to pursue the case, such as assigning other partners to work on the case and/or retaining, at RM & S's expense, skilled antitrust attorneys as co-counsel. Rectifier's officers stated that they wanted C & R to remain on the case and that C & R should do whatever was necessary to achieve that result.

On April 11, 1974, C & R by memorandum to the other partners gave notice of their withdrawal from the firm effective April 30, 1974. During the first week of May 1974, C & R formed the law firm of Cohen and Riordan. At that time Cohen had no prospective clients, but he believed that Rectifier would ultimately discharge RM & S and hire C & R to complete the antitrust action.

On May 14, 1974, Rectifier mailed a letter of discharge to RM & S and on the following day hand delivered a similar letter of discharge to RM & S. On May 16, 1974, Rectifier retained C & R as attorneys in the Rectifier action.

The C & R-Rectifier agreement provided that Rectifier would pay to C & R $250,000 per year and 8¾ percent of the recovery in the Rectifier action. The agreement further provided that C & R would indemnify Rectifier against its total attorney's fees (including fees payable to C & R and RM & S) exceeding ⅓ of Rectifier's recovery in the antitrust action, and that the 8¾ percentage contingent fee would be held in escrow for C & R until the amount of the total fees was resolved.

The C&R-Rectifier agreement permitted C & R to receive approximately two times their RM & S partnership percentage of the Rectifier fee. The 8¾ percent contingent fee provided for equals approximately 26 percent of the fee that Rectifier was obligated to pay RM & S under the RM & S-Rectifier agreement. It is also approximately 2.2 times C & R's claimed 1973 partnership percentage of 12 percent in RM & S's 33⅓ percent contingent fee. Thus, both C & R and Rectifier were to financially benefit by the new C & R-Rectifier agreement.

Trial of the Rectifier action commenced in November 1974, and in August 1975 the action was settled for $33 million. Pursuant to the C & R-Rectifier agreement, Rectifier paid C & R $337,000 in current compensation for the period May 1974 through August 1975, and placed $2.4 million in escrow as C & R's 8¾ percent contingent fee. In October 1975, RM & S commenced the present action.

[RM & S allege] that C & R breached their fiduciary duty as partners of RM & S [(Breach of Fiduciary Duty)] by dissolving RM & S in bad faith to cause Rectifier to discharge RM & S and obtain increased compensation for themselves (Bad Faith Dissolution); further, that the Rectifier action was the unfinished business of the dissolved RM & S partnership and that C & R breached their fiduciary duties by

---

2. *Fracasse v. Brent* (1972), 6 Cal. 3d 784, 100 Cal. Rptr. 385, 494 P.2d 9, permits a client who retains an attorney pursuant to a contingent fee agreement to discharge the attorney with or without cause and to pay the reasonable value of the discharged attorney's services if and when said contingency occurs, rather than the fee specified in the agreement.

failing to complete the case for the dissolved partnership and that they held the sums received from Rectifier for completing the case as constructive trustees for the dissolved RM & S (Unfinished Business).

The [lower court] denied C & R's motion for summary judgment, but found that the following issues regarding the cause of action for breach of fiduciary duty were without substantial controversy: (a) That RM & S was a partnership at will; (b) that RM & S had failed to state a cause of action because a partner in a partnership at will may exercise his right to dissolve the partnership for any reason and in bad faith; and (c) that Rectifier terminated their agreement with RM & S in mid-May 1974, and that the termination of such agreement precluded RM & S from stating a cause of action against C & R for breach of C & R's fiduciary duty to complete unfinished business.

Appellants claim that such rulings were prejudicial because they were precluded from proving that C & R violated their fiduciary duties to RM & S prior to mid-May by: (a) Formulating a secret plan to let RM & S finance the Rectifier action until C & R believed the case was close to trial and then making a joint demand for an unprecedented division of the contingent fee; (b) making disparaging remarks to Rectifier about RM & S which C & R did not disclose to RM & S; and (c) failing to complete unfinished business before the termination of the RM & S-Rectifier agreement.

Was the Rectifier action the unfinished business of the dissolved RM & S partnership so that C & R breached their fiduciary duties by failing to complete the case for the dissolved partnership and thus held the sums received from Rectifier for completing the case as constructive trustee for the dissolved RM & S?

The concept of unfinished business arises from the rule of law that upon the dissolution of a partnership, the partnership is not terminated but continues to exist for the limited purpose of winding up its affairs and completing all unfinished business. [UPA §§ 29, 30, 33]. Thus, on May 1, 1974, the day following the dissolution of RM & S there existed three entities: C & R (comprised of Cohen and Riordan), a new RM & S (comprised of the partners of RM & S remaining on April 30, 1974), and the dissolved RM & S which had not yet been wound up. Until the dissolved partnership was wound up, the partners of the dissolved RM & S continued to owe fiduciary duties to each other, especially with respect to unfinished business.

Two fiduciary duties are particularly relevant to this appeal:

First, each partner of a dissolved partnership has the duty to wind up and complete the business of the dissolved partnership existing prior to its dissolution (unfinished business). [UPA §§ 30, 33]; *Smith v. Bull,* (1958) 50 Cal. 2d 294, 303-304, 325 P.2d 463 ("As to the 'unfinished business,' a duty to perform services rests on the partnership at the time of dissolution and continues thereafter to rest on the partners or the surviving partner."); *Little v. Caldwell,* (1894) 101 Cal. 553, 558-562, 36 P. 107 ("[T]he surviving partner must complete all executory contracts of a firm which remain in force after the death of a partner.").

Second, a partner of a dissolved partnership may not take any action with respect to unfinished business which leads to purely personal gain.

A partner of a dissolved partnership who violates any one of these fiduciary duties is liable to the other partners for this breach.

Notwithstanding the foregoing, the [lower courts] dismissed RM & S's claim that C & R were liable for such breach, reasoning that Rectifier's discharge of RM & S precluded any liability. The [lower courts] focused on the date of RM & S's discharge rather than the date of RM & S's dissolution to determine the duties of C & R with respect to unfinished business. To determine whether business of a dissolved partnership is unfinished business, the court should look to the circumstances existing on the date of dissolution of the partnership, not to events occurring thereafter. Thus, in *Smith v. Bull*, the court states that *Little v. Caldwell*

> clearly indicates the line of demarcation between "unfinished business," being business covered by contracts of employment at the time of dissolution, and other matters, not covered by contracts of employment, but which *thereafter* become the subjects of contracts of employment through the goodwill previously existing between the partnership and the clients. As to the "unfinished business," a duty to perform services rests on the partnership at the time of dissolution and continues thereafter to rest on the partners or the surviving partner.

And in *Heywood v. Sooy*, (1941) 45 Cal. App. 2d 423, 426, 114 P.2d 361:

> [T]he test of what constitutes 'unfinished business' of a partnership upon dissolution is whether there existed, at the time of the dissolution, any contract of employment between the partnership and the clients for the performance by the partnership of the services thereafter claimed to be "unfinished business."

It is clear, therefore, that the RM & S-Rectifier agreement was unfinished business of RM & S on May 1, 1974, the day following the dissolution of RM & S.

Given the facts of this case, the [lower court's] conclusion that Rectifier's discharge of RM & S in mid-May 1974 precluded a cause of action for C & R's breach of duty to complete the Rectifier action for the dissolved partnership was error. A trier of fact could find that C & R dissolved RM & S for the very purpose of voiding its fiduciary duty to RM & S; that Rectifier's mid-May discharge letter was therefore the result of C & R's breach of duty to complete unfinished business rather than a termination of C & R's duty; that it was because of C & R's breach of duty during the period May 1 to mid-May that the dissolved RM & S was discharged by Rectifier and lost the difference between what it would have received under the RM & S-Rectifier agreement and the quantum meruit recovery less attorneys' fees that RM & S would have received from Rectifier.

The [lower court's] conclusion that Rectifier's discharge of RM & S required dismissal of RM & S's cause of action for breach of C & R's fiduciary duty was also erroneous because a partner of a dissolved partnership who attempts to reap personal gain from the unfinished business of the dissolved partnership is liable to his copartners for breach of fiduciary duty, despite any discharge of the dissolved firm. The existence of the fiduciary duty prohibiting partners of a dissolved partnership from entering into contracts for personal gain in connection with unfinished business of the partnership is well established.

In *Little v. Caldwell*, after the dissolution of a law partnership by the death of one of the partners, the surviving partner entered into a contract with a client of the dissolved partnership to appeal a contingent fee case unsuccessfully tried before dissolution. The new contract altered the existing obligations and rights of the parties by relieving the client from the obligation to pay additional costs and increasing the contingent fee from 15 percent to 60 percent. The surviving partner argued that the client's entry into this agreement with him after the dissolution of the partnership extinguished his obligation to share the fee with the deceased partner. But the court in rejecting this argument stated:

> In the discharge of this obligation or duty in relation to the unsettled and unfinished business of the firm, the surviving partner occupies the position of a trustee, and, while he may compromise disputed claims, or modify an existing contract by releasing the other party thereto from some of its obligations, when in the exercise of an honest judgment the best interest of the partnership seems to him to require such action, still, in doing so, he cannot be permitted to make gain for himself at the expense of the estate of the deceased partner, by consenting to the extinguishment of a contract belonging to the partnership, and the substitution therefor of another relating to the same subject matter, and in the profits of which he alone is to participate. Whatever may be the effect of such new or substituted contract as between the immediate parties to it, a court of equity in settling the accounts of the partnership will not treat it as an entire extinguishment of the original contract, or deny the right of the representatives of the deceased partner to an equitable participation in the profits realized from the latter contract, and which may be regarded, so far as concerns the partnership, as only a modification of the former contract.

After *Little v. Caldwell* was retried, the trial court held that the second contract entered into by Caldwell with the client was but a modification of the first. This finding was supported by evidence that the second contract did not provide for a fee of 60 percent but for an additional 45 percent fee and because defendant had asked for a release from plaintiff of plaintiff's rights under the first contract. Since the findings of the trial court were sufficient to dispose of the case, the Supreme Court did not address the consequences which would follow from a so-called termination of the first contract and a substitution of a "new contract." The court did, however, state the trial court was also justified in holding that the contracts were not separate and distinct because

> [t]he consideration moving from the attorneys, that they were to prosecute to a conclusion the litigation in question, always remained; the terms of their compensation and risk in so doing alone were varied.

So in the present case, the consideration moving from C & R—their prosecution of the Rectifier action—continued under the C & R-Rectifier agreement, only the compensation to be paid by Rectifier being varied and this without the acquiescence of RM & S. It is clear that a partner completing unfinished business cannot cut off the rights of the other partners in the dissolved partnership by the tactic of entering into a "new" contract to complete such business.

Given the facts of this case, though Rectifier had a right to terminate the contract with RM & S and hire C & R, C & R could not avoid what was tantamount to a conflict of interest—*i.e.,* the fiduciary duty it owed to RM & S.

Rectifier's purported discharge of RM & S is irrelevant to the issue of C & R's breach of their fiduciary duty to the remaining partners of RM & S. A partner's fiduciary duty to complete unfinished business on behalf of the dissolved partnership arises on the date of dissolution and governs each partner's future conduct regarding this business. Since the Rectifier action remained exactly the same case before and after RM & S's dissolution, C & R's liability for failing to complete the Rectifier case for the dissolved RM & S and for entering into a contract personally to profit from the unfinished business of the dissolved RM & S survived execution of the C & R-Rectifier agreement and Rectifier's discharge of RM & S.

The *Little v. Caldwell* opinions and the other unfinished business cases strike a reasonable balance between a partner's right to pursue his own business after dissolution of a partnership, and his duty of loyalty to his ex-copartners. The partner may take for his own account new business even when emanating from clients of the dissolved partnership and the partner is entitled to the reasonable value of the services in completing the partnership business, but he may not seize for his own account the business which was in existence during the term of the partnership. Clearly, the balance between such competing public policies is upset if a partner may dissolve a partnership to cause a termination of a partnership business, or if a partner may withhold his necessary services from the dissolved partnership to preclude the completion of unfinished business, or if the partner may complete such business and retain the proceeds for himself.

The rulings of the [lower courts] are reversed and the cause is remanded for further proceedings not inconsistent with this opinion.

Notes

1. In *Meehan v. Shaughnessy*, 404 Mass. 419, 535 N.E.2d 1255 (1989), Meehan and Boyle, two partners in the law partnership of Parker Coulter, became dissatisfied and formed their own firm. Before they dissolved the partnership, Meehan and Boyle made arrangements to begin practice in their new firm immediately after dissolution. They leased and furnished new offices. They prepared a list of Parker Coulter clients that they felt would move their business to the new firm. They even approached other Parker Coulter lawyers about leaving with them. When asked if they were planning to leave the firm, they denied it. *After* they announced their departure, Meehan and Boyle refused to identify to the other partners those clients and matters they intended to try to take with them. Although the partnership agreement, as interpreted by the court, permitted them to take partnership clients upon payment of a "fair charge," the court found that Meehan and Boyle had breached their fiduciary duties:

> Parker Coulter argues that the judge's findings compel the conclusion that Meehan and Boyle breached their fiduciary duty not to compete with their partners by secretly setting up a new firm during their tenure at Parker Coulter. We disagree. We have stated that fiduciaries may plan to compete with the entity to which they owe allegiance, "provided that in the course of such arrangement they [do] not otherwise act in violation of their fiduciary duties." *Chelsea Indus. v. Gaffney*, 389 Mass. 1, 10, 11-12, 449 N.E.2d 320 (1983). Here, the judge found that Meehan and Boyle made certain logistical arrangements for the establishment of MBC. These arrangements included executing a lease for MBC's office, preparing lists of clients expected to leave Parker Coulter for MBC, and obtaining financing on the basis of these lists. We believe these logistical arrangements to establish a physical plant for the new firm were permissible under *Chelsea Indus.*, especially in light of the attorneys' obligation to represent adequately any clients who might continue to retain them on their departure from

Parker Coulter. There was no error in the judge's determination that this conduct did not violate the partners' fiduciary duty.

Lastly, Parker Coulter argues that the judge's findings compel the conclusion that Meehan and Boyle breached their fiduciary duties by unfairly acquiring consent from clients to remove cases from Parker Coulter. We agree that Meehan and Boyle, through their preparation for obtaining clients' consent, their secrecy concerning which clients they intended to take, and the substance and method of their communications with clients, obtained an unfair advantage over their former partners in breach of their fiduciary duties.

A partner has an obligation to "render on demand true and full information of all things affecting the partnership to any partner." [UPA § 20]. On three separate occasions Meehan affirmatively denied to his partners, on their demand, that he had any plans for leaving the partnership. During this period of secrecy, Meehan and Boyle made preparations for obtaining removal authorizations from clients. Meehan traveled to New York to meet with a representative of USAU and interest him in the new firm. Boyle prepared form letters on Parker Coulter's letterhead for authorizations from prospective MBC clients. Thus, they were "ready to move" the instant they gave notice to their partners.

On giving their notice, Meehan and Boyle continued to use their position of trust and confidence to the disadvantage of Parker Coulter. The two immediately began communicating with clients and referring attorneys. Boyle delayed providing his partners with a list of clients he intended to solicit until mid-December, by which time he had obtained authorization from a majority of the clients.

Finally, the content of the letter sent to the clients was unfairly prejudicial to Parker Coulter. The ABA Committee on Ethics and Professional Responsibility, in Informal Opinion 1457 (April 29, 1980), set forth ethical standards for attorneys announcing a change in professional association. Because this standard is intended primarily to protect clients, proof by Parker Coulter of a technical violation of this standard does not aid them in their claims. We will, however, look to this standard for general guidelines as to what partners are entitled to expect from each other concerning their joint clients on the division of their practice. The ethical standard provides that any notice explain to a client that he or she has the right to decide who will continue the representation. Here, the judge found that the notice did not "clearly present to the clients the choice they had between remaining at Parker Coulter or moving to the new firm." By sending a one-sided announcement, on Parker Coulter letterhead, so soon after notice of their departure, Meehan and Boyle excluded their partners from effectively presenting their services as an alternative to those of Meehan and Boyle.

Meehan and Boyle could have foreseen that the news of their departure would cause a certain amount of confusion and disruption among their partners. The speed and preemptive character of their campaign to acquire clients' consent took advantage of their partners' confusion. By engaging in these preemptive tactics, Meehan and Boyle violated the duty of utmost good faith and loyalty which they owed their partners. Therefore, we conclude that the judge erred in deciding that Meehan and Boyle acted properly in acquiring consent to remove cases to MBC.

2. Another typical context in which a breach of fiduciary duties occurs in connection with dissolution is a *wrongful continuation* of partnership business without any statutory or contractual right to do so. Wrongful continuation usually happens in partnership at will after a falling out among the partners. One group of partners voluntarily dissolves the partnership, "locks out" another partner or group of partners, then continues business for its own account.

Because the excluded partners have not wrongfully caused dissolution (why?), they have the right to participate in winding up (UPA § 37), and for that purpose have the right to possess partnership property (UPA § 25(2)). The "continuing" partners are wrongfully using partnership property for non-partnership purposes (their own business), as well as wrongfully excluding the other partners from partnership property. Not only must the continuing partners account *to the partnership* for profits under UPA section 21, but UPA sections 22(a) and (c) give the excluded partners a right to an accounting. Of course, the excluded partners may also sue to enforce their right to liquidation by sale (UPA § 38(1)). In addition, they may ask to have the court wind up the partnership (UPA § 37).

C. Effect of Dissolution on Rights of Third Parties

Wester & Co. v. Nestle

669 P.2d 1046 (Colo. 1983)

STERNBERG, Judge.

The plaintiff, Wester & Co., leased a store to defendant Nestle and third-party defendant Ellis, who conducted a partnership business named Red Rocks Meat and Deli on the premises. Nestle assigned his interest in the partnership to third-party defendant Herline. Rent being in default, the lessor sued Nestle. When Nestle prevailed in a trial to the court, the lessor appealed.

Nestle and Ellis leased the premises in June 1978. They signed the lease as individuals, but lessor knew they were operating Red Rocks Meat and Deli as a partnership. Nestle transferred his partnership interest in October 1978 to a third-party, John C. Herline. Included in this transfer was Nestle's entire interest in partnership equipment, leases, and other assets. In return, the new partnership, and Ellis and Herline individually, agreed to assume all liabilities and to indemnify Nestle. In January 1980, lessor and Ellis executed an addendum to the original lease to lease adjacent space, which also altered the rental base for the premises first leased. By May of that year lease payments were in default for both premises, and lessor sued Nestle for breach of the lease.

At the trial, Ellis testified that the assignment and release agreement had been mailed to lessor, thereby giving notice that Nestle was no longer liable on the lease; that he introduced Herline to lessor as his new partner, and the latter did not object to a change in parties, or request that Nestle remain liable; and that when the addendum was executed it was clear to lessor that Ellis was then operating as a sole proprietor. As supporting evidence Nestle submitted the affidavit of the president of lessor in which he acknowledged being advised that Nestle was no longer a partner when the addendum to the lease was executed.

The lessor denied receiving notice prior to January 1980 that Nestle had withdrawn from the partnership and maintains that it had not agreed to look to the remaining partners and the new partnership to satisfy its debts.

Nestle brought in Herline and Ellis as third-party defendants, claiming a right to indemnification in the event he was found liable to the lessor. Nestle was granted summary judgment on this indemnification claim before trial. Herline cross-appeals this ruling.

Following trial on the primary action, the court resolved the factual disputes in Nestle's favor. Finding that the partnership had dissolved when Nestle withdrew, the court applied [UPA § 36(2)] to the facts and concluded, from lessor's knowledge of the situation and the parties' course of dealings, that lessor had consented to Nestle's discharge from liability. It also concluded that provisions in the addendum materially altered the parties' liability on the underlying lease, thereby discharging Nestle from liability by application of [UPA § 36(3)].

The dissolution of a partnership does not of itself discharge the existing liability of any partner. [UPA § 36(1)]. A partner is discharged from existing liability by an agreement to that effect between the withdrawing partner, the remaining partners, and the partnership creditor, and "such agreement may be inferred from the course of dealing between the creditor having knowledge of the dissolution and the person or partnership continuing the business." [UPA § 36(2)]. Or, under [UPA § 36(3)], a material alteration in an existing liability will discharge from liability a partner whose obligations have been assumed.

The trial court found, on conflicting testimony, that the conditions for discharge from liability under both of these subsections existed, and such factual findings, supported by evidence in the record, may not be disturbed upon appeal.

The lessor's argument that this assignment of interest was a breach of the clause prohibiting assignment of the lease is without merit. Even if it is assumed, *arguendo*, that occupancy by the partnership after withdrawal of Nestle was an assignment in breach of the lease, the lessor had waived any objection by accepting the rent for over two years.

Judgment affirmed.

Notes

1. A dissociating partner remains liable to partnership creditors, UPA § 36(1) except to the extent particular creditors may expressly or impliedly agree otherwise. UPA §§ 36(1), (2). Because the continuing partners have agreed that, *as between them and the dissociating partner*, they will be responsible for obligations to partnership creditors, the dissociating partner's liability is similar to that of a surety. *B-OK, Inc. v. Storey*, 79 Wash. 2d 387, 485 P.2d 987 (1971). Thus, UPA section 36(3) gives the dissociating partner the common law *suretyship discharge* resulting from a material alteration in the nature or time of payment by a creditor who knows of the dissociating partner's change in status.

2. RUPA sections 703(a), (c) and (d) are the RUPA provisions equivalent to UPA section 36.

Wolfe v. East Texas Seed Co.

583 S.W.2d 481 (Tex. Civ. App. 1979)

DOYLE, Justice.

East Texas Seed Company (appellee) sued Charles R. Wolfe (appellant) and Nick Wolfe, doing business as Wolfe Construction Company, for certain goods and merchandise sold and delivered to the construction company on an open account from February 9, 1974, through September 30, 1974, for a total amount of $6,323.05. Alternatively, appellee sued the partnership of Charles R. Wolfe and Nick Wolfe, doing business under the firm name of Wolfe Construction Company, for the amount of the debt, claiming that appellee had no knowledge of the dissolution of the partnership in 1973, said partnership having been formed in 1971. Appellee further alleged that if it had been aware of said dissolution it would not have extended credit to the construction company. Appellant defended on the grounds that he was without legal capacity to be sued since his partnership with Nick Wolfe had been dissolved in 1973 prior to the inception of debt made the basis of this suit. The trial court awarded appellee judgment against the defendants, jointly and severally, for $5,318.04 with interest. Only Charles R. Wolfe appealed.

[Appellant] allege[s] that the district court erred in rendering judgment for the plaintiff in that there was no evidence of probative value in the record to show that the plaintiff knew of or relied in any way on the individual credit of defendant Charles R. Wolfe as a partner in the company in selling the merchandise or incurring the account, and that the court also erred in rendering judgment for the plaintiff against defendant Charles R. Wolfe in that the evidence of record clearly shows that this defendant received no value or benefit from any of the items made a basis of this suit.

Appellant argues that pursuant to the [UPA], he is not under any duty to tender notice of dissolution of the partnership to creditors and, further, that he is absolved from all partnership liability under [UPA section 35(2)], stating:

> (2) The liability of a partner under Paragraph (1b) shall be satisfied out of partnership assets alone when such partner had been prior to dissolution:
>
> > (a) Unknown as a partner to the person with whom the contract is made; and
> >
> > (b) So far unknown and inactive in partnership affairs that the business reputation of the partnership could not be said to have been in any degree due to his connection with it.

Appellant cites no authority for his interpretation of this article.

A fair summary of the testimony concerning the partnership and its dissolution is as follows: Appellee's manager, Mr. Kirby, admits he did not know whether appellant's company was a partnership when it first began doing business with them. He stated that he first became aware of the partnership in 1974 after it had been dissolved. He further explained that if he had known of the dissolution he would have investigated the matter and that it would have made a "whole lot" of difference to his company.

Appellant strongly contends that since the partnership had been terminated before the inception of the debt, he should not be personally liable. As a general rule this would be true where notice of the dissolution has been given to third parties who had dealings with the partnership. On the other hand, absent any notice of dissolution, appellant cannot escape personal liability for the subject debt unless he can show that prior to dissolution, he had been "So far unknown and inactive in partnership affairs that the business reputation of the partnership could not be said to have been in any degree due to his connection with it." [UPA § 35(2)(b)].

The facts before us show that appellee did business with the company prior to the partnership dissolution; that appellant was known as Wolfe Construction Company; that the company was composed of two brothers, Nick and Charles R. Wolfe; that either man had authority to purchase seed; and that both men bought and paid for the seed. Appellant denies receiving any benefit from these transactions personally, but admits the partnership could have purchased the seed and benefited from it. Business was continued by appellant under the same name of Wolfe Construction Company, Nick Wolfe still worked for the company and no notice of partnership dissolution was sent to appellee. Appellant's reputation was relied on in transactions with appellee, and even in the absence of any partnership agreement parties may be bound as partners as to third parties.

The judgment of the trial court is affirmed.

Note

The RUPA sections analogous to UPA section 35 are RUPA sections 702, 703, and 704 (dissociating partners), and RUPA sections 804 and 805 (dissolution/winding up). These sections make several substantive changes.

First, the "dormant partner" provision limiting the liability of persons not known to the creditor *and* generally inactive in partnership business has been eliminated. Instead, a dissociating partner will only be liable for new partnership obligations if the persons dealing with the partnership reasonably believed that the dissociating partner was a partner at the time of the transaction. This would change the result in *Wolfe*; because East Texas Seed Company did not know at the time it entered into the transaction that Charles was a partner, Charles would not be liable to it.

Second, the RUPA treats all persons without actual notice of a partner's dissociation in the same manner. That is, the RUPA does not distinguish between creditors and persons entering into contracts. Notice by publication in a newspaper of general circulation is no longer permitted or required. Instead, as to all persons entering into transactions within two years after a dissociation, the dissociating partner retains the power to bind the partnership *and remains liable* to such person. The only way to cut off the dissociating partner's power to bind and liability is by filing a "Statement of Dissociation" under section 704. Note that the Statement of Dissociation is not effective as to third persons until it has been on file for 90 days.

RUPA sections 804 and 805 are generally equivalent to sections 702, 703, and 704, except that only the partnership may file a Statement of *Dissolution*. Of course, even in a dissolution, dissociating partners may protect their interests by filing a Statement of Dissociation under RUPA section 704.

Palomba v. Barish

626 F. Supp. 722 (E.D. Pa. 1985)

JAMES McGIRR KELLY, District Judge.

Presently before this court is defendant Robert C. Daniels' motion [for] summary judgment.

Plaintiffs, a group of seamen, were allegedly injured while the vessel they were on was in navigable waters of the Atlantic Ocean. Plaintiffs engaged the defendant law firm of Adler, Barish, Daniels, Levin & Creskoff (Adler-Barish) to represent them in their action against the ship for damages. Defendant Marvin Barish, a partner of Adler-Barish, was the attorney who handled plaintiffs' claims.

The court which was presiding over the plaintiffs' action against the ship dismissed certain of the plaintiffs' claims (hereinafter "dismissed plaintiffs") because dismissed plaintiffs were not produced for deposition and medical examination and plaintiffs' expert witness medical reports were not furnished for the steamship company as required by an order entered and agreed to by counsel. The remaining plaintiffs' claims (hereinafter "limited plaintiffs") were allowed to proceed to trial as to damages, but a key expert witness was prohibited from testifying . . . due to the alleged failure of defendant Marvin Barish to make the expert witnesses reports available to the steamship company's counsel.

Plaintiffs here allege they suffered injury due to the alleged malpractice of defendant attorneys who had represented them in their claim against the steamship company.

In Count I of the complaint the dismissed plaintiffs assert that because of the negligence of the defendants in the preparation and handling of their claims, they were prejudiced and lost the right to recover damages against the steamship company.

In Count II of the complaint the limited plaintiffs assert that because of the negligence of the defendants they were injured because they were deprived of putting into evidence material and testimony which would have benefited them in their attempt to establish damages.

Count III of the complaint asserts a claim on behalf of all plaintiffs for punitive damages against the defendants for "continual and flagrant disregard of agreed upon scheduling orders."

I have jurisdiction over plaintiffs' action because of diversity of the parties. Accordingly, I must apply Pennsylvania state law. Pennsylvania law is clear that the negligence of one partner acting in the ordinary course of the business of the partnership will be imputed upon the non-acting partners, making the non-acting partners jointly and severally liable for the negligence. [UPA §§ 13 & 15].

Defendant Daniels has contended that he was forced out of Adler-Barish, thus dissolving the partnership two years prior to the time of the purported negligence which gave rise to plaintiffs' claims. While plaintiffs have alleged negligence on behalf of all defendant attorneys, they assert that defendant Marvin Barish was the firm's representative which they dealt with.

A party who has prior dealings with a partnership and without [actual or constructive] knowledge of a subsequent dissolution of the partnership, and continues to deal with a partner, can hold liable the former partners of the dissolved partnership. [UPA § 35].

Thus, a party who is not given notice of dissolution, but continues to transact business with a "partner," can hold liable the former partnership. It should be noted at this juncture that

> even after dissolution, a partnership is not terminated but continues to exist until the winding up of partnership affairs is completed and the authority remains to act for the partnership in winding up partnership affairs and complete transactions begun but not yet finished at the time of dissolution.

North Star Coal v. Eddy, 442 Pa. 583, 586, 277 A.2d 154, 156 (1971). The dissolution of a partnership will not relieve an individual partner of a duty under a contract entered into before the partnership was dissolved. Thus, I find the fact that Daniels' withdrawal from Adler-Barish two years prior to the purported negligent act is of little moment to whether or not Daniels can be held liable for the malpractice of his former partners.

An action of malpractice by an attorney can generally be based upon either tort or contract theory. The action brought by plaintiffs here appears to rest upon tort theory for recovery. Generally a tort by one partner occurring subsequent to dissolution of a partnership cannot be imputed upon the former partners, unless the party who committed the tort was winding up the partnership affairs or completing partnership business. A partner who has not, *inter alia*, wrongfully dissolved the partnership has the right to wind up the partnership affairs. [UPA § 37]. Because no pleadings or material submitted to the court have expressed that defendant Barish wrongfully dissolved the partnership, I must assume that Barish had a right to wind up certain former Adler-Barish commitments.

Defendant Daniels has submitted an affidavit of his counsel, Neil Witkes, to support his position that plaintiffs had actual knowledge of the Adler-Barish firm being dissolved, since Daniels' withdrawal from Adler-Barish. Witkes avers that certain correspondence of various plaintiffs which were addressed to the successor firm of Adler-Barish establishes that these plaintiffs had knowledge of the expulsion or absence of defendant Daniels from the firm. It may be permissible, but not advisable, for an attorney to present his own affidavit for a motion for a summary judgment. However, here the more serious problems arise because of possible hearsay and authentication questions of the documents Witkes has submitted as well as inferences such writings convey. Indeed, the fact that plaintiffs addressed letters to a succeeding firm of Adler-Barish does not dispose of all questions of fact as to whether or not the plaintiffs had knowledge that Daniels was no longer with the law firm which represented them.[12] The letters do not preclude an issue of fact in dispute. Because I find in consideration of the letters, an issue of fact still present, I need not rule as to whether the letters should be excluded because they were not properly authenticated or may contain hearsay. Daniels has submitted an affidavit averring that he was expelled from the partnership and was denied access to the client files to which he could have obtained address information of clients so that notice of his leaving Adler-Barish could be made. Conversely, other partners of the former Adler-Barish firm who are defendants in this action have submitted affidavits averring that Daniels withdrew on his own accord and was not forced out of Adler-Barish; additionally, other defendants aver that Daniels was not prohibited from accessing client files. Thus, I cannot rule as to the absence of a factual dispute concerning Daniels leaving the Adler-Barish firm. Moreover, the fact that Daniels' former partners allegedly wrongfully denied him access to the client files does not release Daniels from his duties to plaintiffs.

---

12. The law firm originally engaged was Adler, Barish, Daniels, Levin & Creskoff, the succeeding law firm was Adler, Barish, Levin & Creskoff. The fact that a person's name does not appear in the firm's name does not necessarily mean that the person is not a partner with the firm. Additionally, I note that the new firm's name may be confusingly similar to the first firm's name so that the plaintiffs were not aware of Daniels' absence.

Daniels' submission of affidavits has not precluded a genuine issue of fact concerning, *inter alia*, whether or not plaintiffs had knowledge of the dissolution of Adler-Barish or that Barish was not charged with winding up Adler-Barish's affairs. Accordingly, I must deny defendant Daniels' motion for summary judgment as to Counts I and II of plaintiffs' complaint.

Last, I turn to defendant Daniels' assertion that the punitive damages claim, Count III of plaintiffs' complaint, is improper because defendant Daniels avers in his affidavit that he was not a partner of Barish when the purported negligence occurred. However, as stated earlier, the fact that a partnership dissolves does not terminate affairs that were current at the time of dissolution; termination of liability occurs once the current matters (at time of dissolution) are resolved or wound up. Moreover, the very fact that Barish was permitted to wind up affairs for the former partnership may in itself be a reckless act. Accordingly, defendant Daniels' motion for summary judgment as to Count III must be denied.

[T]he summary judgment motion must be denied.